The Illustrated
Empathy Gap

The Illustrated Empathy Gap

Challenging public incredulity on the
prejudice against men and boys

Edited writings 2014 to 2023

William Collins

Principia Publications Unlimited

This edition first published April 2024

A catalogue record for this book is available from the British Library.

ISBN: 978-1-8380216-4-1

Cover design by rawb

Principia Publications Unlimited
https://principiapublications.wordpress.com/

Contents

Section 13: Moral Usurpation

Preface

This book does not duplicate the material in my earlier book, *The Empathy Gap*, though the broad topics are, of course, the same – specifically gender issues from a male perspective. However, this book is based on blog articles, the originals of which can still be found on my blog *The Illustrated Empathy Gap* (http://empathygap.uk). Indeed, with few exceptions, the chapter titles are the same as the titles of the corresponding blog articles. But the book has not been compiled simply as cut-and-paste from the blog. All the chapters have been edited, in some cases only slightly and in some cases quite radically.

I had an embarrassment of riches from which to choose. My guiding principle was to avoid duplication with *The Empathy Gap* whilst choosing material which complemented it and illustrated the phenomenon to which the title refers. Consequently, all the material herein relates to gender and from the perspective of male disadvantage.

Like *The Empathy Gap*, this book is heavy with references, which (in the ebook) are hyperlinked in almost all cases. All the references have been reviewed as links do tend to go dead over time. In such cases I have either found the same reference at another URL or found another, equivalent, reference. Unlike the previous book the references appear at the end of the chapter to which they refer, which is easier for the reader.

The original articles date from 2014 to 2023. It was not my intention to carry out a wholesale updating, e.g., by using updated datasets where available (and this is often the case for ONS data, for example). Rather, the original articles are, in part, a testament to the time they were written and I wished this to be maintained. Where this objective is not compromised by also including more recent data I have sometimes done so. In particular, there are some aspects of the original articles that it would be misleading to leave unchanged. For example, in the case of legislation that was planned or in development at the time of the original article it would be very misleading to a reader now to retain the original text if said legislation has now been formally published (e.g., an Act that has received Royal Assent). Consequently, updating may be more extensive in such cases, possibly with the new legislation being quoted. A similar remark applies in the case of changes of government and changes of personnel in the ministries of state, for example. Phrases such as "then Home Secretary" are often deployed for clarity.

The overall purpose of this book is the same as that of *The Empathy Gap*, namely to illustrate the reality of the gender empathy gap and the closely related gamma bias or gynocentrism. The disadvantages or inequalities suffered by men and boys are substantial and to be found across all aspects of life: education, accidents, health and longevity, domestic abuse, suicide, criminal justice, as victims of crime and, most especially, as parents, including in respect of the impact of family breakdown.

To some this may seem quixotic. Indeed, to some people merely having the temerity to mention male disadvantage may invoke fury. "Inequality" is so often linked with women and girls, or with minorities, that it has become an unchallenged axiom that we need not be concerned about males *qua males*. Yet the evidence, as presented in *The Empathy Gap*, presents a radically opposite perspective. The observation that senior positions are still occupied more by men than women – politicians, professors, consultants, high court judges – is not apposite. Nor, I should add, are men so dominant at even these levels as they once were and probably will not remain dominant for much longer. But, in any case, it is not these men who bring down the average male longevity or populate the prisons or swell the ranks of the under-educated. The intersection of men-plus-deprivation is a more virulent combination even than women-plus-deprivation, as the data presented in *The Empathy Gap* demonstrates.

The primary purpose of this book is to complement the case presented in *The Empathy Gap* by presenting a host of specific issues which illustrate the reality, and sometimes the origin, of the gender empathy gap and the resulting male disadvantages.

One issue I perhaps failed to make sufficiently clear in the previous book I now emphasise: none of my writings or talks are intended to make a play for men in the victimhood Olympics. I abhor with every fibre of my being the spurious leveraging of victimhood to gain social advantage. Seeking victimhood is a profoundly false and deeply unethical behaviour which has played a large part in the destruction of our society. In any case, you would need to have failed to appreciate the foundational thesis of my books, namely the empathy gap itself, to think that claims of victimhood could be advantageous for men. The empathy gap precludes the very possibility. That is rather the point. Victimhood works only where there is an antecedent condition of empathy to exploit and plunder.

What, then, *is* the purpose of highlighting the male disadvantages? The purpose is to bring this reality into collision with the approved narrative, and thereby to attempt to convince the reader that the empathy gap is real. What would follow from that revelatory experience is that the approved narrative, including feminism, is actually just an epiphenomenon of the empathy gap. Rather than being empirically based, the approved/feminist narrative is a psychosocial product of the empathy gap (or gamma bias or gynocentrism, if you prefer).

I also wish to emphasise that I have not personally suffered any of the male disadvantages about which I have written so much. I am one of the lucky ones. To my mind this strengthens my position as any detractors wishing to discredit my perspective by claiming that I am a hurt man with a chip on my shoulder simply have no grounds for doing so.

A Guide to the Contents

The articles are not presented in chronological order. Rather the book is structured in 13 sections according to topic. By this means, articles originally published many years apart are brought together in a (hopefully) coherent whole.

It seems appropriate to start the book, and the section on justice, with a review of the law of coverture. This is a subject much beloved of feminists as, in their interpretation, coverture provided the quintessential manifestation of oppressive patriarchy in the legal arena. As usual, however, the full truth is not that.

The Corston Report (chapter two) was the first time I realised just how fraudulent were feminist claims of a desire for equality. It also served as a vehicle for my first crushing realisation that many women, perhaps most women, and not merely self-identified feminists, agreed wholeheartedly with its sexist insistence that women be treated far more leniently than men. And most men agreed. In short, I learnt the reality of gynocentrism.

The remaining chapters in this opening section on "broken justice" are snapshots of the concerted drive to destroy relations between the sexes via the use of lawfare, aided by well-placed feminist activists and professionals. All the resulting changes to legislation and associated practices have been on a one-way ratchet in the direction of fatherlessness and declining birth rate.

The second section on sexual assault starts with my 2018 review of false allegations in the UK. This review serves to demonstrate how trivial are many women's motivations for making allegations which would utterly destroy a man, and, in many cases, this is serial behaviour by the accusing women. The associated miscarriages of justice often result from disclosure failures. This generic failure of the criminal justice process was subject to severe censure by the Justice Select Committee in 2018, whose report stated clearly the attitudes and procedures which the police must adopt - alas, to no avail. The intentions of the Crown Prosecution Service to continue to not just allow but actively to promote a biased approach to sexual offence cases is made explicit in Operation Soteria (chapter 17).

It does not matter how many times I emphasise that a focus in my writings on harms to men does not mean I am denying that bad things – including serious sexual offences and domestic abuse – also happen to women. It does not matter how often I make this statement, there are those who will not – apparently cannot – see books such as this as other than such a denial. This results from the moral infantilism which is now rampant in our culture and which, with some irony, is only able to see issues in binary, black or white, terms.

The third section addresses illustrative cases of the perennially distorted picture of domestic abuse to which the public is subjected, culminating in the culture-wide damage this is doing to our children.

Section four illustrates how boys are treated more harshly than girls, and in non-Western cultures whose designation as "patriarchal" deflects attention from this reality. The focus is again on boys in section five on education in the UK which contrasts the diminishing educational attainment of boys with professional and political attitudes to it. Our culture is one in which an education professional can dismiss any need to address this issue with an insouciant "girls are just cleverer" (chapter 30).

Section six gives some illustrations of the falsity of the feminist conception of "equality". Much of this is older material which I now almost feel no longer needs saying – but unfortunately it does. If you want to wind me up, just mention the WASPIs. Entitlement? Off the scale. Chapter 34 is one of my few forays into the abortion issue, and the hardening of my previously rather liberal opinion.

There is no situation which feminists will fail to use to aggrandise women and castigate men, as section seven demonstrates in the context of the covid period. I also include here, with a considerable level of quantitative detail, the impact on primary healthcare of the majority of General Practitioners now being women. This is followed in section eight with a miscellany of the types of feminist propaganda in which our culture is marinaded.

Section nine is more scientific in tone, with much on the evolutionary origins of our gendered outlook, culminating in a deconstruction of the egregiously misleading Implicit Association Test. Section 10 looks at some of the results of half a century of feminism in respect of the wedge driven between the sexes – as implemented mainly by the vilification of men. In respect of "reactionary feminism" (chapter 52) I really don't care what adjectival rider is prepended to "feminism", it remains too poisonous a term to be applied to oneself for anyone who has acknowledged what destruction feminism has wrought.

Section 11 sees me enjoying myself, talking about books and their authors. I wonder what Henry James (chapter 60) would have made of *The Power* (chapter 61). Section 12 concedes that the culture "war" (i.e., slaughter) was lost, though that should not discourage dissidents from continuing to pour scorn on the brave new culture and all its works.

The final section broadens the subject matter to more general politics and introduces my concept of moral usurpation, which I offer as the psychological basis of the collectivist new culture. These closing two chapters are an introduction to my earlier book, *The Destructivists*, and also add something to it, especially as regards ESG (Environmental, Social and Governance, the corporate index). The last chapter has been extended from the original blog post in respect of ESG, specifically to illustrate how the pressures on financial institutions to conform are enacted coercively from the top down, that is, from the UN down through national legislatures.

My final point is the most important. Despite the reception that work such as this will receive in most quarters now, its purpose is not to advance the cause of the male identity group. That would be deepening the already serious divide in our society. Its purpose is to discredit the identity group perspective entirely by showing how its weaponisation has wrought destruction upon us by creation of fatal division. If there is to be any hope that the growing authoritarianism alluded to in the last two chapters may be avoided, then healing of these divisions is the only means by which this could be achieved. But this cannot come about before the truth of the issues discussed herein is acknowledged. Finally, I emphasise again that my focus on issues affecting men and boys is to redress the imbalance that these are generally neglected, not to pretend that women and girls do not have their own issues.

Style Issues

I confess my sin in using "male" and "female" as nouns, at least in the plural "males" and "females". Blame the English language for having no alternative to the cumbersome "men and boys" and "women and girls". I apologise to those whose grammatical sensibilities are offended. I write "covid" as just that, with a small "c". This is deliberate. I refuse to enhance the disease's significance with a capital. In this I follow Clare Craig

I use English spelling. However, in quotes from non-UK authors, their original spelling is retained without confusing the text with "(sic)". Quotes use the double quote mark and are in italics. Quotes within quotes use the single quote mark. Acronyms are generally explained in each chapter in which they are used, but in addition there is an acronym guide at the end of the book. For ebook readers the hyperlinks are confined to two places; to the References gathered together at the end of each chapter, and in the date of the original blog article which appears immediately below the subtitle to each chapter. The context of each chapter is the UK unless otherwise stated.

Acknowledgements

I take the usual cop-out that there are too many people to whom acknowledgement is due to attempt to name them all, which has the merit of being true. These good people have at least one thing in common: they are content to work for no pay, no plaudits and often outright condemnation. Any errors are my own. Most happily I acknowledge all readers of this book, without whom it would have been pointless.

William Collins, 7 April 2024.

Section 1

Broken Justice

1. Coverture

It seems appropriate to start the book, and the section on justice, with a review of the law of coverture. This is a subject much beloved of feminists as, in their interpretation, coverture provided the quintessential manifestation of oppressive patriarchy in the legal arena. As usual, however, the full truth is not that.

Original posted on 4th December 2018.

I have opined previously that patriarchy, far from being oppression of women by men, was largely a piece of theatre, an illusion. By observing the formalities associated with a man being "master in his own house", the man's blushes were spared: no one need ever acknowledge his domestically subservient position, though everyone really knew. The law of coverture is generally regarded, especially by feminists, as a quintessentially patriarchal device. They are right – but only if we adopt the interpretation of patriarchy as illusion. Looking behind the smoke and mirrors of coverture into how it was interpreted in practice reveals that it too was really a façade of male power concealing a female power within. For the account which follows (which relates to the UK), I have drawn upon the sources listed in the References.

A grossly distorted picture is easy to conjure if one selects only the benefits to one sex and only the disbenefits to the other. Then one can spin a tale of oppression out of straw. The feminist depiction of coverture is such a case (as, indeed, is the feminist depiction of history generally).

Until around the mid-Victorian period, English Common Law had held that a married couple constituted a single legal entity. This was the legal equivalent of the Christian "one flesh". Under the system of coverture, the husband was the manifestation of the legal entity whilst the wife's legal status became covert, i.e., hidden. The law of coverture is a favourite of the feminists as an example of historical female oppression. Whilst an unmarried woman could own property and enter into legal contracts in her own right, this was denied to a married woman under coverture because she was held to be legally tied to her husband who must act for them as a couple in legal matters. I am no apologist for the system of coverture, but feminists will never tell you of the flip side of the arrangement.

Pause to consider for a moment the great boon that being legally non-existent might be to the unscrupulous or the criminal.

Since the man was the manifest legal entity he became responsible for crimes – or torts – committed by his wife. The most common example of this were the Victorian debtors' prisons. Some 10,000 people, 95% to 98% of them men, were imprisoned yearly for debt in the Victorian era, Ref.[1]. This was at a time when 20% of prisoners sentenced for criminal offences were women, and it is reasonable to suppose that women were responsible for incurring around 50% of debts, perhaps more. A debt might have been due to the wife's profligacy or carelessness, but it was the husband who went to prison.

Another aspect of the law of coverture which feminists do not bother to mention was known as the principle of "necessaries". A man was obliged to provide financially for his wife. In fact, it was not only marriage but also cohabitation which created this obligation. The principle of "necessaries" under coverture meant that the wife – or common-law wife – could enter a 'contract' for goods, or purchase any goods, on credit if they were deemed to fall under the aegis of "necessaries". This could be done unilaterally without the husband's knowledge, though he would still be responsible for honouring the debt. This was, of course, a practical necessity because wives were usually charged with maintaining the household and hence spending the bulk of the domestic monies. And, for most people at that time, domestic spending was all their spending.

But what constituted "necessaries" was highly class and social status dependent. Thus, for a woman of high social status such items as a carriage, expensive lace clothing and the hire of servants would be deemed "necessaries" because they were expected of a woman in her position. The law of "necessaries" effectively gave women great powers of consumption without legal responsibility for the consequences.

In practice, though, the bulk of legal cases to recover debt related to the lower orders, inevitably. That wives were supposedly legally invisible under coverture was given the lie by the fact that the courts were full of married women in debt cases. Frequently it was the wife in court representing her indebted husband despite the latter being liable. This was partly so the husband did not lose a day's pay in attending court. But it was also because the wife was recognised as the person who had contracted the debt. And it was also tactically wise since a woman was more likely to gain a sympathetic ear with the court. Records indicate that women were more likely than men to obtain preferential terms for the debt repayment, such as repayment in instalments. Should the wife lose the case, however, it was the husband who might end up in prison, not her.

Wives' legal non-existence was further betrayed as fictional when the creditor was also represented in court by his wife, who was quite likely to have sold the goods in the first place. So the courts might feature two warring women, both of whom were formally representing their husbands, neither of whom were present. Margot Finn, Ref.[2], has described coverture in everyday practice as "existing in a state of suspended animation" as women did, in reality, exercise considerable influence, both legally and financially. When coverture truly was called into play was in deciding who went to prison.

Sometimes the husband was ruled not liable for the debt, but the burden still did not fall upon the wife, who was protected by her legal standing of being incapable of contracting debt. The loss in such cases fell to the hapless tradesman.

Joanne Bailey, Ref.[3], adduces evidence that, in practice, wives maintained during marriage substantial property interests of their own, there being other laws in operation which protected their interests and which were dominant over the common law of coverture, *de facto* if not *de jure*. To quote Margot Finn, Ref.[2], "*seventeenth- and eighteenth-century women enjoyed substantially more economic authority than the literature on coverture would suggest....Maxine Berg's analysis of probate accounts in eighteenth-century Sheffield and Birmingham similarly emphasizes that women played an important economic role as executors and guardians in some cities, where moreover they 'did own real property and, in most cases... disposed of it as they wished*".

Wives frequently took an active part in their husbands' businesses and this also required that they be delegated powers of agency, whether formally or informally. This might, in some cases, extend to legal Power of Attorney. Such arrangements were also a practical necessity if the husband's business required his physical absence from the home for long periods, in which case the wife was effectively left as the business agent in the home town.

Bailey, Ref.[3], asks whether there is any evidence for a great distinction before, during and after marriage in women's purchasing habits, or other financial powers. She concludes there is little evidence of any significant distinction in practice. The ostensible legal annihilation of women in marriage under coverture would appear to be another instance of the largely illusory nature of patriarchy.

The beneficial aspects of coverture for wives did not stop with access to credit underwritten by their husbands whilst the marriage lasted. The law of "necessaries" extended even to separated wives. An estranged wife could continue to run up debts with which to burden her ex-husband. This was commonly used as a tactic to force the husband to agree divorce terms favourable to the wife. Such estranged wives could, and did, push the strategy as far as having the husband imprisoned until he gave them what they wanted.

There are recorded cases such as this one: a man returned home from a business trip to discover that his wife had sold everything he possessed and set herself up in alternative accommodation with the proceeds. He was now destitute but there was nothing he could do. He could bring no case against his wife because she and he were deemed to be legally identified, and one cannot sue oneself.

So, is the feminist portrayal of coverture as patriarchal oppression of women the true and undistorted picture of historical reality? Clearly not.

Even after the 1869 Act for the Abolition of Imprisonment for Debt, imprisonment was still retained for certain cases of debt, including the financial provision for wives – hence the law of "necessaries" continued even after this Act. And this is despite the fact that, starting in 1870, there were a succession of Married Women's Property Acts which reversed the parts of coverture relating to wives' property and allowed married women to own property and capital in their own right.

A common feminist fallacy is that wives enjoyed no legal protection from their husbands' violence in these periods. There were, in fact, many statutes which provided protection (though the stigma around marital violence was undoubtedly not what it is today). With some irony, given its reputation, coverture was itself one of the legal mechanisms for such protection. Under coverture, abused wives could obtain a 'surety for the peace', a bond which obliged a husband to keep the peace towards his wife – a forerunner of today's injunction orders.

The law of coverture effectively placed a legal obligation upon husbands to ensure their wives obeyed the law. In fact, coverture had its origins in common law and hence in ancient custom and practice which had also obliged husbands to make sure their wives behaved themselves. A particularly egregious example of this was the Skimmington Ride, Ref.[4]. It is still the case today that society has a hard time accepting that some men may be the victims of partner abuse, rather than the perpetrators. In historical times things were no better – in fact worse. A man who allowed himself to be abused by his wife would be punished for it by his community. A husband was expected to control his wife. If she beat him, then this was regarded as a failing on his part. The punishment was the Skimmington Ride, in which the man was obliged to ride a donkey through the town facing backwards, and thus looking ridiculous, whilst the populace would bang pots and pans and jeer and mock him by calling out insults. The modern equivalent, I suppose, is the male victim of partner violence who phones the police only to find that he is the one they arrest.

Feminists have held coverture as a clear example of male privilege. But the feminist presentation of the law of coverture and related laws as a great boon for men and oppression for women is a gross distortion. What such laws were truly designed to do was to impose responsibilities upon men, and to provide for the punishment of men should they fail to fulfil these responsibilities. At a time when most paid work, sufficient to maintain a family, was gruellingly hard manual labour which women physically could not do, it is easy to see why society placed these burdens upon men. Coverture does not embody male privilege but male obligation. No doubt feminists would say "patriarchy hurts men too". But if it was patriarchy which imposed these laws, it was the ruling elite that was the patriarch, and they imposed the burden of responsibility on the other men. In reality, it was hardly patriarchy but necessity which truly imposed the burden. This would continue to be the case until technology made all our lives so much easier.

In common with other aspects of what feminists interpret as patriarchal oppression, coverture was part of a system which tied men into obligations of resource provision for their wives (a situation which evolved as a surrogate for the provisioning of children). The ultimate dismantling of coverture, and the full legal independence of the sexes, was part of the process which weakened men's social and legal binding into the family. From the feminist perspective this was part of their overarching program to "smash the patriarchy". Indeed it was. But one's perspective on how desirable that might be hinges upon the meaning one attaches to "patriarchy". From the feminist perspective of patriarchy as oppression of women, its demolition is an unmitigated good. But the alternative perspective is that patriarchy was merely an illusion, a piece of theatre, designed to encourage men to commit to obligations which self-interest would reject. From this perspective the dismantling of coverture was relief of men's obligations and hence more a cause for men's celebration than women's.

So, both parties are happy, then.

Except, of course, that they are not.

References

[1]   Ware, S.J. (2014). *A 20th Century Debate About Imprisonment for Debt*. 54 Am. J. Legal Hist. 351 (April 2014). Also available from *An Early 20th Century Parliamentary Debate 2013 Nov 11.docx (ku.edu)*.

[2]   Finn, M. (1996). *Women, consumption and coverture in England, c. 1760–1860*. The Historical Journal, 39, pp 703-722, September 1996. Full text also available from *Women, consumption and coverture in England, c. 1760–1860 (ucl.ac.uk)*.

[3]   Bailey, J. (2002). *Favoured or oppressed? Married women, property and 'coverture' in England, 1660–1800*. Continuity and Change 17 (3), 2002, 351–372. Cambridge University Press. Also available from *here*.

[4]   George, M.J. (1994). *Riding the Donkey Backwards: Men as the Unacceptable Victims of Marital Violence*. The Journal of Men's Studies, Volume 3, No.2, November 1994, 137-159. Also available from *http://www.fact.on.ca/Info/dom/george94.pdf*.

2. The Corston Report, A Case Study in Gynocentrism

The Corston Report is now an historical document. The overtly sexist sentiments upon which the entirety of the Corston Report is based are now triumphant. It has been declared government policy since 2018 to deflect women away from prison "wherever possible", but with no such directive for male offenders - in fact, quite the opposite. In terms of my own red pill learning history, this report was the first time I realised just how fraudulent were feminist claims of a desire for equality. It also served as a vehicle for my first crushing realisation that many women, perhaps most women, and not merely self-identified feminists, agreed wholeheartedly with the Corston Report's sexist insistence that women be treated far more leniently than men. And most men agreed. In short, I learnt the reality of gynocentrism. I have not attempted to update the various data quoted; let it stand as an historical document.

Original posted on 23 November 2014.

In 2007 the Home Office published a report by Baroness Corston on the treatment of women within the UK criminal justice system, especially prisons, known as *The Corston Report*, Ref.[1]. This report contains my all-time favourite feminist quote,

"Equality does not mean treating everyone the same."

I kid you not. The Baroness liked the sound of that so much, she used it twice. Some animals are more equal than others: it's right there on the page.

The thrust of the report's recommendations was for a more understanding, caring, compassionate treatment of female offenders. I could be persuaded that many of the report's recommendations are good ideas. I tend to think that there must be something more constructive that could be done with offenders than simply have them sit in prison, bored to death, doing nothing for months or years. But I have one little problem with the report. This caring, compassionate and understanding approach is for women only. Of course, the report was commissioned to be about women only – but that only begs the question "why?". Why have a particular concern for just 5% of the prison population and not the other 95%, based solely on sex?

It is clear from the report itself that the furthest thing from the good Baroness's mind was to apply a similar approach to male offenders. As a result I am tempted to say that this vile document is the most gynocentric thing I have ever seen coming out of a formal governmental source – but unfortunately the competition in that respect is very strong.

The report originates from a determined mind-set of gender discrimination. The attempt is made to justify this one-sided concern, as you will see from the extracts below (in italics) which are followed by my comments. Bear in mind throughout that this perspective has proved triumphant and is now established principle within criminal justice in the UK. In short, you are imprisoned for what you are, not for what you have done. And this is only one aspect of the sex-based corruption of justice which is now routine.

"Most women do not commit crime."

What a facile comment to make, you might think. But the effect is subtle. It suggests, subliminally, that most men *do* commit crimes. Preposterous when stated explicitly, but logic is not how psychological suggestion works.

"The biological difference between men and women has different social and personal consequences."

Yes, men and women are biologically and socially different. How does this justify compassion for one sex only?

"Proportionately more women than men are remanded in custody."

"Proportionately more", eh? Proportionately to what? In the year ending March 2013 some 3,631 women were remanded in custody awaiting trial compared with 44,953 men. The bulk of such remands will be for indictable offences, for which about 6 times more men are tried than women. You will note that 44,953 is actually over 12 times more than 3,631. So the truth is that it is men who are remanded in custody disproportionately more often than women – by a factor of 2. You can only contort the Baroness's claim into a semblance of truth by taking the remand figures as a proportion of prisoners. But, as shown in my other posts, Refs.[2-5], men are sent to prison far more often, and for longer, than women for the same crimes, resulting in a gender disparity in imprisonment of at least a factor of 3.5. So what the Baroness claims is disproportionate remand of women is actually disproportionate imprisonment of men – nice, eh?

"Women commit a different range of offences from men. They commit more acquisitive crime and have a lower involvement in serious violence, criminal damage and professional crime."

Even if this were true it would be irrelevant. They get sentenced for what they did. And they are far more leniently sentenced than men for the same offence, see Refs.[2-5]. But it is not even true. The pattern of women's offending is actually fairly similar to that of men, again see Refs.[2-5] and *The Empathy Gap*, Ref.[6]. Note in particular, contrary to the Baroness's claim, that the same proportion of women prisoners are in prison for violent crimes as is the case for men. The most common reason for a woman to be arrested is for violent offences. The proportion of women arrested who are arrested for violence is the same as that for men. For an example of how Baroness Corston was able to distort reality into the shape she wanted, despite the data, see Ref.[4].

"Relationship problems feature strongly in women's pathways into crime."

I expect the same is true for men. Even if it were not, in what way does this justify compassion for one sex only?

"Coercion by men can form a route into criminal activity for some women."

Ah, yes. Nothing is ever a woman's fault. There's always a man to blame somewhere. This is the denial of female agency which typifies feminism. Where is the evidence to support this claim? Anyone? A source?

"Outside prison men are more likely to commit suicide than women but the position is reversed inside prison."

This is a truly vile bit of misdirection. It is outrageous to claim that suicide is a greater problem for women, prisoners or not. From Ref.[7] we learn that between January 2013 and 2 October 2014, 130 men and just 4 women prisoners killed themselves. Even accounting for there being twenty times more male prisoners, this is still a higher per capita rate of suicide for male prisoners – and more than six times the national average. Ref.[6] presents the prison suicide data for the ten years 2008 to 2017. There were 710 suicides of male prisoners and 32 of female prisoners. This is a higher suicide rate per 1000 prisoners for men than for women (0.93 cf 0.80), so Corston's claim is false as well as appallingly lacking in compassion for males.

"Self-harm in prison is a huge problem and more prevalent in the women's estate."

A greater percentage of women prisoners self-harm than male prisoners, true. But a greater number of male prisoners self-harm. In 2009, 5340 male prisoners self-harmed (6.7%) compared with 1356 women (31%). I recall that one male prisoner, in the heat of the 2014 summer, gouged his own eyes out.

"Because of the small number of women's prisons and their geographical location, women tend to be located further from their homes than male prisoners, to the detriment of maintaining family ties, receiving visits and resettlement back into the community."

Oh, this is a good one. The reason why there are few women's prisons, and hence why they are geographically spread out, is because women are 3.5 to 6 times less likely to be sent to prison than men for the same offence. So, men are dead lucky to be sent to prison so much more frequently – so their visitors don't have to travel so far. Barrel scraping, anyone?

"Prison is disproportionably (sic) harsher for women because prisons and the practices within them have for the most part been designed for men."

This says that prison is *harsher* for women because it's *the same* as it is for men. Feminist logic does hurt the brain, doesn't it? But it isn't really a failure of logic; it's a gendered application of concern – the empathy gap, otherwise known as prejudice.

"Levels of security in prison were put in place to stop men escaping."

No kidding.

Is there supposed to be some implication that women's prisons don't need security? Yes, I think so, because the direction of travel in recent years has been to place female offenders in open facilities, with their children.

"The women's prison population suffers disproportionately because of the rapidly increasing male prison population and the pressure to find places for men, leading to re-roling of female prisons."

This is another of my favourites. Let me translate. It says that we are putting more and more men in prison and this is a disadvantage to women. It leaves one open-mouthed in admiration at the shear audacity.

"Custodial sentences for women must be reserved for serious and violent offenders who pose a threat to the public. Community solutions for non-violent women offenders should be the norm."

OK, but why should this not apply to men also? There is little difference in the proportion of the male and female prison populations committed for violent offences. For example, out of the 10 crime categories used in Ref.[8], the most common reason for imprisonment for both sexes was "violence against the person", standing at 28% of the prison population for both men and women. More recent data continues to show that this is persistently the case, e.g., Ref.[6]. So there is no reason for not treating male prisoners in the same way as women based on the frequency of crimes of violence. It is just flagrant discrimination.

"Women must never be sent to prison…to teach them a lesson."

I could not believe I had read this right. Surely there has always been an element of punishment involved in sentencing offenders? Rehabilitation is not the only issue. As far as I am aware the principle of retributive justice, which is expected by society and victims alike, has not been suspended for male offenders – and rightly so. Why is it wrong to teach offenders a lesson if they are female? What more proof of rampant gynocentrism do you need? Princesses must never be punished, but do what you like with the scumbag men. Sarcastic, yes, but this is exactly the sentiment which prevails.

"Women have been marginalised within a system largely designed by men for men."

What does this mean? It means we cannot possibly condone treating women the same way we treat men. It's nasty in prisons, you know. Not a suitable place for women at all. Corston amplifies what it means…

"Treating men and women the same results in inequality of outcome. Equality does not mean treating everyone the same. The new gender equality duty means that men and women should be treated with equivalent respect, according to need. Equality must embrace not just fairness but also inclusivity. This will result in some different services and policies for men and women. There are fundamental differences between male and female offenders and those at risk of offending that indicate a different and distinct approach is needed for women."

Orwell could have learnt something from Baroness Corston. This is both 1984 and Animal Farm at once – both new-speak and "some animals are more equal than others". I wonder what the average member of the public would think about the statement *"Equality does not mean treating everyone the same"*. It defies belief that anyone has the nerve to pass this off as acceptable in a society which is supposed to be egalitarian. But feminists do, because we have been letting them get away with it for half a century, and over that time they have got bolder and bolder and ever more powerful.

"Coercion by men can form a route into criminal activity for some women."

The text of the report amplifies the myriad of ways in which, when women offend, it is really men's fault. Remember when you were at school aged 7 and the teacher didn't accept the excuse "Waa! waa! He *made* me do it"? Well that excuse is now acceptable – for women only, of course.

"Men in general appear better able to cope with institutional life. For men prison is a "bad patch"; for women it is "life stopping". For women, prison is not just an interruption in their lives; it can separate them from their children permanently."

Like the Baroness's suicide claim, this reverses reality. Prison is worse for women because they can lose their children? Hmm, the family courts, part of the same justice system that brings us this stuff, have taken *millions* of children off their fathers, and these men haven't even done anything wrong. But that's OK. They're just men. They don't really feel any sense of loss, it's just a "bad patch", not like real humans who have feelings. No, as far as the Baroness is concerned, men are just Neanderthal clods with no emotions whom you can treat like dogs without inconveniencing your conscience.

"Women's physical and emotional health and well-being is damaged by their experience within the criminal justice system in a way that differs from men's experiences and is beyond the comprehension of some men."

Yes, you're right there, Baroness, your concept of equality is totally beyond my comprehension. Ask yourself whether Corston researched the effects of imprisonment on men's physical and emotional health and well-being. One doubts it. It is so much easier to stick with her simple prejudice that men are Neanderthal brutes – which also extends, it seems, to limited intellectual capacity too.

"We are rightly exercised about paedophiles, but seem to have little sympathy, understanding or interest in those who have been their victims, many of whom end up in prison."

Aargh! I refer you to chapter 20 of Ref.[6] for a thorough account of what that comment misses. In brief, for starters, at least 20% of paedophiles are women, Ref.[9], and they almost always get away with it. (See also Ref.[10]). But worse, this statement could have been made with at least as much veracity of men in men's prisons. Did Corston not know that more than half of male sex offenders against females have a history of having been sexually abused as a child themselves, and most of those specifically by a woman (Refs.[11-15])? Yes, those men who are the most reviled creatures on the planet would, just a few years earlier, have been regarded as victims – if anyone had known – but they almost never do. Erin Pizzey knew this 50 years ago. Why do Corston and the rest of the feminists not know? Because they don't want to know.

"I would add that I do not rule out the need for a separate sentencing framework for women at some time in the future, indeed, the statutory duty from next April to take positive action to eliminate gender discrimination and promote equality under the Equality Act might require this in due course."

Mention of the Equality Act might bring on a whole new rant on my part. Suffice it to say that Harriet Harman's Equality Act allows for positive action to eliminate discrimination where none exists, i.e., to introduce discrimination – in this case by introducing a different "sentencing framework" for women. In other words, one law for men and another law for women. That's equality, folks.

It can hardly make very much difference since women are so advantaged in practice in any case. My blood would boil, but it's all boiled off already.

This is equality and justice brought to you courtesy of feminism.

References

[1] Corston, J. , Baroness (2007). *The Corston Report - review of women with vulnerabilities in the criminal justice system (asdan.org.uk)*.

[2] Collins, W. (2014). *UK Prisoners – The Genders Compared | The Illustrated Empathy Gap*, November 2014.

[3] Collins, W. (2015). *5 in 6 Men? A Response to Ally Fogg | The Illustrated Empathy Gap*, March 2015.

[4] Collins, W. (2016). *Observations on Davies-Corston Disagreement | The Illustrated Empathy Gap*, August 2016.

[5] Collins, W. (2018). *Sex Bias in Criminal Justice | The Illustrated Empathy Gap*, October 2018.

[6] Collins, W. (2019). *The Empathy Gap*. LPS Publishing, June 2019.

[7] Laville, S., and Taylor, M. (2014). *Prisons inspector lays out factors behind high suicide rate | The Guardian*, 21 October 2014.

[8] Berman, G., and Dar, A. (2013) *Prison Population Statistics*, House of Commons Library, Standard No SN/SG/4334, June 2013.

[9] Elliott, M. (2009). *Our blind rage at women who abuse*, The Guardian 11 June 2009.

[10] Collins, W. *Women Sex Offenders Against Children | The Illustrated Empathy Gap*, 12 November 2017. Amongst many other sources this links to a *compilation of 275 female teachers* in the USA convicted of sexual assault (or rape in US terminology) against boys they were teaching, almost all in just a few years, 2007 – 2009.

[11] O'Brien, M.J. (1989). *Characteristics of Male Adolescent Sibling Incest Offenders*. Orwell, VT: Safer Society Press.

[12] Brière, J. and Smiljanich, K. (1993). *"Childhood Sexual Abuse and Subsequent Sexual Aggression Against Adult Women"*. Paper presented at the 101st annual convention of the American Psychological Association, Toronto, Ontario.

[13] Groth, A.N. (1979). *Sexual trauma in the life histories of rapists and child molesters*. Victimology: An International Journal, 4(1), 10-16.

[14] Petrovich, M., and Templer, D.I. (1984). *Heterosexual molestation of children who later become rapists*. Psychological Reports, 54(3), 810.

[15] Murphy, N. (2017). *Are the histories of male prisoners really any less traumatic than those of female prisoners?*. Presentation at the Male Psychology Conference, University College London, 23-24 June 2017.

3. All Hale the Top Dog

This post was a brief résumé of the career and achievements of Baroness Brenda Hale on being made President of the Supreme Court. Things have moved on since 2017. Practice Direction 12J has been revised, more than once. The drive to prevent a man accused of domestic abuse, but without legal representation, to question his accuser in court has been achieved by the Domestic Abuse Act 2021, along with much else. All these changes are on a one-way ratchet in the direction of fatherlessness and declining birth rate. Reference to "coalition" refers to the Conservative–Liberal Democrat coalition government, 2010 – 2015.

Original posted on 21 July 2017

On 20/7/17 it was announced, Ref.[1], that Baroness Brenda Hale had reached the very pinnacle of her profession: she became President of the Supreme Court of the United Kingdom, the most senior judge in the land. Rejoice! Hale had been Deputy President since 2013. She had previously been a High Court Judge in the Family Division, a Lord of Appeal, and Professor of Law at Manchester. Hale was Chancellor of the University of Bristol for 12 years until 2016. Here I review a few highlights of the good Baroness's career, by way of celebration. I have stolen material shamelessly from Nick Langford's *An Exercise in Absolute Futility*, Ref.[2], a book you should read, by the way. All quotes are therefrom unless otherwise stated.

Both Brenda Hale's parents were headteachers, her siblings were two sisters, no brothers. She was educated at the all-girls Richmond High School and Girton, Cambridge – which was then also women only. She had one child, a daughter, with the husband she divorced in 1992 (Anthony Hoggett). Hale spent 18 years in academia, whilst also working part-time as a barrister. I don't think she would object to being labelled a feminist academic by background.

In 1984 Hale became the first women (and the youngest person) ever appointed to the Law Commission. She declared herself, "a feminist of the kind who would like to see changes in the way society is organised". Quoting Langford,

"She seems to have owed her position to a fellow Commissioner, Nigel Farrand, whom she later married 9 days after divorcing her first husband. In a collection of essays she had written,

Family Law no longer makes any attempt to buttress the stability of marriage or any other union....Logically we have already reached a point at which, rather than discussing which remedies should be extended to the unmarried, we should now be considering whether the legal institution of marriage continues to serve any useful purpose (Eekalaar & Kats, 1980)"

One can reasonably ask, if this was her view, why she nevertheless married twice herself, for a total of 49 years so far. Could it be that the ideological drive to eliminate marriage was medicine intended only for others to swallow?

Try telling a blue pill friend that feminism has been against marriage and working towards its destruction from the start. You will simply not be believed. It matters not how many Germaine Greer etc. quotes you throw at them. It is also interesting to reflect that the same body of opinion which is so opposed to heterosexual marriage – or, at least, in favour of its emasculation as a social force – is also so adamant that same-sex marriage is an essential feature of a decent society. How can this apparent contradiction be resolved other than by hypothesising that the true motivation behind both views is the desire to unravel the social fabric?

Noting that Hale was using the surname Hoggett at the time, Langford writes,

"Hoggett was the first Law Commissioner to introduce her personal take on hugely controversial social issues into statute law. A politically savvy feminist who embraced the usual collection of fashionable causes, she used her position as a political soap-box from which to broadcast her contentious views, making her 'the most ideological, politically-correct judge ever to have been appointed to the highest court in the jurisdiction' (Phillips, 2003). She attempted to turn the Law Commission, and thence the law itself, into an instrument of social change. Her Children Act incorporated into statute law the new practices introduced by the judiciary and consolidated the principle that the child's interests were paramount. Hoggett considered the Act her greatest achievement: the law no longer supported marriage because, 'it has adopted principles for the protection of children and dependent spouses which could be made equally applicable to the unmarried' (Amneus, 1999)."

The Act which is referred to above as "hers" is the Children Act 1989. This is the Act which contains the epochal clause,

"The rule of law that a father is the natural guardian of his legitimate child is abolished."

Since equality of opportunity is not enough, and only equality of outcome will do, I have to ask: where is my uterus? It is forbidden to acknowledge that the lack of child gestational and nurturing equipment puts men at a huge biological disadvantage. If society were truly interested in equality, this biological disadvantage would be offset by appropriate cultural and legal arrangements aimed at tying father and child more tightly together – arrangements involving paternal rights and responsibilities to the benefit of the individual father as well as society. This used to be the case, however imperfectly. The above single sentence quote is one of the most significant blows in eradicating these provisions – to the detriment of both the individual father and society as a whole. Dwell upon this the next time you hear the phrase 'deadbeat Dads', or hear news about poverty-stricken single mothers living in man deserts, or debates about the rate of male suicide. Thanks, Baroness Hale.

In contested cases of child contact which come before the Family Courts, the use of domestic violence allegations is a widespread tactic, Ref.[3]. Referring to a 2000 report by Claire Sturge and Danya Glaser, which was instrumental in the development of the CAFCASS practice direction on domestic violence, Langford writes,

"The report is fundamentally driven by the doctrine that the position of the 'primary carer' is unimpeachable and her moral supremacy incontestable. The crime of domestic violence is considered a transgression against her, and so its impact on the child is viewed in the context of the effect on her rather than directly on the child.....Brenda Hale contrived to incorporate this doctrine into the Children and Adoption Act 2002. An application by the father to have contact with his children is viewed with suspicion because access to the children can take place only through the mother, and the impact on the mother of the application is what matters to the authors, whilst the right of the child to have contact with his non-resident parent is secondary.... Contact is reinterpreted not as the child's right but as a father's unreasonable, domineering intrusion into the mother's new life.....The authors conclude that contact within a contested contact case will always be harmful, and should only take place where it is supportive to the resident parent, i.e., the mother."

Langford quotes Sturge and Glaser thus,

"If anything the assumption should be in the opposite direction and the case of the non-resident parent one of proving why he can offer something of such benefit not only to the

child but to the child's situation (i.e., act in a way that is supportive to the child's situation with his or her resident parent and able to be sensitive to and respond appropriately to the child's needs), that contact should be considered."

This battle still rages, the latest attacks upon fathers' contact being via Women's Aid's Child First campaign, Ref.[4], and the attempts to prevent a man facing a domestic violence allegation without legal representation from cross-examining his accuser. The reversal of the presumption of innocence takes on the added urgency in these cases that any ongoing relationship with a man's children may depend upon his success in proving his innocence of invented charges, without the benefit of legal representation, legal aid or (since the Domestic Abuse Act 2021) even being allowed to question his accuser. All this is accepted by the public only because they are kept largely in ignorance – until it happens to them – together with daily reminders from all directions that men are inherently dangerous and undeserving whilst women are their perpetual victims.

The Children Act 1989 Section 1(2A) directs the courts to, "presume, unless the contrary is shown, that involvement of that parent in the life of the child concerned will further the child's welfare". (This was introduced into that Act only in 2014, see Ref.[3] section 12.3 for the full story). Accordingly, judicial Practice Direction 12J states that "the Family Court presumes that the involvement of a parent in a child's life will further the child's welfare, so long as the parent can be involved in a way that does not put the child or other parent at risk of suffering harm". Whether this direction remains within Practice Direction 12J was, in 2017, under debate following the above feminist attacks on the principle. (Update: As of 6 April 2023 it now reads "the court presumes that the involvement of a parent in a child's life will further the child's welfare, unless there is evidence to the contrary", Ref.[5]).

One of the pernicious aspects of allegations of domestic violence in the context of the Family Courts is that the standard of proof required is not "beyond reasonable doubt", as it would be in the criminal courts, but "balance of evidence", i.e., just very slightly more likely than not. Baroness Hale was also influential in consolidating this standard, Langford quoting her thus,

"I would go further and announce loud and clear that the standard of proof in finding the facts necessary to establish the threshold…is the simple balance of probabilities, neither more nor less."

As a lay person it puzzles me that an allegation of a criminal offence is not dealt with in the criminal courts, where the fundamental principle of innocence until proven guilty beyond reasonable doubt would prevail. But Langford tells us that, *"family judges resist the transfer of allegations to the criminal courts: most wouldn't stand up"*. So the allegations remain within the Family Courts in which the standard of proof is far lower but the punishment much harsher: your removal from the life of your children.

Another issue in which Baroness Hale has played a role relates to cases where there is a shared residence order, the child spending a substantial amount of time in the care of the parent, usually the father, who is not the main carer. There are several ways in which the non-resident parent, usually the father, is financially disadvantaged in these circumstances. Many readers will be far better acquainted with the minutiae of these matters than myself, but roughly it is as follows. Firstly, child support payments are exclusively from the parent designated 'non-resident' to the parent designated as the resident parent (these days called "the parent with care"). A reduction in this payment is made if the non-resident parent (NRP) has the child overnight on some days on a regular basis. However, even if the NRP has the child for 3 days a week or even more, up to half the nights in the year, child maintenance payments will only be reduced to between 40% and 57% of the full amount payable if the NRP never cared for the child at all (Ref.[7]). You will read in many places that equal shared care means no child maintenance is payable, but this requires equal split of all responsibilities and all time throughout the day, a requirement which is virtually impossible to meet in practice, especially by a parent who is working full time – and hence overwhelmingly likely to be the father. This becomes a "winner takes all" system because even if a father working full time has the child for half the evenings and nights in the year, he will be designated as the NRP. Who then receives child benefit from the government is usually decided by HMRC to be the mother as she has been declared the parent-with-care by virtue of receiving child maintenance payments. Stitch up? You bet.

In addition to child support and child benefit, a separated mother as a resident parent can also receive chid tax credits (now subsumed into universal credit), none of which the non-resident father can receive. In summary, if both parents share evening/overnight care equally, and perhaps have equal expenses, but only the father works full time, the mother then gets child benefit, child tax credits (or equivalent if eligible), and child maintenance payments from the father because the mother is arbitrarily ruled the "resident parent". The father gets nothing. The vicious effect of this financial strangulation can be to frustrate the father's ability to share care of the child. Quoting Langford again, "*If they are unable to afford appropriate accommodation for their children the family courts will not award fathers overnight staying contact. Coalition changes to housing benefit rules made this situation worse by ensuring that parents not in receipt of Child Benefit were not allowed bedrooms for their children. If there are distances between fathers and mothers – and fathers usually bear the cost of travel – this can mean that fathers end up with little or no contact with their children because they simply cannot afford it*".

A number of legal challenges to these glaringly inequitable arrangements have been made by fathers over the years but with little or no success, the government appearing, as Langford puts it, "*determined to continue grotesque discrimination against fathers*". For example, a legal challenge in 2012 concerned a father who was responsible for the care of his two children for 3 days per week. He had no funds to meet his children's needs, and was seeking the Child Tax Credit payments for them to be split with the mother. Langford again, "*The issue was not that the regulations were discriminatory, which the HMRC could not dispute, but whether the discrimination was justified. In the Supreme Court, Brenda Hale ruled that the Child Tax Credit scheme had been introduced to tackle child poverty which is measured according to household income; Government targets on poverty would be easier to meet if financial support were given to single households and not split*". Nice rationalisation, Baroness.

One does not need to be especially cynical to argue that the financial difficulties of shared parenting faced by the parent who is arbitrarily designated 'absent', despite not being, seems to have been engineered to discourage the arrangement.

It is not only in the Family Courts that Baroness Hale has spread her feminist message. Perhaps her most famous quote relates to the comparative treatment of men and women in the criminal justice system. It originates from her 2005 Longford Trust Lecture and is quoted in the Equal Treatment Bench Book, Ref.[6]. Its appearance in the latter, the guidance to the judiciary on how to treat people equitably, confirms that it is now regarded as official policy – worryingly. Here it is,

"It is now well recognised that a misplaced conception of equality has resulted in some very unequal treatment for the women and girls who appear before the criminal justice system. Simply put, a male-ordered world has applied to them its perceptions of the appropriate treatment for male offenders.… The criminal justice system could … ask itself whether it is indeed unjust to women."

In other words, the Baroness is claiming that it is unjust to women to treat them like men. If women were indeed treated like men in the criminal justice system, this sentiment would still be unacceptable. But women are treated far more leniently than men, as I have covered at length in previous posts (see chapter 2 on *The Corston Report*, Lady Hale's perspective aligns with that document perfectly: "*equality does not mean treating everyone the same*").

It still makes my head reel. This is the mindset of these feminists. Accepting that this is so is a red pill moment. There is a reason why the mantra is "men's rights are human rights". It's because, staggeringly, this principle needs asserting.

References

[1] Austin, H. (2017). *Baroness Hale of Richmond 'to become first woman appointed as Britain's most senior judge'*. Independent, 21 July 2017.

[2] Langford, N. (2015). *An Exercise in Absolute Futility: How feminism, falsehood and myth changed the landscape of family law*, CreateSpace Independent Publishing Platform, 5 Oct. 2015.

[3] Collins, W. (2019). *The Empathy Gap*. LPS Publishing, June 2019. Or see *Legal Aid and Domestic Violence in the Family Courts*, The Illustrated Empathy Gap, 9 February 2017.

[4] Collins, W. (2017). *332 Child Homicides*, The Illustrated Empathy Gap, 3 February 2017.

[5] Justice. (UK government), 2023: *Practice Direction 12J: Child Arrangements and Contact Orders, Domestic Abuse and Harm*, 6 April 2023.

[6] Judicial College (2023): *The Equal Treatment Bench Book*. The link is to the latest, 2023, revision, which still contains the quote given in the text.

[7] Child Maintenance System Calculator (accessed 13/10/24)

4. False Allegations in the Family Courts

I have corrected the claim that the average number of incidents suffered by victims of domestic abuse was "at least 3" to "at least 2.1", and have amended the percentage reporting to the police to be consistent with the same source. The argument is not significantly affected and indicates that more than half, perhaps about two-thirds, of allegations of domestic abuse in the family courts are false. Whilst all estimates of rates of false allegation are highly uncertain, this article definitively establishes that the contrary claim, that the proportion of false allegations in the family courts is "very small", has no basis whatsoever and has arisen merely as a woozle – a claim which has no empirical basis and which has gained acceptance simply through repetition. Unfortunately, the Ministry of Justice continues to find it convenient to believe it (or to pretend to) and as a result a vast number of fathers are sundered from their children's lives.

Original posted on 14 September 2020

In my first book, *The Empathy Gap*, Ref.[1], section 19.6, I discuss false allegations of rape and the difficulty of obtaining a secure estimate of the rate of false allegations due to the extremely wide spread of reported data. However, I also show in that section, using only data from National Statistics, that 77% of allegations of rape made to the police appear to be false. (For a more recent critique of this and other estimates of the rate of false rape allegations see Ref.[2]).

This article addresses a different question: the rate of false allegations of domestic abuse (including rape) made in the context of Private Law Children Act cases in the Family Courts in England and Wales. My conclusion is grossly in conflict with the claims made in the June 2020 Family Justice Review that only a very small proportion of such allegations are false. I show here that this claim by the Family Justice Review is unsupported by any sources claimed in the review itself, despite appearances to the contrary.

Indeed there appears to be no evidence at all to support the contention that the rate of false allegations in the family courts is small. In contrast two simple and independent arguments presented below, and based on National Statistics alone, suggest that *most* such allegations are false.

4.1 The Prevalence of Allegations in the Family Courts

The best data for the percentage of private family law cases involving allegations of domestic abuse were provided by the Ministry of Justice research team as a private communication to the charity FNF-BPM Cymru together with HMCTS (HM Courts & Tribunals Service) and is shown in Table 4.1 below.

	Number of cases with harm alleged			Total cases	
	Start of case	During case	Total	Started	% harm alleged
2011	20,876	3,133	24,009	49,066	48.9%
2012	21,934	3,309	25,243	52,062	48.5%
2013	21,484	3,747	25,231	54,624	46.2%
2014	17,947	2,874	20,821	42,115	49.4%
2015	17,694	3,505	21,199	43,347	48.9%
2016	19,607	4,139	23,746	48,246	49.2%

Table 4.1: Percentage of private family law cases involving allegations of domestic abuse (England and Wales)

The best estimate is therefore that 49.2% of private family law cases involve allegations of domestic abuse. Independent support for a figure close to 50% comes from academic studies, Refs.[3,4], both of which involved allegations of domestic abuse in very close to 50% of their samples of cases. In June 2020 the literature review conducted by Adrienne Barnett for the MOJ's Family Justice Review compiled nine sources which all showed allegation rates in child arrangement cases of about 50% or greater (see Table 4.1 of Ref.[5]).

4.2. Prevalence of Partner Abuse and Domestic Abuse in the General Public

The annual Crime Surveys for England & Wales (CSEW) are generally regarded as the best indicators of the true volume of crimes, including intimate partner abuse. Figure 4.1 has been plotted from the data in Table 6a of the 2019 Crime Survey for England and Wales, Ref.[6].

Figure 4.1 shows all partner abuse against people aged 16 to 74, including sexual abuse, by sex of victim, broken down by marital status: married, cohabiting, single, separated, divorced or widowed. (Recall that partner abuse does not require the partners to be living together, or ever to have lived together). Each bar of the histogram indicates the percentage of respondents with that marital status who reported partner abuse in the survey.

It is clear that partner abuse (and actually domestic abuse generally) is far more prevalent amongst the separated or divorced, and least common amongst married couples (a fact which never seems to emerge in the popular narrative).

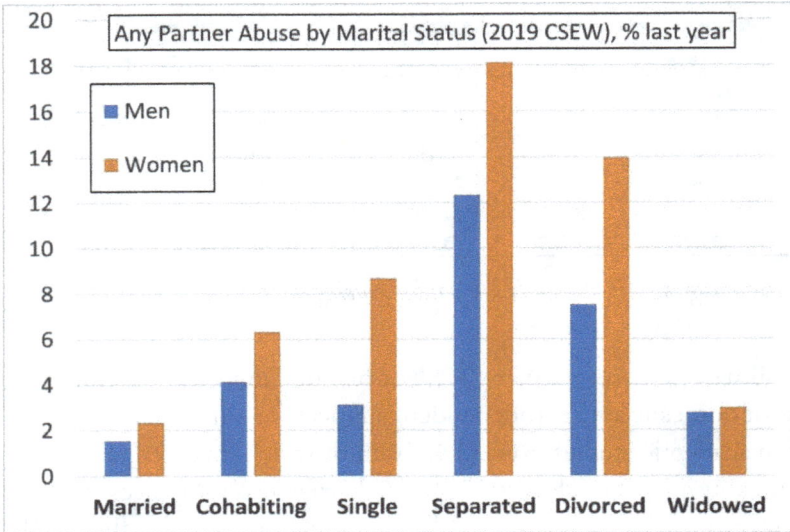

Figure 4.1: Partner abuse by marital status and victim's sex, from Ref.[6].

4.3. Implications for the Rate of False Allegations

As 50% of private law cases involve allegations of abuse, but Figure 4.1 indicates that even for the case of separated couples the true underlying rate of abuse does not exceed 18% according to the CSEW (our best guide) the implication is that 64% of allegations of abuse in the family courts are false.

A potential problem with that estimate needs discussion, namely that the abuse data of Figure 4.1 relate to abuse suffered "in the last year". There is therefore a potential for larger prevalence figures to apply if earlier years were also taken into account. In this respect note that we are interested in counting victims, not counting incidents. Hence, the data will not be affected by earlier abuse suffered by a victim who also suffered abuse in the last year (since that victim is already counted). Any enhanced prevalence can only relate to individuals who suffered no abuse in the last year, but did suffer abuse in earlier years. However, there are likely to be few such cases for separated couples, for the following reason.

The dominant feature of Figure 4.1 is the strong association between the prevalence of abuse and being separated or divorced. The prevalence of abuse is highest in the "separated" category, indicating that abuse tends to peak soon before, or soon after, separation. Consequently, cases of separated couples where there has been no abuse in the last year, but there was abuse earlier, are anomalous in relation to the trend suggesting there will be very few such cases.

In passing I note that the sampling used by ONS/CSEW reproduces reasonably well the proportions of the general population within the various marital status categories (see Ref.[7]).

4.4. Estimate from Police Recorded Domestic Abuse Data

In England & Wales, Ref.[6] Table 13 indicates that the number of offences recorded by the police and flagged as "domestic abuse related" was 746,219 in the year ending 31 March 2019. However, Tables D5 to D7 of the corresponding demographics tables, Ref.[8], indicate that many of these incidents were repeat incidents involving the same victim. The average number of incidents per victim may be estimated from the data in these Tables to be at least 2.1. Hence the number of victims of domestic abuse recorded by police in that year was about 355,000.

In round numbers about 55,000 private law Children Act cases go through the family courts in England & Wales per year (having continued to increase beyond the dates covered by Table 4.1), hence involving about 110,000 parents. This is 0.23% of the adult population of England & Wales (which is about 48 million aged 16 and over). Hence, if these 110,000 parents were a random cross-section of the adult public we could expect 0.23% x 355,000 = 817 parents in private family law to have reported domestic abuse to the police in the year.

However, these 110,000 parents are not a random cross-section of the public. We have seen from Figure 4.1 that separated partners experience far higher levels of abuse. For partner abuse, the largest figures are for separated women, being 18%, or 15% of both sexes combined. These figures compare with the population average partner victimisation of women of 5.6%, or 4.2% for both sexes combined (Ref.[6], Table 1a). Hence, separated people experience 3.6 times the prevalence of abuse compared to the average. Hence, in round numbers we could expect that, say, 3.6 x 817 ≈ 2,940 parents in private family law would have reported domestic abuse to the police. This compares with about 27,500 allegations of victimhood being made within the family courts (i.e., 50% of 55,000).

The huge gap between the expected 2,940 people reporting domestic abuse to the police, and the 27,500 allegations of victimhood made in court is reduced when account is taken of the known under-reporting of domestic abuse. The point here is that domestic abuse is generally under-reported but is likely to be reported in the context of a family court case. Ref.[8] Table D8 indicates, for the years ending March 2017 or 2018, that between 27% and 46% of people reported the offence to police. Hence the 2,940 reports to police would correspond to between 2,940 / 0.46 = 6,391 and 2,940 / 0.27 = 10,888 actual offences. [It is worth noting that for those that did not report abuse to the police, the most common reason was that the abuse was too trivial or not worth reporting, 45.5%].

Finally, then, a generous estimate is that about 11,000 of the 55,000 cases in private law per year might be expected to involve domestic abuse. This compares with about 27,500 allegations being made, so we conclude that 60% of allegations of domestic abuse made in private family law are false. This is indeed very close to the estimate made without using police data in section 3 (i.e., 64%).

Moreover, based on the CSEW survey evidence, 45.5% of the (genuine) 11,000 victims would have regarded the offence in question to be "too trivial to report" – before they were involved with the family court, that is. This suggests that 78% of allegations of domestic abuse made in the family courts are either false or too trivial to have a bearing on court proceedings.

4.5. The MOJ's Family Justice Review

This was a "consultation" commissioned by the MOJ to address the risk of harms to children and parents in private law family cases. The Family Justice Review Panel, and the associated report authors, are known to be partisan with a record of advocacy on behalf of mothers. There were no balancing voices speaking for fathers at all. The Family Justice Reports were published in June 2020, Refs.[9,10]. The main report makes this statement,

"The literature suggests that there is a perception amongst some professionals that mothers in child arrangements cases make false allegations of domestic abuse as part of a 'game playing' exercise to delay or frustrate contact. However, research suggests that the proportion of 'false' allegations of domestic abuse is very small."

The Main Report references section 7.2 of the companion Literature Review by Adrienne Barnett, Ref.[5], in support of this contention. (For a critique of the partisan nature of Dr Barnett's work see Ref.[11]). Only one paragraph of that section addresses the issue of false allegations. It is this,

"Hunter and Barnett (2013) noted that whenever objective efforts are made at quantifying 'false allegations' of domestic abuse, the proportion of unfounded allegations turns out to be very small. Allen and Brinig (2011) found not only that 'false' allegations in divorce proceedings (including in applications for protective injunctions) constituted only a very small proportion of domestic violence claims, but that the ratio of men to women making false claims was 4:1. Some professionals interviewed by Harwood (2019) commented that the prevalence of false allegations is hard to gauge because they are so rarely tested."

The last sentence is true. Findings-of-Fact are held very seldom to examine domestic abuse allegations in the family courts (Ref.[5] indicates typically fewer than 10%, often far fewer). Even when fact finding hearings are held, they are rarely conclusive.

The above quote appears to include two sources of support for the contention that false allegations constitute "only a very small proportion of domestic violence claims", namely Refs.[12,13]. Actually there is only one, Ref.[13], because, when one takes the trouble to read Ref.[12], one finds that all it contains on the matter is this,

"The spectre of false allegations is a recurrent trope in all discussions of domestic violence, but whenever objective efforts are made at quantification, the proportion of unfounded allegations turns out to be very small."

…and Ref.[12] then cites Ref.[13] in support of this claim. It would appear that after many years devoted to these studies, these leading "experts" in the field have only that one source to support their contention that false allegations constitute "only a very small proportion of domestic violence claims" (and that reference is from North America, not the UK).

I note that the authors of Ref.[12], Rosemary Hunter and Adrienne Barnett, were the authors of the Family Justice Review Final Report and the associated Literature Review respectively (Ref.[9]). Both these authors have been partisan advocates on these matters for many years. They are guilty here of trying to big-up the support for their contention that false allegations are rare by circular referencing – to hide the extreme sparsity of such support.

It turns out that the support for their contention that false allegations are "only a very small proportion of domestic violence claims" is not merely sparse but non-existent because Ref.[13] does not provide it either.

Let us note immediately that this reference uses data from the State of Oregon in 1997: a different jurisdiction, a different Nation State, and 27 years old. There is a rather obvious question mark over the relevance of this work to England & Wales in 2024. That this is the best 'evidence' that Hunter and Barnett can dredge up is telling in itself.

But the key issue is the definition of "false allegation" used by Ref.[13]. The definition is given in this quote.

"the divorce records contain information on whether accusations of domestic violence (abuse) were made and whether or not the court issued protective orders based on these accusations. We call cases where an abuse claim was made but no order issued a 'false claim'."

But this is an utterly preposterous measure of false allegations. Protection orders are issued based on the complainants' claims – essentially as a precaution pending later investigations (which generally never come). This definition presupposes that all cases where a Protection Order was issued were valid allegations. But that is the very claim which is in dispute. It is circular logic which assumes what it purports to prove.

This ridiculous definition of "false allegation" explains the extraordinary claim, based on Ref.[13], that "the ratio of men to women making false claims was 4:1". If that claim did not make the MOJ question the veracity of the source, one wonders if they read their own reports at all. Now we see that all that statement really means is that Protection Orders are refused four times more often when the complainant is male. *Quelle surprise!*

Similarly, in the context of female complainants, the very low rate of what Ref.[13] calls "false allegations" actually means only that female complainants are virtually always granted a protection order. But this does not imply anything about the validity of the allegation because orders are not made on the basis of any investigation or finding of facts, but upon a principle of precaution.

We can be sure that if any real evidence existed to support the claim that the proportion of false domestic abuse allegations in the family courts is small, then Hunter and Barnett, and the rest of those involved in the Family Justice

Review, would certainly have found it and reported it. We can conclude there is no such evidence.

4.6. Conclusions

Two independent methods, based on National Statistics alone, imply that about 60% to 64% of allegations of domestic abuse made in private law cases in the family courts are false.

Moreover, 78% of such allegations are either false or too trivial to have a bearing upon the court proceedings.

Claims made in the Family Justice Review that "the proportion of 'false' allegations of domestic abuse is very small" are unsupported, the apparent support provided in the Literature Review of Ref.[9] being fatally flawed, if not actually fraudulent.

4.7. Recommendations

The magnitude of the impact of the above findings on the Family Justice Review, and the fact that this high rate of false allegations has been ignored, invalidates the Family Justice Review, which should therefore be withdrawn.

The simple arguments presented here cannot be unknown to the authors of the Family Justice Review reports, given their many years' experience in these matters. This implies that the gross misrepresentation of false allegations within the Family Justice Review reports must have been done deliberately to mislead the MOJ on this key issue. Authors who set out deliberately to mislead should not be employed in future reviews.

Needless to add, none of this has had any impact on the direction of travel of the MOJ since the original article was written in 2019.

References

[1] Collins, W. (2019). *The Empathy Gap*. LPS Publishing, June 2019.
[2] Bradford, R. (2022). *False allegations of rape: the true extent remains unknown*. Male Psychology / The Magazine, 1 March 2022.
[3] Hunt, J. and Macleod, A. (2008). *Outcomes of applications to court for contact orders after parental separation or divorce*. Ministry of Justice, Family Law and Justice Division. September 2008. Authors from the Oxford

Centre for Family Law and Policy Department of Social Policy and
Social Work University of Oxford.

[4] Harding, M. and Newnham, A. (2015). *How do County Courts Share Care
of Children between Parents*. The universities of Reading and Warwick,
May 2015.

[5] Barnett, A. (2020). *Domestic abuse and private law children cases A literature
review*. Ministry of Justice Analytical Series, 2020. Author from Brunel
University.

[6] Office for National Statistics (2019a). *Domestic abuse prevalence and victim
characteristics*. This web page links to several years' data, see the 2019
dataset, though others will be very similar.

[7] Office for National Statistics (2019b). *Population estimates by marital status
and living arrangements, England and Wales*. (The 2019 dataset would have
been used in the original post).

[8] Office for National Statistics (2019c). *Crime in England and Wales:
Annual Trend and Demographic Tables*. (The February or July 2019 dataset
would have been used in the original post).

[9] Ministry of Justice (2020 update). *Assessing risk of harm to children and
parents in private law children cases* (a consultation).

[10] Hunter, R., Burton, M., and Trinder, E. (2020). *Assessing Risk of Harm to
Children and Parents in Private Law Children Cases: Final Report*. Ministry of
Justice, June 2020. The authors were Professor Rosemary Hunter,
University of Kent, Professor Mandy Burton, University of Leicester,
and Professor Liz Trinder, University of Exeter.

[11] Bradford, R.A.W. (2020). *The Language of Deceit, Division and Dominance*.
New Male Studies, Vol 9, Issue2 (2020) 1–21.

[12] Hunter, R., and Barnett, A. (2013). *Fact-Finding Hearings and the
Implementation of the President's Practice Direction: Residence and Contact
Orders: Domestic Violence and Harm*. A Report to the Family Justice
Council, January 2013. Rosemary Hunter and Adrienne Barnett on
behalf of the FJC Domestic Abuse Committee.

[13] Brinig, M., and Allen, D.W. (2011). *Do Joint Parenting Laws Make Any
Difference?* Notre Dame Law School. Journal of Empirical Legal Studies,
Vol 8, Issue 2, 304–324, June 2011

5. Vetting? What Vetting?

This is a shortened version of the original blog post. As far as I am aware the 2019 3rd edition of the Respect Toolkit remains the current version at the time of writing. It is worth readers noting that, in practice, what happens when a male domestic abuse victim phones a helpline (whether the Dyn Project or another) will depend upon the individual answering the phone. There are decent people out there who do not necessarily conform to the inequitable policies their organisations would support in principle. Nevertheless, surveys continue to find that male victims seeking help are overwhelmingly disbelieved. (NB: In the context of the time, my usage of "Welsh Assembly Member" is correct. This would become "Member of the Welsh Parliament" only the month after the original blog post).

Original posted on 22 April 2020.

In 2017, Welsh grandmother Anne O'Regan complained to the EHRC (Equality and Human Rights Commission) about the Dyn Project, a Welsh domestic abuse service for men operated by Safer Wales and supported by the Welsh government. She complained that the service was discriminating against men by subjecting callers to a vetting procedure, something not done for female callers to similar helplines. Despite the complaint being directed through her Welsh Assembly Member, the EHRC's initial reaction was that there was no basis for the complaint. The EHRC Wales Commissioner's office initially replied, Ref.[1],

"The Dyn Project provides support to Heterosexual, Gay, Bisexual and Trans men who are experiencing domestic abuse from a partner. The Dyn Project has developed five guiding principles for its work with men. These include that a clear screening protocol is essential in order to identify, and respond appropriately, to counter-allegations. Screening is not commonplace within services for women because women constitute the overwhelming majority of those abused."

The informed reader will spot some problems with this, one being that the repeated claim that "women constitute the overwhelming majority of domestic abuse victims" by a cabinet minister in parliament has been criticised by the UK Statistics Authority. They stated, Ref.[2], *"The phrase 'overwhelming majority' is a subjective statement. However, it may imply that a larger proportion of victims are female than the statistics show."* But more fundamentally the argument is spurious anyway, and actually quite horrible. Would those proposing this preposterous rationalisation agree that screening ethnic minority callers to helplines would be justified on the basis that they are just that – minorities?

But, helpfully, the above quote does tell us this: *"screening is not commonplace within services for women"*. Also very usefully it confirms, in the context of the Dyn service for male complainants, that *"a clear screening protocol is essential"*. You will not be surprised, but it is useful to have it confirmed.

Mrs O'Regan and her Welsh Assembly Member persisted. The persistence paid off, the EHRC being persuaded to seek independent legal advice. The result was, it seemed, clear enough. In a further communication later in 2017 the EHRC Wales wrote, Ref.[1],

"...our view is that a policy of screening male but not female callers to an advice line is likely to constitute direct discrimination, in breach of section 13 of the Equality Act 2010. Although women comprise the overwhelming majority of victims of domestic abuse, this does not mean that a comparison between the way men and women are treated by the providers of the helpline is not a comparison between similarly situated individuals."

Great Scott – logic! In these benighted times this constituted quite a triumph and so hit the press, e.g., Ref.[3].

If you expected that this would be the end of vetting male callers to domestic abuse helplines, think again. This was not the final word. The final word was that any service offering support to both sexes which treated the two sexes differently based on their sex would be in breach of the Equality Act. But a helpline may legitimately provide support to one sex only, such as the Dyn Project. There is then no breach of the Act if their procedures differ from the procedures applied by another service providing support to the other sex. You didn't imagine the forces of institutionalised prejudice would be defeated so easily, did you?

The screening of male complainants can be traced to the charity Respect, which provides guidance on how male callers to domestic abuse services are to be treated. I had something to say about this matter in Ref.[4]. At that time Respect's *Toolkit for Work with Male Victims* was in its second edition, dated 2013. The principal author of that second edition of the Toolkit was none other than Thangam Debbonaire, Labour MP for Bristol West and a shadow minister, who was then (in 2012/13) the Research Manager at Respect. Immediately prior to that, Debbonaire was an officer in the Women's Aid

Federation of England. We must assume that, with her background, Debbonaire would have been familiar with the procedures employed with female callers to Women's Aid charities. And we already know what that is from the EHRC's response: *screening is not commonplace within services for women.* Well, of course not, because Women's Aid is the very organisation which promoted the dictum *"believe the victim"* – in the context of women only, of course.

Imagine, then, you are in Debbonaire's position in Respect in 2012/13 having been asked to author guidance on the treatment of male callers. As a person dedicated to equality, what could one possibly do but recommend the same procedure already familiar from its use with female victims? Instead what Debbonaire and her co-workers produced was the *Toolkit for Work with Male Victims 2nd ed*, some 81 pages of hurdles for male victims to clear before being believed. I'll say a little more about what the Toolkit contains when I get to its more recent edition shortly.

However, Respect also accredit perpetrator programmes and you may want to see what I had to say about their approach to this in Ref.[4]. I note that the Respect Standard has been reissued since that blog article and I have not deconstructed it. However, it requires that programmes to be accredited share their Principles, one of which is,

"Organisations work in a way that is gender informed, recognising the gender asymmetry that exists in the degree, frequency and impact of domestic violence and abuse. They understand that men's violence against women and girls is an effect of the structural inequality between men and women and that its consequences are amplified by this."

This ideological position is at variance with empirical reality which shows that, on the contrary, the degree, frequency and impact of domestic abuse on men is comparable to that on female victims, and the cause is not structural inequality, Ref.[6].

Nothing fundamental has changed in the feminist mindset which underpins all Respect's advice and operations, although they may now be better at disguising it. That being the case, the perceptions which inform their work will be just as they expressed in their 2008 Position Statement, long since removed from their site (but recorded in my original blog post). You should not expect equitable treatment of men and women to emanate from this source. If equitability were intended, why would there be a need for a 107 page Toolkit for men whilst needing nothing at all for female complainants other than "believe the victim"?

The bulk of Respect's 107 page 2019 *Toolkit for Work with Male Victims 3rd edition*, Ref.[5], is focussed on screening out male callers who cannot prove their case. Here are some extracts,

Section 2.4: "*...you will find that perpetrators of domestic violence perceive themselves to be the victims. This is a very common strategy (unconscious or conscious) for perpetrators to use and one which they may use very effectively if we don't have ways of identifying who is doing what to whom and with what consequences. Commonly perpetrators whose partners have used some form of self-defence or violent resistance will identify themselves as primary victims in that moment.*"

Section 4: "*Victim who is actually a perpetrator. Sometimes, if the person using intimate partner violence has experienced force used by their victim as self-defence, defence of children, resistance or retaliation they may be wrongly identified – or wrongly present – as a victim.*"

Section 4.2: "*The dangers of incorrectly identifying someone: ....if men are incorrectly identified as the victim when they are in fact the perpetrator, this will mean that their partner/ex is identified incorrectly as the perpetrator or as part of a 'mutually violent couple'.*"

Section 7: "*Given that the majority of perpetrators are male and that perpetrators are often prone to manipulation or minimisation of the violence they have used, practitioners are rightly concerned that they may be approached by men who present as victims but are in fact perpetrators. Evidence from current male victims' services confirms that this happens. A significant number of men calling the Men's Advice Line who initially identify as victims change their own identification by the end of the call or provide information about the violence in their relationships which strongly suggests that they are either not a victim or in fact are the perpetrator....practitioners are also concerned that they don't make situations more dangerous for the partners of men who present as victims but are actually perpetrators.*"

Section 7.3: "*During the course of a relatively short conversation, men provide a great deal of information in response to the questions put to them, which help staff to make an initial assessment of who is doing what to whom and with what consequences....It will also help to inform them about when it is appropriate to ask a man to consider some of the effects of his behaviour on his partner or to challenge him more directly.*"

One of the most surprising claims in the 2019 Toolkit is in Section 5: *"Most research indicates that mutual violence is very rare, some even suggests that there is never an equal use of violence and abuse"*. This is in flat contradiction with the PASK Project, Ref.[7], which concluded, based on a vast meta-analysis, that most of domestic abuse is bi-directional.

One of the tools provided to carry out the recommended vetting of male callers is the Checklist of 23 questions in Section 4.4. The striking thing about this checklist is that it requires recording of evidence, or absence of evidence. Quite what constitutes evidence in the context of a telephone call is something I find mystifying, but apparently *"professionals who are skilled and experienced in working with responses to intimate partner violence will be able to use their experience, clinical judgement and sense of authenticity"*. Oh, righto. If the person answering the phone believes you or not – OK, understood.

The first 5 questions in the Checklist are about forms of violence which the caller might have experienced, as one would expect. Question 7 asks whether the caller's accounts of violence appear to be "authentic". (That'll be about being believed again, then). The other 17 questions all relate to the caller's potential abusive behaviours or issues which would undermine his credibility.

No vetting then – just a checklist that concentrates far more on discrediting than believing. And to be believed you must have evidence.

On this basis the caller is assigned to one of five categories, only one of which is "victim of domestic violence", the others all include, to varying extents, a degree of culpability.

So how does Respect's *Toolkit* get around the little awkwardness posed by the Welsh EHRC's legal ruling, quoted above? This is how the *Toolkit* gives the casual reader assurance,

Section 4.1: *"Organisations supporting female and male victims of domestic abuse must ensure that their assessment processes are consistent and cohesive. Respect does not recommend the use of a separate assessment process for male and female victims, as there is a risk that one client group might inadvertently be discriminated against, by having to overcome added barriers to receive a service. For example, the organisation should decide that both female and male service users are proactively asked about their use of violence and abuse when assessed, or that neither male or female service users are asked."*

Section 5: "*The assessment tools and forms that follow are designed for agencies offering a face-to-face service to male victims of domestic violence, ideally in a multi-agency setting. Respect does not recommend the use of separate assessment processes for male and female service users to organisations supporting both client groups. Before using this assessment tool with male service users, the organisation should consider what assessment is carried out with female service users, and ensure that neither client group is disadvantaged by processes that may be disproportionately onerous.*"

Got that?

Happy now?

I did forewarn you about the loophole in the EHRC's ruling. And note how carefully the above paragraphs are phrased. The casual reader will be reassured. But the principle of equal treatment only applies to an organisation providing services to both sexes.

Respect's Men's Advice Line, and Safer Wales's Dyn Project, provide services only to men. They are not obliged to adopt the same processes as another service supporting women. The above paragraphs are a smokescreen. My guess is that they were included in the 2019 revision of the Toolkit specifically to avoid falling foul of the EHRC's 2017 ruling. But, make no mistake, the purpose of the Toolkit is explicitly to present a process for male complainants which differs radically from how women are usually treated by women's helplines. And this remains legal for single-sex services.

In 2020 the threat of domestic abuse during covid-19 lockdowns was bigged-up by politicians who claimed that, irrespective of sex, victims should phone the 24 hour *National Domestic Abuse Helpline* (a service run by the uber-feminist charity Refuge). Deborah Powney repeatedly asked what actually happens when a man calls that helpline. She also repeatedly asked Respect about screening male callers to their Men's Advice Line. Eventually she got a response from Respect, Ref.[8]: "*we wanted to confirm that the Men's Advice Line doesn't screen callers, no one has to prove they're a victim to get a service*".

In what way can Respect's insistence that "*the Men's Advice Line doesn't screen callers, no one has to prove they're a victim to get a service*" be regarded as anything other than mendacity? Their own Toolkit requires male callers to provide evidence that they are victims, and this is precisely a requirement to prove they are a victim.

References

[1] All the original correspondence to and from the EHRC Wales Office is in my personal possession but not publicly available.

[2] Bell, D. (2019). *Stats Watchdog Upholds MBC Complaint over Government's Misleading Description of Proportion of Domestic Abuse Victims Who Are Female*. Men and Boys Coalition, 11 November 2019.

[3] Western Mail (2017). *Helpline's 'discriminatory' policy against males changed*. Western Mail, 21 November 2017.

[4] Collins, W. (2017a). *UK PV Perpetrator Programmes – Part 1*, The Illustrated Empathy Gap, 29 July 2017.

[5] Martin, L. and Panteloudakis, I. (2019). *Toolkit for Work with Male Victims of Domestic Abuse*. Respect (charity), 3rd edition, 2019.

[6] Collins, W. (2017b). *UK PV Perpetrator Programmes – Part 2*, The Illustrated Empathy Gap, 4 August 2017.

[7] Hamel, J. (2012). *Partner Abuse State of Knowledge Project Findings At-a-Glance*. November, 2012.

[8] The Glass Blind Spot. *What Happens When Someone Calls The National Domestic Abuse Helpline? [Short Answer]*. YouTube 26 November 2021.

6. Misogyny Hate Crime: How the Trick is Performed

The burden of this article is to outline the process by which well-planned and well-resourced activism can result in the desired outcome being implemented in legislation. In this case, making misogyny a hate crime in the UK, they have not succeeded (yet). I have shortened the original post and brought up to date (as of October 2023) the legislative position.

Original posted on 4 October 2020.

At what point do we draw the line?

And when that line is crossed, what next?

What is a "Consultation" for? For those who think it is to test public opinion so that said opinion may be used to steer government policy, you really haven't been paying attention. A Consultation is an announcement to the activists that the endgame of this particular play is near at hand, in this case a Law Commission Consultation.

Does anyone think that when the government, under Theresa May as Home Secretary, called in September 2014 for "Consultation" on the proposed criminalisation of coercive and controlling behaviours that this was anything other than a charade? I didn't, even at the time, despite making a 100+ page submission (under J4MB cover), Ref.[1].

Then there was the hilarious Consultation on the 2020 Divorce, Dissolution and Separation Bill. 80% to 83% of people who responded disagreed with the key proposals of the Bill, a fact that was raised by more than one member of the House of Lords during the Bill's passage, Ref.[15]. What difference did it make? None.

Need I mention the various Consultations leading up to the Domestic Abuse Act 2021? I hope not. I haven't the strength.

Consultations give activists the opportunity to formalise their policy opinions in a form that gives legitimacy to the relevant government ministry's adoption of them. As such, they come near the end of the activists' campaign.

These things are planned and prepared many years in advance. So it has been with the drive to make misogyny a crime within primary legislation. It has not suddenly popped up in 2023 or 2020, or even since the 2018 Bracadale report, Ref.[2]. It probably first came to public notice in July 2016 when Sue ****, after just three weeks in the job as Chief Constable of Nottinghamshire, announced that, *"Nottinghamshire Police, in partnership with Nottingham Women's Centre, has become the first force in the country to recognise misogyny as a hate crime."*

You may be puzzled. You should be. The police cannot simply create new crimes. That is the job of parliament. Let me spell out how a pressure group can create new primary legislation from nothing.

You don't start from now, you start from at least 6 years ago, Ref.[3], probably much longer back than that. "You" in this case means Nottingham Women's Centre. They started by creating a bit of advocacy research funded by the Nottinghamshire Police and Crime Commissioner.

On the strength of that, Nottingham Women's Centre invited Nottinghamshire Police to a series of *Safer for Women Conferences* where the coppers were regaled with suitably worrisome stories illustrating *"the breadth of violence and intimidation that women experience on a daily basis"* in the communities they police. This is Women's Aid training the police. It is routine in the VAWG context. Nothing new here, move along.

But the real purpose of these training sessions is to *"encourage more women to come forward and report offences"*. They are not so foolish as to lobby immediately for primary legislation against misogyny. They prepare the ground first. The plan is to get data showing how huge is the problem of misogyny. But they, i.e., Women's Aid, do not do this themselves; they get the police to do it. By this means it attains the aura of independence (no need to mention that the police have been trained by Women's Aid). But even better, as police data, the "hate crime statistics" appear to be real crime data.

They are not, of course. Because the police cannot create new crimes. The term "hate crime" is used to conjure the impression of a statutory offence; it's all part of the manipulation of perception and opinion. But the definition that Nottinghamshire Police adopted (and one can be certain where it came from), was,

"A hate crime is simply any incident, which may or may not be deemed as a criminal offence, which is perceived by the victim or any other person, as being motivated by prejudice or hatred."

The alert may spot that this does not align with the official CPS definition of hate crime which is now in force, Ref.[4], which does require the incident to be a crime. But you miss the point. The adoption of the above interim definition was to cast the net as wide as possible. The purpose here, you see, is to inflate the statistics as much as possible. The CPS definition of hate crime is,

"Any criminal offence which is perceived by the victim or any other person, to be motivated by hostility or prejudice, based on a person's disability or perceived disability; race or perceived race; or religion or perceived religion; or sexual orientation or perceived sexual orientation or transgender identity or perceived transgender identity."

The aim of the activists in this case is to get "women and girls" added to the list. The CPS add,

"There is no legal definition of hostility so we use the everyday understanding of the word which includes ill-will, spite, contempt, prejudice, unfriendliness, antagonism, resentment and dislike."

You may recall that in the CPS VAWG reports, Ref.[5], "Violence" does not mean violence, "Women" does not mean women, and "Girls" does not mean girls. Similarly, "hate" has morphed into "unfriendliness". Hate, of course, would be the state of mind of the supposed villain. But that's irrelevant. It is only the perception of the alleged "victim" – or, indeed, some bystander – which matters in the classification as a Hate Crime. If anyone on the planet perceives you as unfriendly, or detects a hint of dislike, you're toast. You may need to take acting lessons. Do you think being subject to such traps might cause you to be resentful? Oops, not allowed. Send him down.

You see how this works? The definition, especially the interim one, casts the net as wide as possible. The sole purpose is to maximise the number of "incidents" recorded by the police as hate crimes. And a key part of the police training is that they must ask about the potential for any incident they attend having been motivated by "prejudice or hatred". Your house was burgled? Could it have been motivated by hate, madam? Well, it wasn't motivated by love, I suppose.

In short, just as research may be woozled, so also police statistics can be woozled so long as you can get at them for a spot of "training". The end result is an alarming picture of rampant male vileness, oppressing women and making women fearful as a matter of everyday routine – and the police have hard statistical evidence to prove it.

Following Nottinghamshire Police recognising misogyny as a hate crime (even though it isn't) in July 2016, it was inevitable that other forces would follow suit. North Yorkshire was next in May 2017, pushed in that direction by Police & Crime Commissioner for North Yorkshire, Julia ********, and announced by Deputy Chief Constable for North Yorkshire, Lisa *******.

Just as the Nottingham Women's Centre was behind the move in that county, so in North Yorkshire there were also women's organisations in the role of *éminence grise*, specifically the Sheffield Women's Network and "women from York St John University". Who the latter individuals might be I know not, but I note that, at the time, the Pro-Chancellor and Chair of York St John University was Ann Margaret *****, CBE, and the Governor and Vice Chancellor of the University was Professor Karen *******. Whether they had any involvement I do not know.

Not to be outdone in their feminist credentials by Nottinghamshire, North Yorkshire cast the net even wider still, Ref.[6]. The offence could only be committed by men or boys, and only women and girls could be victims. Examples of offending behaviour classed as misogyny hate crime included,

- unwanted or uninvited sexual advances;
- physical or verbal assault;
- unwanted or uninvited physical or verbal contact or engagement;
- sexually graphic and explicit obscene language;
- use of mobile devices to send unwanted or uninvited messages or take photographs without consent.

"Uninvited verbal contact" means a man is not permitted to speak to a woman or a girl until spoken to. As for "uninvited messages", that applies to virtually every email or text you ever send or receive.

Taken literally, this outlaws any pro-active interaction by a male with a female.

Recall that this is a police invention, not a crime at all. Its purpose is to gather and record data to use to motivate later calls for primary legislation. Being an open invitation to regard anything as a hate crime is entirely deliberate.

Note also that, because it is an invention – essentially just some data gathering which the police choose to carry out – it is not subject to any equality restrictions. For this reason it can be done for just one sex, without any statistics on "misandry hate crimes" being gathered. (Not that men are socialised to recognise such things).

By October 2020, seven of the 43 police forces in England and Wales had classed misogyny as a hate crime (even though it isn't), some sources say eleven police forces, e.g., Ref.[16].

Whether further police forces, indeed all of them, have since adopted misogyny hate "crime" is unclear. Ref.[17] stated, in November 2021,

"Baroness Williams of Trafford, Minister of State for the Home Office, said that the Government believed it necessary to await the outcome of the Law Commission's review before making changes to police recording practices. However, she agreed that the collection of data is helpful, so committed to asking police forces to record on an experimental basis those offences perceived by victims to be based on hostility towards their sex. The minister said this would help to inform longer-term decisions once the recommendations from the Law Commission's review had been published and considered."

But then Ref.[17] concludes, citing Ref.[16],

"In October 2021 it was reported that the National Police Chiefs' Council had not yet received guidance from the Home Office about how the recording should be done."

And so to the present (October 2023).

Firstly Scotland. The *Bracadale Report*, Ref.[2], recommended that "gender" be added to the list of characteristics which would exacerbate offences. Leading feminist organisations argued against that in favour of a sex-specific misogyny ruling. In the event, the *Hate Crime and Public Order (Scotland) Act 2021*, Ref.[7], hedged its bets by giving the power over to Scottish Ministers to decide later ("Scottish Ministers may by regulations add the characteristic of sex to the list of characteristics"). As far as I am aware, this has not been done. Moreover, this clause does not empower ministers to make a sex-specific offence category.

Turning now to England & Wales. The private members' Bill, the Hate Crime (Misogyny) Bill, proposed by Wera Hobhouse MP (Lib Dem, Bath)

never got past its first reading in the Commons on 13th November 2020. This is the usual fate of private members' Bills.

However I shall concentrate here upon the Hate Crime Consultation, Ref.[9], published by the Law Commission on 23 September 2020 as this is more likely to be the prelude to primary legislation.

A Consultation might be expected (by those innocents not versed in the arts of political manipulation) to simply pose neutral questions for respondents to address, without biasing the likely responses in one direction or another. The Law Commission's "Consultation" was far from that. It actually presented the case for making misogyny a hate crime. It is a wildly partisan political position statement, with a Con-Con-Consultation tagged on.

The word "misogyny" appears in the Consultation Paper 73 times. The word "misandry" appears just once.

A report commissioned by our old friends the Nottingham Women's Centre was cited six times in the Consultation Paper, they liked it so much, Ref.[10].

But the Law Commission's favourite author was Hannah Mason-Bish of the Department of Sociology, University of Sussex. She got 28 citations, for such belters as *"Some men deeply hate women, and express that hatred freely: Examining victims' experiences and perceptions of gendered hate crime"*, Ref.[11]. The Abstract starts,

"Extensive debate about the place of gender within the hate-crime policy domain has been fuelled by national victimisation surveys indicating people's experiences of 'gender hate crime' coupled with Nottinghamshire Police's decision to begin categorising misogynistic street harassment as a form of hate crime."

Bit of a common factor in evidence, isn't there? But do you see how this "academic" journal paper is built upon the prior activism? In turn, this "academic" publication has been used to influence the Law Commission, *en route* to primary legislation (they hope).

One of the repeatedly cited works of Hannah Mason-Bish was published in *Feminist Criminology*, Ref.[12]. I'm sure readers must be familiar with that august organ. Well, you certainly won't be familiar with *White Male Criminology*.

It is difficult to convey the tenor of the Consultation Paper without quoting a great deal of it. But to avoid cluttering these pages I refer you to the original blog article, Ref.[13]. It is not just the content of these extracts which is revealing, but also the language used, which clearly emanates from the feminist lexicon. The irony is palpable as the contributions are a torrent of man-hating dressed up as a desperate need to protect women from woman-hating men. Feminists are masters at table-turning and projection.

But don't worry, there is balance…there is that one mention of misandry, remember. It was taken from that very same Nottingham Women's Centre Misogyny Hate Crime Evaluation Report, Ref.[10]. The quote reads,

"A male respondent in the Nottinghamshire Evaluation suggested that gender-based hate crime reform would fail if it didn't conform to formal equality: 'I think it should include misandry as well. 100%. Absolutely… I don't think it could ever succeed unless it was inclusive. It will absolutely fail if it only gives women protection and men not because that's not equality before the law.'"

Do note how they mention that this was the opinion of a male respondent, as if to discredit it as an example of the very misogyny they battle against. There was no need to mention the sex of other contributors, such as those quoted at length in Ref.[13]: all female and feminist.

And after the phrase "formal equality", which the respondent did not actually use, they link to the 1966 paper in *Ethics* by D Lyons *The Weakness of Formal Equality*. For those not yet versed in the corruption of the concept of "equality" this is an allusion to the brave new view that "equality does not mean treating everyone the same" (see chapter 2). It is now established in legal practice that equality may mean treating some people better, and our hapless male respondent is so behind the curve that he is unaware of this.

However, the Law Commission have now published their final report on the Consultation, Ref.[14]. Their Recommendation 8 stated,

"We recommend that sex or gender should not be added as a protected characteristic for the purposes of aggravated offences and enhanced sentencing."

Finally, we come to the Online Safety Act, Ref.[18], which received Royal Assent on 26 October 2023. The Act does not contain the word "hate". Despite that the government has stated that "illegal content that platforms will need to remove includes hate crime", Ref.[19]. But the Act does not explicitly state to what categories of persons the provision of "hate crime" relates, that is it makes no mention of "protected characteristics" in relation to hate crime provisions. Instead, the Act includes a range of priority illegal offences that social media companies must remove from their platforms.

The Act creates a new harm-based communications offence to capture communications sent to cause harm without a reasonable excuse. This offence will make it easier to prosecute online abusers by abandoning the requirement under the old offences for content to fit within proscribed yet ambiguous categories such as "grossly offensive," "obscene" or "indecent". Instead it is based on the intended psychological harm, amounting to at least serious distress, to the person who receives the communication, rather than requiring proof that harm was caused.

Ref.[20] advises that, "The new offence will consider the context in which the communication was sent. This will better address forms of violence against women and girls, such as communications which may not seem obviously harmful but when looked at in light of a pattern of abuse could cause serious distress."

However, there is no misogyny hate crime as such, nor a specific sex-based hate crime category. As always, though, the interpretation of terms like "psychological harm" and "pattern of abuse" will skew the interpretation towards females and away from males.

References

[1]   Collins. W. (2014). *Con, not Consultation*. The Illustrated Empathy Gap, 22 September 2014.

[2]   The Scottish Government (2018). *Tackling misogyny* (The Bracadale Report). 7 October 2018.

[3]   Collins, W. (2016). *The Law is a Joke*. The Illustrated Empathy Gap, 18 July 2016.

[4]   Crown Prosecution Service (accessed October 2023). *Definition of Hate Crime*. Undated.

[5]   Collins, W. (2015). *The Desolation of VAWG*. The Illustrated Empathy Gap, 4 July 2015.

[6]   Police, Fire and Crime Commissioner, North Yorkshire (2017). *Misogyny recognised as a hate crime in North Yorkshire*. 10 May 2017.

[7]   Scottish parliament (2021). *Hate Crime and Public Order (Scotland) Act 2021*.

[8]   Hobhouse, W. (2020). *Hate Crime (Misogyny) Bill - Parliamentary Bills - UK Parliament*, 4 May 2021.

[9]   Law Commission (2020). *Hate Crime Laws, A Consultation.* 23 September 2020.

[10]   Mullany, L. and Trickett, L. (2018). *Misogyny Hate Crime Evaluation Report,* 9 July 2018. The authors were Professor Louise Mullany and Dr. Loretta Trickett, of Nottingham University and Nottingham Trent University, on behalf of Nottingham Women's Centre.

[11]   Mason-Bish, H. and Duggan, M. (2019). *Some men deeply hate women, and express that hatred freely: Examining victims' experiences and perceptions of gendered hate crime*. International Review of Victimology 26(1) 112-134, 5 September 2019.

[12]   Mason-Bish, H. and Zempi, I. (2019), *Misogyny, racism and Islamophobia: Street Harassment at the Margins*. Feminist Criminology 14(5) 540-47, May 2018.

[13]   Collins, W. (2020). *Misogyny Hate Crime: How the Trick is Performed*. The Illustrated Empathy Gap, 4 October 2020.

[14]   Law Commission (2021). *Hate crime laws: Final report*. 7 December 2021.

[15]   Hansard (2020). *Divorce, Dissolution and Separation Bill [HL], Volume 801: debated on Wednesday 5 February 2020*.

[16]   Topping, A. (2021). *Tory peers to defy Boris Johnson with push to make misogyny a hate crime*. The Guardian, 8 October 2021.

[17]   House of Lords Library (2021). *Misogyny: a new hate crime?* 22 November 2021.

[18]   UK parliament (2023). *Online Safety Act 2023*. 27 October 2023.

[19]   UK government (2023). *A Guide to the Online Safety Act 2023*. 30 August 2023.

[20]   UK government (2022). *Online safety law to be strengthened to stamp out illegal content*. 4 February 2022.

7. Baroness Hale Retires

I look back on more of her achievements.

Original posted on 22 December 2019

Baroness Brenda Hale, the chief architect behind the pivotal Children Act 1989 and one-time feminist academic, retired on 10th January 2020. In chapter 3 I gave my version of her biography (admittedly partisan) when she was appointed to that role in September 2017. I will not repeat myself beyond a couple of quotes, but it would surely be discourteous not to recognise the occasion. Readers will, no doubt, be keen to watch her valedictory ceremony and speeches, Ref.[1].

I neither mourn nor celebrate her going. If it had not been her, it would have been some other feminist.

Hale was the first woman President of the Supreme Court, though that is less significant than it might appear given that the Supreme Court, a creation of the Blair/Brown governments, came into being only in October 2009. The Supreme Court assumed the judicial authority previously enjoyed by the House of Lords. This acquires an interesting political spin when one recalls their Judicial Lordships' recent (and, it now seems, remarkably pointless) ruling that Boris Johnson's proroguing of parliament was unlawful.

I disagree. In a Constitutional Monarchy, one meaningful action which the Monarch can, and is required, to take is to dissolve parliament if the so-called representatives of the people have demonstrably deviated from being representative of the people. This was already the case when the Supreme Court made their ruling, and it is even more clear now. Their ruling was, "*the decision to advise Her Majesty to prorogue was unlawful because it had the effect of frustrating or preventing the ability of Parliament to carry out its constitutional functions*". But this is incorrect. In a democracy, the ultimate sovereignty lies with the people. And in a Constitutional Monarchy the Monarch is charged with protecting that sovereignty against usurpation by errant parliamentary representatives, as was the case here. The Supreme Court, under Hale's presidency, has proved to be a highly partisan political body and this experimental appellate court should be disbanded. However, I digress.

Though I will not reprise chapter 3, there are two quotes which are worth repeating and which serve to illustrate whence she cometh,

"It is now well recognised that a misplaced conception of equality has resulted in some very unequal treatment for the women and girls who appear before the criminal justice system. Simply put, a male-ordered world has applied to them its perceptions of the appropriate treatment for male offenders.... The criminal justice system could ... ask itself whether it is indeed unjust to women."

Even more importantly, from the 1989 Children Act, para 2(4), this killer stroke is Hale's greatest achievement,

"The rule of law that a father is the natural guardian of his legitimate child is abolished."

I will return to that.

There are those who would pour praise upon Hale on the basis that the 1989 Children Act enshrined in law the Paramountcy Principle, namely that the welfare of the child should be the courts' paramount consideration. I am indebted to a commenter on the original post putting me right on that score. I quote, "The paramountcy principle was enshrined in law in the 1925 Guardianship of Infants Act and was maintained in the 1989 Act. Arguably, the principle itself is very much older; a similar principle has been used for at least 1,000 years."

Perhaps few would disagree with the principle, though it is possible to do so. The same commenter wrote of the principle, "Its great advantage is simplicity: no one else's rights need to be considered, and to all intents and purposes, parents have no rights in family law at all. Thus it keeps the decisions of the courts (and others) focused and relatively straightforward, but dismissing the rights of all other parties is a long way from justice.... Critics have suggested that the rights of the whole family should be considered, but that would vastly complicate the law."

However, I would argue that it is not that laudable principle which is contentious, but the manner by which it may be achieved.

What we have here is yet another deployment of Moral Usurpation, Ref.[2]. This is a tactic in which a valid moral concern is used to blindside us to policies which are enacted under its cover. It is a form of verbal legerdemain whose purpose is to deaden critical faculties. For example, it may seem good for a court to listen to "the voice of the child" – if it's said quickly. But that is not a policy which any parent would indulge in overmuch at home, otherwise it would be all video games and no school.

One of the many things for which the Family Courts can be criticised is the lack of monitoring of the outcomes of their own decisions – and I include Public Law as well as Private Law cases. There should be a database of millions of longitudinal case histories stretching back half a century, something any social scientist would give their right arm for. But it does not exist. Instead we are obliged to rely on "studies" coming out of an academia which is so ideologically skewed as to make most such reports worse than valueless.

How convenient it is that the feminists insist everything is a social construct and biology counts for nothing. Yet motherhood is firmly and inviolately embedded in the biological, whereas fatherhood is entirely dependent upon social approbation and reinforcement. By denying this, the feminists hide women's natural privilege. Reversing the social endorsement of fatherhood in primary legislation – abolishing the rule of law that a father is the natural guardian of his legitimate child – is the action of a bully. It is the action of the powerful and secure upon those who have not the means to defend themselves. It emanates from a mindset which still wants to extract benefit from men without giving anything back in return. There is no longer a deal on the table. There is only coercion. Then fools cry that young men today lack "commitment". But, as C.S.Lewis (or Geoff Dench) might have put it, there is a more ancient magic which men possess: in the end, they can just walk away. And now they are doing so (see chapter 54).

What lies behind all this is towering arrogance. The feminists believe that men are unnecessary. More specifically, they believe that fathers are unnecessary. The weight of evidence to the contrary cuts no ice. The feminist project is to "free" women from dependency upon men, and marriage is, in their view, the quintessential embodiment of that dependency. Ergo, the principal aim of feminism is, and always was, to smash marriage. Despite this being espoused openly in a vast outpouring of feminist literature – and being carried out very successfully in practice – the public remain unaware of this central policy objective, bamboozled as they are by the smoke screen of "equality". Here's a quote from Baroness Hale (plain Mrs Justice Hoggett at the time, I think),

"Family Law no longer makes any attempt to buttress the stability of marriage or any other union.....Logically we have already reached a point at which, rather than discussing which remedies should be extended to the unmarried, we should now be considering whether the legal institution of marriage continues to serve any useful purpose (Eekalaar & Kats, 1980)" (quoted in Ref.[3]).

...an opinion which did not prevent her marrying twice herself.

The trend away from marriage, and the related loosening of the bonds between fathers and their children, was not the sole creation of Baroness Hale – but she was part of the feminist-driven process which caused it and she had a larger part in it than most. The project of demonising men and making women fearful of men is part of the same policy direction. That fatherlessness is related to severe adverse outcomes for children is now undeniable – but that does not stop it being denied. And the blame is also so wonderfully deniable: it is all the fault of feckless men. What an odd coincidence that men have become feckless at exactly the same time that feminism successfully engineered society in accord with their ideology.

And with the decrease in marriage, and the rise in transient cohabitation and single living, comes, not only fatherlessness, but also a destruction of communities. It will not wash to lay the blame for the divisions in our society, now so painfully evident, at the door of "Tory austerity". This has been building for fifty years, across many governments of both political complexions. The one constant, and always the driver of social change, has been feminism: the Teflon ideology which is never held to account.

The beneficiaries of this social engineering are not only the two million or so men who have been mangled by the Family Courts' child arrangements over the last forty years, but also the single parents struggling to raise children alone. These single parents are not only the product of divorce, but also – and mainly – the product of the decline of marriage. Welcome to the urban man deserts. Even fifteen years ago one could identify many city postcodes – perhaps some in every major city – in which one in three families with dependent children were single parent families. And 50% - 60% of families with dependent children in these districts do not have two married (or civil partnered) parents.

Marriage is not for the benefit of men or women. It never was. It is not a lifestyle choice. Marriage was devised as a structure for the raising of children.

The attack on marriage is therefore an attack on children. But most crucially it is stable marriage that creates stable fatherhood, which is precisely why the feminists set about smashing it.

The destruction of marriage goes hand-in-hand with the drive to get women working more hours outside the home (the true objective behind the ceaseless focus on so-called pay gaps). This is to be achieved (in the minds of those who advocate this policy) by state-controlled childcare. It is fully consistent with the morphing of state education from academic education into social re-education. This is the "progressive" agenda. Brenda Hale has done her bit to push it along. To anyone who knows anything about the psychology of child development, it is a horrifying prospect.

Even those people who prefer to remember Hale mostly as a children's rights campaigner and as "the judge who tried to put children first in court settings and cases involving child welfare issues" are obliged also to recall that her creation, the 1989 Children Act, includes "the right to remove children from parents without their consent (forced/ non consensual / involuntary adoption)" and that this is presented as justified on the basis of the nebulous test of 'risk of future harm'.

Those who sup with the Devil should be aware that one's spoon can never be long enough. Once you have let the state into your family, you have compromised your authority to protect your own children. The same weapons that may seem to assist you now can later be used against you. This same nebulous risk of "future harm" has been used in the Family Courts for decades to sunder fathers from their children – and in far greater numbers than involuntary adoptions.

Researching Reform commented on this issue in the context of guidance on human rights law published by the British Association of Social Workers, Ref.[4]. The article reacts to the guidance's referring to "dispensing of parental consent to adoption" as merely "controversial" with some incredulity. The author notes that, "*Forced adoption is no longer seen as controversial by experienced academics, politicians and campaigners in this field. It is seen as a phenomenon which breaches the human rights of children and families without good reason*". The author further notes that, "*social work practice is to a very large extent not backed up by science or data*". The article also claims that covert surveillance via social media is being used by social workers, observing that, "*a spike in child welfare professionals using platforms like Facebook to spy on families and children has been particularly concerning, after a study carried out by Lancaster University confirmed that social workers were breaking the law by accessing users' personal information"*.

Non-consensual adoption is the subject of Family Court Judge Stephen Wildblood's 2019 play, as reported by **Louise Tickle in the Guardian, Ref.[5]**. Having noted that both the father and the mother are present in the Court, the play has the judge rule "I therefore dispense with the consent of the mother and of the father to the placement of Kye for adoption". But then Tickle writes,

"Listening to the words that will remove a baby from its mother, for ever, feels akin to what it must once have been like to hear a judge pronounce the death sentence. It is hard to think of a more serious act – even imprisonment – that the state can now impose than extinguishing the relationship between a parent and their child."

Yes, quite. But only the mother, it seems, will be so affected according to Tickle. And where was the Guardian's concern these last 50 years when exactly this treatment was meted out to fathers in numbers vastly greater? Empathy gap, at all?

All this has been but a precursor to an examination of the statistics of children in care (which I subsequently published in a following post, Ref.[6]). For now, consider Figure 7.1 which shows the increased numbers of children "in care" (England only) since Hale's creation, the 1989 Children Act, was passed. Figure 7.2 shows the increased number of children being adopted from care (in England) over that same period. Nearly 90% of the latter are enforced adoptions in which the parents' consent is "dispensed with".

A legacy to be proud of? I think not.

Numbers of children starting and ceasing to be looked after in the year, and numbers at 31 March

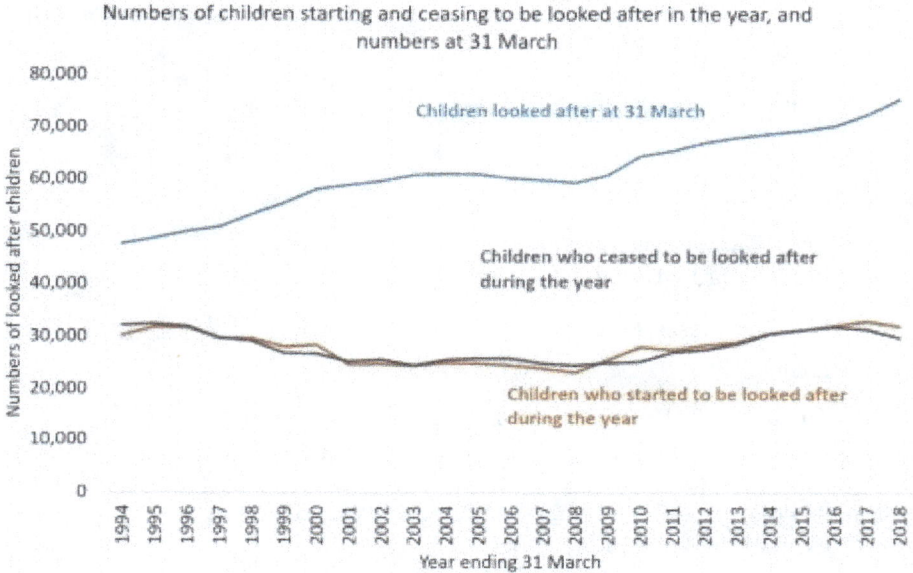

Figure 7.1: Total number of children "in care" in England (top curve)

Looked after children who were adopted during the year

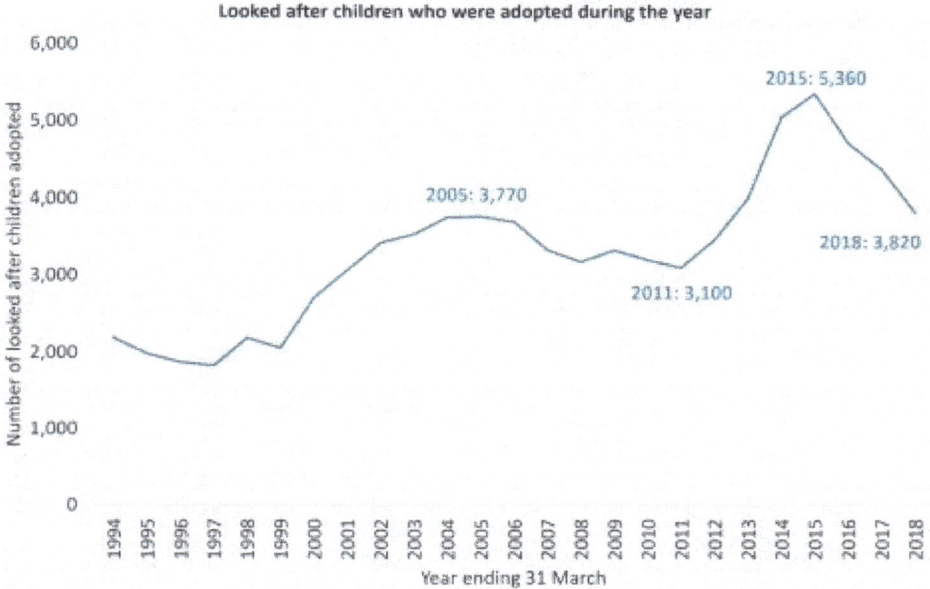

Figure 7.2: Number of children in care who were adopted, per year (England)

References

[1] Supreme Court (2019). *Lady Hale's Valedictory Remarks*. 18 December 2019.

[2] Collins.W. (2022). *The Destructivists*. Principia Publications Unlimited, 20 February 2022. (See also chapter 70).

[3] Langford, N. (2015). *An Exercise in Absolute Futility: How feminism, falsehood and myth changed the landscape of family law*. CreateSpace Independent Publishing Platform, 5 October 2015.

[4] Natasha, Researching Reform (2019). *Leading Social Work Body Publishes Human Rights Handbook*. 16 December 2019.

[5] Tickle, L. (2019). *'It's a very harsh environment': judge's play shines light on family courts*. The Guardian, 18 December 2019.

[6] Collins, W. (2019). *Children in Need: Statistics (England)*. The Illustrated Empathy Gap, 24 December 2019.

Section 2

Rape / Sexual Assault

8. A Study of False Allegations of Rape

This chapter is a shortened form of three blog posts combined. It summarises my findings from a search, in early 2018, of news media for reports of demonstrably false rape or serious sexual assault allegations among the general public. This yielded some interesting information on the reasons why people (mostly women) make false allegations, the reasons why men are sometimes falsely convicted, and the frequency of serial accusers. A separate exercise was to examine news reports of sexual assault allegations against senior politicians or celebrities, with a view to examining what proportion turned out to appear false. That, also, was salutary, especially in view of the continuing stream of male MPs (and celebrities) who lose their positions or their livelihoods as a result of untested allegations. One of the blogs starts with this quote from a lawyer,

"This isn't a story of a few rogue cops gone bad, or a crumbling, underfunded criminal justice system overwhelmed by national austerity (though both get blamed daily in courts and the press to cover a wider, more difficult truth). This is a story of a state funded system designed with political ends in mind to convict those accused of crime, because once a person is charged they must be guilty, if only the Crown can prove it." (Ref.[1]).

Originals posted on 28 January 2018, 12 February 2018, 28 February 2018

In late 2017, following the well-publicised collapses of the rape cases against Liam Allan, Isaac Itiary and Samuel Armstrong, and the exoneration of Danny Kay after four years in prison, I conducted a search of news reports for other cases of false allegation, Ref.[2]. I confined my search to the UK and to serious sexual assault, mostly rape. In this initial investigation I deliberately excluded well-known names, that is: senior politicians and celebrities. I carried out a separate search to address those cases later.

I wanted to focus on reasonably recent cases. In the event I easily found 146 cases among the general public, 106 of which were dated between 2013 and January 2018. The earliest case was 1997, but there were only 15 cases before 2010. The smaller number of cases found in earlier years will almost certainly be due simply to the difficulty of retrieving older material (especially before newspapers appeared on the internet), and cannot be assumed to be due to any lesser underlying frequency. Because I was reliant on news media, the 146 cases found will be but a tiny proportion of those that have occurred. Most will simply never attract the attention of reporters. Nothing can be concluded regarding the frequency of false allegations of rape from the number, 146, of cases I found.

Ref.[3] records my summaries of the case histories of these 146 cases of false allegation, mostly of rape but all of serious sexual assault. Ref.[4] records the data extraction categories I used and the resulting detailed data tables. Below I give a brief summary of the findings.

The actual case histories are an essential component of the overall picture. They drive home the message that, whatever their frequency, when false rape accusations are made they are a very serious crime – though they are not always treated as such by the authorities.

Rape allegations are mud that sticks indelibly. Consider a totally innocent man – he need not even have met the accuser. But not only does the accused have his life ruined for perhaps two or three years whilst the case comes up – during which time he may be suspended from work, or actually sacked, prevented from access to children – which may mean he is separated from his own family, and possibly subject to a curfew and made to wear an electronic tag – and not only might he end up bankrupt in paying for his defence – not only will he be subject to abuse and social ostracising by his friends, relatives and neighbours – not only will his name be forever linked by search engines with the rape accusation – but he may find his employers refuse to re-employ him even after he is exonerated, and when he attempts to get a new job, the DBS process may very well reveal his acquittal at a rape trial because the police "think he might have been guilty" – see Ref.[5], for example.

Once accused, the social stain of a rape accusation is never entirely eradicated. If a man accused of murder is, in the end, not even charged, there is usually no lingering stain. People just assume it was a mistake. But when the accusation is of rape, for reasons which have nothing to do with logic, people will tend to think that the man just got away with it and the stigma remains. The extreme stress caused by rape accusations is illustrated by those cases in which the accused ultimately kills himself, even though entirely innocent.

Feminists will insist that rape is rape, there are no 'degrees of rape'. But that is not so. A rape committed with monstrous violence is not the same as a case of disputed consent following an instance of mutually drunken monkey sex. A malicious false rape accusation is worse than the latter form of rape, by far. And yet this is not recognised in law.

The striking thing about virtually all the cases is the triviality of the reasons for lying about something with such serious consequences for the accused. This is the empathy gap yet again. What else can account for those who think that an accusation which will blast a man into hell is legitimised by being stood up, or as a stratagem to avoid being dumped, or to excuse bad exam grades, or simply to get a lift home?

Before I present the results of my researches, let me emphasise the key factor which leads to false allegations going all the way to court, and perhaps a wrongful conviction: disclosure failure.

Disclosure Failure

It is important to realise that the whole criminal justice process is entirely reliant on the police finding all the relevant evidence, and disclosing it to the legal counsel.

Disclosure failure refers to exculpatory evidence which is not disclosed by the police, or only disclosed very late when earlier disclosure would have avoided charges. This may be because the police have failed to be duly diligent (e.g., not bothering to search the mobile phone of the accuser) or have done so but do not disclose the evidence to the legal counsel. Categorisation as disclosure failure also applies when the police have been in possession of definitive exculpatory evidence from early in the investigation, but charges are nevertheless brought and the prosecution finally offer no evidence within days of the trial date, or at trial.

How frequent are such disclosure failures? The answer, I'm afraid, is "very". Ref.[1], a firm of solicitors, tells us,

"Most of us would expect the police to want to catch the criminals. The people that have done it. The guilty ones. And that is exactly what most police officers, perhaps understandably, think is their job as well. But you and they would be wrong, profoundly wrong, and it is this basic, fundamental error that lies at the heart of the problem."

"Because who decides who's guilty? The job of the police is to investigate whether or by whom an offence has been committed. They have a legal duty to investigate all reasonable lines of enquiry, whether they point towards the guilt or innocence of a particular suspect. It sounds simple, but if you are a suspect in a criminal case you need to understand that this isn't how it works. … Inconvenient evidence that would undermine a prosecution or assist a suspect doesn't achieve either of those aims, so it doesn't have any real importance.

As soon as the police think it is their job to catch the criminals, the system goes wrong, because it is they, not a court or a jury or anyone independent, who is deciding on who is a criminal and then setting about proving it. As soon as a police officer goes about the job of investigating all lines of enquiry, and simply properly presents that evidence, the system will work so much better."

"This description is not the cynical rant of a defence lawyer embittered by the constant failure of the police, CPS or Judges to apparently care one bit about due process in investigations and disclosure. It is a summary of legal policies, and the everyday experience of practice in police stations and courts."

Across all crimes, Ref.[6] indicated a 70% increase in cases collapsing due to disclosure failure in the two years between 2015 and 2017.

Part A: The General Public

Bail

Most of the accused men were released on bail after being held for questioning. However sometimes bail was refused and such men would then be retained in custody (on remand). Four of the 146 cases involved men being retained on remand, for periods between one month and 12 months. A woman can get a man locked up immediately simply by making out he is dangerous – e.g., "he came at me with a Samurai sword – he has other weapons at home". That will get the man arrested by a car-load of armed police and held without bail.

False Conviction and Imprisonment

Of the 146 cases, 15 involved men initially being convicted and imprisoned. Several served their full term before being exonerated. The number of years they actually spent in prison was,

10 weeks, 6 months, 1 year, (2 cases), 18 months, 2 years (6 cases), 3 to 4 years (3 cases), 4 years (2 cases), 17 years and 25 years.

Serial False Accusers

A complainant is classed as a serial false accuser if accusations have been made falsely regarding two or more separate incidents involving different alleged perpetrators. Of the 146 cases listed, 25 involved serial false accusers. The total number of people (almost all men, of course, but one or two women) accused by these 25 complainants were (in the order listed in Ref.[3]),

8, several, 2, 15, 3, several, 5, 2, 3, 2, 2, 3, 3, 5, 2, 2, 4, 2, 2, 2, 8, 3, 7, 2, 2

In addition, there were a further 15 complainants who made allegations against more than one person as part of the same single allegation or incident.

Failures of Disclosure

From news reports I was able to identify that disclosure failures were evident in 28 of the 146 cases listed. This does not mean that disclosure failures did not contribute to the remaining 118 cases, only that this could not be ascertained from the news reports.

24 cases of disclosure failure were identified from the 92 cases listed since Alison Saunders took up the position as Director of Public Prosecutions (DPP) in November 2013 (26%), compared with 4 cases of disclosure failure in the 54 cases listed before that date (7%). A t-test indicates this increase in disclosure failure rates after Alison Saunders' became DPP is statistically significant. However, that does not prove causal connection of the two things.

Potential Police or Professional Malfeasance

Cases where a police officer or the prosecution services appear to have been beyond negligent and have either been subject to formal complaints, been sued, or appear to have been potentially criminal include the 11 cases,

17/22, 16/6, 16/14, 16/25, 16/26, 15/1, 15/7, 14/2, 10/9, 6/1, 5/1

where the case reference refers to that defined in Ref.[3].

In addition, case 16/5 involved a female QC gaming the system to her advantage, changing her status from 'accused' to 'victim', hence guaranteeing anonymity and securing her career.

Associated Deaths

The 146 cases involved 16 deaths. 12 of these were the suicide of the wrongly accused, one was the suicide of the falsely accused's mother, one was the suicide of the alleged false accuser, one was a homicide due to vigilante action, and one was the death in prison of an innocent man. The names of these dead are included in Ref.[4].

Guilty Until Proven Innocent

The most shocking thing about these 146 cases is how they undermine your faith in British justice (if you had any, I used to). The judiciary and the criminal justice process have allowed a situation to develop in which an allegation alone is sufficient to get you convicted and banged up for a very long stretch – in the case of sexual assault. This does not mean you will necessarily be convicted in such cases – but it does mean you are at the mercy of the jury (if there is one).

In such a circumstance the burden of proof is shifted to the defence because the default position has shifted from "innocent until proven guilty" to being a lottery. Unlike most criminal cases, where most evidence is prosecution evidence, in sexual assault cases there is a need to find exculpatory evidence to put up against the allegation. So, even if the police and prosecution are efficient and do their job, there is inevitably an element of "guilty until proven innocent" about sexual assault cases, Ref.[7].

This is why then-DPP Alison Saunders' statement, Ref.[8], that it is not practical, or necessary, to trawl through all the complainant's social media, etc., seeking evidence is so appalling. Evidence which emerges from such sources is more likely to be exculpatory than condemnatory – and the defence stands more in need of evidence to offset the prosecution's head-start, namely the allegation. Saunders reveals her concern only with erecting a prosecution case and not with justice. This is the endemic mindset within the Crown Prosecution Service (CPS), see chapter 17.

Reasons for False Allegations

Reasons for making the false allegation were apparent in 94 of the 146 cases. The number of cases out of 94 corresponding to the various causal categories were as follows,

Regret (19): This was the commonest category. The woman regrets her behaviour sometime after the event and projects the blame onto the man by changing her mind about consent. This is typical of the 'drunken monkey sex' type of situation, common amongst students and other young people.

Rejection (14): This category applies to women who decide to punish a man for dumping them (hell hath no fury like a woman scorned).

Revenge, Anger (14): This category applies when the accusation appears to have been a calculated act of aggression for revenge or retaliation when the reason for the anger is other than being dumped.

Infidelity (10): This category refers to women who are married or have a regular boyfriend and seek to excuse themselves for their infidelity by transmogrifying consensual sex with A.N.Other into rape.

Attention (10): Some women seem to enjoy the police attention, and the sense of importance it gives them.

Extortion/blackmail/fraud/compensation (9): In general it is not possible to tell from news reports whether an alleged victim received victim compensation. However, financial gain by some means or another – generally not via victim compensation, e.g., blackmail – was identified in 9 cases. It is likely that victim compensation is a far more significant motivator than can be discerned from the news reports of these cases, especially as compensation is not dependent upon a conviction. Indeed, there are cases where the allegation has been exposed in court as false, but compensation has still been paid.

Rivalry (4): This category relates to cases where false accusers appear to have been motivated by a desire to topple the accused from an influential position, e.g., due to ideological opposition, professional jealousy, or to enhance their own career advancement, protected by anonymity. This category will be more significant in cases involving celebrities and politicians, which are excluded here.

Delusional (4): This is self-explanatory – some women go to extraordinary lengths to fake claims. The characteristic of these cases is they appear obviously bonkers – but are often treated seriously anyway.

Sympathy (3): Some women experiencing a bad patch with their boyfriends, possibly rejection, decide to accuse someone other than the boyfriend as a strategy to gain the boyfriend's sympathy and re-cement their relationship. In such cases the woman may accuse a man she had never even met.

Jealousy (3): If she can't have him, no one will! Put him in prison! Or it may be jealousy over financial, rather than amorous, advantage.

Academic (2): These cases refer to students making an excuse for the lateness of a coursework assignment or seeking mitigation against poor exam performance. Yes, it happens.

In addition to the above there was one case of an unfounded belief in the target's paedophilia (case 16/22) and one case where the motivation was to get a lift home in a police car (15/4). Ruining a man's life for a £20 cab fare – incredible, isn't it?

Part B: Senior Politicians

My intention in the case of politicians was different from that of the preceding study among the general public. The latter were confined to false accusations. Here my aim is to compile *all* allegations of sexual misdemeanours, above a certain level of severity, against national government officers – whether false or otherwise. Most allegations are less serious than rape. Some are less than criminal. Again I confine attention to the UK.

The bar as regards "sufficient severity" was set at those cases in which the police have been involved, whether or not charges were forthcoming, plus cases which have led to sackings or enforced resignations or suspensions. The latter sets the bar well below the criminal level. However this criterion also excludes the myriad of allegations emerging from #MeToo pogrom.

I confine attention to MPs, peers and people working in the Houses of Parliament, plus senior figures in major government departments who may be taken to be political figures. Hence, Bishops are included, but lower-ranking priests are not (so the bulk of accusations within the Churches are not considered here).

Local government officials, Mayors and local Councillors, are excluded. It is worth noting in passing that there have been a surprisingly large number of people in local government convicted of (criminal) sexual offences, averaging around 10 per year. This seems alarming until one recalls that there are 20,811 local councillors, so this is a yearly rate of 0.048%, which is essentially the same as the rate amongst the population as a whole.

I have not adopted any strict cut-off on date, though I did not wish to go back into ancient history (the Neil & Christine Hamilton case is perhaps an exception due to its extraordinary nature). Nevertheless, whilst most cases relate to relatively recent years, this is in respect of the accusations, not the alleged incidents. Many of the alleged incidents are historical, in some cases dating back as far as the 1960s – or even 1951 in one case.

Several of the cases reviewed here may be cases of political intrigue, i.e., destroying a political opponent through allegation. It is worrying that we have handed to the unscrupulous a virtually risk-free means of subverting the democratic process by being able to destroy anyone at will. Sorry – that should be any *man*.

For the specific cases considered, and my brief case histories, see the original post, Ref.[9]. Of the 25 people whose cases I reviewed, my summary is as follows, though I refer you to Ref.[9] for the names of the accused other than in the case of convictions and sackings,

- Only two resulted in criminal convictions (Phillip Lyon and ex-Bishop Peter Ball, both imprisoned);

- A further two remain unresolved and relate to alleged perpetrators who are dead. One was almost certainly guilty, the other not so clear, but I shall count both as guilty for sake of argument;

- Four cases remain unresolved but my reading of them at the time was that they would ultimately exonerate the accused of *criminal* wrongdoing, or remain unresolved;

- Four men were sacked for alleged misdemeanours which were not criminal (Sir Michael Fallon, Damian Green, David Mellor and Lord Mendelsohn);

- The remaining 13 people are no longer under suspicion for the accusations.

Of the 13 people effectively declared not guilty, only five involved a scheduled trial, resulting in exoneration of the accused or conviction of a false accuser. The remaining eight cases never had charges brought.

In summary, if pushed to judge the 24 men and one woman as either "guilty of a criminal offence" or "not guilty of any criminal offence", I'd say 4 guilty and 21 not guilty. You may come to your own view, but it is beyond doubt that the bulk of allegations against senior politicians were either false or below the criminal level (and do recall how low that bar is now).

Part C: Celebrities

The scope in this case was the same as that for politicians: including all cases of sexual assault or misconduct against a celebrity, whether apparently true or false, and confined to the UK. Who qualifies as a 'celebrity'? I define this simply as "a person of whom most people would have heard".

One of the most egregious habits of the police in sex cases is the tendency to trawl for additional accusers – especially a feature of celebrity cases. Paul Gambaccini described it as being *"used as human fly paper to encourage other people to come forward and make allegations against him"*. At one time I would have assumed – like everyone else – that multiple accusers must surely indicate the accused's guilt. No longer. Not when the police pro-actively seek additional accusers and even mention the possibility of victim compensation.

It is a great wheeze to accuse celebrities. The police will find it ever so much easier to trawl for other willing accusers. And the police seem to have a particular delight in bringing down the famous, which is not entirely a post-Savile effect, though that is certainly a major exacerbation. It is also a great boon to lawyers when celebrities are accused, because they are the very people who can afford to pay their defence teams six figure sums – pretty much the going rate to prove to the system's satisfaction that a lunatic fantasist with no evidence is a lunatic fantasist with no evidence.

One of the most pernicious aspects of sex offence allegations is that, once accused, a man's reputation can never fully recover unless the accuser is prosecuted and shown conclusively to be a liar, which is rare. Merely having no charges brought, or even being found not guilty at trial, still leaves an indelible taint. And many men will be sacked as soon as they are accused, and never re-employed even when exonerated.

The form of words used by the CPS does not help: "We keep all our cases under constant review and in this case it was decided that based on the strength of the evidence there is no longer a realistic prospect of a conviction". Note the "no longer", suggesting there once was a realistic prospect of conviction. This form of words is inevitably interpreted by the public as meaning "we think the bastard did it but we just don't have enough evidence". In truth it is more likely to mean there is not a shred of independent evidence whatsoever, and never was – and we've just been keeping the poor bugger on a leash for a couple of years in case some other accuser might turn up with some evidence.

Such is the nature of the animus directed at men now that it is not only the famous that 'the system' delights in bringing low, but also those whose reputation was especially pristine hitherto. So, the avuncular Rolf Harris was a big scalp. I remain less than convinced that he did anything illegal. Similarly, I find it hard to regard Dave Lee Travis as a public menace. After attempting 15 charges, and being cleared of 14, they finally nailed him on a breast squeezing incident.

In Victorian times a woman could ruin her reputation simply by allowing herself to be left alone with a man. Following #MeToo, are we nearing the point where the same is now true with the sexes reversed? It is becoming common for men to avoid being left alone with a woman or girl – especially in schools and universities. I certainly wouldn't want to be a male GP or physiotherapist seeing women patients.

I refer you to the original post, Ref.[10], for the list of 45 celebrities whose cases I briefly reviewed.

Of the 45 cases, in my opinion 12 men were guilty, 29 men were innocent, and in 4 cases the matter is not clear. You may judge it differently. However, it is clear that the innocent out-number the guilty by some considerable margin.

The 45 celebrities whose accusations I reviewed join the 25 politicians I reviewed earlier, making 70 in all. Combining politicians and celebrities that is 50 innocent men out of 70 accused, a false allegation rate of 71%. Whilst we cannot read this across to the general public, it is interesting how similar this figure is to false allegation rates estimated in a different context, see chapter 4.

Ref.[11] told us that, in May 2015, "*Some 261 celebrities and politicians, including sports, TV and music stars, are being investigated for alleged child sex abuse, police have revealed…The rogues gallery includes 135 TV, film and radio stars, 43 musicians and seven sports figures as well as 76 politicians, the officer in charge of the issue has disclosed.*"

Well, 261 is far bigger than the 70 I have identified. One presumes that the other 191 – or at least the vast majority of them – were never progressed very far, i.e., they turned out to be unreliable accusations. Have we really ended up with only 20 guilty out of 261? I hardly dare suggest a false allegation rate quite so extreme as that.

References

[1] Stone King Solicitors. *Disclosure Failures in Criminal Trials*. (I originally attributed this to solicitor Matthew Graham on 24 January 2018. But the web page now bears the name Nicholas Wragg with a date 13 May 2021).

[2] Collins, W. (2018a). *Rape – Part 1 (Statistics)*. The Illustrated Empathy Gap, 22 December 2017.

[3] File of *False Rape Case Histories*

[4] File of *False Rape Case Histories' Data Extraction Categories*

[5] Gibb, F. (2017). *Teacher 'lost two jobs over rape acquittal'*. 22 November 2017.

[6] Cowling, P. (2018). *Hundreds of cases dropped over evidence disclosure failings*. BBC News, 24 January 2018.

[7] Hewson, B. (2016). *The feminising of justice that makes it hard for men charged with rape to get a fair trial*. Mail Online, 14 April 2016.

[8] Maidment, J. (2018). *Police do not need to fully check photographs and social media accounts in rape cases, head of CPS suggests*. The Telegraph, 18 January 2018.

[9] Collins, W. (2018b) *Rape – Part 3 (Politicians)*. The Illustrated Empathy Gap, 12 February 2018.

[10] Collins, W. (2018c). *Rape – Part 4 (Celebrities)*. The Illustrated Empathy Gap, 28 February 2018.

[11] Whitehead, T. (2015). *76 politicians, 178 celebrities and 7 sports stars: the scale of VIP child sex abuse inquiry*. The Telegraph, 20 May 2015.

9. The Chris Crabtree Case

As a spin-off from my investigations into false rape cases in January/February 2018 I read a great many news reports of such cases. Most were appalling and I could not dwell long on all of them. However, I thought it worth posting on some specific cases. This chapter, and the five that follow, are examples of just that. This one is extraordinary by any standards.

Original posted on 9 February 2018.

In 2012, Chris Crabtree, 43, then in a parachute regiment, rather regretted taking Emily Checksfield, 41, as his partner, Ref.[1]. He was ultimately to discover that she had previously been known as Nadine Milroy-Sloan, but only after he had become her victim. They had met on a dating website and had a relationship lasting nine months. But then Mr Crabtree discovered that she had been defrauding two military charities for which she had been assisting him in raising funds. He told her the relationship was over and that she had to pay back the money or he would tell the police.

She was never tried on that charge. Immediately she realised her game was up, she contacted the police and claimed that Mr Crabtree had threatened to kill her with a samurai sword. She fooled the police into believing that Crabtree was mentally unstable, had PTSD from his time in combat, that he had access to weapons and was likely to resist arrest. As a result Mr Crabtree was arrested at gunpoint by armed officers, denied bail and spent the next three months in prison on remand, with his 25-year military career in jeopardy. He was completely innocent of any wrongdoing. He was entirely her victim.

To those who caution against exaggerating the dangers of false accusations, do internalise this lesson in the power of a woman to get a man incarcerated immediately with no evidence at all.

While in custody, it dawned on Mr Crabtree that anyone who rejected Checksfield "had to pay". And he was paying.

While locked up, Mr Crabtree was subjected to further wild and untrue accusations which, he later said "could have reduced a lesser man to suicide". Checksfield concocted more and more lurid tales in an endeavour to keep Mr Crabtree imprisoned, including claims that his laptop contained child porn and evidence he had been torturing prisoners in Afghanistan. At this point Checksfield's story began to unravel when experts found no such material on the laptop, and eventually Mr Crabtree's innocence was proven. However, it was to take action from Mr Crabtree himself to get Checksfield prosecuted and brought to book.

But first.....so-called Emily Checksfield's back story – when she was known as Nadine Milroy-Sloan, Ref.[2]. Then 29, she already had a criminal record before she claimed that she had been raped by former Tory MP Neil Hamilton, together with his wife Christine. In truth, she had never even met the couple.

Milroy-Sloan – or Checksfield, if you prefer – said she had been lured to a flat by Barry Lehaney who had told her he was the Hamiltons' chauffeur. There she claimed the sex attack had taken place. Two days before the date of the fictitious attack, Milroy-Sloan offered the publicist Max Clifford a story about the Hamiltons being involved in a vice ring and a tax scam. Clifford told Milroy-Sloan she could expect about £100,000 from the media if she could prove her vice ring claims.

Milroy-Sloan then set out to "get the evidence" and arranged to see Mr Lehaney, with whom she had been exchanging explicit e-mails. She told Lehaney that she wanted him to arrange a meeting with Neil and Christine Hamilton for the purpose of a sexual encounter.

In court, Milroy-Sloan denied making false rape allegations against the Hamiltons and Mr Lehaney. She told the court she "apologised" if she had made an "honest mistake". The court didn't buy it and in 2003 Checksfield – or Nadine Milroy-Sloan – was jailed for three years after a trial that cost an estimated £1 million.

So back to 2012 and poor Mr Crabtree who had had no idea initially with whom he was entangled...

Even with Emily Checksfield's notorious past, the police and the CPS decided to prosecute Mr Crabtree over the samurai sword claim. Fortunately for him, her story fell apart. But even then, the CPS did not proactively prosecute this appalling serial liar.

Instead, on returning home from prison, Mr Crabtree found his home ransacked and his belongings missing. He launched a burglary allegation against Checksfield and some of his belongings were found in her new home.

Though she was later acquitted of the burglary charge, it was to prove her undoing anyway. Checksfield begged Mr Crabtree to meet her so she could persuade him to drop the charge. He did meet with her – and secretly recorded their conversation. Unknowingly she condemned herself, admitting she had lied about the whole thing. Mr Crabtree later remarked, "Seeing her again after everything, I had to ignore every sense of loathing I had for her because I knew getting that confession was gold dust. She is so convincing. I think she is a sociopath. She has no conscience."

Two years later that recording finally cleared Mr Crabtree's name for good and secured her conviction and a four-year jail term. Be careful, gentlemen, she's on the loose again now, and heaven knows under what name. And do not be so foolish as to expect the agencies of criminal justice to protect or assist you.

References

[1] Robson, B. (2014). *Army veteran speaks of prison ordeal at hands of Hamiltons' rape claim liar Emily Checksfield after she is jailed for more lies*. Kent Online, 2 October 2014.

[2] Paterson, M. (2003). *Hamiltons' rape accuser faces prison sentence*. 17 May 2003.

10. The Victor Nealon Case

This is the second of my case histories of men accused of rape. Bear in mind throughout these case histories that these stories, appalling though they are, are actually relatively common. But you don't hear about many of them.

Original posted on 11 January 2018.

I bring you the case of Victor Nealon, former postman. Most of the false allegation cases in my compilation relate either to events which never happened, or to consensual sex which was later claimed to be non-consensual. In this case, however, there has been no suggestion that the complainant was untruthful or that her claims were inaccurate. This is simply a case of convicting the wrong man. Though the story starts in 1997 it is not until mid-2015 that this case reaches its final appalling conclusion...

I quote from Ref.[1] by solicitor advocate Mark Newby: "*The judgment and the back story behind this case serves as a depressing epitaph for the criminal justice system and its complete lack of progress since the notorious miscarriages of the late 1980s and early 1990s*".

Mr Nealon had been unjustly convicted of attempted rape and wrongfully imprisoned for life. He had been in jail for 17 years. In 2014, after his conviction was finally quashed, Mr Nealon was discharged from Wakefield prison with £46 and nowhere to stay. He spent his first night of freedom as a homeless man on the streets, Ref.[2]. Makes you proud to be British, doesn't it?

The victim was subjected to an attempted rape outside a nightclub. The attacker had been seen in the night club hours before and was described as having a noticeable lump to his forehead and a strong Scottish accent. After the attack he made his escape.

Victor Nealon had never been to the nightclub in question. Mr Nealon is of Irish extraction and has a strong Irish accent. Although he has a facial disfigurement, this is due to serious acne. He has no 'lump'. His misfortune was to be living in the area and to have, in the past, been convicted of offences. So he was arrested.

Some weeks after his arrest, Nealon was asked to stand in an ID parade which he readily volunteered to do. The ID parade failed to follow the required procedures. The police officer leading the case was present at the ID parade and spoke to at least one of the witnesses. This contravenes procedure because of the possibility of influencing the witness, deliberately or accidentally. Oddly, the complainant herself did not attend the ID parade. One witness picked out Mr Nealon but stressed that the man involved had a strong Scottish accent. Other witnesses failed to pick out the applicant, including the victim's friend who helped compile an e-fit picture.

Mr Nealon was at home with his partner and daughter at the time of the offence. He thus had two alibis, but the prosecution mounted an attack on these alibis in court over the alibis' error in correctly naming the videos they had watched that night. The defence team were unaware of this evidence before trial and so had not the opportunity to present their own version of the issue.

But the most serious failure was in respect of DNA evidence. Mr Nealon had provided DNA samples to the police officer involved with leading the case and understood this was to facilitate testing against the woman's clothing. Not only did that testing not occur but the exhibits, apart from a skirt, remained in their sealed evidence bags. Staggeringly, the court was not given the true position over the lack of forensic testing in the case.

In other words, it was a disclosure failure that led to an innocent men being imprisoned for 17 years, combined with a litany of procedural failings.

The DNA testing was finally done only in 2009, twelve years after Mr Nealon had been convicted and sent to prison. The DNA present in all key intimate areas was that of an unknown male and not Victor Nealon. Incredibly, despite that, it would be another five years before his conviction was quashed by the Court of Appeal. Finally, in 2014, the Court of Appeal concluded in its judgment: 'the jury may reasonably have reached the conclusion, based on the DNA evidence, that it was a real possibility that the "unknown male" – and not the appellant – was the attacker.'

If the DNA testing had been done in 1997 then a man would not have lost 17 years of his life. But in 1998 and 2002 the Criminal Cases Review Commission had refused to carry out the DNA tests. Why? One cannot escape the suspicion that bolstering the apparent integrity of the system was of greater priority than justice. This is how the system itself colludes with disclosure failure – of which I will have more to say in chapter 17.

It is worth noting that Nealon's serving of 17 years was because he continued to protest his innocence, which thus denied him parole. Ask yourself how many innocent men would ultimately "admit" their guilt in order to get out of prison. Almost all, I would think. And this is part of the mechanism by which miscarriages of justice are kept hidden. The system protects its reputation by piling up procedural barriers. But the system is now too broken for such subterfuge to be sufficient camouflage.

Quoting solicitor Mark Newby again, Ref.[1], "*All of this conduct – the failure to undertake the DNA assessments, the misleading of the court, the collection of late rebuttal evidence and presence of the officer at the ID Parade – are all indicative of a disturbing approach to building a case against Victor Nealon at all costs. Had those involved with the case chosen instead to investigate the case in a fair and open manner then the result would have been very different.*"

I wrote the following denouement in January 2018: The euphoria of his release now some years past, Victor Nealon's life is grim. His parents died while he was in jail and his partner and daughter moved on. He lives alone. Prospective employers treat him with suspicion. He lives on benefits. After 17 years in prison for a crime he did not commit, Mr Nealon's application for compensation was turned down, Ref.[3]. He appealed, but to no avail. He was turned down again, Ref.[4].

"*It's one thing to lose your friends, family, freedom, money and job. It's quite another to be told that if you don't confess to the crime you'll never be released,*" he said. He maintained his innocence even though it cost him an extra seven years in prison.

He had three hours' notice of his release, was given a train ticket and £46.

References

[1] Newby, M. (2014). *The case of Victor Nealon: 17 wasted years*. The Justice Gap, 3 April 2014.

[2] Topham, G. (2013). *Wrongly jailed Victor Nealon spends first night as free man on streets*. The Guardian, 16 December 2013.

[3] Robins, J. (2015). *Wrongly convicted men launch new case against the Justice Secretary*. Independent, 18 January 2015.

[4] Jordan's Solicitors (2015). *Victor Nealon - Miscarriage Compensation Refusal Statement*. 8 June 2015.

11. A Criminal Investigation

This is the third of my case histories of false rape allegations.

Original posted on: <u>3 January 2018</u>.

The full facts of this case emerged only in 2017, though its origin goes back to 2014. Many, many times in compiling my list of false rape accusation cases (chapter 8) I thought "my goodness, that was surely the worst yet". Here's one of those. Whilst we can all enjoy getting mightily indignant about malicious false accusers, there are times when the alleged victim does need protecting – and I don't mean from the alleged rapist. I mean from the police and the CPS – and from false "friends". Can I be prosecuted for suggesting that the actions of the police and the CPS drove this young woman to kill herself?

Hannah S, 22, then a student at university, accused Mr V, 33, of rape in 2014, Ref.[1]. After making the allegation she became depressed and ultimately killed herself in August 2015. There had been no charge brought against Mr V up until that time, and he was only charged with rape in April 2016. Mr V was "removed from his attempts at education", to quote his defence counsel. In March 2017 the CPS announced they were dropping the prosecution because there was no realistic prospect of gaining a conviction. The stock phrase used in these situations is "we have no evidence to present". In this case it rather belied the fact that there was, and always had been, a mountain of evidence – all of it exculpatory.

After the announcement Mr V said, "*The news of Hannah's death made me physically sick. I cared about her. It was shocking and difficult to process. I was confused, sad and angry all at the same time. I will sadly never know the exact reasons for Hannah's actions. My anger and frustration is directed at the police and the CPS who have had overwhelming evidence from the outset that no crime was committed.*" He saw the trial as the only chance to clear his name. He had hoped to expose serious flaws, not just in his own case, but in the wider legal system – failings that let down both parties, himself and the vulnerable young woman who accused him and ended up dead.

Why had the CPS not charged Mr V by August 2015, for an allegation relating to 2014 when both parties had been interviewed by the police in

March 2015? One has to assume it was because they knew there was no realistic prospect of conviction from the start. This is consistent with, though not the same as, Mr V's claim that they had "*overwhelming evidence from the outset that no crime was committed*". So why did the CPS raise the charge in April 2016, eight months after the young woman's suicide? What role exactly did the police and the CPS play in her suicide? Did she perhaps come under pressure to continue with her accusation after having doubts herself? Did the CPS decide to charge Mr V as a means of deflecting attention from their own culpability?

Let's take a closer look. And do note that during the hearing the prosecutor said the decision not to continue the prosecution had been taken at the "highest level" of the CPS. Can we assume that meant Alison Saunders, the DPP at the time?. Why?

The defending QC described the aborted prosecution as "terribly disturbing and distressing". He too had been looking forward to the facts of the case coming out at trial. It was, he said, "perhaps an unrivalled case study in how a false allegation can come about". Indeed, and that, I suggest, is precisely why the CPS played their cards so as to prevent the details emerging.

You see, there was indeed a mountain of evidence in Mr V's favour – including thousands of social media messages suggesting there was no assault, information indicating his accuser had serious mental health issues, and even evidence from her computer suggesting the allegations had not only been false but that she had considered withdrawing them.

It was after Mr Va made it clear he did not want his relationship with Hannah to continue that the complaints were made. (Look back at chapter 8 which identified rejection as the second most common reason for false allegations of rape). And here the story becomes complicated. The full backstory can be read in Ref.[2], from which I have extracted the following (the account opens after Hannah had had a fall at the gym and been taken to hospital),

"*Other students joined them at the hospital and one, James (not his real name), drove everyone home after Hannah was given the all-clear at 3am. It was in the course of that evening that Hannah made an allegation of assault, telling James that (Mr V) had touched her inappropriately. James messaged his friend Michelle (not her real name), who had written in a blog about being raped the previous year.*"

"A few days later Michelle spoke to Hannah. The day after that, Mr V received a disturbing Facebook message. 'due to what happened last week when I came over to yours I have decided that I don't want any contact with you,' wrote Hannah. 'I don't feel like you respected me or how I feel. I had been clear with you on the phone that I didn't want things to happen again, and yet you still went ahead.'"

"Had Hannah written this entirely by herself? Not according to their friend Steven (not his real name), who had been present when the message was sent, as was Michelle. Indeed, in his witness statement, he talks about the message being 'formulated by Michelle', saying 'it seemed that Hannah had little input into this'. Elsewhere in the statement he says: 'I was shocked by this. I recall that Michelle soon became heavily involved with Hannah and seemed to have a lot of influence over her. I fully believe that [Hannah] was not raped or sexually abused by (Mr V),' he concludes."

"He was not the only one to think that way. Numerous students were prepared to go to court to speak on Mr V's behalf."

"The role of Michelle was significant. She had been with Hannah when she contacted the university authorities with her allegations and it was Michelle who rang the police on Hannah's behalf."

"Hannah eventually accused Mr V of raping her on unspecified dates, once in the autumn of 2014 and again in February 2015. There was no forensic evidence of rape. The only evidence against Mr V was in a statement made by Hannah to the police six months before her death, and even this was contradictory and bore no relationship to the allegations she originally confided to university friends."

"It is also undermined by more than 10,000 Facebook and WhatsApp messages between them that have now been transcribed and analysed. Seen by The Mail On Sunday, they showed the pair continued to have an amicable relationship after the alleged rapes."

"The following evening the pair exchanged a stream of messages, with no mention of a mild disagreement let alone sexual assault. Hannah implored (Mr V) to come over, clearly struggling with his decision to end their relationship. His replies were polite and the exchange ended on good terms. 'Have a good match tomorrow [smiley face],' she said."

"'Not one message supports the prosecution case or Hannah's account,' said Mr V's solicitor Mark Newby. 'It is striking all their exchanges are entirely good-natured on both sides. They reveal nothing at all untoward about Mr V's conduct'…. 'If the police had looked at the correspondence they could have arrived at no other conclusion than Hannah wasn't telling the truth'."

"Also disclosed by the prosecution in the case files for the inquest was her internet search history. This included multiple searches in August 2015 on false allegations and on how to withdraw prosecutions – as well as research into the kind of personality disorders that drive such allegations."

"Two weeks before her death, Hannah twice downloaded CPS guidance on perverting the course of justice."

Ref.[2] adds, *"she was also questioned about previous allegations of rape she had made against another man."*

Ye Gods, one despairs.

Another of Mr V's solicitors, Anna O'Mara, said: *"I had never before seen a person charged with an offence when there existed such strong evidence pointing to his innocence."* She was further shocked by the manner in which the police conducted their interview of Hannah, when this evidence later emerged. She described it thus: *"Hannah initially was reluctant to commit herself to making an allegation against Mr V. This eventually led to the officer pointing out to her what the police would need to prove a case. It was only after Hannah had received prompts from the officer that she hesitantly developed a disjointed allegation against Mr V"*.

It would appear that the combined actions of her "friend", Michelle, together with subtle police pressure, precipitated an allegation which Hannah later regretted – but felt trapped and unable to retract. Was it this, on top of a history of mental illness and suicidal thoughts, that caused her suicide? We will never know for sure, but it seems likely that the existing criminal investigation procedures were hardly Hannah's friend – let alone Mr V's.

Where are the wise grandmothers and grandfathers of yesterday who could, calmly but firmly, have got to the truth of these allegations without the heavy-handed involvement of Mr Plod and Ms feminist-pseudo-friend? We have banished them. They are no longer required in this brave new world. The Authorities will deal with it. Take that line, and this is what you get.

References

[1] Rudgard. O. (2017). *Student whose rape accuser killed herself before his trial says he has been through a 'horrendous ordeal' as his case is dropped by prosecutors*. The Telegraph, 20 March 2017.

[2] Robins, J. (2017). *'I don't blame my troubled friend for crying rape - just those who put her up to it'*. Mail Online, 6 May 2017.

12. Anonymous v Anonymous

This is the fourth of my case histories of false rape allegations.

Original posted on: <u>24 January 2018</u>.

The boy was 12 in 2014 when he lost his virginity and was subsequently accused of rape by the 13-year-old girl in question, Ref.[1].

He had been at a sleepover at a friend's house. The boy was a first-rate pupil, getting top grades, and had not previously been in trouble. He was arrested by police in his pyjamas and placed in an adult cell. Adult male prisoners were later placed in the adjacent cell. He had to give a semen sample, a DNA sample, a sample of pubic hair and had his fingerprints taken. He was finally released in the middle of the night. His Mum took him home and put him to bed. But he had to return at 10:00 the next morning to be 'interviewed'.

Upon being accused, the boy was thrown out of school and forbidden to be around females under the age of 16 – despite being only 12 himself. His mother's entire world collapsed as she realised that 'guilty until proven innocent' was the order of the day. She would get no assistance from the police or the social services.

It took 14 months for the trial to be held, a trial which lasted four days! We hear a great deal about grown women in rape trials having to be protected from the trauma of a court appearance by being allowed to give evidence by video. But subjecting this (now 13-year-old) to four days of trial in which his life was in the balance – that's OK, it seems. Any comment from the rape activists on that at all? Of course not, because he is of the sex which deserves the worst the world can throw at him. And, remember, there is no such thing as an innocent male, of any age.

For God's sake, why did the trial last four days when his accuser admitted in court that the sex between them was consensual and she had said it was rape only so her boyfriend would not be angry that she had had sex with someone else?

The boy was acquitted in 2016 and left the court in tears. He had lost a year of schooling and felt so stigmatised that he preferred to move to the other end of the country to start a new life afresh, living with his father.

A woman police officer compassionately commented after the case, "*It is not uncommon for a child to be placed in a cell for a serious crime, as the age of legal responsibility is 10. It is not unusual for us not to tell an adult prior to a child's arrest what the child is being arrested for. This is to protect the integrity of the investigation.*" I see.

This case reminds me of a caller to James O'Brien's programme on LBC radio (circa 2016 – unfortunately no longer online). A mother told the story of her 12-year-old autistic son who had been accused of rape by a 15-year-old girl. He too was carted away by the police to a cell, to his mother's great distress and amazement. The girl eventually admitted that she'd made it up to punish the boy for refusing to take her to the cinema.

It's a good job males are powerful and privileged, isn't it?

Rape, in English law, is an explicitly gendered crime. It is, by definition, the possessor of the penis doing the penetrating who is guilty. And this is justified – how? Because the possessor of the convex genitalia is "powerful", feminism tells us, whereas the possessor of the concave genitalia is a powerless, innocent victim. Irrespective of one's views about this when applied to adults, how does it play out when applied to a 12-year-old boy and a 13-year-old – or 15-year-old – girl? It is possible, even likely, that the 12-year-old boy would be physically smaller than these girls – and could hardly be said to be in a dominant social position, as feminists will often claim in the adult context. Why, then, should we not equally regard the 12-year-old boys in these cases as having been raped by the girls?

How can the existing law be interpreted as anything other than the most flagrant institutionalised prejudice in such circumstances?

References

[1]   Hewitt, S. (2016). *My son is 12 - how can he be a rapist? Nightmare ordeal of boy's 'sleepover sex'*. The Mirror, 28 March 2016.

13. Two More False Rape Cases

This is the fifth of my case histories of false rape allegations; two different cases in this chapter.

Original posted on: *26 January 2018*

Darryl Gee, John H and an Anonymous Woman

There was good news and bad news for Darryl Gee in 2006, Ref.[1].

The good news was he had been exonerated of the rape for which he was jailed in 2000.

The bad news is he was dead.

He'd died in prison four years before, after serving two years as an innocent man. He died shortly after his second appeal had failed, Ref.[2].

Mr Gee had been a music teacher. A woman had accused him of raping her as a 10-year-old girl in a school classroom and in the school staff room ten years earlier. There was no corroborating evidence or adverse witness testimony, despite the helpline set up by the local council to flush out further evidence against Mr Gee. Gee could not deny that he and the pupil had been alone (she was the only member of her class who was learning French horn). But unlocked rooms where anyone could catch an attacker *in flagrante delicto* were hardly the typical location for a violent attack.

Nevertheless, Mr Gee was sentenced to 8 years in prison.

More damningly, the same complainant had made virtually identical allegations against another man, John H, who was jailed for 12 years. This appears not to have perturbed anyone. (Mr H's conviction was also later overturned).

But the additional evidence which eventually earned Mr Gee's exoneration, albeit post-mortem, came about due to a friend of the family who was a consultant physician. This doctor knew that Mr Gee had a serious spinal curvature problem (having two more ribs on one side of his body than the other). As a consequence Mr Gee was slow and awkward in his movements. It was difficult to see how he could have been physically capable of doing what was alleged – in fact, impossible, the doctor argued.

Mr Gee should never have been tried let alone convicted. His 88-year-old mother was more concerned about how her son could have been convicted with no corroborating evidence. Me too, yet the case histories I have compiled show time after time that men are regularly sent to prison for very long stretches based on nothing but the allegation. This is a lesson that men have yet to learn, and boys have yet to be taught, about our society now: you will have to prove your innocence of an allegation that might come out of left field many years later.

Mrs Gee senior said "*I still don't understand why that girl said what she did*". No, that, too, is often a mystery, though chapter 8 sheds light on the usual reasons, which are remarkable for their triviality compared to the devastation they wreak upon the accused men – death in this case.

Shannon Taylor and Warren B

Warren B, 40, spent three years and four months in jail as a convicted sex attacker until his 'victim' was unmasked as a fantasist who had accused other blameless men, Ref.[3]. We only know the name of the false accuser, Shannon Taylor, because she was named under parliamentary privilege, Ref.[4].

She was never prosecuted despite having made seven other false sex attack allegations before that of the unfortunate Mr B, including one against her father. Taylor apparently kept changing her name and moving, so police forces did not realise they were dealing with the same woman.

Taylor said Mr B seized her at knifepoint outside a village club early on New Year's Day, marched her down an alleyway and indecently assaulted her. Mr B was jailed, initially for three years but later increased to five, despite no forensic evidence to back up the claims. Mr B was jailed simply on the word of Taylor. That is always a very bad basis for justice – but particularly so in this case. Mr B understandably reacted with fury after learning that police knew all along that the woman was unreliable. A report revealed that officers were told that Taylor was unreliable, unstable and craved attention – but they failed to disclose that at his trial.

Shannon Taylor's own mother has described her as "*a persistent liar, very manipulative and a bully*" who frequently claimed to have been beaten, sexually attacked and raped – all of which were untrue. Taylor's own daughter said, *"she is a danger and the public needs to be warned. She needs prosecuting for what she did. She is every man's worst nightmare."* As far as I am aware Taylor was never prosecuted despite Lord Campbell-Savours calling for her prosecution.

After Mr B was released from prison, the Home Office sent him a bill for £6,800 for his Board & Lodging whilst inside, Ref.[4]. You really couldn't make this up, could you? It's OK, though, they changed their minds later…..they actually charged him £12,500!

Note added in proof: It is standard practice by the MOJ to charge the falsely imprisoned for their bed and breakfast whilst inside. As of March 2024 there is a petition in circulation which is demanding that this practice is stopped and calling for reimbursement to individuals subjected to this monstrous piece of heartless injustice, Ref.[5].

References

[1] Herbert, I. (2006). *Jailed for a crime he didn't commit*. Independent, 8 June 2006.

[2] Yorkshire Live (2006). *Mum, 88 sees rape conviction quashed for son who died in jail*. Original 1 April 2006, updated 13 July 2013.

[3] Camber, R. (2010). *Innocent man jailed for 3 years over false rape claim - despite police knowing 'victim' was a fantasist*. Mail Online, 18 June 2010.

[4] The Standard (2012). *Sex attack liar named by Peer*. 12 April 2012.

[5] O'Brien, M. (2024). *Demand Reimbursement for Wrongfully Convicted Individuals Charged for 'Bed and Board'*. Change.org, accessed 17 March 2024.

14. Rolf Harris v Women Sex Offenders

This is the last of my accounts of sexual assault cases, but this one is different. I do not claim that Rolf Harris was innocent. Indeed, he was found guilty in court. My personal opinion is that Harris was probably more guilty of stupidity than criminality, but that is my guess and was not the outcome of the trial. My purpose here is to contrast the treatment of Harris with that of contemporaneous female sexual abusers of minors. The latter behaved at least as badly, and often far worse, than Harris, even assuming all allegations against Harris were true. Yet Harris was declared a non-person and thrown into the furthest regions of hell, whilst in contrast the public insist on regarding female abusers as having done nothing terribly heinous. Some people even believe that boy victims of such women should be grateful for the attention. This is the empathy gap in its most stark and disgraceful form. It manifests both in the public mind and in the criminal justice system, both of which will punish you for what you are, not for what you have done. This chapter is lengthy for a reason: I wish to drive home the message that adult women sexually offending against minors is not rare.

Original posted on: *15 November 2015*.

Rolf Harris's guilt or innocence is not the main point of this article. Its main purpose is to contrast the extreme difference between the treatment of Harris, even if his guilt be assumed, and that of female sex offenders against minors. Consequently, I make no attempt to deconstruct the conduct of the trial or the evidence presented or the performance of the police, though there are others who have done so, e.g., Refs.[1,2,3,4]. Here I just flat-footedly present the charges and outcome of the trial. Personally, I am far from convinced that the case against Harris was proved beyond reasonable doubt, but I am not privy to what transpired in court and I will not present here the arguments to support that view, but see Refs.[1-4].

My purpose is to contrast the public attitude, and the attitude of the courts, to male and female sex offenders. The concentration on female offenders is not intended to deny or disguise the prevalence of male offenders. The issue addressed here is the perception of the offence and how this differs according to the sex of the perpetrator. Nor am I arguing, necessarily, for harsher treatment of female offenders – or for more lenient treatment of (genuine) male offenders. I am arguing only that in an equitable society the treatment of both should be the same, and independent also of the sex of the victim. What punishment – or treatment – is appropriate does not fall to me to decide, thankfully.

In June 2014 Rolf Harris was initially found guilty on 12 counts of indecently assaulting four girls between 1969 and 1983, Ref.[5]. Harris denied all 12 charges on which he was found guilty. They were,

- Count one: A woman said Harris touched her inappropriately when she was just seven or eight while he was signing autographs in 1969.
- Count two: Harris was accused of fondling a teenager's bottom at a charity event in Cambridge in 1975.
- Counts three to nine: A childhood friend of Mr Harris' daughter, Bindi, said he repeatedly indecently assaulted her from the age of 13, starting in 1978, including once when his daughter was asleep in the same room.
- Counts 10 to 12: Australian woman Tonya Lee, who waived her right to anonymity, said Harris touched her inappropriately one day while she was on a theatre group trip to the UK at the age of 15.

In Count One the woman claimed Harris touched her intimately when she was seven or eight after she queued to get his autograph at a community centre near Portsmouth in 1969. On 16 November 2017 the Court of Appeal cleared Harris of this charge. You can read the account of how insecure was the original conviction in Ref.[6]. The Court of Appeal upheld the guilty verdicts on the other 11 charges.

In February 2017, Harris was cleared of three charges relating to other women, but the jury failed to reach a verdict on four other charges, Ref.[7]. In a retrial in May 2017, the jury again failed to reach a 10:2 majority verdict and Harris was cleared of these charges also, Ref.[8].

Hence, of the total of 19 charges for which he was tried, Harris was cleared of eight. In brief, the 11 charges on which he was found guilty were,

In Count Two the complainant, then aged 14, claimed that Harris fondled her bottom outside a Celebrity It's a Knock Out event in Cambridge.

In Counts 10-12 Tonya Lee, then 15, claimed that Harris asked her to sit on his lap before moving his hand up her leg and thigh. "*He was moving back and forth rubbing against me,*" she said. "*It was very subtle, it wasn't big movements.*" She told the jury that Harris had then patted her on the thigh and moved his hand upwards. She said she had "started to panic" and rushed to the toilet. When she came out, she said, Harris was waiting for her and gave her "a big bear hug" before putting his hand down her top and then down her skirt. Harris said he had no recollection of ever meeting Ms Lee.

So far all the charges have involved claims of one-off incidents of inappropriate touching. Counts 3-9 were potentially more serious, involving alleged grooming and actual sexual congress with a minor. The complainant was a childhood friend of Harris's daughter, Bindi. The burden of the complainant's testimony was as follows,

Harris took his daughter's friend with them on a holiday to Canada, Hawaii and Australia in 1978 when she was 13. As she came out of the shower wearing only a towel, she said that Harris put her hands over her and touched her intimately. She claimed that two days later Harris touched her again as she emerged from the sea, just feet from his sunbathing wife and daughter. He wrapped a towel round her and fondled her crotch, she said. She claimed that similar incidents happened throughout the holiday. On one occasion two years later, when she was 15, she said that Harris performed a sex act on her in Bindi's bedroom while his daughter slept in a single bed beside them. During another sleepover, he was said to have sexually abused her in Bindi's bedroom after Bindi had left the room. She claimed the abuse continued throughout her teenage years. On one occasion, when she was 19, she said that Harris sexually assaulted her in his swimming pool at his home in Bray, Berkshire. From this point, she started to go along with his demands. She said he went on to take advantage of her at his home, her family home, in his Mercedes while driving along the M4 and in his dressing room just before he was due to perform in Cinderella at Wimbledon Theatre in 1994. In 1987, when aged 22, she performed a sex act on Harris in his red Mercedes car on the M4. She said she was drunk at the time.

Harris admitted having a relationship with the woman, but said it began after she turned 18. It was not disputed that Harris and the complainant had a consensual sexual relationship from when she was 18 or 19 in 1983 until it was ended in 1994 when she was 29. They therefore had an adult, consensual sexual relationship for 10 or 11 years following the claimed period of abuse whilst the complainant was underage. It was not disputed that the affair ended acrimoniously. It was not disputed that the alleged victim had asked Harris for $45,000 although she disputes it was an attempt at blackmail as Harris claimed.

At the first of his trials, Rolf Harris was found guilty on all 12 charges and was sentenced to prison for five years and nine months. He was 84. There were 150 complaints that the sentence was too lenient. His clearance of one of those charges came only after he was released and hence too late to change his sentence.

Harris suffered from ill-health in prison, not surprisingly for a man of his age. When he required hospital attention, presumably fearing public demonstrations, he was sneaked into a secure ward in Royal Stoke hospital through a side door – into the "Ebola Ward" where he could be retained in a secure, private room, Ref.[9].

Harris was 87 when he was released from prison on parole on 19 May 2017 whilst his final trial was still in progress, and hence with the threat of going back to prison still hanging over him. He died on 10 May 2023. When the two-part documentary *Rolf Harris: Hiding In Plain Sight* premiered on the UK-only streaming service ITVX on 18 May 2023, it was not public knowledge that he was already dead. His death was announced only on 23 May, apparently to prevent unseemly interference with his funeral. News outlets' accounts of his death all had the general tenor "good riddance to the disgraced paedo".

But imprisonment is only part of the punishment. The public demanded that Rolf Harris be absolutely destroyed. All his achievements would be made void, his reputation turned to dross. It is obligatory in our times that his name be rendered synonymous with utter evil, with no hope of redemption. His punishment must continue after his release from prison in the form of being forever a social pariah with no reprieve possible. He was stripped of his Bafta fellowship. He was stripped of his CBE. He was stripped of his honorary degree from the University of East London. Galleries were reputed to have destroyed his art (or, at least, to have removed it from public view). His famous portrait of the Queen was quietly disappeared.

Harris's 11 million pound fortune was expected to be exhausted on legal costs as well as compensation claims, Ref.[10]. There was no shortage of other complainants coming forward, thanks to vigorous police trawling. On his release from prison he would have been close to broke, aged 87 and utterly vilified. He went to the grave knowing that he would be regarded as a monster after death and for as long as his name is remembered. Perhaps the public would like to have seen him face some lions in a modern Colosseum by way of a grand finale?

And so to the contrast between Harris's treatment and that of women sex offenders. I will draw the reader's attention to the extreme contrast between the vilification of Harris, by the court and public alike, and the following cases of adult female sexual offenders against minors. Please be aware that these are merely a few examples, confined to the UK and roughly contemporaneous with Harris's case. Do not imagine that female sex offences against minors are rare.

In years up to 2012, the 44-year-old woman and ex-teaching assistant EW had sex with a string of underage schoolboys in Wokingham, Ref.[11]. The latest offences against two boys took place in her own home, in her car and at the boys' school. She assaulted boys of 15 and 16 with no previous sexual experience. At her trial in 2014 the court was told these events were "a disgraceful abuse of her power".

The court heard that EW texted the boys, telling them to leave lessons, and would lead them to a deserted maths classroom at the Wokingham school where she worked. There she performed oral sex on them. The news accounts report that on one occasion she lured a 16-year-old around to her house for a sex session after messaging him via Facebook, telling him her husband was out. In another instance she texted the boy telling him to excuse himself from class, before dragging him into an empty maths room and asking: "Are you going to fuck me or not?" One day she offered to give him a lift home but she pulled her Jeep into a deserted car park and told him "before I go, I just want to do something" and unbuttoned his trousers and performed oral sex on him. After she had finished she performed a sex act on herself, groaning loudly.

It was also reported that EW asked a 15-year-old boy to keep the Bluetooth function on his phone activated so she could send him pictures of herself in her underwear playing with sex toys. The pair would kiss on the stairs at school and then have sex. In another instance, she drove the youngster to a secluded area of woodland, where they had sex on the back seat of her car. EW told the boy it did not matter about using a condom because she was unable to have children.

The judge was told that the boy had been reluctant to report the affair to the police because EW had threatened him with her husband, who was a black belt in karate. He feared a reprisal attack.

Her punishment?

She escaped jail being given only a suspended sentence and was ordered to undergo two years of supervision by the probation service and to pay a £100 victim surcharge. Mr Recorder John Gallagher told her she was only avoiding prison because she had already been punished for previous offences.

That's right. She avoided prison because she had previously been jailed for 32 months after admitting sexual assault of five other pupils at the same school.

Having let her off prison, the judge said, "this is your last chance, there can be no more of this". That's telling her, judge!

Not quite the same treatment as meted out to Rolf Harris, was it?

And if you think EW's behaviour was less reprehensible than Harris's, ask yourself: is that just because of the culture in which you have been raised – namely one in which women are always essentially harmless whatever they do, whereas men will be declared dangerous monsters after a far slighter offence. The test of this prejudice, this sex-bias, is revealed by reversing the sex of all involved in EW's case. How does it look now?

Note that, in all newspaper reports of sexual assaults by women, rather than using words like "assault" or "abuse" words like "affair" or "crush" or "sex romp" or "having a fling" are used. Here's another contemporaneous case.

According to the newspapers, CP, a 32-year-old married woman and teaching assistant, had a "torrid two-year affair" with a male pupil, starting when he was 14, Ref.[12]. According to the judge, though, the word "affair" did not cut it. He said,

"Let me make this abundantly clear, this is a case of gross child abuse. People who work as teaching assistants, whatever their gender, who take advantage of victims, of any gender, commit very serious offences indeed. It makes no difference that the victim was a boy. It makes no difference he may have thought he was in a relationship with you. The law is there to stop people taking advantage of children."

Quite, well said, judge – but he still gave her only a suspended sentence.

At the time of the offences (the newspapers used the word "affair"), CP was employed at a school in Chelmsford, Essex, and the teenage boy was a student in her class. The abuse (the phrase used in the newspapers was "illicit dalliance") reportedly started after the 14-year-old boy sent his teacher an innocent Christmas card. Soon after the boy turned 15, the pair embarked on a physical relationship. For two years, CP managed to keep her abuse of the boy secret. During that time she sent him several thousand lewd texts. When his parents found out about the abuse CP threatened to kill herself.

Explaining his decision to issue a suspended sentence, the Judge stated that although the boy was underage, he was a willing participant in the affair. Really? But, judge, are you not aware that the law says an underage person cannot give consent? That's why it's called "the age of consent". Bit of a clue, that. It seems to me that the judge was actually rationalising a disinclination to send her to prison which originated, not in any legal consideration, but in his own socially conditioned psychology.

And here's another case from around the same time.

In 2013, 35-year-old married mother of three and teacher, **BS**, had "an affair" (that word yet again) with her 16-year-old pupil, Gary after she confided in him about her marriage breakdown, Ref.[13]. **It's been illegal since 2000 for a teacher to have sex with a pupil under 18, even if it's consensual.** Gary was described in the newspapers as "fresh faced". The photos show someone you would unhesitatingly describe as a child (see Ref.[13]). According to the news reports, the pair started meeting in the local park (nothing shady there at all) and their relationship soon turned physical, although BS insisted that 'nothing sexual happened' beyond kissing. And yet she spent the night with him in his bed in jeans and a bra after the "affair" was discovered. BS looked surprised as the sheriff decided not to jail her and she left Stirling Sheriff's Court with a broad grin across her face. **Gary's parents were not impressed.** His father said, "It's not right. She's a sex offender, pure and simple", Ref.[14].

Here's another from the same year. Female babysitter, MEM, then 18, forced a 13-year-old boy to perform sex acts on her when she was supposed to be looking after him, Ref.[15]. In 2014, MEM, from Milton Keynes, was reported as having rubbed the boy's thigh and sat on top of him, straddling him face to face. She kissed him on the lips. He described it as open and closed mouth. She put his hand down her pyjamas, then placed her hand over his through the clothing. MEM committed sex acts on the boy on three separate occasions.

Later, MEM was reported to have sent a number of sexually explicit messages to the boy through Facebook. The court was told the messages read: *"We should meet up, just me and you. Keep it hush hush – don't tell [a friend]. You are fairly mature for your age and you're not bad looking. I have got a really soft spot for you, babe. I think you have a hidden talent. I think you could handle me. You are going to take control of me and show your dominant side. It isn't about size, it's the way you use it."* During the exchange she also said she 'could get into trouble' if anyone else read the messages. Clearly MEM was well aware that what she was doing was wrong.

Her defence barrister said MEM should have any jail sentence suspended so that she would benefit from one-to-one courses aimed to teach defendants appropriate sexual behaviour – something the defence claimed is not made available to serving prisoners. Personally, I have no great difficulty with such a suggestion, except, of course, that few people would extend such consideration to male offenders. To prison with the wicked men and to hell with any constructive treatment. Indeed, to hell with the men.

The judge, Karen Holt, said "The law reflects the seriousness of this abuse of trust on a child so young. As far as you are concerned, it is right I take into account your background – you have a sad background. You have not got into trouble despite your poor parenting. Bearing in mind your age and lack of previous convictions, your case doesn't meet the criteria for any form of imprisonment for public protection. A custodial sentence is appropriate. I have spent some time, bearing in mind all the circumstances, on whether that has to be an immediate custodial sentence. I am just about persuaded I don't need to send you to prison today." Again one wonders whether this same judge would have been "just about persuaded" against a custodial sentence if an 18-year-old male (a man) had done the same things – especially to a 13-year-old girl. The statistical evidence suggests not. I suggest that the judge would never have considered anything other than a custodial sentence for a male. In the case of a male, a disadvantaged background would not have been sufficient mitigation. Also, the judge would not have been so likely to dismiss the issue of "public protection" in the case of a male defendant, I suspect. To which public did she refer? Not the public of 13-year-old boys, I think. MEM was given a two-year prison sentence suspended for two years.

And here's another from the same year as Harris's conviction. Married, 35-year-old female teaching assistant HT was cleared by a jury of three allegations of sexual activity with a 16-year-old pupil but admitted sexual activity with a child by a person in a position of trust, Ref.[16]. She sent pictures of herself in lingerie to the 16-year-old, asked him what colour knickers she should wear to a meeting and told him he would be a legend if he had sex with her on her school desk, Ref.[17]. She was sentenced to four months in prison but suspended for two years by judge Peter Armstrong. Her husband said, after the hearing, that he had caught her 'in a clinch' with another boy, aged 17, previously, Ref.[18]. He realised where her priorities lay when she replaced a picture of their daughter with a picture of herself together with a boy pupil.

HT must be able to charm judges. She escaped prison again after she ran down a motorist and damaged two cars while drunk, Ref.[17]. Teesside Crown Court was shown video of her slurring words in her car. She even failed to give a breath sample to the police and failed to stop at the site of the crash. After such an offence one might have expected the previously suspended sentence to be activated. But, no. The judge told her "I am satisfied that there is ample protection to the public". Really, judge? As long as you are not a teenage boy or a road user?

And another from around the same time. 30-year-old female teaching assistant CB admitted having oral and penetrative sex with a boy she was teaching, Ref.[19]. In 2015 CB was given a two-year suspended prison sentence for three crimes: two counts of sexual activity with a child, and a third count of sexual activity in a position of trust. The boy was 15 at the time. CB was suspended then dismissed from a school in Manchester. After sentence was passed the boy criticised her suspended two-year sentence as 'atrocious', Ref.[20]. He said their relationship grew to such an extent that her two-year-old daughter started calling him 'dad'. He claimed they had unprotected sex at least 50 times and that CB tried moral blackmail on the boy, telling him she was pregnant and demanding he run away with her "or it would break my daughter's heart". There seems to have been an element of coercive control in their "relationship", and the boy ended up phoning Childline.

And another court case from the same year as Harris's. KAMB, 26, a woman teacher from Newport, pleaded guilty to four counts of the sexual offence "abuse of position of trust by engaging in sexual activity with a child", Ref.[21]. The offences, spanning a period of seven months, concerned a sexual relationship KAMB had had with a pupil aged under 18, whom she was teaching at the school where she worked. We are not told the actual age of the pupil. The matter came to light when the pair visited a sexual health clinic. More than 1,200 text messages between the pair were found on KAMB's phone, including sexually explicit content. Police also recovered naked pictures of the pupil stored on her phone. The court heard how the pair went away together on two separate occasions. In January 2013, the pupil accompanied KAMB on a teacher training weekend. There the pupil stayed in a hotel with her, paid for by the school as part of a training course. The two went away again in July 2013 on a camping weekend where sexual activity again took place. KAMB admitted to seeing the pupil at least once a week outside of school for the purposes of sex. She was sentenced to ten months for each count, to be served concurrently and suspended for two years. She was ordered to complete 200 hours of unpaid work. She has been added to the sex offenders register and automatically barred from working with young adults or children.

Then, again from the same year, there was the delightful KA, divorced 44-year-old mother of two, who took advantage of being offered a bed in a friend's house after a party to sexually assault her friend's son, aged 14, Ref.[22]. KA pounced on the boy as he got ready for bed and used him as her "sex object" – only to be rumbled when his older brother heard her making sex noises. The boy later told a friend: "I went to get into my trackies and she stripped naked in front of me. We had sex but it was really weird. She kept asking me to spit on her and all these weird things". KA initially tried to claim that the boy initiated the sex, but changed her plea to guilty at the last minute. In 2014 she was sentenced at Canterbury Crown Court to a nine-month jail sentence – but yet again suspended. The boy's mother was not impressed, noting "he was just a child". She opined that female offenders should be treated the same as male offenders: that KA should have gone to prison.

And I haven't mentioned yet the 'celebrated' case of JH, the 21-year-old woman babysitter from Swindon whose idea of 'looking after' an 11-year-old boy included full sexual intercourse, Ref.[23]. According to the news reports, she simply stripped off, then stripped him, then straddled him.

Judge Tim Mousley QC said it was an exceptional case that allowed him to step outside the rigours of the sentencing guidelines. He claimed that, because the boy was a mature 11-year-old and JH was an immature 20-year-old at the time, *"that narrows the arithmetic age gap between you"*. Yet again we see, in my opinion, a judge's rationalising his innate reluctance to see females as abusers. On the stated grounds he imposed a six-month sentence…you guessed, suspended for two years. Despite appeal against this sentence that many, including the boy's mother, saw as too lenient, the appeal court upheld the original sentence, Ref.[24].

Are you still having difficulty with your socially conditioned perspective that it's not very serious when women do it to boys? Try reversing the sexes on the last couple of cases. The complainants in the Harris case were described in the newspapers as "brave victims" who had undergone "terrifying ordeals". The boy victims of the above women were never described in such terms in the newspaper reports.

It is not only men who are subjected to historical allegations of sexual abuse. A woman, MMcC, was tried in 2015 for sexual offences against a 15-year-old boy 29 years earlier when she was 33, Ref.[25]. In 1986 MMcC visited the boy's mother and when he came downstairs in a towel to get something for his bath she wolf-whistled at him. As he left the room he heard her telling his mum that if she went after him he "would go up the stairs as a boy and come down as a man". While he was in the bath she came in, plunged her hand into the water and grabbed his private parts and after making a sexual remark she left laughing.

A week later he was at her Huyton home looking after her young son when she sat next to him wearing a tight nightdress and after saying everything would be all right began stroking different parts of his body. She helped him undress, before they had sexual intercourse. "He did not fancy her but did not know how to stop what was happening," said the prosecutor. Over the next six weeks MMcC orchestrated about 30 other occasions for various sexual activities and the boy felt coerced into taking part. Eventually he told his mother's partner who said he would sort it out but MMcC continued her abuse of the boy. She would say, "I have to have you" and "I can't stop myself."

Judge Watson summed up as follows. "*You manipulated him for your own sexual advantage, you groomed him....You used him as your sexual plaything. I hope you now realise your behaviour has cast a shadow over his life for the last 29 and a half years. An appalling shadow which has had a real impact upon him. If anyone thought it was the sort of behaviour a 15-year-old boy would fantasise about, this case gives the lie to that very false picture. You deserve to go to prison for what you did, it was not a one off but a string of different sexual acts against him that summer. The very fact that he came forward last year to tell someone tells you it is not something he has been able to leave behind at all.*"

Then the judge sentenced her to 21 months in prison – suspended for two years. Yet again, no jail for the female offender. Her victim "stormed angrily" out of the courtroom.

Is this lenience to women sex offenders because the victim is male? There may be an element of that, but it is certainly not the only factor. Women sexually offending against girls are also treated leniently. Take the case of 27-year-old Cumbrian teacher HS, Ref.[26], again from the same year as Harris's trial. According to the judge, she groomed a 15-year-old girl pupil, including the use of a large number of "intimate and explicit" text messages and moving images. They 'counted down the days' until her 16th birthday after which the teacher admitted they had had a sexual relationship (it would seem in ignorance of such an act being illegal between a teacher and a pupil aged 16). The judge said the explicit texts and images were a significant aggravating feature. Nevertheless, he gave HS only a suspended sentence on the basis that "the relationship appeared to be a case of mutual affection". Hmm, I think we can conclude there was some mutual affection between Rolf Harris and his daughter's friend, given that their adult affair lasted 10 or 11 years. But what's mitigation for the goose is not mitigation for the gander, clearly.

And here's another from the same year as Harris's conviction and involving a female victim, in this case no older than 12. CH, a 25-year-old woman, was a beauty pageant judge when, the reports state, she intensively groomed and ultimately sexually assaulted a young girl, plying her with cigarettes and alcohol, Ref.[27]. CH sent 1,200 texts and social media messages to her victim – who was under 13 years old. But she was spared jail. She was given an 18-month jail sentence suspended for two years after she admitted four sexual assaults on the girl and "being an adult who met a girl following grooming".

Then there is the 2015 trial of the female PE teacher, SB, 31, from Coventry who admitted sex acts with two teenage girl pupils from her school, Refs.[28,29]. The news reports say she groomed the girls, the offences taking place over a period of three years. One of the girls was 13 or 14 when the abuse started, the other 16. SB engaged in sex in a storeroom with one of her victims after befriending her on an internet messaging site. There was one occasion when she was in bed with both girls at the same time. One of her victims said she felt "that she was groomed into thinking that she was gay when she had never looked at the same sex in that way before". SB was sentenced to 18 months in prison, this time immediate custody.

In 2013, female teacher RS, 41, from Caerphilly, denied indecent assault and sexual activity on a female pupil starting when the girl was 14, Ref.[30]. RS started the "relationship" after kissing the girl in a stationery cupboard at the school where she taught her. The court heard the girl had sleepovers at RS's house several times a week. Their liaisons continued for four years until the girl's parents found out and put a stop to it. But, after starting university, the girl ultimately went to the police. RS's defence counsel argued that it was a "genuine loving relationship", but she was found guilty and given an 18-month prison sentence.

So we see that female sex offenders do not always escape gaol. Where the victim is male, however, cases awarded an immediate custodial sentence are generally more heinous than those reviewed above. For example, the young woman, LM, was jailed for a nominal two years in March 2014, Ref.[31]. LM had full sexual intercourse with an eight-year-old boy at least 50 times, starting when she was 16. She continued having sex with the boy until he was 10. At trial LM was 21 and had a child of her own.

And there was the case of CL, the 48-year-old female music teacher from Leeds, who was jailed in 2015 for 6 months for sex offences against a vulnerable 17-year-old boy at the special needs school where she worked, Ref.[32]. The boy was described as having learning difficulties, a general developmental delay and a lack of stranger-danger awareness. CL kissed and exchanged flirty messages with the vulnerable teenager and they also engaged in sexual activity in her bed on two occasions.

Then there was a woman, AL, who was tried in 2015 for historical sex offences and sentenced to eight years in prison. AL denied all the allegations but admitted having a legal, sexual relationship with the older complainant when he was 18. AL, aged 55 when convicted, was a nationally acclaimed head teacher in the 1980s. Earlier in her career, starting at age 28 when she was a history teacher, she groomed two boys, aged 13 and 15. While she was married to the second of three husbands, AL had groomed the younger victim. He was encouraged to expose her breasts during a dare game at her home before she let him watch her bathe. She then took his virginity on the marital bed while he was still in his school uniform. She seduced the other boy in a tent at a camp in the middle of the night after she encouraged him to sneak over. The teacher had told her husband to sleep in a separate tent before asking the boy to visit her. She had repeated sexual relations with the two boys over several years.

Oddest of all in respect of female-on-female sex offences are those which involve the abuser pretending to be male. A case which came to trial in 2015 was that of 25-year-old GN of Cheshire, Ref.[34]. Her victim, though, was another adult woman, also 25. The complainant and GN were friends, as women. But the complainant claimed that GN had also taken the persona of a man and had tricked her into wearing a blindfold whenever they met, including the ten or so times they had sex – with GN wearing a prosthetic penis. The defendant claimed, unsuccessfully, that there was no blindfold and her partner was both consenting and knowing regarding her true gender. False accusation? Who knows, but I suspect that impersonating a man made GN's position in court far more problematic for her defence. She got eight years – clearly her male impersonation was good enough to get a man's sentence.

A similar case in 2013, and involving underage girls, did not result in a custodial sentence for female perpetrator CW of Aberdeen. She was 19 to 21 when the offences took place; her victims were 13. Presenting herself as a 17-year-old male, CW "used a sex toy to persuade the girls of her sex". Unlike the case of GN, the virginal girls in question would be easier to fool. Unusually one of the victims has identified herself, Megan A. She was unaware of the deceit until the police told her and was outraged at the sentence CW received: probation and 240 hours community service. Megan said, "*She will be able to go back to her own house and lie in her own bed again. I will also be lying in mine, still trying to deal with what she has done to me. I really hope the judge has thought this sentence through because if C does this again, I hope he knows it's on his conscience"*. Judges don't think like that, Megan.

The judge said that CW's gender identity disorder led her to genuinely feel that she was male and that significantly lowered her culpability. My mind just refuses the fence on that one. Had CW felt authentically like a man she would have had a heightened sense of culpability, not the reverse. Moreover, her feelings are not the issue. If I genuinely believe I deserve that BMW 7-series I just stole, does that justify my theft? The issue, in any case, is unlawful sexual activity with a minor – regardless of CW's sex or sexuality. What do we pay these judges for?

These male-impersonator cases may not be as rare as you'd think. There was a documentary on UK TV circa 2013 in which a late-teenage girl had fooled a younger girl into believing she was a boy. She ended up in bed with her and raped her with a 6 inch wooden dildo. A woman acquaintance who watched the documentary with me opined, "she's not a rapist, she's just a poor confused girl". Well, of course, those two statements are not mutually exclusive. My annoyance at the remark lies, as always, in the double standard. Had the girl been a boy and behaved in exactly the same way, there would be no qualification of the designation "rapist". Having the nerve to suggest that a male perpetrator might be a "poor confused boy" would not be well received, and might meet with screeches of "rape apologist".

All these court cases were within a year of Rolf Harris's conviction and all in the UK.

I have not included the far more serious cases of Marie Black and Vanessa George who were each instrumental in separate organised paedophile rings, involving other abusers, both men and women. Marie Black's case was tried the same year Harris was convicted. She faced 24 charges against five children under 13, including five counts of child cruelty, four of rape and seven of causing children under 13 to engage in sexual activity, as well as several counts of sexual assault, Ref.[36]. She was at the centre of a "gruesome" child sex abuse ring which passed children round "like toys". The children were abused at parties arranged for the purpose and are believed to have been offered as prizes in raffles. She was given a life sentence, Ref.[37]. Several years earlier, Vanessa George, 40, from Plymouth, was jailed for a minimum of seven years after admitting abusing toddlers at the nursery where she worked and photographing it, Ref.[38]. Vanessa George admitted seven sexual assaults and six counts of making and distributing indecent pictures of children. She used a mobile phone to take pictures of herself abusing toddlers and shared them with others on the internet.

The few cases reviewed above are certainly the tip of the iceberg as regards illegal sexual activities between women and underage boys or girls. Ref.[39] is a list of women teachers in the USA who were convicted of sexual offences against boys. It is a very long list, despite being mostly from only a five-year period, 2005 to 2009.

I will not reiterate the statistics of women's sexual offending but refer you to my previous book, Ref.[40]. I will only note here that the academic literature of female perpetrated sexual abuse is both extensive and of long standing, as you can see from Ref.[41] for which the first entry is 1857. That list was discontinued in early 2016.

Jenni Murray, Ref.[42], has difficulty understanding why women do it. She would have no such difficulty understanding why men do it, I suspect, though, as a feminist, her understanding of that too might be badly wrong. Her difficulty with women sex offenders originates from the feminist conceit that all women are invariably benign. They are not. Women are just as flawed as men. This is the opinion of Anthony Beech, Ref.[43], criminological psychology professor at the University of Birmingham on female teacher sex offenders: *"The teachers feel entitled. They think they can have sex with anyone they want. It's power imbalance and manipulation. There's a narcissism – I can do what I want because I'm the most important person going."*

The above examples demonstrate that women's offending commonly displays the following characteristics: persistent grooming which continues for years, offences against multiple victims, offences against either pre-pubescent victims (hence physically as well as legally children), as well as against pubescent victims, and threats in the event of disclosure. The words used by judges in their summing-up at the trials have included statements such as, *"a disgraceful abuse of power"*, *"a case of gross child abuse"*, and *"very serious offences indeed"*.

And yet the women whose offences were described in these terms often receive only suspended sentences, and generally fail to attract public opprobrium except in extreme cases. When women are imprisoned for sex offences against underage but pubescent boys (hebephilia), many people struggle to interpret this as just. Many (most?) people simply do not believe that the sexual exploitation of pubescent boys by women is damaging. Barbara Ellen, responding to the case of female offender MM, wrote in the Guardian, Ref.[44], *"do we seriously think that a female teacher sleeping with a male pupil is on a par with a male teacher sleeping with a girl pupil? I don't. And neither, I'd wager, would most 15-year-old boys....If anything, one would have thought they might be jealous. The internet is awash with sites dealing with "older woman teacher-pupil" fantasies. And there lies the rub – should the law be treating male and female pupil victims equally when male and female teenagers are so different?"*

Barbara Ellen can rest assured that, in general, the judiciary reflects her (overtly sexist) position, as do most of society. Barbara Ellen's position, simply put, is that "he enjoyed it and he should be grateful for the attention". Barbara Ellen's views are obnoxious, but, I suspect, distressingly common. In her world view only females are precious and vulnerable. Males are neither. It never crosses her mind that a teenage boy's facade of sexual bravado has been imposed upon him by a gynocentric society – because the assumption of braggadocio is the role which boys have been allotted. It is no accident that this psychological trap then gives spurious justification to female preferencing. That sexually exploited boys suffer damage is not something in which Barbara Ellen and her kind believe or have any concern. Even given their concern only for females, they may have a different opinion if better informed. The proportion of adult male sex offenders against females who have been sexually abused as minors specifically by women is extremely high (see Ref.[40]).

This is the empathy gap: the source of most male disadvantage. It is this same empathy gap which permits male victimisation to be vanished away. This vanishing away of male victimisation is official CPS VAWG policy, Ref.[45]. It is reflected in, for example, the public being unaware that not all the victims of the grooming gangs of Rotherham and Oxfordshire were girls – at least 50 and 80 respectively were boys. The Rotherham report, Ref.[46], noted that none of the boy victims had been flagged by social workers as "risky business" and stressed the importance of *"making sure that judgments about child sexual exploitation are consistent and gender neutral, for example by asking if the same level of risk would be acceptable if the child was the opposite gender".*

This is not a new observation. In the USA, a 2008 report revealed that, in New York City, 53.5% of the victims of commercial sexual exploitation of children were boys, Ref.[47]. In 2013 a report by the organisation End Child Pornography and Trafficking, Ref.[48], similarly reported about 50% of children trafficked and sexually exploited to be boys in the USA as a whole. In 2014 in the UK Barnardo's criticised the stereotypical belief that boys are less vulnerable to child sexual exploitation, observing that this has led to boys receiving insufficient protection from front-line services, Ref.[49]. Barnardo's stated that new findings indicate up to a third of child victims are male.

I may seem to have strayed from my brief, namely the different treatment of male and female sex offenders, by both the public and the courts. But my point is that the invisibility of male victims of sexual abuse, and the harsher treatment of male perpetrators of sexual abuse, have a common cause: the empathy gap for males. And "empathy gap" is a polite term for prejudice.

The public are deeply sexist, men and women both. This is why they can demand that Rolf Harris be thrown into the nethermost pit of hell, whilst simultaneously regarding women who commit very similar offences, or worse, as merely "having an illicit fling". This anti-male sexism has been inflamed to neurotic proportions by feminism. Masculinity is intrinsically toxic. Male sexuality is essentially nasty. Any expression of male sexuality, however mild, will be seen as threatening and abusive. Women's sexuality, on the other hand, is benign – even when they do exactly the same thing, or far worse.

The ambient mythology of women's perpetually caring and compassionate nature protects them from being seen as sexually predatory. The myth trumps reality at every turn. Reality is perceived through the filter of society's preconceptions. This is what sexism is. Everything a man does is exploitative, predatory, damaging, dangerous and an expression of his male power. Nothing a woman does can possibly be any of these things, even when it is.

A man touching a woman's bottom is a monstrous predator. But if a woman were to fondle my behind in a public place (and, yes, it's happened, more than once) it is not something that I could even complain about without being mocked. Not that I have the slightest wish to. I'm not playing the victim here. I have not been socialised to regard myself as so precious that I need the fainting couch over such trivia. But the feminist victimhood mentality is precisely such pretension. It is convenient for feminists to appear vulnerable, because their illusion of vulnerability is their strength, their power.

And this is what the vilification of the likes of Rolf Harris is really about: female power. This, and the ocean of propaganda in which we swim, is to remind us constantly that all men are dogs and we need to remember our place.

References

[1] Elsie and Vi (undated). Rolf Harris is Innocent.

[2] Merritt, W. (2022). *Rolf Harris: The Defence Team's Special Investigator reveals the Truth behind the Trials*. UK Book Publishing, 5 May 2022.

[3] Davis, M. (2014). *Rolf Harris trial: 'no independent evidence' to prove entertainer was at scene of alleged sexual assaults, defence claims*. The Standard, 23 May 2014.

[4] Smith, V. (2014). *Rolf Harris 'victim' Tonya Lee denies making up sex assault claims to pay off debts*. Mirror, 21 May 2014.

[5] BBC News (2014). *Rolf Harris guilty of indecent assaults*. 30 June 2014.

[6] Camber, R. (2017). *'Youngest victim' of Rolf Harris may have to pay him back £22,000 in compensation after his conviction for groping her is overturned on appeal*. Mail Online, 17 November 2017.

[7] England, C. (2017). *Rolf Harris cleared of three sexual assault charges at Southwark Crown Court*. Independent, 8 February 2017.

[8] BBC News (2017). *Rolf Harris trial: Jury discharged as no verdicts reached*. 30 May 2017.

[9] Wheatstone, R. and Murphy, I. (2015). *Rolf Harris 'admitted to Ebola ward' after being sneaked into hospital side-entrance*. Mirror, 12 Nov 2015.

[10] Evans, M. and Hollywatt (2014). *Compensation claims could see Rolf Harris lose his £11 million fortune*. The Telegraph, 1 July 2014.

[11] Thorne, L. and Gutteridge, N. (2015). *EW: Ex-teaching assistant had sex with schoolboys at family home while husband was at work*. Mirror, 14 March 2015.

[12] Mullin, G. (2014). *Married teaching assistant, 32, sent thousands of lewd texts after starting two-year affair with 14-year-old schoolboy - and threatened suicide when his parents found out*. Mail Online, 14 October 2014.

[13] Moncur J. (2014a) *Married teacher BS spared jail term after admitting affair with schoolboy, 16*. Daily Record, 1 March 2014.

[14] Moncur, J. (2104b). *Married teacher BS grins as she's spared jail term after admitting affair with 16-year-old schoolboy*. Mirror, 26 February 2014.

[15] Thornhill, E. (2015). *Babysitter who forced a 13-year-old boy to perform sex acts on her at a onesie party avoids jail*. Mail Online, 10 November 2015.

[16] Armstrong, J. (2014). *Teaching assistant cleared of having sex with schoolboy but guilty of kissing him*. 20 November 2014.

[17] Corcoran, K. (2015). *Teaching assistant whose life was left in tatters after a fling with a pupil is spared prison AGAIN after she ran down a motorist and damaged two cars while drunk*. Mail Online, 18 September 2015.

[18] Wellman, A. (2014). *Ex-husband of teaching assistant who admitted kissing teenage pupil 'walked in on her canoodling another'*. 22 November 2014.

[19] Corcoran, K. (2015). *Shamed teaching assistant, 30, escapes jail after she admitted having sex with a teenage student*. Mail Online, 23 September 2015.

[20] Duell, M. (2015). *Schoolboy seduced by disgraced teaching assistant reveals they had sex 50 times - and she told him he had made her pregnant*. Mail Online, 29 September 2015.

[21] Lea, L. (2014). *Newport teacher who slept with pupil spared jail*. South Wales Argus, 7 April 2014.

[22] Kent Online(2014). *Deal mother's betrayal by former friend KA who seduced son of 14 three decades her junior*. 1 August 2014.

[23] Ward, V. (2015). *Babysitter spared jail after having sex with boy aged 11*. The Telegraph, 5 October 2015.

[24] Twomey, J. (2015). *Mother's fury as baby sitter who seduced her son avoids jail again*. Express, 9 December 2015.

[25] Siddle, J. (2015). *Gran who groomed and stole virginity of schoolboy comes face-to-face with victim in court 30 years later*. 16 October 2015.

[26] BBC News (2014). *Cumbria teacher HS sentenced for affair with schoolgirl*. 12 August 2014.

[27] Williams, A. (2014). *Female beauty pageant judge, 25, groomed pre-teen girl with 1,200 texts and social media messages before sexually assaulting her*. Mail Online, 6 August 2014.

[28] Robinson, M. (2015). *Female PE teacher, 31, is facing jail after admitting sex acts with two teenage girl pupils from her school who she was caught in bed with at same time*. Mail Online, 26 October 2015.

[29] BBC News (2016). *SB jailed over child sex offences in Coventry*. 29 January 2016.

[30] BBC News (2013). *Fairwater High teacher RS jailed over sex with pupil*. 22 November 2013.

[31] Corcoran, K. (2014). *Female paedophile, 21, is jailed for two years after she had sex with an eight-year-old boy 50 times, starting when she was 16*. Mail Online, 21 March 2014.

[32] Glanfield, E. (2015). *Music teacher, 48, who had sex with a 'vulnerable' boy of 17 who she taught at a special needs school is jailed*. Mail Online, 16 July 2015.

[33] Cockcroft, S. (2015). *Branded a 'dirty pervert' and sentenced to eight years: Headteacher once hailed a visionary is jailed for taking the virginity of two underage boys in the 1980s*. Mail Online, 25 June 2015.

[34] Robson, S. and Wheatstone, R. (2015). *Fake penis woman jailed for 8 years for tricking female pal into sex using prosthetic*. Mirror, 12 November 2015.

[35] Cramb, A. (2013). *Teenage victim of woman who pretended to be a man speaks out*. 9 April 2013.

[36] Mail On Sunday (2014). *Woman, 33, appears in court accused of raping and abusing children*. 15 June 2014.

[37] BBC News (2015). *Marie Black gets life term for child abuse*. 28 September 2015.

[38] BBC News (2010). *Little Ted's was 'ideal' place for Vanessa George abuse*. 4 November 2010.

[39] WND. *Women teachers sexual offending against underage boys in USA*. Compiled from wnd.com circa 2016.

[40] Collins, W. (2019). *The Empathy Gap*. LPS Publishing, 2019. See chapter 20.

[41] *Bibliography Female Sex Offenders and Their Victims Chronological.docx*, and see also *Bibliography Female Sex Offenders and Their Victims Alphabetical.docx*. Do not try to access the site from which this list was originally downloaded. It closed in 2017 and the URL has been taken over by a porn site.

[42] Murray, J. (2015). *Disturbing rise of the women child sex predators: How sickening slew of babysitters and teachers are abusing young boys and girls – but would they be punished so leniently if they were men?* Mail Online, 15 October 2015. I wrote a personal reaction to this article in 2015 which has since been removed from my web site but which I can supply privately on request.

[43] Sanghani, R. (2015). *Underage sex conviction: Why older women have sex with young boys*. The Telegraph, 23 June 2015.

[44] Ellen, B. (2009). *This shameful liaison does not deserve prison*. The Guardian, 29 November 2009.

[45] Collins, W. (2105). *The Desolation of VAWG | The Illustrated Empathy Gap*. 4 July 2015.

[46] Jay, A. (2014). *Independent Inquiry into Child Sexual Exploitation in Rotherham 1997 – 2013*. 21 August 2014.

[47] Curtis, R. et al. (2008). *Commercial Sexual Exploitation of Children in New York City, Volume One: The CSEC Population in New York City: Size, Characteristics, and Needs*. Report Submitted to the National Institute of Justice, United States Department of Justice, September 2008.

[48] Logan Keziah, L. (2019). *Boys: The Under-mentioned Victims of Child Sex Trafficking and Sexual Exploitation*. Social Worker web site swhelper, 7 April 2019.

[49] Malik, Z. *Barnardo's: Sexual exploitation of boys 'overlooked'*. BBC News, 27 August 2014.

15. Rape Trial Juries and the Erosion of Justice

Here I combine a couple of posts on feminists' attempts to hold rape trials without juries as a means of gaining more convictions. The actual guilt of the men in question is of no concern to them. This would be unacceptable under any circumstances, but when combined with the large proportion of rape allegations which are false (chapter 8 and Ref.[6]) and the corruption of the disclosure process (chapter 17) what we are looking at is systemic corruption of justice.

Originals posted on: 28 May 2021 and 30 April 2023

Feminists have an implacable determination to put more men in prison for rape. That objective is now being progressed by the SNP – well known for their upholding of strict personal standards. (The SNP is the Scottish National Party, the ruling party in Scotland as I write in March 2024).

In my May 2021 article, Ref.[1], I addressed the growing feminist determination to achieve more rape convictions by promoting the idea that jurors are unsuitable to make judgments on these sex offence cases. Mere lay persons, the hoi polloi, the riff-raff, the deplorables (that'll be us) have not the wisdom to decide upon such matters. Any similarity to the reaction of the establishment to the Chartists' petitions of the early nineteenth century is entirely apposite.

But what has that got to do with our former Deputy Prime Minister, Justice Secretary and Lord Chancellor who was ousted from these posts in April 2023? I'll come to that.

The feminists' proposed policy on the matter revolves around either doing away with juries in rape trials, or subjecting juries to "training". One knows who would do the "training". No doubt juries would be told that women rarely lie about rape, perhaps presenting some of the spurious statistics which abound. Such "trained" juries would be a sham, an obvious undermining of the principle that juries should be drawn, uncontaminated, from the general public. But focus has, it seems, shifted to calling for juries to be scrapped entirely in rape trials by those who interpret any not-guilty verdict as the jury's error, for example Julie Bindel, Ref.[2], and Labour MP Ann Coffey, Ref.[3]. Coffey claimed that juries were "reluctant to convict young men" apparently because of "the dominance of rape myths in society and shockingly low conviction rates". She repeated these claims in a parliamentary debate, Ref.[4]. Both are untrue as we shall see.

In happier times, one might have had confidence that Members of Parliament would have the wisdom, and historical appreciation, to protect jury trials with great passion. No longer. Feminism is now the dominant caucus across all parties. Feminists have no truck with nasty patriarchal wisdoms. They can contemplate the abolition of juries in rape trials with nothing but approbation. But justice, like freedom, is indivisible.

You may be inclined to dismiss this whole issue, wondering why you should waste time or concern upon rapists, who are, after all, the scum of the earth. The issue here is, of course, whether the accused actually are rapists. If you incline to the belief that women never lie about rape, then all that stands between you and a horrible awakening is an accusation. Do not be too confident that that cannot happen: being innocent is not a guarantee. There are cases, e.g., Ref.[5], where a man ends up in court on a rape charge made by a woman whom he has never met. The percentage of rape allegations which are false is, perhaps, almost quantum mechanical in its uncertainty, for example see Ref.[6]. The only thing one need appreciate is that, regardless of the unknowable percentage, false allegations are common not rare.

Consequently, in a decent society with a decent criminal justice system, it is essential that the rights of the accused (of rape or anything else) are protected. Irrespective of some people's opinion to the contrary, (e.g., Ref.[7]) it is a sound principle that it is better to let ten guilty men go free than to incarcerate a single innocent man (probably for 10 years or more in the case of rape). This is what "beyond reasonable doubt" is about. And, as barrister Matthew Scott has emphasised, Ref.[8], scrapping juries in rape trials may well be the precursor to scrapping juries altogether – they are expensive, after all.

Moreover, with the CPS determined to subvert the disclosure process (see chapter 17), the very problem that resulted in the collapse of some celebrated rape cases, the last thing our trial system needs is the abandonment of juries too.

To impose some patriarchal wisdom on you: when the criminal justice system becomes highjacked by a political power, you are on the path to tyranny, if not already there.

The 2018 debate in parliament, Ref.[4], was held as the result of a petition, Ref.[9]. The petitioners claimed that,

"Research shows that jurors accept commonly held rape myths resulting in many incorrect not guilty verdicts. Rapists are walking free from court, although evidence is robust."

And that,

"Research by Rape Crisis and Alison Saunders, Director of Public Prosecutions, finds that jurors often accept rape myths and thus acquit rapists who are in fact guilty. 66% of jurors do not understand judges' legal directions which attempt to dispel rape myths, but fail. Jurors need proper rape myth training prior to and throughout trials."

Leaving aside that Alison Saunders is hardly one's first choice if the objective is to bolster credibility, the petitioners' claims were followed by three links, as if to material reporting the ostensible "research". Not so. All the links merely list the supposed rape myths (e.g., Ref.[10]); none provide any evidence whatsoever that there is widespread public belief in them or, more specifically, that jurors believe these myths.

There is no such research.

I can be pretty confident about that for two reasons. Firstly, had there been any, it would certainly have been linked.

More fundamentally, though, to support the contention regarding rape trial jurors' views it would be necessary to interview such jurors. This is problematic because jurors are prohibited from discussing cases. Special dispensation would be required to permit jurors to answer questions put to them by specifically authorised researchers. To date the only researcher granted this permission in England is Professor Cheryl Thomas and her team. (Thomas is Professor of Judicial Studies at UCL and Director of the UCL Jury Project).

In her 2020 report, Ref.[15], Thomas was scathing about the petitioners' claims…

"At the time of the petition there had been no research in England and Wales with real jurors on the issue of whether they accepted commonly held rape myths or understood judges' directions on such myths. This meant that the petition's claim that research showed jurors accepted commonly held rape myths and did not understood judges' directions on these myths could not have been correct."

That's polite academic speak for "they made it up". But I get ahead of myself; I'll return to Thomas's 2020 report shortly.

Readers may recognise the name Cheryl Thomas. She has previous form in respect of upsetting the feminist position on rape juries. In her 2010 review of this subject, Ref.[11], she concluded that, contrary to popular belief and previous official reports, juries in rape trials convict more often than they acquit. In fact, in 2010 she concluded that jury conviction rates in rape cases exceed that in other serious crimes (attempted murder, manslaughter, GBH), adding that *"Juries are not primarily responsible for the low conviction rate on rape allegations"*. In 2010 Professor Thomas also concluded that,

"Jury conviction rates for rape vary according to the gender and age of the complainant, with high conviction rates for some female complainants and low conviction rates for some male complainants. This challenges the view that juries' failure to convict in rape cases is due to juror bias against female complainants."

In other words it is men, not women, who get short-changed by the justice system when complaining about rape. In Tables 19.4a-c of *The Empathy Gap*, Ref.[12], I compare conviction rates for all ages of male and female complainants of sexual assault, data which is fully consistent with Thomas's conclusion. This is worth noting because the data in CPS VAWG reports on rape prosecutions and convictions does not disaggregate by sex of victim – and, notoriously, the CPS VAWG reports classify male victims as victims of Violence Against Women and Girls (see Ref.[13]).

I'll not burden this post with rape conviction statistics, though you can find a compilation in the original posts, Refs.[1,14].

Before I return to Professor Thomas's work, what is the Scottish parliament up to? Well, as Stuart Waiton, lecturer at Abertay University, put it *"the Scottish government, aided and abetted by the judiciary, is mounting an elitist assault on the justice system"*, Ref.[16].

Lord Advocate Dorothy Bain KC, Scotland's top prosecutor, declared her support for juryless trials for rape and attempted rape cases, Ref.[17]. She said she regarded politicians as "morally obliged" to consider it. Bain based this opinion on the claim that research shows there is "overwhelming evidence" that jurors hold "prejudicial and false beliefs" about rape that affect their evaluation of evidence presented at trial, and that this research has found "considerable evidence of the expression of problematic attitudes towards rape complainers" among jurors. In other words, the usual "rape myths" argument.

The research Bain was referring to was that of Glasgow University's Fiona Leverick and co-workers published in March 2021, Ref.[18]. Leverick has given a description of her research in Ref.[19]. Leverick, with Glasgow University colleague Professor James Chalmers, and Professor Vanessa Munro of Warwick University, were commissioned to carry out the work by the Scottish Government. (Is that a paymaster who is neutral? Note that the former justice secretary and current First Minister, Humza Yousaf, has a history of advocating for juryless trials in an even wider context, Ref.[17]). Here's the key extract regarding how Leverick et al acquired their data,

"The team used professional polling companies to recruit hundreds of volunteers, via public and door-to-door work. Videos of trials were made and mock juries were set up in buildings made to resemble courts."

In other words, real jurors were not involved. The point is crucial because the November 2020 report by Cheryl Thomas contains a devastating critique of the use of such methods – of which Leverick et al **must** have been fully aware before publication. The same newspaper report, Ref.[19], rightly alludes to this, quoting Tony Lenehan, president of the Scottish Criminal Bar Association,

"The research from Fiona Leverick and colleagues involved pretend jurors hearing pretend cases as the law doesn't allow research with real jurors in real cases. Important academic voices add to our own doubts about the validity of this type of limited inquiry. It is disappointing to see the Lord Advocate embrace uncritically the stated findings of the mock jury work, where academic peers have expressed substantial misgivings....No type of High Court trial needs the input of our society more than rape trials....Jury-less trials in rape cases is a terrible idea. It seems to prioritise the voices of an emotionally invested minority, undermined by, rather than supported by, evidence and experience. It will dilute public confidence in justice and, in the long term, is likely to achieve the opposite of what it hopes."

Quite. And there are plenty of other authoritative legal voices speaking out against this feminist crusade (e.g., Refs.[20-24]. But there were plenty of authoritative medical voices speaking out against the government's covid-19 impositions, but to no avail. Dorothy Bain's wishes have triumphed, at least in political circles. Lady Dorrian's review , Ref.[25], has provided the basis for the SNP government to instigate a pilot juryless trial system, now given the green light, Ref.[26]. The political view may not triumph, however, as lawyers are resisting it. Trials cannot take place without legal counsel and the boycott of juryless trials looks solid at present, Ref. [27].

And so, at last, to the 2020 report by the UCL Jury Project led by Professor Cheryl Thomas, Ref.[15]. It is such an emphatic demolishing of the Bain-Dorrian-Leverick feminist position that I quote it at some length. Thomas sets the background to her research thus,

"The 21st century jury in England and Wales has recently come under attack on the grounds that jurors are biased against complainants in rape cases and refuse to convict defendants in rape and sexual offences cases because they believe myths and stereotypes about rape and sexual behaviour. Until now there has been no empirical evidence based on research with real jurors at court in England and Wales to either substantiate or refute these claims. But this has not deterred the making of assertions about jury bias in rape and sexual offences cases, including calls for the removal of juries in rape cases.

None of these claims were based on any research with actual juries in England and Wales. Instead they have relied on public opinion polls, a single study that used students and volunteers to act as proxy ("mock") jurors and anecdotal views of prosecutors in rape cases who were asked post-acquittal why they thought they did not achieve a conviction in their cases."

Despite the lack of any empirical evidence from research with real jurors, the insubstantial claims Thomas alludes to led to the petition discussed above. I believe these remarks pre-dated the publication of Leverick et al's Glasgow research, but that research was also based entirely on mock juries not real ones. Thomas goes on to observe, referring back to her 2010 report, Ref.[11],

"It is unclear what the source could be of the statistic cited (in association with the 2018 petition) that the conviction rate in rape trials is 21 per cent lower than other crimes. Detailed research on all jury verdicts in all courts in England and Wales over a substantial period of time had already shown that juries convict in rape cases more often than they acquit, and that the jury conviction rate in rape cases is higher than it is for other serious crimes such as attempted murder, GBH, and threatening to kill."

Anomalously low conviction rates continue to be cited by those promoting the Bain-Dorrian-Leverick feminist position, namely they claim that the conviction rate for those rape cases that reach court is 43% compared to

88% for all crimes (see Refs.[19,26]). In Refs.[1,14] I present CPS data which shows the 43% figure to be incorrect and instead supports the Thomas position, quoted above.

However, the beneficial spin-off from the 2018 petition, and the associated monoculture of (feminist) opinion expressed in parliament, was the commissioning of Thomas's new research.

The UCL Jury Project undertook the research in 2018–19, basing it on real juries and real trials, immediately post-verdict. A total of 65 discharged juries (771 jurors) in 4 different court regions took part in the research. The cases the juries tried covered a range of offences, including sexual and non-sexual offences. There was a 99 per cent participation rate. The findings regarding what jurors really believe were,

"…hardly any jurors believe what are often referred to as widespread myths and stereotypes about rape and sexual assault. The overwhelming majority of jurors do not believe that rape must leave bruises or marks, that a person will always fight back when being raped, that dressing or acting provocatively or going out alone at night is inviting rape, that men cannot be raped or that rapes will always be reported immediately. The small proportion of jurors who do believe any of these myths or stereotypes amounts to less than one person on a jury."

It is worth taking a look at Figure 8 of Thomas's report to see just how very emphatic is that conclusion, reproduced below as Figure 15.1.

Figure 15.1: Figure 8 from Ref.[15]: Juror attitudes to rape myths and stereotypes

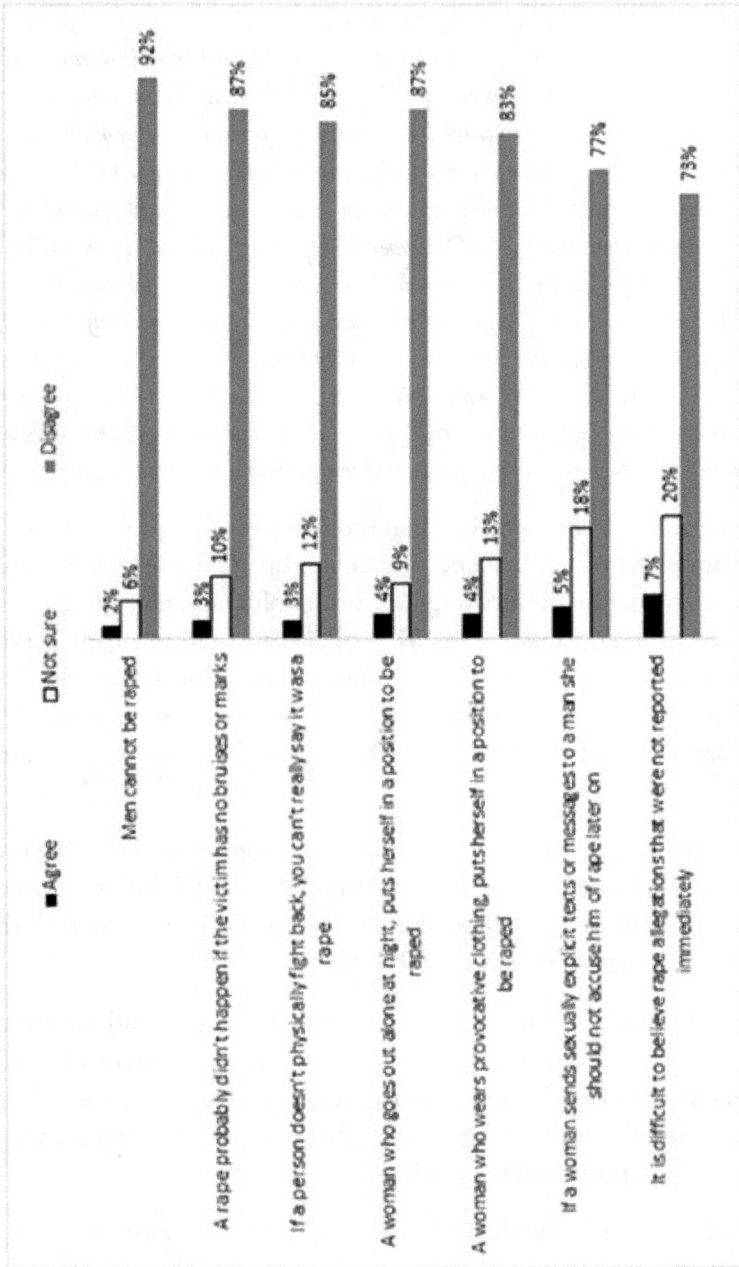

Thomas sums up the implications of the UCL research thus,

"This first ever empirical research assessing the attitudes of actual jurors serving on real cases in England and Wales reveals that the claim made in the petition to Parliament that "Research shows that jurors accept commonly held rape myths resulting in many incorrect not guilty verdicts" is incorrect. The research also reveals that previous claims of widespread "juror bias" in sexual offences cases are not valid. Jurors at court do not hold the same views on these issues as reported in public opinion polls and "mock" jury research using students and volunteers. For example, a December 2018 End Violence Against Women survey reported that 33 per cent of Britons said there must be violence for rape to occur. But the UCL Jury Project research conducted with actual jurors shows that only 3 per cent of jurors said rape had to result in bruises or marks and only 3 per cent of jurors said it was not rape unless a person fought back. Not only does this demonstrate that public opinion polls cannot be a proxy for what real jurors believe, but the small percentages of real jurors who believed these rape myths amounted to less than one person on any jury."

Thomas then goes on to ask why it is that mock juries and opinion polls are so unrepresentative of real juries. The answer is simple: sample bias. Thomas asked 1,175 jurors whether, if jury duty had been voluntary, they would have chosen not to serve. The answer was 87% of them would not have served on the jury. So, by using volunteers in mock juries one is sampling an uncharacteristic 13% of the population (at best, assuming there are no other biases in the sampling, which, as anyone who has conducted survey research knows well, is darned hard to avoid).

So, there we have it – Thomas's research provides the only reliable data on the issue of juries believing rape myths. Data based on mock juries is known to be grossly unreliable. The valid outcome of the UCL work is that the widespread belief in rape myths is a myth.

[Incidentally, Thomas's jurors went on to state that they had benefited considerably from their experience as jurors, despite the fact that most would have avoided jury duty had it been optional. Ref.[15] is worth reading on this finding as it consolidates the main finding that the real jury experience is unlike what can be reproduced by mock juries or surveys].

So, finally – what about Dominic Raab, then – our former Lord Chancellor, Secretary of State for Justice and Deputy Prime Minister who was ousted in April 2023? Rabb was obliged to resign following allegations of "bullying". An independent review by a KC cleared him of all but two "charges". As

Rabb said in his resignation letter, Ref.[28], setting the threshold for bullying so low is a dangerous precedent. For years we have seen inconvenient politicians being removed from parliament by allegations of sexual misconduct. This provides yet another mechanism for the removal of those with Incorrect views.

As Brendan O'Neill wrote in The Spectator, Ref.[29], "*I know the story is that he was a monster in his various departments, allegedly barking instructions and wagging a finger at his stressed-out minions. But the anti-Raab revolt smacks far more of bullying to me. Civil servants clubbing together to drum an exacting minister out of his job? It definitely has a whiff of Mean Girls to it.*" O'Neill has it right – Raab was just doing his job, dealing firmly with civil servants who jolly well needed it.

Raab must surely have been in the sights of the progressives for a long time. A few of his sins can be read in Refs.[30-32]. He thought there should be a consistent standard in regard to sexism against either men or women. He actually had the nerve to say that some feminists were now amongst the most obnoxious bigots – and repeated it when challenged. Raab highlighted the wide range of sex discrimination he said was faced by males including anti-male discrimination in rights of maternity/paternity leave, young boys being educationally disadvantaged compared to girls, and how divorced or separated fathers are systematically ignored by the courts. He claimed (rightly) that from the cradle to the grave, men are getting a raw deal. Men work longer hours, die earlier, but retire later than women (this being before the state pension age reforms).

These remarks were early in his career, but the progressives do not forgive or forget. His cards were marked.

But it was Raab's pressing for a UK Bill Of Rights that I suspect led to his removal becoming an urgent priority for the progressive axis. This Bill, if enacted, was intended to replace the Human Rights Act. That's bad enough from the left's perspective. But there's worse. It would also have ended the duty on UK courts to take into account the case law of the European Court of Human Rights, a body which Raab was right to emphasise has no legislature (and hence, by implication, no legitimacy). "We'll make crystal clear", Raab said, "that the UK Supreme Court, not Strasbourg, has the ultimate authority to interpret the law in the UK".

Oh dear, that's rather too much "taking back control", isn't it? Well, Raab **was** a leading light in Brexit, another of his sins. Removing the UK from the jurisdiction of the European Court of Human Rights is again topical, having been promoted by the Home Secretary in October 2023, Suella Braverman, who received flack for it, as one would anticipate, and has subsequently resigned. On the heavyweight legal side, Lord Sumption is also calling to leave the European Court of Human Rights, arguing (rightly) that we do not need to be subject to its rulings in order to ensure human rights, Ref.[33].

Raab's Bill of Rights would also strengthen the right to freedom of speech, another area which the progressives regard as merely "right-wing" (oddly). So, you see, Raab's crimes are many and deep.

But the relevance to this chapter is that Raab's Bill of Rights would also have enshrined in primary legislation the right to trial by jury in England and Wales. Raab wrote in The Times *"Trial by jury is another ancient right, applied variably around the UK, that doesn't feature in the ECHR (European Court of Human Rights), but will be in our bill of rights"*.

Raab duly sponsored the Bill of Rights in June 2022, Ref.[34], which progressed only as far as its second reading in the Commons before Liz Truss, briefly Prime Minister, shelved it. But under the new Prime Minister, Rishi Sunak, Dominic Raab regained his post. As would be anticipated, the Bill of Rights was back on the agenda. In the state opening of parliament in 2023, it was indeed announced that the Bill would be brought back.

On 28 March 2023 Raab said that the Bill of Rights was "ready to go", Ref.[35].

A few weeks later, Raab was gone. You may reasonably ask who is running the UK: our elected representatives or unknown, nameless civil servants who refuse to be accountable to anyone?

What happens to the Bill of Rights now remains to be seen. However, it looks hopeful. The new Lord Chancellor and Justice Secretary, Alex Chalk, appears to back it – at least if the contents of his web site as a constituency MP is any judge, Ref.[36]. On that site he appears to support the Bill, though there's no saying how he may modify it from Raab's version. In particular he states that the United Kingdom would remain in the ECHR and that the UK would uphold the rulings of the Strasburg court. However, of note for this chapter, he states: "it will also recognise that trial by jury is a fundamental element of fair trials in the UK". So, perhaps England and Wales will escape the debacle descending upon the Scots. As I write, it remains to be seen.

References

[1] Collins, W. (2021). *The Myth About Rape Myths | The Illustrated Empathy Gap blog*. 28 May 2021.

[2] Bindel, J. (2016). *Juries have no place at rape trials – victims deserve unprejudiced justice*. The Guardian, 12 August 2016.

[3] Topping, A. (2018). *Scrap juries in rape trials, Labour MP suggests*. The Guardian, 21 November 2018.

[4] Hansard, Commons (2108). *Rape Myths and Juries*. Volume 649, 21 November 2018.

[5] Graham, P. (2018). *Sex offence fantasists, and their police enablers*. International Conference on Men's Issues (ICMI18), 21 July 2018.

[6] Bradford, R. (2022). *False allegations of rape: the true extent remains unknown*. The Centre for Male Psychology, The Magazine, 1 March 2022.

[7] Maugham, J. (2021). *No, the legal system isn't biased against men – it allows them to rape with near impunity*. New Statesman, 4 May 2021.

[8] Scott, M. (2018). *Rape juries: Jolyon Maugham hits the wrong target*. Barrister Blogger, 2 June 2018.

[9] Petitions to UK government and parliament (2018). *All jurors in rape trials to complete compulsory training about rape myths*. Closed 17 July 2018.

[10] Rape Crisis (undated, accessed 5/11/23). *Myths versus Facts*.

[11] Thomas, C. (2010). *Are Juries Fair?* Ministry of Justice Research Series 1/10, February 2010.

[12] Collins, W. (2019). *The Empathy Gap*. LPS Publishing, June 2019.

[13] Collins, W. (2015). *The Desolation of VAWG*. The Illustrated Empathy Gap, 4 July 2015.

[14] Collins, W. (2023). *Rape Trial Juries and the Erosion of Justice*. The Illustrated Empathy Gap, 30 April 2023.

[15] Thomas, C. (2020). *The 21ˢᵗ Century Jury: Contempt, Bias and the Impact of Jury Service*. Criminal Law Review (11) pp. 987-1011.

[16] Waiton, S. (2023). *The SNP's elitist attack on trial by jury*. Spiked Online, 26 April 2023.

[17] Taylor, M. (2021). *A fresh approach: An interview with Lord Advocate Dorothy Bain QC.* Holyrood, 15 December 2021.

[18] Chalmers, J., Leverick, F. and Munro, V. E. (2021*). The provenance of what is proven: exploring (mock) jury deliberation in Scottish rape trials*. Journal of Law and Society, 48(2), 226-249, 29 March 2021.

[19] McDonald, C. (2021). *Influential academic warns Scotland's juries are failing rape victims and judge-only trials must be considered*. The Sunday Post, 26 December 2021.

[20] Summan, K. (2021a). *Judiciary imperils right to a fair trial with renewed attack on juries*. Scottish Legal News, 18 March 2021.

[21] Summan, K. (2021b). *Fifty-three shades of grey*. Scottish Legal News, 11 May 2021.

[22] Lenehan, A. (2021). *Who will limit the limiters?* Scottish Legal News, 28 July 2021.

[23] Summan, K. (2021c). *Faculty defends juries against 'baying' special interest groups*. Scottish Legal News, 22 September 2021.

[24] BBC News (2023a). *Senior judges raise concerns over juryless trials in Scotland*. 24 September 2023.

[25] Scottish Government (2022). *Lady Dorrian Review Governance Group: Consideration of a Time-Limited Pilot of Single Judge Rape Trials Working Group Report*. Justice Directorate, 12 December 2022.

[26] BBC News (2023b). *Not proven verdict to be scrapped in Scottish courts*. 26 April 2023.

[27] BBC News (2023c). *Lawyer boycott of juryless rape trials 'to be unanimous'*. 9 May 2023.

[28] Raab, D. (2023). *Dominic Raab: Resignation letter and Rishi Sunak's response in full*. BBC News, 21 April 2023.

[29] O'Neill, B. (2023). *Is Dominic Raab really a 'bully'?* The Spectator, 21 April 2023.

[30] Raab, D. (2011). *We must end feminist bigotry*. Politics Home, 24 January 2011.

[31] Prince, R. (2011). *Dominic Raab: men should 'burn their briefs' in protest at 'obnoxious feminist bigots'*. The Telegraph, 24 January 2011.

[32] BBC News (2011). *MP Dominic Raab says men victims of discrimination*. 25 January 2011.

[33] Hymas, C. (2023). *Lord Sumption backs calls for Britain to leave European Convention on Human Rights*. The Telegraph, 28 September 2023.

[34] Ministry of Justice (2022). *Bill of Rights: Bill documents*. UK Government, 22 June 2022.

[35] Duffy, J. (2023). *The Bill of Rights Bill is Back*. Law Pod UK, 28 March 2023.

[36] Chalk, A. (undated). *Bill of Rights*. Alex Chalk MP for Cheltenham's blog. Undated.

16. Charlotte Proudman on the Liam Allan Case

Familiarity with the Liam Allan case would be helpful to the reader, but not essential as long as you know this: Liam Allan was about to stand trial for rape when the prosecution barrister (yes, the prosecution) insisted that the police hand over the complainant's mobile to the defence team. The police either hadn't bothered to search it, or had deliberately withheld a key text message on that phone. The defence council was given until the next day to examine the phone. She searched the phone herself, overnight, and found a number of messages to Mr Allan pestering him for sex, and fantasising about "rough sex and being raped". Whatever you may think, messages such as those will not result in exoneration. Indeed, the judge would probably disallow them to be used as evidence. But the defence council also discovered this message from the complainant to a friend, "it wasn't against my will or anything". Slam dunk? Yes, and the case immediately collapsed, but only after dragging Mr Allan through nearly two years of hell. He was saved from 10 years in prison and the irreversible destruction of his life only by the good fortune of ethical action by the prosecution barrister.

Original posted on 29 December 2017.

On the 21st December 2017, barrister Charlotte Proudman, Ref.[1], had published in the Guardian, Ref.[2], an article on the Liam Allan case, Ref.[3], and its ramifications. She appeared rather upset about it. Well, as a barrister she might very reasonably be upset about the issues that case raised around disclosure. But that is not what seemed to upset her. What did upset her was "the dampening effect" the case might have on encouraging other women to allege rape, and, of course, obtain convictions. (She does not use that phrase, but I believe that is the expression commonly used in this context).

I'd like to examine just three sentences in Ms Proudman's article. The first is this,

"(However) the reporting on cases such as these, with a focus on a few text messages out of 40,000, may leave future victims less likely to come forward."

I am all admiration.

I do appreciate the noble art of misdirection.

Note how that sentence acts like Novocaine on the intellect. Its grammatical structure suggests that it contains a logical inference. But actually it is a logical miasma, a piece of verbal hypnosis. It gives the false impression that "*a focus on a few text messages out of 40,000*" acts to logically connect "*the reporting on cases such as these"* so as to make *"future victims less likely to come forward"*. But let's pull it apart.

"a focus on a few text messages out of 40,000": The subliminal suggestion here is that because only a few text messages were pertinent to the Liam Allan case, and that constitutes only a tiny percentage of 40,000, that that somehow diminishes their importance.

Eh? What?

If there were a billion messages, all totally irrelevant bar one, but that one was "the sex was entirely consensual" – that's all one need know, isn't it? The allusion to *"a few text messages out of 40,000"* is merely an attempt to fog the reader's brain.

"the reporting on cases such as these.....may leave future victims less likely to come forward.": Let us examine what *"the reporting on cases such as these"* means. It means the reporting of the fact that clear documentary evidence of the consensual nature of a sexual encounter will be taken by a court to negate a claim of rape. But that could only be a deterrent to potential complainants if such clear documentary evidence of consent existed. And that could only be the case if the person in question was considering making a false allegation, not a true one. So there is no way that *"the reporting on cases such as these"* could possibly *"leave future victims less likely to come forward"* as long as "victims" means strictly that: true victims. What Charlotte Proudman appears really to mean is that the Liam Allan case might leave future dishonest claimants less likely to make a fraudulent rape allegation – but, oddly, she regards this as a bad thing.

The sentence is a double non sequitur. But it is a masterpiece of verbal legerdemain which purports to present the exposure of a callous liar as contrary to justice.

That sentence is immediately followed by a short paragraph,

"The reporting of the Allan case sends a message to women that your allegation of rape might not be believed if you claim that a sexual encounter was consensual and later report rape..... This contrasts with the law, which says a woman can withdraw her consent to sexual intercourse at any time."

Now, I do not have Ms Proudman's legal training. However, I strongly suspect that when the law says *"a woman can withdraw her consent to sexual intercourse at any time"*, if indeed it does, it is actually referring to any time during the incident in question. I don't think the law is intended to legitimise **retrospective** withdrawal of consent – days, weeks, months or years later.

And yet this is apparently what Ms Proudman has in mind.

Look closely at the tense of the verb. She is positing a case in which *"you claim that a sexual encounter **was** consensual"*. This clearly indicates an antecedent condition of a state of consent existing during the encounter. And yet, Ms Proudman appears to interpret the law in such a way that this would not invalidate an allegation of rape – because *"a woman can withdraw her consent to sexual intercourse at any time."*

This is precisely apposite to the Liam Allan case because one of the text messages was "it wasn't against my will or anything". Note the tense.

Simply put – to the ordinary man and woman in the street – whose wisdom I generally hold in substantially higher regard than that of barristers – the existence of clear and unambiguous evidence that the complainant considered that the sexual encounter was consensual is sufficient to invalidate any allegation of rape. As long as this applied during the encounter itself, I think the courts would take that view too – I certainly hope so.

Staggeringly, and chillingly given that this woman is a barrister, Ms Proudman is arguing otherwise. She **does** seem to believe that a woman (but seemingly not a man) should be able to withdraw consent retrospectively.

Ms Proudman appears to believe that women should be able to re-characterise any sexual intercourse as rape, unilaterally, at will, after the event.

If this is the way the law is to go, I suggest the public should be made more clearly aware of the fact. Perhaps it could be part of Sex and Relationship Education in schools. Of course, under such conditions, sex with a woman would not be legally advisable for men – at all, ever.

References

[1] Delingpole, J. (2015). *The Guilty Secrets of Man-Hating Feminazi Charlotte Proudman.* Breitbart, 11 September 2015.

[2] Proudman, C. (2017). *Why does police mishandling of evidence only make headlines in rape cases?* The Guardian, 21 December 2017.

[3] Collins. W (2017). *Rape – Part 1 (Statistics)*, The Illustrated Empathy Gap, 22 December 2017.

17. Operation Soteria

This final chapter of the section on sexual offences shows that the injustices and anti-male biases of the preceding chapters are not accidental but driven by political and ideological pressures which act via the Crown Prosecution Service to misdirect the police away from their true task of pursuing the truth to a false objective of maximising convictions at the expense of the truth.

Original posted on: 22 December 2022.

If a week is a long time in politics, five years is sufficient to induce total amnesia.

About what? Here's a hint: in Greek mythology, Soteria is the goddess of safety and deliverance from harm. Bear with me, though, as I reprise the background before getting to the latest shenanigans of the Crown Prosecution Service (CPS) and Operation Soteria.

2017/2018

In late 2017 there were several rape prosecutions in which serious disclosure failures caused public concern. Only very late in the day was it revealed that the alleged victims' accounts were unreliable, the cases therefore being dismissed or previous convictions quashed, including the cases involving Liam Allan, Isaac Itiary, Danny Kay and Samuel Armstrong, Ref.[1].

The most well-known was the Liam Allan case, in which text messages on the complainant's mobile indicated conclusively that the sex had been consensual. The police had not bothered to search the phone, though it was in their possession – or, perhaps they had, but failed to disclose their findings. Mr Allan avoided a likely 10-year prison sentence only because the prosecution barrister insisted the police hand over the mobile to the defence council to examine.

It was later revealed that this glaring disclosure failure was not recorded as such by the CPS even when the prosecution had been stopped as a result. Moreover, even months later, Alison Saunders, then the DPP, was unaware that the Liam Allan case had not been classed as a disclosure failure, despite it having become a *cause célèbre*.

All the cases against Liam Allan, Isaac Itiary, Danny Kay and Samuel Armstrong collapsed within a week or so of each other due to the very late disclosure of mobile phone evidence which disproved the complainants' claims. Liam Allan, Isaac Itiary and Samuel Armstrong narrowly avoided long prison sentences. Danny Kay was not so lucky – the evidence which exonerated him came to light only after he had served four years of a four and half year sentence. But none of these men need ever have been charged if the police had done their job.

These disclosure failures led to the CPS being obliged to conduct an investigation. The resulting report was a disgraceful exercise in obfuscation (for details see Ref.[2]). However, the Justice Select Committee, whose job it is to oversee matters independently of the Ministry of Justice, did very much better in their investigation, Ref.[3]. Here are some key extracts from the Select Committee's report,

"...*disclosure errors have led to miscarriages of justice and...some people have gone to prison as a result.*"

"*It is disappointing that we have heard the same issues raised throughout this inquiry as have been noted by inquiries as far back as 2011, and it is further disappointing that the Attorney General in place at the time of inquiry stated to us that he was aware of problems going back as far as 1996 but yet the problem had persisted and apparently worsened under his watch.*"

"*We conclude that disclosure failures have been widely acknowledged for many years but have gone unresolved.... This was not aided by data collected by the Crown Prosecution Service which might have underestimated the number of cases which were stopped with disclosure errors by around 90%.*"

"*The Code for Crown Prosecutors is clear 'Prosecutors must be fair, independent and objective...* **Prosecutors must always act in the interests of justice and not solely for the purpose of obtaining a conviction'.**" (my emphasis)

"**It is fundamentally important that all police officers recognise both that they are searching for the truth; and that they have core disclosure duties which are central to the criminal justice process.**" (my emphasis)

"*It is important that those who come forward to report serious offences, particularly those of a sexual or otherwise sensitive nature, are treated by investigators with respect and sensitivity. Their personal information should be handled in the same way and in accordance with their rights to privacy, where that is consistent with the interest of justice.* **The law is clear in that the right to a fair trial is an absolute right which cannot be violated to protect the right to privacy.**" (my emphasis).

"We expect the next Director of Public Prosecutions (DPP) to proactively address disclosure throughout their tenure."

The Select Committee were to be disappointed in that last expectation. The DPP who replaced Alison Saunders in November 2018 was Max Hill. In his first public speech he said this, Ref.[10],

"Rape complainants must have their personal privacy, including mobile phone records, protected."

"We are very clear that seeking to examine the mobile telephones of complainants and witnesses is not something that should be pursued as a matter of course in every case. It is of vital importance that the personal information of those who report sexual offences is treated in a way that is consistent with both their right to privacy and with the interests of justice."

Hill added that there needed to be a lasting change in culture when it came to disclosure but he insisted that prosecutors were not obliged to trawl through the mobile phone records of all rape complainants as they struggled to cope with the rise in the volume of digital evidence. (This is a peculiar assertion as it is the job of the police to do the trawling for evidence).

Do note how flagrantly Max Hill's stated position – and hence that of the CPS – conflicts with the statement quoted above from the Select Committee's report: the right to a fair trial is an absolute right which cannot be violated to protect the right to privacy. Moreover, note that this statement is not merely the Select Committee's opinion, but a statement of how the law stands. The DPP's position is, therefore, contrary to a fundamental principle of justice.

2020

The Select Committee did their job. But making progress against the feminist state is like brushing water uphill: inevitably it comes right back again. The public's memory, and hence concern, rapidly evaporates. Having given it a couple of years, the feminists were on the march again, demanding that more men are sent to prison. Enter Vera Baird, committed feminist, one-time Solicitor General, one-time Police and Crime Commissioner of

Northumbria, and then the Victims' Commissioner. She suggested to ministers that they take rape prosecution decisions out of the hands of the CPS, Ref[4]. The Prime Minister, then Boris Johnson, all but acceded to Baird's demands, Ref.[5]. He promised that the cross-government crime and justice task force, which he led, would impose targets on the police to refer more "high quality" rape cases. He also promised to impose targets on the CPS to prosecute both a greater volume of cases and a greater proportion of cases. Absolutely no political interference in the justice process there then.

What is a "high quality" rape case? It is one with a high probability of gaining conviction. And how, exactly, are the police supposed to improve the "quality" of rape cases, in that sense? There are two ways: one consistent with the principles of justice and one in direct conflict with principles of justice. The first way involves referring to the CPS only those cases which the totality of evidence more strongly indicates guilt. But achieving greater quality of referred cases in this way would inevitably lead to a reduced volume referred. This would be contrary to the political pressure which insisted on both increased "quality" *and* increasing volume of cases.

Arising from that political demand was a pressure on police to adopt the second alternative, which is simple enough. They try hard to build a prosecution case, but they put no effort into finding exculpatory evidence. In other words they revert to the negligent practices which led to the debacles of the recent past – disclosure failures. And whilst this is strictly a police failure, one sees clearly now how the political system pushes the police in that direction. In this instance by a Prime Minister with insufficient wisdom, insufficient awareness and insufficient bravery to stand up to the feminist lobby – powerfully represented by the Victims' Commissioner. In that respect he differs from the rest of parliament not one bit.

And so we come to…

2022: Operation Soteria

In July 2022, the DPP, Max Hill, with Chief Constable Sarah Crew, National Police Chiefs' Council Lead for Rape and Adult Sexual Offences, issued a press release, Ref.[6]. I include extracts below. In reading these, bear in mind the conclusions of the Select Committee in 2018, above.

Quote: "*Close joint working from the very start of an investigation means we can build the best possible cases more quickly. With police going to the CPS earlier in the process and more often, the rise in charging decisions will lead to more trials and more convictions. Early advice in these cases has been key in helping us use our joint resources more effectively and narrow the gap between the number of offences reported to the police and cases going to court.*"

Note how flagrantly this contravenes the Select Committee's guidance. The clear intention, openly declared here, is that the prosecution service shall direct the police investigation in order to "build the best possible case". This means the best case for the prosecution. The Select Committee make abundantly clear that that is NOT what the police should do. I quote the latter again: "It is fundamentally important that all police officers recognise that they are searching for the truth". But political pressure, acting through the CPS, impinges upon the police and is instrumental in encouraging their failure to investigate or disclose exculpatory evidence. This is political corruption of the criminal justice process.

Quote: "*An ambitious programme of work called Operation Soteria is testing new ways of working to transform how the CPS and police handle rape investigations and prosecutions, centring on the conduct of the suspect as opposed to the victim. It is already in action in five police force areas and work is ongoing to roll it out to a further 14 forces with the aim of this being complete by March 2023.*"

Sexual assault cases hinge upon consent. Is the conduct of the **alleged** victim relevant to the issue of consent? Clearly the answer is "yes". Indeed, because the DPP has already stated his reluctance to investigate IT equipment thoroughly, the complainant's behaviour and conduct is about all there may be to go on – beyond the testimony of the two involved parties. The defendant is already being placed in a position of having to demonstrate his innocence, despite this being contrary to the accepted principle of justice, and now all means of doing so are being denied him – deliberately.

Quote: "*Operation Soteria drives a strong focus on closer joint working between the police and prosecution teams across the country to drive up the number of successful prosecutions. A wide-ranging plan of action is underway to improve this crucial relationship, working together closely from the very start of an investigation to advise on lines of enquiry and actions to strengthen the evidence.*"

Here "successful prosecutions" means convictions. The CPS has adopted a policy which is directly contrary to what the Select Committee directed, namely to act 'in the interests of justice and not solely for the purpose of obtaining a conviction'". Similarly, "strengthen the evidence" means strengthening the prosecution evidence only, in order that the prosecution be "successful".

It could not be clearer: there is a deliberate policy to operate directly contrary to the Select Committee's guidance. Their guidance was specifically to avoid disclosure failures, as well as serving the wider interests of true justice. Operation Soteria is the name given by the CPS to their drive to do exactly the opposite, implementing a process of deliberately undermining true justice.

Quote: *"The Operation Soteria pathfinder projects will give clear evidence of which approaches have the biggest impact. We will evaluate good practice then work with police forces to roll them out across England and Wales ahead of a new national operating model from June 2023."*

Again, "biggest impact" means largest increase in convictions. Whether the man convicted is guilty or innocent is irrelevant.

Quote: *"A key shift has been a move to increase early advice where police can consult a prosecutor on investigative strategy from the beginning to talk through the evidence needed to build and strengthen the case."*

Yet again: consulting a prosecutor "to talk through the evidence needed to build and strengthen the case" will not relate to exculpatory evidence, will it? They are setting up a process to drive disclosure failure. This is knowing and deliberate. And note that it is the CPS exerting this pressure on the police, albeit upon a police force now very willing to comply, led in many cases by feminist chief constables perhaps with the blessing of an ideologically aligned PCC. (15 chief constables in England and Wales were women as of July 2021, Ref.[7], and this had risen to 19 out of 49 by January 2023, Ref.[8]).

It is quite staggering that neither the DPP nor the Chief Constable of Avon and Somerset seem to have grasped that what they are doing is profoundly wrong. Or perhaps they have?

A familiar feature of totalist regimes is their capture of the justice process. Totalist regimes are generally held in power by an ideology which permeates the whole culture. This is necessary if the justice process is to be corrupted, because the enactment of injustice in myriad cases requires many individuals to comply. Ideology is the means by which this is achieved – including the knowledge that ideological alignment is key to promoting selfish interests. To this end, feminism will serve just as well as Marxism or Fascism.

Soteria Connections

The name "Soteria" has a significance beyond Greek mythology. There is an American organisation named Soteria Solutions, Ref.[9], whose ethos aligns with Operation Soteria. A legal professional in the USA has advised on Soteria as follows,

"Soteria Solutions comes out of the University of New Hampshire (UNH) and was funded by grants from the Department of Justice for 'Bystander' and 'Know Your Power' training. The people running the program, Sharyn (redacted) and Jane (redacted), are feminists. Partnered with UNH is the New Hampshire Coalition Against Domestic and Sexual Violence who work with police and prosecutors to create the narrative for state wins."

Here "state wins" means convictions. Note that the MO of feminist organisation Soteria Solutions aligns precisely with the CPS's press release and declared policy on Operation Soteria.

A Suggestion Regarding Process

The formal position is that the prosecution is in charge of disclosure, though the prosecution is obliged to pass everything disclosed to the defence council. That, however, is grossly insufficient if the prosecution has directed the police (who do the legwork) to focus entirely on prosecution evidence.

The solution is simple. Take disclosure out of the hands of the prosecution. Either put the defence in formal charge of disclosure – or have an independent body charged with that responsibility. That needs to be combined with training the police to understand that their duty is to the truth, not to the prosecution.

But at present, under the influence of feminist lobbying, the political process puts pressure of the CPS which in turn directs the police, with the result that justice is undermined in the service of an ideology which is defined by its sex-based prejudice.

We are used to the vilification of men. What receives less attention, but is actually even more destructive, is the refusal to accept that femaleness does not confer blameless innocence; women and girls are just as flawed as men and boys. So long as systemic gynocentrism continues to disguise that simple fact, the feminist steamroller will continue to destroy justice.

References

[1] Collins, W. (2017). *Rape – Part 1 (Statistics)*, The Illustrated Empathy Gap, 22 December 2017.

[2] Collins. W. (2019). *The Empathy Gap*. LPS Publishing, June 2019. See section 19.7.

[3] Justice Select Committee (2018). *Disclosure of evidence in criminal cases*. UK parliament, 20 July 2018.

[4] Barrett, D. (2020). *Rape 'has been decriminalised': Watchdog makes damning claim as hard-hitting new report reveals number of cases taken to trial has plunged by 52% in just two years*. Mail Online, 14 July 2020.

[5] Barr, C., and Topping, A. (2020). *Downing Street plans rape prosecution targets for police and CPS*. The Guardian, 9 August 2020.

[6] Crown Prosecution Service (2022). *CPS publishes latest statistics on all crime types showing steady increase in rape convictions*. Press Release 21 July 2022.

[7] Weston, K. (2021). *Third of police chiefs are women: Record 15 forces now have a female leader as experts say they have become less like The Sweeney and more like Line of Duty*. Mail Online 2 July 2021.

[8] SecurityWomen (2023). *Record 40 per cent of chief constables are now women amid anti-misogyny drive*. 17 January 2023.

[9] Soteria Solutions (accessed 9 November 2023). *Soteria Solutions - Violence and Harassment Prevention Training*.

[10] Gibb, F. (2018). *We shouldn't be trawling rape victims' phones, says law chief*. The Times, 14 November 2018.

Section 3

Domestic Abuse

18. Domestic Abuse: The Latest Lie

Here I show how Ministers of State can get away with stating the most outrageous untruths in parliament, so long as it conforms to the approved narrative, namely the vileness of men and the universal innocence of women.

Original posted on: 19 July 2019.

In the context of a debate in the House of Commons on the Domestic Abuse Bill on 16 July 2019, Victoria Atkins, then Parliamentary Under Secretary of State for Crime, Safeguarding and Vulnerability, made this statement, Ref.[1],

"…of the 2 million victims, we estimate that around 1.3 million are female and around 695,000 are male, and within that 695,000 we believe – it is very difficult to identify this, and there are problems in doing so – that the majority of perpetrators are male."

The statement is false. It is wildly incorrect. It has been known to be false for decades. It is doubly false, in fact, because it is neither difficult nor problematic to identify statistics and hence to confirm that it is false.

A weight of evidence, both recent and going back decades, confirms that the overwhelming bulk of partner abuse against men is perpetrated by women. In addition, the majority of all domestic abuse of men is also perpetrated by women. In this chapter I present the data. It is beyond credibility that an Under Secretary of State for Crime did not have ample access to all these data sources, and more. So, was Victoria Atkins' remark gross incompetence or deliberate misinformation? (Or, perhaps, was she misled by ideologically motivated researchers?).

If there is one thing which gets the parliamentary Opposition fired up, it's a government minister misleading the House. Usually they smell blood. There are precedents aplenty that the sequence of events immediately following 16 July 2019 should have gone like this,

- The Opposition feign outrage at parliament being misled;
- The minister is eventually obliged to retract and eat humble pie;
- That may not be enough, and the minister may finally be drummed out of office.

Does anyone think that any of these things will happen in this case? Of course not. Because ministers may tell porkies of any magnitude with impunity so long as the tale aligns with the approved narrative. And the approved narrative always approves of vilifying men and reinforcing the myth that all women are perpetual angels.

The Data

Attention should be paid to where evidence relates to *partner* abuse or *any domestic* abuse. Where partner abuse is specified, sexuality will imply the sex of the perpetrator given the sex of the victim (other than for bisexuals). This cannot be assumed in the case of other forms of domestic abuse.

(A) Survey Data and Police Reports from the UK

For interest I give some older data as well as more recent data, to confirm my claim that the truth of this matter has been known for a long time. In chronological order…

A.1 Home Office (1999)

Ref.[2], Quote, in the context of domestic abuse: *"95% of assaults against men were by women"*.

A.2 British Crime Survey, 2007/8 and 2008/9

The data from Ref.[3], Table 3.07 is reproduced here as Table 18.1.

Category of abuse	Heterosexual Male Victims	Gay Victims	Heterosexual Women Victims	Lesbian Victims
All domestic abuse	4.1%	8.9%	5.9%	17.3%
Non-sexual partner abuse	3.3%	6.2%	4.3%	12.4%
Non-sexual family abuse	1.5%	3.3%	2.2%	8.5%
Sexual assault or attempts	0.3%	4.2%	2.6%	8.7%
Number of respondents	20,892	512	24,795	473

Table 18.1: Data from Ref.[3]

From Table 18.1 it follows that 689 heterosexual men who were surveyed reported that they had experienced non-sexual partner abuse, i.e., by a woman, and that 32 gay men who were surveyed reported non-sexual partner abuse, i.e., by a man. Hence, non-sexual partner abuse against men was perpetrated by women in 95.6% of cases. For partner abuse including sexual assaults the figures are 752 heterosexual men and 53 gay men, i.e., women were the perpetrators in 93.3% of cases. For sexual offences committed by a partner, there were three times as many heterosexual men assaulted sexually by their female partner as gay men assaulted by their male partner.

In the case of family abuse, the sex of the perpetrator cannot be concluded on the basis of sexuality. However, it is noted that most domestic abuse is partner abuse, hence it can be concluded that most domestic abuse against men is perpetrated by women. [To spell this out, assume that all domestic abuse against men which is not committed by the partner is perpetrated by men. Even under this assumption the above tabulated data show that there were 213 men suffering domestic abuse by other men, and 752 men suffering abuse by women. Thus even with this extreme assumption, women account for at least 78% of domestic abusers of men].

A.3 Scottish Government, 2012

Data on police reports of domestic abuse in Scotland, 2000 to 2012, are given in Ref.[4], page 21, and summarised here in Table 18.2. This shows, over that 12-year period in Scotland, the proportion of men reporting domestic abuse to the police who reported female perpetrators was quite consistent year-on-year, between 91.8% and 94%.

A.4 Crime Survey for England and Wales, 2015

Data was provided by ONS in response to an *ad hoc* request in July 2016, Ref.[5], and is reproduced here in Table18.3. The data are percentages of those reporting partner abuse (ages 16 to 59). Of the 283 men reporting partner abuse in the 2015 Crime Survey for England and Wales, only 150 provided the sex of the perpetrator. Of these 19 reported male perpetrators and 126 reported female perpetrators (plus 5 reporting both). Hence, of those men reporting partner abuse who specified the sex of their abuser, 84% reported a lone female perpetrator and 87% reported abuse including a female abuser.

Year	Male victim female perpetrator	Male victim male perpetrator	Percentage female perpetrators
2000-01	2,696	173	94.0%
2001-02	2,976	231	92.8%
2002-03	3,243	287	91.9%
2003-04	3,695	328	91.8%
2004-05	4,532	380	92.3%
2005-06	4,932	400	92.5%
2006-07	5,482	455	92.3%
2007-08	6,199	530	92.1%
2008-09	7,361	548	93.1%
2009-10	7,938	666	92.3%
2010-11	8,889	693	92.8%
2011-12	9,569	659	93.6%

Table 18.2: Data from Ref.[4]

Perpetrator	Male Victim	Female Victim
Male	7%	59%
Female	45%	2%
Both male and female	2%	1%
Don't know/can't remember	15%	6%
Don't wish to answer	32%	32%
Number of respondents	283	834

Table 18.3: Data from Ref.[5]

A.5 Scottish Government, 2018

Ref.[6] gives data for domestic abuse reported to the police in Scotland in the year 2017/18. In that year, 16% of domestic abuse reports to Scottish police were men reporting abuse by women, whilst only 2% were men reporting abuse by men. Hence, 89% of men reporting domestic abuse reported a female perpetrator.

In the same year the Scottish Government published findings from their Crime and Justice Survey, Ref.[7], Figure 9.11 of which provides the following data. Of male respondents reporting partner abuse, 88% reported perpetration by their female partner and 9% by their male partner, i.e., 90.7% of men who reported the sex of their abuser reported abuse by a woman. Quote, *"abusive partners were overwhelmingly of the opposite gender"*.

A.6 Crime Survey for England & Wales, 2018

The data in Ref.[8] relates to people ages 16 to 59 and is presented here in Table 18.4.

Sexuality	Any DA		PA Non-sexual		Number of Respondents	
	Men Victims	Women Victims	Men Victims	Women Victims	Men	Women
Heterosexual or straight	4.0%	7.2%	2.2%	5.1%	4,361	5,037
Gay or lesbian	8.2%	10.0%	5.1%	8.4%	108	83
Bisexual	5.7%	25.3%	5.6%	14.1%	56	106

Table 18.4: Data from Ref.[8].

From this it follows that 96 heterosexual men who were surveyed reported that they had experienced non-sexual partner abuse, i.e., by a woman, and that 6 gay men who were surveyed reported non-sexual partner abuse, i.e., by a man. Three bisexual men reported partner abuse, by a perpetrator of unknown sex. Hence, between 6 and 9 men who were victims of partner abuse were victimised by other men, and between 99 and 96 were victimised by women. Hence, non-sexual partner abuse against men was perpetrated by women in 91.4% to 94.3% of cases.

In the case of domestic abuse perpetrated by a person other than the victim's partner, the sex of the perpetrator cannot be concluded on the basis of sexuality. However, it is noted that most domestic abuse is partner abuse, hence it can be concluded that most domestic abuse against men is perpetrated by women. [To spell this out, even if it is assumed that all domestic abuse which is not committed by a partner is perpetrated by men, the tabulated data still shows that there are more female abusers of men than male abusers of men].

A.7 Survey of Male DA Victims by Charity FNF-BPM Cymru, 2018

This unpublished survey requested input from males who had experienced domestic abuse. 92.6% of respondents were resident in the UK; 97.8% of respondents identified as male; 85% of respondents stated they were white and 94.7% that they were heterosexual.

Outcome: 95.0% of abusers identified as female (671 out of 706)

(B) Academic Studies (Worldwide)

B.1 Partner Abuse State of Knowledge Project (2013)

The Partner Abuse State of Knowledge Project (PASK), Ref.[10], is the most comprehensive review of domestic violence research literature conducted to date. This three-year research project was conducted by 42 scholars at 20 universities and research centres and combines the results of hundreds of studies into domestic abuse, worldwide. Headline conclusions were,

- *Rates of female-perpetrated violence are higher than male-perpetrated (28.3% vs. 21.6%)*

- *Among large population samples, 57.9% of inter-partner violence reported was bi-directional, 42% unidirectional; 13.8% of the unidirectional violence was male to female (MFPV), 28.3% was female to male (FMPV).*

- *Among school and college samples, percentage of bidirectional violence was 51.9%; 48.1% was unidirectional; 16.2% was male-to-female (MFPV) and 31.9% was female-to-male (FMPV).*

Given that most perpetrators of partner abuse against women are men, the above conclusions can only be consistent with the overwhelming majority of perpetrators of partner abuse against men being female perpetrators.

B.2 Compilation of Studies by Martin Fiebert (2014)

Fiebert has been publishing updates of his bibliography specific to female on male partner violence for many years, one of which is Ref.[10]. Quote,

"This annotated bibliography describes 343 scholarly investigations (270 empirical studies and 73 reviews) demonstrating that women are as physically aggressive as men (or more) in their relationships with their spouses or opposite-sex partners. The aggregate sample size in the reviewed studies exceeds 440,850 people."

There are reams of other peer reviewed academic journal publications backing up the incontrovertible fact that domestic abuse and partner abuse is suffered by men at comparable rates to women. But this does not prevent the narrative that women are "the overwhelming victims" continuing to be cited in political circles, including in influential documents which affect policy – including which parent becomes estranged from their children after parental separation. The barriers in the way of accepting this well-established fact are political, evolutionary, psychosocial and ideological, further entrenched by powerful vested interests. One despairs of ever penetrating the crania of those who will not hear, especially when it remains expedient to be deaf and politically hazardous to be anything else.

References

[1]   UK parliament (2019). *Domestic Abuse*. Hansard Volume 663: debated on Tuesday 16 July 2019.

[2]   George, M. (199). *An Analysis of Male Victimisation*. A report for Parity, based on the Home Office Research Study 191 (HORS 191), *"Domestic Violence: Findings from a new British Crime Survey self-completion questionnaire"*, Catriona Mirrlees-Black, Home Office 1999.

[3]   Home Office Statistical Bulletin, "Homicides, Firearm Offences and Intimate Violence 2008/09: Supplementary Volume 2 to Crime in England and Wales 2008/09 (Third Edition)", Table 3.07.

[4]   Dempsey, B. (2013). *Men's experience of domestic abuse in Scotland: What we know and how we can know more*. University of Dundee School of Law (2013), page 21 [data derived from Scottish Government (2012a), *Domestic Abuse Recorded by the Police in Scotland, 2010-11 and 2011-12*].

[5] Crime Survey for England and Wales, (2015). *Sex of perpetrator of partner abuse, by sex of victim, year ending March 2015 CSEW*, Office for National Statistics, 12th July 2016.

[6] Scottish Government (2018). *Domestic Abuse Recorded by the Police in Scotland in 2017-18*. 27 November 2018.

[7] Scottish Government (2019). Scottish Crime and Justice Survey 2017-2018: main findings. Justice Directorate, 26 March 2019. (Figure 9.11).

[8] Crime Survey for England and Wales (2018). *Domestic abuse: findings from the Crime Survey for England and Wales, year ending March 2018*. See Appendix Tables November 2018, Table 8.

[9] Hamel, J., project lead (2013). *The Partner Abuse State of Knowledge Project*. (See also *Gender-Inclusive Treatment of Intimate Partner Abuse*).

[10] Fiebert, M.S. (2014). *References Examining Assaults by Women on Their Spouses or Male Partners: An Updated Annotated Bibliography*. Sexuality & Culture, volume 18, pages 405–467 (2014)

19. Invisible Dead Men

A list of men killed by their female partners in Great Britain in the period 2011 to 2023.

Originals posted on: 25 February 2017 and 19 November 2023

This piece was posted on International Men's Day 2023 (19th November). For my contribution I thought I'd emulate Jess Phillips MP. Every International Women's Day (IWD) she reads out in parliament a list of female victims of partner homicide. I'm sure her omission of the male victims must be just an accidental oversight. To save her the trouble of finding them (her usual sources will not have done so) I have provided a list below. I suggested at the time that perhaps she could read these out too, in the debate for International Men's Day the following Tuesday.

I was joking, of course. I'm not in favour of such public readings, by anyone anywhere. It only promotes the nasty flavour of some sort of unholy competition. The number of women **directly** killed by male partners is undoubtedly larger than that in the reverse sense. So, if there were such a grisly competitive game, it is conceded. (Do note the word **directly**, and see below).

No, my interest in compiling a list goes back to the first time I did so, in early 2017. The reason is that, when it comes to male victims, there is a suspicion in some quarters that the statistics are somehow misleading; there are no dead men behind the data really. "Show us the bodies", they cried. Men dying just isn't the same as women dying. I don't need to labour for the audience of this book how that perception arises – through the empathy gap or gamma bias. It becomes harder to deny, though, when specific cases are identified, and especially when one reads the case histories.

Ah, but the usual culprits will opine, women only kill their male partners when they have been driven to it by years of abuse. Well, there are such cases, though I suspect the courts may not always discriminate between mutual partner abuse (which, let us not forget, is the most common sort) and the cases of women-only victimisation. However, in many cases the courts DO identify mutual abuse. Moreover, and this is what certain parties are most keen to keep submerged, there are many cases where the man has been subject to persistent abuse by his female partner, and his eventual death is the result of its, almost inevitable, escalation. In other words, exactly the sort of case which rightly excites so much ire when the sexes are the other way around.

Below I list just the names of the dead and the manner of the killing involved in the partner homicides of men by women. (The method I used for searching means I did not pick up men killed by gay partners). I found 168 cases between 2011 and November 2023 (including a handful earlier).

For the period 2011 to 2016 you can find my brief case histories for each killing in Ref.[1]. For the period 2017 to November 2023 you can find the case histories in Ref.[2].

The list below relates to women who killed their male partners. I also record, in a list that follows the main list, (i) cases of attempted murder of a man by his female partner, and, (ii) lesbian or bisexual women who killed their female partners, or a lesbian couple killing another woman.

I do not include other domestic homicides. I found many cases of women who killed their mothers, or their fathers, or their sisters or brothers, or their grandmothers or grandfathers, but these are not included.

Cases of women killing other people, including children, are omitted. (There are many).

All cases of death due to careless/reckless driving are omitted. (There are many).

I also did not include cases where a jealous woman, rather than killing her partner, killed the female love rival. I noted several of these.

The issue of what constitutes being a "partner" is fraught. Before the mid-20th century, this could be identified with "spouse" as the prevalence of partners living together without being married was low. Obviously, this will no longer serve. Indeed, in most cases the partners listed below were not married. In some cases it is clear, e.g., if reports use the term "partner" or "boyfriend", etc. In other cases I have taken a sexual involvement to be sufficient, or where the couple were living together, even without a known sexual involvement if the woman was financially dependent on the man (which, in the cases below, sometimes means "leeching off him"). However, living together alone would not be sufficient without those other qualifiers, thus excluding lodgers, etc.

This is a list of those convicted. There may well be others that were not convicted, or even discovered.

There are many cases where the killing was instigated by the female partner but she got one or more men to assist in carrying out the deed. I have only been able to capture those cases where the woman was convicted as well as the man/men. (It is typical in such cases that the woman is convicted of manslaughter but the man is convicted of murder and gets the longer sentence). There may be other cases where a woman's "commissioning hand" failed to be identified. Such cases would appear in reports to be "man kills man" cases and so I will not have identified these.

This is a list of direct killings which resulted in homicide trials. Hence, suicides resulting from partner abuse, including suicides resulting from a fathers' estrangement from his children by belligerent actions by the mother, are not included as I have no means of identifying them. This is a major omission because the total incidence of male suicide per year is massively greater than their deaths by direct partner homicide, by a factor of 200 or so. Consequently, any sizeable proportion of these suicides which result from domestic abuse or parental alienation has the potential to completely swamp the direct partner homicide deaths. In fact, I can state that this must definitely be the case. But reliable statistics are not known. Domestic abuse induced suicides have become topical of late, but you can be sure that the usual suspects will only be presenting half the story.

The date stated in the list refers to the date of conviction, not the date of the killing. The latter will be one or two years earlier in most cases, and sometimes many years earlier. The ages of the victim are at death, obviously.

Finally, the list will not be complete. It is merely what I found, which is ultimately reliant on news reports and the amount of effort I expended.

So, for the period 2010 to 2023, here is a list of 168 cases of men who were the victims of homicide by their female partners (possibly with others), plus 19 attempted murders of men by their female partners (or soliciting for a murder) and 7 lesbian homicides of women.

1.   2023: Rees Howarth stabbed to death.

2.   2023: Kasey Anderson, 24, stabbed to death.

3.   2023 Dylan Bacon, 39, stabbed to death.

4.   2023: Paul Hanson, 54, stabbed to death.

5.   2023: Saqib Hussain, 21, and Hashim Ijazuddin, 21, car rammed into a tree by another vehicle.

6.   2023: Paul Wagland, 52, stabbed to death.

7.   2023: Liam Smith, 38, shot dead.

8.   2023: Vishal Gohel death by blunt instrument.

9.   2023: Samuel Mayo, 34, stabbed to death.

10. 2023: Andrew Smith, 70, strangled to death.

11. 2023: Jonathan Gibbons, 50, stabbed to death.

12. 2023: Kevin Caster, 43, drugged and stamped to death.

13. 2023: Tai Jordan O'Donnell, 19, stabbed to death.

14. 2023: Frankie Fitzgerald, 25, throat cut and stabbed.

15. 2023: Thomas Campbell, 38, beaten, scalded and stabbed.

16. 2023: Saul Murray stabbed to death.

17. 2022 Steven Davies, 39, stabbed to death.

18. 2022: Keith Green, 40, stabbed to death.

19. 2022: Giovanni Wallace, 29, stabbed to death.

20. 2022: Gary Morgan, 36, stabbed to death.

21. 2022: Bradley Lewis, 22, stabbed to death.

22. 2022: Anthony Dunn, 81, smothered.

23. 2022: Paul Searing, 57, stabbed to death.

24. 2022: Matthew Wormleighton, 45, stabbed to death.

25. 2022: Mohammed Mukhtar, 53, bound and strangled.

26. 2022 Nigel Johnson, 55, stabbed to death.

27. 2022 Christopher Higgs, 21, stabbed to death.

28. 2022: Paul Fletcher, 31, stabbed to death.

29. 2022: Oliver O'Toole, 31, stabbed to death.

30. 2021: Adam Kroliowski, 32, stabbed to death.

31. 2021: Nigel Chapman, 62, stabbed to death.

32. 2021: David Jackson, 78, stabbed to death.

33. 2021: William Middleton, 38, stabbed to death.

34. 2021: Lee McKnight, 26, beaten, tortured and drowned.

35. 2021: Michael Baines, 80, scalded with boiling sugar water, died of severe burns.

36. 2021: Warren Glover beaten to death.

37.   2021: Joe Pooley, 22, drowned.
38.   2021: Piotr Lacheta, 55, kicked and stamped to death.
39.   2021: Raymond Cullen, 55, blunt instrument to head.
40.   2020: Mark Fisher, 33, stabbed to death.
41.   2020: Kieran Brown, 18, stabbed to death.
42.   2020: Zygimantas Kromelys, 26, stabbed to death.
43.   2020: Nigel Wright, 64, kicked to death.
44.   2020: Wayne Coventry, 36, stabbed to death.
45.   2020: Craig Morse, 33, stabbed to death.
46.   2020: Ronald Portz, 30, stabbed to death.
47.   2020: Paul Tong, 54, beaten to death.
48.   2020: Giedrius Juskaukas, 42, stabbed to death.
49.   2020: John Carroll, 52, stabbed to death.
50.   2019: John Robinson, 37, stabbed to death.
51.   2019: William Taylor, 69, strangulation/suffocation.
52.   2019: Paul Taylor, 45, stabbed to death.
53.   2019: Gary Cunningham, 29, stabbed to death.
54.   2019: Paul Gillet, 54, beaten to death.
55.   2019: John Maclean, 35, stabbed to death.
56.   2019: Steven Donaldson, 27, severance of spinal cord with machete.
57.   2019: Atakan Atay stabbed to death.
58.   2019: Kanagusabi Ramanathan, 76, beaten to death.
59.   2019: Kevin Nix, thrown from a car.
60.   2019: Martin Welsh stabbed to death.
61.   2019: James Field, stabbed to death.
62.   2019: Jack Delany stabbed to death.
63.   2019: Filip Jaskiewicz stabbed to death.
64.   2019: Alan Grayson, 85, stabbed to death.
65.   2019: Stephen Grant, 49, stabbed to death.
66.   2019: Haider Hayat, beaten and throat cut.
67.   2019: Mark Evans, 54, stabbed to death.
68.   2019: Alan Cowie, 65, Asphyxiated by standing on throat.
69.   2018: Conner Cowper, 18, stabbed to death.
70.   2018: Raul Chiriac, 26, stabbed to death.
71.   2018: Christopher Pearson, 39, stabbed to death.
72.   2018: Khalid Safi, 18, stabbed to death.
73.   2018: Neal Jex, 52, stabbed to death.

74. 2018: Keith Robinson, 59, arson causing petrol vapour explosion.
75. 2018: Kai Gareth Prothero, 47, stabbed to death.
76. 2018: Philip Rolph, 65, stabbed to death.
77. 2018: Paul Lavelle, 50, cut to face with sharp implement.
78. 2017: Matthew Birkinshaw, encouraged suicide.
79. 2017: Pietro Sanna, 23, stabbed to death.
80. 2017: Man Limbu, 75, strangled to death.
81. 2017: Mark Shaw, 29, stabbed to death.
82. 2017: Henry Wilson, 70, smothered to death.
83. 2017: John Poole, 50, stabbed to death.
84. 2017: Mohammed Yousaf, 65, throat cut and beaten.
85. 2017: Derek Taylor, 71, struck with hammer and axe.
86. 2017: David Butterfield, 43, stabbed to death.
87. 2017: Douglas Anderson stabbed to death.
88. 2017: Jimmy Prout, tortured to death over a period of months.
89. 2017: Anthony Culley, 56, stabbed to death.
90. 2017: Romualds Baluls, 32, stabbed to death.
91. 2017: Michael Beckwith, 44, beaten to death.
92. 2017: Fred Payne, 78, killed in fire (arson).
93. 2017: Alan Allan 34, stabbed to death.
94. 2016: Jonathan Baines 44, stabbed to death.
95. 2016: James Knight 26, stabbed to death.
96. 2016: Jason Capper 45, stabbed to death.
97. 2016: Jolyon Wray 46, stabbed to death.
98. 2016: Tanveer Iqbal 33, strangled to death.
99. 2016: Karl Bloxham 39, stabbed to death.
100. 2016: Shenol Erol Ali 32, stabbed to death.
101. 2016: Mark Hopes 45, beaten to death.
102. 2016: Stephen Burton 50, stabbed to death.
103. 2016: Alexander Duncan 59, stabbed to death.
104. 2016: Glyn Evans 58, stabbed to death.
105. 2016: David Edwards 51, stabbed to death.
106. 2016: Lee Gillespie 26, stabbed to death.
107. 2016: Norasab Hussain 33, stabbed to death.
108. 2016: Damon Searson 23, stabbed to death.
109. 2016: Marc Hastings 43, stabbed to death.
110. 2015: Phillip Nicholson 22, stabbed to death.

111. 2015: Richard Brown 47 and Sophia Christopher, 4, stabbed to death.
112. 2015: Louis Spires 68, suffocated to death.
113. 2015: David Butterworth 38, stabbed to death.
114. 2015: Graham White 38, beaten to death.
115. 2015: Norman Bruce 64, stamped to death.
116. 2015: Peter Hedley 49, beaten to death.
117. 2015: Kyle Farrell 21, stabbed to death.
118. 2015: Robert Dobinson 33, stabbed to death.
119. 2015: Mark Cannon 44, stabbed to death.
120. 2015: Ashley Meadowcroft 18, stabbed to death.
121. 2015: Jamie Belshaw 36, stabbed to death.
122. 2014: Alan Easton, stabbed to death.
123. 2014: Scott Blackwood 30, tortured to death.
124. 2014: John Fletcher 53, stabbed to death.
125. 2014: Leonard Pollen 58, pills & wrist slashing carried out by partner in suicide pact which she then failed to carry out on herself.
126. 2014: Geraint Hughes 60, stabbed to death.
127. 2014: Geoffrey Carter 58, stabbed and then death by smoke inhalation following arson on his flat.
128. 2014: Majid Khan 15 and Anum Khan 8, (siblings of intended target Amjad Khan) killed by arson.
129. 2014: Scott Dunne, stabbed to death.
130. 2014: Peter Davegun 42, beaten to death.
131. 2014: Barry Wilkins 71, stabbed to death.
132. 2014: Czeslaw Zawadzki 58, stabbed to death.
133. 2014: Martin Ackroyd 50, suffocated and strangled.
134. 2013: Richard Sherratt 57, battered to death.
135. 2013: Darren Orrett 32, stabbed to death.
136. 2013: Peter McMahon 68, beaten to death.
137. 2013: Nusrat Begum 36 (intended victim was Dawood Hussain) death in fire by arson.
138. 2013: Lukasz Slaboszewski 31 stabbed to death by Joanna Dennehy.
139. 2013: Kevin Lee 48, stabbed to death by the same Joanna Dennehy, 31 (she also killed non-partner John Chapman and attempted the murder of two other men chosen at random)
140. 2013: Michael Kerr 30, stabbed to death.

141. 2013: John Sampford 83, strangled to death.
142. 2013: Michael Moss 48, beaten to death.
143. 2013: Gareth Matthews 32, stabbed to death.
144. 2009: Piotr Rafacz, stamped to death.
145. 2012: Don Banfield 63, method unknown.
146. 2012: Lionel Morl 49, beaten to death.
147. 2012: Winston Fernandez 69, beaten to death.
148. 2012: Sean Martin 21, stabbed to death.
149. 2012: Alan Kopp 30, stabbed to death.
150. 2012: James Dornan 33, "glassed" leading to death.
151. 2012: John Whyte 50, stabbed to death.
152. 2012: Colin Ballinger 66, suffocated.
153. 2012: Ian Graham 51, stabbed to death.
154. 2012: Alan Clinch 48, stabbed to death.
155. 2012: Darren Dempsey 37, stabbed to death.
156. 2012: Karl Jones 37, blunt force beating.
157. 2011: Kevin Carter 30, stabbed to death.
158. 2011: Paul Norfolk 77, beaten to death with hammer.
159. 2011: Shaun Corey 42, drugged, tied up, strangled and suffocated.
160. 2011: Carlos Vilela 45, burnt alive with petrol (also crippling injuries to his daughters).
161. 2011: Arunas Ramanauskas, stabbed to death.
162. 2011: Martin Rusling 44, stabbed to death.
163. 2011: Alan Meeking 49, deliberate car crash.
164. 2011: David Twigg, fire/smoke inhalation (locked in store cupboard by the perpetrator who then lit a fire outside the door).
165. 2004: Kenneth Quy killed by the same murderer who went on, six years later, to kill…
166. 2010: Carl Everson 41, stabbed and stamped to death.
167. 2010: Andrew Oates 44, beaten to death with hammer.
168. 2010: Lakhvinder Cheemac 39, poisoned.

In addition, here are 19 cases of attempted murder of a man by his female partner, where the man was lucky to survive, or a conspiracy to murder that did not come off…

- Douglas Patrick 70, survived poisoning.
- Alexander Cameron, survived stabbing.

- Leng Hie Tiong 38, survived stabbing.
- Unnamed ex-husband, survived stabbing.
- Richard O'Rourke, survived stabbing.
- Stephen Watt 52, survived stabbing.
- Andrew Lyle, 47, survived being drugged, doused in petrol and set alight.
- Carl Gallagher, contract killing which didn't come off.
- Paul Belton, 50, whose murder was solicited, but the police intercepted.
- David Harrison, 59, attempted murder by stabbing by female partner after her long campaign of domestic violence against him.
- Unnamed boyfriend aged 25 who was the victim of an attempted murder by shooting.
- Unnamed ex-boyfriend was the subject of a botched murder attempt by a woman despite her written plan and careful preparation.
- Rob Parkes, unharmed, but the subject of three attempts by his ex-wife to have him killed.
- Michael Coen, attempted murder by stabbing by his female ex-partner (who also stabbed his new partner).
- Anonymous boy, 14, attempted murder by blunt instrument and stabbing by a 14-year-old girl and her 14-year-old boy accomplice.
- Ray Weatherall survive poisoning, shooting and electrocution/burning in an attempt to murder him by his wife and her lover.
- Iain Fullerton was repeatedly stabbed by his wife of 29 years in an attempt to murder him
- Jonathan Ingham was stabbed multiple times by his ex-partner in an attempt to murder him
- Daniel Rotariu, 31, survived being doused in sulphuric acid as he slept by his girlfriend who was convicted of attempted murder.

And finally, seven cases of lesbian killers, or would-be killers,

- Wendy Thorpe 42, battered to death by her lesbian lover.
- Lisa Ann Quigley 30, stabbed to death by her lesbian lover.
- Leng Hie Tiong 38, survived stabbing by her lesbian lover.
- Another lesbian killer did not kill her partner but she killed on behalf of her partner.
- A lesbian stabbed a female love rival, Sahkira Loseke, 22, through the heart after being accused of flirting with her girlfriend.

- A lesbian couple were both jailed, in association with the murder of Nadine Burden, 36.
- A lesbian committed serious and sustained violence on her 30-year-old female partner, Lyndsey Vaux, over many years. Vaux ultimately died of the combined effects of 90 separate injuries.

References

[1] Collins, W. (2017). Period 2011 to 2016 *WomenKillingTheirMalePartners 2011 to 2016*

[2] Collins, W. (2023). *Women Killing Their Male Partners 2017 to 2023*

20. Measuring Coercive Control

Here I examine some ONS research from 2019 which investigated how the phenomenon of coercive or controlling behaviours within the domestic context or between intimate partners could be measured. Unfortunately, the research is badly tainted by the evident ideological bias of its Steering Group.

Original posted on: 26 July 2019

On 29 December 2015, the government introduced the offence of controlling or coercive behaviour in an intimate or family relationship as Section 76 of the Serious Crime Act 2015, Ref.[1]. The creation of this legislation, under feminist Theresa May as Home Secretary, followed a government "consultation" the outcome of which was decided before the call for views was published, Ref.[2].

The Office for National Statistics (ONS) reports crime statistics annually, including domestic abuse: the Crime Surveys for England and Wales (CSEW). At the date of the research, surveys included questions relating to non-physical domestic abuse, as well as violence, but these did not align with the definition of coercive control as legislated in December 2015 (nor with later 2021 amendments). Indeed, how coercive control consistent with the legal definition is to be measured is an open question. Accordingly, the ONS carried out research into possible measures of coercive control, trialling new survey questions starting in April 2017. On 18th April 2019 the ONS published the results of their research based on survey responses obtained in the period April 2017 to March 2018, Ref.[3]. This article discusses their findings, limitations, and actions. It is worth noting that this research pre-dated the Domestic Abuse Act 2021 which, amongst other things, amended the legal definition of coercive and controlling behaviours.

The ONS findings are of considerable interest in at least two aspects: (a) the relative prevalence of this type of domestic abuse experienced by men and women, and, (b) the significance of preventing contact with children being classified as a form of coercive control. The actions taken by the ONS in the context of these two issues is of some concern.

Legal Definition of Controlling or Coercive Behaviour

I quote below from the Serious Crime Act (2015) Section 76, Ref.[1], as amended by the Domestic Abuse Act 2021, Ref.[4], (extracts only),

"Controlling or coercive behaviour in an intimate or family relationship

(1) A person (A) commits an offence if (a) A repeatedly or continuously engages in behaviour towards another person (B) that is controlling or coercive, (b) at the time of the behaviour, A and B are personally connected, (c) the behaviour has a serious effect on B, and (d) A knows or ought to know that the behaviour will have a serious effect on B.

(4) A's behaviour has a "serious effect" on B if (a) it causes B to fear, on at least two occasions, that violence will be used against B, or (b) it causes B serious alarm or distress which has a substantial adverse effect on B's usual day-to-day activities."

(6) A and B are 'personally connected' if any of the following applies: (a) they are, or have been, married to each other; (b) they are, or have been, civil partners of each other; (c) they have agreed to marry one another (whether or not the agreement has been terminated); (d) they have entered into a civil partnership agreement (whether or not the agreement has been terminated); (e) they are, or have been, in an intimate personal relationship with each other; (f) they each have, or there has been a time when they each have had, a parental relationship in relation to the same child; (g)they are relatives."

Prior to the changes brought about by the Domestic Abuse Act 2021, the original wording of the Serious Crime Act Section 76, as it was introduced in 2015, defined 'personally connected' as,

"A and B are 'personally connected' if—

(a) A is in an intimate personal relationship with B, or

(b) A and B live together and—

(i)they are members of the same family, or

(ii)they have previously been in an intimate personal relationship with each other."

The change is important because the original definition makes clear that the criminal offence of controlling or coercive behaviour requires that the parties in question are, at the time of the incidents, either in an intimate relationship or live together. Thus, incidents occurring only post-separation could not be counted as controlling or coercive offences. This contrasted markedly with other forms of partner abuse for which status as an ex-partner is sufficient. Indeed, the overwhelming bulk of partner abuse recorded by the crime surveys relates to separated or divorced couples or single people (see chapter 4, Figure 4.1). It was therefore a bald anomaly to define controlling or coercive behaviour differently. The effect was that, prior to 2021, controlling or coercive behaviour occurring post-separation, and hence whilst child contact or other family court disputes were proceeding, did not meet the legal definition. The significance of this to the ONS's research will be brought out below.

However, the wording of the Serious Crime Act Section 76 was amended, to that shown above, following the passing of the Domestic Abuse Act 2021. You will note that clause (6) does now admit the offence of coercive and controlling behaviours to relate to incidents occurring post-separation. Hence, alienating behaviours (parental alienation) would no longer be excluded as a S76 offence. Unfortunately, as we will see in chapter 22, what the Domestic Abuse Act 2021 gave with one hand it took away with the other.

ONS/CSEW Existing Measure of Non-Physical Domestic Abuse

In 2016 the CSEWs already contained questions relating to Non-Physical Domestic Abuse, namely, respondents were asked whether they have been,

- prevented from having their fair share of the household money
- stopped from seeing friends and relatives
- repeatedly belittled to the extent that they felt worthless

The questions are asked both in the context of a partner, and separately in the context of any other family member. Whilst there is some overlap between these questions and coercive or controlling behaviour, they do not conform to the required definition. This fact motivated the ONS's research into a measure which conforms better to the legal definition. (It should be noted that the questions now asked in the CSEW Intimate Partner Abuse surveys are far more extensive, Ref.[5].)

ONS's Trial of a Measure of Controlling or Coercive Behaviour

The measures of controlling or coercive behaviour trialled from April 2017 consisted of two parts: behaviours and impacts. A key issue is that at least one controlling or coercive behaviour had to be reported in order for the questions about impact to be addressed. In the abstract this may seem only sensible, but there is an important issue lurking therein, as we shall see.

Trial Behaviour Questions

These are the questions asked in the trial,

"In the last 12 months, has a partner or ex-partner ever repeatedly or continuously done any of the things listed below? By partner we mean a boyfriend, girlfriend, husband, wife or civil partner. Please select all that apply.

1. Unfairly controlled how much money you could have or how you spent it
2. Isolated you from your friends and family
3. Monitored your letters, phone calls, emails, texts or social media
4. Enforced rules or activities which humiliated you
5. Controlled how household work or childcare is done
6. Kept track of where you went or how you spent your time
7. Bullied or intimidated you, for example by punching walls or destroying property
8. Forced you to engage in sex or certain sexual acts against your will
9. Threatened to harm children in the household"

A welcome aspect of this is that the ONS trial does not restrict controlling or coercive behaviours to people living together at the time, and hence, in this respect, it is consistent with the post-2021 legal definition. It should be noted that the questions now asked in the CSEW Intimate Partner Abuse surveys cover most of the behaviours addressed in the trial questions, some in far more detail, Ref.[5]. However, question 5, which might be expected to be a controlling behaviour more prevalent amongst women controlling men than the reverse, is not asked. (I would go as far as to opine that almost all men living with a woman in an intimate relationship will experience item 5).

Impact

If a respondent reported being subject to at least one of the controlling or coercive behaviours, they were asked to respond to the following impact questions,

"Thinking about these actions you experienced in the last 12 months, to what extent did you suffer any of the following as a result?

[A] Fear that violence would be used against you
[B] Feeling unable to leave the relationship/household due to fear of coming to harm
[C] Constantly living in fear which affected your day-to-day activities
[D] Significant changes in routine, behaviour, or appearance to try to avoid the abuse
[E] Forced to give up work, education, or volunteering due to fear of coming to harm
[F] Fear that you would lose contact with your children"

For each impact category the respondent indicates if they suffered it very much, quite a lot, a little or not at all. It is in respect of Impact F, "fear that you would lose contact with your children" that the plot thickens. More on this key issue below.

ONS Research Results

For half of respondents (chosen at random), the new controlling or coercive behaviour questions replaced the original non-physical abuse questions at the same point in the CSEW survey. The other half of respondents received the original non-physical abuse questions. This permitted a comparison of the two measures.

Abuse Category	Non-Physical	Controlling or Coercive
These behaviours (partner)	3.0%	1.7%
These behaviours (family)	1.3%	0.6%
All domestic abuse	6.1%	4.5%

Table 20.1: Comparison of Trial Controlling or Coercive Behaviour Questions with Existing Non-Physical Abuse Questions in 2017-2019

The trial controlling or coercive behaviour questions indicated significantly lower prevalence than the existing non-physical abuse questions, Table 20.1.

Also of interest is that the sex difference in partner victimisation prevalence rates was found to be substantially reduced by the trial controlling or coercive behaviour measure, Table 20.2.

Abuse Measure	Women	Men
Abuse by partner, current non-physical measure	4.5%	1.5%
Abuse by partner, trial controlling or coercive measure	2.2%	1.2%
Family abuse, current non-physical measure	1.5%	1.2%
Family abuse, trial controlling or coercive measure	0.8%	0.4%

Table 20.2: Sex Differences in Victimisation using the Trial Controlling or Coercive Behaviour Questions and the Existing Non-Physical Abuse Questions in 2017-2019

ONS Reaction to the Research Results

The ONS research direction was guided by a Domestic Abuse Statistics Steering Group. This group was chaired by ONS and included representatives from across government, academia, the voluntary sector and Kantar Public who run the CSEW. The membership is given in Annex A of the ONS research report, Ref.[3]. All of those members who might be considered as "experts" in domestic abuse, as opposed to representatives of governmental organisations, were of a clearly feminist ideological background (with the exception of the Chairman of Mankind Initiative). The Group was well placed to block any changes to ONS domestic abuse measures which would reduce its apparent prevalence or reduce the sex difference in its prevalence, such outcomes being contrary to the (dominant) feminist narrative. The trialled questions for controlling or coercive behaviours, if used in place of the existing non-physical abuse questions, would do both. It was therefore unsurprising that the ONS – under the influence of their Steering Group - concluded that, *"the questions require further development before we can be confident that they are fit for purpose. To allow for this, the questions tested in the split-sample experiment were removed from the survey in April 2019".* They were explicit about the reasons,

i. The considerable extent of the difference in domestic abuse prevalence estimates generated by the two questions requires more in-depth research and exploration.

ii. The difference between men and women in the prevalence of domestic abuse changed with the introduction of the controlling or coercive behaviour questions – the extent of this difference and the reasons why such a change occurred needs further investigation.

iii. The wording and other aspects of the questions may be drawing in people who are not victims, or be missing those who are.

iv. Therefore, we have agreed that further development is needed and have removed the trial questions from the CSEW from April 2019 whilst further research is conducted.

Does anyone believe that if the trial questions had shown an apparent increase in prevalence rates and a greater ratio of female to male victimisation compared to the existing non-physical abuse questions that *i* and *ii* would have been a problem for the adoption of the new questions? No, the difficulty was not that the results changed but that they changed in the wrong direction. A greater apparent female victimisation would have been perfectly acceptable, indeed desirable.

Similarly, objection *iii* betrays that the Steering Group had a preconception regarding "people who are victims" quite independent of the definition via the questions. Upon what else could they take the view that people who were not true victims were being "drawn in"? The truth, one suspects, was that the "drawing in" of "people who are not victims" refers simply to men, whose victimisation must always be minimised by disbelief or being defined away altogether.

Contact with Children

Despite the inclusion within the Impact questions of "fear that you would lose contact with your children", the issue of child contact denial was minimised by the conditions of the trial. The reason is that none of the "Behaviour" questions related to the respondent having experienced child access denial. Recall that the trial protocol required at least one "Behaviour" to apply in order for the Impact questions to be asked. The absence of a Behaviour question relating to child contact will therefore have minimised responses to the Impact question relating to child contact because that question would be addressed only to people who happened to suffer one of the other Behavioural abuses. In view of this, it is not so surprising that ONS wrote,

"Two impacts elicited a higher proportion of 'does not apply' responses than others, for behaviours experienced both by a partner or ex-partner and by a family member:

- 'Forced to give up work, education or volunteering due to fear of coming to harm'
- 'Fear that you would lose contact with your children'

From this, we concluded that these two impacts should be removed from the definition of a victim for this initial stage of the research."

One wonders what the response to this Impact category would have been had the Behaviour question "prevented you from having contact with your children" been included.

However, even putting this aside, the reasoning is spurious. It is not the frequency of "does not apply" for different questions that matters, but the frequency with which it was reported as being suffered. As regards the question "fear that you would lose contact with your children", and in reference to partners/ex-partners, more than twice as many men answered this question with "suffered to some extent", than the number who stated "does not apply".

Furthermore, according to Tables 4a and 4b of the ONS's results (see links in Ref.[3]) this was the only impact category in which more men than women suffered to some extent. Moreover, this category is precisely that for which men report suffering most (both as regards partners/ex-partners and other family members) – despite the absence of an appropriate Behaviour question. Therefore, by omitting this impact category the impact results will be seriously gender-skewed, and one cannot escape the feeling that this is what truly motivated its exclusion.

Loss of Contact with Your Children is Not a Harm and Fear of it is Not a Real Fear

But it gets worse. The ONS Steering Group were guilty of an enormous and insupportable value judgment which explicitly minimises men's suffering. The ONS write,

"Responses to 'Fear that you would lose contact with your children' impacting the respondent 'to some extent' were marginally higher in relation to behaviours experienced

among men by a partner or ex-partner. There was concern among some members of the Domestic Abuse Statistics Steering Group that this impact was likely to illicit (sic) a relatively high response among men, which may not truly reflect controlling or coercive behaviour but rather a relatively common outcome in dissolved relationships. As such, at this early stage of the research, we took the decision not to include this impact in the definition of a victim. This is something we will investigate in later stages of the research."

This is logically incoherent. The intention is to measure impact. How can an impact be ruled as insignificant or unreliable on the grounds that it is more common? One must suspect that the desire of the Steering Group was to avoid eliciting "a relatively high response among men", contrary to their ideological narrative. (Amusingly, their misspelling of "elicit" as "illicit" is perhaps a Freudian slip, betraying their mindset that "a relatively high response among men" must be declared illicit).

Moreover, in as far as the impact is the *fear* of the harm in question being realised, is it reasonable to regard the fear as being reduced because the realisation of the harm is more common? The opposite surely applies. That the loss of contact of a non-resident parent, usually the father, with his children is a common outcome only makes fear of it more reasonable.

The ONS position appears to have been badly skewed by a value judgment which is insupportable, and, in fact, easily refuted. It relates to whether losing contact with one's children constitutes a harm. The answer is already available because the ONS note that the statutory guidance *"states that any level of fear experienced would be considered serious under the offence"*. But it seems that the feminist advisers, always ready with some verbal legerdemain, have provided a slippery get-out. In Section 5 Note 3 of Ref.[3] the ONS claim that,

"The word 'fear' is used differently in 'fear that you would lose contact with your children' in that it is not connected to a fear of violence or a fear of coming to harm, therefore this consideration (i.e., that the guidance would indicate that this constitutes a harm) does not apply. Future research will consider careful use of the word 'fear'".

This is utterly outrageous. It asserts that losing contact with one's children does not constitute a harm. This is a remarkable position to adopt and easily refuted. Consider asking any parent if they would prefer being punched in the face or never seeing their children again. How many parents would choose the latter? But recourse to such analogies is unnecessary. The legal definition of Controlling or Coercive Behaviour, quoted above, states that the "serious effect" criterion is met if the behaviour, *"causes B serious alarm or distress which has a substantial adverse effect on B's usual day-to-day activities"*. Being forcibly estranged from one's children certainly does just that.

In fact, losing contact with one's children is a harm of a particularly high order. Removing it as an impact is insupportable. And that is before consideration is given to the fact that, alone of the putative impact questions, this one involves a third party, namely the child. The interests of the child are paramount in family law, and yet the one category of impact which involves the child was dismissed.

The discussion relating to the definition of a victim of coercive control is also disconcerting. Having rejected two impact categories which contain the word "fear", the ONS then propose that the word "fear" is made the basis of accepting any degree of harm, including only "a little", as sufficient evidence of impact. In contrast, the one impact category which does not include the word "fear", namely "significant changes in routine, behaviour, or appearance to try to avoid the abuse", is required to be reported at the level "very much affected" in order to qualify.

This is again a strange value judgment which appears to elevate fear of an outcome above an actually realised outcome. Thus, for example, if "constantly living in fear which affected your day-to-day activities" is reported to apply "a little", then the impact criterion is satisfied regardless of whether there is actually any effect on your daily activities. In contrast, for a real change in your daily activities due to coercive control to qualify as evidence of victimhood the change would have to be at the "very much affected" level.

This elevates to a higher level of significance a subjective hypothetical of X which may never have happened over an objective actual occurrence of X. It is difficult not to see this as an attempt to cook the books. By focussing on fear, and only fear of certain possibilities and not others, the recommended definition of coercive control would be gender-skewed from the start, because women tend to be more fearful than men despite empirical evidence that men may be more often subject to the feared event.

The reality is that the coercive control of men by their female partners is common, Refs.[6,7]. Yet, lamentably, the prejudice against recognising this is far more widespread than this ONS research, including the criminal justice system in which 97% of those convicted under the Serious Crime Act Section 76 are men.

References

[1] UK Government (2015). *Serious Crime Act 2015 (Section 76)*.

[2] Collins, W. (2014). *Con Not Consultation*. The Illustrated Empathy Gap blog, 22 September 2014.

[3] Office for National Statistics (2019). *Developing a measure of controlling or coercive behaviour*. 18 April 2019.

[4] UK Government (2021). *Domestic Abuse Act 2021*.

[5] *CSEW IPA questions*

[6] Graham-Kevan, N., and Powney, D. (2021). *Male Victims of Coercive Control, Experiences and Impact*. University of Central Lancashire and Mankind Initiative.

[7] Bradford, R.A.W. (2022). *Association of partner abuse with loneliness and impaired well-being of separated fathers in Wales*. New Male Studies, Volume 11, Issue 1, 1-20, June 2022.

21. The Great Covid Domestic Abuse Epidemic That Never Was

During the covid-19 lockdowns we constantly heard that rates of domestic abuse were soaring. After reviewing what the narrative was on this topic over that period (roughly March 2020 to September 2021) I present an analysis of police reports of domestic abuse across England and Wales. The latter, obtained by FOI and disaggregated by sex, tells a very different story. The impatient reader can skip straight to the Conclusions.

Original posted on: 25 September 2021.

The Narrative

During the covid period, not only was the Angel of Death stalking the land with unprecedented slaughter, so we were told, but a by-product of covid lockdowns was a surge in domestic abuse, so we were told.

As the first English lockdown started, Women's Aid were already predicting dire consequences for victims of domestic abuse. In August 2020 a joint Panorama/Women's Aid "investigation" reported that domestic abuse surged in lockdown. The Guardian reported it thus, *"The coronavirus crisis has dramatically compounded domestic violence against women, new research has revealed. Two-thirds of women in abusive relationships have suffered more violence from their partners during the pandemic"*, Ref.[1].

In a fine example of arguing both ways, not only lockdowns but also the ending of lockdowns have been blamed for rises in domestic abuse. In November 2020, Ref.[2] told us,

"ONS statistics out today reveal a rise in domestic abuse related offences during the first UK national lockdown when compared to the same period in previous years. They also reveal a huge increase in numbers of calls to support services....The number of offences flagged as domestic abuse-related increased each month from April to June 2020, with the largest month-on-month increase (9%) between April and May 2020. This increase coincides with the easing of lockdown measures from 13 May 2020, when it may have been safer for victims to contact the police, painting a worrying picture for what the women's sector have predicted will be another spike as the second bout of national lockdown measures are eased this December....Labour is calling on the Government to outline its plan to protect victims of gender-based violence and provide sustainable support for the women's sector to help them cope with the rise in domestic abuse."

To anyone of a vaguely empirical bent, observing a data signal that persists whether or not lockdowns are in progress might suggest that lockdowns are irrelevant to the issue – but not when one's politically driven conclusions come first and "evidence" is the arrangement of words to suit it.

In June 2020, Human Rights Watch, Ref.[3], exposed the political motivation behind this narrative,

"'The government of the United Kingdom is stalling on establishing a robust legal framework to address violence against women and girls even as reported domestic abuse spikes during the pandemic', Human Rights Watch said today. 'Insufficient measures to ensure critical support and services for survivors of violence – especially those least likely to get help – before and during the covid-19 pandemic have left organizations that help some of the most vulnerable women scrambling to meet needs.'

'The pandemic has exposed longstanding flaws in the UK government's approach to domestic violence,' said Hillary Margolis, senior women's rights researcher at Human Rights Watch. 'Erosion of support for specialist domestic abuse services was already a national crisis, and this is a critical moment for the government to demonstrate commitment to long-term investment in these services for every woman and girl.'

'The government has repeatedly said it prioritizes protection and support for women and girls experiencing violence, but it has yet to ratify a landmark European treaty on violence against women signed by the government eight years ago today. The Domestic Abuse Bill before Parliament fails to ensure protection for all women and girls.'"

All this is political pressure, not analysis. In the last paragraph Margolis was referring to the Istanbul Convention, Ref.[4], which was subsequently ratified on 24 July 2022 (see chapter 23).

Not to be outdone in the representation of domestic carnage, on 1 February 2021, Under-Secretary of State for Justice, Alex Chalk, told us that *"charities have reported a 200% increase in calls and people accessing webchat services since the first lockdown"*, Ref.[5].

On 3 February 2021, The Sun confidently informed us that, *"the covid pandemic fuelled a 10 per cent annual rise in domestic violence, it emerged yesterday as MP's heard of a looming crisis in services for victims"*, Ref.[6].

One can hardly blame journalists for being confused about correlation versus causality when people who call themselves researchers do the same – when it suits. I have given only a small selection of the reports that abounded in news outlets over the period March 2020 to September 2021 linking domestic abuse statistics to covid lockdowns. None actually established any such link, they only asserted one.

A strong candidate for the nastiest misreporting on this issue is the article in inews on 24 September 2021, Ref.[7], which carried this headline, *"Covid-19 and domestic violence: abusive men deliberately exposed wives and partners to virus, study finds"*. The article informs us that *"survivors of domestic violence and abuse have been at an increased risk of contracting suspected or confirmed covid-19, according to University of Birmingham researchers who pinned the blame on male behaviour"*. I will resist the temptation to critique the study in question, Ref.[8], but it does not say what the title of the inews article claims.

Now for the cash…

In early April 2020, before the first covid-19 peak, Priti Patel, then the Home Secretary, announced £2 million to "immediately bolster" domestic abuse helplines and online support, Ref.[9]. In parallel, Priti Patel also announced the awareness campaign, #YouAreNotAlone, Ref.[10], whose purpose was, *"to reassure those affected by domestic abuse that support services remain available during this difficult time"*. A male victim might ask "what support services?".

At the start of May 2020, towards the end of the first covid-19 wave, the government announced a further £35M to fund domestic abuse services and safe accommodation. In November 2020, during the second major English lockdown, the government provided a further £10.8M to rape and domestic abuse support services.

In December 2020 the government launched the "Ask for ANI" (Action Needed Immediately) scheme whereby people could ask for emergency assistance at their pharmacy (those which had signed-up for it), including a Safe Space arrangement in pharmacy consulting rooms, Ref.[11].

Then on 1 February 2021 the Ministry of Justice announced a further £40M funding boost for specialist rape and domestic abuse support services, Ref.[5]. The same source gives a figure of £125M as the extra funding provided to local authorities for the provision of safe accommodation for victims of domestic abuse and their children.

That's a grand total of an **extra** £213M government funding to domestic and sexual abuse services over a 10-month period. This will be on top of the approximately £300M funding received by Women's Aid affiliated charities in the UK annually, Ref.[12].

The Reality

Let me say straight away that the ONS have been more measured in their reporting of the recent domestic abuse statistics than have many of those commentators who have used ONS statistics to support their pre-established political, ideological or financial interests. In a data release on 25 November 2020, Ref.[13], ONS states immediately,

"Police recorded crime data show an increase in offences flagged as domestic abuse-related during the coronavirus (covid-19) pandemic, however, there has been a gradual increase in police recorded domestic abuse-related offences over recent years as police have improved their recording of these offences; therefore it cannot be determined whether this increase can be directly attributed to the coronavirus pandemic."

Finally! Someone states the bleedin' obvious. You cannot conclude anything about lockdowns from a greater level of police reports of DV in 2020 compared to 2019.

A greater prevalence of reports of DV in 2020 compared to 2019 was expected anyway, irrespective of covid, because the volume of DV reports to the police has been increasing for ten years (at least). This is unlikely to be because of an increase in the number of victims of DV because the CSEWs have been showing either a decreasing prevalence of DV by victim, or a roughly flat prevalence trend, over the same period (see Figure 21.1). An increasing number of incidents per victim may be part of the explanation for the increasing police record data, though an increasing propensity to call the police together with better police record keeping will also be part of the explanation.

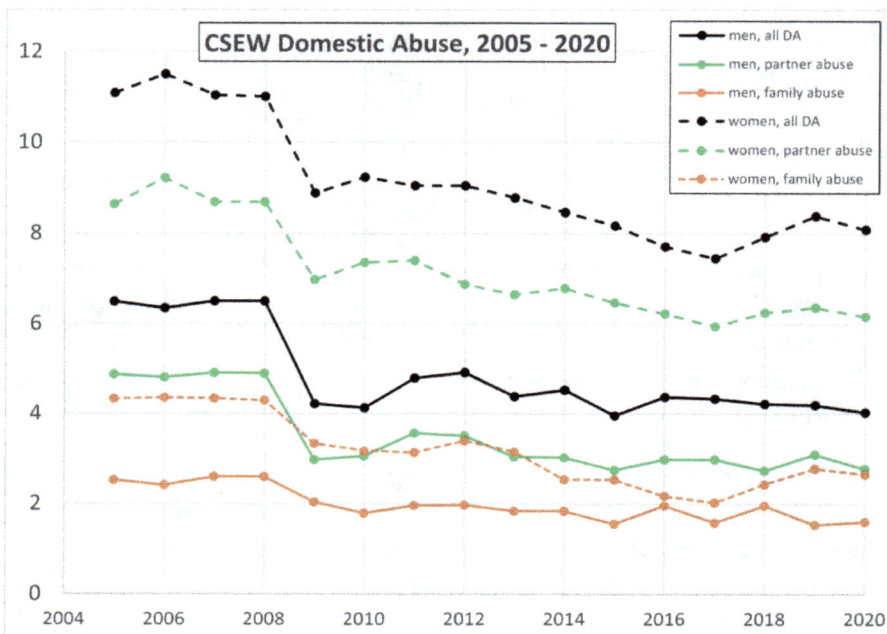

Figure 21.1: Plotted using data from the 2020 CSEW, Ref.14]. The Figure plots the percentage of people of the same sex who were victims once or more in the preceding year. Data relates to the 12 months ending 31 March of the plotted year.

I have obtained data on the numbers of reports of domestic abuse recorded by police in the calendar years 2018, 2019 and 2020 via Freedom Of Information enquiry. The following words were used, raising an FOI on each of the 42 police forces in England and Wales,

"Please provide the total number of reports recorded by you and categorised as domestic abuse or domestic violence in each of the last three calendar years (2018, 2019, and 2020), disaggregated by sex of complainant or victim."

I obtained responses from 38 police forces (one with incomplete 2018 data). These data, for 2018, 2019 and 2020, can be augmented by the comparable data for years 2012 to 2018 reported by Mankind Initiative, Ref.[15]. I have addressed two objectives,

• Demonstrate that police reports of domestic abuse have been trending up for a decade across virtually all police regions, and,

• Analyse whether the volume of reports in 2020 was or was not larger than expected based on the trends.

For the first of these I use my own FOI data for 2018, 2019 and 2020, covering 38 police forces, plus the Mankind Initiative data for all 42 forces between 2012 and 2018. I have performed a simple linear regression against year of the total recorded crime incidents categorised as domestic abuse. 38 of the 42 police forces' data have positive regression coefficients (slopes), indicative of a trend of increasing numbers of domestic abuse reports to each of these 38 forces over the period 2012 to 2020. Of the 4 forces which have a negative regression coefficient (trend of decreasing reports), three are not statistically significant ($p > 0.05$). Of the 38 forces with positive regression coefficients (increasing trend), the coefficient is significant at the 95% confidence level ($p < 0.05$) in 25 cases. In 16 of these cases significance is at the 99.9% confidence level.

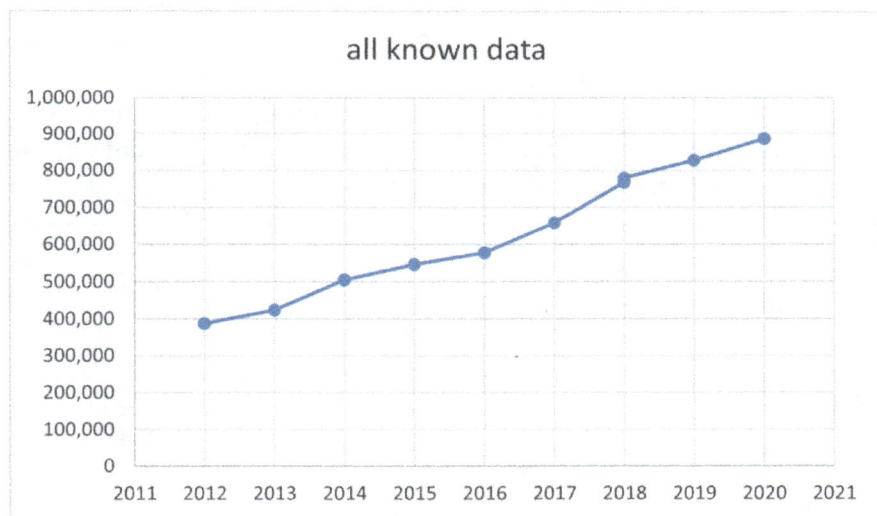

Figure 21.2: All Police Recorded Incidents, 2011 – 2020 (5 forces missing in 2019, 2020)

Summing all domestic abuse incidents over England and Wales shows a positive upward trend significant at the one-in-ten-million level. The corresponding graph is shown as Figure 21.2.

This establishes that police recorded DV-related incidents have been trending upwards over the period 2012 - 2020, and hence that a larger number of such reports in 2020 compared to 2019 means nothing as regards the effect, or otherwise, of covid lockdowns. This immediately discredits all the claims of the prevailing narrative, summarised above.

To address my second objective I need to establish a means of detecting whether the number of police reports in 2020 was in excess of what might have been expected based on a continuing upward trend. In fact, Figure 21.2 almost clinches the issue already as there is no sudden 'blip' in 2020, rather the 2020 data continues the previous trend, the slope of the data between 2018 and 2020 being broadly similar to that earlier.

However, to address this question with greater precision, I examined individually all 38 Forces' responses for which I have complete data. To do so I defined an 'Index of Change' (IOC) which has the following properties. The Index of Change is positive if the number of victims in 2020 exceeded what would have been expected based on the trend between 2018 and 2019. Conversely, the Index of Change is negative if the number of victims in 2020 was less than what would have been expected based on the trend between 2018 and 2019. The magnitude of the Index of Change is the extent of the deviation from expectation expressed as a percentage of the number of victims in 2019. For algebraic details of the definition of the Index of Change I refer the reader to the original post, Ref.[16].

Victims	Number of forces with negative IOC	Number of forces with positive IOC	IOC for whole of England and Wales (38 Forces)
Female victims	25	13	-2.9%
Male victims	23	15	2.4%
Total victims	26	13	1.3%
Percentage of victims who were male	16	22	3.3%

Table 21.1: Index of Change (IOC) Results

Table 21.1 shows how many of the individual police forces produced negative or positive Indices of Change. For male victims, female victims or the total victims, there are more negative than positive Indices, indicating that the number of police forces which reported smaller numbers of victims than expected based on the 2018 to 2019 trend exceeds the number of forces which reported larger numbers of victims than expected.

In contrast, if we look at the number of male victims expressed as a percentage of all victims of known sex, $m/(m+f)$, the Index of Change is positive for more forces than it is negative, i.e., the number of police forces which reported a larger proportion of male victims than expected based on the 2018 to 2019 trend exceeds the number of Forces which reported a smaller proportion of male victims than expected.

The last column of Table 21.1 is based on the total number of victims summed over the 38 police forces who responded to my FOI (or, in the case of the percentage of male victims, the average of this percentage over the 38 Forces). The overall Index of Change is negative for female victims, but positive for male victims, total victims and the percentage of male victims.

Finally, the percentage of police reports of domestic abuse which relate to male victims continues to trend upwards, as it has for years, Figure 21.3.

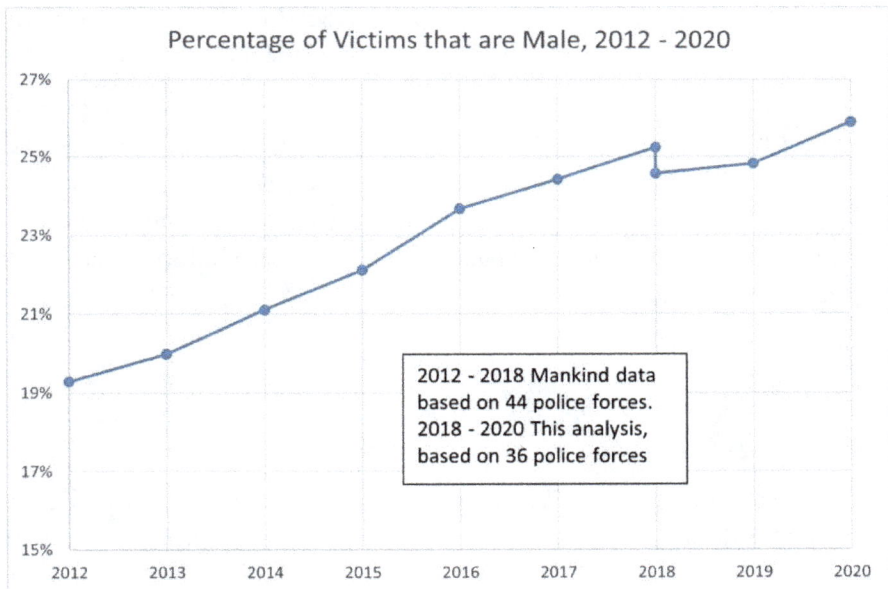

Figure 21.3: Percentage of police reports of domestic abuse relating to male victims, trend

Conclusions

[1] The police recorded data on numbers of reported incidents classified as domestic abuse have been trending up across almost all police forces for at least a decade.

[2] This contrasts with crime survey data on numbers of domestic abuse victims which has not been trending up, but either trending down or roughly static.

[3] A larger number of police recorded domestic abuse incidents in 2020 compared with 2019 cannot be taken as indicative of a covid lockdown effect as this was expected, without covid, based on prevailing trends.

[4] The question of whether 2020 brought an unexpectedly large volume of domestic abuse incidents must be explored by measuring any exceedance of reported incidents from that expected based on trends. This measure is provided here by an Index of Change (Ref.[16]).

[5] More police forces reported data which indicated that the volume of incidents in 2020 was less than expected based on trends than the number of forces reporting greater volumes than expected. This suggests there was no significant "covid lockdown" enhancement of domestic abuse prevalence in 2020 across England and Wales as a whole.

[6] Based on summing incidents across the 38 police forces responding to my FOI, the overall Index of Change for women victims was negative (-2.9%) whilst for male victims it was positive (+2.4%). These are only small deviations from expectation, but if there was a "covid lockdown" enhancement of DV across England and Wales as a whole it would apply only to male victims.

References

[1] McDonald, H. (2020). *Domestic abuse surged in lockdown, Panorama investigation finds*. The Guardian, 17 August 2020.

[2] Thomas-Symonds, N. (2020). New statistics reveal spike in domestic violence during lockdown. Website Labour.org.uk, November 2020 (since taken down).

[3] Human Rights Watch (2020). *UK Failing Domestic Abuse Victims in Pandemic*. 8 June 2020.

[4] Collins, W. *Istanbul Convention: Approaching UK Ratification | The Illustrated Empathy Gap*. 15 December 2016.

[5] Rt Hon Alex Chalk (2021). *Extra £40m to help victims during pandemic and beyond*. Ministry of Justice, 1 February 2021.

[6]   Sullivan, M. (2021). *ABUSE UP Covid lockdown fuels 10 per cent annual rise in domestic violence*. The Sun, 3 February 2021.

[7]   Gallagher, P. (2021). *Covid-19 and domestic violence: abusive men deliberately exposed wives and partners to virus, study finds*. inews, 24 September 2021.

[8]   Singh, J., et al. (2021). *The risk of COVID-19 in survivors of domestic violence and abuse*. BMC Medicine volume 19, Article number: 246 (2021).

[9]   Havard, T. (2021). *Domestic abuse and Covid-19: A year into the pandemic*. House of Commons Library, 11 May 2021.

[10] Rt Hon Priti Patel (2020). *Home Secretary announces support for domestic abuse victims*. Home Office, 11 April 2020.

[11] Home Office (2023). *Ask for ANI domestic abuse codeword: information for pharmacies*. (This is an update of the scheme introduced in 2020). 17 February 2023.

[12] Collins, W., *UK Domestic Violence Charities' Finances*. The Illustrated Empathy Gap, 16 September 2016.

[13] Office for National Statistics (2020a). *Domestic abuse during the coronavirus (COVID-19) pandemic, England and Wales*. 25 November 2020.

[14] Office for National Statistics (2020b). *Domestic abuse prevalence and victim characteristics*. See Appendix Table 3b of the March 2020 dataset.

[15] Mankind Initiative (2018). *Reports of Domestic Abuse to Police Disaggregated by Sex of Victim, 2012 – 2018*.

[16] Collins, W. (2021). *The Great Covid Domestic Abuse Epidemic That Never Was*. The Illustrated Empathy Gap, 25 September 2021.

22. Throwing Children to the Wolves: Part 1

I have split the original post with this title into two parts. This first part addresses those aspects of the Domestic Abuse Act 2021 which concern alienating behaviours (or parental alienation if you prefer). The second part addresses the issues which appeared in a sequence of Appendices in the original post. Neither part gets close to doing full justice to all the aspects of the Domestic Abuse Act 2021. For further details I refer you to the numerous earlier articles in my blog, The Illustrated Empathy Gap (empathygap.uk). A thorough account would require a long, tedious and depressing book to itself. It was the latest episode in the ongoing exercise in utter futility.

Original posted on: <u>*8 November 2022*</u>

The Domestic Abuse Act 2021 became law on 29 April 2021. The long sorry saga of this parade of discrimination masquerading as care and protection began in 2018. But it did not end when the Act became law. The grand finale, or to be more precise, the grand nadir, came only in July 2022.

I had not the heart to blog about it at the time. After several years of DA Act related posts and submissions, I had rather run out of steam – and there was nothing to celebrate and nothing further to be done in the context of that Act. I reprise the sequence of events and some of the key issues in Part 2 (chapter 23).

What I wish to draw to your attention in this chapter is the extent to which ministers have the power to define law virtually unilaterally in certain circumstances. These circumstances occur when primary legislation, duly passed by parliament, requires "clarification" in the form of Statutory Guidance. This effectively devolves the power of defining the *de facto* law to an individual minister. So it was for the DA Act.

As the DA Bill was on its long journey through parliament, the associated Statutory Guidance was first published as a draft in July 2020. It was later re-issued in draft in July 2021, after which yet another public "consultation" was held, which closed 14 September 2021. After that all was quiet, as far as I am aware, until the government's response to that consultation. Ref.[1], was published alongside the formal Guidance itself in July 2022, Ref.[2]. The final version of the Guidance was a shock; it omitted key paragraphs which we had expected to find there based on the July 2021 draft.

The point of this article is to highlight how the one possible benefit to be gained from this sorry episode, namely the recognition in law of parental alienation (PA) as a form of child abuse, was snatched away at the last moment – by the minister, not parliament.

The Statutory Guidance was issued by the Home Office under Home Secretary Priti Patel. She was also the Home Secretary who just managed to ratify the Istanbul Convention before losing her job. Whether a different Home Secretary might have produced a different outcome I rather doubt, but one cannot be sure.

Here are some key extracts from the July 2021 draft Guidance, not the final version of the Guidance. These extracts are taken from the Section "Recognising Domestic Abuse", intended to provide Guidance on what constitutes domestic abuse.

"*Controlling or coercive behaviour*

56. Controlling or coercive behaviour also forms part of the definition of domestic abuse in section 1(3)(c) of the 2021 Act.

57. Below is a list of behaviours that are within the range and continuum of coercive or controlling behaviour. This list is not exhaustive. (I include just the relevant examples below)…

> *Using children to control their victim, for example, threatening to take the children away or manipulating professionals to increase the risk of children being prevented from having contact with the victim or having children's social care involvement;*

> *Alienating behaviours [footnote 26], including invidious drip feeding of negative views to a child by one parent about the other parent, or any attempt by one parent to frustrate or limit the child's contact with the other parent, other than for reasons based on concern about the risk to that child;*"

Footnote 26 read: "*Whilst there is no single definition of alienating behaviours (sometimes referred to as 'parental alienation'), the Children and Family Courts Advisory and Support Service (Cafcass) defines parental alienation as when a child's resistance or hostility towards one parent is not justified and is the result of psychological manipulation by the other parent.*"

The July 2021 draft Guidance also included this,

"Emotional or psychological abuse

60. Domestic abuse often involves emotional or psychological abuse. This can include: (relevant examples here only)…

> *Turning children and friends against the victim (which may have a subsequent impact on children) including falsely and without justification telling a child that the other parent abandoned them, never loved them, or never wanted them;*

> *Distorting a child's memories about the victim parent, including telling a child the other parent will pick them up/meet them, when that was not true, falsely telling medical/school staff they have sole custody of a child so that no information is provided to the other parent, painting the other parent in a negative light to the child, including mocking their personality characteristics, job, friends, family and belittling them (including in front of the child);"*

Hence, in the July 2021 draft Guidance it was clear that Parental Alienation was explicitly included as a form of controlling or coercive behaviour and a form of emotional or psychological abuse (both being forms of domestic abuse, of both the alienated parent and the child).

But then, suddenly, it wasn't.

All the above extracts were removed from the Statutory Guidance as published in July 2022. The only part which remains has been robbed of its specific allusion to parental alienation in respect of its relation to child contact denial, now reading "using children to control their victim, for example, threatening to take the children away".

Some might argue that the examples of controlling or coercive behaviour, and of emotional or psychological abuse, within the Guidelines are sufficient to cover PA. I beg to differ. Certainly, PA is indeed a form of controlling or coercive behaviour, and also a form of emotional and psychological abuse, Ref.[3], but the words remaining within the Guidance do not reflect the specific characteristics of PA which make it PA. The text that remains within the Guidance was never intended to do so, quite the contrary. Suitable wording that does specifically reflect the phenomenon of parental alienation – the words quoted above – were removed. This was not an accident.

This change was given spurious legitimacy by the government's response to the consultation on the draft Guidance, Ref.[1]. In one of my earliest posts I noted that it was the government which put the "Con" into "Consultation", Ref.[4]. The government's response to the consultation submissions in respect of parental alienation is contained in Ref.[1] paragraphs 3 to 8. They note that they were presented with two diametrically opposed schools of thought. One was aligned with the above extracts from the 2021 draft Guidance. The other was the feminist position on PA. The latter promotes the view that claims of PA are an abuser's strategy to discredit allegations against them. Paragraph 6 makes the decision, thus,

"The consultation responses highlighted a lack of shared understanding of 'parental alienation' – its definition and implications, and how to approach it in practice. Therefore, explicit references to 'parental alienation' and 'alienating behaviours' have not been made in the finalised draft."

I invite you to critically examine that reasoning. How does the "lack of shared understanding" lead to a decision to exclude PA as a form of abuse? Could one not equally argue that, to err on the side of caution, PA should be included as a form of abuse? After all, the behaviours described in the extracts above are indisputably undesirable. It is not only the contentious term "parental alienation" but the words that describe these behaviours which have been removed.

The reality is clear enough. There was always a determination to remove PA from the Guidance and the consultation was a vehicle for giving it apparent legitimacy. The game is given away by para 7 which starts,

"This approach to finalising the guidance reflects findings from 'Assessing Risk of Harm to Children and Parents in Private Law Children Cases' Report (June 2020), often referred to as the Harm Panel Report (Ref.[5])."

Yes, well, it would. The panel, Ref.[6], that was responsible for that so-called Harms Report was so one-sided in terms of their views on these very issues that the nature of their eventual report was inevitable. The sole author of the influential Literature Review which forms a key part of the overall Harms Report was Adrienne Barnett, a feminist barrister turned academic, whose views on parental alienation are well-known and uncompromisingly partisan. "PA's intended purpose", she has written in an academic publication, is "to shut down domestic abuse in private family law". I have deconstructed her perspective in Ref.[7]. Just to orient readers on Dr Barnett's views, here is an extract from the Abstract of her PhD thesis,

"This study concludes that in order to regain a valid and authoritative voice for women in current family law we need to expose and disrupt law's construction of the 'scientific truth' about children's welfare".

Are you happy with "disrupting scientific truth", i.e., radically changing or undermining scientific truth? Especially where it impacts children's welfare? And this is the axis of opinion which has been used to imbue with ostensible legitimacy the removal of PA as a form of domestic abuse (of parents and children).

By Section 8 of the consultation response, in a section titled Alienating Behaviours, the discussion has, bewilderingly, moved onto perpetrator programmes – and they don't mean for alienators.

But what is the true scientific status of PA? I'm not about to attempt a literature review of parental alienation in this post – though the reason is telling in itself: the academic literature on PA is too vast for me to address in less than many months of work. By 2016, parental alienation and alienating behaviours in separated or divorced families had been well documented in over 500 references drawn from the professional literature across 30 countries, Ref.[8]. By 2018 there were more than one thousand research and clinical studies reported in scientific and professional journals, books and book chapters, Ref.[9].

A recent systematic review of the literature on PA by Portilla-Saavedra et al, Ref.[10], has concluded that *"parental alienation is a phenomenon with a significant prevalence in the population and has been linked to a deterioration in the mental health of people who experience it or have experienced it"* and that *"the 11 selected studies established relationships between the experience of parental alienation and mental health indicators, both in children, adolescents, and adults who experience or experienced these dynamics. It was also related to psychological abuse."* The paper also identified a need to *"place it as a form of child abuse".*

Moreover, PA is not a rare phenomenon but appallingly common, Ref.[11].

It is tempting to express this as the political establishment, irrespective of political party, having been captured by the partisan feminist lobby. But in truth it is not a capture but an alliance, a symbiosis. Feminism is a tool for those of an authoritarian bent – which tends to be everyone in positions of power unless that power is closely monitored, severely restricted, and frequently curtailed by democratic sovereignty. But the political process is also a tool for feminism. This is the feminist establishment. It operates on the basis that feminism gifts the establishment with ostensible moral legitimacy, whilst in return the establishment yields some policy influence to feminism.

The result is that a serious and very widespread social ill is being hidden and effectively condoned. The feminist establishment is throwing vast numbers of children to the wolves.

References

[1] UK Government Home Office (2022). *Domestic Abuse Act 2021 Statutory Guidance Consultation Government response*. Published 8 July 2022.

[2] UK Government Home Office (2022). *Statutory guidance: Domestic Abuse Act 2021*. Published 8 July 2022.

[3] Parental Alienation UK (2022). *Domestic Abuse Act 2021 – Statutory Guidance.*

[4] Collins, W. (2014). *Con Not Consultation*. 22 September 2014.

[5] UK Government Ministry of Justice (2020). *Assessing risk of harm to children and parents in private law children cases (Final Report, Literature Review and Implementation Plan)*. June 2020.

[6] Collins, W. *Family Justice Review Panel*. The Illustrated Empathy Gap, 1 July 2019.

[7] Bradford, R.A.W. (2022). *The Language of Deceit, Division and Dominance*. New Male Studies, Volume 9, Issue 2, December 2020.

[8] Harman, J., et al (2016). *Prevalence of parental alienation drawn from a representative poll*. Children and Youth Services Review, Volume 66, July 2016, Pages 62-66.

[9] Kruk, E. (2018). *Parental Alienation as a Form of Emotional Child Abuse: Current State of Knowledge and Future Directions for Research*. Family Science Review, Volume 22, Issue 4, 2018.

[10] Portilla-Saavedra, D., et al (2021). *Perspectivas y tendencias actuales del concepto de alienación parental: una revisión sistemática de la literatura (Current perspectives and trends of the concept of parental alienation: a systematic review of the literature)*. Ter Psicol vol.39 no.2 Santiago July 2021.

[11] Harman, J., et al (2019). *Prevalence of adults who are the targets of parental alienating behaviors and their impact*. Children and Youth Services Review, Volume 106, November 2019, 104471.

23. Throwing Children to the Wolves: Part 2

I have split the original post with this title into two parts. The first part addressed those aspects of the Domestic Abuse Act 2021 which concern parental alienation. This second part addresses the issues which appeared in a sequence of Appendices in the original post, (i) a timeline of the progress of the DA Bill, its associated Guidance and MOJ "research", (ii) the ratification under false pretences of the Istanbul Convention, (iii) the government's opinion, contrary to law, that there is no automatic right to contact between a parent and their child.

Original posted on: 8 November 2022

The Recent Timeline of the Ongoing Exercise in Utter Futility

The harm to children done by parental alienation (PA) is facilitated by the narrative that domestic abuse is overwhelmingly perpetrated by men against female victims. But men, too, are victims of partner abuse, 95% of such being heterosexual, i.e., with perpetration by female partners (chapter 18). If you doubt it see Ref.[1]. Moreover, domestic abuse has serious impacts on men, contrary to what is often claimed, as is demonstrated by the study of Ref.[2] based on non-resident fathers.

There is a steadfast refusal by society as a whole, and feminists in particular, to believe that partner abuse of men by women is comparable in impact and prevalence to the reverse. For feminists, maintaining the fiction that partner abuse is "overwhelmingly perpetrated by men on women" is not only a cornerstone of their perception of the world, but also crucial to maintaining their influence which constantly levers this perception.

September 2014 (Ref.[3]): I start with my commentary on the government's "Consultation", under Theresa May as Home Secretary, on making coercive and controlling behaviours in intimate relationships an explicit criminal offence. They did, via an amendment to the Serious Crime Act, and it became law on 29 December 2015 (see chapter 20). This would have been acceptable were it not for the totally sex-skewed narrative around it…and, of course, Homo sapiens' innate sex bias. As a result, 97% of convictions for this new offence are men, despite the coercive control of men by women being extremely common, at least as common as the reverse, and its impacts severe, see Refs.[1,4].

September 2014 (Ref.[5]): This was the first of several posts on the appalling sexism of the Istanbul Convention prior to its ratification by the UK government.

July 2015 (Ref.[6]): This post exposed the fact that the Crown Prosecution Service (CPS) reports ostensibly on Violence Against Women and Girls (VAWG) actually hide male victimisation by redefining any male victims as a VAWG statistic. This persists to this day, despite the CPS being shamed into making a note of the fact on the title page of their reports.

August 2017 (Ref.[7]): This post presents a brief summary of the academic work refuting the feminist "patriarchal power and control" aetiology of domestic abuse. The literature is far vaster than indicated in that post, long though it is. An associated issue is that "Duluth"-type perpetrator programmes do not work.

July 2019 (Ref.[8]): The government raised a Consultation in 2018 on their ideas for the pending Domestic Abuse Bill. The draft Bill then went forward to the Public Bill Committee who then invited evidence from the public, as is normal. In this post I link to male-friendly submissions to both the Consultation and the Public Bill Committee. I submitted one on behalf of Parity. I also summarised some of the key features in the draft Bill, which sets the agenda for the next three years on this matter.

18 April 2019: The ONS published its research on the problem of measuring coercive control with the flaws, arising from the ideological bias of their Steering Group, already discussed in chapter 20.

16 July 2019 (Ref.[9]): the Parliamentary Under Secretary of State for Crime, Safeguarding and Vulnerability, Victoria Atkins, made her wildly false statement that the majority of perpetrators of domestic abuse of men are other men, which I have already deconstructed and refuted in chapter 18. The minister was informed of her error. No correction has been made.

October 2019 (Ref.[10]): The second reading of the DA Bill. I'm not going to go into chapter and verse (see also Ref.[8]) but here are some major aspects of the Bill...

(i) the creation of a worryingly powerful Domestic Abuse Commissioner, chosen, of course, from the most culpable of the usual culprits. Nicole Jacobs was appointed to the £140,000 pa part-time post nearly two years before the

DA Act received Royal Assent. She was therefore able to give evidence to the Bill Committee which led to the Act which created her post. Eh? That's some trick they pulled.

(ii) the creation of domestic abuse protection notices and orders (DAPNs and DAPOs), which make it even easier to eject men from their homes on an allegation. Breaking the terms of these new protection notices/orders is now a criminal offence, thus undermining yet another fundamental principle of law. A man can be given a criminal record without ever being tried or admitting guilt.

(iii) prohibition of cross-examination of (alleged) victims by the respondent (viz the accused), often with no professional representation either – a triumph of justice, I'm sure you'll agree. Victimhood status now automatically confers "special measures" such as being permitted to give evidence by video.

(iv) The promise of loads of money, but I invite you to try to discover how much of this largesse ends up in the hands of organisations that genuinely assist male victims.

All this comes about because of innate and institutionalised prejudice. The government reiterated in their formal response to the Bill Committee that *"We fully recognise that domestic abuse is a gendered crime, which disproportionally affects women"* (in case you had any lingering doubt). This perspective informs the entire issue, but it is empirically false and has been known to be so for decades. It is not statement of fact but a statement of political position.

June 2020 (Ref.[11]: The Ministry of Justice published the review they had commissioned ostensibly addressing "assessing the risk of harm to children and parents in private law children cases", the so-called "Harms Report", actually three reports. The authors were such that the nature of what would be produced was inevitable. This "report" was so biased it defies my vocabulary. So bad, indeed, was it that Terrence White and Benjamin Garrett applied for a judicial review of it. Unsurprisingly, permission for a judicial review was rejected and the attempt now wallows in perpetual appeal, I believe. Terry summarised the Harms Report thus: "It has no technical merit. It misquoted and mischaracterised the technical papers that it relied upon. Its process was technically flawed to the extent its internally-generated indicia cannot be relied upon". I return to this matter below. Since June 2020 this

"Harms Report" continues to motivate "reforms" to the family courts and ancillary services, in the intended direction.

June 2020 (Ref.[12]): Following the change of government the DA Bill went through the Public Bill Committee again. I compiled evidence again, this time on behalf of the charity Both Parents Matter Cymru, Ref.[13]. In practice only those people whom the Bill Committee invite to give evidence in person really matter. 17 people or organisations were invited, every single one feminist or a female victim. They did not even bother to pay lip service to male victims, and it wasn't because no representatives of male victims submitted written evidence – there were plenty, and not for the first time. Both male victims and organisations and individuals with professional knowledge submitted on behalf of the male victim - all ignored.

August 2021 (Ref.[14]): Then we get to the Consultation on the draft Statutory Guidance, the DA Bill having become an Act by this point. I submitted a very detailed response. I pointed out that the claim "women are more likely to experience repeat victimisation, be physically injured…" was contradicted by the government's own Crime Surveys. I note it was dropped from the issued Guidance, so perhaps they actually read my submission. (Stunned, falls off chair). If you want to get a feel for how pervasive is the skewed representation of the whole subject of domestic abuse, I flatter myself that my submission, Ref.[14]), might assist you. The length and detail are the point. But the final published version of the Statutory Guidance was a disappointment as regards parental alienation (see chapter 22).

February 2022 (Ref.[15]): Despite the "exercise in utter futility" summarised above, some good people are trying to promote the male victims' interests by pushing for a strategy to address violence against men and boys.

May 2022 (Ref.[16]): A last-ditch attempt to head off the ratification of the Istanbul Convention by writing to my MP arguing that ratification would contravene the 2010 Equality Act – what with it being flagrantly sexist and everything. Fat chance of any assistance from Chocolate Teapot, MP.

July 2022 (Ref.[17]): The DA Act Statutory Guidance is published, see chapter 22. Rejoice.

24 July 2022 (Refs.[18,19]): The Istanbul Convention (IC) is ratified by the UK. Rejoice some more.

24 July 2022 (Ref.[20]). With the ratification of the IC the UK becomes subject to compliance examination by a body called Grevio within the Council of Europe. Wild rejoicing! What could possibly go wrong?

The Ratification of the Istanbul Convention was Carried Out under False Pretences

Refs.[19,20], from 24 July 2022, alluded to an MP's concerns over ratification of the IC. One of the issues he raised was its applicability to male victims. On 14 July this MP received a reply from a Minister of State at the Home Office. The relevant extract is,

"I would like to reassure you that my ministerial colleagues and I are satisfied that the Convention applies to male victims of these crimes as well as female ones."

The letter goes on to reassure us that otherwise they *"would not have signed up to it and would not now be ratifying it."*

One might suppose that this claim was to head off further questions about the conflict between a Convention which applies to only one sex and the 2010 Equality Act. The question that arises is this: what was the basis of the Home Office's claim that the IC also applies to male victims? The IC itself gives no hint that it could apply to male victims, Ref.[19], and every indication to the contrary. Similarly, Grevio's Third Report, Ref.[20], gives no hint of having any interest or concern for male victims.

The Home Office's claim that the IC also covers male victims is without any visible means of support.

The clincher is this. The IC is a product of the Council of Europe. It must be the Council of Europe that is empowered to give a definitive answer to the key question: Does the IC also apply to male victims?

So we asked. And on 28 July, four days after ratification, we got an answer by email from conventionviolence@coe.int

"Thank you for your inquiry about the "Council of Europe Convention on preventing and combating violence against women and domestic violence", also called the Istanbul Convention. Article 2 of the convention sets out its scope: This Convention shall apply to all forms of violence against women, including domestic violence, which affects women

disproportionately'. This means that it is only applicable to women victims of violence, including women victims of domestic violence.

However, the preamble of the convention recognizes that "men may also be victims of domestic violence", and explicitly encourages its state parties to apply its provisions to all victims of domestic violence (Article 2, paragraph 2). Therefore, state parties to the Istanbul Convention are under a legal obligation to apply its provisions to women victims of all forms of violence as covered by the scope of the convention, but it is left to the discretion of each member state whether or not to apply the convention also to male victims of violence.

Kind regards, Secretariat."

So there we have it. The IC does not apply to male victims, and there has never been any reason to think it did. The ratification of the IC by the UK was carried out under false pretences.

The Government Owns Your Children – They Think

The application for a judicial review of the Harms Report, Ref.[11], was led by Terry White. I'll not attempt a summary of the issues he raised due to their length, but you can see for yourself in the following document trail: the Statement of Facts, Ref.[21], the Grounds for Judicial Review, Ref.[22], the MOJ's "Grounds for Resistance", Ref.[23], i.e., the basis of their rejection of the application, Terry's Response to the Grounds for Resistance, Ref.[24], and his Addendum to that Response, Ref.[25], the Bundle relating to the application for appeal and its Skeleton Argument, Ref.[26], and the principal document from it, Terry's summary of the exchanges relating to whether parents have an automatic right to contact with their own children, Ref.[27].

Terry summarises the reasons for rejection of his application for a judicial review as follows,

"My submission was rejected at the High Court on the basis of amenability (ostensibly) because the Report has no legal effect. I have appealed to the Court of Appeal. I was listening to this case and heard the "Harms Report" referred to a number of times as if it were a reliable source of information to decide these matters before the court. The use of the Report in the Court of Appeal to affect the outcomes of real cases, and then to shape the recommendations coming from the Court of Appeal for the lower courts, means it is part of the chain to legal effect and there is no opportunity to examine the Report's merits before legal effect.

On the other hand, if there is an opportunity to examine the technical merits of the Report before legal effect, it would be this case. So I ask that you alert the Court of Appeal to my JR submission and ask that the technical merits of the Harms Report are examined before any recommendations are made to the lower court. I am very wary that there are real fathers without contact with their children in this matter so whatever is done, those cases must be progressed.

But someone has to look under the hood at this thing, urgently."

To put it more simply, the claim that the Harms Report has no legal effect is preposterous. It is instrumental in deciding the fate of children and their parents in the family courts. That is legal effect, QED.

But the issue that emerged in Terry's struggles with the government Legal Department is the government's presumption of powers they do not legally possess in respect of child contact by their natural parents. Here are Terry's words again...

"In specific regard to the UNCRC review, one of the peculiar things that popped out from my Judicial Review submission was the government's declaration that 'There is no automatic right to contact between a parent and child.'" (This is stated in the Grounds for Resistance, Ref.[23]).

Terry continued,

"I put to the Government Legal Department that surely they meant there is no "absolute" right – that is, there is a right but it can be defeated, say for welfare reasons.

The confirmed government position is that, no, there is no "automatic" right – that is to say, there is no right until some permission or authority is granted: in other, more sensational words, a "parenting licence". To be clear: the UK government is claiming there is no right for a child to have contact, even with their happily married, stable and competent parents, or with his or her mother, unless and until there is some sort of governmental intervention to grant or create that right.

They haven't provided any source law for this. Just a declaration. Now it's going to the Court of Appeal.

I argue that this is a repudiation of Articles 7-9 of the UNCRC. I summed up the position in this attachment which formed part of my submission to the Court of Appeal."

Do note there is nothing sex-specific about this. Children are not their mothers' any more than they are their fathers', according to the government. Only the government has children now. The children are not yours, so they claim.

References

[1] Bradford, R. (2020). *FNF Both Parents Matter Cymru, Survey of Male Victims of Domestic Abuse*. Presentation at the conference "Domestic Abuse is a Mens' Issue, Too", 7 June 2020.

[2] Bradford, R.A.W. (2022). *Association of partner abuse with loneliness and impaired well-being of separated fathers in Wales*. New Male Studies, Volume 11, Issue 1, 1-20, June 2022.

[3] Collins, W. (2014a). *Con, not Consultation*. The Illustrated Empathy Gap, 22 September 2014.

[4] Graham-Kevan, N., and Powney, D. (2021). *Male Victims of Coercive Control, Experiences and Impact*. University of Central Lancashire and Mankind Initiative.

[5] Collins, W. (2014b). *Compulsory Feminism from the Council of Europe*. The Illustrated Empathy Gap, 24 September 2014.

[6] Collins, W. (2015). *The Desolation of VAWG*. The Illustrated Empathy Gap, 4 July 2015.

[7] Collins, W. (2017). *UK PV Perpetrator Programmes – Part 2*. The Illustrated Empathy Gap, 4 August 2017.

[8] Collins, W. (2019a). *The Domestic Abuse Bill*. The Illustrated Empathy Gap, 4 July 2019.

[9] Atkins, V. (2019). In the House of Commons Hansard record: *Domestic Abuse, Volume 663: debated on Tuesday 16 July 2019*.

[10] Collins, W. (2019b). *Domestic Abuse Bill (2nd Reading, October 19)*. The Illustrated Empathy Gap, 9 October 2019.

[11] UK Government Ministry of Justice (2020). *Consultation outcome, Assessing risk of harm to children and parents in private law children cases*. June 2020.

[12] Collins, W. (2020a). *Domestic Abuse Bill, 4th June 2020*. The Illustrated Empathy Gap, 4 June 2020.

[13] O'Regan, A. (2020). *Written evidence from FNF Both Parents Matter Cymru (Charity No. 1134723) in relation to the Domestic Abuse Bill*. Submitted to the Public Bill Committee, June 2020.

[14] Collins, W. (2021). *Consultation on Domestic Abuse Act Draft Guidance*. The Illustrated Empathy Gap, 22 August 2021.

[15] Collins, W. (2020b). *#BAMS4NI*. The Illustrated Empathy Gap, 12 February 2022.

[16] Collins, W. (2022a). *Ratification of the Istanbul Convention*. The Illustrated Empathy Gap, 24 May 2022.

[17] UK Government Home Office (2022). *Statutory guidance: Domestic Abuse Act 2021*. Published 8 July 2022.

[18] Council of Europe. *The United Kingdom ratifies the Istanbul Convention*. Strasbourg, 21 July 2022.

[19] Collins, W. (2022b). *Istanbul Convention Ratified by UK*. The Illustrated Empathy Gap, 24 July 2022.

[20] Collins, W. (2022c). *Grevio Third Report, June 2022*. The Illustrated Empathy Gap, 24 July 2022.

[21] White, T., and Garrett, B. *Statement of Facts* (in the application for a judicial review of the "Harms Report", Ref.[11].

[22] White, T., and Garrett, B. *Statement of Grounds* (in the application for a judicial review of the "Harms Report", Ref.[11].

[23] Vincent, L. (2022). *Summary Grounds for Resisting the Claim* (in the application for a judicial review of the "Harms Report", Ref.[11].

[24] White, T., and Garrett, B. *Supplementary Response to Defendant's Grounds for Resistance*. (in the application for a judicial review of the "Harms Report", Ref.[11].

[25] White, T., and Garrett, B. *Second Supplementary Response to Defendant's Grounds for Resistance*. (in the application for a judicial review of the "Harms Report", Ref.[11].

[26] White, T., and Garrett, B. *Skeleton Argument* (in the application for a judicial review of the "Harms Report", Ref.[11].

[27] White, T., and Garrett, B. *Skeleton Argument Continues in Respect to Appeal Ground C* (in the application for a judicial review of the "Harms Report", Ref.[11]).

Section 4

Boys

24. Afghan Boys

A lot has happened in Afghanistan in the 10 years since I wrote the original of this article. But I wonder if anything of substance has really changed as regards the issues discussed here?

Original posted on: 22 September 2014

I acknowledge Ali Mehraspand, an Iranian engineer, whose writings have provided much of the culture-specific content of this article. Any mistakes are my own.

I have no wish to be a woman in Afghanistan. On the other hand, I have no wish to be a man or a boy in Afghanistan either. My original 2014 article started with a brief look at the status of women in Afghanistan at that time. Since the UK and the USA left the country in 2021 I have no doubt that, under Taliban rule, the status of women has nose-dived from the improving conditions of some years ago. At that time, Shabnam Nasimi, Ref.[1], wrote that, "*Afghanistan is a patriarchal society where all the major institutions are controlled by men*" and that, "*Almost every woman in Afghanistan is hidden and isolated from the outside world.*" These are the things we expect to hear about an Islamic country. And yet the same author also then wrote,

"*Securing women's rights has been one of the main goals particularly of the UK's intervention in Afghanistan. Over the past decade, the UK government has helped achieve much, including a new constitution which enshrines equal rights for women and men and a landmark Elimination of Violence Against Women (EVAW) law. Just over 27% of members of parliament are female and women fill a quarter of government jobs. Over two million girls are now in school – four in ten of all pupils – and many women are free to participate in public life and to work outside their homes, as doctors, teachers, entrepreneurs and lawyers.*"

Hmm, that's different. And, in 2014, the country had already had a female Minister of State, e.g., Ref.[2]. Nevertheless, I expect that has all gone into reverse since the resurgence of Taliban control. My difficulty was, and remains, my usual difficulty: what about the other half of the story? Am I alone in finding it strange to talk about *Elimination of Violence Against Women* in a country which had been a war zone for decades?

The virulent combination of western feminism and Islamic legal tendencies to protect women excessively have led, according to Ali Mehraspand, Refs.[3,4], to these cultures being prime exemplars of male disposability.

Recall that in Islamic law it is the male of the household who is responsible to provide for the family. There is no such responsibility placed on women. The male householder is obliged to supply the women of the house with their due *Nafaqah*, the money for all domestic expenses. Now imagine how many Afghan households are without any able-bodied adult male, due to the fighting. If the husband is not dead or seriously hurt, he may be away fighting. In this situation the responsibility for providing the *Nafaqah* falls to the sons. There must, I suppose, be an age limit. But whatever it is, it is certainly very young indeed. It is common for boys as young as 9 or 10 to be placed in that position of responsibility.

Nor is this merely a ceremonial or formal responsibility. It is an actual obligation to acquire money – enough for the family to live on. There is no obligation on the women of the household to provide for themselves. The culture is such that women feel entitled to be provided for. They feel no shame about this, even though it may involve a very young boy providing for several far older women.

So it is that a 10-year-old boy may be obliged to prostitute himself in order to provide for his own mother and several able-bodied, and perhaps far older, sisters. This is not rare. This is commonplace.

How could women in this position not be ashamed? The answer is that their culture does not necessitate any shame – it is the accepted norm. You will do well to recall this reality when western feminists describe such women as the victims of a patriarchy. Their freedoms are curtailed, certainly, but on the other hand they are also the beneficiaries of a system which places the really arduous task upon the male – of however tender an age.

And there is a further twist. Quite possibly the women would not even be allowed to seek work under regimes as harsh as that of the Taliban. But if they were (and it seems that many Afghan women did work in 2014, though that has probably changed) the Islamic law allows such a woman to keep all her earnings for herself. She is under no obligation to use her own money to support her family. That obligation always lies with the male – to provide the *Nafaqah*.

And it gets worse. In the case of Afghanistan, due to the endless wars, huge numbers have fled to neighbouring countries as refugees. This includes Iran, where refugees have been fleeing since the Soviet invasion of Afghanistan in 1979. The total number of Afghan refugees, or other immigrants, in Iran is difficult to know accurately. Just short of one million are legal, but there will be a large contingent of illegals. Every year the order of hundreds of thousands of Afghans repatriate from Iran. There are approximately three million Afghan citizens in Iran as of January 2023, but many of these will have been born in Iran since the start of the conflicts over 40 years ago. A clear majority are male, and 47% are under 20 years of age. Visit Tehran, or most other Iranian cities, and you will see boy refugees occupied in hard labour. In 2014 Mehraspand, Ref.[4], put the number of boy labourers in Afghanistan itself at 1.9 million, and probably more than that number again in neighbouring countries.

Mehraspand, Ref.[4], states that 60% of rape victims in Iran are male. Iran's chief of police said that the victims were mostly child labourers. There is a long tradition of rape or sexual exploitation of boys in Afghan culture. Where such things are organised they are known as Bacha Bazi or "dancing boys". Popular but discreet, "being into kids" or "boy play" happens all over Afghanistan. Unlike in the west, paedophilia against boys, though not officially approved, does not carry heavy stigma. (Girls, in contrast, are protected by their families. A deflowered girl becomes a marriage problem). A documentary on the phenomenon can be found at Ref.[5]. It is strongly recommended viewing. I should add that it is possible that the practice will have been banned under Taliban rule. But when the ever-so-liberal western powers were in Afghanistan the traditional practice of Bacha Bazi enjoyed a resurgence.

But the truly awful thing is that these poor boys are suffering the dreadful life of hard labour, or prostitution, simply so that they can give virtually all their meagre earnings to their mother and sisters. The labour work is viciously hard and deaths are commonplace. Ali Mehraspand, Ref.[4], says he has known 6 Afghan men personally who have died on the job, one of them whilst working on his parents' house. He observes their parsimonious habits thus: "*When they take a little time to have lunch under the red-hot sun, I have witnessed the painful scene of their shopping for lunch: some soda and some bread. They tear up the bread to pour in the soda. They then fill their spoon with the soda-dipped bread to eat as if it was a steak sandwich. Why? You see, because the money is not to be wasted on luxuries like food while their mother and sisters back in Afghanistan expect it."*

Quoting Mehraspand again, *"Every now and then, self-righteous idiots remind us that they would rather be a man in Afghanistan. They of course do not have the slightest clue what they are talking about. Being an Afghan man means to continue to be a sweat machine to provide where provision is so difficult that 50% of children suffer from malnutrition. Being an Afghan boy means to be a child labourer, perhaps in some other country, just so you can send back the money for female family members. Being an Afghan boy means facing more threats of sexual abuse and forced labour. And labour in the minds of Afghan men and boys is extreme labour."*

This is what the international feminist machine keeps hidden. Their agenda to pursue female advantage is prosecuted by pedalling half-truths that are whole lies. Where the resulting injustice is to males, it does not matter; not even if the males in question are millions of small boys. So next time you hear some privileged, western woman whinging about their imagined oppression recall this example of real gender-based disadvantage.

References

[1] Nasimi, S. (2014). In 2014 Shabnam Nasimi was a law student working for the UK Home Office as an Afghan women's development officer. The quotes were taken from articles on the web site open.democracy.net, since removed.

[2] Jalal, M. (2014). In 2014 Dr. Massouda Jalal was a political activist, former Minister of Women in Afghanistan, and founding President of the Jalal Foundation. Material taken from open.democracy.net, since removed.

[3] Mehraspand, A. (2014). *Indentured servitude for men in Iran: The myth of patriarchal oppressive divorce*. A Voice For Men, 13 August 2014.

[4] Mehraspand, A. (2014). *Afghanistan is the hotbed of male disposability, boy or man. World's reaction? Help women and girls!*. A Voice For Men, 15 August 2014.

[5] Quraishi, N., Director (2010). *The Dancing Boys of Afghanistan*. Clover Films, premiered in the UK at the Royal Society of Arts on March 29, 2010.

25. Child Exploitation and Modern Slavery: It's a Gender Issue

Guess which gender. I have not updated the data from that quoted in the original 2020 post.

Original posted on: 15 January 2020.

Modern Slavery, Adults

You will recall the annual Violence Against Women and Girls reports published by the Crown Prosecution Service (the CPS VAWG reports), e.g., Ref.[1]. These are the reports in which Violence does not mean violence, Women does not mean women, Girls does not mean girls, and conviction for a rape-flagged charge does not mean convicted of rape. VAWG, you will recall, is a category of crime. The victims may be men or boys. The offence may not be violence. You may think that there is an intention to mislead here. I couldn't possibly comment.

One of the categories of crime within the VAWG umbrella is Modern Slavery and Human Trafficking. You may think that this mostly involves women and girls being exploited as prostitutes. Well, a lot of it does, but most does not. The 2018/19 CPS VAWG report, Ref.[1], includes data from the National Referral Mechanism (NRM) which records potential victims (you have to dig deep into the Appendices to find it). In 2018/19 men and boys outnumbered women and girls by 52% (3,874 cf 2,544).

In the Modern Slavery and Human Trafficking category, between 2017 and 2018, the number of women and girls sexually exploited increased by 7% to 1,725. But the number of men and boys exploited for their labour increased by 71%, to 3,525 – twice as many. Bear in mind these data are within a report titled "Violence Against Women and Girls".

In 2018/19 there were 219 convictions for Modern Slavery and Human Trafficking. This is a larger number of convictions than in previous years.

In July 2019, eight people – five men and three women – were convicted and sentenced to prison, Ref.[2], for an average of nearly eight years each. The gang were described as the biggest modern-day slavery network ever exposed in the UK. Their victims were mainly Roma, from Poland. The gang came to the UK specifically to traffic their fellow countrymen. The number of witnesses (i.e., victims who were identified and testified) was variously reported as being between 80 and 92. Different reports estimate different total numbers of victims, most of whom were not identified, up to 440 in total.

How many of these 440 victims were men? I recall radio news reports at the time referring to the victims as "people". You should always be suspicious when victims are described in gender-neutral terms; it probably means a predominantly male victimisation is being hidden. So it was in this case. It would seem that all but one were men, to quote Ref.[3],

"The only woman known to have been enslaved by the gang sits in a red parka, her arms clamped between her legs, as she relates a trafficker's threat to her......"

Child Exploitation

In 2020 the ONS first released a compendium of data on child abuse, Refs.[4,5]. The report combines data from several different sources. One of these is the CSEW (Crime Survey for England & Wales). This survey is completed by adults (16 and over) and hence relates to adults recalling abuse to which they were subject as a child (i.e., historical abuse). I have some major misgivings about such data, especially as it relates to relative male and female victimisation, of which more below. However, in this section on child exploitation, the data is taken from the NRM, as reported in Ref.[6]. This relates to contemporaneous reports of child victimisation. "Child" in these data means someone aged 17 or younger. "Exploitation" within the context of NRM data can be taken as synonymous with "a victim of modern slavery".

Figure 25.1 shows the numbers of exploited children identified in the UK in calendar years 2016, 2017 and 2018 by category. As for adults, it is the forced labour category which is largest and has increased fastest (by far).

Table 25.1 breaks this down by sex (for 2018). Boys are ten times more likely to be involved in exploited labour than girls. Girls are five times more likely to be involved in sexual exploitation than boys. But, overall, the number of exploited boys exceeds the number of exploited girls by 155%. These are not all children trafficked from abroad. 45% were UK nationals.

Whether children or adults, it seems that modern slavery is a gender issue to the net disadvantage of males. Once again, and entirely predictably, this is not something one hears the media promulgating.

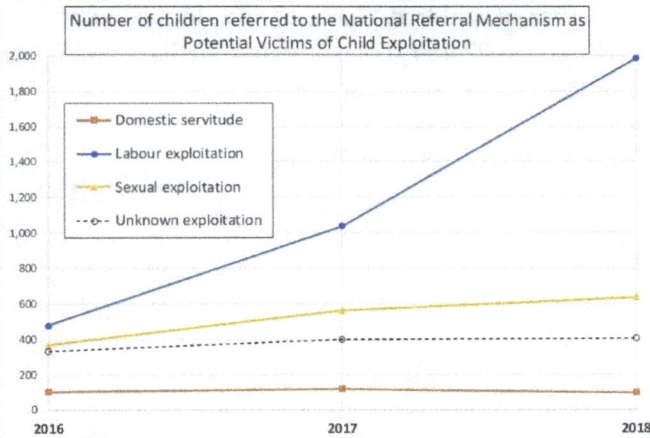

Number of children referred to the National Referral Mechanism as Potential Victims of Child Exploitation

— Domestic servitude
— Labour exploitation
— Sexual exploitation
- -o- - Unknown exploitation

Figure 25.1: from Ref.[5] Table 35

Type of Exploitation	Boys	Girls
Domestic servitude	52	44
Labour exploitation	1,805	182
Organ harvesting	4	0
Sexual exploitation	105	532
Unknown exploitation	282	122
TOTAL	2,248	880

Table 25.1: Number of children in UK referred to the NRM as potential victims of exploitation, by sex, year ending December 2018 (total regardless of nationality), from Ref.[5] Table 36.

Child Abuse

I will focus here on contemporaneous data from children themselves, not testimony from adults reporting historic child abuse (for reasons I will elucidate shortly).

The number of children with a protection plan, by category of abuse which made it necessary, is shown against year in Figure 25.2, from Ref.[5]. Figure 25.3 gives the breakdown by sex. Boys outnumber girls by 8%.

The latest data on the number of children "in care" (i.e., looked after by a local authority) is 30,770 boys and 27,450 girls (summing England and Wales from Tables 23 and 31 of Ref.[5]), an excess of boys of 12%.

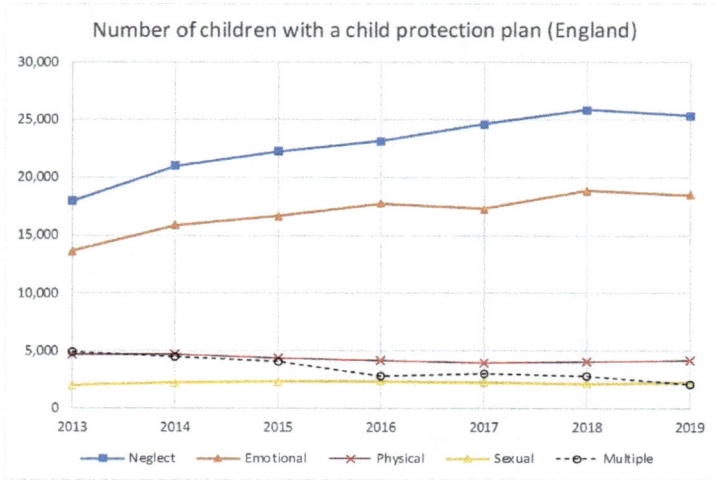

Figure 25.2: data from Ref.[5] Table 13

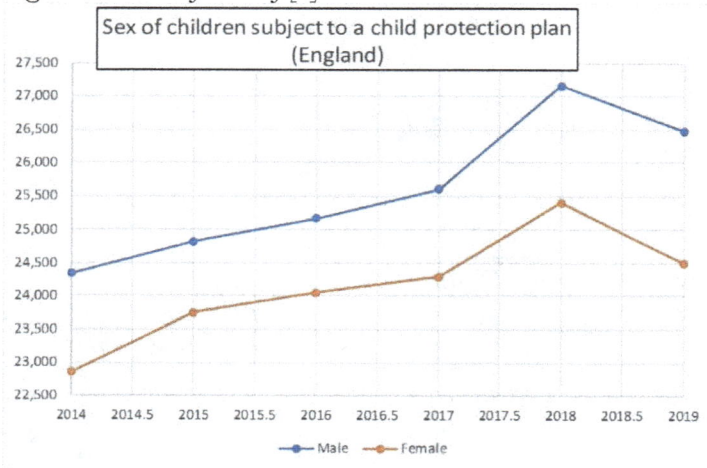

Figure 25.3: data from Ref.[5] Table 14

I have drawn attention to these care and protection plan statistics because I wish to point out the contrast with Figure 25.4. This plots the number of counselling sessions delivered by Childline as a result of abuse issues, by sex of recipient. In 2010 there were twice as many sessions delivered to girls: by 2019 this had become nearly four times as many. In view of boys outnumbering girls in the care and protection plan data, this is odd. For "odd" you may wish to read "prejudice".

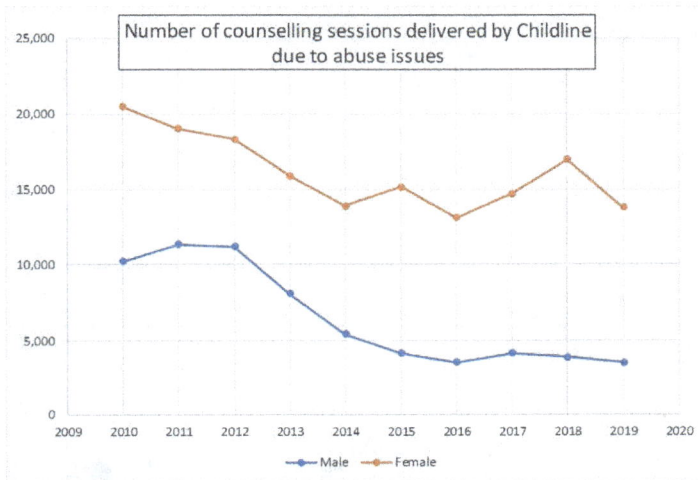

Figure 25.4: date from Ref.[5] Table 38

Perpetrators of Child Abuse

This is the one case where I use data from adult reports of their abuse as children. The data in Table 25.2 was again taken from Ref.[5] whose source was NAPAC (the National Association of People Abused in Childhood). It indicates that there is little difference between perpetration of child abuse by mothers and fathers. Mothers were responsible for 24% and fathers for 27%. So parents as a whole account for about half of child abuse.

However, the striking thing about Table 25.2 is that adult women report well over three times as much historic childhood abuse as do adult men. This stands in stark contrast to the evidence from protection plans (Figure 25.3), where there are more boys than girls. This *may* indicate that adult women are more likely to recall childhood abuse – or that men are less likely to interpret childhood experiences as abuse. For this reason I regard the gender-split of adults reporting historic abuse as unreliable, and this would be expected to apply to CSEW data too. (I will be happy to hear alternative interpretations).

Alleged Perpetrator	Male Complainant	Female Complainant
Mother	200	806
Father	242	881
Stepmother	8	15
Stepfather	33	243
Others	467	1,217
TOTAL	950	3,162

Table 25.2: data from Ref.[5] Table 46

References

[1] Crown Prosecution Service (2019). *Violence Against Women and Girls Report 2018/19*.

[2] BBC News (2019a). *UK slavery network 'had 400 victims'*. 5 July 2019.

[3] BBC News (2019b). *How I became a victim of a modern slavery gang*. 5 July 2019.

[4] Office for National Statistics (2020a). *Child abuse extent and nature, England and Wales: year ending March 2019*. 14 January 2020.

[5] Office for National Statistics (2020b). *Child abuse extent and nature: Appendix tables*. 14 January 2020.

[6] UK Government, Home Office (2019). *2019 UK Annual Report on Modern Slavery*. October 2019.

26. Children in Custody: It's a Gender Issue

Readers familiar with The Empathy Gap, either the book or the blog, will be aware of the discrimination against men in the UK criminal justice system, and boys too. Indeed this is a universal phenomenon. Here I review a 2019 report from the UN on children in custody globally. Remarkably for a UN report the discrimination against boys is clearly emphasised.

Original posted on: 27 November 2019.

Figure 26.1: Boys in detention centre, Togo, from Ref.[1]

In 2019 the United Nations published a major study on children in custody worldwide, Ref.[1]. The main report, by Manfred Nowak, is 767 pages long. It identifies 7 million children in various types of custody, including police cells, prison, and detention centres. 94% of them are boys.

The panel which led the study consisted of 170 non-governmental organisations working directly or indirectly on children's deprivation of liberty. Information was collected from every region of the world: 41 inputs from Europe; 27 from Africa; 20 from Asia, 19 from North and South America; and 11 from Oceania.

The treatment meted out to many of these children, overwhelmingly boys, is extremely distressing, and I do not intend to go into those details here. One may hope, and expect, that boys in custody in the UK do not experience such brutality. Unfortunately one would have been disappointed in that expectation in the past, e.g., in the 1970s and 1980s, Refs.[2,3].

In terms of the gender ratio of children in custody, the worldwide data and UK data are similar, except that the UK is rather worse, with 97% to 98% of children in custody being boys.

The UN is hardly noted for being a male-friendly organisation. It drives a host of feminist agendas. That only makes what follows even more noteworthy. I quote firstly the UN Secretary-General's own words, Ref.[4], commenting on the publication of Ref.[1] in 2019,

"The data collected for the study indicate significant gender disparities in the situation of children deprived of liberty. Altogether, there are far more boys deprived of liberty worldwide than girls. In the administration of justice and in the contexts of armed conflicts and national security, 94% of all detained children are boys; in migration detention the figure is 67% and in institutions it is 56%. The number of boys and girls who live with their primary caregiver (almost exclusively mothers) in prison is similar."

"Compared with the overall crime rate for children, the data gathered for the study show a tendency of the child justice system to be more inclined to apply diversion measures to girls than boys. While approximately one third of all criminal offences worldwide committed by children are attributed to girls, only 6% receive a prison sentence. There may be various reasons for this phenomenon. Most importantly, girls usually commit less violent offences and are more often accused of status offences. Girls are generally first-time offenders and more receptive to the deterrent effect of incarceration. Another explanation is the "chivalrous and paternalistic" attitude of many male judges and prosecutors in the child justice systems, who assume, according to traditional gender stereotypes, that girls are more in need of protection than boys."

"Although most States allow convicted mothers to co-reside with their young children in prison, only eight States explicitly permit fathers to do so. Even in places where fathers as primary caregivers are allowed to co-reside with their children, there are (almost) no appropriate "father and child units" in the prisons, which means that there are practically no children co-residing in prison with their fathers."

*"Children from poor and socioeconomically disadvantaged backgrounds, migrant and indigenous communities, ethnic and religious minorities and the LGBTI community, as well as children with disabilities and, **above all, boys, are largely overrepresented in detention and throughout judicial proceedings**."* (my emphasis)

"Deprivation of liberty constitutes a form of structural violence against children."

In view of the latter observation, and the overwhelming preponderance of boys in custody, can one not reasonably conclude that here we have an instance of gendered structural violence – against boys? And yet you will find no mention of this in the Istanbul Convention.

In the complete report, Ref.[1], the section on Discrimination Against Boys puts England and Wales amongst the top few countries in terms of gender ratio: "*In some States, the percentage of boys detained in the context of the administration of justice is close to 98% (England and Wales, Argentina) or even 99% (South Africa, Georgia)*". Did we want to be in such company?

Almost all you need to know is the title of one of the report's sub-sections: "*Penal System is the Most Gendered Institution in Society*". Quite. But what follows in that section is something I never thought to see in a report from the UN.

"*Most research on the gender dimension of deprivation of liberty relates to the administration of criminal justice and primarily addresses cases of discrimination against girls, not against boys. Yet in 2006, Paulo Sergio Pinheiro noted that 'millions of children, particularly boys, spend substantial periods of their lives under the control and supervision of care authorities or justice systems, in institutions such as juvenile detention facilities and reform schools.*

According to research conducted by Bruce Abramson in the same year, the 'penal system, adult and juvenile, is the most heavily gendered institution in society, even more so than the military, given current trends. He adds that **the human rights movement, and the children's rights movement in particular, is contributing to this male-female gender gap by discriminating against boys**" (my emphasis)

It continues with this quote from Bruce Abramson,

"*Whether we look at the CRC* movement, or at the broader human rights movement, or at the specialized juvenile justice advocacy, we find the same pattern of avoiding the gender dimension of juvenile justice. Some adults are in deep denial of the gender issue when boys are at the losing end of the disparities. But most people recognise that there is a gender issue. The problem is that no one has found an effective, positive way to address it. I think that juvenile justice professionals and CRC activists are paying a dear price in credibility for their failure to address gender: the public knows – at some level of awareness – that the advocates for reform are not addressing the problem when they duck the gender dimension of delinquency…..Sad to say, there is outright sex discrimination against boys in the CRC movement.*" (*CRC is the UN Convention on the Rights of the Child)

Wow! Let me just check this is really a UN report. But it may be significant that Nowak had to go back to research reported in 2006 for this evidence, Ref.[5]. He goes on to note,

"Although girls are less likely to commit serious criminal offences than boys, the detention rate does not reflect the crime rate. More than one-third (35-40%) of all criminal offences worldwide are attributed to girls. However, only one fourth of all children (25%) who come in formal contact with the criminal justice system are girls. Finally, only 11.6% of all convicted children are girls, and only 6% of all children who end up in detention are girls."

Nowak concludes that the data show that girls receive more lenient sentences, usually non-custodial, and tend to benefit from diversion away from custody through all the stages of the process. These observations are depicted in Figure 26.2.

Share of Boys and Girls at Different Stages of the Child Justice System

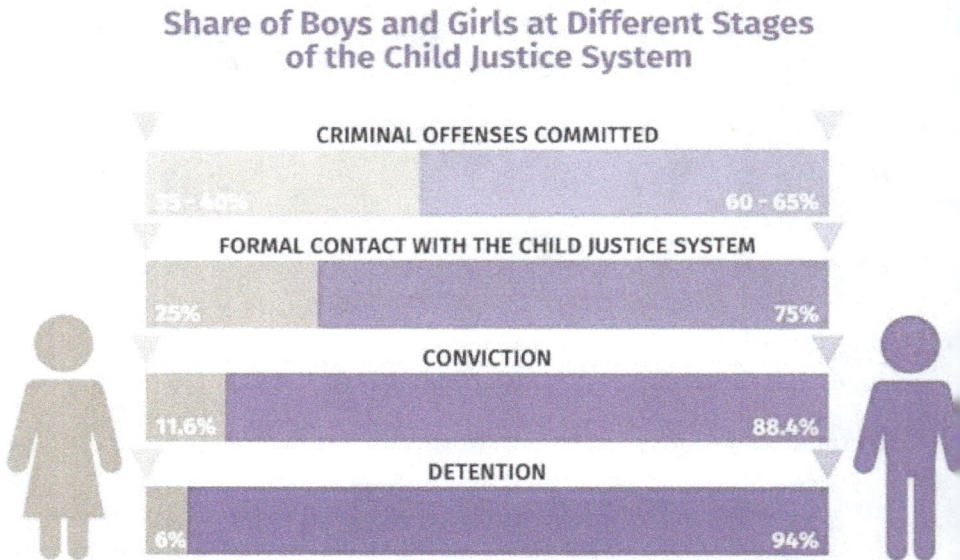

Figure 26.2: taken from Ref.[1]

Share of Boys and Girls in all Situations of Deprivation of Liberty

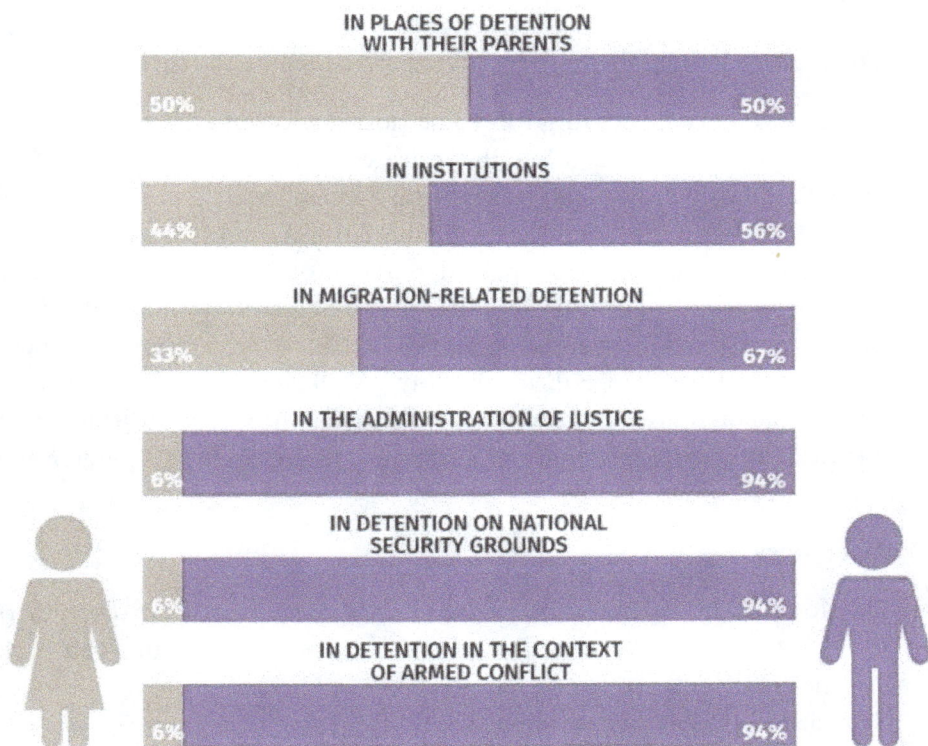

**IN PLACES OF DETENTION
WITH THEIR PARENTS**

50% — 50%

IN INSTITUTIONS

44% — 56%

IN MIGRATION-RELATED DETENTION

33% — 67%

IN THE ADMINISTRATION OF JUSTICE

6% — 94%

**IN DETENTION ON NATIONAL
SECURITY GROUNDS**

6% — 94%

**IN DETENTION IN THE CONTEXT
OF ARMED CONFLICT**

6% — 94%

Figure 26.3: taken from Ref. [1]

The similarity with adult imprisonment in the UK is striking. It appears that neither age nor culture greatly ameliorates the huge sex-bias in incarceration. In the case of adults in the UK, we are surely long past any debate about the overwhelming male dominance in prison being largely due to discrimination; the progress of men and women through the UK criminal justice system is remarkably similar to Figure 26.2. It is reasonable to suppose that discrimination is responsible also for the overwhelming preponderance of boys in the juvenile facilities.

Nowak's chapter on gender issues ends in Recommendations which include this,

"Address over-representation of boys in detention by various means, above all by promoting diversions at all stages in the criminal justice system and by proportionally applying non-custodial solutions to boys, as it is more widely practised with girls."

Who is going to hold the relevant UK minister's feet to the fire on this one?

It seems we have a way to go in some quarters. As of March 2018 there were 972 boys and just 32 girls in the secure estate in England & Wales (97% boys), Ref.[6]. (The latest data as I write in September 2023 is 606 boys and 7 girls (99% boys), Ref.[6]). Also in March 2018, Anne Longfield, then the Childrens' Commissioner for England, reported on a visit to some of these children "to learn about their lives before entering custody and understand the factors that led to them being imprisoned and what, if anything, could have been done to change their trajectory". Well, very laudable. It's exactly what a Children's Commissioner should do. I have no difficulty with that...except that from a choice of 972 boys and 32 girls, the 10 children she chose were all girls.

References

[1] Nowak, M. (2019). *United Nations Global Study on Children Deprived of Liberty*. *Global Study on Children Deprived of Liberty.* From the web page choose the pdf version for the graphics used herein).

[2] Allison, E., and Hattenstone, S. (2012). *A true horror story: The abuse of teenage boys in a detention centre*. The Guardian, 13 April 2012.

[3] Dearden, L. (2019). *Almost 1,800 boys abused at detention centre, police reveal as 'brutal' prison officers jailed*. Independent, 18 April 2019.

[4] Guterres, A., UN Secretary General (2019). *Global study on children deprived of liberty: Note by the Secretary-General*. UN General assembly, paper A/74/136, 11 July 2019. (Take care to access the 23-page original version). In case of local difficulty of access there is a copy here.

[5] Abramson, B. (2006). *Juvenile Justice. The Unwanted Child*. In E.L.Jensen and J.Jepson (eds) *Juvenile Law Violators, Human Rights and Development of New Juvenile Justice Systems*, Oxford, Hart Publisher, 2006

[6] UK Government (2023). *Youth Custody Data*. Last update 10 November 2023.

[7] Longfield, A., UK Children's Commissioner (2018). *Voices from the Inside: The experiences of girls in Secure Training Centres*. March 2018.

Section 5

Education

27. Teachers' Sex Bias Revealed

I have been blogging on the measurable bias by teachers in the UK in favour of girls for the last ten years. Educationalists are aware of this bias but are unconcerned. This chapter refers to what happened during the "covid years", 2020 to 2022, specifically in respect of A Levels and how the pro-female bias went into overdrive in that period. The government denied there was any bias via a report from Ofqual which provided a case study in how truth is obfuscated. Statistical analysis is an aid to thinking, not a replacement for it. Statistical analysis, like words, can be used to reveal the truth or to hide it.

Originals posted on: 11 November 2020, 29 August 2021, 16 September 2022 and 20 August 2023.

In the peak covid years of 2020 and 2021, when schools were shut for much of the time, A Levels were awarded without the benefit of any exams. The government's first idiotic mistake was thinking they could bestow graded awards without exams and without controversy (give me strength). But at least to begin with there were sane people somewhere within the process who moderated the teachers' assessments so that the latter's predictably and preposterously inflated grading was brought down to something vaguely credible. These initial examless grades were published in September 2020.

Never missing an opportunity to make politics out of education, there followed a media blitz about an "algorithm", which the Opposition were delighted to refer to as a wicked plot by the government to swindle pupils out of their deserved grades. They were referring to the moderation of teachers' assessments to render them reasonable. This media storm was bolstered by whinging from aggrieved pupils who also claimed they had been swindled (surprise!). So, the ever steadfast and imperturbable Johnson government capitulated and replaced the initially moderated results with the raw teacher assessments. What could possibly go wrong? Or, rather, what could possibly go wrong that a child of ten could not foresee?

Reliance on teachers' assessments alone opens the door to subjective bias, personal animosities and ideological motives. To that one can add, perhaps, the fear that other teachers would bump up their pupils by a grade or two and so, if they did not also do so, their pupils would effectively be unfairly treated. The result, inevitably, was grade inflation of ridiculous proportions.

In 2020 the A Level awards were, bluntly but honestly stated, essentially just made up by teachers. The one good thing about this debacle is that it has provided statistically unambiguous evidence of teachers' bias by sex, as I will show. Having got away with massive grade inflation, and sex bias, in 2020, both the inflation and the sex bias were even worse the following year, in 2021, which was also examless. The grade inflation was widely reported in the press. The sex bias, needless to say, was not.

In 2022 exams returned, but do not assume that meant a return to fairness. There was always going to be a problem returning to the grade percentages of 2019. Ofqual therefore opted to attempt to do so only by 2023. In contrast, the 2022 grade boundaries were set at "a mid-point between 2019 and 2021", Ref.[1]. With no irony intended, the subtitle of that reference was "Ofqual's approach to grading for GCSE, AS and A levels to be fair to students: a transition year in 2022". Exactly what "a mid-point" means is not clear to me, though – as we shall see – the results speak for themselves. It's all very well to refer to this as "grading more generously", Ref.[2], but that completely misses the fact that this generosity is biased by sex, and hence, in competitive university entry, it means reduced chances for young men. Ask yourself, what is the "mid-point" between fair and grossly unfair?

I can now present the compiled A Level award data from all the "covid" years 2020, 2021 and 2022, together with data for 2023 when some sort of normality was resumed based on exams without additional fiddling by Ofqual. Crucially, I also include the comparable data from years 2010 to 2019 which can be used as a benchmark for exam-based awards.

Figure 27.1 shows the percentage of candidates of the same sex who were awarded the top A* or A grades against year, 2010 to 2023. The three "covid years" are immediately apparent. Two results are given for 2020. The lower data point was the interim award which was moderated to offset the teachers' grade inflation (and did so quite successfully, retaining only a slight degree of inflation). The higher point is the final award, based on teachers' assessments unmoderated. The awards based on teachers' assessments in 2020 and 2021 were preposterously inflated for both sexes, and the same is true for the "mid-point" year, 2022. Whilst both sexes saw huge grade inflation, the girls' awards were significantly more inflated than the boys' awards. In the years preceding covid, there was negligible difference in the percentage of boys and the percentage of girls being awarded A or A* grades. In the covid years, the percentage of girls awarded these top grades exceeded the percentage of boys by up to 5%. This was contrary to all precedent.

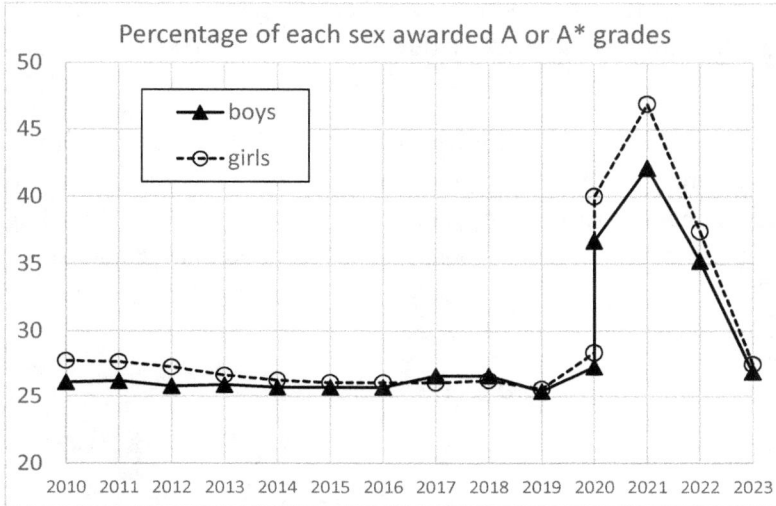

Figure 27.1: Percentage of each sex awarded A or A* grades, 2010 – 2023

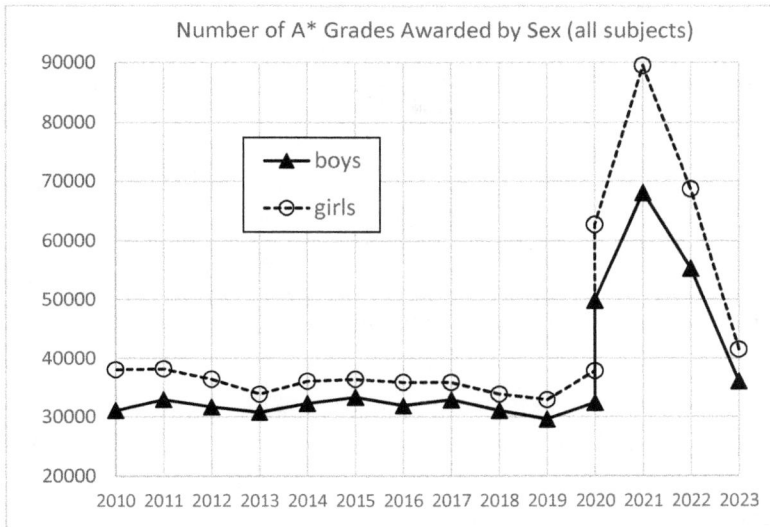

Figure 27.2: The number of A* grades awarded by sex

The bias is even clearer when the numbers of top awards are compared rather than the percentages. Thus, Figure 27.2 plots against year the number of A* grades awarded to girls and boys separately. Because more girls than boys take A Levels, the number of girls awarded A* grades has been greater than the number of boys awarded A* grades for many years despite the percentages being within a fraction of a percent. However, prior to covid, the number of A* grades awarded to girls exceeded the number to boys by less than 5,000. During covid in 2021 this leapt to over 20,000, more than four times as many.

Figure 27.3 shows the same phenomenon for A* and A grades combined, plotting the difference between the number of A or A* grades awarded to girls and the number awarded to boys. Prior to covid this had been trending down and was running at about 20,000. In 2021 it peaked at 58,000, some three times larger.

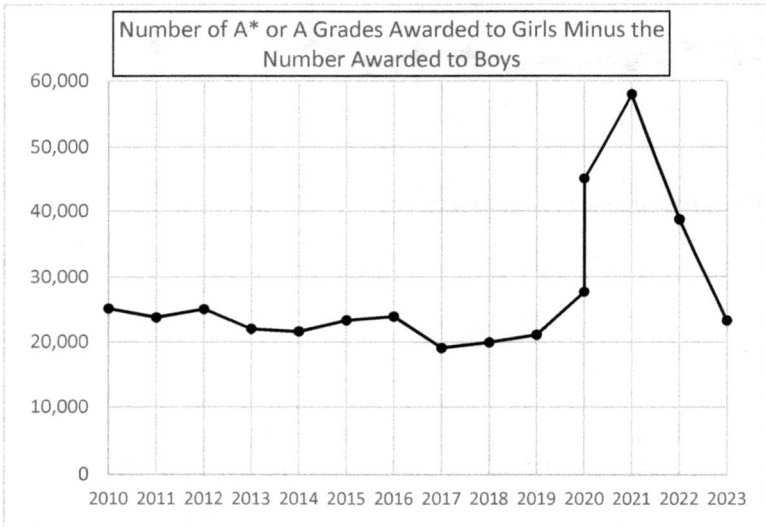

Figure 27.3: The number of A or A grades awarded to girls minus the number awarded to boys*

Do note that Figures 27.1-3 all show that, in 2023, when awards were once again based on exams without further Ofqual interference, the data returned to something close to where it lay pre-covid, in 2019 and before. This establishes definitively that the obviously anomalous spikes in the data, and the bias by sex, originated from the teachers.

Nor was the sex bias minor. In terms of the number of top awards, this bias increased the gap between the sexes by a factor of between three and four. This is massive bias.

This does not mean that all teachers are biased. Nor does it mean that the bias is displayed by one sex of teacher only. Nor does it mean that the bias is conscious, or that it results from ideological convictions. Nevertheless, as a statistical phenomenon overall it is clearly very real. And since this bias has been revealed so clearly by the data, one must ask what more insidious effects might this bias be having on boys' performance throughout their schooling? Evidence recently provided to the All-Party Parliamentary Group (APPG) on issues affecting men and boys supports the contention that the lower attainment of boys is created by the way boys are treated by the adults in their lives and that, when given a level playing field and appropriate support, boys achieve as well as girls and enjoy their time at school more, Ref.[3].

It is worth perusing the data in Table 1 of Ref.[4] to gauge how preposterous was the A* grade inflation in the covid years. In 2019 just 3.7% of girls were awarded A* in Computing; in 2021 that became 25.7%. In 2019 just 6.1% of girls were awarded A* in Sports & PE; in 2021 that became 27%. Similarly, in Further Maths 22.1% became 50.7%, and in Physics 8.5% became 25.3%, and so on. Boys' awards were inflated also, but not by quite so much.

As a result, in the covid years, girls became dominant in almost all subjects as regards the percentage being awarded A* grades. Based on exams in 2019, a larger percentage of boys than girls attained A* grades in English Literature, Chemistry, French, Maths, Further Maths, Physics, Classics, German, Music, Religious Studies and Other Sciences. In 2021, based on teachers' assessments, this list shrank to just Chemistry, French and Other Sciences. In that year a larger percentage of girls than boys were awarded A* in the male bastions of Maths, Further Maths and Physics.

The sex bias can be quantified based on the assumption that 2019, based on exams, can be taken as the equitable datum. Bias is then defined as the excess of the percentage of girls over the percentage of boys gaining A or A* grades in 2021 (based on teacher assessments) minus the excess of the percentage of girls over the percentage of boys gaining A or A* grades in 2019 (based on exam results). Expressed algebraically,

bias = (GTA - BTA) - (GEx - BEx)

where G and B denotes girls and boys respectively, and TA and Ex denote teachers' assessments (in 2021) and exam-based results (in 2019) respectively. In other words, the bias is defined as how much the girls' advantage has increased as a result of being assessed by teachers rather than by exam. A positive bias is to girls' advantage, or to boys' disadvantage, and a negative bias vice versa.

Subject	% bias 2020	% bias 2021	Subject	% bias 2020	% bias 2021
Art & Design	3.4	4.0	Law	0.8	3.6
Biology	0.8	2.4	Maths	6.1	7.3
Business	2.5	4.1	Further Maths	5.0	6.3
Chemistry	1.9	4.2	Media & film	6.6	9.6
Classical studies	5.4	4.6	Music	4.3	5.5
Computing	8.4	8.6	Physics	4.8	5.4
Design & Tech	5.2	10.6	PE / Sports	8.4	11.7
Drama	2.8	5.1	Politics	1.9	3.6
Economics	4.5	5.6	Psychology	4.8	7.4
English Lit	2.9	3.5	Religious Studies	2.0	2.3
English Language	4.3	5.2	Sociology	4.1	5.6
Engl. Lit & Lang	2.7	3.0	Spanish	0.8	-0.4
French	1	2.2	Other Sciences	-1.1	7.8
Geography	6.1	7.1	OML	-1.3	-3.4
German	0.3	-1.8	Other Subjects	2.3	4.0
History	5.7	7.5	**All Subjects**	**3.2**	**4.7**

Table 27.1: Percentage sex bias by subject based on A Level awards at grades A or A*, 2021

Table 27.1 lists the bias for all subjects separately. ("All subjects" means all subjects where the total number of candidates was in excess of 2,500. This only excludes Welsh, Irish, ICT, and Performing Arts). Of the 31 subjects listed, the bias is in girls' favour in all but three. Moreover, in all but one of the 28 subjects where the bias is in favour of girls, the bias has increased since 2020. Across all subjects, the average bias in 2020 was 3.2%. In 2021 this has increased to 4.7%. The bias is greater than 5% in 16 subjects, and in double figures for two subjects.

Whilst the present author is easily ignored, it is not so easy to ignore Mary Curnock Cook, the former head of UCAS (the University and Colleges Admissions Service). She had an article in *The Times*, Ref.[5], and another with detailed statistics in FENEWS, Ref.[6]. The former quotes the latter where Curnock Cook opines that *"this goes further than the usual concerns about boys' underachievement in education compared to girls and needs a convincing explanation to eliminate what seems, on the face of it, to indicate systemic bias against boys"*.

The Department for Education, responding to the allegations by Curnock Cook, and at the end of her *Times* article, Ref.[5], claimed that any evidence of systemic bias against boys was ruled out by an analysis by Ofqual. This is factually incorrect, as I demonstrated in Ref.[4]. The Ofqual analysis, Ref.[7], does identify the bias but expresses it in such an anodyne and technical manner that the casual reader would not notice. The Ofqual report plots the key results using a graphical scale so small that the 4.36% bias identified becomes invisible to the naked eye. This is an embarrassingly crude method of burying an important result. Yet that result of the Ofqual analysis is there in the report, Ref.[7], if you take the trouble to unearth it and can interpret the document. Moreover, their 4.36% bias is quite close to my result, 4.7% bias (Table 27.1). For details of my critique of the Ofqual analysis I refer you to Ref.[4].

Do I detect political pressure being brought to bear on the author of Ref.[7]? I ask because the same author, Ming Wei Lee, with a co-author, also produced a relevant report earlier in 2021, Ref.[8], which identified a need to conduct a literature review "on systematic divergence between results from teacher- and test-based assessments" in order to "raise awareness of potential risks to the dependability of assessment results which are based entirely on teacher judgements". With respect to gender bias in teachers' assessments, Ref.[8] concluded *"evidence of teacher bias in relation to gender is mixed, but a slight bias in favour of girls (or against boys) is a common finding"*. As we have seen, though, whether this bias can be called "slight" depends upon what metric is used. Based on the comparative numbers being awarded top grades the bias was enormous, as we have seen. 4.36% represents a very large number of individuals.

There is more to honesty than merely never being untruthful. Here is an example of dishonesty: "any evidence of systemic bias against boys was ruled out by the analysis by Ofqual". Here is an example of an honest depiction of what happened in the covid years: the excess of top A/A* grades awarded to girls over boys in 2021 was nearly triple that in the last exam year, 2019.

All the A Level data I have used here and in the original blog articles were taken from Brian Stubbs' site, Ref.[9].

References

[1] Saxton, J. (2021). *Ofqual's approach to grading exams and assessments in summer 2022 and autumn 2021*. Ofqual, 30 September 2021.

[2] Edexec (2022). *GCSEs and A Level exams in 2022 will be graded more generously*. Education Executive, 9 February 2022.

[3] APPG Men and Boys (2023). *Closing the attainment gap for boys at secondary school*. YouTube, 2 December 2023. See also the associated report from the APPG: Inquiry No 4: *Boys' Educational Underachievement*, 13 November 2023.

[4] Collins, W. (2021). *A Level Awards 2021 and Their Obfuscation*. The Illustrated Empathy Gap, 29 August 2021.

[5] Paton, G. (2021). *Boys losing out at A Level is a 'sign of bias' in grading system*. The Times, 23 August 2021.

[6] Curnock Cook, M. (2021). *'Systemic bias against boys'? Unexplained differences in Teacher Assessed Grades between boys and girls in this year's A level results*. FENEWS, 23 August 2021.

[7] Lee, M.W. (2021). *Summer 2021 student-level equalities analysis - GCSE and A level*. Ofqual, 20 August 2021.

[8] Lee, M.W., and Newton, P. (2021). *Systematic divergence between teacher and test-based assessment: literature review*. Ofqual, 17 May 2021.

[9] Stubbs, B. (2023). *Student Performance Analysis*. Summer 2023 update.

28. Education UK: The Intersection of Race and Sex

The dependence of educational disadvantage on sex, ethnicity and socioeconomics is addressed here using government data. Sex is the dominant factor. While ethnicity is also important this is also misleading as, for example, Black Africans and Black Caribbeans are at opposite ends of the achievement distribution. This suggests that it is culture rather than race per se that is the relevant factor. But the most educationally disadvantaged are White British Boys and Black Caribbean Boys. The intersection of Black and Female is not an indicator of educational disadvantage, but the opposite, especially if Female is combined with Black African.

Original posted on: 8 April 2021.

The government's *Independent Report from the Commission on Race and Ethnic Disparities*, Ref.[1], published 31 March 2021, caused a bit of a stir. It was refreshing to see ethnicity factors across various issues addressed with empirical honesty rather than ideological skew. If you didn't catch Andrew Neil's interview of Mercy Muroki, one of the team that produced the report, then it's worth viewing, Ref.[2]. A government report which identifies family structure and culture as more important determinants of outcomes than race bears more than passing notice. It challenges head-on those who remain, so destructively, in control of the race narrative. That narrative has little basis in empirical fact, as this report demonstrates in the context of education. Muroki even refers to single-parent families as culprits in underperforming offspring. The usual belligerents will be out to get her now, rest assured.

However, back to sex. Here I confine myself to the topic of education and what we can glean from the government's report on the interplay of ethnicity and sex as regards educational attainment.

It is hardly the first time that official sources (or my blog) have pointed out that it is the intersection (ha!) of sex and race in which the educational nadir is to be found. And the intersection in question is not black/female but either white/male or male/socioeconomics, rather inconveniently for the approved narrative. For example, see Ref.[3] or many of the UCAS end of cycle reports while Mary Curnock Cook was still in charge.

Let's turn firstly to the Independent Report on Education and Training, Ref.[4], which forms one part of the government's review. References to "Tables" in the text below relate to that.

Key Stage 4 (Age 16, Year 11, mostly GCSEs)

The data here actually derive from the University of Oxford's 2020 report by Professor Steve Strand *Effects of Ethnicity and Socioeconomic Status on Attainment*, Ref.[5]. He used data from exams in 2015 (I don't know why more recent data were not used, though obviously the covid years would have to be avoided).

Table 2 addressed Key Stage 4 results by ethnicity, sex and parental socioeconomic classification. It uses so-called Level 2 attainment. In terms of GCSE equivalents, this means grades A* to C in old notation, or grades 4 to 9 in the newer numerical system. For readers more familiar with the national exams before 1986, this is supposed to be broadly equivalent to an O Level pass. From the data in that Table I have plotted the histogram of Figure 28.1, which shows the percentage of each ethnic group reaching this level of attainment in both English and mathematics. For comparison, the averages for all girls and for all boys, i.e., all ethnicities combined, are also shown.

The sex-based disparity (roughly 10%) is broadly similar to the spread between the ethnic mean and the ethnic extremities. In other words, very roughly speaking, ethnicity and sex disparities are of similar magnitude – if one compares on the basis of the means of these groups. It gets more interesting when the intersection of ethnicity and sex is considered. But Figure 28.1 alone is sufficient to discredit agonising over race whilst ignoring the sex disparity.

On the purely ethnicity issue, Figure 28.1 illustrates why BAME is a misleading categorisation. Even "Black" is misleading, as the Black African group consistently tends to do better than the White group, whilst the Black Caribbean group is consistently bottom of the heap – if one ignores Irish Travellers, Gypsies and Roma, that is.

Data disaggregated by both ethnicity and sex was provided in Table 3 which uses the "mean Best 8 score". The Best 8 score is a measure of attainment which uses the total score across the best 8 examination results achieved by the pupil. Each GCSE scores equal to its grade (i.e., a grade 9 counts 9, grade 8 counts 8, etc.). The "mean Best 8" is the average of the Best 8 scores across the ethnic and sex group in question.

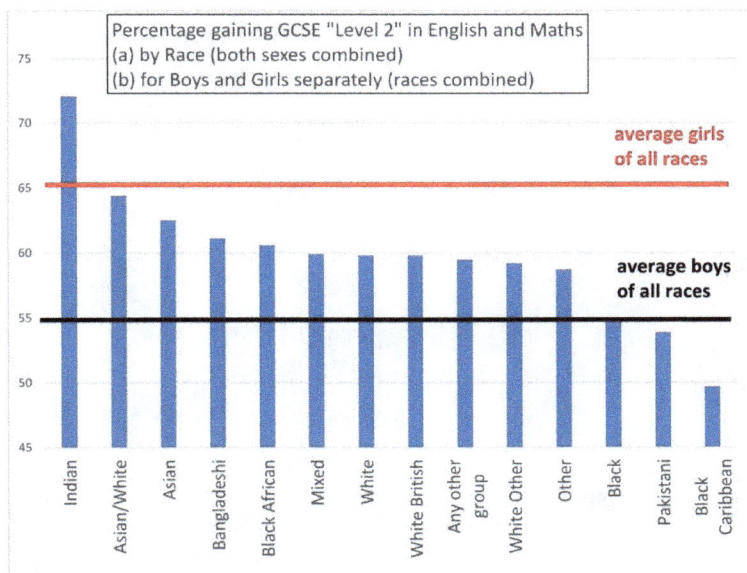

Figure 28.1: Percentages gaining GCSE Level 2 in English and Maths by Ethnicity

However, the data in Table 3 is normalised using the standard deviation of the whole dataset (all ethnicities, both sexes). Hence the units in Table 3, and in my Figure 28.2 below, are "numbers of standard deviations above the mean". Negative values, therefore, are achievement levels below the mean.

Figure 28.2 provides this "mean Best 8" attainment measure for a sub-population of each ethnic group of average socioeconomic status, disaggregated by sex. The sex disparities are now stark. For all ethnicities the average girl lies above the whole-population mean. In contrast, the groups which lie substantially below the mean are White British boys and Black Caribbean boys. The latter are the bottom of the heap (Gypsy, Roma and Irish Traveller groups would be lower still but excluded due to very low statistics). Note again that Black African boys do far better (close to mean, and Black African girls are well above the mean).

Figure 28.3 is a similar plot for the sub-populations defined at one standard deviation below the mean socioeconomic status. Very few boys from this economically disadvantaged background make it above the mean attainment. In contrast, the average girl of the Bangladeshi, Indian, mixed Asian/White or Black African groups still attains well above the mean, even with this economic disadvantage. In contrast, the average boy of Pakistani, White British, "other" White, or Black Caribbean groups does woefully badly – and it is the White British and Black Caribbean groups which are emphatically the worst underachievers for both sexes.

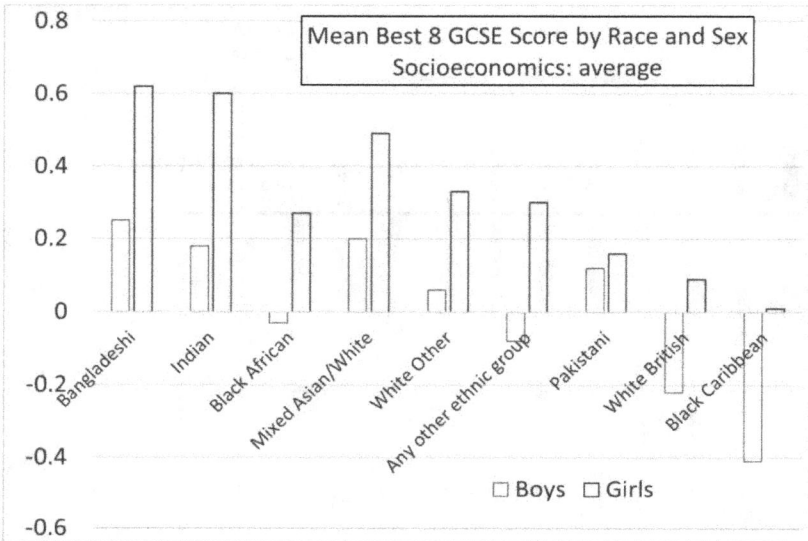

Figure 28.2: Mean Best 8 Scores by Ethnicity and Sex (Socioeconomic Average)

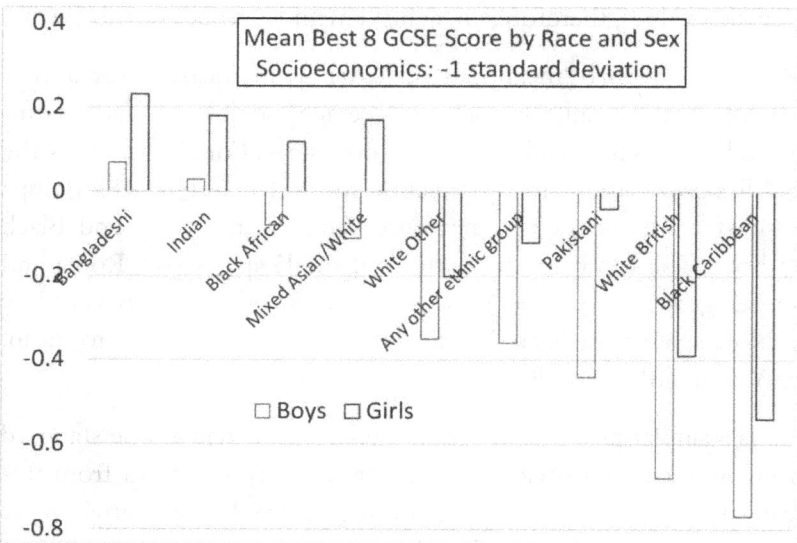

Figure 28.3: Mean Best 8 Scores by Ethnicity and Sex (Socioeconomic Minus One Standard Deviation)

Exclusion from School

Ref.[4] includes data on permanent exclusions from school, which is usually due to persistent disruptive behaviour. In the 2018 to 2019 school year there were 438,300 temporary exclusions, and 7,900 permanent exclusions. The permanent exclusions are considered here. However, the report does not disaggregate exclusions by sex. But boys are excluded far more frequently than girls. Government data, Ref.[6], tell us, *"Boys have more than three times the number of permanent exclusions, with 6,000 permanent exclusions, at a rate of 0.14 compared to 1,900 for girls in 2018/19 (0.05)"*.

Assuming that sex ratio holds for all ethnic groups, I used the exclusion data from Ref.[4] to produce Figure 28.4. This shows the odds ratio of permanent exclusion by ethnic group and sex compared to the White British group of both sexes. The effect of sex swamps that of ethnicity. For almost all ethnicities, boys are more likely to be excluded than the average White British pupil, but that is because the average White British pupil includes girls as well as boys. In short, it is sex which is by far the dominant feature, not ethnicity.

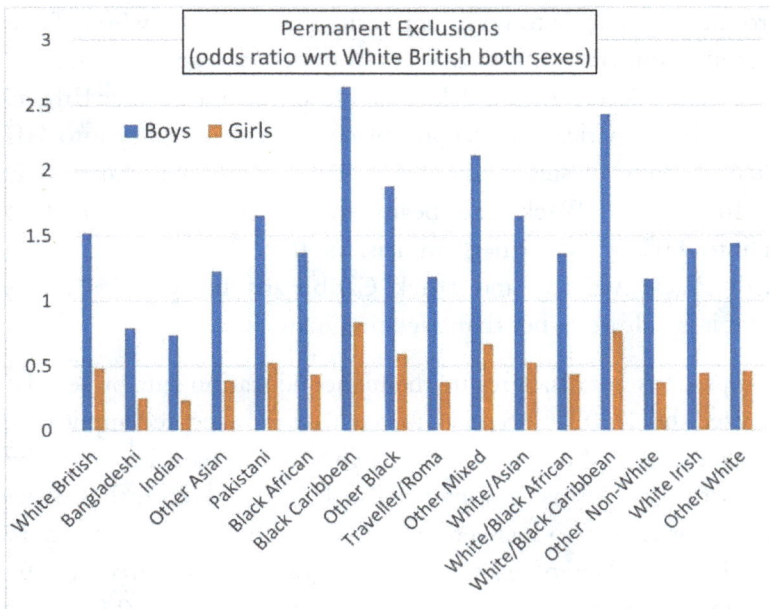

Figure 28.4: The Odds Ratio of Permanent Exclusion from School by Ethnicity and Sex (relative to all White British of Both Sexes)

Higher Education (HE)

The government report, Ref.[4], again does a good job of dispelling misconceptions about race and progression to higher education. The data in Table 7 have been plotted below as Figure 28.5. This shows how terribly badly the White British group does compared to all other major ethnic groups, even being outperformed by the Black Caribbean groups (again only Travellers/Roma do worse).

In Figure 28.5 "FSM" stands for Free School Meals and is a marker for those from a poor background. The Figure shows that, for ethnicities that have a high progression rate into higher education, socioeconomics has little effect. But as one moves down to the ethnicities with lower progression rates into higher education so the disadvantageous effects of socioeconomics also become more marked. In short, there is a synergistic intersection between ethnicity and socioeconomic status. This effect is worst for White British and White Irish.

But, nevertheless, even a White British 18/19-year-old who is not from a poor background is less likely to go to university than a person who is from a poor background but from any one of seven non-White groups: Chinese, Black African, Bangladeshi, Indian, Pakistani, Other Asian or Other Ethnic. The position of Black Africans in second place in terms of entry into HE (broadly equal to Bangladeshis, Indians and Other Asians) is particularly noteworthy. In contrast, Black Caribbeans wallow at the lower end of progression into HE. This further emphasises that BAME is a useless category, with Black Africans and Black Caribbeans being poles apart, suggesting that it is culture rather than race that matters.

However, Ref.[4] does not disaggregate the higher education data by sex. To do so I have used the 2020 UCAS end-of-cycle data for accepted applicants, Ref.[7]. This source gives the actual number of acceptances broken down by sex and by most of the ethnic groups used in Figure 7. Hence these data provide the ratio of female to male entrants into HE by each ethnic group. Armed with this, the data of Table 7 can be used to deconvolute the progression rates separately for each sex and each ethnic group. (I included a correction for the different numbers of male and female 18-year-olds, this being the dominant age at entry).

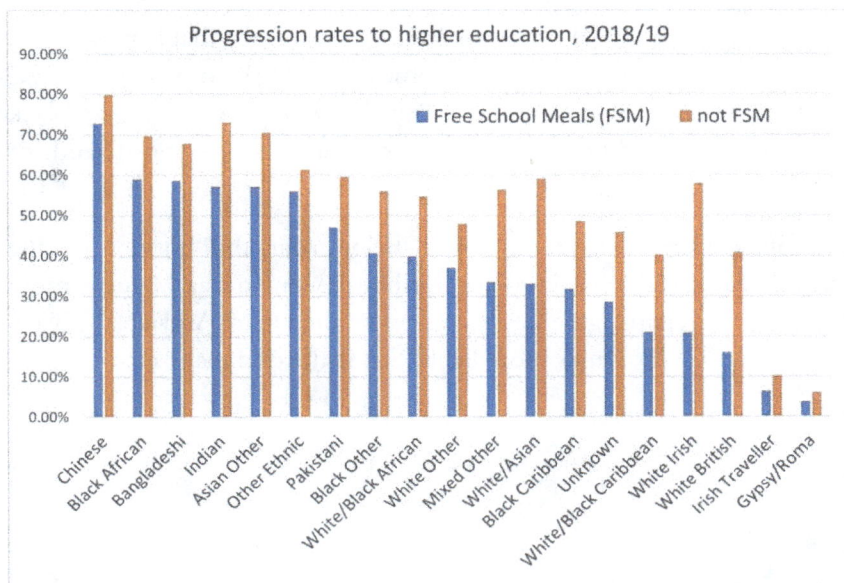

Figure 28.5: Progression Rates to Higher Education by Ethnicity and Socioeconomics

Figure 28.6 is the resulting histogram of progression to HE for the sexes separately and for non-FSM. Figure 28.7 is the equivalent for FSM. Comparing the spread due to ethnicity in the two Figures, it is immediately clear that this is far greater for FSM individuals, i.e., socioeconomics accentuates ethnic disparities (as is also clear from Figure 28.5). Where ethnicities do well, socioeconomics matters little.

Men have lower progression into HE than women in every ethnic group without exception, and irrespective of socioeconomics.

Finally, Figure 28.8 plots the percentage by which the number of UK domiciled women accepted into HE exceeds that of men in 2020, against ethnic group. This is based on UCAS data alone and is not disaggregated by socioeconomics. The sex disparity is greatest for Whites and Blacks, especially Black Caribbean, and least for the several Asian groups including Chinese.

Note that all the HE data here relates to UK domiciled students only, not to the total UK HE entrants (many of whom are from abroad). Consequently the ethnicity, sex and socioeconomic dependencies are specific to the UK.

If you look at the graphic which heads Ref.[3] you will see that it shows that, in 2015, a poor black woman was three times more likely to progress to HE in the UK than a poor white man. But that data did not disaggregate Black Africans and Black Caribbeans, which we now see to be at opposite ends of the achievement distribution.

Despite Black Caribbeans as a whole being near the bottom of the educational heap, in 2020 a poor Black Caribbean woman was 3.3 times more likely to go to university in the UK than a poor white man. And a poor Black African woman was 5.5 times more likely. Sex is the dominant factor again.

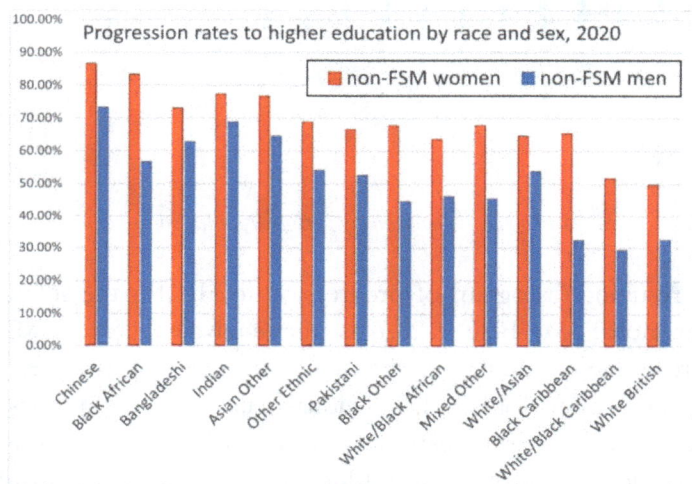

Figure 28.6: Progression Rates to HE by Ethnicity and Sex (non-FSM)

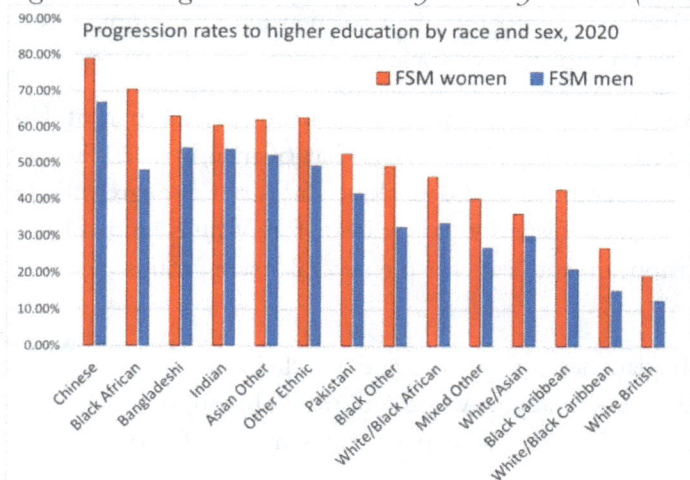

Figure 28.7: Progression Rates to HE by Ethnicity and Sex (FSM)

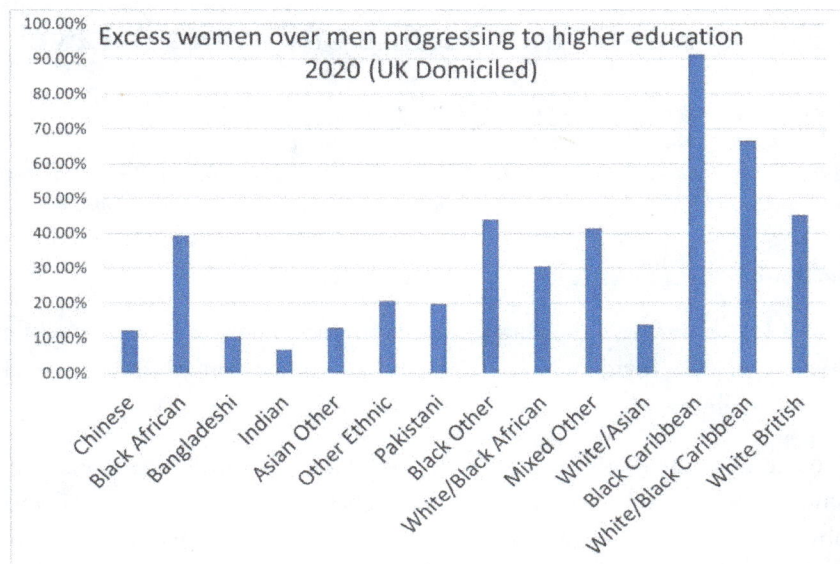

Figure 28.8: Excess of Women over Men Progressing to HE by Ethnicity

References

[1] UK Government (2021a). *Independent report of the Commission on Race and Ethnic Disparities*. Commission on Race and Ethnic Disparities, 28 April 2021

[2] Spectator TV (2021). *How racist is Britain?* Mercy Muroki and Andrew Neil, 5 April 2021.

[3] Collins, W. (2016). *HEPI Report on Male Underachievement in Higher Education*. The Illustrated Empathy Gap, 12 May 2016.

[4] UK Government (2021b). *Independent report on Education and training. Commission on Race and Ethnic Disparities*. 28 April 2021.

[5] Strand, S. (2021). *Ethnic, socioeconomic and sex inequalities in educational achievement at age 16*. Commission on Race and Ethnic Disparities, 28 April 2021.

[6] UK Government (2023). *Permanent exclusions and suspensions in England*. The dataset for 2018/19 was used.

[7] UCAS (2020. *Undergraduate Sector-Level End of Cycle Data Resources 2020*. University and Colleges Admissions Service, December 2020

29. Feminisation and Decline of Physics A Level

This is one of my earliest posts. You can tell this from the angrier tone which I tended then to adopt. I thought it would be of interest because it is a rare example of how the deliberate feminisation of an academic subject can be traced and the mechanisms driving it exposed. The latest versions of physics A Level may differ from what is described here, dating from 2015.

Original posted on: 10 February 2015.

We hear a lot about the feminisation of schooling. Here I present a specific example, with clear evidence: the deliberate feminisation of the A Level physics curriculum.

In 2006 the Institute of Physics commissioned a study into the reasons why girls choose not to study physics at A Level, resulting in Ref.[1] by Patricia Murphy and Elizabeth Whitelegg. The key findings of this report were discussed in a Department of Education and Skills report Ref.[2]. Some key quotes from these reports are as follows.

"Murphy and Whitelegg refer to studies that have shown that physics and other sciences are measured to be up to a whole grade more difficult compared with most other subjects at A Level and GCSE."

I don't see that as a bad thing. It means that standards are high. (Actually, they are not, as I show below – but this suggests that the standard is truly woeful in other subjects).

"These findings have been challenged, but there is still a perception of physics as a difficult subject, which may act as a deterrent, particularly to girls."

Why should a subject being hard be a deterrent to girls? If it's hard, it's hard for everyone. I hope they were not suggesting that girls are not clever enough? I don't believe that. (By the way, of those girls who do study physics at A level, a greater percentage get an A grade than boys).

"Girls are more likely than boys to give value to the social context in which tasks are posed in defining a problem; boys are more likely than girls not to 'notice' the context….some students, particularly boys, see little value in a focus on social contexts and problems."

Fair enough. That may explain why physics is less popular with girls, then. Because physics is about inanimate matter and has no social context.

But to the authors of Refs.[1,2], having identified the "problem", the next step is to overcome it. If physics is not to girls' liking, then physics will have to change, like this,

"The Murphy and Whitelegg report describes the need for curriculum change and change in the teaching and assessment of physics in order to engage girls better. The curriculum should be 'context based' or 'humanistic'. It should: Use a variety of social situations and contexts to organise and determine the scientific content of the course; Represent science as something that people do, influenced by historical, political, cultural and personal factors, not just as a body of knowledge; Use values inherent in science as topics for discussion and critique."

Speaking as a physicist myself, this is a monstrous travesty. I cannot conceal my outrage at having some utter moron piss on my subject (forgive my French). You're going to use "social situations" to determine the scientific content of a physics course? This makes as much sense as suggesting you use a proton synchrotron to write a literary critique of *Pride and Prejudice*.

Grasp this: the whole power of science, and physics in particular, is its strict objectivity. By adhering to rigorous objectivity we can uncover absolute facts about the world. Objectivity is achieved by the exclusion of the subjective. Therein lies the power of the experimental method, prior to which sophists would simply debate their prejudices endlessly.

There is no social context in physics, you fools. It's about electrons. It's about the motion of planets, which is not noticeably influenced by the existence of *Homo sapiens*. It's about the primordial fireball in the first fraction of a second of the universe's existence. It's about pure mathematical constructs of awesome elegance which turn out, amazingly, ineffably, numinously, to align with the behaviour of inanimate matter. It is gloriously austere and deeply mysterious.

It's supposed to be forbidding for it reveals the face of God, in as far as it can be apprehended by mortals.

It is, in fact, one of the few things that lifts human life a little above the level of the mundane and utilitarian.

And these idiots have confused it with technology.

Of course, to the *faux*-intellectual post-modernist there is no such thing as absolute truth. They tell us that science is a social construct. I don't see them throwing themselves off high places in the belief that gravity is a mere social construct, more's the pity.

Here's an illustration of what you get if you let post-modernists loose on science: from Sandra Harding, Ref.[3], a so-called feminist philosopher and philosopher of science,

"Why is it not as illuminating and honest to refer to Newton's laws as 'Newton's rape manual' as it is to call them 'Newton's mechanics?'"

Well, Sandra, without wishing to dive too deeply into rigorous analysis, that'll be because it's utter bollocks. No, on reflection, it's worse: it gives genuine, well thought-out utter bollocks a bad name.

Or consider that other feminist philosopher, Luce Irigaray, Ref.[4], who regards $E = mc^2$ as a "sexed equation" because she argues that,

"...it privileges the speed of light over other speeds that are vitally necessary to us."

Thanks for explaining that one to me, Luce. To be fair, the invariance of light speed came as a great surprise to physicists, too. But, you see, that's the point. To the scientist, once the experimental evidence has accumulated sufficiently, it becomes incumbent upon one to accept reality, whether it conforms to one's preconceptions or not – and relativity definitely did not. To the post-modernist, though, the dictum is, "if I don't like it, then it isn't so".

Recall that wonderfully dismissive expression of Wolfgang Pauli's: "not even wrong"? Well, these people are of an entirely different order. They are not even not even wrong.

But back to A Level physics. What Murphy and Whitelegg recommended is that physics be changed to suit girls better. To hell with the subject, let's just replace it with some drivel on which girls can get a good mark. Who cares about real education, as long as we can provide a vehicle to further the feminist objective of female dominance in everything?

But no one paid them any mind, surely?

Dream on.

When feminists say "jump", people jump. And jump they did.

What Murphy and Whitelegg, Ref.[1], advocated in 2006 was a change to the A Level physics curriculum to introduce or emphasise context and the human element. But Murphy and Whitelegg's report was a review of earlier reports dating predominantly from 1990 to 2005. The changes needed to make physics more appealing to girls had already been well publicised. Consequently, the Exam Boards were already ahead of the game in terms of providing the required revised curriculum.

Exam Board AQA had already introduced in 2002 a "Physics B" curriculum called "Physics in Context". The use of the keyword "context" ties this modified syllabus unambiguously to the agenda exemplified by Ref.1 but actually in currency for years before this report. In a page now unavailable, the web site of exam board AQA advocated for Physics B in these terms,

"Physics B: Physics in Context' places the subject firmly in a range of contemporary contexts. It introduces students to new and exciting areas of physics and develops essential knowledge and understanding – all through a context and applications led approach to capture the interest of students."

For "capture the interest of students" we can read, in the light of Ref.[1], "capture the interest of girls".

Similarly, the exam Board OCR introduced their alternative A Level "Physics B (Advancing Physics)" in 2005. The OCR web site, Ref.[5], recommends this new curriculum in these words,

"The Advancing Physics course provides a distinctive structure within which candidates learn both about fundamental physical concepts and about physics in everyday and technological settings. It shows the usefulness of the subject and illustrates the impact that discoveries in physics have had on the way people live... In Advancing Physics there are opportunities for candidates to..... use their imagination... and, place physics in a social or historical context and argue about the issues that arise."

I think this establishes that the changes align with what Refs.[1,2] identify as specifically designed to appeal to girls, but not necessarily to boys, i.e., deliberate feminisation.

The Exam Board Edexcel retained a single exam but modified the corresponding pedagogy so that it may be either concept-led or context-led. The context-led approach was based on the Salters Horners Advanced Physics Project and has been in use since 2000. An extract from the Edexcel syllabus guide as it was in 2015 describes the context-led approach thus,

"The context approach begins with the consideration of an application that draws on many different areas of physics, and then the laws, theories and models of physics that apply to this application are studied. The context approach for this unit uses three different contexts: sports, the production of sweets and biscuits and spare part surgery."

Again the keyword "context" clearly aligns it with the intent of Refs.[1,2]. Although there is only one set of exams in this case, the teacher is given two different ways in which to approach the material, and we see that the context-led approach is aligned with feminised pedagogy.

You might imagine that no harm is done by the options introduced by the Exam Boards since only an *alternative* to the more traditional, concept-led, approach has been offered. But this is illusory. How many schools can resource teaching one group of pupils "Physics A" and another group of pupils "Physics B"? None, I suggest. A choice of one or the other has to be made. Even if the exam is the same (Edexcel), the teacher must choose one or other of the teaching styles, concept-led or context-led.

So which is it to be? Well, which do you think? I have no data for the country as a whole. But I can tell you the position at my local secondary school (a state comprehensive). They have opted for Exam Board OCR and are studying Physics B, the context-led, or feminised, syllabus. And how many girls are taking the subject at A level? In the lower sixth (AS year) just 4 girls out of a class of 40. And that is despite the head of physics being a woman (a proper physicist, by the way, with a PhD in particle physics).

So, 90% of the candidates, the boys, are being taught a curriculum which has been optimised for the remaining 10%, the girls, because this is what has resulted from a political driven desire to encourage more girls into the subject. The girls have duly, and unsurprisingly, declined to oblige. And the boys are left with the feminised syllabus.

Hey ho.

I have one final observation to make regarding the relative popularity of physics with boys. Whilst physics does exert a positive attraction to many boys, both for its intrinsic interest and because of the perceived employment benefits, it is incorrect to assume that these are the only reasons for physics (and maths) being popular with boys. There is also a less appreciated and more disturbing reason. I know this is so because my own sons were a case in point. Many boys suffer from poor verbal skills, possibly, but not necessarily, as severe as dyslexia. Having suffered this major disadvantage throughout their school experience, when choosing their A Level subjects they are keen to minimise any further exposure to the dreaded *word*. Subjects that involve much reading or writing are avoided. Hence maths, physics, and ultimately engineering and other 'hard' sciences, rise to the fore. From this perspective the male dominance of STEM subjects can be seen, not as a privilege, but as a symptom of boys' general educational disadvantage in other areas.

Whilst on the subject of physics A Level I'd like to expose a separate issue (or is it?), namely the decline of standards. This is unlikely to mean much to non-physicists, but I invite you to compare the 2008 OCR Physics B exam papers, linked at Ref.[6], with the A level physics papers from 1962 (NUJMB), linked in Ref.[7]. Note firstly that whilst the 1962 papers were three hours long, the 2008 papers are just an hour and 15 or 30 minutes. The 2008 papers lead the candidate by the nose through questions, requiring very little in terms of knowledge. And the calculations are almost always merely multiplying two numbers, and perhaps dividing by a third number. Most intelligent people could have a good stab at these questions without knowing any physics. The 1962 papers are entirely different. They often involve deriving algebraic expressions from scratch. Sixth form students today would probably have a nervous breakdown if faced with something like those 1962 papers. Also, these days candidates are given a sheet of formulae, so very often they don't even need to know (say) the equation for the couple acting on a magnetic dipole in a magnetic field. In the sixties you'd be expected to either know it or to derive it from first principles.

Overall it is clear to me that the standard has dropped dramatically. In 2005 the Qualifications and Curriculum Authority did not agree, but they looked at far too short a timebase, Ref.[8]. I am a zealot in the matter of physics, admittedly, but I'd like to see the subject made more demanding again (though not necessarily being so reactionary as to have a syllabus quite like that of the 1960s).

It rather raises the question as to why standards have dropped. It is a broader question than just the feminisation issue. I have not researched the matter and make no definitive statement. However, the answer seems rather obvious. Since the 1960s we have seen the introduction of school league tables and a massive expansion of universities, hungry for students who are now paying customers. How can so many more university places be filled unless standards were dropped? Schoolteachers are judged on their performance, and the schools themselves are judged upon their performance, and both of these are gauged by exam results. The schools therefore have a vested interest in exam grade inflation, whilst the universities are keen to collaborate so as to acquire more paying customers. The Qualifications and Curriculum Authority is, perhaps, too feeble a regulator to resist pressure from The Blob, which will all be one way. Pity the teaching staff at the universities who have to live with the result. It is notorious that the maths ability of new physics undergraduates is often below the required standard and so many universities offer what is effectively a remedial maths course for new physics students.

References

[1] Murphy, P., and Whitelegg, E. (2006). *Girls in the physics classroom: a review of the research on the participation of girls in physics*. Institute of Physics, London, UK, June 2006.

[2] UK Government (2007). *Gender and Education: the Evidence on Pupils in England*. Department of Education & Skills, 2007

[3] Harding, S. (1986). *The Science Question in Feminism*. Cornell University Press 1986

[4] Sokal, A. (1997). *Fashionable Nonsense: Postmodern Intellectuals' Abuse of Science*. St Martin's Press, English translation edition October 1999.

[5] OCR Exam Board (2013). *Physics B Specification Version 4 September 2013.*

[6] OCR Physics B A Level Exam Papers 2008: paper 1, paper 2, paper 3

[7] NUJMB Physics A Level Exam 1962: all papers.

[8] Qualifications and Curriculum Authority, "Review of standards in physics: GCSE 1997 and 2002; A level 1996 and 2001", 2005. http://dera.ioe.ac.uk/8912/1/12888_physicsreport.pdf

30. Girls Are Just Cleverer

"Girls are just cleverer" concluded a certain professional educationalist. Here I lay out the reasons why he was wrong.

Original posted on: *13 August 2021*.

"After years of trying to explain comparative female academic success, a leading education expert has concluded that girls are simply cleverer than boys", so read an article in The Times on 12 Aug 2021, Ref.[1].

The leading education expert in question was Professor Alan Smithers, a man who has spent a long working lifetime in the field of education, for the 17 years prior to that article as Director of the Centre for Education and Employment Research, University of Buckingham.

"When girls leapt ahead at GCSE", he said, *"this was attributed to the modular structure of the course, which favoured their conscientious approach, and when GCSEs were reformed to be more like O Levels, the girls' lead was dented only slightly"*.

The "leap ahead" experienced by girls when O Levels were replaced by GCSEs is shown in Figure 30.1, below. Many people have attributed this "leap ahead" to the change in the nature of the award, e.g., the move to a modular structure or the inclusion of course work. It is to this that Smithers refers. However, it tends to be forgotten that, prior to the introduction of GCSEs, not all pupils took O Levels at all. In schools with less academic pupils, there was also a lower tier of national exams at age 16, the CSEs. It was said that a top grade at CSE was equivalent to an O Level pass. With the introduction of GCSEs, both sets of pupils would now take the same exams.

So an alternative explanation for the "leap ahead" is that it fails to compare like with like. After 1986 a larger cohort of pupils would be taking GCSEs compared to those who would previously have taken O Levels, although the new influx would be of generally lower academic standard. However, to accommodate this it must have been made easier to obtain A*-C at GCSE than the comparator used for O Levels. This must surely have been the case because the percentage gaining 5 or more A*-C GCSEs was immediately greater than the percentage gaining 5 or more O Levels. So the explanation for the "leap ahead" by girls may be that a A*-C graded at GCSE was easier to obtain than the comparator used at O Level and this "lowering of the bar" brought in more girls than boys because this refers to the lower levels of attainment (where there are more disengaged boys than girls). So the "leap ahead" says little or nothing about pupils of average or above average ability. One might have thought that a career educationalist would have known this.

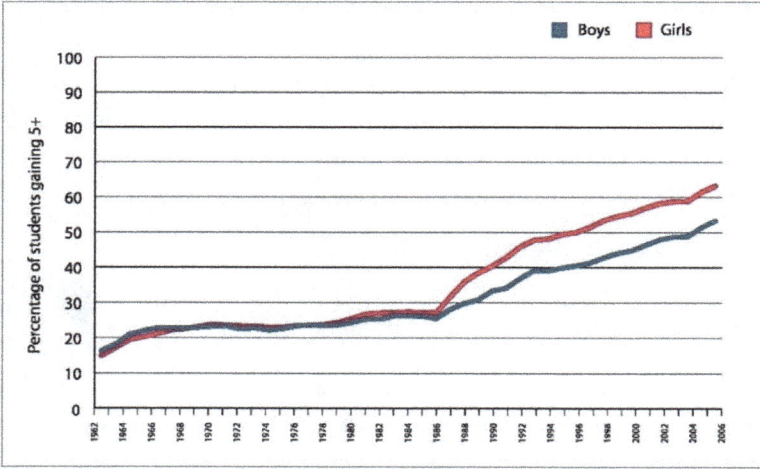

Source: Department for Education Statistics of Education

Figure 30.1: Percentage of School Leavers Achieving 5+ A-C (or Pass) O levels or A-C GCSEs, by Sex (1962 – 2006) from Ref.[2].*

But there is a more glaring problem with Smithers' simplistic claim that "girls are just cleverer": girls did not always outperform boys. This is also clear from Figure 30.1. Ref.[2] notes that *"Boys were slightly more likely than girls to reach the 5+ threshold between 1962 and 1967. Between 1968 and 1986 the difference between the sexes was either around zero or 1-2 percentage points in girls' favour."*

Professor Smithers continues,

"Now with teacher assessment girls have gone further ahead and it has been suggested that this is because teachers favour them. On the strength of their superior performance in schools, girls are more likely to go to university. In 1980, they were outnumbered by three to two but 40 years on that has been a complete reversal."

It is not a "suggestion" that teachers' assessments favour girls, but established by clear and unambiguous evidence from the data. I have been pointing this out in the context of Key Stage 2 Standard Attainment Tests (KS2 SATS, taken at age 10/11) for a decade. Also, the covid years provided clear evidence that this bias also exists in A Level results when based on teachers' assessments (see chapter 27). My latest update of the KS2 SATS analysis is given in Figures 30.2 and 30.3. (For the definition of "bias" see chapter 27. Positive bias means in favour of girls). What is concerning about this evidence of bias is not only the few percentage points difference it makes in these cases but what it might imply for a more pervasive and insidious discrimination that colours a boy's whole perception of learning and social ethos.

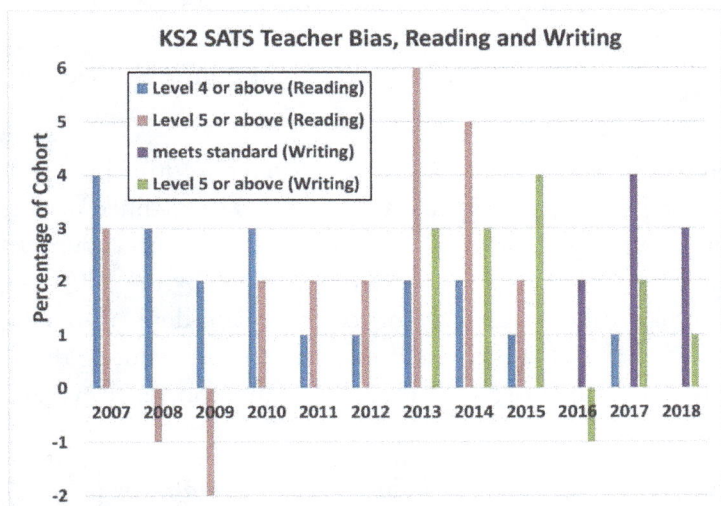

Figure 30.2: Teacher Bias in KS2 SATS (reading & writing)

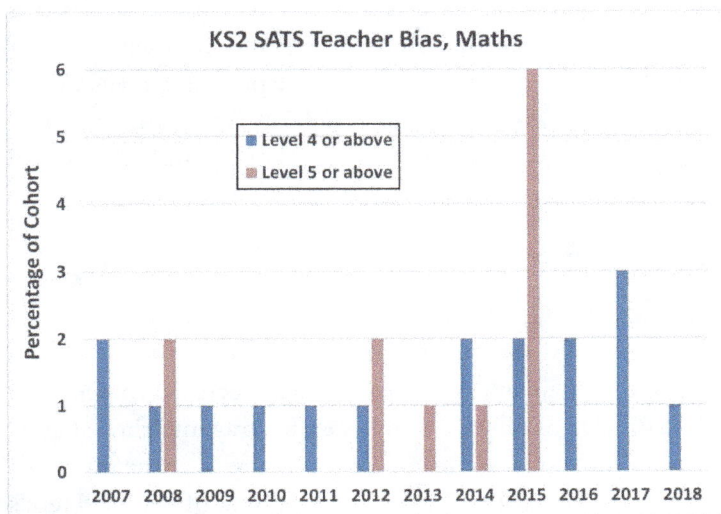

Figure 30.3: Teacher Bias in KS2 SATS (maths)

The good professor asks, *"Why then does it seem so difficult to accept that females are cleverer?"* But I could equally well ask: why is it so difficult to accept that boys are disadvantaged?

One might have thought that a man with an MSc and a PhD in the Psychology and Sociology of Education might have had a suspicion that psychology and sociology could have an impact on education. But it seems not. Perhaps it's with his being male – he's just not very bright. Oh dear, what a pity, never mind, allow me to assist. Just why *is* it difficult to accept that females are cleverer?

Well, what on earth does the Professor mean by "cleverer". With a PhD in a psychological subject he should know that such terms are undefined until a measurement procedure is specified. If the measurement procedure is defined by the attainment of education awards sanctioned by the JCQ (the Joint Council for Qualifications) then I grant you, it's a slam-dunk. (Do note I write "awards", not "exams"). Girls are doing very well in attaining these awards, in comparison with boys, so if that's the definition of "cleverer" that's the end of the matter.

But hold on – the good Professor is claiming that the **reason** why girls are doing better in these awards is **because** they are cleverer. I declare a foul. The explanation is void if you use circular logic. In order for the Professor's claim that girls are cleverer to provide an explanation of their superior attainment of awards, there must be some independent measure of "cleverness" which makes the assertion meaningful. What the Dickens could it be? Hmm…what might a person versed in psychology and educational matters think could be a measure of "cleverness". Tricky, eh?

Not really, no. IQ, of course (or, better, "g" – General Intelligence).

There is a vast literature on IQ, much of it on sex differences. And whilst there is some contention around sex differences in IQ, these pale into insignificance compared to the contention around the effects of ethnicity and country-of-origin on IQ. Thankfully we don't need to stray into those highly charged areas. And in respect of sex, the controversies are over the minutiae, not the broad perspective – at least as regards the vast bulk of people. Here's a short lecture on sex differences in IQ.

Firstly there is the thorny issue of whether IQ is a well-defined quantity. There are many different variants of test, and differences in results between test types are inevitable. However these differences are notable, in general, for being small, the test results being very strongly correlated. Nevertheless, there will remain a reasonable concern that, where only very small sex differences are apparent, that these differences are an artefact of the particular tests used.

This situation is exacerbated by the one finding that appears consistent over time, consistent across cultures, and broadly (if not invariably) consistent between test variants: namely that sub-categories of test question show sex differences. This is illustrated by Table 30.1, taken from the meta-analysis by Hedges and Nowell, Ref.[3]. The magnitudes of the sex differences illustrated by Table 30.1 will vary between studies, but the signs of the sex differences are pretty robust (positive denotes male superiority, negative female superiority). Some aspects of verbal skills/comprehension, perceptual speed and associative memory tend to favour women and girls, whereas mathematics and visuospatial skills favour men and boys.

Table 2. Sex differences on seven types of ability test (from Hedges & Nowell, 1995)

Test	Reading comprehension	Vocabulary	Mathematics	Perceptual speed	Associative memory	Spatial ability	Mechanical reasoning
Median effect size*	−0·09	+0·02	+0·17	−0·23	−0·26	+0·19	+0·77

*Effect size in *d* (standard deviation units), with a positive sign indicating male superiority, and a negative sign female superiority. The results shown are the median of the studies surveyed by Hedges & Nowell (for different types of test, the number of studies ranged from two to five).

Table 30.1: taken from Ref.[3]

Sex differences in cognitive ability are greatest in mechanical reasoning and spatial ability, and especially in mental rotation, where males outperform females by almost a standard deviation in some studies. To quote N.J.Mackintosh, Ref.[4], *"The largest, most reliable and most persistent difference between the sexes is that observed in tests of spatial ability. As already noted, tests of three-dimensional mental rotation yield a difference of some 13-14 IQ points – a difference which, unlike many others, has shown no signs of decreasing in the past 20 years…. and while the determined environmentalist will obviously be able to dismiss this, it does suggest that the difference is not simply a consequence of cultural attitudes."*

Standard IQ tests contain a mix of question types, with the overall IQ score being determined by the aggregate result. Obviously, then, whether a sex difference is apparent in the resulting IQ score will depend upon the particular mix of question types adopted. Quoting Mackintosh, Ref.[4], again,

"Although the overall difference between the sexes was trivial, there were some items or sub-tests on which females consistently did better than males, and others on which males consistently obtained higher scores than females. The two happened more or less to cancel each other out to yield approximate overall equality. But it now seems obvious that a judicious choice of sub-tests for inclusion in one's test battery could yield any outcome one wanted. Indeed, feminists inclined to see male conspiracies lurking everywhere may think that this is just what has happened with the revisions of the Wechsler tests, for both the WISC-R and WAIS-R now yield a significant overall male superiority."

Those last-mentioned test types feature large in the analyses which I quote below. However, this ambiguity, due to the arbitrariness of weighting between question types, is minimised in what is referred to as General Intelligence, denoted "g" rather than IQ. This is measured by essentially the same types of test but analysed differently. The general ability factor, g, is technically defined as the unrotated first factor or principal component of a factor analysis or principal components analysis. However, whilst g minimises dependence on the arbitrary mix of questions it does not eliminate it entirely. Some authors claim that g is *"very close to the IQ calculated from a battery of diverse tests"*, for example Lynn and Meisenberg, Ref.[5].

For the consensus view of sex differences in intelligence as it stood in the mid-90s we can again quote Mackintosh's review, Ref.[4].

"The differences in the original standardisation samples for the two tests were small, 1.7 points for the WISC-R and 2.2 for the WAIS-R. But Lynn (1994) reviewed a number of other large scale studies of the Wechsler tests which consistently found a significant male superiority, averaging 2.35 points on the WISC and 3.08 points on the WAIS. There can be little doubt that the sex difference on these tests is reliable – and slightly larger for adults on the WAIS than for children on the WISC. But is it real, or at least, typical? One might suppose that the best way to answer the question is to look at the results obtained with other general IQ test batteries on large, representative samples of the population. The answer turns out to be somewhat equivocal. Thus Herrnstein and Murray (1994) obtained the test scores of some 12,000 teenagers and young adults on the AFQT test and found a difference of 0.9 IQ points in favour of men. But Lubinski and Humphreys (1990) analysed the test scores of some 100,000 16-year-old American schoolchildren, and found

a difference of 0.3 IQ points in favour of girls; while the 1980 standardisation of the Differential Aptitude Tests, on a representative sample of American 14-18-year-olds, yielded an overall difference of 0.8 IQ points in favour of females (Feingold, 1988)."

The latter, apparently conflicting results, would seem to be an age effect. Introducing the special edition of Mankind Quarterly in September 2016, Richard Lynn and Gerhard Meisenberg in Ref.[4] note that the consensus position is for negligible sex difference in IQ (or g), but state that, *"This special issue presents a number of papers challenging the widespread consensus that there is no sex difference in general intelligence"*. They opine that, *"while there is virtually no sex difference up to the age of 16 years, from this age onwards males develop an advantage that increases with age reaching approximately 4 IQ points among adults (Lynn, 1994). Further data documenting this male advantage was given in Lynn (1999) and in a meta-analysis of sex differences on the Progressive Matrices by Lynn and Irwing (2004) concluding that among adults males obtain a 5 points higher IQ than females."*

Richard Lynn had been a bullish proponent of adult male advantage in general intelligence for 30 years or so before he died in 2023. He had a particular theory of cognitive development. The theory states that boys and girls mature at different rates such that the growth of girls accelerates at the age of about 9 years and remains in advance of boys until 14–15 years. At 15–16 years the growth of girls decelerates relative to boys. As boys continue to grow from this age their height and their mean IQs increase relative to those of girls.

If correct, this theory would caution against drawing any conclusions for adults from tests on school-age children. This is important because some papers on sex differences are indeed based on school-age children and so potentially misleading. The theory seems to have some merit in respect of the commonplace observation that girls at primary school have always outperformed boys, but that as adults men (used to) catch up and potentially exceed women in ability (see, for example, Figures 5 and 6 of Ref.[6]).

In support of this theory, Colom and Lynn, Ref.[7], conclude,

(Abstract extract) *"This paper presents new evidence for the theory from the Spanish standardization sample of the fifth edition of the DAT. 1027 boys and 924 girls between 12 and 18 years were tested. The general trend shows that girls do better at the younger ages and their performance declines relative to boys among older age groups, which supports the developmental theory. The sex difference for the DAT as a whole for 18 year olds is a*

4.3 IQ advantage for boys, very close to the advantage that can be predicted from their larger brain size (4.4 IQ points). The profile of sex differences in abilities among the Spanish sample is closely similar to that in the United States and Britain, which is testimony to the robustness of the difference in these different cultures."

The Abstract of the influential, if now rather old, meta-analysis by Hedges and Nowell, Ref.[3] appears supportive. It reads,

"Sex differences in central tendency, variability, and numbers of high scores on mental tests have been extensively studied. Research has not always seemed to yield consistent results, partly because most studies have not used representative samples of national populations. An analysis of mental test scores from six studies that used national probability samples provided evidence that although average sex differences have been generally small and stable over time, the test scores of males consistently have larger variance. Except in tests of reading comprehension, perceptual speed, and associative memory, males typically outnumber females substantially among high-scoring individuals."

I now present the results from the special issue of Mankind Quarterly, September 2016, 57(1), but with a warning that many of the papers include Richard Lynn as a co-author. I do not suggest that this impacts on their reliability, but it may well have a bearing on the type of testing and analysis performed which might introduce a skew. However, do notice the range of different cultures over which broadly consistent results were obtained.

Davide Piffer, Ref.[8],

Abstract: *"Data are reported for the scores of men and women in the standardization of the American WAIS-IV. Men obtained a significantly higher Full Scale IQ than women by 2.25 IQ points and on the General Ability Index by 4.05 IQ points. Men obtained significantly higher scores on the index IQs of Verbal Comprehension, Perceptual Reasoning and Working Memory, and women obtained a significantly higher score on the Processing Speed index IQ. Men showed greater variability than women on the Full Scale IQ, the General Ability Index and on twelve of the fifteen subtests."*

Salaheldin Bakhiet et al, Ref.[9],

Abstract: *"The intelligence of 1936 engineering students in three universities in Sudan was tested with the Advanced Progressive Matrices. The sample obtained an average British IQ of 93. Males obtained marginally higher average scores than females, equivalent to approximately 1.2 IQ points."*

George Spanoudis, et al, Ref.[10],

Abstract: *"Sex differences on the Standard Progressive Matrices are reported for 10- to 17-year-olds in Cyprus. There were no significant differences among 10- to 16-year-olds but among 17-year-olds males obtained a mean IQ 4.4 points higher than females."*

Yoon-Mi Hur, et al, Re.[11],

Abstract: *"Sex differences in intelligence have been much disputed for many decades. The present study examined the issues of whether sex differences in intelligence change during development. In total, 11,164 children (mean age = 13.5 years; SD = 2.6 years) completed the Standard Progressive Matrices Plus (SPM+). From age 8 to 19 years, sex differences in the total score of the SPM+ increased from -0.06d (favoring females) to 0.46d (favoring males), with an average of 0.23d. Our findings support Lynn's developmental theory of sex differences in cognitive abilities."* (NB: 0.23d is about 3.5 IQ points).

Hsin-Yi Chen, et al, Ref.[12],

Abstract: *"Sex differences on the WISC-III are reported for the 13 subtests, the Verbal and Performance IQs, the four Index IQs and the Full Scale IQs in Taiwan and the United States. The sex differences are closely similar in the two samples with a correlation of .87 (p<.001) in the 13 subtests. Males obtained significantly higher Full Scale IQs in the two samples of .21d and .11d, respectively."* (NB: 0.21d corresponds to about 3.2 IQ points).

Flores-Mendoza et al, Ref.[13],

Abstract (extract): *"... we reviewed and compiled intelligence data from Brazil, and found evidence for a male advantage in adulthood in most dimensions of intelligence. We then analyzed new adult data on three unidimensional IQ tests for the measurement of general intelligence (the g factor), and found evidence of a male advantage in two, but a female advantage in the third. However, scores on two tests appeared to be highly confounded with education level, and once this variable was controlled, the female advantage in one test and the male advantage in another were not noticeable. In general, our results were mostly in line with the male advantage hypothesis, although this did not appear to be uniformly consistent or of high magnitude in Brazil."*

I am not attempting to present a definitive case for male advantage in intelligence, despite the clear direction of the above studies. My aim is the more modest one of definitively answering Professor Smithers' question

"Why does it seem so difficult to accept that females are cleverer?" That great pile of academic studies makes it difficult, Professor, and it doesn't end there.

To put an alternative to Richard Lynn's 'male advantage' point of view I refer you to the above quote from Mackintosh, Ref.[4], and some further observations of his which are probably still apposite despite their vintage…

"…it will be argued that performance on any one of these tests is correlated with performance on any other: hence, general intelligence, (may be) defined as g, or the first principal component of any suitably diverse battery of mental tests. Is there not a sex difference in g? The answer is still: it depends. The general factor extracted from the Wechsler tests yields a difference between the sexes, in favour of males, that is actually some 40% larger than their difference in average scores (Jensen & Reynolds, 1983). Thus the 2.3-point advantage for males in overall IQ on the WAIS would again, to Lynn's satisfaction, translate into a 4-point male advantage on the general factor extracted from the test. The reason for this is that the various sub-tests of the WAIS differ rather widely in their loadings on this general factor and there is some tendency for males to do better on sub-tests with higher g-loadings."

Mackintosh also takes a dim view of the claims for a larger male variance,

"…there would then be equally little reason to believe in that other hoary explanation of greater male eminence – greater variability in general intelligence. Neither Raven's matrices nor the DAT reasoning tests reveal reliable evidence that the variance of male scores is greater than that of females (Court, 1983; Feingold, 1992)."

All this might seem like much ado about nothing as the differences in question are so small, and this is indeed the case as regards the vast bulk of the populace. Many of the above sex differences are fractions of an IQ point, and even the larger ones are just a few IQ points. To the general population this is hardly going to be perceptible. However, where these small differences become amplified into a major effect is in the tail of the distribution. The IQ Comparison Site, Ref.[14], illustrates this nicely. I illustrate it in Figure 30.4 in an alternative manner using the ratio of men to women at high IQ for the assumed cases of male advantage defined by,

- Sex difference in means of 5 IQ points (same standard deviation)
- Sex difference in means of 1.7 points plus difference in standard deviation of 1 point.

Only 1% of the public has an IQ above 135, but, based on results like that of Richard Lynn and others quoted above, there would be more than twice as many men as women at such high IQ levels.

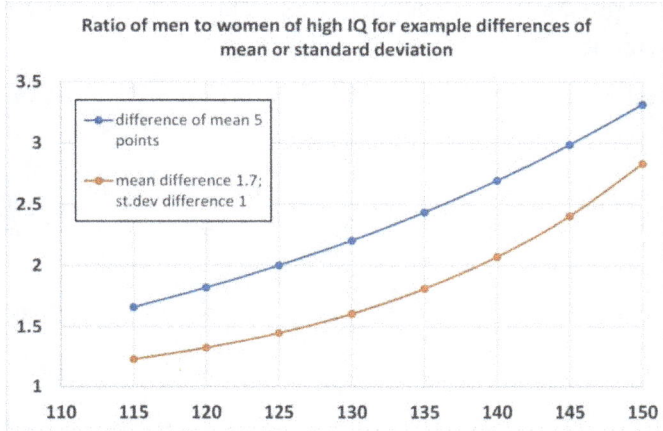

Figure 30.4: The ratio of men to women at high IQ given illustrative small differences in population means and/or standard deviations

The small sex difference in IQ which Lynn and others assert might, via its amplified effect on the tail of the distribution, provide an explanation for a remarkable observation by Olson, Ref.[15]. In the USA there is a clear correlation between the average IQ of students studying a given subject and the gender ratio of that subject. Subjects dominated by men have high IQ averaged across all people studying the subject, whilst subjects dominated by women have relatively lower IQ averaged across all those studying the subject, see Figure 30.5. (Note that "relatively lower" means closer to the national population average, but still above average (>100) because we are dealing with college students in all cases).

Before concluding, I must add some further evidence that comes, not from academic studies, but from the sharp end of educational practice: the experience of schools. In 2023 the All-Party Parliamentary Group (APPG) on issues affecting men and boys (secretary Mike Bell) ran a campaign on boys' education and the reasons for boys' underperformance relative to girls. What emerged, and you can hear this from the teachers themselves in Ref.[16], is that when a school focuses on boys rather than merely accepting their underperformance, then the boys can do as well as the girls, or even better. What emerged is that the lower attainment of boys is created by the way boys are treated by the adults in their lives and that, when given a level playing field and appropriate support, boys achieve as well as girls and enjoy their time at school more. In other words, just as girls' historical under-achievement can be aligned with low cultural expectations, so can boys' current under-achievement.

U.S. college majors: Average IQ of students by gender ratio

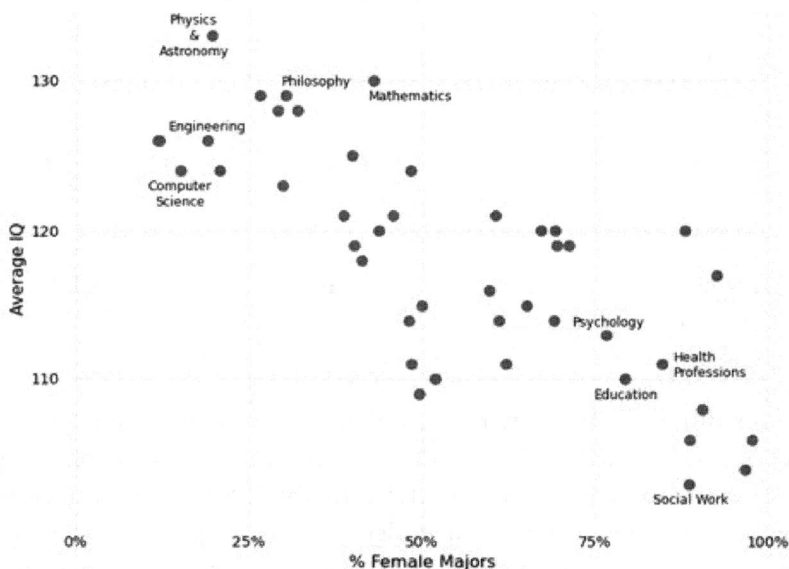

Figure 30.5: Average IQ of USA Students by College Major Gender Ratio, taken from Ref.[15]

So, finally, to answer Professor Smithers, ***all that*** is why I find it so difficult to accept that females are cleverer. Not only does the best available (and extensively researched) measure of "cleverness" not support it, but there is ample evidence that the prevailing anti-male culture is the source of boys' underperformance in those awards which Smithers regards as a measure of "cleverness". One might have expected an educationalist to be aware of the potential impact of psychological, sociological and cultural issues on school attainment irrespective of innate ability. That Smithers prefers to opt for "girls are just cleverer" is symptomatic of the culture of which he is typical.

The education machine is stuffed full of people like Professor Smithers who are entirely comfortable with making public statements along the lines that "girls are cleverer" whilst also waxing lyrical about the dangers of "stereotype threat" to educational attainment, and yet failing to realise that they themselves constitute such a threat.

I look forward to the Professor's next article about the educational underachievement of black Caribbeans or pupils from poor backgrounds, exhorting us to embrace the obvious truth that "they are just a bit stupid". But there will be no such article because, in those cases, the Professor will not be doing as he advises in the context of sex – taking the data at face value rather than addressing why there might be a bias or sociological disadvantage lurking somewhere. Instead he will suddenly have an urgent need to explain away the data. The difference arises because some groups may be denigrated with impunity, while others must not be – and this is an expression of the prevailing approved prejudices.

There is nothing progressive about views such as those expressed by Smithers; actually they are embarrassingly atavistic. It is bad enough that power-hungry and male-hating female feminists have become so common, but let's not forget that this feminist power has been granted by men. A cheap trick that advances a man, unjustified, on the male hierarchy, is to make himself look good by trashing other males. Badmouthing males is always safe and can only assist the ambitious, of either sex, regardless of ideology. We deplorables are no longer fooled. Feminism is the servant of the elites, and we know it now.

References

[1] Woolcock, N. (2021). *GCSE results suggest girls are just cleverer, says expert*. The Times, 12 August 2021.

[2] UK Government (2007). *Gender and education: the evidence on pupils in England*. Department for Education and Skills, 2007 (Section 3.5.1).

[3] Hedges, L., and Nowell, A. (1995). *Sex Differences in Mental Test Scores, Variability, and Numbers of High-Scoring Individuals*. Science 269 (issue 5220) 41-45, 7 July 1995.

[4] Mackintosh, N.J. (1996). *Sex differences and IQ*. Journal of Biosocial Science. 28(4) 558-571, 1996.

[5] Lynn, R. and Meisenberg, G. (2016). *Sex Differences in Intelligence*. Mankind Quarterly 57(1) 5-8, September 2016.

[6] Collins, W. (2015). *Teachers' Unfairness to Boys?*. 14 March 2015.

[7] Colom, R., and Lynn, R. (2004). *Testing the developmental theory of sex differences in intelligence on 12–18 year olds*. Personality and Individual Differences 36(1) 75-82, 2004.

[8] Piffer, D. (2016). *Sex Differences in Intelligence on the American WAIS-IV*. Mankind Quarterly, 57(1), 25–33, September 2016.

[9] Bakhiet, S.F.A., et al (2016). *Sex Differences in the Intelligence of University Engineering Students in Sudan*. Mankind Quarterly, 57(1), 95–98, September 2016.

[10] Spanoudis, G., et al (2016). *Sex Differences for 10 to 17 Year Olds on the Standard Progressive Matrices in Cyprus*. Mankind Quarterly, 57(2), 283–290.

[11] Hur, Y.-M., et al (2017). *Testing Lynn's Theory of Sex Differences in Intelligence in a Large Sample of Nigerian School-Aged Children and Adolescents (N>11,000) using Raven's Standard Progressive Matrices Plus*. Mankind Quarterly, 57(3), 428–437, September 2016.

[12] Chen, H.-Y., et al (2016). *Sex Differences on the WISC-III in Taiwan and the United States*. Mankind Quarterly, 57(1), 66–71, September 2016.

[13] Flores-Mendoza, C., et al (2016). *Cognitive Sex Differences in Brazil*. Mankind Quarterly, 57(1), 34–51, September 2016.

[14] de la Jara, R. (2007). *Sex Differences in IQ*. Personal web site, September 23, 2007.

[15] Olson, R.S. (2014). *Average IQ of Students by College Major and Gender Ratio*. 26 June 2014.

[16] APPG Men and Boys (2023). *Closing the attainment gap for boys at secondary school*. YouTube, 2 December 2023. See also the associated report from the APPG: Inquiry No 4: *Boys' Educational Underachievement*, 13 November 2023.

Section 6

"Equality"
for some

31. The Wrong Sort of Equality

In 2015 I responded to the Equality and Human Rights Commission (EHRC) regarding their Consultation on their Strategic Plan. I suspect they were not grateful for my trouble. This chapter is that submission, with a few suitable updates to avoid being misleading.

Original posted on: 18 December 2015.

I responded to the EHRC by email because their tick-box menus of choices did not cut it for me. I preferred to start further back, with the EHRC report *Is Britain Fairer (2015)*, Ref.[1].

What am I to say when the arbiters of fairness are themselves unfair?

In Section 4.7 of the report (Access to Higher Education) we are told that,

"In 2008, men were more likely to have a degree than women (22.3% of men compared with 20.5% of women). By 2013, women had overtaken men, with 27.7% of men holding a degree compared with 28.4% of women."

So, a gender gap in HE attainment in favour of females then, but of negligible magnitude and of only recent occurrence.

Really?

No. This is an example of what I call "constructive mendacity": a statement which can be defended as correct but which is grossly misleading.

I presume the EHRC's statement must relate to degrees held by the whole population – including people whose degrees were awarded more than forty years ago and whose educational qualifications ceased to have any significance decades ago. Is this a fair reflection of the current relative status of the genders in Higher Education (HE) attainment? No. The truth is that women have been awarded more degrees than men in the UK every year since 1993, now over 30 years. Most people gaining degrees in the last ten years were not born when men dominated in HE. Moreover, the gender gap in degree attainment widens year-on-year. By 2020 it stood at 37% more women gaining degrees than men. The number of first- and upper-second class degrees awarded to women exceeds that awarded to men by a similar percentage.

The report recognises that poor white boys are the most disadvantaged in terms of school educational attainment. But it fails to acknowledge that this had been the case also at HE level for over twenty years by 2015 (and now over thirty years). This has prompted then-UCAS chief Mary Curnock Cook to say that "poor white males should now be the focus of outreach efforts", Ref.[2]. It will make no difference. She said much the same last year. Despite that, in replying to an FoI enquiry raised by J4MB, "*Does the DfE recognize boys' underachievement as a problem to be addressed, and if so, what initiatives are in place, and how much is budgeted for them in 2015/16?*" the Department for Education responded on 30th July 2015 thus, "*The Department does not fund any initiatives that just focus on addressing boys' underachievement*". The DfE have responded in essentially the same way to similar FoI queries several times since.

In 2015 the DfE also volunteered the information that, "*The DfE funds the Further Mathematics Support Programme and the Stimulating Physics Network...they do place some additional emphasis on addressing the low proportion of girls progressing to these A levels.*" Do note that, contrary to popular belief, women dominate as undergraduates in STEMM subjects (science, technology, engineering, maths, medicine and subjects applied to medicine). They have done so since 2015, and to an increasing degree each passing year. This is despite men dominating in technology, engineering and maths and because women dominate in science and in both medicine and subjects allied to medicine. And yet the political mind still insists on giving gender-specific assistance to girls in STEMM, and this skewed concern persists at university level with the operation of Athena Swan (see Ref.[6], section 2.8).

The fact that in 2015 the Education Secretary, Nicky Morgan, was also Minister for Women and Equalities would hardly help. Indeed, the fact that "Equalities" is elided with "Women" is the source of the problem (though entirely deliberate).

No doubt Nicky Morgan, as a good feminist, might expect that when boys are raised to be "confident feminists" this will make all the difference. Others may think that, since 7-year-old boys already expect to fail, what we have here is a case of low-expectations-breed-low-achievement, Ref.[[3]. From whom do these low expectations emanate? Surely not from society as a whole, Ref.[4]? A society which now regards, not merely young men, but specifically young *white* men as the most derided socio-ethnic group, Ref.[5].

(It's worth noting that the second most derided group were young Caribbean males. So the two most derided groups are also the two groups at the bottom of educational attainment, see chapter 28).

Next we turn to longevity. When it comes to disadvantage, being dead takes some beating – and dying is the one area in which male supremacy remains unchallenged. Substantially more males than females die in every age range from the tiniest babies to over 80-years-old, Ref.[6]. It is well-known that men's life expectancy is shorter than women's, the gap being some 3.7 years (UK wide). You might have expected this to be worth mentioning in a section on longevity and inequality. But no. Instead the report states only that,

"The gap in life expectancy between men and women narrowed in all three countries between 2007/09 and 2011/13, with the greatest decrease in Scotland."

It's almost as if the EHRC do not want to mention male disadvantages and so do their best to obfuscate them. And for an organisation so keen on intersectionality one might have thought that the intersection of "poor" and "male" might have provoked some comment in the context of longevity – the gender gap in life expectancy increasing in the lower socioeconomic strata. This also appears to have escaped the attention of the EHRC.

The report rightly raises the high rate of male suicide. But on the subject of effects of gender on health care we are told only that,

"A higher proportion of women than men in England reported having bad or very bad health."

This is a most peculiar statement given that the total number of deaths of males under 75 in 2013/14 exceeded that of females by 32,014 and 3,032 more men than women died of cancer, Ref.[6]. One might have thought this worth mentioning in a section on health care disadvantage, but no. Similarly the 110% excess male deaths due to cardiovascular diseases, Ref.[6], might have been thought pertinent here. Also, this section of the report would have been an ideal place to raise the disparity in research funding into gender-specific diseases. But no, none of those things were even hinted at.

Then we have the gender pay gap (oh God, here we go again). I refer you to Ref.[6] chapter 7, because any fewer than those 49 pages will not do justice to the issue. In particular, any discussion about the "pay gap" that does not take on board tax, pensions, hours worked and who spends more is perpetrating a constructive mendacity.

At this point the political nature of the so-called *Fairness* report is exposed most clearly. We read that, "*Women were less likely than men to be employed… Women were over-represented in part-time work*". But by what objective measure is this a disadvantage to women? British Social Attitudes surveys have revealed for decades that women would prefer looking after home and children, and working part-time or not at all, rather than going out to work full-time. Women with partners who earn enough generally have the choice. Their partners, in contrast, generally do not have a choice. They must work full-time in order to provide that choice to their female partners.

The presentation of women's working patterns as inequality or unfairness reflects only the political agenda behind the EHRC report, not an objective assessment of the population. Throughout most of my 37 years of full-time working, with no breaks at all, I worked around 55 hours per week compared with my wife's 12 hours per week. Was my wife disadvantaged? I don't think so – and nor did she. She often expressed it herself thus "one of us might as well be happy". It was a sentiment I was content to endorse, not least because the option of me being the happier one did not arise.

In the section on sexual violence the report stated simply,

"The UK has not ratified the Istanbul Convention on preventing and combating violence against women and domestic violence."

We have now (see chapter 23). But the so-called Istanbul Convention is the most egregious piece of sexism, a child of ten could see that. For those who have difficulty appreciating this sexism, try changing "women" to "white people", "men" to "black people" and "gender" to "race". Extracts from this Council of Europe convention then become,

"Protect white people against all forms of violence, and prevent, prosecute and eliminate violence against white people; design a comprehensive framework, policies and measures for the protection of and assistance to all victims of violence against white people; promote international co-operation with a view to eliminating violence against white people; provide support and assistance to organisations and law enforcement agencies to effectively co-operate in order to adopt an integrated approach to eliminating violence against white people."

and,

"Parties shall pay particular attention to white victims of race-based violence in implementing the provisions of this Convention."

and,

"Special measures that are necessary to prevent and protect white people from race-based violence shall not be considered discrimination under the terms of this Convention."

and,

"Parties shall take the necessary measures to encourage all members of society, especially black people, to contribute actively to preventing all forms of violence covered by the scope of this Convention (i.e., against whites)."

Nasty, isn't it? But the nastiest part is that, not only are adult men excluded from equal compassion in the event of being the victims of violence, but boys of however tender an age are also excluded.

Support for this vile Convention by the EHRC is totally incompatible with an organisation supposed to uphold either equality or human rights.

In the Section on child sexual abuse, the EHRC *Fairness* report states,

"A number of high profile independent inquiries have highlighted serious issues in relation to child sexual abuse and exploitation in England and Wales. These include: The Jay inquiry into child sexual exploitation in Rotherham (Jay, 2014), and the Serious Case Review into child sexual exploitation in Oxfordshire, concerning the grooming and abuse of vulnerable girls (Bedford, 2015)."

Either the authors haven't actually read these reports or they have deliberately obscured the victimisation of boys. They have reinforced the false impression that the press, and the BBC, have promulgated – that the victims were all girls. But at least 70 of the Rotherham victims were boys in 2007 alone, Ref.[8], and about 50 of the Oxfordshire victims, Ref.[9], were boys. The Jay report on Rotherham explicitly cautions against the very error which the EHRC makes in overlooking the boys. It stresses *"the importance of making sure that judgments about child sexual exploitation are consistent and gender neutral, for example by asking if the same level of risk would be acceptable if the child was the opposite gender"*.

Next up: prisons. There is no mention in the report of the 20:1 male:female ratio in prisons, nor that this ratio is due, in part, to the far harsher treatment meted out to men (see Ref.[6] chapter 8). This is not surprising since there is no public acknowledgement of the fact, despite it being obvious on perusing the sentencing data. But it is one of the more flagrant discriminations against men (or leniencies towards women) and its omission from the EHRC report further undermines its credibility.

The report rightly mentions the appalling suicide rate in prisons. What it does not mention is that these are almost all men. This would inevitably be the case even if the per capita rate of suicide amongst male and female prisoners were the same, simply due to the 20:1 ratio. But it isn't. The male per capita rate is worse. Despite the rate of male suicide in the population at large being a distressing 3 to 4 times that of females, the per capita rate of suicide amongst male prisoners is nearly six times higher still (so a male prisoner is at least 18 times more likely to kill himself than a free woman). There is no mention of these glaring gender disparities in the report. The EHRC simply does not want to highlight any male disadvantages. The entire report is an exercise in prejudice.

Lastly, but emphatically not least, there are many major issues which the report fails to recognise as issues at all. These include,

- the inequity of tolerating the practice of male genital mutilation in contrast to the (rightly) illegal status of female genital mutilation;
- the scandalously inequitable provisions for male victims of partner abuse compared with those for female victims (and, worse, the fact that statutory services still tend to disbelieve male victims);
- the deep-seated blindness of society to sexual victimisation of males, especially that of adult men by adult women;
- the gendered nature of homelessness;
- the *de facto* absence of a man's right to know if a child is biologically his, and the whole area of paternity rights – notable for their almost complete non-existence in practice;
- the operation of the family courts and the devastation they wreak commonly on fathers, sometimes on mothers, and always on the children. What about the inequality imposed on children raised without two live-in parents?

These things are, I know, the Wrong Sort of Equality.

References

[1] Equality and Human Rights Commission (2015). *Is Britain Fairer? The State of Equality and Human Rights 2015*. EHRC 30 October 2015.

[2] Coughlan, S. (2015). *Women take record number of university places*. BBC News, 17 December 2015.

[3] Hartley, B.L., and Sutton, R.M. (2013). *A Stereotype Threat Account of Boys' Academic Underachievement*. Child Development 84(5) 1716-1733, October 2013.

[4] Collins, N. (2013). *Boys 'worse at school due to stereotypes'*. The Telegraph, 12 February 2013.

[5] Kellner, P. (2015). *Introducing the most derided ethnic group in Britain: young white men*. YouGov, 14 December 2015.

[6] Collins, W. (2019). *The Empathy Gap*. LPS Publishing. (See chapter 3).

[7] Dugan, E. (2015). *Life expectancy in the UK: Wealthy men living longer than the average woman for the first time*. Independent, 21 October 2015.

[8] Jay, A. (2013). *Independent Inquiry into Child Sexual Exploitation in Rotherham 1997 – 2013*. 21 August 2014.

[9] Pettifor, T. (2015). *Oxfordshire child abuse: Authorities 'turned blind eye' as hundreds were abused by paedophile gangs*. Mirror, 3 March 2015.

32. Dear Nicky

In 2014 I wrote an open letter to Nicky Morgan, now Baroness Morgan of Cotes and then Secretary of State for Education and Minister for Women and Equalities. The context was her support for compulsory sex and relationship education (SRE) in schools. An equivalent missive today would have a whole lot more to condemn. Here I critique the lobbying in support of SRE by the End Violence Against Women and Girls Coalition (EVAWGC), which is a UK-wide coalition of more than 85 women's organisations focussed on VAWG and this includes FGM (female genital mutilation). I have updated several aspects of the article. Fortunately, the ultimate government guidance, when SRE was indeed made compulsory in schools in 2020, was not so one-sided as EVAWGC would have liked. There are, however, other issues with that guidance, and indeed the practice which followed, which raise different concerns beyond the scope of this piece.

Original posted on: 30 September 2014.

Dear Nicky,

Re: Your support for compulsory Sex and Relationship Education in schools.

The End Violence Against Women and Girls Coalition (EVAWGC) in Ref.[1] quotes you as saying, *"As both Secretary of State for Education and Minister for Women I am wholly committed to tackling violence against women and girls."*

As Secretary of State for Education you must surely be mindful that you have charge over an area in which the disadvantaged sex are boys and young men.

Forgive my asking, but are you not embarrassed to be the minister with a portfolio which explicitly acknowledges only disadvantage to females whilst also having the education remit, in which it is emphatically males that are disadvantaged?

Of course, it is not only in education that males are disadvantaged but in all walks of life – including many of those areas which are falsely considered the domain of female disadvantage alone.

(In the original article I continued by summarising boys' educational disadvantage, for which I now refer the reader to section 5 of this book or chapter 2 of *The Empathy Gap*, Ref.[4]).

As Secretary of State for Education, are you content with this situation?

If not, are you "wholly committed" to tackling it? If so, perhaps you have given some thought as to its cause? I hope this has gone beyond "it's the boys' own fault", for this fails to explain why it was not always thus. That boys start their primary schooling already expecting to fail, whilst girls start expecting to succeed might have something to do with it, don't you think? I recollect a suggestion in other contexts that societal expectations have substantial influence on educational attainment. Do you agree?

But instead of a positive campaign to encourage boys in school it appears that you are intent on adding to their difficulties. Ref.[1] begins, "*Following Rotherham…*" and quotes you as follows, "*Recent events have brought into sharp focus the crucial importance of teaching young people to understand the abuse women and girls can face.*"

Are you unaware that over 70 of the abused children in Rotherham were boys (Ref.[2]), or is it that you do not regard it as so "crucially important" to understand the abuse of boys? Perhaps it is because the very title of your office recognises only disadvantage to females? This is a pity in view of the "*relatively low reporting of sexual exploitation of young males*" (Ref.[2]). The Rotherham report is particularly critical of the high threshold adopted in the case of male victims as regards being recognised as at high risk and in need of social care – even when the boy had been raped. The report pointedly emphasises "*the importance of making sure that judgments about child sexual exploitation are consistent and gender neutral, for example by asking if the same level of risk would be acceptable if the child was the opposite gender*". Do you agree? If so, how is this consistent with espousing the explicitly gender-biased agenda promoted by the End Violence Against Women and Girls Coalition?

It appears that there is an intention, by both the EVAWGC and yourself, to lay the blame for Rotherham on all men. The fact that it is well-known that the perpetrators of the Rotherham abuses were from a very specific demographic, namely Pakistani-heritage Muslims, is to be ignored, it appears. The reason is easy to see. It is because it is politically problematical to even talk about the specific demographic without attracting the taint of racism or of belonging to the far-right. In contrast, blaming all men is perfectly consonant with the approved narrative. The actual problem is thereby ignored. It seems that serving the diktats of a certain agenda is more important than actually protecting working-class girls (let alone boys).

The report into the Rotherham abuses, Ref.[2], states that, "*Seminars for elected (council) members and senior officers in 2004-05 presented the abuse in the most explicit terms. After these events, nobody could say 'we didn't know'.....*

By far the majority of perpetrators were described as 'Asian' by victims, yet throughout the entire period, councillors did not engage directly with the Pakistani-heritage community to discuss how best they could jointly address the issue.....Several staff described their nervousness about identifying the ethnic origins of perpetrators for fear of being thought racist; others remembered clear direction from their managers not to do so."

This is what being "in care" means, it would appear – not being cared for at all. Even when, in two of the cases, fathers tracked down their daughters and tried to remove them from houses where they were being abused, they were arrested themselves.

The scandal of Rotherham is that political correctness prevented a known problem from being tackled, for many years. This is clearly conveyed by the report, Ref.[2], which states, "*frontline staff appeared to be confused as to what they were supposed to say and do and what would be interpreted as 'racist'. From a political perspective, the approach of avoiding public discussion of the issues was ill judged."* And also, "*Several councillors interviewed believed that by opening up these issues they could be 'giving oxygen' to racist perspectives that might in turn attract extremist political groups and threaten community cohesion."*

This is what happens when a particular demographic is given special protected status at the expense of another. Political correctness then distorts a proper sense of justice and compassion.

You appear to be intent on repeating this mistake in the context of gender.

What does EVAWGC advise the Minister for Women and Equalities? They fall back upon blaming their usual demographic of choice: the one that enjoys no protected status, the demographic which is uncomplicated by PC constraints, the demographic which no one will object to being blamed: all males. And in the case of schools, this means that all boys – of however tender an age – will have the guilt laid on their heads.

How convenient that this also aligns with the long-standing ideological agenda of the so-called 'experts' behind EVAWGC. In view of the number of boys amongst the abused, this is beyond unjust and into the realms of the obscene.

This agenda and ideological slant is summarised in EVAWGC's so-called Factsheet, Ref.[3]. This includes the advice to include material in school curricula "acknowledging the scale of violence against women and girls" and the need to "challenge notions of male sexual entitlement".

That males are substantially more often the victims of violence is indisputable, but unacknowledged in the Factsheet. This is true of all levels of violence, up to and including homicide. And just as men are the main victims of adult homicide, so the homicide of boys exceeds that of girls (see *The Empathy Gap*, Ref.[4], Figures 9.2 and 9.4 and Table 9.2). Feminists have scant interest in this except in one respect: they will happily remind us, correctly, that, outside the home, it is men who are the majority of perpetrators of this violence against other adult men. What this reveals is that feminists are not primarily interested in protecting victims at all; they are primarily interested in vilifying males.

Similarly, feminists never cease to remind us that the majority of domestic homicides of adults are women killed by men (though there is no shortage of the reverse, as chapter 19 demonstrates). The numbers, though, are small compared with homicides outside the home, hugely dominated by male victims. And very small indeed compared with suicide, of either sex.

But feminists are strangely quiet about the killing of children. The reason is simple: it does not play well with their agenda. Data from the UK, the USA and large international studies all show that parents are responsible for around 75% - 80% of child killing, and that mothers are responsible for the killing of children significantly more frequently than fathers (see *The Empathy Gap*, Ref.[4], section 9.2.7). This is true whether a single perpetrator is considered or joint perpetrators. This again demonstrates how the feminist mindset works. The motivation is not primarily concern for the victim, but the demonisation of males. The killing of children is not a suitable topic for that purpose.

Even confining attention to partner violence, which the EVAWGC Factsheet, Ref.[3], presents as exclusively the victimisation of women, in truth men are comparably often the victims of partner abuse, perpetrated by women (see *The Empathy Gap*, Ref.[4], section 9.2). This has been known for half a century but is denied for the same reason that the Rotherham abusers were not exposed: women, like Pakistani Muslims, are a demographic against which it is not politically correct to raise accusations.

A further purpose of the EVAWGC Factsheet was to *"unpick harmful stereotypes that place responsibility on girls to protect themselves from violence and abuse".* In view of the even greater victimisation of boys, it is worth considering whether it would be sensible or desirable to, *"unpick harmful stereotypes that place responsibility on boys to protect themselves from violence and abuse."* It would not be sensible or desirable to do so because boys have no choice other than to attempt to protect themselves – often in vain – since no one else is going to assist them – certainly not the authors of this appalling Factsheet with its unidirectional compassion.

In short, there is simply no rational basis for confining attention to "violence against women and girls", nor basing countermeasures on the presumption of male perpetration alone. The EVAWGC Factsheet is wilfully blind to half of human suffering, the motivation being ideological gender prejudice.

The Factsheet lists a range of other forms of abuse, every one of which is just as pertinent to male victimisation as to female – but this is not mentioned. I make just a few brief points as illustrations of the issues.

FGM is indeed an abomination which needs stamping out. But we live in a culture in which genital mutilation of boys is not merely tolerated but regarded as benign, even beneficial. The truth about male genital mutilation (MGM) is that it does, and was always intended to, result in diminished sexual function, see *The Empathy Gap*, Ref.[4], chapters 5 and 6, and Ref.[5]. In the West, MGM is invariably carried out on babies or children too young to give meaningful consent and is therefore a human rights violation – a fact which is being universally ignored. Circumcision of males is completely unregulated in the UK. Anyone – you, me or the local barber – can set up a business cutting off baby boys' foreskins (£100 was the going rate in 2014). Even in the USA, where the mutilations are generally carried out in clean conditions, boys do die each year from a procedure which is entirely unnecessary, see *The Empathy Gap*, Ref.[4], section 5.3.1.

And in Africa the situation is so bad as to defy comprehension. Adult men who have escaped the practice can be forcibly circumcised in the street by mobs formed for the purpose. In the Eastern Cape and Limpopo regions of South Africa alone, at least 419 boys died and more than 456,000 were hospitalised as a result of brutal genital mutilation over a 6-year period, Ref.[6]. Some people in the West think that ritual mutilations are a suitable subject for tourism, Ref.[7]. But well done to The Daily Mail for publishing the photographs in Ref.[8] which show the reality of MGM of small boys – albeit only from the waist up. If you want to see what it really looks like, search YouTube, though they have a habit of taking down the videos as being rather too much reality.

A further purpose of the EVAWGC Factsheet is to "challenge notions of male sexual entitlement". The presumption that there is a specifically male attitude of sexual entitlement is a political credo which is flatly contradicted by research data, for example Refs.[9-18]. These academic studies make clear that men are subject to unwanted sexual encounters, including intercourse, to a comparable degree as women. The past inaccurate perspective on male sexual victimisation has been largely a result of ingrained gender biases. For example, from a survey sample of 993, roughly equal numbers of men and women, Ref.[9] concludes that more men (62.7%) than women (46.3%) had experienced unwanted intercourse.

Ref.[12] was based on women's self-reported use of sexual aggression against men. The (female) authors concluded, "*Almost 1 in 10 respondents (9.3%) reported having used aggressive strategies to coerce a man into sexual activities. Exploitation of the man's incapacitated state was used most frequently (5.6%), followed by verbal pressure (3.2%) and physical force (2%). An additional 5.4% reported attempted acts of sexual aggression.*" Were the sexes treated equally in law, at least 7.6% of these women would effectively have admitted to being rapists.

Ref.[15] is a review of 42 research papers addressing the sexual coercion of both women and men. In virtually every case the level of sexual coercion against both men and women was remarkably high. Whilst that against women tended to be higher, that against men was comparable, ranging from 10% to 90% depending upon type (from rape at one end to unwanted sexual attention at the other). Virtually all of these behaviours were heterosexual. Women admitted indulging in sexual coercion at a prevalence of 16% to 43%. Women used physical force against men to achieve intercourse with a prevalence of 15% to 20%.

Ref.[16] reports that 43% of US high school boys have had an unwanted sexual experience, 95% with females.

Ref.[17] is based on incidence data on sexual victimisation over a 12-month period from five federal surveys in 2010 to 2012 in the USA. The authors conclude that, "*...surveys detect a high prevalence of sexual victimization among men - in many circumstances similar to the prevalence found among women...We recommend changes that move beyond regressive gender assumptions, which can harm both women and men.*"

The presumption of the EVAWGC Factsheet is an example of just such a "regressive gender assumption", namely that only men perpetrate sexual offences. It needs to be borne in mind that if men were treated equitably in law, "unwanted intercourse" would be rape.

The Factsheet states, "*Sexual violence is perpetrated overwhelmingly by men and boys against women and girls they know.*" Whilst the association of sexual assault and rape exclusively with female victims is in line with public perception, for this very reason any programme of education should be aimed at correcting this false belief. The essence of sexual offences in English law is consent, or rather lack of consent. And yet, in practice, the issue of consent in a heterosexual encounter is only ever questioned as regards whether the female consented. So ingrained is our cultural bias in sexual matters that even the notion that the consent of the male might be required appears quixotic.

Type of offence	Female victims	Male victims
Rape (completed) or Made to penetrate	0.5% to 0.7% (1.1% including attempts)	1.1%
Sexual coercion	2.0%	1.5%
Unwanted sexual contact	2.2%	2.3%
Non-contact unwanted sexual experiences	3.0%	2.7%

Table 32.1: From Ref.[18] tables 2.1 and 2.2 (percentages in 2010)

In some jurisdictions and offence categories, the skew between the sexes is given spurious legitimacy by focussing on "penetration". This introduces culpability based on who has the concave genitalia and who the convex genitalia. It appears to be based upon the assumption that convexity implies agency, and hence the consent of the possessor of the convex genitalia can be assumed. This is both psychologically and physiologically false. Hence, "being made to penetrate" should be interpreted as equivalent to non-consensual penetration. I would quote the comparable UK data but the corresponding surveys in this country are not sufficiently concerned about males to even ask the relevant questions.

Data from the USA revealed, at least as early as 2011, that males are coerced into penetrative sex with females against their wishes with comparable frequency to that in the reverse direction, see Table 32.1 based on Ref.[18]. And the long-term impact of childhood sexual abuse on boys is similar to that on girls, Ref.[19].

The Factsheet details the incidence of sexual violence against women and girls. But no consideration is given to that in the reverse direction. This merely reflects societal prejudice that male sexual victimisation by females does not happen. But "prejudice" is the right word here. There is a steadfast refusal by society as a whole to recognise male sexual victimisation by females because the very idea runs counter to perceived gender roles. The perception is that women and girls are precious and vulnerable, whereas men and boys are neither. This pernicious untruth is reinforced by the EVAWGC Factsheet and this is typical of feminist sources.

References

[1]   End Violence Against Women (2014a). *Education secretary Nicky Morgan backs new EVAW schools factsheet on VAWG*. 24 September 2014.

[2]   Jay, A. (2013). *Independent Inquiry into Child Sexual Exploitation in Rotherham 1997 – 2013*. 21 August 2014

[3]   End Violence Against Women (2014b). *Factsheet on VAWG for Schools (pdf)*. 7 October 2014.

[4]   Collins, W. (2019). *The Empathy Gap*. LPS Publishing, June 2019.

[5]   Leonard B Glick, *Marked in Your Flesh: Circumcision from Ancient Judea to Modern America*. Oxford University Press, 2005.

[6]   Gonzalez, L.L. (2014). *Over Half a Million Initiates Maimed under the Knife*. The South African Health News Service, 25 June 2014.

[7]   Fisher, A. (2016). *Tribal circumcision ritual becomes Africa's latest tourist attraction*. ABC News, 31 December 2016.

[8]   Pleasance, C. (2017). *Brace yourself, this might sting a bit*. Mail Online, 27 June 2017.

[9]   Muehlenhard, C., and Cook, S. (1988). *Men's self-reports of unwanted sexual activity*. Journal of Sex Research **24**, 58-72, 1988.

[10]   Struckman-Johnson, C. (1988). *Forced sex on dates: It happens to men, too*. Journal of Sex Research, 24, 1988, 234-241.

[11]   Coxell, A., et al (1999). *Lifetime prevalence, characteristics, and associated problems of non-consensual sex in men: cross sectional survey*. British Medical Journal, **318**, 846-850 (March 1999)

[12]   Krahe, B. et al (2003). *Women's sexual aggression against men: prevalence and predictors*. Sex Roles 49, 219–232 (2003).

[13]   Philip Cook and Tammy Hodo, *When Women Sexually Abuse Men: The hidden side of rape, stalking, harassment and sexual assault*. Praeger, Oxford, 2013.

[14]   Hines, D.A. (2007). *Predictors of sexual coercion against women and men: a multilevel, multinational study of university students*. Arch Sex Behav. 36(3):403-22, 2007.

[15]   Fiebert, M.S. *References Examining Men as Victims of Women's Sexual Coercion*. Sexuality and Culture 4, 81–88 (September 2000)

[16]   French, B.H. et al (2014). *Sexual Coercion Context and Psychosocial Correlates Among Diverse Males*. Psychology of Men & Masculinity, 17 March 2014.

[17]   Stemple, L., and Meyer, I.H. (2014). *The sexual victimization of men in America: New data challenge old assumptions*. American Journal of Public Health, E1-E8 (2014) 301946.

[18]   Black, M.C., et al (2011), *National Intimate Partner and Sexual Violence Survey (NISVS) 2010 Summary Report*. National Center for Injury Prevention and Control, Centers for Disease Control and Prevention, November 2011.

[19]   Dube, S.R. et al (2005). Long-Term Consequences of Childhood Sexual Abuse by Gender of Victim. American Journal of Preventive Medicine 28, 430-438, 2005.

33. The WASPIs and Female Entitlement

For many decades in the UK the State Pension Age (SPA) for men was 65 whilst for women it was 60. Moreover, men had to pay five more years than women into National Insurance before getting the full pension. The shorter life expectancy of men coupled with a later retirement age meant that, in the 1960s, even men who lived to retire could expect to draw the pension for only half the number of years as the average woman, despite having paid substantially more into the system. The government's decision to end this pension inequality was, undoubtedly, driven more by the desire to save money than any concern about unfairness. Nevertheless, to end it was right. Accordingly, the SPA for women was gradually raised from 60 to 65 over a nine-year period between 2010 and 2018. Hence it took nine years to reach equality. By then the SPA for men was scheduled to increase to 66 and so too was the SPA for woman, both reaching 66 in 2019/20. To anyone whose psychology was not steeped in the necessity of female preferencing this change was inevitable and fully justified. To the WASPIs (Women Against State Pension Inequality) it was injustice.

Original posted on: 26 November 2019.

"I'll scream and scream 'til I'm sick!", quoth Violet Elizabeth, William Brown's tiny nemesis (see chapter 57). It seems that strategy for getting one's own way is still favoured in some quarters.

The September 2019 News Briefing published by UK charity Parity, Ref.[1], reported on the failure of the "Back to 60" campaign's judicial review. This group of women had sought redress for what they claimed was unfair treatment in the raising of the State Pension Age (SPA) for women from 60 towards equalisation with men. The WASPIs (Women Against State Pension Inequality) are a similar group campaigning for compensation to be given to women born in the 1950s. The exact arguments and objectives of the WASPIs have morphed over time, Ref.[2]. The latest incarnation of their claim centres around inadequate warning given to these "1950s women" about the SPA increases.

Despite this claim being emphatically rejected - not only by government, Ref.[3], but also by judicial review , Refs.[3,4] - in the 2019 election campaign then-leader of the Labour Party, Jeremy Corbyn, committed to giving the WASPIs what they were asking for, calling it a "moral debt". Some sources put the cost as high as £58 billion, Ref.[5]. The reader may think that this is just another instance of bribing people for votes, I couldn't possibly comment.

Let us leave aside that men have had a later SPA than women for many decades prior to last year. Let us leave aside that, even with the same SPA, men will typically enjoy fewer years of retirement due to shorter longevity (a life-gap of 3.6 years on average). Let us instead examine whether the specific WASPI claim of inadequate warning about SPA increases is valid, and if so, if it is particular to women.

Chapter and verse on the time-line of changes in SPA can be found in Ref.[3]. This timeline is nicely summarised by Figure 33.1, taken from Ref.[6].

Figure 1 – State Pension Ages, 2010-36

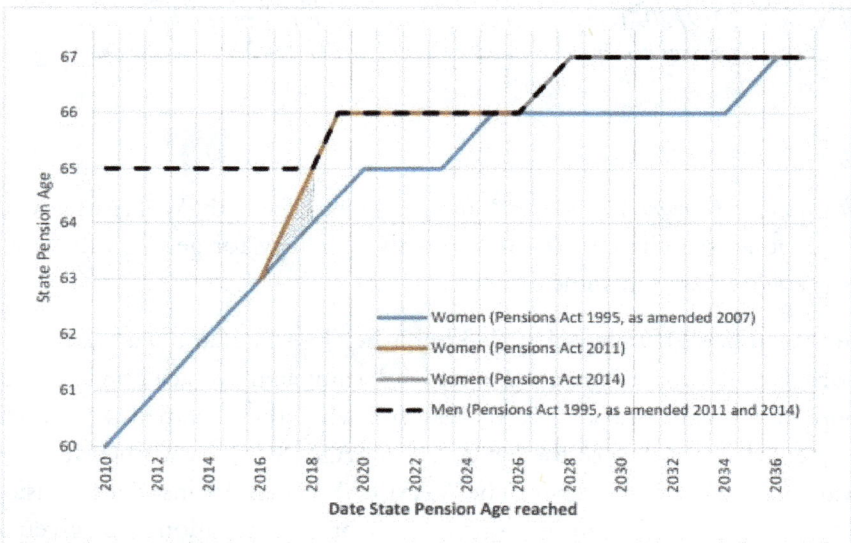

Figure 33.1: Changes in SPA over time by sex (taken from Ref.[6])

The 1995 Pensions Act was the first to recognise equalisation of the SPA for men and women as the objective, and undertook to raise the SPA for women from 60 to 65 in a phased manner starting in 2010 and completing that process by 2020. Hence women had between 15 and 25 years warning of the intended SPA increase in 1995.

As Brexit was also topical (in 2019, the date of the original post), it is worth noting that this 1995 legislation was, in part, a result of EU pressure. The ruling by the European Court of Justice in 1986 that the UK's gendered approach to retirement ages was incompatible with the 1976 European Commission's Equal Treatment Directive required 'progressive implementation' of equalisation of pension rights. Ironically, this landmark European Court ruling related to a case brought against HM Government by a woman. She had complained that the Area Health Authority for which she worked required her to retire at the age of 60, despite her desire to go on working. (Just when you thought it was the EU being nice to men, eh? Not at all, just a good illustration that the globalists' advocacy of "women's rights" is actually a cover for getting women working more hours).

In 2007 the (Labour) government first instigated a planned rise in SPA, for both sexes, first to 66 by 2024 and then to 67 by 2036, and then to 68 by 2046.

This was superseded in 2011 by the (Con-Lib Coalition) government which made two changes to the timetable. It accelerated the final phase of the equilibrating of the SPA for the sexes by accomplishing the increase in women's SPA from 63 to 65 between 2016 and 2018 rather than between 2016 and 2020, i.e., bringing its completion forward by two years. But the 2011 Pensions Act also brought forward achieving the SPA of 66, for both sexes, from 2024 to 2019. Hence, this change was brought forward by 5 years and was to be implemented in a single year, 2018.

Figure 33.1 is the clearest depiction of all this.

The women most severely impacted by the 2011 changes are those who turned 64 in 2018 who might have expected to receive their state pension that year, but will now have to wait two more years, receiving their pension at age 66 in 2020 (along with men of the same age). Note that the greatest impact is a two-year delay, not five years. These most impacted women therefore had 7 years warning that they would not receive their pension in 2018 (the changes having been enacted, recall, in 2011). Is this not reasonable warning?

In any case, men were in a similar position. A man turning 65 in 2018 would have expected to draw his pension that year, but the same 2011 Act meant that he would have to wait another year until he was 66 to do so. Such men also had the very same 7 years warning of this change. This is sufficient to obliterate the WASPI's claim – unless the same claim of inadequate warning were to be made also for men. But the WASPIs were blind to the position of men, as these entitled sort of women always are.

[As it happens, the author is a case in point. I turned 65 in the year this article was posted but did not get my state pension until the following year. However, there is no WASPI campaign for me, I note – not that I want one].

If the 2011 Act were implemented for men – but the situation for women remained as it was in 2007 under the Labour government – Figure 1 shows that equalisation of the pension age for the two sexes would have been pushed out to year 2036. This illustrates graphically how fraudulent is the WASPI claim to be based on "equality". It is actually inspired by "women's equality", which by now we all know is code for preferencing.

Having started by ignoring the starkly obvious state pension inequality which has prevailed for decades prior to last year, namely that to men's disadvantage, it is perhaps relevant to note that it is men who continue to pump the overwhelming bulk of the monies into the exchequer which pays for pensions, and indeed all public expenditure. The taxation, benefits and pensions systems form a mechanism for the transfer of money from men to women. That is the rather large elephant which goes unnoticed.

This raises another, and more egregious, pension inequality: that between the public and private sectors. The disparity between the two is now quite obscene as the public sector continues to live in a never-never land of unfunded "defined benefit" Ponzi pension schemes, underwritten by the taxpayer, Refs.[7,8]. With twice as many women as men in the public sector, this is another aspect of the men-to-women money syphon. But this one is unsustainable, and public sector workers are in for a shock as inevitable as arithmetic.

And finally, all this highlights yet another genuine equality issue: that between the generations. Just as all government promises, funded by borrowing or taxation, are a burden upon the younger generations, so the WASPI claim is also. I doubt that Corbyn would have delivered on his promise, even had he become Prime Minister. But if he had, even the most cursory attention to balancing the books would require passing the bill onto younger people, of both sexes, in the form of further accelerations in SPA increases.

Added in proof: On 21 March 2024 it was announced that the Parliamentary and Health Service Ombudsman (PHSO) has found that women born in the 1950s *"may have been affected by DWP's failure to adequately inform them that the State Pension age had changed"*. The Ombudsman claimed that *"the DWP's handling of* the changes meant some women lost opportunities to make informed decisions about their finances. It diminished their sense of personal autonomy and financial control". The announcement also states that "*to date, DWP has not acknowledged its failings nor put things right for those women affected. DWP has also failed to offer any apology or explanation for its failings and has indicated it will not compensate women affected by its failure*". The PHSO Chief Executive is Rebecca Hilsenrath who was previously the CEO of the EHRC – enough said? (See chapter 31).

References

[1] Parity (2019). *Parity News Briefing – September 2019*. Published by the UK charity, Parity.

[2] Coppola, F. (2016). *The WASPI campaign's unreasonable demand*. Coppola Comment blog, 31 July 2016.

[3] UK parliament (2021). *Research Briefing: Increases in the State Pension age for women born in the 1950s*. House of Commons Library, 19 November, 2021.

[4] Courts and Tribunals Judiciary (2019). *R (on the application of Julie Delve and Karen Glynn) -v- the Secretary of State for Work and Pensions*. High Court of Justice, Queen's Bench Division, 3 October 2019.

[5] Bartlett, N. (2019). *Jeremy Corbyn says WASPI women payout is a 'moral debt' owed by Britain*. Mirror, 26 November 2019.

[6] Pemberton, H. (2017). *WASPI's is (mostly) a campaign for inequality*. Political Quarterly, 88(3), 510-516.

[7] TaxPayers' Alliance (2018). *Pensions Inequality*. 27 August 2018.

[8] Collins, W. (2019). *The Empathy Gap (section 7.9.1)*. LPS Publishing, June 2019.

[9] Parliamentary and Health Service Ombudsman (2024). DWP failed to adequately communicate changes to Women's State Pension age. 21 March 2024.

34. Women Trump Children

In June 2022 the overturning by the Supreme Court of 1973's Roe v Wade ruling in the USA reignited the abortion debate in that country. In truth, the debate had never cooled much in the USA which has always retained a strong pro-life lobby. In contrast, there is no public debate on abortion in the UK. It lies well outside the Overton Window and hence falls to social pariahs like MRAs or (real) Christians to make the case for the most vulnerable imaginable.

Original posted on: 1 February 2019.

Introduction / Evolution

So-called "men's rights" are not really just about men's rights but also about children's rights and about societal health. It has been apparent for some time that feminists set women ahead of children. I thought I couldn't get any more implacably opposed to feminism. It seems I was wrong.

Let me remind you of the evolutionary origin of our difficulties. The preferencing of women (call it chivalry, call it matricentrism or gynocentrism, call it the empathy gap, call it gamma bias, call it what you will) has its origin in the pair-bond, a key *Homo sapiens* adaptation, one of the keys to the overwhelming success of the species. In this regard, women – as mothers – are a proxy for children. Evolution cares only for reproductive success, which is manifest in children and their survival to reproductive age. When women's primary concern was the domestic, they functioned as a suitable proxy for children. What was beneficial for the mother could be assumed to also be beneficial for the child.

But in respect of women in a non-domestic role, such as in the external workplace, their preferencing is an anomaly: such preferencing is not conducive to evolutionary success. Indeed, in as far as it diminishes the birth rate (as it has), it is counter-evolutionary. And when it comes to killing babies, there can be no clearer departure from an evolutionary optimum: no clearer indication that feminism has subverted and invalidated the proxy status of women.

Background: Women Before Children

Where I'm heading in this chapter is abortion, and, in particular, the moves to permit abortion without time limit. But first, a brief reminder of how feminism has been putting women's rights ahead of children's rights for decades. This has long been apparent in the context of the safeguarding of children. This arises in the context of custody/contact after parental separation. For example, Karen Woodall, Ref.[1], wrote,

"For four decades since the change in divorce laws, the needs of women in the family have usurped the needs of children…"

More seriously still, the same focus on mothers to the exclusion of their children also occurs when social services are actively involved in a dysfunctional family. Here is Woodall again, writing in 2013, Ref.[2], the emphasis is in the original,

"The reports of Filicide, the murder by a mother of her child, are all over the news this week. Baby P, Daniel Pelka, Hamzah Khan, Keanu Williams being just four names that are engraved upon our consciousness, not just because of their untimely deaths, but because of the nature of the suffering inflicted upon them before they died.

Collective handwringing is in evidence up and down the land and who is to blame is being widely discussed. The sight of the Head of Birmingham Children's Safeguarding Board attempting to squirm out of the reality of her responsibility for allowing yet another death of a child to happen on her watch, was excruciating on the BBC news last night. Her words, in a statement released this week scream out the reality of why children are dying,

'I wish, on behalf of all the statutory agencies who sit on the Board to express very deep regret and distress about Keanu's death. We apologise unequivocally for what were totally unacceptable and unnecessary failures both collectively and individually in every organisation which had contact with Keanu. We fully accept all the findings of the Serious Case Review and the recommendations made.

*Keanu died because there was failure across every agency to see, hear and respond to him in the context of what he was experiencing at any one point in time. **Staff were distracted by his mother's needs and by taking what she was telling them at face value.'** "*

Woodall continues, *"**Staff were distracted by his mother's needs and by taking what she was telling them at face value!** In other words, a systemic use of gender biased practice which focuses practitioners not on the needs of children, but on the rights and needs of women. If ever there was proof needed that social work and our children and family services are, as a very senior social worker said recently, a 'feminist industry', this is it. Gender biased family services, upholding the rights and needs of women* *above those of children, are killing those children in a neighbourhood near you and until we name it, we are never going to stop it.*"

The four cases named above are not isolated. Ignoring the danger to children posed by mothers is an endemic problem. This was further exposed in a November 2017 report from the Children and Family Court Advisory and Support Service (Cafcass), Ref.[3]. This report derives lessons to be learnt from the 97 Serious Case Reviews (SCRs) to which Cafcass contributed between 2009 and 2016. These SCRs involved known or suspected abuse or neglect of a child where the child died or was seriously harmed. The key findings were,

- Both this study, and the Triennial Review, found that equal numbers of fathers and mothers are responsible for deliberate (child) homicides;

- Allegations of domestic abuse had been made in 71% of cases, and almost all allegations of domestic abuse were against men, or included men, usually fathers;

- Of those cases where domestic abuse allegations had been made, only in about half of the cases was the person thought to have killed or harmed the child the alleged domestic abuse perpetrator;

- In some cases, the authorities' concentration on the alleged risk posed by the father or male partner may have masked a greater risk posed by the mother. Quote, *'In some cases where index incidents were perpetrated by the mother, SCRs found that the mother's history had not been sufficiently analysed, concerns about her being overshadowed by concerns about the father or other male. It is interesting to note that such SCRs do not show a simple relationship between male domestic abuse and the fatal / serious maltreatment of children.'*

One might have hoped that after a sequence of very high-profile cases, the acknowledgement of the issue by Cafcass, and repeated assurances that "lessons would be learnt" that lessons would indeed be learnt. But no. To think that lessons would be learnt is to underestimate the depth of resistance that exists within the social services and other authorities to the notion that mothers, too, can pose a risk to their children – not just men.

As Karen Woodall has identified, the root cause of the problem in acknowledging the potential risk to children from women is that the mother's wellbeing is actually being placed ahead of that of the children. To demonstrate that lessons have not been learnt, consider the London Safeguarding Children Board (and I expect much the same will hold for other Safeguarding Children Boards). Their advice on safeguarding children affected by domestic abuse, Ref.[4], runs to 58 pages and over 18,000 words. In all those 58 pages there is not even a hint that mothers might pose a risk to their children. Bear in mind this advice was still current in 2019, six years after the promise that "lessons would be learnt". The advice is entirely based on the assumption that the danger, to both mother and children, is from the father or male partner. For example, the primary purpose of the advice is,

- *"To support <u>the mother</u> to assist her to protect herself and the children; and,*
- *To hold the abusive partner accountable for the violence and provide <u>him</u> with opportunities to change."* (My emphasis)

Symptoms of abuse uniformly assume a male perpetrator and include, for example,

i. *"...controlling who the mother or children see or where they go, what they wear or do, stalking, imprisonment, forced marriage;*

ii. *...the severity of the violence against the mother is predictive of the severity of abuse to the children;*

iii. *The child being abused as part of the abuse against the mother:*

iv. *The children are often reliant on their mother as the only source of good parenting, as the abusive partner will have significantly diminished ability to parent well."*

Note how *ii* and *iii* are directly contradicted by the 2017 Cafcass findings, Ref.[3], and yet these same empirically false claims continue to be made, decade after decade, despite their acknowledged contribution to the deaths of children.

One needs to imagine this sort of stuff continuing over 58 pages. Where there is an oblique nod to a potential for mother's culpability, the blame is redirected at the nearest man, the mother having no recognised capacity for reprehensible agency, for example,

- *"Being forced to participate in the abuse and degradation by the abusive partner"*.

Since drugs and alcohol play major roles in domestic abuse, any culpability of a mother who so indulges is also explicitly deflected to the nearest man,

- *"Mothers may have started using legal drugs prescribed to alleviate symptoms of a violent relationship. Mothers may turn to alcohol and drugs as a form of self-medication and relief from the pain, fear, isolation and guilt that are associated with domestic abuse. Alcohol and drug use can help eliminate or reduce these feelings and therefore become part of how she copes with the abuse.*
- *Mothers can be coerced and manipulated into alcohol and drug use. Abusers may often introduce their partner to alcohol or drug use to increase her dependence on him and to control her behaviour."*

None of this has any empirical basis. It is made up. It stems from a determination that women must never be held responsible – for anything, either child abuse or their own drug abuse. It is prejudice. And it is prejudice which results in child abuse and death. And this is in official advice on child safeguarding.

The reality is that mothers are at least as likely to perpetrate child abuse as men, including being responsible for child deaths. My own article *332 Child Homicides*, Ref.[5], concluded that, where culpability was established, the mother was the lone perpetrator in 36% of cases and either a lone or a co-perpetrator in over half of cases (58%).

But there is a steadfast refusal – as evidenced by the Child Safeguarding Boards – to acknowledge that women are not all angels, and, in fact, are no better than men. The price for this conceit is paid by children, whom the so-called Safeguarding Boards prefer not to safeguard if it means knocking women off their pedestals. But off their pedestals they must go, or this perversion of morality will only worsen. It already is doing.

And this brings me to the latest horror in the abortion saga.

Abortion Without Time Limit

Unlike many within the men's movement, I was never against abortion – before. I could not go along with the Catholics, or many other Christians, who maintained that even a zygote is a sacred life. I was of the view that abortion, within some time limit, is the lesser evil compared to bringing an unwanted child into the world. To me, the issue was viability. If the embryo is not viable outside the uterus, then abortion could be tolerated, though regrettable. The current 24-week limit (in Great Britain) could, admittedly, do with review, since a 24-week-old foetus can be viable with modern medical technology. So the time limit needs revising down.

But in January 2019, New York state passed a law allowing abortions without a time limit, Ref.[6]. This breaks new ground, though it is an objective which feminists have been pursuing for a long time, in the UK as well as the USA and elsewhere, Ref.[7]. In May 2016, the Royal College of Midwives announced their decision to support a campaign to scrap the time limit on abortion and sweep away all current legal restrictions, Ref.[8]. Thankfully, there was a storm of protest, both from rank-and-file midwives and also MPs. It appeared that the Royal College's chief executive, Cathy Warwick, had "ridden roughshod" over majority opinion. The new law proved more popular in New York, where the passing of the Act was greeted with an "eruption of applause" in the Senate, Ref.[9].

The ethical disintegration in the USA is not confined to New York. A Bill in Virginia, proposed by Fairfax County's Kathy Tran, Ref.[10], was headlined to permit abortion up to birth. There was initially a suggestion that her Bill would permit "abortion" even after the women in question had already gone into labour, but she later retracted any remark to that effect.

The so-called "moderate" Democratic Virginia Governor, Ralph Northam, deepened controversy by suggesting that the baby in question might be born, alive, but then killed subject to the mother's wish and agreement by two doctors. To be accurate, in the video recording of this statement, Ref.[11], Northam alluded to the foetus being severely deformed and perhaps non-viable. He also suggested the baby, once born, might be resuscitated, if necessary, before a discussion between the mother and doctors took place. He does not say what this discussion would be about, but the context implies it would be a discussion regarding whether the baby should be dispatched if the mother so wished.

Kathy Tran's Bill did not get passed by the State legislature. But the attempt proves what is in the mind of some influential actors, and hence what is likely to recur. The Bill would not have made late abortion, even at the point of delivery, conditional upon non-viability, or even any problem at all with the baby. Instead either severe foetal abnormality or a claimed adverse impact on the mother's health would suffice to justify the killing. And what would constitute a challenge to the mother's health? Answer, *"all factors – physical, emotional, psychological, familial, and the woman's age – relevant to the wellbeing of the patient"*

We need look no further than our own law of abortion in Great Britain to expose the paper-thin fraudulence of this pretence at protection. This would actually be abortion on demand, without time limit.

Here is the existing law in Great Britain according to the Abortion Act 1967. Abortion is legal in Britain up to 24 weeks if either of the following holds: (a) continuance of the pregnancy risks injury to the physical or mental health of the pregnant woman or any existing children of her family; or, (b) there is a substantial risk that if the child were born it would suffer from such physical or mental abnormalities as to be seriously handicapped. After 24 weeks abortion is legal only if there is a substantial risk to the woman's life or there are serious risks of foetal abnormalities.

In 2017 there were 197,533 abortions in England & Wales. Only 1.68% (3,314) of these were due to "the risk that the child would be born seriously handicapped", Ref.[12]. Hence, over 98% of abortions (194,219 in 2017) are carried out ostensibly due to the risk to the physical or mental health of the women. How credible is this? In fact Ref.[12] states that 98% of abortions were carried out "under Ground C" and that "ground C abortions have consistently accounted for over 97% of abortions over the last 10 years". It goes on to clarify,

"The vast majority (99.4%) of abortions carried out under ground C alone were reported as being performed because of a risk to the woman's mental health. These were classified as F99 (mental disorder, not otherwise specified) under the International Classification of Disease version 10 (ICD-10) and therefore no further breakdown is possible within the report."

In 2017 there were 679,100 live births in England & Wales. Had the 194,219 babies been permitted to be born, we are being asked to believe that 22% of the total births would have resulted in harm to the mother serious enough to motivate the abortion. In reality the actual implied percentage would be far bigger because this would imply that quite a sizeable proportion of the 679,100 babies actually born would cause their mothers harm too.

For comparison, just 0.008% of mothers die in childbirth in the UK, Ref.[13].

And just 0.4% of babies are stillborn or subject to natural foetal death in utero, Ref.[14].

In truth it is clear that ideological sympathy for "a woman's right to choose" leads practitioners to interpret frustrating the mother's wish for an abortion as a challenge to her mental health. The issue of harm to the mother is really a ruse, a subterfuge. The existing British law is, *de facto*, abortion on demand before 24 weeks.

The NHS makes abortion on demand unambiguous. In their guidance on the conditions applying to abortion, the NHS makes no mention whatsoever that there are supposed to be medical grounds to justify it. Instead the NHS states bluntly, Ref.[15],

"The decision to have an abortion is yours alone"

"Some women may be certain they want to have an abortion, while others may find it more difficult to make a decision".

There is no mention of the two GPs who are supposed to sanction the abortion based on one of the grounds stated above. The NHS's statement is therefore *de jure* false, though perfectly accurate *de facto*.

A few years ago the NHS guidance used to add, *"you may also want to speak to your partner, friends or family, but you don't need to discuss it with anyone else and they don't have a say in the final decision"*. But all mention of the father (never referred to using that term) has now been removed.

The NHS add,

"If you're under 16, your parents do not usually need to be told. The doctor or nurse may encourage you to tell a parent, carer or other adult you trust, but they will not make you. There are organisations, usually known as crisis pregnancy centres, that offer counselling around pregnancy. They do not refer people for abortion, and may not offer balanced or accurate advice."

So, we should not be fooled by the new law in New York, or that which was proposed in Virginia, as regards the medical proviso. That is a mere sop. What these laws will be, in reality, is abortion on demand without time limit, and even up to, including and beyond the point of labour.

This is murder.

This is no longer a matter of opinion.

There is no functional difference between a baby which is just days, or a few weeks, from full term and a newborn baby. The only difference is their location in space.

Feminist moral corruption and self-aggrandisement have now reached the point at which they present women as deities who may decide life and death over others. They need to be stopped.

References

[1] Woodall, K. (2019). *Digging up the Feminist Past to Develop a Family Focussed Future.* Karen Woodall blog, 27 January 2019.

[2] Woodall, K. (2013). *Gender Biased Family Services: Killing Children in the UK*. Karen Woodall blog, 4 October 2013.

[3] Green, R., and Halliday, E. (2017). *Learning from Cafcass submissions to Serious Case Reviews*. Cafcass, June 2017 (This version of the report has been adapted for sharing with external agencies, and case examples have been anonymised to protect identities, November 2017).

[4] London Child Protection Procedures (2017). *Chapter 28. Safeguarding children affected by domestic abuse. 5th edition, 2017*. (This version captured February 2019).

[5] Collins, W. (2017). *332 Child Homicides*. The Illustrated Empathy Gap, 3 February 2017.

[6] O'Kane, C. (2019). *New York passes law allowing abortions at any time if mother's health is at risk*. CBS News, 24 January 2019.

[7] Valenti, J. (2014). *There is absolutely no reason to restrict women's options for abortion access*. The Guardian, 6 May 2014.

[8] Bingham, J. (2016). *Abortion is part of our calling, says Royal College of Midwives chief Cathy Warwick*. The Telegraph, 20 May 2016.

[9] Maule, W. (2019). *New York Senate Erupts in Applause After Passing Horrific Late-Term Abortion Bill*. Faithwire, 23 January 2019.

[10] McBride, J. (2019). *Kathy Tran: 5 Fast Facts You Need to Know*. Heavy, 30 January 2019.

[11] Allahpundit (2019). *"Moderate" Dem Virginia governor: Our new late-term abortion bill would allow babies to be killed ... after they're born; Update: Northam responds*. Hot Air, 30 January 2019.

[12] Department of Health and Social Care (2018). *Abortion Statistics, England and Wales: 2017*. June 2018, revised December 2018.

[13] The Guardian Datablog (2010). *Maternal mortality: how many women die in childbirth in your country?* 12 April 2010.

[14] Office for National Statistics (2021). *Births and infant mortality by ethnicity in England and Wales: 2007 to 2019*. Dataset release 26 May 2021.

[15] NHS (2020). *Overview: Abortion*. 24 April 2020.

Section 7

Health
& Death

35. Covid-19 and Female Leaders

Readers will recall that covid-19 did not cause any cessation in feminist propaganda. On the contrary it merely provided another context in which to claim that women were both more victimised and also generally superior. It was bleakly amusing to witness how the feminist mind could continue to assert, without embarrassment, that the pandemic was worse for women despite it being clear from the start that the disease was more deadly for men. In June 2020 a 'study' appeared which purported to show that women-led countries performed better in covid-19 outcomes. In August 2020 I deconstructed the claims of the paper and showed them to be invalid – even with the data available at that time.

I have retained the data from the original post though I have shortened the presentation and details. I have resisted the temptation to update the analysis using the far greater volume of data that became available later. That would be to miss the point, which is that even with the data available at the time the claims being made were erroneous. But it is worth bearing in mind that the UK had experienced only its first wave of covid-19 in August 2020, and many parts of the world had yet to experience their worst waves of the disease. It would be of interest to repeat the analysis now – though if I did I would be far more interested in the implied efficacy of lockdowns, or lack thereof, than the sex of the political leadership.

Original posted on: 20 August 2020.

When the feminists are not busy vilifying men and presenting women as their perpetual victims, they are indulging in self-glorification instead.

On 19 August 2020 The Guardian ran a story titled, *"Female-led countries handled coronavirus better, study suggests"*, Ref.[1]. They linked to a study by Supriya Garikipati and Uma Kambhampati at the universities of Liverpool and Reading respectively, Ref.[2]. Both have PhDs in economics from Cambridge.

The Guardian describes the study as "published by the Centre for Economic Policy Research and the World Economic Forum", which I interpret as meaning those bodies funded the work. At the time of The Guardian article, and my own blog piece, the study had appeared on the SSRN (Social Science Research Network) preprint repository. Since then it has been published by Feminist Economics, see Ref.[2]. The conclusions of the study claim that,

"Our findings show that covid-outcomes are systematically and significantly better in countries led by women and, to some extent, this may be explained by the proactive policy responses they adopted. Even accounting for institutional context and other controls, being woman-led has provided countries with an advantage in the current crisis.

The original preprint also concluded that "…*the gender of leadership could well have been key in the current context where attitudes to risk and empathy mattered as did clear and decisive communications……women leaders seem to have emerged highly successful.*" The published paper includes closing sections which read as a paean to female superiority in leadership.

The Guardian article included the graphic reproduced here as Figure 35.1,

Reported Covid-19 deaths in countries led by women were lower than those led by men

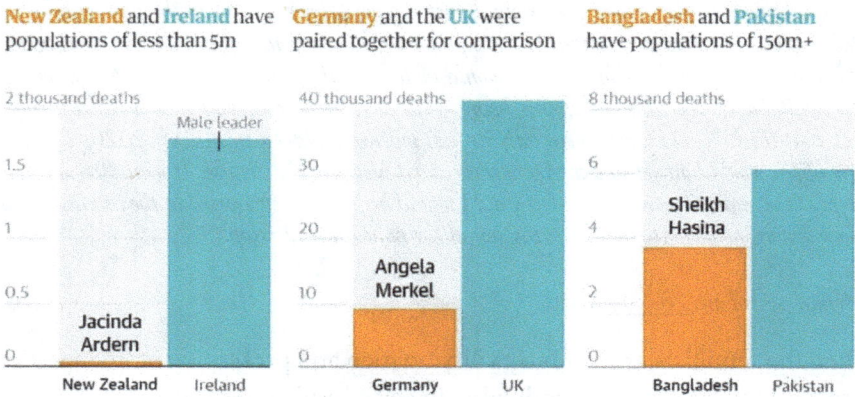

Guardian graphic. Johns Hopkins University. Numbers rely on public data from multiple sources (data correct to 17 August 2020). Note: Researchers created 'nearest neighbour' countries to offset the small sample size, pairing countries with similar characteristics

Figure 35.1: From Ref.[1]

It is not that the authors' geography has gone so awry as to believe that New Zealand and Ireland are literally 'nearest neighbours' – the term is used in a different sense, see below. (I shall resist the temptation to elaborate on how badly Jacinda Arden's and Angela Merkel's halos have tarnished since the summer of 2020).

I am rather proud of having had the insight in August 2020 to write: "I have been keeping well away from covid-19 statistics in general, other than the occasional reminder to the wilfully obtuse that male mortality is roughly double that for women. There are a number of reasons for my reticence in getting involved in covid stats, one being that we have yet to see if the statistics at present bear any relationship to the final out-turn in, say, a year or two's time. Draconian lockdowns now may mean more deaths later – who knows. Another reason is that I have been sceptical about the value of the statistics, both of the numbers of cases and the numbers of deaths."

However, I couldn't let Garikipati and Kambhampati's study pass without examination, as I'm sure you will appreciate. I have analysed the data myself. As a by-product I find my previous scepticism in respect of the data to be justified.

In common with Garikipati and Kambhampati I take the covid-19 data from Worldometer, Ref.[3]. Specifically, I took the data as they were on 19 August 2020. Garikipati and Kambhampati's data extended only up to 19 May 2020, some three months fewer data than I have used. In both cases the data refer to cumulative quantities, i.e., cases, tests and deaths up to the date specified above.

Worldometer issues due warnings about the data. Data for total cases in a given country refer to the sum of confirmed cases and those that are merely suspected. However, as testing covers only a fraction, generally a tiny fraction, of populations, Worldometer warn that *"most estimates have put the number of undetected cases at several multiples of detected cases"*. In other words, no one really knew how many people had been infected with the virus in any given country (with a very few exceptions).

Total deaths are defined simply as the cumulative number of deaths among "detected" cases (noting that "detected" might mean a positive test result, or merely a suspected case). Hence the death data could be wildly too small or wildly too large. Since the death data is drawn only from detected cases, and since it is acknowledged that the number of people infected is probably "several multiples" larger, that potentially biases the death data down by a substantial factor. However, one might argue that this is less important than it appears because, where deaths occur, the case is likely to be counted as "detected". In other words, those instances of infection which are not "detected" are likely to have extremely low mortality rates. Instead the death data may be over-estimated if large numbers of deaths within the "detected" cases are attributed to covid-19 simply because the person was infected and died. In other words, how many people counted within the covid dead actually died *with* the virus rather than *of* it?

On top of those major uncertainties, there are many reporting issues listed by Worldometer. Countries are constantly changing their methodology for reporting. Worldometer's list of reporting issues seemed not to be complete (at that date) as the UK was not listed despite having recently revised down their death data. Finally, data collection and analysis will be inconsistent between countries – and that is rather damning since the present exercise is precisely a comparison between countries.

In short, the quality of the data was woeful. However, that did not frustrate my objective which was not to draw any definitive conclusions based on the available covid-19 statistics. My objective was only to examine the veracity of Garikipati and Kambhampati's claims given the data available to them. The observations made above are already several nails hammered into the coffin lid of absolute veracity. But the rest of my analysis asks what we find even if we are happy to take the data at face value.

Worldometer lists 180 countries with covid-19 data for all three of tests, cases and deaths attributed to covid (with all the provisos noted above). There are several more with data for some but not all these quantities, a total of 210 locations being listed. I use all the data available and confine attention to (i) cases per million population, and, (ii) "covid deaths" per million population. Comparison between countries would be meaningless unless data per million of the population were used. Henceforth I may fail to stipulate "per million" for brevity, but this is to be understood throughout.

Figure 35.2 plots "covid deaths" versus cases, where each point is a different country. The graph uses a log-log scale in which a straight line indicates an underlying power-law relationship. The Pearson correlation between deaths and cases is 0.88, suggesting a simple linear proportionality. This is confirmed by the log-log plot whose trend line has a slope which is close to unity.

This makes sense, indicating that the number of deaths is proportional to the number of cases, as one would expect. Note that this says nothing about the accuracy of either the death data or the data for cases. Both could be wrong by some factor – and the factor could be different for deaths and cases – but proportionality would still be found if these factors were broadly the same between countries. (There were, however, other aspects of the data which were anomalous, for details of which see the original post. These anomalies do not detract from what follows).

Now let's examine the claims of Garikipati and Kambhampati, Ref.[2]. The following lists countries in which the most powerful executive politician was female at the time in question. This is clear in 17 cases. I have listed a further 9, making 26 in all, these being cases of a woman president with a male prime minister. The UK is listed in the Worldometer data as UK, not as four separate nations, so you won't find Nicola Sturgeon below (though it would have been valid to include Scotland as the Scottish parliament had jurisdiction over covid policy in Scotland.)

- Bangladesh   Prime Minister – Sheikh Hasina
- Barbados   Prime Minister – Mia Mottley
- Belgium   Prime Minister – Sophie Wilmès
- Bolivia   Interim President – Jeanine Áñez
- Denmark   Prime Minister – Mette Frederiksen
- Estonia   President – Kersti Kaljulaid
- Ethiopia   President – Sahle-Work Zewde
- Finland   Prime Minister – Sanna Marin
- Gabon   Prime Minister – Rose Christiane Raponda
- Georgia   President – Salome Zourabichvili
- Germany   Federal Chancellor – Angela Merkel
- Greece   President – Katerina Sakellaropoulou
- Iceland   Prime Minister – Katrín Jakobsdóttir
- Myanmar   State Counsellor – Aung San Suu Kyi
- Namibia   Prime Minister – Saara Kuugongelwa
- Nepal   President – Bidhya Devi Bhandari
- New Zealand   Prime Minister – Jacinda Ardern
- Norway   Prime Minister – Erna Solberg
- San Marino   Captain Regent – Grazia Zafferani (joint)
- Serbia   Prime Minister – Ana Brnabić
- Singapore   President – Halimah Yacob
- Slovakia   President – Zuzana Čaputová
- Switzerland   President of Federal Council – Simonetta Sommaruga
- Trinidad & Tobago President – Paula-Mae Weekes
- Taiwan   President – Tsai Ing-wen
- Belarus   President-elect – Sviatlana Tsikhanouskaya

Figure 25.2 shows the above 26 female-led countries as red squares. It is immediately obvious that the red points are broadly similar to the rest of the data. The red line is the best fit to the red data (for female-led countries). This is the best straight line fit to the log-log data, i.e., the best power law fit to the data itself. Also shown are the upper and lower 95% confidence bounds on the total (blue) data.

The red line lies comfortably within the blue dashed upper/lower 95% confidence limits, indicating that the red data is not significantly different from the total (blue) dataset.

The obvious red outlier at abnormally low deaths per million in Figure 25.2 is Singapore. The two countries with the largest number of deaths per million (San Marino and Belgium) also had female leaders, though I regard this as quite irrelevant. The red point with the greatest deaths per million (1,237) is San Marino, which has a population of only 33,941 and only 42 deaths, and so is hardly very indicative. However, similar observations apply also to many countries led by men. (Recall that these data relate to 19 August 2020 and I expect the situation changed radically later. I'm not trying to prove anything about covid here – other than the fact that Ref.[2] is profoundly misleading).

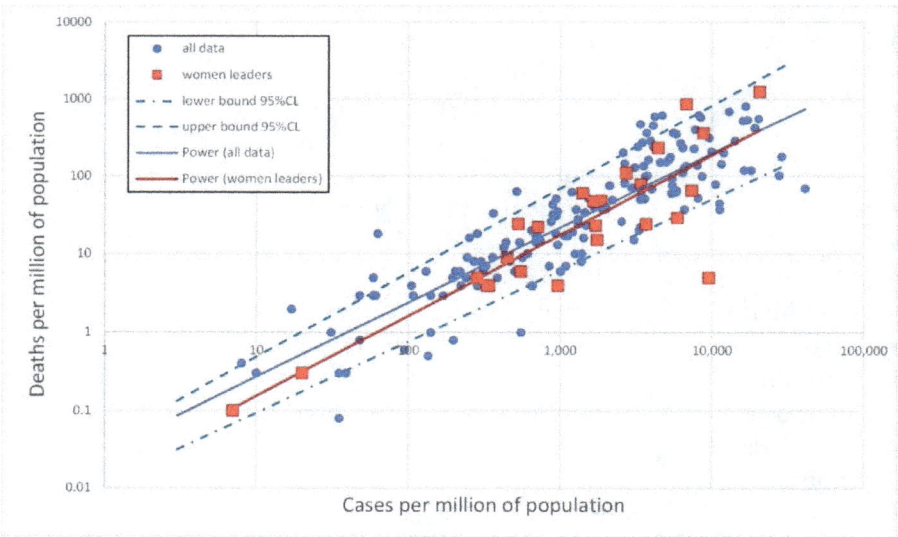

Figure 35.2: Cumulative Worldometer data to 19 August 2020 of deaths per million versus cases per million. Each point is a different country. Red squares indicate countries with female leadership as defined in the text.

Conclusion

The claim made by Garikipati and Kambhampati, Ref.[2], namely that "*covid-outcomes are systematically and significantly better in countries led by women*", is not supported by the data source they used at around the time their preprint was published. On the contrary, there was no statistically significant difference between female-led countries and the totality of countries. It would be of interest to repeat the analysis now (though, personally, I doubt any difference would be seen and hence I am hardly motivated to bother).

The methodology used in Ref.[2] was to compare male- and female-led countries by pair-wise comparison, i.e., one female-led country is paired with one male-led country. This is illustrated by the Guardian graphic reproduced as Figure 35.1. It is clear from the huge scatter in the data shown in Figure 35.2 that how one chooses the pairs in question will dictate the answer one gets. In other words, Garikipati and Kambhampati have indulged in a particularly crude form of cherry-picking and referring to it as "nearest neighbour matching" does not improve its validity. It is readily seen from Figure 35.2 that one could easily pick pairs of countries which would seem to support the idea that women leaders were poor compared with men – if anyone were so silly as to wish to do so.

References

[1]   Henley, J. (2020). *Female-led countries handled coronavirus better, study suggests*. The Guardian, 18 August 2020.

[2]   Garikipati, S., and Kambhampati, U. (2020). *Leading the Fight Against the Pandemic: Does Gender Really Matter?* SSRN, Written 3 June 2020 (last revised 28 Nov 2022, after my blog post – I have not examined for changes). It was later published in Feminist Economics, 27:1-2, 401-418, doi: 10.1080/13545701.2021.1874614, 1 March 2021.

[3]   Worldometer (see text for dates of access). *Covid-19 Coronavirus Pandemic*.

36. Filthy Men Deserve to Die

I am proud of the fact that I committed to print as early as 19 April 2020 my view that the government had failed to properly consider the morality of lockdowns as a response to covid-19, or the broader implications of such draconian action, Ref.[1]. With the covid inquiry still underway as 2023 draws to a close, the line that poor excuse for an inquiry is taking is that the only possible criticism of the lockdown policy is that it was not pursued early enough and severely enough. I tried hard to avoid immersing myself in covid statistics in 2020, knowing it to be premature, to which I allude in the opening paragraph, though I ultimately succumbed. However I could not resist publishing some justifiably angry blogs such as this one, which I have left largely unchanged.

Original posted on: 31 May 2020.

I have been paying scant attention to the statistics on covid-19. For one thing, it seems that everyone else is obsessing over them. But more importantly, it's a couple of years premature yet. I suspect that lockdown will ultimately prove responsible for increasing the number of deaths, by inhibiting herd immunity and as a result of its economic impact – but time will tell.

Figure 36.1: World War 1 recruitment poster employing shaming and moral coercion.

One thing was predictable: when times are hard, people double-down on their prejudices. London's burning? Blame the Jews. Inevitably the virus merely presented another opportunity for a spot of man-bashing. One of the more disgusting tendencies of feminists is using their access to media outlets, newspaper columns (and even parliament) to criticise their own husbands. Then-Prime Minister, Boris Johnson's, beloved sister, Rachel, did just that recently, Ref.[2]. Apparently, men are enjoying being at home and don't much want to get back to work. Women, on the other hand – at least those who agree with Rachel Johnson – want their men to bugger off back to work asap. What does that tell us about how much the two sexes enjoy their usual lifestyles? With all the tact and self-awareness one usually associates with feminists, Johnson concluded her piece with "Women of Britain say GO!". Very revealing, Rachel. Riff on that one, readers.

The ever-lovely Janet Street-Porter has usefully summed up the thrust of the narrative on covid-and-gender claiming that it's women who bear the brunt of the misery whilst being ignored. (We know that women's voices are silenced because they tell us so daily on a hundred mainstream news and media outlets). Here's what Street-Porter wrote, Ref.[3].

"The vast majority (60%) of coronavirus victims are male – probably because men are more likely to suffer from high blood pressure, heart disease and chronic lung conditions.

To be blunt, more men than women have chosen risky behaviour – booze, fags and drugs, all of which makes them vulnerable.

Plus, there's plenty of evidence that men aren't so bothered about hand washing and general cleanliness and up to 50% of young males are now flouting social distancing and meeting their mates. In this crisis, women have toed the line, done everything we've been asked – and yet we've been treated appallingly.

This crisis continues to be navigated by men and on current evidence, they haven't a clue. Our macho Prime Minister continues to use the language of war to 'fight' this disease, when what we need is emotional intelligence – empathy, soothing words to build community support through exhausting and trying times."

Did you spot all the empirical sources which underpin those claims? No? And did you spot Street-Porter's own "empathy and soothing words"?

The "more men die, women suffer most" narrative is everywhere. Actually, it can be worse than that: the first part of that statement is often omitted entirely and we just get "women suffer most". This is the variant most common in the corridors of power. I refer you to the Glass Blind Spot's summary of a two-hour-long meeting of the Women and Equalities Committee, Ref.[4], which included just 51 seconds on men. (Incidentally, given that – leaving aside age - the two fairly clear correlates with mortality to emerge so far are (i) men, and, (ii) ethnic minorities, the fact that nine of the 11 members of the WEC are white women rather raises the question: why do the WEC think they are the appropriate body to discuss the impact of covid-19? This is a rhetorical question – the purpose of the WEC is to spin any issue into a woman's issue).

Another example of an official body which ignores the "more men die" part of the story is the EHRC Wales in their recent parliamentary briefing paper, written by Hannah Wharf and Angharad Price, Ref.[5]. Their depiction of the unequal impact of covid-19 is that it applies to, "*older and disabled people, some ethnic minorities, some women and people living in socioeconomic disadvantage*". (Elephant in the room? Where? Where?). Obviously there's lots in their paper about VAWG, and space to give Gypsy, Roma and Traveller communities their obligatory mention – but men? No. Nada.

Here's another example of the "women most affected" narrative coming from people in positions of authority. This one is Debora Price, Professor of Social Gerontology, University of Manchester, and President of the British Gerontology Society. She speaks in this video, Ref.[6], at 40:00 minutes, or you can see her slides here, Ref.[7]. It's worth listening to the video (or a glance at the slides). Pay gap and other financial disadvantages figure large. One of my favourites is the claim that older women are particularly impacted, and care home deaths "are a gendered issue". Well, bloody obviously. Anyone who's visited a care home knows that they are overwhelmingly dominated by women. Those cunning men manage to wangle their way out of being disadvantaged by covid-19 by sneakily being already dead. Male privilege again, see.

But the part of Price's talk I'd like to draw to your attention is,

"*Covid-19 seems to be making men sicker and leading to greater male mortality at all ages. Focus so far in the public domain has been very much on men – Including some discussion of exaggerated masculine behaviours in the face of catastrophic threats, e.g., less hand washing, less social distancing (war metaphors = a real man can fight and defeat the virus).*"

See how "more men die" is immediately followed by "it's men's own fault". It always is. Male suicide, male failure in education, male victims of domestic abuse, men's mental illnesses, men's health disadvantages, men's alienation from their own children...they are all men's own fault. (Unlike women's disadvantages, of course, which only a hateful sexist bigot would suggest was their own fault).

The psychology of this came home to me forcibly when street-campaigning against male genital mutilation. Feminist types are wont to react to you, not merely by disagreeing, but with passionate anger. I was quite baffled. Whilst I can understand that some people may have a different opinion, where does that anger come from? I could understand anger if I were campaigning in favour of cutting body parts of babies – but why should anyone be so cross about campaigning against it? The answer, I believe, is that such people – feminists – cannot bear the spotlight of concern being turned on males – even male babies. The spotlight of concern must always be upon females. It's more than just the empathy gap; women must be granted the monopoly of concern, not merely most of it.

But I want to focus on the hand washing thing.

As soon as hand washing became the cause *du jour* I knew where this would go. Janet Street-Porter has informed us that *"men aren't so bothered about hand washing and general cleanliness"* and Debora Price confidently asserts that there is *"less hand washing"* by men because of their *"exaggerated masculine behaviours"*.

"Dirty Jews" is it?

Sources, at all?

The "men are filthy beasts" narrative is just another part of "it's men's own fault". It's the only reaction to male disadvantages that is possible within feminist psychology.

Dr Sara Kayat, a UK GP, shared some of her theories as to why covid-19 appears deadlier for men. Top of her list is hand-washing habits. She wrote,

"The World Health Organisation has continually advised to frequently wash your hands with soap as the best and most cost-effective method to control the spread of covid-19. However, studies suggest that men tend to wash their hands with soap less often than women. While a recent study concluded that on average, most countries' hand-washing habits increased, there was still a noted difference as 57% of women were more likely to adopt increased hand-washing and hand-sanitising behaviour, compared to just 51% of men."

Not all that much difference, I note.

Here's another from the USAPP (American Politics and Policy) whose central mission is, they tell us, "to increase the public understanding of social science". In a piece titled, *How men's misplaced sense of masculinity in the face of covid-19 may be killing them*, Ref.[8], we read,

"The evidence and messaging are clear – one of the most important ways that people can protect themselves and others from the spread of covid-19 is to frequently wash their hands. And yet, according to survey data, men are still washing their hands less often than women. Using survey data, Dan Cassino finds that men who feel that they have the same chance of dying from covid-19 as women are less likely to wash their hands, potentially because they are doubling down on their masculine identities in the face of a threat that they can't control."

"potentially because", eh? So, that bit was just made up, then. They continue,

"In survey after survey, we see that American men just aren't washing their hands at the same rates as American women. At a moment when health experts are begging Americans to wash their hands frequently in order to help stop the spread of the coronavirus, why are American men lagging? In recent data – collected between March 10th and 16th by USC's Understanding America Survey – 91 percent of women say that they're washing their hands more frequently because of the covid-19 pandemic, compared with only 85 percent of men."

Again, the difference is not that marked (and was the difference statistically significant?). But anything will do to motivate man-bashing. And all these sources depend upon the accuracy of self-reporting. Could there be a gender effect in that accuracy? Might one sex be particularly keen to appear clean? Wash my mouth out for even suggesting it!

(The same source goes on to state: *"Democrats are more likely to report washing their hands frequently than Republicans"* – absolutely no bias there, I'm sure).

Ref.[9] is another example of the dirty men narrative. It was a pandemic of blaming dirty men.

But even if the identified 6% difference between the sexes in hand washing is correct, it hardly contributes much to a roughly 100% greater male mortality rate. (NB: This was the figure I estimated at the time, I have not examined it using more recent data). And, in any case, it's not men's *infection* rate which is greater – it's their mortality. This obvious point is conveniently ignored by all those commentators desperate to neutralise male disadvantage and turn it into "women most affected" as quickly as possible.

The reason why I alighted on the hand-washing topic is that I had a distant memory of reading a paper on bacteria assays carried out on hand swabs, disaggregated by sex – and a finding that ran counter to the "filthy men" narrative. I'll get to that shortly. But the reason why, many years ago now, I had an interest in the topic bears a short digression.

I used to work in a large office. The management were very safety conscious and kept meticulous records of accidents and near-misses. Like virtually everywhere else, the overwhelming majority of accidents were due to slips, trips and falls – especially on staircases. The company instituted a policy of making holding the handrail on stairs obligatory. One woman complained on the grounds that at the bottom of the staircase was the gents' toilet. She did not elaborate, but the implication was clear. She did not want to touch a handrail which some filthy man emerging from the toilet had touched before her. The women's toilet was in the same place, by the way, but obviously no one made an objection on those grounds (because that would be the most hateful misogyny – yes, it would).

So, that's when I initially researched the facts on bacteria-on-hands-by-sex. (Incidentally, urine is virtually sterile, but I find no one is ever very impressed by that observation). I emphasise that the sources below refer to bacteria, not viruses. How indicative they may be for viruses I leave to your judgment.

Consider firstly Ref.[10], Fierer et al (2008), extracts from which are,

"The diversity of skin-associated bacterial communities was surprisingly high; a typical hand surface harboured >150 unique species-level bacterial phylotypes, and we identified a total of 4,742 unique phylotypes across all of the hands examined." (27 men, 24 women).

"Men and women harbour significantly different bacterial communities on their hand surfaces…. Interestingly, the palms of women were also found to harbour significantly greater bacterial diversity than those of men, whether diversity was assessed by examining

the overall phylogenetic structure on each hand (Fig. 2A) or the average number of phylotypes per hand (Fig. 2B).

We do not know what drives these differences in overall diversity, but differences in skin pH may be influential. Men generally have more acidic skin than women and work from other microbial habitats has shown that microbial diversity is often lower in more acidic environments. Other explanations for why men and women appear to harbour distinct hand bacterial communities may include differences in sweat or sebum production, frequency of moisturizer or cosmetics application, skin thickness, or hormone production."

Personally I find it entirely unsurprising that women's hands tend to have a greater range of bacteria. Women's hands tend to be warmer and more moist than men's hands, and these are the conditions which promote bacterial growth. It has little to do with hygiene.

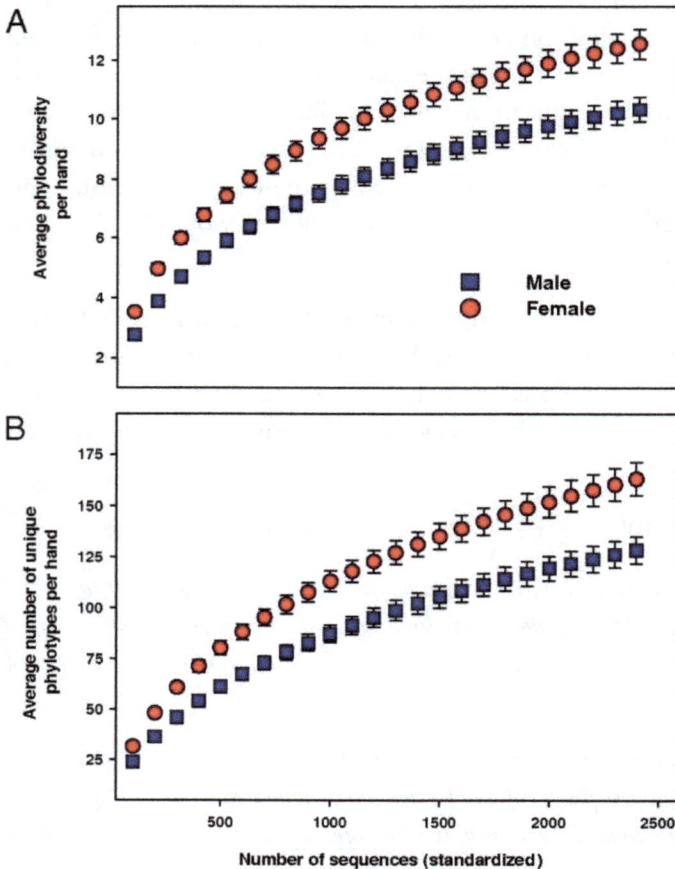

Figure 36.2: Taken from Ref.[10].

Turning now to Ref.[11] by Judah et al (2010), the authors took hand swabs from 404 members of the public using public transport (buses and trains). Data was gathered at five major cities and concentrated upon bacteria of faecal origin. Bus users were more contaminated than train users. Data from three cities (London, Cardiff, Birmingham) indicated that a greater percentage of women than men had contaminated hands. Data from two cities (Liverpool, Newcastle) indicated that a greater percentage of men than women had contaminated hands. Overall there was no significant difference, see Table 36.1.

City	Men	Women
London	6%	20%
Cardiff	15%	29%
Birmingham	23%	26%
Liverpool	36%	31%
Newcastle	57%	31%
Overall	28%	27%

Table 36.1: Prevalence of faecal organisms by city and gender, from Judah et al, 2010. Percentages with contaminated hands.

Covid-19 being worldwide, Ref.[12] may also be relevant. This study was conducted to determine the prevalence of bacteria and intestinal parasites among food handlers in Ethiopia. Table 4 of the paper indicates that 27% of men and 31% of women were found to test positive.

In conclusion, covid-19 provided yet another opportunity for the man-bashers to indulge their prejudice. It is familiar that times of social stress enhance existing prejudices. Claiming that men's greater mortality may be related to their less frequent hand washing is illogical as the gendered effect of covid-19 is on mortality, not infection. In any case the quoted differences in hand-washing frequency were too small to explain anything, and probably not statistically significant. Men do not appear to have higher levels of hand-borne pathogens than women, at least as judged from bacterial assays. (I leave aside whether covid-19 was, in any case, transmitted by contact).

In short, the anti-male narrative was, as usual, a result of endemic prejudice and was without any empirical basis. The popularity of the dirty-men narrative was yet another emphatic underwriting of the reality of the empathy gap and male disposability.

References

[1] Collins, W. (2020). *The Morality of Lockdown* The Illustrated Empathy Gap, 19 April 2020.

[2] Johnson, R. (2020). *Is it just me or are men milking the lockdown? asks FEMAIL's guest columnist Rachel Johnson*. The Daily Mail, 27 May 2020.

[3] Street-Porter, J. (2020). *Coronavirus kills more men than women but it's women who are bearing the brunt of the misery while our incompetent macho leaders have consistently side-lined and ignored us*. Mail Online, 13 May 2020.

[4] The Glass Blind Spot (2020). *Covid-19: Karens Most Affected?* The Glass Blind Spot YouTube channel, 11 May 2020.

[5] Wharf, H., and Price, A. (2020). *Rebuilding a more equal and fairer Wales: Focus on the unequal impact of the coronavirus pandemic May 2020*. Equality and Human Rights Commission Briefing Paper 1, May 2020.

[6] Manchester Institute for Collaborative Research on Ageing, MICRA (2020). *MICRA Webinar: The Impact of COVID-19 on Health and Social Inequalities in Older People*. University of Manchester School of Social Sciences, 19 May 2020.

[7] Price, D. (2020). *Gender, Ageing and Covid-19*. Presentation at the MICRA webinar, Ref.[6], 19 May 2020.

[8] USAPP, American Politics and Policy (2020). *How men's misplaced sense of masculinity in the face of Covid-19 may be killing them*. Blog article, 9 April 2020.

[9] Brueck, H. (2020). *Women say they're washing their hands significantly more than men as the coronavirus spreads around the world*. Business Insider, 28 February 2020.

[10] Fierer, N., et al (2008). *The influence of sex, handedness, and washing on the diversity of hand surface bacteria*. PNAS 105 (46) 17994-17999, 18 November 2008.

[11] Judah, G., et al. (2010). *Dirty hands: bacteria of faecal origin on commuters' hands*. Epidemiol. Infect. (2010), 138, 409–414. Published online 2 September 2009.

[12] Mengist, A., et al (2018). *Bacterial and Parasitic Assessment from Fingernails in Debre Markos, Northwest Ethiopia*. Canadian Journal of Infectious Diseases and Medical Microbiology, Vol 2018, 6532014, 18 October 20.

37. GP Meltdown? What Few Will Say

This book is full of things that one is not allowed to say in "polite" society, but this is one of the most unsayable of all. The claim is that the diminishing of GP services to the public is a result of the dominance of female GPs and their extremely high proportion of part-time working. The contentious nature of the claim obliges me to include rather more tabular and graphical evidence than in most chapters. For non-UK readers a GP is a General Practitioner who is contracted to the National Health Service (NHS) and provides primary health care via surgeries which are based locally. GPs do not usually work in hospitals. Serious cases requiring hospital care are referred to a hospital by the GP.

Original posted on: 7 June 2022.

Many people will have noticed that GPs' surgeries never returned to their pre-lockdown arrangements. Moreover, for some years prior to covid it had been notoriously difficult to get a GP appointment, especially in some areas and especially in less than a few days.

Commentators are becoming more outspoken regarding the reason for this diminishing performance of general practice: it is due, they claim, to the increases in the proportion of GPs who work part-time. Writing in *The Spectator* on 4 June 2022, Meirion Thomas, Ref.[1], observed,

"Currently, an astonishing 58% of GPs work three days or fewer per week. We're told that seeing patients is such a stressful business that part-time working is the only way to prevent burnout. In my 33 years working as an NHS consultant surgeon, I don't remember this ever happening to heart, brain, cancer or other specialists who take life and death decisions every day. GPs' work is far less complicated. Why should they be so badly affected by burnout?"

However, only the bravest commentators will proceed to the next step – that the increase in part-time working by GPs in recent decades is a result of the huge increase in the proportion of GPs who are women. Kathy Gyngell did so in an interview on GB News, Ref.[2], to the visible discomfort of the presenter. Even GB News, it seems, does not want to air anything that sounds supportive of the idea that the old workaholic patriarchy might have been a social good – and still less can any implied criticism of the feminist equity obligation be voiced.

Here I do my usual thing and examine the data. Is it true that the pressure on GPs has increased over recent decades? Is it true that GPs' part-time working has increased markedly? And is it true that this is attributable mostly to women GPs? The answers are no, yes and yes respectively, and very clearly so, as we will see.

One issue that must be mentioned immediately in the context of the pressure on GPs is the Blair-era revised GP contract (2004). In simple terms this made being a GP a 9 to 5 job (or, often, less than this). Out went the idea of GPs "doing their rounds" after hours and at weekends – essentially working whatever hours it took to get through the workload. This was, at a stroke, a massive diminishing of pressure on GPs. This is forgotten now. The attention span of the feminist-progressive mind is conveniently short: historical reality does not play well with their narrative. But there can be little doubt that in the bad old days when GPs were overwhelmingly men who worked very long hours indeed, those old patriarchs represented very good value for money.

Readers may like to skip the details and proceed straight to the Summary, but the proof is in the details.

Ambiguities in the Data

I will use several different sources below, in order to piece together the full picture. There will be inconsistencies between sources and ambiguities in defining what is measured. The bulk of the inconsistencies between sources probably result from said ambiguities, i.e., they relate to different definitions of the measured quantity. The matter is exacerbated by politicians who spin the data according to their political prejudice. Some of the issues are as follows,

- Exactly who is counted as a "GP"? Is it only those fully qualified, or does it include GP trainees who are already doctors and are currently working in practices as the final step towards qualification? Does it include locums? Does it include "GP Partners" or salaried GPs? Does it include "Registrar GPs"? Sources will differ; some give data for all the above, some just one number without clearly stating what it is.

- Also numerically very important is whether we are counting all registered GPs, or only those for whom there is evidence that they are currently working as a GP. Do GPs on the specialist register count as "registered"? Basing a definition on evidence of being currently employed as a GP depends upon one of two things, both unreliable. The first is surveying GP practices, which inevitably results in only a proportion of practices responding, and so will always be incomplete. The second method is to use the NHS Practice History Records for individual registered GPs. Unfortunately, as of 2016, only 87% of registered GPs had a practice history record, and only 79% had both a practice record and a valid practice history entry, see Ref.[3].

- A GP may have more than one contract, and some sources may count contracts rather than GPs.

- If you are a politician of the Party in power you will most likely quote headcount numbers of GPs. If you are an opposition politician seeking to demonstrate how the government is running down the NHS, you will quote either FTE (Full-Time Equivalent) or the number of GPs per 100,000 of the population. The latter is as much a measure of population increase as of GP numbers. The bleakest picture is provided by FTE per 100,000, but this is also the best measure of how much GP time is available per patient.

However, despite all these opportunities for political obfuscation or inconsistent definitions, we shall see that all sources indicate the same qualitative answers to the questions posed above, i.e., the pressure on GPs, the issue of part-time working and the increasing proportion of women GPs.

I address the three GB nations in turn: England, Scotland and Wales.

England

Most of the data used here derives from NHS Digital's publications on workforce, current or historical, plus some data from the General Medical Council, Refs.[3-5].

Ref.[5] indicates that over the period 1995 – 2005 the number of male GPs remained constant while the number of women GPs increased substantially (hence an increasing total number of GPs). Over this period there were around three times as many female part-time GPs as male, even when male GPs outnumbered female GPs by more than two-to-one.

Figure 37.1 shows that the total number of fully qualified permanent GPs in England hasn't varied much over the period 2015 to 2022, but has risen slightly.

Figure 37.2 shows that the number of fully qualified permanent female GPs increased steeply over the period 2015 to 2022 whilst the corresponding number of male GPs reduced. The number of fully qualified permanent female GPs exceeded the number of fully qualified permanent male GPs in 2014. By 2022 the number of fully qualified women GPs exceeded the number of male GPs by 35%. We will see that this dominance of women GPs is certain to increase far above that level.

Figures 37.3 shows that more than twice as many female GPs work less than 15 hours/week than male GPs. Figure 37.4 confirms that the number of female GPs working part-time has continued to considerably exceed the number of male GPs working part-time. However, this Figure under-estimates the issue because it fails to disaggregate full-time working (37.5 hours/week) from part-time working between 15 and 37.5 hours per week.

Figure 37.5 shows that fewer male and female GPs are choosing to work over 37.5 hours per week, but nevertheless there are still two-and-a-half times more men doing so than women. The rapidly reducing number of male GPs, and hence the reducing number of GPs working in excess of 37.5 hours, is a contributor to the overall reduction in working hours being delivered by GPs now compared with the past.

Figure 37.6 plots against year an estimate of the percentage of GPs working part-time, by sex, between 2015 and 2022. This uses the data for total headcount (N) and full-time equivalent (FTE) from Ref.[4] Sheets 1a and 1b and estimates the percentage of part-time working based on the simplifying assumption that (a) all part-time working is exactly half full-time, and, (b) working in excess of full-time can be neglected. The fraction of part-time workers is then $2(N - FTE)/N$. Both sexes have shown an increase in part-time working. 30% of male GPs worked part-time in 2022. For women GPs this was a staggering 86.5%. Overall, 62% of GPs were working part-time in 2022. Part-time working male GPs are likely to be nearing, or beyond, retirement age. In contrast, most part-time working female GPs are in their 30s or 40s.

Figure 37.7 shows that the number of patients per GP has not changed much over the period 2015 – 2022. In contrast the number of patients per full-time equivalent GP has increased by 15% over the period, due to a combination of the increased population and the decreased number of FTEs. The latter is despite the increase in the number of GPs and is due to the decrease in the average number of hours worked per GP.

Using General Medical Council data for England and Scotland in 2016, Ref.[3], Table 37.1 shows how GPs working patterns break down. Fewer than 20% of GPs have a single contract for permanent full-time working, compared with 46% who have a single contract for part-time working (either permanent or locum). The low percentage of single-contracted full-time GPs is only partly due to the large number of single-contracted part-time GPs. It is also due to the large percentage (34%) of GPs with two or more contracts. (Some GPs with multiple contracts may work more than one FTE, but many will still work less than one FTE in aggregate). The majority of GPs holding multiple contracts are women (roughly twice as many as men).

This GMC source indicates that in 2016, in England and Scotland, the number of licensed female GPs under 50 exceeded the number of licensed male GPs under 50 by 55%.

In 2016 in England and Scotland, of those GPs with a single, permanent, part-time contract, 61% were women. However, single contract part-time working, whether permanent or locum, accounts for less than 46% of the total number of GPs. The full extent of part-time working is obscured in these data due to multiple-contract working, much of which will also be part-time even in aggregate.

Working Pattern	Number of GPs	Percentage of those with known contract type(s)
All registered GPs	54,024	–
Part-time permanent, only	11,441	27.2%
Part-time locum, only	7,811	18.6%
Full-time, permanent	8,341	19.8%
Two contracts, permanent + locum	8,077	19.2%
Two contracts, other types	3,438	8.2%
Three contracts	2,942	7.0%
No valid data or incomplete data	11,974	–

Table 37.1: GP Working Patterns in 2016, England and Scotland. Data from Ref.[3]

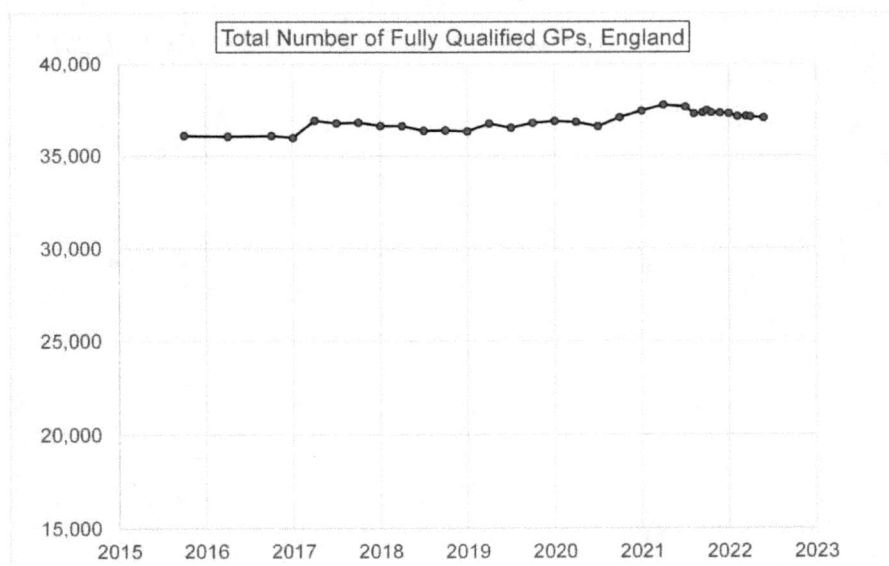

Figure 37.1: Number of Fully Qualified Permanent GPs, England, 2015 – 2022. Data from Ref.[4]

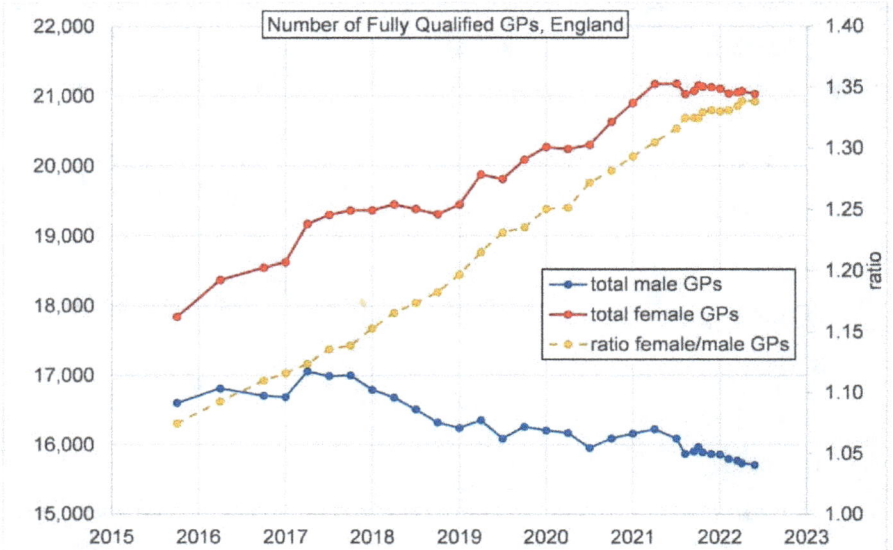

Figure 37.2: Number of Fully Qualified Permanent GPs, by Sex, England, 2015 – 2022. Data from Ref.[4]

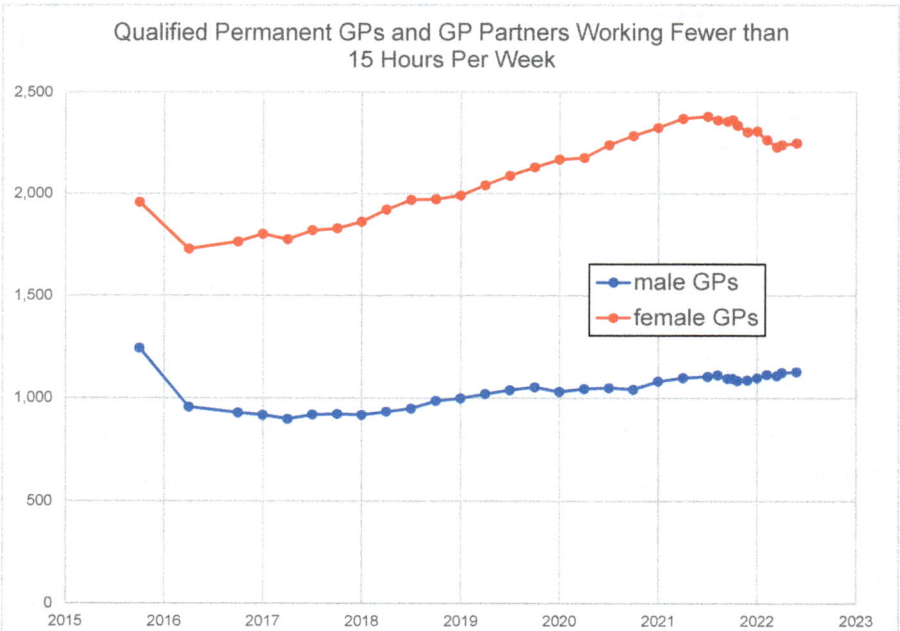

Figure 37.3: Number of GPs Working < 15 Hours/Week, England, 2015 – 2022. Data from Ref.[4]

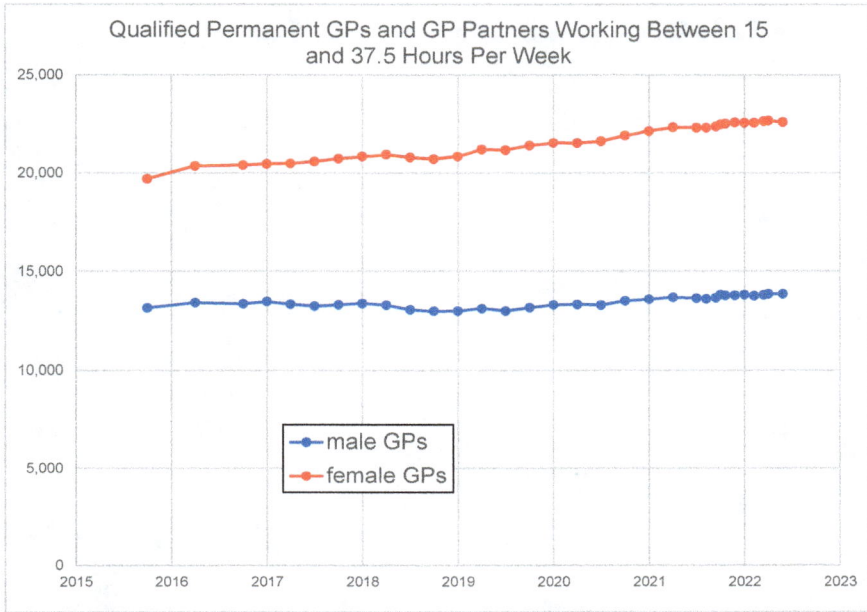

Figure 37.4: Number of GPs Working More Than 15 and Up To 37.5 Hours/Week, England, 2015 – 2022. Data from Ref.[4]

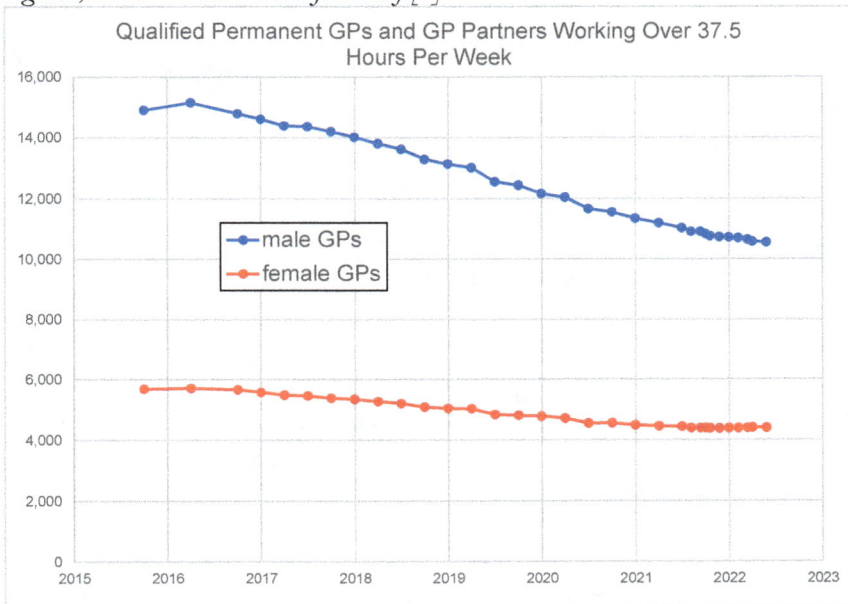

Figure 37.5: Number of GPs Working Over 37.5 Hours/Week, England, 2015 – 2022. Data from Ref.[4]

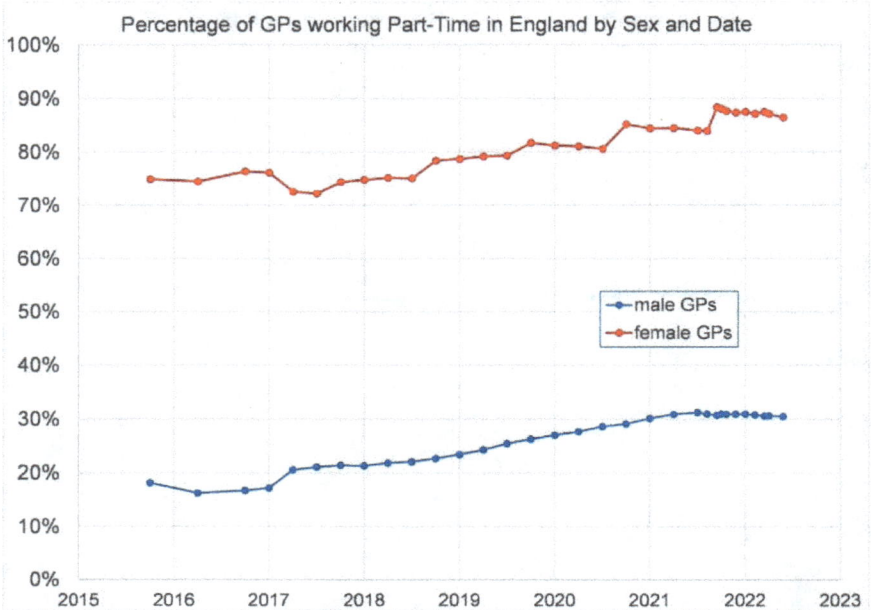

Figure 37.6: Percentage of GPs Working Part-Time by Sex, England, 2015 – 2022 (estimated – see text for methodology). Data from Ref.[4]

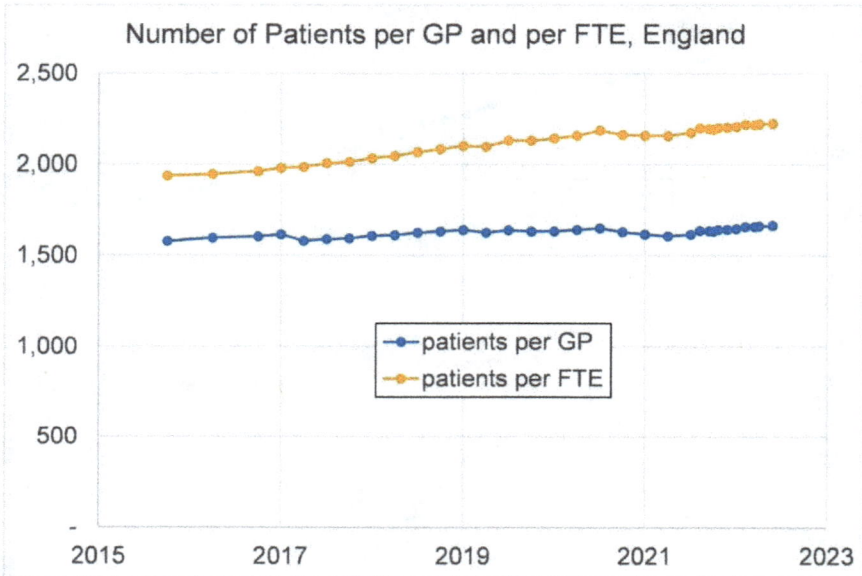

Figure 37.7: Number of Fully Qualified GPs per Patient of Number of FTEs per Patient, England, 2015 to 2022. Data from Ref.[4]

Wales

Data has been taken from Ref.[6]. The main source of data used in that report was the General Medical Services (GMS) census, which is generated from the Exeter (GP payments) system, provided to the Welsh Government through a contract with NHS Digital. The number of GPs in Wales gradually increased from under 1,800 in the mid-1990s to around 2,000 in 2010. Since then the number of GPs has remained largely stable, with small year-to-year changes. The number of patients per GP has remained stable over the period 2000 – 2018 at about 1,600 (similar to that of England over the last decade or so). FTE data was not obtained.

Figure 37.8 shows the GP headcount in Wales by sex, from 2000 to 2018. Women became the majority of GPs in Wales in 2015. In 2000 there were 2.5 male GPs to every female GP. Between 2000 and 2018 the number of male GPs decreased from 1,280 to 873, whilst the number of female GPs increased from 515 to 1,091 (excluding GP Registrars). If GP Registrars are included, in 2018 the number of female GPs exceeded the number of male GPs in Wales by 32%.

Figure 37.9 shows how the number of female GPs in the younger age range, 30 to 44, has overtaken the number of male GPs in this age range. Just before 2000 there were twice as many men GPs as women in this age range. By 2018 there were twice as many women GPs as men GPs in this age range.

The number of male GPs in the next age band, 45 to 54, has also been falling and 2018 saw the number of female GPs in this age band overtake the number of male GPs. As of 2018 there were more male GPs only in the oldest age band, 55 to 64. Inevitably this will shortly cease to be the case as they retire.

Figure 37.10 displays the sex-age distribution in Wales as of 2018. It is clear that the dominance of female GPs is certain to increase as the oldest GPs (mostly men) retire and the younger GPs (mostly women) work through the system. New GPs will certainly continue to be strongly dominated by women, partly because female medical students outnumber male by 85% now, and partly because women will remain attracted to the part-time working opportunities with high salary. In 2017/18, for every male GP joining practices in Wales there were 2.1 female GPs.

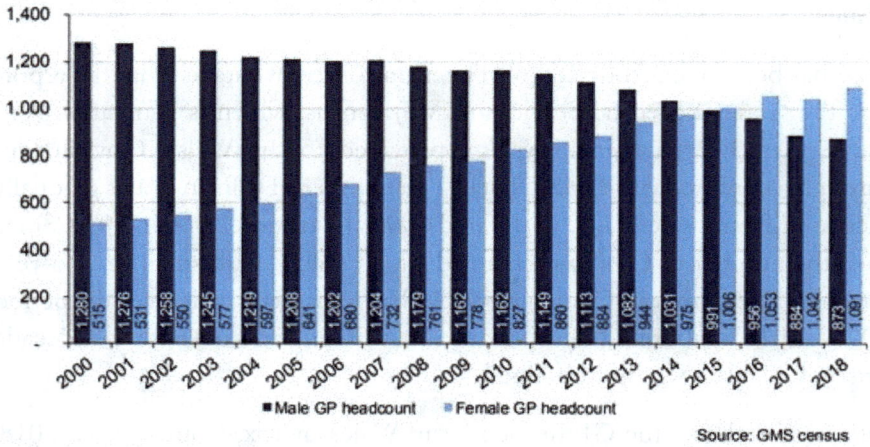

Figure 37.8: GP Headcount in Wales by Sex, 2000 – 2018, Ref.[6]

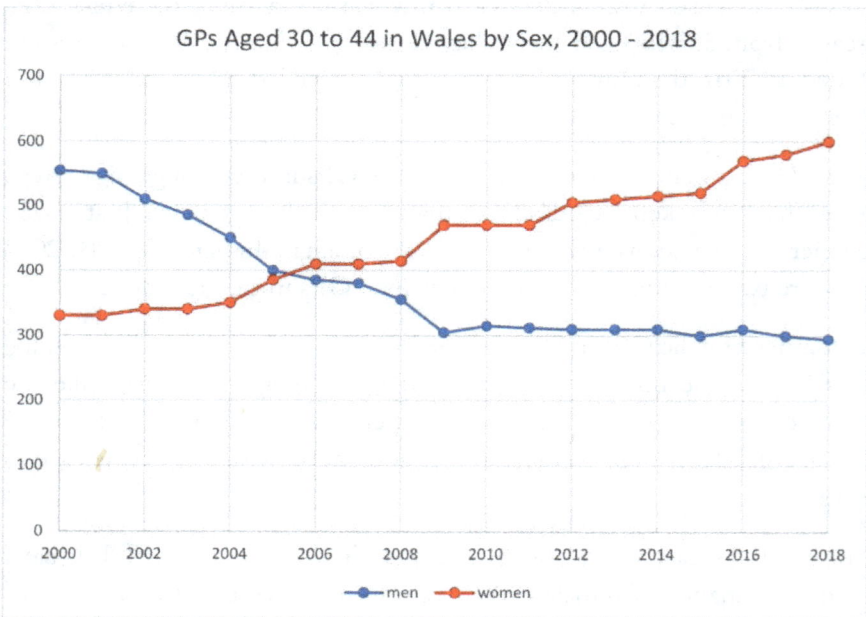

Figure 37.9: GPs Aged 30 to 44 in Wales by Sex, 2000 – 2018, Ref.[6]

GP age pyramids

Chart 8: GP Practitioners by gender and age, at 30 September 2018

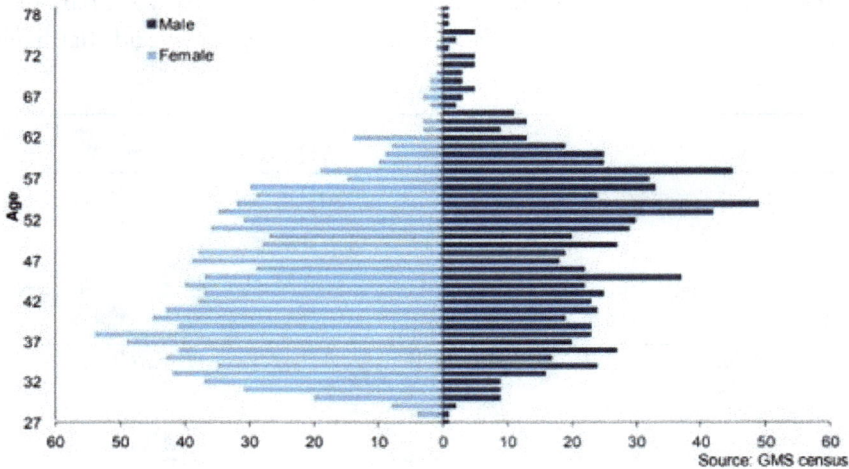

Figure 37.10: GP Practitioners in Wales by Sex and Age in 2018, Ref.[6].

Scotland

Data was taken from Ref.[7]. GP headcount in Scotland was fairly constant between 2009 and 2017 at around 4,453. The number of registered patients per GP in 2015 – 2017 in Scotland was about 1,250, substantially fewer than in England and Wales.

The dominance of women GPs in the younger age ranges is even more emphatic than in England and Wales, with three times more female than male GPs in the youngest age range, Figure 37.11. In 2017 there were 40% more women GPs than male GPs, but this will now be substantially greater and is set to reach twice as many women GPs in the next 10 years or so.

GPs' contract working time is measured in "sessions" which are roughly half-days, or 4 hours. In 2017 in Scotland, despite there being 40% more female GPs, the total number of sessions worked by male and female GPs was the same, a total of 13,300 sessions per week in total by each sex.

On the basis that working more or less than 8 sessions defines full-time versus part-time working, the number of GPs working part-time by sex is given by Table 37.2. A staggering 82.7% of female GPs in Scotland were working part-time in 2017, compared to 34.3% of male GPs. Overall, 62.5% of GPs in Scotland worked part-time.

Figures 37.13 to 37.15 show that women GPs' tendency to work part-time persists across all the age ranges (e.g., even in age ranges beyond that likely to be associated with childcare).

	Part-Time	Full-Time	Percentage Part-Time
Women	1,812	379	82.7%
Men	538	1,027	34.3%
All	2,350	1,406	62.5%

Table 37.2: Number of GPs in Scotland Working Part-Time v Full-Time, 2017, Ref.[7]

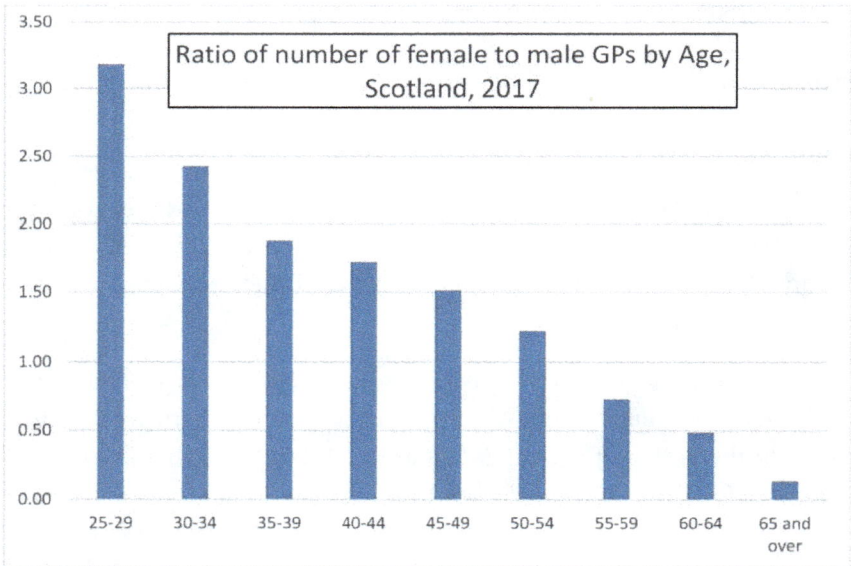

Figure 37.11: Ratio of Female to Male GPs by Age in Scotland, 2017, Ref.[7]

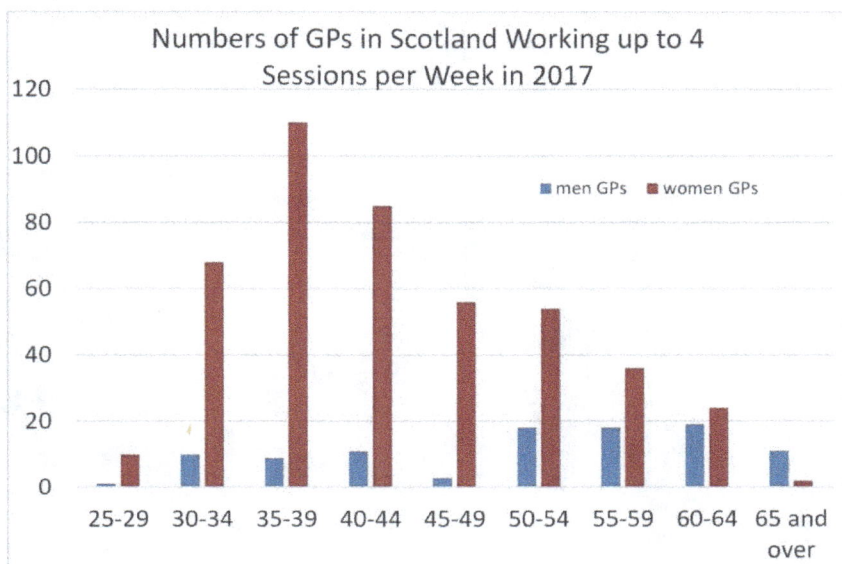

Figure 37.12: Numbers of GPs in Scotland Working Up To 4 Sessions (16 Hours) per Week, 2017, Ref.[7]

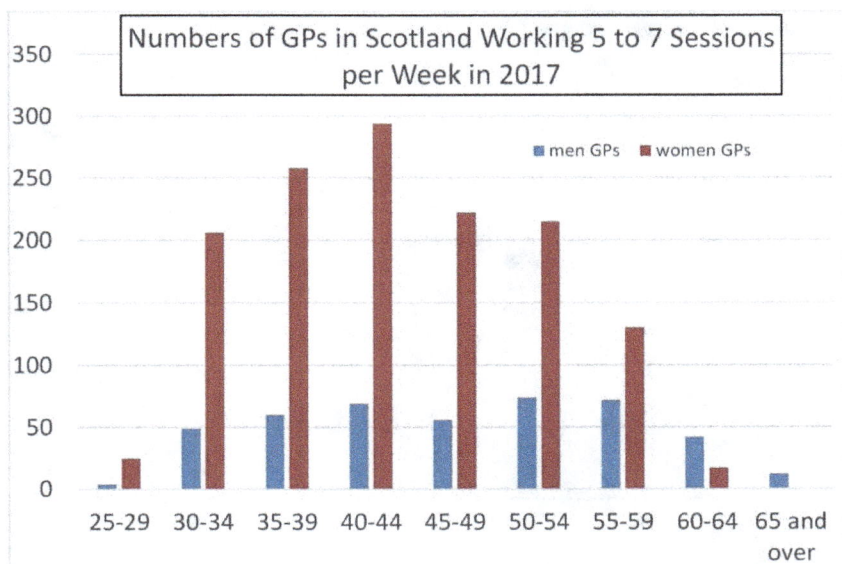

Figure 37.13: Numbers of GPs in Scotland Working 5 to 7 Sessions (20 to 28 Hours) per Week, 2017, Ref.[7]

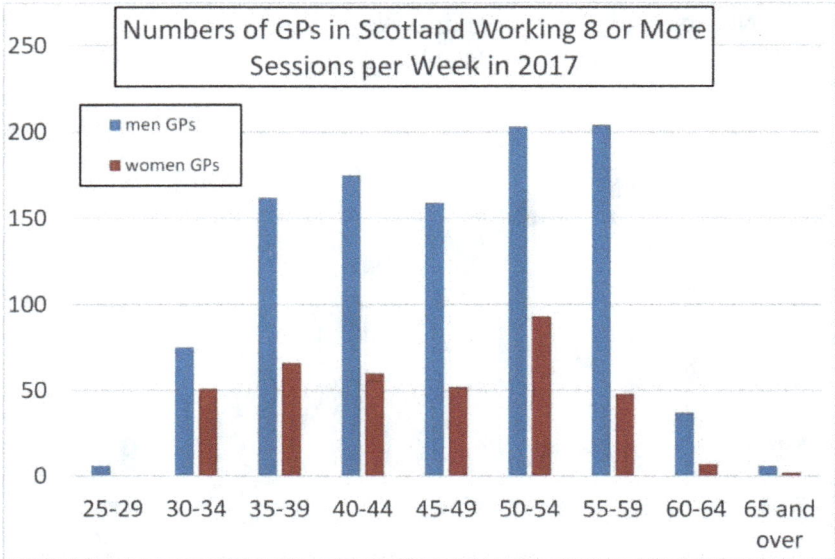

Figure 37.14: Numbers of GPs in Scotland Working 8 or More Sessions (32 or More Hours) per Week, 2017, Ref.[7]

Number of qualified, permanent GPs* per 100,000** across the regions of the UK (headcount), 1964 to 2018

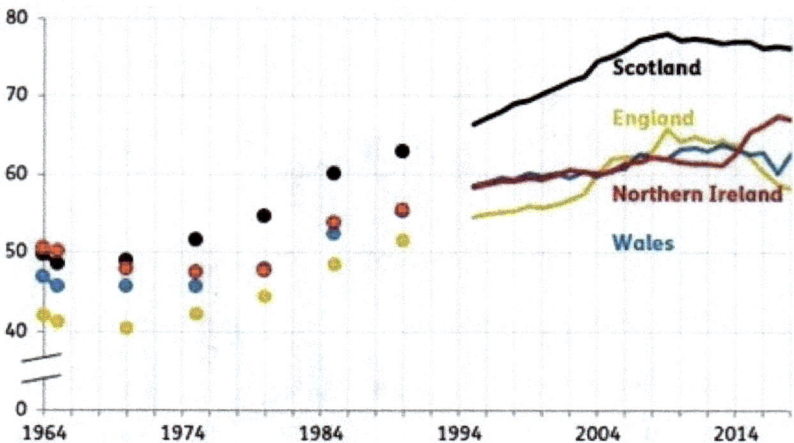

* all GPs excluding locums, retainers and registrars

** population figures are based on GP registered patients rather than UK population

*** trends should be interpreted with caution due to multiple changes in the data over time and differences in how data is collected in different regions of the UK

Figure 37.15: Number of fully qualified, permanent GPs in the UK per 100,000 of registered patients, 1964 – 2014. Copied from Ref.[8] which cites Ref.[9].

Whole UK

Figure 37.15 presents data over a longer time-base, from 1964 to 2014. It shows that the number of qualified GPs per registered patient has increased markedly over this period, though there has been a small drop-off over the last decade. Nevertheless, in 1970 in England there were 2,500 registered patients per qualified GP compared with around 1,600 in 2022.

It cannot be claimed that the pressure on GPs is greater now than it was historically. The opposite is the case. This does not stop politicians putting this spin on the data by using FTE rather than headcount, e.g., Refs.[8,9]. But this is a consequence of decreased working hours per GP. One cannot reasonably claim that the pressure on GPs is greater because they work fewer hours.

The pressure is, in fact, being displaced to hospital A&E departments – where male doctors still predominate, incidentally.

Summary

In England in 2014 the number of fully qualified permanent female GPs exceeded the corresponding number of male GPs for the first time. By 2022 the number of fully qualified permanent female GPs exceeded the corresponding number of male GPs by 35%. In 2022 in England the overall percentage of GPs working part-time was 62%. For women GPs the figure was 86.5% and for male GPs 30%.

In Scotland in 2017 the figures were similar, with 82.7% of female GPs working part-time compared to 34.3% of male GPs. Overall, 62.5% of GPs in Scotland worked part-time.

In England and Scotland combined in 2016, fewer than 20% of GPs had a contract for permanent full-time working as their sole contract. In England and Scotland combined, in 2016, the number of women GPs under 50 years old exceeded the corresponding number of male GPs by 55%.

In Wales, women became the majority of GPs in 2015. In 2000 there were 2.5 male GPs to every female GP. By 2018, the number of female GPs had exceeded the number of male GPs in Wales by 32%. By 2018 the number of female GPs in Wales in the age range 30 to 44 was double that of male GPs of the same age.

In England the number of patients per GP has not changed much over the period 2015 to 2022. In contrast the number of patients per full-time equivalent GP has increased by 15% over the period, due to a combination of the increased population and the decreased number of FTEs. The latter is despite the increase in the number of GPs and is due to an increased proportion of GPs working part-time (hence reducing the average weekly hours worked).

Over a long time-base, 1964 to 2014, the number of GPs per registered patient increased markedly in all UK nations, though there has been a small drop-off over the last decade in England. Nevertheless, in 1970 in England there were 2,500 registered patients per qualified GP compared with around 1,600 in 2022.

In summary, a far larger proportion of women GPs work part-time than male GPs. Also the proportion of women GPs has increased steeply over the last few decades, especially in the younger age ranges. The proportion of GPs who are women is certain to continue to increase markedly as the oldest GPs, mainly men, retire, and the new GPs will be strongly dominated by women because female medical students exceed male medical students by 85%. The average hours worked per GP will therefore also continue to fall, thus further degrading the service to the public (if total GP numbers remains constant).

So, to answer the question posed in the introduction – yes, it is true that GPs' part-time working has increased markedly and this is indeed attributable mostly to women GPs. But the pressure on GPs has reduced, on average, as their individual working hours have reduced markedly.

So – what few will say is this – next time you can't get a GP appointment you might like to reflect on its causes. One contributory cause, though not the only one, is the ideological neglect of boys' education over many decades which has led to the dominance of women as medical students.

You can have feminist "equity", but there is no law of the universe that says you can also have a functioning healthcare system or a thriving national economy.

References

[1]   Meirion Thomas, J. (2022). *Medical emergency: general practice is broken*. The Spectator, 4 June 2022

[2] Gyngell, K. (2022). *Today's talking point: Should the NHS stop its GP part-time work culture?* TCW Defending Freedom, 4 June 2022. (See also the linked video clip from GB News, https://youtu.be/BfDJyHggYBc)

[3] General Medical Council (2018). *What our data tells us about general practitioners working for the NHS in England and Scotland*. GMC Working Paper 6, May 2018.

[4] NHS Digital (2022). *General Practice Workforce, 30 April 2022*. Official statistics, published 26 May 2022.

[5] NHS Digital (2006). *General and Personal Medical Services, England - 1995-2005*. Official statistics published 24 Apr 2006.

[6] Welsh Government, Statistics for Wales (2019). *GPs in Wales, as at 30 September 2018*. Data release 27 March 2019.

[7] Public Health Scotland (2017). *National Primary Care Workforce Survey 2017*. Data and Intelligence (Previously ISD Scotland). The 2017 dataset is no longer online so that link is to a privately held copy. The corresponding data from 2019 onwards is currently still online *here*.

[8] Full Fact (2019). *GP Numbers: Up or Down?* 13 May 2019.

[9] Palmer, B. (2019). *Is the number of GPs falling across the UK?* Nuffield Trust, 8 May 2019.

38. Rough Death

I used to volunteer in a night shelter for rough sleepers. I do not have a rosy-eyed view of these people, the very bottom of our demographic heap. Their problems are usually more intractable than can be cured by just giving them somewhere to live. From informal personal experience I'd say about a third of them are addicted – to anything that comes along. Another third have severe mental health problems or are just of low intelligence. A large proportion have been in prison. The final third are those who are unfortunate. These are the ones that can more easily be helped. None of them deserve to die alone on the streets, sometimes so devoid of any connection to society that even their names are unknown.

Original posted on: 27 December 2018.

Data here have been taken from The Bureau of Investigative Journalism, who obtain their data via crowd sourcing. When I wrote the original blog article in December 2018 the Bureau had been collecting data for just over a year. Their data, including the list of names, is summarised in the original post. In some cases there was a brief biography, some of which I include below as illustrations.

There is no obligation on either national government or local authorities to record data on the deaths of rough sleepers. The Bureau is therefore to be commended in being proactive in compiling these data. Despite many vulnerable people being known to the authorities, local journalists and charities are often the only ones that report these deaths. To compile their list, the Bureau makes use of their extensive network of local journalists to report to the Bureau's central register what appears in local papers. In addition, the Bureau speaks to councils, hospitals, coroners' offices, police forces, charities, GPs and NGOs.

The result is a set of definitely identified deaths, but there is no guarantee that all are captured; realistically many will not be. The total number of rough sleeper deaths identified by the Bureau between 1 October 2017 and 27 December 2018, some 15 months, namely 546, will therefore be an under-estimate. (Of these 294 were in England or Wales).

The ONS estimates a far larger total figure for the number of rough sleeper deaths in England and Wales in 2017 (namely 597, about double the number of individuals specifically identified by the Bureau). This serves to illustrate how hard it is to capture rough sleeper deaths with the current *ad hoc* arrangements.

The Bureau's database does not always identify the name of the deceased. The labels "unknown" and "anonymous" are used. I take "unknown" to mean only that their source did not provide the name, though it might be known by someone. However, I interpret "anonymous" to mean the deceased's name was simply not known at all.

Half the Scottish cases and all the Northern Irish cases were labelled "unknown". The number of deaths in England and Wales labelled "unknown" was 109 out of 294 (37%).

The number of people in England and Wales who died "anonymous", or for whom only a first name or nickname was known, was 87 (30%). Some of those labelled "unknown" would undoubtedly fall into this category also, so the actual figure of "anonymous" deaths is greater still. To die without anyone even knowing your name is the ultimate in social isolation.

The Bureau's main list includes all the cases from England and Wales, and about half the cases from Scotland (mostly those in Glasgow). This list totals 351 deaths, and comprises 223 men, 38 women, and 90 cases where the sex is unknown. The rest of the Scottish data and all the Northern Irish data does not specify the sex.

Hence, where sex has been recorded, 85% were men and 15% women. This is in good agreement with ONS estimates, below (84% men). There are nearly 6 men dying on the streets for every woman who dies on the streets.

The ONS have been estimating rough sleeper deaths only since 2013. The methodology deployed by ONS starts with death registration records and searches on terms like "no fixed abode", "homeless" and "night shelter" or the name or address of a known homeless hostel or project. Coroners' inquest reports are also used as a source. In common with the Bureau's approach, the ONS searches include homeless people who had been found in need of medical attention in the street and subsequently died in hospital, or other places of medical assistance. The ONS also deploy sophisticated statistical tools to include allowance for more deaths not captured by the direct searches. They state that, "this is a robust but conservative (lower bound) model, so that the figures produced should be taken as the lowest probable estimates."

The ONS approach is "top down", whereas the Bureau's list is "bottom up".

Key findings from the December 2018 ONS report, Ref.[2], were,

- There were an estimated 597 deaths of homeless people in England & Wales in 2017 (an increase of 24% since 2013);

- Men accounted for 84% of these deaths;

- The top three causes of deaths of the homeless in 2017 were drug poisoning (32%), suicide (13%) and alcohol-specific (10%);

- Although there is a concentration of homeless in London, and hence a concentration of homeless deaths in London, the rough sleeper death rate per million people (15.4) is not the largest, being exceeded by the West of England (21.0), Liverpool (20.5) and Greater Manchester (17.8);

- The peak age for the deaths of rough sleeping men is 45-49, and for women 35-39 (see Figure 1). You don't live to be old on the streets.

A Few Case Histories

Data are all very well, but the specifics of cases tell another story. Here are a random few, in no particular order.

Chris Conlin, who died in Leigh, on November 5, 2017, aged 31, became homeless after the death of his mother and brother. Local residents who knew him said he prioritised food for his dog over himself.

Brodie Rippindale died aged 31 in the closed doorway of a shut Salvation Army office in Falmouth, on 6 December 2017.

Istvan Kakas died in Bath, on 16 October 2018, aged 52. He had been a chef working for both Gordon Ramsay and Michael Caine and had completed more than 250 parachute jumps while on military service. He received a heroism award from the mayor of Bath after he helped save a man and his daughter from drowning. He began selling the Big Issue in 2010.

Craig Cunningham died sleeping rough in Chester, on October 25, 2018. He used to manage a Kwik Save store before falling on hard times.

Ben, of unknown surname, died in Retford, on 27 February 2018, aged 53. He died in his tent in freezing weather conditions. He had only recently been discharged from hospital after being treated for pneumonia. According to a local woman who knew him, Ben had worked as a bricklayer but had stopped working after the death of his partner seven years earlier.

Rob O'Connor died in Chelmsford, on 23 February 2018. He died in a shop doorway on a night when temperatures dropped to -2°C. Rob had recently undergone treatment for cancer and had his voice box removed.

An unidentified man died in Barnsley, on 12 February 2018. His body was found in the woods outside Barnsley in freezing cold temperatures. A local homeless charity told the press: "It is unbelievable the conditions they are living in out there, where they are sitting outside absolutely frozen. And there are two or three who have dogs and they would wrap them up rather than themselves. They are wearing four or five layers of clothing just to survive, not only through the night but through the day too."

Kenneth Howson died in Leeds, on 5 January 2018, aged 65. Kenneth's decomposed body was found in a field where he lived in a tent.

Jean Louis du Plessis died in Bristol, on 3 January 2018, aged 41. He was found unresponsive and in a "sleeping position" in a car park during the freezing weather of Storm Eleanor. An inquest found him to be in a "state of prolonged starvation".

Colin Ellis was found dead behind the steering wheel of his car, in which he lived, in late autumn 2017. By the time he was discovered, he had been there for several days. Charity workers recalled Mr Ellis regularly bought food and gave his own cash to other people on the streets.

Darren Greenfield died in Edinburgh in December 2017, aged 48, after years of sleeping rough. He had served with the 2nd Royal Tank Regiment, the Royal Army Pay Corps and the Adjutant General's Corps. He became homeless after leaving the army.

Anthony Barnard died in Lowestoft, on 28 December 2017, aged 57. Mr Barnard was found dead in the garden of his former home.

Allan "Scotch" Alexander died while sleeping rough in a car park in Taunton, on Boxing Day 2017. A fellow rough sleeper told local news: "We went to sleep on the top layer of the car park. I had a quilt, but Alan didn't have anything except the clothes he was in. It was really cold and raining heavily. We were wet through.". The day before his death Allan was seen giving away a Christmas meal to a homeless woman by a member of the public.

Henryk Smolarz died in Plymouth city centre, on 12 March 2018, aged 62. His name was provided by a fellow rough sleeper. He was believed to have been Polish and friends say he was a physicist and mathematician.

Hamid Farahi died in Church Langley in March 2018, aged 55. Hamid, a physicist who fought in Iraq, was living in the back of his car in a Tesco car park. He moved to a shelter during the cold weather and passed away there.

Stephen Kinghorn was born in South Shields, Country Durham. He attended a sailing school in Hull for five years where he took part in the 93/94 Tall Ships Race, coming third with his team. The team also helped to build a school in a remote village in Zimbabwe and sailed to various other places. Stephen left as a fully qualified skipper of small vessels. Things started going downhill when his first child was stillborn and continued to slip further downwards. Stephen went to London and was involved with Love Activists and a homeless kitchen trying to get food for fellow homeless. He was proud of being part of that. Then his second child died, which was the catalyst to sending him rock bottom. Stephen died in London on 19 March 2018. He was 39 years old.

Ryan McGurgan died in Leeds on 10 April 2018, aged 33. He was found dead in a hostel for homeless men on the morning he was due to be recalled to prison.

Mary Lane died in Gravesend on 22 April 2018, aged 53. Her body was found in a sleeping bag in the woods. She was not identified for many weeks and it was apparent she had been there for some time.

Only known as "Tibby", this Romanian man died in his wheelchair after volunteers reported he looked frail and very neglected (Stratford, 7 June 2018, aged 50).

Paul Williams was found frozen to death by a homeless-outreach officer on the streets outside the Bullring Shopping Centre in Birmingham on 17 December 2017, aged 38.

An unnamed 22-year-old woman was found on fire at an emergency shelter hostel in Derby on 25 August 2018. She was taken to hospital where she died. A city support worker told the press "She had her issues in life but the most tragic thing in all of this is that she was getting better."

An unnamed 31-year-old man was found dead in Wakefield on 20 August 2018. The manager of the Community Awareness Programme said "we are watching them die – you end up getting used to it and we don't want that to happen."

Remigiusz Boczarski had been living in a bus shelter in Malvern when he died, apparently from suicide, on 30 October 2018, aged 40. A local woman who befriended him told press: "He would turn up at my door and I would wash his clothes and give him a meal. He was always a really nice guy. He never overstayed his welcome." It seems he decided not to overstay his welcome on this mortal coil either.

Gyula Remes was the man who died outside the MPs' entrance to the House of Commons on 19 December 2018. He gave the MPs an opportunity to wring their hands in anguish – for a bit.

References

[1] McClenaghan, M. and Boutaud, C. (2018). *Dying Homeless: Counting the deaths of homeless people across the UK*. The Bureau of Investigative Journalism, 23 April 2018.

[2] Office for National Statistics (2018). *Deaths of homeless people in England and Wales: 2013 to 2017*. Release date 20 December 2018.

Section 8

Feminist Propaganda

39. Global Gender Gap Report

This was one of my earliest posts. It was the first time I'd stumbled across the World Economic Forum (WEF) and their role in promoting international feminism. It bewildered me utterly at the time. What's in it for them? I have kept the article essentially as it appeared at the time. It exposes that the WEF's Global Gender Gap Index (GGGI) is actually blatant feminist propaganda and utterly fraudulent as a measure of gender inequality. It's one of my angry posts, as my early posts tended to be. Red Pill rage, I suppose.

Original posted on: 8 November 2014.

In November 2014 the press had been reporting on the World Economic Forum's Global Gender Gap Report 2014, Ref.[1]. The WEF publishes such a report annually. As I write the latest is Ref.[2]. It claims that "gender equality is stalling; 131 years to close the gap". That'll get the ladies all riled up, eh? But I shall stick here to the 2014 version which I used in my original post.

It's a big fat report. Very big. In fact it's 385 pages of utter nonsense.

It is almost insulting that the authors do not even try to hide their fraudulence. They are so arrogant in their power that they openly admit they have cooked the books. They know that they will get no challenge from the movers and shakers, the press, the media and the politicians. They know that they could fill 384 of those 385 pages with copy-and-paste from a telephone directory – so long as the conclusion on page 385 is that women are being disadvantaged. Then the media and the politicians will report just that. Who cares whether it's based on garbage.

No, not garbage. Garbage would be neutral.

But I get ahead of myself. Darn it, I've given away the punch line – and you'd never have guessed.

The report purports to measure quantitatively the 'gap' between the sexes for each country. It uses 'gaps' across four areas: Economic Participation and Opportunity, Educational Attainment, Health and Survival, and Political Empowerment. These 'gaps' are defined as the ratio of the number of women in the desired state to the number of men. For example, it might be the number of women attaining some educational level divided by the number of men attaining that same educational level. Or it might be the number of female government ministers divided by the number of male government ministers. Or it might be the ratio of female-to-male earned income. An overall 'gender gap' for a given country is defined as the simple average of the four contributing 'gaps'.

In each case, equality is represented by a ratio of 1. A ratio of less than 1 indicates female disadvantage.

So, you expect me to add, a ratio great than 1 indicates male disadvantage.

No, sorry. That's simply not allowed.

If the ratio turns out to be greater than 1, i.e., indicating male disadvantage, they just set it back to 1.

Eh?

That's right.

All male disadvantage is simply vanished away.

All male disadvantage, however severe, is defined as equality.

It really is as blatant and as outrageous as that. Honestly. I'm not making this up. As I said – they rely on no one actually reading the report.

They are entirely upfront about it. The report states that,

"the Index rewards countries that reach the point where outcomes for women equal those for men, but it neither rewards nor penalizes cases in which women are outperforming men..."

In case you failed to understand that, it continues,

"Thus a country, which has higher enrolment for girls rather than boys in secondary school, will score equal to a country where boys' and girls' enrolment is the same."

In other words, male disadvantage is equality. You cannot accuse them of not making it clear. It is abundantly clear. But just in case you haven't got the message yet, there's this,

"To capture gender equality, two possible scales were considered. One was a negative-positive scale capturing the size and direction of the gender gap. This scale penalizes either men's advantage over women or women's advantage over men, and gives the highest points

to absolute equality. The second choice was a one-sided scale that measures how close women are to reaching parity with men but does not reward or penalize countries for having a gender gap in the other direction. We find the one-sided scale more appropriate for our purposes.….."

I'll bet you do. And "one-sided" is an apt description. In case you haven't grasped it, the "negative-positive" scale would have recognised cases of male disadvantage. The "one-sided" scale simply airbrushes away ratios greater than one (male disadvantage), leaving only cases of female disadvantage. The nature of the "equality" measure employed in the report mathematically guarantees that it can only appear to indicate female disadvantage. The last sentence in full reads,

"We find the one-sided scale more appropriate for our purposes, as it does not reward countries for having exceeded the parity benchmark."

Do you see how twisted is the mindset of the authors? The only thing that crosses their minds in respect of cases of male disadvantage is that this might be worthy of a reward. They consider themselves ever so egalitarian that they are willing to eschew the reward. What noble people they are.

Before I proceed to specific examples, do note that as long as men and women are different in any respect (which they always will be) this will always be perceived under this measure as female disadvantage. Equality on this measure could only be attained if women were advantaged over men in absolutely everything.

Let me give some illustrations. In the Educational Attainment category virtually all Western European and Anglophone countries are given a "gap" index of 1.0, or a tiny bit below such as 0.998 or 0.9996, essentially indicating equality. This deliberately hides away the indisputable and notorious fact that boys are sinking without trace in the educational systems of pretty much all these countries. Certainly in the USA and the UK, women dominate emphatically as undergraduates and have done for 30 years. According to this ever-so-erudite report, this is equality.

This is deliberate, not an oversight. It is a counterfactual so severe as to be a lie. It corresponds directly in terms of mindset with the UK's Department for Education which has no intention of doing anything to address boys' education.

Here's another example of the preposterous nonsense that the WEF's GGGI promotes. The Health and Survival category is based upon the ratio of female healthy life expectancy over that for males. The authors of this propaganda spotted that this one would give them trouble. Heck, it's going to be greater than one: women live longer than men in just about every country in the world. No problem, they did this…

"the healthy life expectancy benchmark is set to be 1.06"

Yep, they simply redefined inequality of men as equality again. If women have on average a 6% longer life expectancy than men, this is regarded as equality in the "Survival" category. So by this shifting of the meaning of equality the report massages the score in the Health and Survival category to be just a tiny bit less than one – almost equality with a little disadvantage to women – apparently.

Really? Well, let's see now. When it comes to disadvantage, being dead takes some beating. And when it comes to being dead, men have pretty much cornered the market compared to women. The vast majority of war dead are men. The vast majority of deaths at work are men. Men are over three-quarters of suicide victims. Men are the majority of homicide victims. And most importantly, men have a shorter life expectancy worldwide. In the UK and most Western countries this is due to cardiovascular diseases and cancers. Yes, there are lifestyle issues, but there are also biological factors. More men die prematurely (before age 75) than women of every type of cancer, bar the sex-specific cancers. Overall, men are 44% more likely to die prematurely (before age 75) than women.

All that is equality – in fact, a slight disadvantage to women, as far as the WEF's GGGI report is concerned. And this damnable report is lapped up by feminists everywhere as gospel. It is obscene.

Here's an example of the scoring for the UK in 2014,

- Economic Participation and Opportunity = 0.7140
- Educational Attainment = 0.9996
- Health and Survival = 0.9699
- Political Empowerment = 0.2698
- Overall score (the average of the above) = 0.7383

The Economic Participation and Opportunity "gap" is just our old friend the pay gap. Let's not go there again. Suffice it to say that men doing most of the paid work and women doing most of the spending is disadvantage to women, apparently. But they have bumped up the apparent disadvantage by also including the "ratio of women to men among technical and professional workers". Yes, they've managed to squeeze their STEM gripe in there too. Never mind that women dominate as undergraduates in STEMM now. Never mind the under-representation of men in teaching and health care. That doesn't count – even though (and this may not be mere coincidence) it is in education and health that men are disadvantaged in terms of outcomes for the population as a whole, not just in terms of employment.

The UK Educational Attainment and Health and Survival scores should, of course, be substantially bigger than 1, but this has been airbrushed out.

Then there's the Political Empowerment 'gap'. This is defined essentially as the ratio of female to male Members of Parliament. Actually there is another measure too, which involves looking back 50 years – so even strict equality now would appear as disadvantage to women because of the sins of the past. This "historical disadvantage" is a favourite feminist trick to spuriously justify anything. But the true fraudulence is that political empowerment is not measured by the number of women in the legislature, because male politicians are obliged to be feminists too (even to the point of literally wearing the tee shirt). That the feminist lobby is the dominant political orthodoxy is proved by the press reception of this very report. Any rational journalist with a free hand would savagely excoriate this preposterous nonsense. That this has not happened is all the proof you need as to where the power lies in our country and has done for decades.

And finally, there is the overall "gap", defined as the average of the four contributing "gaps". Do note how ridiculous it is to take a simple, unweighted average of these "gaps". Let me illustrate. Suppose the Political Empowerment "gap" was 0.5. By including this in a simple average with, say, the Health and Survival "gap" the implicit assumption is that not being a Member of Parliament is a disadvantage equivalent to being dead. Moreover, a "gap" of 0.5 would be equivalent to one sex having half the life expectancy of the other. Really? If there were twice as many men in parliament as women, this is as serious a problem as if women's life expectancy was only 40? And no weighting is applied for the number of people actually affected by the disadvantage. There are only 650 members of the UK parliament, whereas the Health and Survival "gap" (which is actually to men's disadvantage) affects the whole population.

I run out of suitable vocabulary to describe how utterly moronic it all is – except, of course, it isn't. It's actually brilliant propaganda. That it is, academically speaking, sheer buffoonery is irrelevant.

So, is the Global Gender Gap Report an example of sexism? No. This report has grown out of an anti-male sexist culture, of course. And cultural sexism leads to systemic bias and myriad random acts of misandry. But sexism *per se* is not goal directed. What we see in this report is an example of a long-standing coordinated campaign driven by political ideology with cold-blooded deliberation. This is beyond mere sexism; it is far worse.

Before closing I draw readers' attention to a more reasonable measure of gender inequality which does admit that the disadvantage can go either way. This is BIGI – the Basic Index of Gender Inequality, which was devised by two academic psychologists, Gijsbert Stoet (University of Essex) and David Geary (University of Missouri), Ref.[3]. Being an unprejudiced measure you will appreciate that the authors had to develop it unfunded. You can read about it in a couple of my other posts, Refs.[4,5]. The latter is particularly interesting in that it shows that the more developed a nation becomes, the more it disadvantages men.

References

[1]   World Economic Forum (2014). *The Global Gender Gap Report 2014*.

[2]   World Economic Forum (2023). *The Global Gender Gap Report 2023.*

[3]   Stoet, G. and Geary, D.C. (2019). *A simplified approach to measuring national gender inequality*. PLOS ONE, 3 January 2019.

[4]   Collins, W. (2019). *BIGI v GGGR*. The Illustrated Empathy Gap, 5 January 2019.

[5]   Collins, W. (2019). *Measuring Gender Equality*. The Illustrated Empathy Gap, 5 December 2019.

40. Photograph 51 – Rosalind Franklin

Here's one of feminists' favourite stories of a wronged woman in science; nearly a Nobel prize winner but neglected and unknown. But wait up a minute. You have heard of Rosalind Franklin, haven't you? Whereas if she had been called George Smithers you would never have heard of him. He would just be another also-ran man in a scientific race. And you've never heard of Raymond Gosling either, have you? He was the young man who actually took Photograph 51. Just saying.

Original posted on: 7 October 2015.

In October 2015, when I wrote this blog article, there was a play showing in London's West End, "Photograph 51", starring Nicole Kidman. She plays the role of Rosalind Franklin, the scientist who did groundbreaking work on the structure of DNA in the 1950s. Kate Mulcahy, Ref.[1], tells Franklin's story thus: "*Marginalised during her research in the 1950s, ostracised by male peers and ultimately overlooked by the establishment, Franklin's data was used without her permission and her contribution to science was drastically under-acknowledged.*" Mulcahy claims that Franklin is "*the latest forgotten female scientist to be thrust into the limelight*" and that she is "*a quintessential example of the maligned woman in science*". In similar vein, Nicole Kidman has said she wants to "*shine a light on the role of Franklin and women like her whose quiet hard work has been overshadowed by pushier men*", Ref.[2]. And again, Anita Singh, Ref.[2], opined of Franklin that she "*played a key role in discovering the structure of DNA while working at King's College London, but was effectively written out of history.*"

I beg to differ. There is something more insidious at work here. It is claimed that Rosalind Franklin is forgotten. But that is odd. Surely she is a household name? And yet if she had been called George Smithers, a man, you would indeed never have heard of him, unless you were a specialist in the field. We, non-specialists, have heard of Rosalind Franklin precisely, and solely, because she was female.

It is often the case in science that several people, or several teams, are racing to answer a certain question. Generally, only one crosses the finishing line first. He, she or they get the accolades. Blokes who finish second are forgotten. It's tough, but that's life. And yet it is often the case that the winning team will be influenced by the work of others in developing their ideas. Well, of course – that's how science works. That's why people publish papers in journals – to communicate with others in the field. So it may very well be that the winners have made good use of the work of the poor saps who came second, and the latter get scant credit for being 99% of the way to the answer. It's a hard life, but there it is. Move on, chaps. Onwards and upwards!

Unless, that is, the person who came second was a woman. Then we are permitted to take a different view. Then it is unfair, it is sexism.

Mulcahy's article claims that Franklin was *"left out of the Nobel Prize to which her work was essential"*, thus giving the impression of outrageous unfairness. Yet the author of the article will be aware, but did not see fit to mention, that Franklin died four years before the Nobel Prize for the structure of DNA was awarded in 1962, and that the Nobel Prize is never awarded posthumously. This is not honest journalism; it is propaganda. It intentionally manipulates public perceptions by creating a false impression, reinforcing the feminist oppression myth. Had Franklin been alive in 1962 we simply do not know if she would also have been awarded a Nobel. Her work was certainly well-known and fully appreciated as significant in the achievement of unravelling the structure of DNA, so she might well have got a Nobel.

But let me reprise the actual history of the discovery of the structure of DNA. For this I am indebted to Matthew Cobb, Refs.[3,4].

When Rosalind Franklin joined King's College, London, in late 1950 she was already an expert in the use of X-ray diffraction for the purposes of determining crystallographic structure. From the start there was a misunderstanding between her and an existing member of King's, Maurice Wilkins, as to whether Franklin was working under Wilkins or independently. Much has been said about the difficult relationship between Franklin and Wilkins. What is not disputed is that they did not get on. This was unfortunate given that they were both working on X-ray crystallography at the same college. Some commenters have attempted to portray this dysfunctional relationship as due to Wilkins' authoritarian or domineering attitude. This seems to be far from the truth. From all accounts Wilkins was a most diffident chap, shying away from confrontation – whilst Franklin was a much more forthright character. Cobb quotes Rosalind's friend Norma Sutherland as recalling, *"her manner was brusque and at times confrontational – she aroused quite a lot of hostility among the people she talked to, and she seemed quite insensitive to this.*" Arguably, Franklin found it necessary to be forceful as a woman in science in those days. But it is more likely that she was simply fiercely protective of her independence and had no great desire to collaborate with Wilkins. Rather oddly this communication breakdown led to parallel working on the same subject, namely the structure of DNA, within the same college (culminating in a pair of independent papers in the 1953 issue of Nature, one by Wilkins and co-authors, and one by Franklin and co-author).

Francis Crick and James Watson, at the Cavendish laboratory in Cambridge, were also trying to figure out the structure of DNA. Unlike Wilkins and Franklin they were not doing experimental work but were attempting to figure out the structure purely theoretically. In 1952 they embarrassed Lawrence Bragg, the Director of the Cavendish, by presenting a model of DNA to Wilkins and Franklin which the latter were able to immediately dismiss as obviously incorrect. Note the inevitable academic rivalry which would exist between Cambridge and King's College London. Consequently, Bragg temporarily banned Crick and Watson from working on DNA. However, Bragg changed his mind when his great rival in the USA, Linus Pauling, also published an obviously incorrect model of DNA. Knowing that Pauling would soon realise his error, but now knowing that his rival was hot on the trail of DNA, Bragg authorised Crick and Watson to recommence work. In just a few frenetic weeks they had the correct DNA structure complete with a ball-and-stick molecular model.

So how did they do it? Well, the idea of a helix being involved was in their minds from the start, simply because it had already been established by Linus Pauling that a helix (the so-called alpha-helix) formed the backbone of proteins. Their method of working was to attempt to build stick-and-ball models of the right atoms and chemical groups, constrained to have the correct bond angles and bond lengths. The process was hampered by not knowing what all the bond angles and lengths actually were. Theoreticians need data. Crick and Watson needed X-ray diffraction information. Looking at what was available they discovered work by the English crystallographer W.T.Astbury from five years earlier, which was a start. (Incidentally it was William Astbury's X-ray work in the 1930s which assisted Pauling's discovery of the protein alpha-helix. So, in William Astbury we have one of the myriad of genuinely unknown and unsung heroes who contribute in a major way to scientific progress – most of them male).

But Crick and Watson needed more, and better, X-ray diffraction pictures. They knew they needed Maurice Wilkins at King's. Unexpectedly Wilkins turned out to be very amenable, and even agreed that a helical structure was probably involved right from the start (in 1951). However, according to James Watson's account in "The Double Helix", Wilkins' difficulties with Franklin had reached the point where she had tried to insist that he stop work on DNA. To keep the peace, Wilkins had handed over to Franklin all his best crystalline samples of DNA, thus hampering his own work. This does not align well with the "sexist male scientist undermines female colleague" trope, does it?

Let's make one thing clear: Rosalind Franklin was a first-rate X-ray crystallographer. She was certainly one of the best, if not *the* best, in the field at the time – though Wilkins was comparable. It is also true that the famous "photograph 51", which forms the title of the play, was pivotal in consolidating the idea of the helical structure. The key to photograph 51 was not just good X-ray technique. The photo was taken using a new crystalline form of DNA, the so-called B form, created under conditions of full hydration. Franklin was the first to identify the B form of DNA (though I'm not clear if she or Wilkins made the sample). There are several issues here which are often elided in popular accounts.

Firstly, recall that Crick and Watson had been working on the assumption of a helical structure for some time, so photograph 51 was confirmation rather than revelation.

Secondly, photograph 51 was published in the famous 1953 issue of *Nature* under joint authorship: Franklin and Gosling. Who was Gosling? Well that would be Raymond Gosling. Contrary to almost every popular account it was not Franklin who did the hands-on work to produce photograph 51, it was Raymond Gosling. But we need not concern ourselves with Gosling. He was just some male research student whom we can ignore completely. (The poor chap was rather buggered about. He initially had Wilkins as a supervisor, but was transferred to work with Franklin, only to be passed back to Wilkins again when Franklin left King's). Of course, had Franklin been a man and Gosling a woman, it would be Gosling who would be the focus of all this fuss. As it is, Gosling doesn't matter at all. Please forget I mentioned him.

Third: it was Maurice Wilkins who first showed photograph 51 to James Watson (though Wilkins himself, with co-workers, would soon produce essentially equivalent pictures). Rosalind Franklin was keeping this latest result to herself at the time. That part of the popular account is true.

Finally, the really crucial issue is this: Franklin was, for a long time, vehemently opposed to the hypothesis of a helical structure for DNA. Be aware that the interpretation of X-ray diffraction patterns is a very tricky business. Do not imagine they are anything like a medical X-ray. They are, in effect, an encrypted version of the physical object photographed (technically they are related to the object's Fourier transformation). Franklin failed, at least initially, to correctly interpret her own X-ray photos. Her experimental technique was impeccable, but her mathematical analysis was no match for Francis Crick.

Crick and Watson had shared with Franklin their hypothesis of a helical structure, but she had been against the idea from the start. Crick and Watson were of the opinion that a helical structure could be seen even in Franklin's earliest X-ray photos (using the A form of DNA), even though the interpretation in that case was fraught. When Watson – and later Crick – saw the B form photo, the helical structure leapt out at them. Franklin, however, failed to see it – initially, though she did eventually.

Photograph 51 had been taken by Ray Gosling in May 1952 but (according to Cobb, Ref.[3]) had not been studied at King's and had lain in a drawer for months. With Rosalind Franklin's departure from King's immanent, responsibility for supervising Gosling's PhD had passed to Wilkins. Under this new arrangement Gosling had given photograph 51 to Wilkins. Gosling was adamant that Wilkins had every right to it. That he chose to show it to Watson was his prerogative.

Earlier the same day that Wilkins showed Watson photograph 51, Watson had had yet another argument with Franklin regarding the helical hypothesis. She was even more dismissive of the idea than ever. So convinced was she that her own work disproved the helical hypothesis, rather than supporting it, she even went to the lengths of posting a notice in the King's college physics department saying, "it is with great regret that we have to announce the death, on Friday 18th July 1952, of DNA helix (crystalline)". This was based on the A form of DNA which fails to show the helical structure so clearly as the B form. Note that Franklin posted that notice two months after photograph 51 had been taken by Gosling.

However, photograph 51 was not enough. Indeed the significance of it has been overblown, probably because of how James Watson wrote his own account in *The Double Helix*.

Crick and Watson needed numbers. They needed data which would constrain key bond angles and lengths. Much has been made of how Crick and Watson acquired this key data. It originated from Franklin, of course. But it was not stolen. Actually Franklin had made this data public in a talk in 1951 which Watson had attended. Stupidly, though, he failed to note down the key data. But Franklin had also written the data in a report to Max Perutz at Cambridge, who had passed it, in February 1953, to Lawrence Bragg, who in turn gave it to Crick and Watson (since Bragg was now keen to beat his old rival Linus Pauling to the big prize). This was what Crick and Watson had been waiting for: the Rosetta Stone which permitted them within a few weeks of intense work to produce a complete model of the DNA molecular structure.

Franklin was close behind. But it was only on 24 February 1953 that Franklin finally realised that both the A and the B forms of DNA were double helices. She would not have the chance to complete the structure because, by then, Crick and Watson had already done so.

There was no impropriety in what Crick and Watson did, though their failure to tell the King's people that they were using their data was impolite. More importantly there was no sexism in this behaviour. It was irrelevant that the data originated from Franklin; it could equally well have come from Wilkins who was duplicating the same work.

The key issue, though, was the interpretation in terms of chemical structure. Here Francis Crick's greater mathematical sophistication came up trumps, though Franklin realised just too late that Crick and Watson had been right all along. To quote Cobb, Refs.[3,4],

"Franklin's laboratory notebooks reveal that she initially found it difficult to interpret the outcome of the complex mathematics – like Crick, she was working with nothing more than a slide rule and a pencil – but by 24 February (1953), she had realised that DNA had a double helix structure and that the way the component nucleotides or bases on each

strand were connected meant that the two strands were complementary, enabling the molecule to replicate. Above all, Franklin noted that 'an infinite variety of nucleotide sequences would be possible to explain the biological specificity of DNA', thereby showing that she had glimpsed the most decisive secret of DNA: the sequence of bases contains the genetic code. To prove her point, she would have to convert this insight into a precise, mathematically and chemically rigorous model. She did not get the chance to do this, because Watson and Crick had already crossed the finishing line – the Cambridge duo had rapidly interpreted the double helix structure in terms of precise spatial relationships and chemical bonds, through the construction of a physical model."

In other words, she ran the Cambridge men a very close race, but finished second. The reason she was second was that she was slower to interpret her own data than they were, partly because her maths was less strong and partly because she failed to appreciate the value of model building. To quote James Watson, *"affecting Rosy's transformation was her appreciation that our past hooting about model building represented a serious approach to science, not the easy resort of slackers who wanted to avoid the hard work necessitated by an honest scientific career".*

It is worth noting that, had Franklin been willing to cooperate with the Cambridge men, the final structure of DNA would have emerged earlier, because her key data was available in 1951. Even if photograph 51 were deemed essential, this was available in May 1952 – suggesting that collaboration would have led to the final structure in June or July 1952, some eight months earlier than it actually emerged. But Franklin did not want to collaborate; she wanted to discover the answer herself.

Again quoting Matthew Cobb, the dénouement was…

"In the middle of March 1953, Wilkins and Franklin were invited to Cambridge to see the model, and they immediately agreed it must be right. It was agreed that the model would be published solely as the work of Watson and Crick, while the supporting data would be published by Wilkins and Franklin – separately, of course. On 25 April there was a party at King's to celebrate the publication of the three articles in Nature. Franklin did not attend. She was now at Birkbeck and had stopped working on DNA."

What we have here is an everyday story of scientific folk. Well, OK, perhaps the importance of the subject was hardly "everyday", but the nature of the groping towards the truth, and the interactions between the personnel, is fairly typical. There is no compelling reason to put a gendered spin on the matter. Had Franklin been male, but otherwise of the same character, the story would have unfolded exactly the same.

In part the claims of gender bias have arisen as a result of the Nobel Prize, but Franklin was no longer eligible, being dead, so that is a completely spurious perspective. There is no way of knowing what the Nobel Committee would have decided had she still been alive. Without any doubt Franklin made a major contribution to settling the structure of DNA. Indeed, she would have solved the problem on her own eventually, had she not been beaten to the answer. Had she been alive, the Nobel Committee's problem would have been that no more than three people can be awarded a given Nobel. Crick and Watson's claim was beyond doubt, so Franklin would have been in competition with Wilkins – especially since they produced essentially equivalent work. Who knows what the Committee would have done. One option would have been to award Crick and Watson the prize for Physiology or Medicine, and award Franklin and Watkins the prize for Chemistry. But who knows.

What I emphatically disagree with is Kate Mulcahy's claim, Ref.[1], that Rosalind Franklin should be a feminist icon. I don't agree that anyone should be a feminist icon. Such a thing is fundamentally divisive. I'm happy for Franklin to be regarded as a *scientific* icon – that, after all, is what she would have wanted.

Anita Singh, Ref.[2], quotes Nigel Franklin, the scientist's nephew, as saying that his aunt has been misinterpreted in the play. *"I think there were little things that annoyed her, like the fact that when she was at King's the common room was men only. But she got on with her work and she would have been astonished at being considered a feminist icon. She didn't think of herself as being different for being a woman. I don't think she felt, other than those social things, in any way held back. It wasn't something she felt, that she was hard done by. The feminist movement has picked her up as an icon and used her in that way. But as far as she was concerned, she loved her work – she was brilliant at what she did – and I really, really don't think that this feminist business that's attached to her was an issue for her at all. Even if she had lived to see Crick and Watson collect the Nobel Prize, she would not necessarily have felt hard done by."*

But Kate Mulcahy will not accept that. Any woman insisting that she is not a victim must be persuaded that she is. Where Kate Mulcahy is coming from is betrayed by her straying into women-in-STEM at the end of her article.

"Men outnumber women in many university science courses", she tells us. One grows weary. Women have been the majority of undergraduates in the UK for 30 years. They dominate in 75% of subjects. There are more women than men as undergraduates in science subjects, and there are more women than men in STEMM subjects (note the two Ms).

But despite those facts there are vast resources extended to encourage more women in STEM, not least by Athena Swan but also by the hordes like Kate Mulcahy who are interested only in advancing women with no regard whatsoever for the other sex, or empirical reality. There are no initiatives to address the male disadvantage which is emphatically apparent in the statistics. Instead, the persistent focus of attention, effort and funding is to encourage more women into TEM, the dwindling island in which men remain dominant. This partisan focus on the educational attainment of the sex that least requires assistance is presented to us as being the pursuit of "equality". No, it is prejudice.

And this is the reason that the play "Photograph 51" and the feminist narrative around Rosalind Franklin is so pernicious. It isn't really about Rosalind Franklin. It isn't really about science. It's all part of maintaining the myth that men are powerful and privileged and women are oppressed. And this myth provides their power, the power to promote female advantage – not equality, but advantage.

References

[1] Mulcahy, K. (2015). *Rosalind Franklin should be a feminist icon - we women in science need her more than ever*. The Telegraph, 15 September 2015.

[2] Anita Singh, A. (2015). *Rosalind Franklin would be 'astonished' to be cast as feminist icon in play starring Nicole Kidman*. The Telegraph, 13 September 2015.

[3] Cobb, M. (2016). *Life's Greatest Secret: The Race to Crack the Genetic Code*, 2 June 2016.

[4] Cobb, M. (2015). *Sexism in science: did Watson and Crick really steal Rosalind Franklin's data?* The Guardian, 23 June 2015.

41. Woman Takes First Picture of a Black Hole (apparently)

The previous chapter was about the feminist myth-making to present women as unsung heroes. Here's another. When will they ever tire of presenting women as wonderful but wronged? Never.

Original posted on: 11 April 2019.

On 11 April 2019, if you had not actually been living in a black hole yourself, and hence out of contact with the rest of the universe, you would have been aware that astronomers had just reported the first picture of a black hole, specifically the supermassive black hole at the centre of galaxy Messier 87. (To be pedantic, it's the first picture of stuff falling into a black hole, the black hole itself being, well, black. Actually, it isn't, quite, but never mind).

One is used to experts interviewed on the BBC about anything scientific (well, about anything at all really) being women on every occasion it proves possible. This was no exception, with local women astronomers being pressed into service yesterday to comment on the achievement. Annoyingly obvious propaganda. One groans and moves on. But press articles appeared such as that by the BBC, Ref.[1], and The Daily Mail's offering, Ref.[2]. The caption to the leading image in Ref.[1] reads "Katie Bouman designed an algorithm that made the image possible".

Ref.[2] included tweets from the usual culprits. Ivanka Trump told us it was "an amazing accomplishment made possible by Scientist Katie Bouman". AOC (Alexandria Ocasio-Cortez) tweeted "take your rightful seat in history, Dr Bouman". Kamala Harris gave us "Katie Bouman proved women in STEM don't just make the impossible, possible, but make history while doing it". Etc. etc.

Indeed, a whole bunch of female celebrities (not noted for knowing anything about science, and caring less) flooded social media to "claim the black hole for woman-kind". My sarcastic words, sorry, but really that's a fairly accurate description of the tweets, e.g., "Let's holla for women in STEM!!", etc. You get the picture. One person - obviously a vile misogynistic troll - complained that they were unnecessarily making a purely scientific achievement a matter of gender. Well, they were. Indisputably. The Twitterati didn't see it that way. Surprise!

Knowing that this was a large international collaboration, I expected that the team involved would be very large. It is often the case in these situations that the leader of the collaboration acts as a figurehead to take the credit (and who then will invariably emphasise that it was a team effort). But that wouldn't do. You see, the Director of the Event Horizon Telescope Collaboration, Shep Doeleman, is a bloke. That wouldn't do at all. Somewhere along the line the media lighted upon a suitable female candidate for glory (led by Twitter, I expect). As leader of the image algorithm team, Katie Bouman was a suitable choice.

Bouman, in best tradition, immediately deflected the credit to her team of computer scientists. Quite right too. She was quoted as saying, "No one of us could've done it alone. It came together because of lots of different people from many backgrounds". The media hype was not Bouman's doing. But the media, and social media, were determined to make her their hero of choice, whether she liked it or not.

Anyone who has worked in teams knows that there tends to be one or two people who are the linchpins. Is Katie such a person, or was it members of her team that better fit that description? Outsiders will never know, and nor does it much matter – to outsiders. Those in the know, know. But even if we knew who were the key players in the algorithm team, that leaves....everyone else. And how many people were there in the Event Horizon Telescope Collaboration? Rather a lot.

Let's take a look at the scientific papers themselves, should we? Six papers were published in Astrophysical Journal Letters on the 10 April 2019, Refs.[3-8]. Click on any of those links and you will find, after the list of the first eight or nine authors, "show full author list". Click on that. Are you getting the message now? That's how many people were involved. And that's how grossly distorted was the media messaging.

All six papers are formally authored by the Event Horizon Telescope Collaboration. In the original blog post I included the complete list of names. I have omitted them here because it would take more than nine pages. There were 348 people in the Collaboration. Not just one woman. I wouldn't be at all surprised if some women astronomers in the team were a bit pissed off that a computer scientist was getting all the credit. In practice, interdisciplinary jealousies can be much more significant than anything to do with gender.

Anyone who wants to work out the male: female ratio in the complete list of authors (using Refs[3-8] or my original post) be my guest. I can't be bothered. I really don't care.

One social media spin, Ref.[9], was to compare Katie Bouman with Margaret Hamilton, who, apparently, "wrote the code that put a man on the moon". I vaguely recall there were some other people involved in that too.

References

[1] BBC News (2019). *Katie Bouman: The woman behind the first black hole image*. 11 April 2019.

[2] Apen-Sadler, D., and MacDonald, C. (2019). *Revealed: The female MIT graduate, aged just 29, who created the algorithm that captured the first ever direct image of a black hole*. Mail Online, 11 April 2019.

[3] The Event Horizon Telescope Collaboration (2019a). *First M87 Event Horizon Telescope Results. I. The Shadow of the Supermassive Black Hole*. Astrophysical Journal Letters, 875(1) L1, 10 April 2019.

[4] The Event Horizon Telescope Collaboration (2019b). *First M87 Event Horizon Telescope Results. II. Array and Instrumentation.* Astrophysical Journal Letters, 875(1) L2, 10 April 2019.

[5] The Event Horizon Telescope Collaboration (2019c). *First M87 Event Horizon Telescope Results. III. Data Processing and Calibration.* Astrophysical Journal Letters, 875(1) L3, 10 April 2019.

[6] The Event Horizon Telescope Collaboration (2019d). *First M87 Event Horizon Telescope Results. IV. Imaging the Central Supermassive Black Hole* Astrophysical Journal Letters, 875(1) L4, 10 April 2019.

[7] The Event Horizon Telescope Collaboration (2019e). *First M87 Event Horizon Telescope Results. V. Physical Origin of the Asymmetric Ring* Astrophysical Journal Letters, 875(1) L5, 10 April 2019.

[8] The Event Horizon Telescope Collaboration (2019f). *First M87 Event Horizon Telescope Results. VI. The Shadow and Mass of the Central Black Hole* Astrophysical Journal Letters, 875(1) L6, 10 April 2019.

[9] Tweet MIT CSAIL, 4:58 PM · Apr 10, 2019

42. Stealing Our Clothes

More examples of the feminist rewriting of history to aggrandise themselves.

Original posted on: 5 April 2015.

The feminist rewriting of history is a familiar phenomenon. The gross misrepresentation in the public mind of the history of universal suffrage is an example, Refs.[1,2]. More generally, so is the preposterous fabrication of "centuries of oppression" of women by men. That society was based on rigid gender roles is indubitable. This involved limitations of freedom, but on both sides not just one. To interpret the gendered social structure of history as oppression of one sex by the other is to wilfully ignore half the story. More recently the tendency to distort the history of the genders has been amplified by the embedding of academic feminism within postmodernism. A doctrine which denies the existence of truth is a great fillip to the propagandist. If there is merely my truth and your truth, and his truth and her truth, then what are we to believe? The answer is that might is right in this pernicious doctrine of the anti-rational. You will believe whoever gets to shout loudest; whoever has the most successful propaganda machine. One of the postmodernist feminist deceits is to claim that the nearest woman was, in fact, the true author of – well, anything impressive done by a famous man.

Twenty or thirty years ago it was in vogue to claim that the first Mrs Einstein, Mileva (née Marić), was, in fact, a contributor to the development of the theory of relativity. To any physicist this immediately seems crazy. The 1905 paper on special relativity is based on a single, blindingly brilliant, insight. It's the sort of thing that, by its nature, arises in one mind – not from a committee. I'm tempted to call it a quantum of perception. It would have been particularly remarkable if the idea for relativity had been Mileva's – she wasn't a physicist. Contrary to popular belief, she was not really a mathematician either. She studied mathematics but failed her exams. In any case, the suggestion that Mileva "helped Einstein with his mathematics" is otiose because the mathematics of the 1905 paper is pretty simple (unlike the mind-bending 1916 general theory). And, if the idea for relativity had been Mileva's, isn't it odd that she did nothing else in physics?

Who would you say was the most likely author of special relativity: the man who wrote two other epoch making papers that same year, one of which won the Nobel prize and kick-started quantum theory, another of which finally clinched the issue of the existence of atoms; the man who successfully generalised relativity to include gravity, and who spent the next 50 years doing a remarkably good impression of being the greatest physicist since Newton – or the woman who appears never to have done any physics at all, even as a student? Tricky one, isn't it? It shouldn't be necessary to refute such silliness at all, but if you must, try Ref.[3] for example.

Oh, and of course, it was the second Mrs Bach who wrote much of Johann Sebastian Bach's music we are now told by the BBC, Ref.[4], based on the claims of Martin Jarvis. You would be hard-pressed to find another musicologist in the world that would agree with Martin Jarvis's baseless assertions. Notwithstanding that, the BBC has seen fit to present the case for Anna Magdalena Bach with all the propagandist's finesse. I was so impressed I watched it twice. It is an excellent study in how to con the public, leaving the viewer with the impression of a sound case when in truth there is nothing to it at all. In a programme lasting 56 minutes there were just 2 minutes of counter-argument, but they are the only 2 minutes that matter. The unwary would be bludgeoned by the preponderance of pro-Anna Magdalena polemic with its constant appeals to poor subjugated women.

The particular pieces which Anna Magdalena is supposed to have composed were: the cello suites, the aria from the Goldberg variations, the first (C major) prelude from the Well-Tempered Clavier, the Credo from the B minor mass, and, in 1713, the Perpetual Canon for Four Voices (BMV1073) as well as an aria for soprano. (For the true authorship and date of BMV1073 see Ref.[5]). It seems not to bother the proponents of the Anna Magdalena thesis that she was only 12 in 1713. At that tender age she was apparently able to impersonate the work of the greatest musical genius of all time at the height of his powers. A canon is not the easiest of musical forms. And the canon in question is a 'puzzle canon' in which only one voice is notated and the rules for determining the remaining parts and the time intervals of their entrances must be guessed. It is the sort of thing that a mature composer might do to challenge players with whom he was familiar. But a 12-year-old? Only if Anna Magdalena was another Mozart (or, rather, a pre-Mozart) – but a Mozart who sounded remarkably like J.S.Bach!

The greatest part of the "argument" for Anna Magdalena as a composer consists of manuscripts in her hand. This is built up in the programme as a matter of profound significance. They brought in a manuscript and handwriting expert to testify that certain pieces, either of text or musical score, were written by Anna Magdalena. The uncritical viewer can easily be taken in by the triumphal tone in which it is "proved" that various manuscripts were written by Anna Magdalena. It is easy to lose sight of the fact that this is neither disputed nor of any significance. It has been known virtually forever that many Bach works are not in his hand, being either copied or scribed by another. There were no photocopiers! Of course Bach gave the tedious task of creating copies to others.

Martin Jarvis's only argument relates to a manuscript of the cello suites. At the end it states "written (écrite) by Anna Magdalena Bach". But Martin Jarvis chooses to be less impressed by what is written on the front page of the manuscript (twice) namely "composed by J.S.Bach". The word "écrite", used of Mrs Bach's contribution, would appear to mean that the manuscript was physically written or transcribed by her. This is the meaning of écrite given in a contemporary dictionary. And we all surely know what is meant by "composed" – though Martin Jarvis insists that it means merely "compiled", like an editor. Yes, we are meant to believe that the man whose name appears on the front page as "composer" was in fact merely the editor of his wife's music. And this is all the "evidence" that Jarvis has.

Oh, and there is the fact – perhaps worth mentioning in passing – that the cello suites do *sound* so very much like Bach, don't they? Just a thought.

Now I confess to being a cloth-eared musical moron, but surely to God the claim that someone else wrote *one of* the preludes of "the 48" (the Well-Tempered Clavier), and just *one part of* the B minor mass, is preposterous. The Well-Tempered Clavier consists of two sets of 24 preludes and fugues, one in each of the major and minor keys. The first pair is in C major, the second in C minor, the third in C-sharp major, the fourth in C-sharp minor, and so on, the rising chromatic pattern continuing until every key has been represented, finishing with a B-minor fugue. It is almost OCD in its mathematical precision. If you were intending to produce a work with this degree of rigorous structure, would you want just one part being composed by someone else?

The same obsessive mathematical completeness is seen in the Goldberg Variations. There are 30 variations. Every third variation in the series of 30 is a canon, following an ascending pattern of intervals. Thus, variation 3 is a canon at the unison, variation 6 is a canon at the second, variation 9 is a canon at the third, and so on until variation 27, which is a canon at the ninth. But we are to believe that the Aria, which opens and closes the piece and upon which all the Variations are based, was written by Mrs Bach. It's not impossible, and in fact this suggestion is less unlikely than the others. But the fact that the manuscript of the Aria is in her hand does not constitute any evidence whatsoever. And so there isn't any.

As for the B minor mass, the maestro's crowning glory, we are to believe that the Credo, just the Credo, was written by someone other than JSB? Really? And managing to sound so integrated, and so – well, like Bach.

Martin Jarvis undermines his own credibility further in some arguments which are completely vapid. It is well-known that Anna Magdalena was a singer of some note, and was hired as such at the court of Köthen. Jarvis attempts to make much of the fact that she was one of the highest-paid musicians at court. "*She must have been doing something other than copying*", he argues. Indeed she was. She was singing. Jarvis conveniently forgets that singers were frequently the most highly paid musicians, more so than mere composers. Another illustration of the tenuousness of his reasoning is his claim that the first Mrs Bach committed suicide. There is no evidence for this whatsoever. His case is based entirely on the fact that Bach's second marriage, to Anna Magdalena, did not take place in church. He claims that this indicates some scandal surrounding the first Mrs Bach's death – obviously suicide through jealousy, he concludes, based on nothing. In truth, second marriages generally did not take place in church at that time, so he has no grounds for suspicion at all.

Why, you have to ask yourself, does the BBC see fit to screen a one-sided defence of Jarvis's claims when they have been solidly refuted by the entire community of musicologists? Christoph Wolff has said "*I am sick and tired of this stupid thesis. When I served as director of the Leipzig Bach Archive from 2001 to 2013, I and my colleagues there extensively refuted the basic premises of the thesis, on grounds of documents, manuscript sources, and musical grounds. There is not a shred of evidence, but Jarvis doesn't give up despite the fact that several years ago, at a Bach conference in Oxford, a room full of serious Bach scholars gave him an embarrassing showdown*". His nonsense was too much even for The Guardian, cellist Steven

Isserlis, Ref.[6], wrote there, *"I'm afraid that his theory is pure rubbish. How can anybody take this shoddy material seriously?"*

But that does not stop the BBC concluding that,

"We will have to take a close look at female relatives of other composers."

Yes, I bet they will.

But let's turn back to physics. I have been motivated to do so by a comment left on a Conservative Woman article by "Mez", Ref.[7]. We can discern her position on gender politics from this comment,

"Leadership corruption requires power and testosterone. Corruption around the world is one of the major contributors to poverty, and that it seems is connected to testosterone."

This is the sort of blatant prejudice which is tediously familiar. "Mez" then quotes at length from a 2002 article in Discover Magazine, Ref.[8]. The article decries women's lack of recognition in science, despite their sterling contribution. The article starts,

"A woman physicist stopped light in her lab at Harvard. Another woman runs the linear accelerator at Stanford. A woman discovered the first evidence for dark matter. A woman found the top quark."

It was these claims that attracted my attention. Let's examine their truth, and, if true, whether the women in question have received due recognition. Firstly, *"a woman physicist stopped light in her lab at Harvard"*.

The woman in question is, I presume, Lene Hau. She led a Harvard University team who, by use of a Bose-Einstein condensate, succeeded in dramatically slowing a beam of light, ultimately in stopping it altogether for a short period. Without doubt this is truly first-rate physics. As is almost always the case, she did not do the work alone. In fact Lene Hau was the leader of a small research group. Her principal co-workers, who appear as co-authors on the relevant papers, were Naomi Ginsberg and Sean Garner.

This work was reported in the period 2001 – 2007. By that time Hau was already a tenured professor at Harvard and had been since 1999. It seems her academic standing was recognised even before she did her most groundbreaking work, though undoubtedly she did much valuable work previously also. So there is no evidence whatsoever for any lack of recognition here. Quite the contrary, in fact. Just look at this woman's accolades,

Honorary Alum 2011 from Aarhus University; the Carlsberg Foundation's Research Award from the Royal Danish Academy of Sciences and Letters, 2011, worth one million kroner; she won a $500,000 MacArthur Fellowship; the H.C. Ørsted Lectureship 2010; recipient of World's Best Dane award, 2010; selected National Security Science and Engineering Faculty Fellow by the United States Department of Defense in 2010; honorary appointment to the Royal Danish Academy of Sciences and Letters; made Fellow of the American Association for the Advancement of Science, 2009; ditto, the American Academy of Arts and Sciences, April 20, 2009; foreign member of the Royal Swedish Academy of Sciences, 2008; won the George Ledlie Prize in September 2008; won the Richtmyer Memorial Award, by the American Association of Physics Teachers, 2004; won the Ole Romer Medal, Danish Natural Science Research Council, 2001; awarded an Honorary Degree in the presence of Her Majesty, Queen Margrethe II of Denmark, 2001; as well as numerous prestigious public lectures and research grants.

Professor Lene Hau, the invisible woman? I think not.

Now let's examine this claim: *"a woman found the top quark"*. I can attach no meaning to this claim at all. It is complete nonsense.

You can read the history of the hunt for the top quark in many places, e.g., Ref.[9]. The last two quarks, the so-called "bottom" and "top" quarks, were predicted by two Japanese men, Makoto Kobayashi and Toshihide Maskawa, in 1973. They won the Nobel Prize in Physics in 2008, although the existence of both these quarks had been established by 1995. The experimental work which discovered the last quark, the "top" quark, was carried out at Fermilab in the USA by two separate teams of workers.

Experimental particle physics is notorious for involving massive teams of people. It is easy to see why. The vast accelerators need to be designed, built and operated. That takes large teams of civil, mechanical, electrical, and instrumentation engineers. The data produced by these machines is acquired at such a pace that no human could ever analyse it. It is analysed by computer. Cutting edge computational facilities are crucial. Enter teams of IT specialists. Oh, and then there's the physicists who direct all the work, and who know what it's all for and understand what the heck is going on (sometimes). That's why you can immediately spot a publication on experimental particle physics without even reading the title: the list of authors often occupies the whole of the first page.

The two Fermilab papers published in 1995 and announcing the discovery of the top quark are a perfect example. The paper from the CDF collaboration, Ref.[10], had about 440 authors whilst the DZero collaboration's paper, Ref.[11], had about 380 authors. (You will have to click on the tab to expand the author list if you want to see all the names).

So, in excess of 800 people discovered the top quark. I've no idea how many of them were women, though some certainly would be. The majority would certainly be men. Who cares? The salient point here is that the claim that "a woman found the top quark" is not merely wrong, it's a profoundly stupid thing to say.

The only way in which you could accredit a single person with the discovery is if you (unjustly) gave all the credit to the Director of Fermilab. But at the time the discovery was announced in 1995 the Director was John Peoples, not a woman. Moreover it was Peoples who presided over the development of the Tevatron, the machine in which the discovery was made. As of 2015 when I posted this article originally there had been no woman Director of Fermilab. The facility's first woman Director, Lia Merminga, was appointed only in April 2022. So the claim that "a woman found the top quark" cannot be given any meaning whatsoever. It is nonsense on stilts.

Which brings me to the next quote: "*Another woman runs the linear accelerator at Stanford*". What image does this conjure? A lone woman, toiling away in her lab and wrestling unaided with the giant monster that is Stanford's linear accelerator. Err, no. The Stanford Linear Accelerator Centre (SLAC), renamed in 2008 the SLAC National Accelerator Laboratory, is another huge establishment, like Fermilab, and employs many hundreds of people. It is this team of many hundreds of people, of both sexes, which "runs the linear accelerator". To claim that any single individual "*runs the linear accelerator at Stanford*" is as silly as claiming that a single person put a man on the moon.

At the time the Discover Magazine article was written, in 2002, the SLAC Director was Jonathan Dorfan. However, a woman, Persis Drell, was Director of Research at Stanford. In fact Persis Drell was later made Director of the whole lab in 2007 and remained in that post until 2012. I presume it must be Drell to whom the Discover Magazine article refers. Recall that the magazine article was presenting us with a picture of a poor, but brilliant, woman scientist doing great scientific work but without recognition. How in God's name is Persis Drell, a Director at SLAC for 11 years, an example of lack of recognition? Do be aware that being Director of SLAC is a long way higher up the food chain than a mere professor. There are dozens, perhaps hundreds, of professors at SLAC (including Drell's own Dad).

And let's not forget that Persis Drell was also Dean of the Stanford School of Engineering for three years and then Provost of Stanford University for six years. She is a member of the National Academy of Sciences, the American Academy of Arts and Sciences, the German National Academies of Sciences Leopoldina, and a fellow of the American Physical Society and a fellow of the American Association for the Advancement of Science (AAAS).

So, Persis Drell – an example of a major woman player in science? Yes. An example of a woman not receiving recognition for her contribution? Err, emphatically not. So, please tell me – what's the gripe?

Finally, the claim, "*a woman discovered the first evidence for dark matter*". The woman in question can only be Vera Rubin. Without doubt Vera Rubin played a major role in providing evidence for dark matter from galactic rotation curves in the period from the mid-60s to the earlier 80s. In 1965 she was the first woman to observe at Mount Palomar. I have her book, *Bright Galaxies, Dark Matters*, Ref.[12] It's a good read, I recommend it.

However, many ideas in physics and astronomy cannot really be attributed to a single individual. Rather they emerge from scientific endeavour and gradually gain ground in terms of credibility. Many astronomers in the early twentieth century attempted to estimate the total mass in various regions of the cosmos from the motions of stars they could see. (Motion is related to gravity, and gravity is caused by mass, so measuring velocities tells you something about mass distributions). The possibility that there might be more mass than could be accounted for by visible stars was always recognised. Rubin cannot be credited with precedence for either the idea or the evidence for dark matter.

Probably the first person to publish evidence of a large discrepancy between visible and gravitational apparent mass was Fritz Zwicky. Zwicky was a difficult chap, he treated his assistants abominably. However, he was a good astronomer. In papers published in 1933 and 1937 he reported measurements of the velocities of galaxies in the Coma cluster of galaxies. Zwicky found that orbital velocities are almost a factor of ten larger than expected from the summed mass of all galaxies belonging to the cluster, e.g., Ref.[13]. Some sources claim that Kapteyn has precedent, in 1922 (Ref.[15]). And papers by Smith and Holmberg in 1937 were also drawing similar conclusions.

Throughout the 1930s and 1940s papers by many authors hinted at missing "dark" mass. In 1957 van de Hulst reported a high rotation curve for the Andromeda galaxy, a forerunner of the type of work to be done later by Rubin. Most significant, though, was the 1959 paper by Kahn and Woltjer, Ref.[14]. These authors found clear evidence for the presence of additional mass in the Local Group of galaxies.

This was the background which forms the context of Rubin's work. So it is not true to assert that *"a woman discovered the first evidence for dark matter"*. Nevertheless, in the 60s and 70s Rubin did some of the best work to consolidate knowledge of galactic rotation curves and related issues, thus providing a considerable enhancement to the credibility of the dark matter hypothesis.

She was not alone in working in this area at that time, though. Other notable authors who published observational evidence for missing mass in the 1970s included Ostriker & Peebles (1973), Einasto, Kaasik, & Saar (1974), Ostriker, Peebles & Yahil (1974), Roberts (1975), Matthews (1977), Bosma (1978) and Faber & Gallagher (1979). And then there were a whole bunch of theoreticians working on the cosmological implications of dark matter, a truly stellar cast of names including Hawking, Rees, Guth, Pagels, Peebles, Preskill, Wilczek and many others. It was hardly a one-person party, though Vera Rubin may have been the only woman involved at that time. (A decade or two later there would be a far greater proportion of women in astronomy). You can read more of the history of dark matter in Refs.[15,16].

There is a spin to the Vera Rubin story of which I was unaware until I did a bit of background reading prior to penning this screed. All her major papers on the subject included the same co-author, one W Kent Ford. He appears as co-author on the 1970 paper, Ref.[17], the 1978 paper, Ref.[18], and the

1980 paper, Ref.[19]. Their key observation is that galactic rotation curves are abnormally flat, a signature of excess mass. This is known in astronomical circles as the "Rubin-Ford" effect, and rightly so. Whilst Vera Rubin's name has become associated with this area of work, that of her male colleague is not so visible – except perhaps to experts in the field. Curious. It's an inversion of the "invisible woman" effect, showing it can cut both ways. Not that I would make a big deal about it. I doubt that either of the parties is in any way aggrieved, and nor am I. (One Norbert Thonnard also appears on two of those papers. Who he? No idea. He's just another anonymous member of the vast army of male scientists and technologists).

As a technical aside, Kent Ford's contribution to their joint work included making the image-tube spectrograph. This was a state-of-the-art instrument in the 1960s, which, like a prism, spread the light from the stars into their component colours which could then be analysed. The importance of this to the Rubin-Ford collaboration can hardly be overstated. The velocity of stars is measured by their red/blue-shift, the change in apparent colour caused by their motion. Hence a spectrograph was the key bit of kit required, without which no galactic rotation curves would have been possible. Reading between the lines we might guess that Kent Ford was the essential techno-nerd in the collaboration.

So, the more balanced truth about Vera Rubin is that she made a major contribution to astronomy and has been widely recognised for it, both within the astronomy community and in the public more widely. However, she was not the first to posit dark matter nor the first to publish observational evidence for it. Nor was she alone in addressing this subject during her most active period; there were dozens (hundreds?) of others also working on it – virtually all of them men.

Conclusive proof that Rubin was hardly an invisible woman is that she has been on Desert Island Discs, proof positive of celebrity status, surely. Was she invited because of her astronomical work, or because she was a woman astronomer? Well, they didn't have Kent Ford on, did they?

References

[1] Collins, W. (2014). Universal Suffrage in the UK. The Illustrated Empathy Gap, 10 December 2014.

[2] Collins, W. (2017). *Centuries of Oppression: The Road to 1918*. YouTube playlist of 26 videos, 8 October 2017 to 26 November 2020.

[3] Weinstein, G. (2012*). Did Mileva Marić assist Einstein in writing his 1905 path breaking papers?* arXiv 1204.3551, 16 April 2012.

[4] BBC Four (2015). *Written by Mrs Bach*. 21 March 2015.

[5] Wolff, Christoph. 2014. *The Bach Canon at Harvard and its dedicatee: a riddle finally solved*. Harvard Library Bulletin 24 (3): 104-109.

[6] Isserlis, S. (2014). *Suite scandal: why Bach's wife cannot take credit for his cello masterwork*. The Guardian, 29 October 2014.

[7] Perrins, L. (2015). *Premature declaration of female victory in the gender wars. Clinton, Sandberg and Mrs Clooney don't hack it*. The Conservative Woman, 31 March 2015.

[8] Svitil, K.A. (2002). *The 50 Most Important Women in Science*. Discover Magazine, 1 November 2002.

[9] Higgins, V. (2020). *Twenty-fifth anniversary of the discovery of the top quark at Fermilab*. Fermilab News, 2 March 2020.

[10] F. Abe et al. (CDF Collaboration) (1995). *Observation of Top Quark Production in $p\bar{p}$ Collisions with the Collider Detector at Fermilab*. Phys. Rev. Lett. 74(13), 2626-2631; 3 April 1995.

[11] Abachi, A. et al. (DZero Collaboration) (1995). *Observation of the top quark*. Phys.Rev.Lett. 74(13) 2632-2637, 3 April 1995.

[12] Rubin, V. (1997). *Bright Galaxies, Dark Matters*. American Institute of Physics, September 1997.

[13] Zwicky, F. (1937). *On the Masses of Nebulae and of Clusters of Nebulae*, The Astrophysical Journal, 86(3), 217, October 1937.

[14] Kahn, F.D., and Woltjer, L. (1959). *Intergalactic Matter and the Galaxy*. The Astrophysical Journal 130(3) 704 November 1959.

[15] Primack, J. (2007). *A Brief History of Dark Matter*. SLAC Summer Institute, 30 July – 10 August 2007.

[16] Bertone, G., and Hooper, D. (2018). *History of dark matter*. Rev. Mod. Phys. 90, 045002, 15 October 2018.

[17] Rubin, V.C., and Ford, W.K. (1970). *Rotation of the Andromeda Nebula from a Spectroscopic Survey of Emission Regions*. The Astrophysical Journal 159, 379 February 1970.

[18] Rubin, V.C., Ford, W.K., and Thonnard, N. (1978). *Extended rotation curves of high-luminosity spiral galaxies. IV - Systematic dynamical properties, SA through SC*. The Astrophysical Journal, Part 2 - Letters to the Editor, 225 L107-L111, 1 November 1978.

[19] Rubin, V.C., Ford, W.K., and Thonnard, N. (1978). *Rotational properties of 21 SC galaxies with a large range of luminosities and radii, from NGC 4605 /R = 4kpc/ to UGC 2885 /R = 122 kpc/*. The Astrophysical Journal, Part 1, 238, 471-487, 1 June 1980.

43. Goodbye, Spectator

Here I describe how I finally lost patience with The Spectator newspaper and cancelled my subscription.

Original posted on: 21 November 2020.

Ben Bradley, MP, is a hero, not a villain. It takes no courage whatsoever to write the sort of stuff that Ditum and Hardman wrote in The Spectator the day after International Men's Day, 2020, Refs.[1,2]. But it does take courage to speak up for men and boys – even when all one is doing is calling for equal treatment.

"No, Ben Bradley: we don't need a minister for men", opined Sarah Ditum, Ref.[1] reacting to Mr Bradley's speech in the House of Commons on International Men's Day.

I fully support Sarah Ditum's right to make her views known. I support Isabel Hardman's perfect right to publish her objectionable piece too. Indeed, I welcome both because it is useful to be reminded of the depth of prejudice which is acceptable in our culture.

However, I do not have to pay to read such views – I can read much the same in The Guardian for free, not that I would. Consequently, I am cancelling my subscription to The Spectator.

There is an extremely good, and equally simple, reason why International Men's Day – and the now annual debate in parliament – are required. The reason is Ms Ditum and Ms Hardman themselves, and the millions of similarly prejudiced individuals who endlessly repeat the same ignorant and compassionless stuff.

On the ignorance front, Hardman writes that, to appease irritating men who asked why she only fund-raised for a women's domestic abuse charity (Refuge) and not for men, she "even set up a fundraising page for a charity which helps male victims of domestic abuse". Hilariously, she means Respect (see chapter 5). Oh, dear. This is, of course, what we are up against.

More seriously, Hardman had the opportunity to learn something which she missed. She raised £20,000 for Refuge but only £330 for the ostensibly-male-supporting Respect. This is the issue, Ms Hardman. People, of both sexes, will support initiatives to help women, but neither sex is inclined to do anything for men. This is why it is totally irrelevant to male welfare that most MPs are men. Men do not have in-group preference, Ms Hardman.

I know that The Spectator wants to present a broad church of opinion, but the Ditum article oversteps the bounds of what is acceptable. It is yellow journalism. And Hardman's article hit a nerve with me because she referred to Diane Abbott's "campaign", Ref.[3], in which Abbott referred to a "crisis of masculinity", consisting – in her opinion – of a generation of young men who are, apparently, Viagra chomping, Jack Daniels quaffing, porn addicts. I have reason to recall Abbott's "campaign" because it was the final straw that turned me into a men's issues blogger in 2013. *"Both of us believe that women have historically been oppressed by a patriarchal society and that this oppression has in no way ended today"*, wrote Hardman. Yes, I know you believe that – but I don't, you see. I believe there are some women who are incapable of any empathy for men and that this blindness leads to a distorted, unbalanced view of reality. After all these years I should be inured to it. But I'm not. It makes me despair.

But Ditum's article is also incompetent journalism because its central tenet includes an error so basic that the Spectator should withdraw the article and never employ Ms Ditum again. I'll come to that.

Ben Bradley's crime was this statement,

"Why have a minister for women and not for men? Why single out one characteristic for special mention? Can we ensure that equality means just that, rather than positive discrimination at the expense of certain groups? Male as equally protected as female."

Ms Ditum takes great exception to this impudence, apparently unaware that Mr Bradley's claim that "males are equally protected as females" is the correct interpretation of the Equality Act 2010, though, of course, it is not the Correct interpretation in Ms Ditum's circles.

She then tries to make hay out of the fact that the only other person in screen shot when Mr Bradley committed his sacrilege was another man. Err…excuse me, but in what way does the conspicuous absence of female MPs (30% of the House) during the International Men's Day debate reflect badly on men exactly? It is an absolute disgrace that there were only three women present, though it does usefully display female MPs' touching commitment to equality.

One woman was apparently there to make an interjection and left the debate before it was half-way through. Another was the relevant minister (who was obliged to be present). And finally, the third woman was the opposition Shadow Spokesperson (who was also obliged to be present). She was the only Labour MP present. Likewise there was just one SNP MP present – they who, as an avowedly feminist Party, put up such a strong representation on International Women's Day. Apart from these, all the other speakers were male and Conservative.

Let me pass over that Ms Ditum spends most of a paragraph criticising Ben Bradley's clothes – a thing which, if the sexes were reversed, would be certain death to a male MPs political career – such is the world of double standards we now inhabit. (By the way, the dress code for MPs is explicitly sexist. Men are supposed to wear shirt, tie and jacket – and have to ask permission to remove their jackets even if the day is sweltering. Women are given far greater latitude in their attire.)

Let me also pass over that Ms Ditum claims that, in Ben Bradley's imagination, "*the political system that exists is one where women are privileged while men are ignored*". He said no such thing, nor did any of the other speakers.

However, I will say it. As the author of a near-700 page book on male disadvantages, Ref.[4], I do assert that women in Western countries are privileged compared to men. It is inconceivable that society would tolerate women and girls suffering the litany of disadvantages which are the norm for men and boys – whilst being told that they are privileged.

However…to get to the burden of my post: Ms Ditum's staggeringly ignorant howler, of direct relevance to the very title of her article, was in response to Ben Bradley's question, "*Why have a Minister for Women and not a Minister for Men?*"

Ditum wrote.

"*Well, and this really is the funny bit… we don't! There's a Minister for Women and Equalities, who has responsibility for addressing all forms of discrimination. At the moment that's done by Liz Truss as a sideline to the trade brief, which I'm sure leaves her lots of time to spare because it's not like there's anything going on at the moment with huge, consuming implications for trade. So the interests of women are represented by part of one department that doesn't even merit a whole minister."*

Err…wrong. Totally, utterly, embarrassingly, wrong. At the time in question, November 2020, the actual position as regards ministers and their portfolios was as follows.

There was indeed an under-Secretary of State whose title was Minister for Women. The post holder at the time was Baroness Berridge of The Vale of Catmose. Baroness Berridge was preceded in that role, Minister for Women, by Victoria Atkins. It was true that Liz Truss then had the twin portfolio of trade and also the title Minister for Women and Equalities. But in the latter role she was assisted by two under-Secretaries, the aforementioned Minister for Women and the Minister for Equalities, the latter being Kemi Badenoch who spoke in the debate. Got that, Ms Ditum?

Perhaps Ms Ditum has not yet mastered Google. If she had she could soon have discovered the remit of the Government Equalities Office, within which all three of the above ministers' portfolios reside, Ref.[4]. In January 2024 this remains unchanged. Whilst it includes a catch-all reference to "reducing discrimination and disadvantage for all", the specific instances all relate to women or LGBT. In particular it makes specific reference to supporting the UN policies exemplified by CEDAW and the Beijing Platform (which I will not expand upon but which are full-on feminist, extreme partisan policy positions). The opening sentence on their web site is,

"The Government Equalities Office leads work on policy relating to women, sexual orientation and transgender equality."

Hence, the remit of the Government Equalities Offices is misaligned with respect to the requirements of the Equality Act 2010, because the protected characteristic is actually "sex", not "women". The Government Equalities Office could be argued to be in violation of the Equality Duty (and I do so argue).

The Government Equalities Office web site, Ref.[5], lists their Priorities thus,

- Helping women to fulfil their potential in the workplace and helping businesses get the full economic benefit of women's skills;

- Eliminating the Gender Pay Gap (GPG) by introducing regulations requiring larger employers to publish their gender pay data, and working with other government departments to address the causes of the GPG;
- Improving female career progression, increasing the number of women on government boards, and in the FTSE 350;
- Addressing the discrimination and inequalities that LGB&T people face;
- Eliminating homophobic, biphobic and transphobic (HBT) bullying in schools;
- Promoting the rights of British citizens abroad and using our influence to promote international equality;
- Supporting cross-government strategies, such as; increasing female participation in the labour market, and preventing violence against women and girls (VAWG).

In conclusion, Sarah Ditum was factual wrong: there was indeed a Minister for Women in 2020. There still is in January 2024, and there had been incumbents in that post for many years before 2020. Moreover, the remit of the Government Equalities Office is explicitly sex specific. Based on that declared remit there is every reason to regard men and boys as being ignored and this raises an issue as regards the consistency of the Equalities Office remit with the 2010 Equalities Act. Hence Ben Bradley's call for a Minister for Men was clearly fully justified, long overdue and increasingly urgent.

References

[1] Ditum, S. (2020). *No, Ben Bradley: we don't need a minister for men*. The Spectator, 20 November 2020.

[2] Hardman, I. (2020). *A minister for men would help solve one problem*. The Spectator, 20 November 2020.

[3] Abbott, D, (2013). *Diane Abbott to warn of British 'masculinity crisis'*. BBC News, 15 May 2013.

[4] Collins, W. (2019). *The Empathy Gap*. LPS Publishing, June 2019.

[5] UK Government (2024). *Government Equalities Office*. Accessed 1 January 2024.

44. Letter to New Scientist

Having had a subscription with New Scientist for decades, this is one example (but not the first) of how I became irritated with the publication going feminist-woke.

Original posted on: <u>14 December 2014</u>.

This is a letter I sent to New Scientist on 13 December 2014.

Re: Complaint regarding article *"Fight back against the hate"* by Aviva Rutkin, Ref.[1]. (That was the title of Rutkin's article I used in my original blog post and which I will have taken from the print magazine version. But I note the title is different in the online version now available, see Ref.[1]).

I am immensely distressed that New Scientist chose to print this article. It is not science and it is not honest. What is it doing in New Scientist?

If New Scientist really had to descend into the fetid mess that is gender politics – and it would be best advised not to – then it is incumbent upon it to take an objective approach. This article fails to do so. In fact the article is simply the same gender-biased stuff that one can read in all the mainstream newspapers and news sites. So why bother? Is New Scientist going into competition with Jezebel?

The article presents the phenomenon of online harassment as if it relates exclusively to female victims. Moreover, by emphasising sexual threats it deliberately gives the uninformed reader the impression that perpetrators are invariably male. Both these impressions are false. Against this backdrop the recent Pew Research report , Ref.[2], is cited as stating that 40% of internet users have been harassed online. This unqualified statistic, following the preceding material, invites the unwary reader to believe that it applies to women being harassed or threatened by men.

But this is an appallingly egregious misrepresentation of the Pew Research report, Ref.[2]. The conclusion of that report is that "men are somewhat more likely than women to experience at least one of the elements of online harassment, 44% vs. 37%", see Figure 44.1 taken from Ref.[2]. Specifically, being called offensive names, being purposefully embarrassed, being physically threatened, and being harassed for a sustained period are all experienced more by men. Whilst more women experience sexual harassment and stalking, the difference between the genders even in these categories is not as marked as implied in the article, namely 10% of men and 16% of women.

Among all internet users, the % who have experienced each of the following elements of online harassment, by gender...

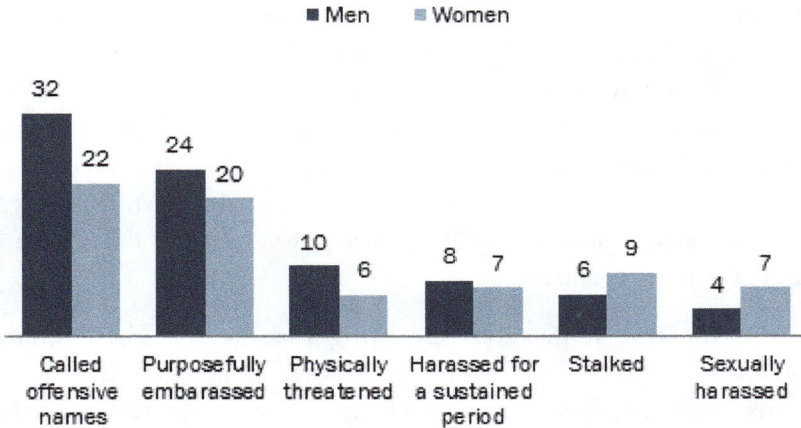

Figure 44.1: The actual results of the Pew Research survey

That the Pew Research report has been used spuriously to support a perspective which is diametrically opposed to its actual findings is outrageously dishonest.

The issue as to who the perpetrators of this online abuse may be is less clear. But if it follows the pattern of adolescent bullying online then same-sex perpetrators will be nearly twice as common as opposite-sex perpetrators (see Table 3 of Ref.[3]). Certainly, severe online threats by women against other women do occur. The first person jailed in the UK for online bullying was a woman, Keeley Houghton, Ref.[4], and one of the two people imprisoned in the infamous Caroline Criado Perez affair was a woman, Ref.[5]. The distressing popularity of such sentiments as #KillAllMen is testament to there being no shortage of women willing to threaten men online.

But there is more to this issue than an argument as to which gender is subject to more online verbal abuse. It is actually a bid by those of a certain political ideology to control what views may be expressed online. The group cited in the article, WAM (Women, Action and the Media) have already successfully coerced Facebook and Twitter into removing material of which they, WAM, disapprove. They have also had suspended the Twitter accounts of people who expressed opinions contrary to WAM's politics. These incidents did not involve abuse or threats. But once the principle of Twitter handing over the role of censor to organisations such as WAM is established, the way is open for political censorship. In this respect, online abuse of women is merely a Trojan Horse being cynically exploited as a power play by those with a authoritarian political agenda.

That this is the true motivation underlying the clamour about online harassment is betrayed by the chillingly frank quote in the article from Mary Anne Franks, *"They (the likes of Twitter and Facebook) are not required to enforce free speech, but can instead set their own rules for what is permissible on their platform"*.

(I would add, for this book in 2024, that these issues have become even more acute now. My words, above, regarding external influence on social media platforms to exercise censorship was to prove prescient during the covid-19 debacle in 2020-23. And the UK's Online Safety Act 2023 may be found to have consolidated the establishment control over information, see Ref.[6]).

Of course my own gender political complexion will be apparent. I do not expect New Scientist to share it. But that is not the point. The point is that this article is not science. Nor is it objective. Nor is it honest. It is propaganda.

I would urge New Scientist to re-examine its editorial policy on this matter. There is every chance that if it does not do so then the good name of the journal will ultimately become besmirched. It seems a pointless risk to take given that these matters are beyond the journal's natural remit.

I had no response from New Scientist.

References

[1] Rutkin, A. (2014). *The fight back against rape and death threats online*. Original version *Fight back against the hate,* New Scientist Vol.224, No.2999, 13 Dec 2014, P.20-21. Online version linked dated 10 December 2014.

[2] Duggan, M. (2014). *Online Harassment*. Pew Research Center, 22 October 2014.

[3] Sourander, A., et al (2010). *Psychosocial Risk Factors Associated With Cyberbullying Among Adolescents: A Population-Based Study*. Archives of General Psychiatry, 67(7):720-728, 1 July 2010.

[4] Carter, H. (2009). *Teenage girl is first to be jailed for bullying on Facebook*. The Guardian, 21 August 2009.

[5] The Guardian (2014). *Two jailed for Twitter abuse of feminist campaigner*. 24 January 2014.

[6] Collins, W. (2023). *The Online Safety Act 2023*. The Illustrated Empathy Gap, 15 December 2023.

[7] Logan. L. (2014). *Putting Anita Sarkeesian in the public square*. A Voice For Men, 28 December 2014.

45. Goodbye New Scientist

Here I record my final break with New Scientist. I wasn't going to pay for this divisive rubbish anymore.

Original posted on: 28 April 2018.

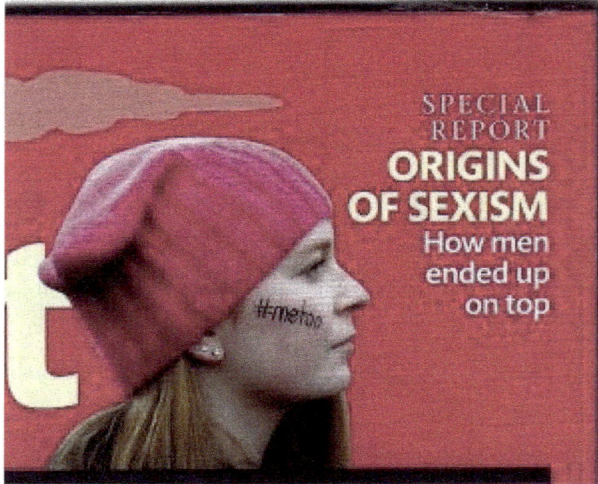

Figure 45.1: Extract from the Front Cover of New Scientist 21 April 2018, Ref.[1]

After looking at the above picture, you will not be surprised to hear that I cancelled my subscription to New Scientist in April 2018 (after too many decades to recall). Five of the featured articles in the 18 April 2018 online edition of the magazine were about gender from the feminist perspective. I link to two of them in Refs.[2,3].

Emily Wilson took over as Editor-in-Chief only the week before the issue in question. Immediately thereafter feminist patriarchy theory, pink pussy hats and #MeToo were the order of the day. She is still in that post as of January 2024. Prior to joining New Scientist she was at The Guardian.

There is nothing in the April 2018 New Scientist articles that you haven't heard before, repeatedly. Placing such material in New Scientist is a coup for the feminists, conveying as it does an aura of scientific respectability on their patriarchy narrative – though they must be getting blasé now that they have total control of the media and can mob, vilify and destroy anyone who stands against them.

In truth, the origins of sexism lie in the female monopoly of the uterus, and the evolved pair-bond which involves the ceding of moral authority to the woman as a surrogate for the offspring, see chapter 48 or Ref.[4]. As the gatekeepers of sex, and hence the wielders of selection pressure, women have moulded men to their requirements. The result is resource provision flowing from men to women, for which men are now vilified in the form of the pay gap. The pay gap mantra and #MeToo are to be interpreted as women changing their required male specification. They have previously bred the Doberman, now they want a King Charles Spaniel. And all the while they are herding men in the direction of their choice, they hold the banner of Patriarchy in front of them to blindside men into believing that men are in charge: Patriarchy that great bugaboo, that Wizard of Oz, that charade, that act of mutual conning, that saviour of men's blushes. The whole of my web site, and this book, is testament to the sexist disadvantage of men, and how well it is hidden under the Patriarchy fig leaf.

Unacceptable gender-political articles had started appearing in New Scientist many years before this. I did blog on a few, for instance those reproduced as chapters 44 and 49 and also Tim Hunt, Ellen Pao and the Reddit Debacle, Ref.[5], and That Google Memo, Ref.[6]. In truth, there has been an objectionable article in virtually every edition for years now.

The edition previous to the "final straw" edition, that on 7 April 2018, included a dreadful Leader Editorial on the PSA test, Ref.[7]. The article lambasted famous men (e.g., Stephen Fry), who, after recently being diagnosed with prostate cancer, had been publicly urging men to get a PSA test. Like others who decry the PSA test, the New Scientist editorial had nothing to offer in its place. The effectiveness of the mammogram test for breast cancer has also been questioned in some quarters, e.g., Ref.[8], but I doubt that you will ever see New Scientist advising women not to bother with one – they wouldn't dare. But they are content to leave men with no test at all for a disease which is notoriously asymptomatic – until it is too late.

The fact that I attended the funeral of a college friend who died of prostate cancer a couple of weeks ago sharpens my opinion, as does the fact that the number of my friends who have, or have had, prostate cancer is getting too large to count.

This terrible article even trotted out the oft repeated and flagrantly callous *"men usually die with prostate cancer rather than of it"*. You might have expected better of a scientific publication. Indeed you would, but then New Scientist is no longer a scientific publication. The fact that, if a man lives long enough he can expect to contract prostate cancer, but to die of something else, has no bearing whatsoever on the fact that in 2015 in the UK some 11,819 men died *of* prostate cancer – more than the number of women who died from breast cancer, Ref.[9]. That's *of* not **with**, please note, New Scientist.

But I digress. Back to edition 21 April 2018, and those feminist articles of which Refs.[2,3] are examples. It was simply the stuff that you can read on a billionty web sites and a great many newspapers and magazines every day of the week. I hardly need describe the contents of the articles, do I? Ref.[3] is about violence against women, of course. The articles praise #MeToo and the related Times Up as part of a positive movement for change. I had a rather different take on these developments in posts reproduced here as chapters 64 and 65.

To 'prove' male privilege there was an article on the opinion of one trans woman. This has no place in any organ pretending to be scientific. Had they gathered personal experiences from a statistically meaningful sample of both trans women and trans men, and properly controlled for other effects such as race, family background, socioeconomics, etc., then it would have been an interesting piece of social research. As it is, all I can say is that I could quote trans women with the opposite opinion to that presented in the article. So what?

Here we have yet another article claiming to have identified the reason for the high male suicide rate. Guess what? *"Seeking help could be construed as a threat to masculinity"*. Ah! I felt sure it would be the fault of masculinity, i.e., men's own fault. And as for male suicide being due to *"a loss of power, control and autonomy"* (i.e., their own fault), those words would be perfectly apposite to describe the typical man's experience of the Family Courts. There is ample evidence that men's suicide peaks rather spectacularly after separation, especially if child contact issues are involved. And as for these macho fools' failure in the help-seeking department, just where do the delightful authors of this piece of secondary feminism suggest that men can go to get help with defeating the monsters which feminism has prepared for them in the form of the Family Courts, the judicial system and the domestic violence industry?

Unconscious bias features as a heading. You can read my take on that masterpiece of manipulation in chapter 50.

James Damore's famous Google Memo, Ref.[6], is quoted by New Scientist. Oddly they don't see fit to mention that the feminist hegemony had him summarily sacked. Well, it would hardly play well against the all-powerful Patriarchy narrative. Heaven forbid that our feminist overlords should be seen to be powerful, let alone tyrannical. That would wreck everything. (I recall hearing a feminist interviewed on Radio 4 use Damore's memo as a refutation that the feminist-left were censorious – a truly impressive display of pretzel logic). The New Scientist article states that Damore "*cited the influence of prenatal testosterone on developing brains as one possible cause*" – that is, a cause of gender differences leading to a greater propensity of males to go into the tech sector. "*Unfortunately for Damore*", it continues, "*the science is not so clear cut*". Err, yes it is – see the references at the end of Ref.[6] or watch the video linked as Ref.[10] featuring Helena Cronin and Simon Baron-Cohen.

Amusingly, the New Scientist attempt to support their claim that "*the science is not so clear cut*" starts with two observations which actually support Damore, including the quote from Larry Cahill, "*there are biologically based sex differences at all levels of mammalian brain function*". The only support for their own claim that "the science is not so clear cut" is to cite "*a study of 1400 human brains which found that they can't be simply classified into male and female*". They gave no reference, but it is clear from the "1400 brains" that they are referring to the work of Daphna Joel which I deconstruct in chapter 49. Joel is such an ardent apologist for social constructivism that she seems to wilfully misinterpret her team's own brain scan findings. This was another case of both the New Scientist and Daphna Joel falling over themselves to align their empirical findings with a feminist interpretation. But they just don't. It's as if they've been shown a picture of a rabbit but they insist it's a dog, because it's a dog they want.

New Scientist is now collaborating with the anti-scientific, social-constructivist, feminist-leftist propagandists. What use is a science magazine which promotes anti-science? None.

References

[1] New Scientist (2018). *Front Cover*. 21 April 2018 (number 3174).

[2] Ananthaswamy, A., and Douglas, K. (2018). *The origins of sexism: How men came to rule 12,000 years ago*. New Scientist, number 3174, online 18 April 2018.

[3] Ananthaswamy, A., and Douglas, K. (2018). *The hidden reasons why societies are violent towards women.* New Scientist, number 3174, online 18 April 2018.

[4] Collins, W. (2016). *Emotion and the Pair-Bond*. The Illustrated Empathy Gap, 11 December 2016.

[5] Collins, W. (2015). *Tim Hunt, Ellen Pao and the Reddit Debacle*. The Illustrated Empathy Gap, 27 July 2015.

[6] Collins, W. (2017). *That Google Memo*. The Illustrated Empathy Gap, 19 August 2017.

[7] Collins, W. (2017). *Prostate Cancer Developments (re-post)*. The Illustrated Empathy Gap, 2 February 2018.

[8] Gilbert Welsh, H. (2014). *Vast Study Casts Doubts on Value of Mammograms*. The New York Times, 2 December 2014.

[9] BBC News (2018). *Prostate cancer deaths overtake those from breast cancer*. 2 February 2018.

[10] Cronin, H., and Simon Baron-Cohen, S. (2018). *Sex Differences - the Real Research is Very Clear*. ZeroFox Given YouTube channel, 26 April 2018.

Section 9

Evolution / Psychology

46. Sexual Crypsis

The original post was titled "Paternity Fraud and Sexual Crypsis". I omit the paternity fraud part here as this was addressed in detail in The Empathy Gap *(section 15.2). Sexual crypsis in humans is, however, worth discussing as few sources do so despite its direct relevance to the sociology of gender.*

Original posted on: 23 January 2017.

Across species in general, the term "sexual crypsis" refers to a female's ability to influence, in a covert manner, whether a specific male will cause her to become pregnant. There are a range of mechanisms in different species that can implement sexual crypsis, and this can occur before, during or after copulation. Detering copulation from occurring is the most obvious strategy, but in many species the female has means by which pregnancy due to an undesired male can be prevented, or its likelihood reduced, even after copulation and insemination.

One mechanism of sexual crypsis, and the one of relevance in humans, refers to the phenomenon whereby oestrus in the female is secret rather than advertised. To quote Matt Ridley, Ref.[1], "women's genes seem to have gone to inordinate lengths to conceal the moment of ovulation".

In short, males do not know when a female is "on heat", i.e., fertile. Here I shall discuss this form of sexual crypsis exclusively. In particular, I address the relevance of sexual crypsis in human reproductive strategy.

It is worth emphasising the oddness of human sexual crypsis. In most mammals, oestrus is advertised in order to attract male mates. Think bitches on heat. Dogs are in no doubt about the matter. Think female chimp. A female chimp in oestrus is embarrassingly obvious even to us humans. So it is reasonable to suppose that the adoption of sexual crypsis in humans carried evolutionary advantage, and, moreover, an evolutionary advantage peculiar to humans. What is the main difference between chimp and human reproductive strategies? Well, that would be the pair-bond. In humans, who exploit sexual crypsis, a long-term pair-bond has evolved, helping to ensure the survival of offspring who take many years to mature. In contrast, in non-cryptic chimps, the mother chimp raises the child essentially unaided.

So what is the link between sexual crypsis and the pair-bond? One suggestion is mate guarding. In a non-cryptic species, in which a female's fertile period is easily recognised, a male wishing to ensure that he gets her pregnant, not another male, need repel other suitors only for the short time she is "on heat". In a cryptic species, on the other hand, he needs to mate-guard all the time because he cannot know when she is fertile. It is easy to envisage this full-time mate guarding as a precursor to the pair-bond. Indeed, this may be part of the explanation. However, it's not the only hypothesis. The other involves the cuckolding strategy. But first, an entertaining diversion.

Consider this suggestion: males are the product of a selective breeding programme, the selection being done by females.

Well, of course, because women are the gatekeepers of sex.

Because women get to choose with whom they have sex, they get to control the direction of human evolution. Providing that you accept that women do indeed decide if procreation takes place (mostly), this conclusion is inevitable. The advent of the pill and elective abortion has only strengthened the female hold on reproduction.

Yes, yes, I know it isn't that simple. But there is a strong tendency in that direction. It is not true that men are always up for sex with any female at any time. That is one of our modern misandric myths. But nevertheless, there is a strong tendency for men to be happy to take advantage of an opportunity to have sex with a women who makes herself available. The reverse is far less often the case. In typical situations it is the woman who is in control. Our society insists that this should be so. Heterosexual rape is, after all, defined in UK law as sex in violation of the woman's consent – specifically the woman's consent. Our society legislates, literally, to ensure that women remain the gatekeepers of sex. I believe that all societies have done so in varying ways.

It is quite amusing really. You see, ladies, every time you complain about men's nature, remember, it's your own fault. If we are monsters, then we are the monsters you created.

No, I'm not entirely serious. There is an element of choice by men too. And evolution does not negate the individual's obligation to moral conduct. I remain responsible for my actions. But nevertheless there is an element of truth in the observation.

What I want to address now is cheating. The pair-bonding scenario is all very nice and cosy, but surely a man's best evolutionary strategy is to spread his seed as widely as possible (in addition, of course, to said pair-bonding arrangement). Men have an advantage here because they could get dozens of women pregnant simultaneously, whilst a woman can incubate only one pregnancy at a time. Men's cheating is a threat to women's evolutionary strategy because his ability to provide resources for her child will be diluted by having to juggle competing claims from other women and their children. So there is a puzzle here: why have women not exploited their control over the evolutionary direction to breed the wandering tendency out of men? Men could have been made to develop so as to be strictly monogamous, a race of utterly faithful men. So why has this not happened?

The answer is that it takes two to cheat. If women have not exploited their control over the evolutionary direction to stop cheating it can only be because cheating favours the promulgation of their genes. It does.

In attempting to optimise their choice in a male, women have a dilemma. On the one hand they would naturally wish to choose a high-status male who, by virtue of his position on the male hierarchy, is flagged as having good genes – Mr Alpha. On the other hand, women also need to choose a male who is going to stick around long term for resource provision purposes – Mr Commitment. The problem is that these two characteristics tend not to occur together in the one bloke. There are exceptions but in general Mr Alpha is too busy prioritising his status – and exploiting his status to indulge in mating opportunities - to be desperately reliable. In contrast, whilst Mr Commitment is lower in status, and hence in genetic fitness, he looks willing to commit to sticking around by way of compensation. So, what's a girl to do?

Cheat, obviously. The optimal strategy for women is to capture Mr Commitment for marriage purposes (read 'resources'), whilst keeping a weather eye out for mating opportunities with Mr Alpha (read 'genes'). So long as Mr Commitment doesn't realise, he'll provide the resources for the raising of the cuckoo in his nest. And this – finally – is where sexual crypsis comes in.

In a species which advertised female oestrus, Mr Commitment would need to guard his potentially errant wife only at such times. But the phenomenon of sexual crypsis gives him no clue to her fertile periods, and he is left with the near impossible task of being on permanent watch. She, on the other hand, does know when her fertile periods are, and can, should she wish, exploit this to maximise the potential for bearing Mr Alpha's child. This might be entirely subconscious on her part. Some quotes from Matt Ridley, Ref.[1], illustrate the point.

"…her husband is, almost by definition, usually not the best male there is – else how would he have ended up married to her? His value is that he is monogamous and will therefore not divide his child-rearing effort among several families. But why accept his genes? Why not have his parental care and some other male's genes?"

"…deep in the mind of a modern woman is the same basic hunter-gather calculator, too recently evolved to have changed much: strive to acquire a provider husband who will invest food and care in your children; strive to find a lover who can give those children first-class genes. Only if she is very lucky will they be the same man….It continues with a rich tycoon's wife bearing a baby that grows up to resemble her beefy bodyguard. Men are to be exploited as providers of parental care, wealth and genes. Cynical? Not half as cynical as most accounts of human history."

One man's philandering is another man's paternity fraud. If the theory is valid you would expect paternity fraud to be more prevalent where Mr Commitment was in a lower socioeconomic class, because then it is so much easier for him to be trumped on the male hierarchy by another bloke. Similarly, you would expect paternity fraud to be less common when Mr Commitment is in a higher socioeconomic class, since in that happy circumstance Mr Commitment is hard to better, being himself something of an alpha male. This is indeed the case; all sources agree that mispaternity is far more common in the lower socioeconomic classes. Similarly, falsely attributed paternity is far less common amongst married couples than unmarried couples. This will partly reflect the socioeconomic dependence as unmarried mothers are far more prevalent in the lower socioeconomic groups.

The rate of mispaternity in the population as a whole is uncertain but the data in Refs.[2,3] suggest a median prevalence of around 6% even when there is no prior suspicion of paternity fraud. Where there is such suspicion, a prevalence of 25% or even higher is likely. However these data disguise the huge demographic dependence of paternity fraud. In the highest socioeconomic classes the rate is probably less than 2%, whilst in the lowest it can be as high as about 30%.

Sexual crypsis is an aid to the cuckoldry apparent in these high rates of paternity fraud. This is evolutionary because men who successfully cuckold achieve more progeny without the burden of resource provision, whilst the women get children with better genes. Only the cuckolded man loses out. This is yet another aspect of male disposability, his loss being the tribe's gain.

One of the more infuriating features of this phenomenon is the degree of explicit or implicit support this situation receives from medical and so-called ethical professionals. There is enthusiasm for promoting "social paternity" over mere biological paternity. Men who are exercised by "whose genes are in this child" are castigated as having a "thin view of fatherhood". In this way society is instructing men to accept being cuckolded. Society benefits, of course, just as society benefits from other products of male disposability. The sex bias is palpable: no one is about to criticise mothers as having a thin view of motherhood because they prefer to raise their own child, rather than being sent home from the maternity ward with any baby.

References

[1] Ridley, M. (1994). *The Red Queen: Sex and the Evolution of Human Nature*. Penguin, 6 October 1994.

[2] Bradford, R.A.W. (2018). *Database of Sources for Mispaternity Rates*. Academia, 23 December 2018.

[3] Colins, W. (2019). *The Empathy Gap (section 15.2)*. LPS Publishing, June 2019.

47. The Bottom of the Rabbit Hole

In many posts I alluded in passing to the evolutionary origins of the empathy gap. In chapter one of The Empathy Gap I emphasised this repeatedly, as I did also in my interview with John Barry for the Male Psychology magazine, Ref.[1]. The posts on which this chapter and the next are based are the most complete account I have written of that perspective. This is a long chapter but justifiably so in view of the significance of the subject, namely the biological basis of male disposability. For the uninitiated the title refers in allegory to the journey people take when discovering the reality of the empathy gap, and allied issues such as male disposability, for the first time. What follows that initial discovery is a succession of revelations which leads to such people asking "how deep does this rabbit hole go?". Here I provide the answer.

Original posted on: 13 January 2017.

How deep does the rabbit hole go?

Many have asked. There is an answer.

The answer is: the rabbit hole is several hundred million years deep.

Male disadvantage is as old as anisogamous sex itself. Ever since males became distinguished from females, males have been disadvantaged. And that happened not long, in evolutionary terms, after the dawn of multicellular organisms.

If males are privileged, or even if we are equal, where is my uterus?

The question is not facetious but central to the issue.

Feminists promote the view that the possession of a uterus is a burden. Certainly, it was when the occupational hazard of being female was a succession of unwanted pregnancies and the curtailment of individual freedom which that imposed, plus substantial risk. In evolutionary terms, the female invests heavily in reproduction.

By the same token, in evolutionary terms, males might appear to have a lot of catching up to do as regards contribution to the reproductive endeavour. But too naive a view of these matters can lead otherwise sound scientific expositions into a pejorative, even misandric, view of male contribution, such as this quote from Lukas Schärer, Ref.[2],

"The male sex can be seen as a parasite of the investment by the female sex."

Here I take a closer look at these evolutionary matters and opine that the origins of male disposability can be traced all the way back to the origin of maleness itself. I shall suggest that our society's blasé indifference to male disadvantage is an evolved trait (albeit one that has also been culturally amplified).

The thesis is this: the evolutionary purpose of males is to be disposable.

In genetic terms, the male contribution to reproduction, which balances the female's greater obvious investment, is the high risk of being surplus to requirements – the benefit of which is the eradication of deleterious genes from the species' gene pool.

That's right, the protective function of males operates even at the genetic level.

The above quote may be turned on its head: the female sex may be seen as parasitic on male disposability – and this is true at great evolutionary depth, not just in human society.

And *that* is the bottom of the rabbit hole.

So, let's throw ourselves down that rabbit hole…

Firstly - what is sex for?

No, no, no. If you thought "for having babies" or "for having fun", go to the bottom of the class. You were thinking of copulation, weren't you?

Sex is a biological reproductive strategy defined by the recombination of genes, the offspring sharing genes from two parents. This is usually accomplished by diploid cell meiosis followed by fusion of the resulting haploid gametes to form the new, and unique, first diploid cell of the offspring, the zygote.

Don't worry if you struggle with that last sentence; I shall now decipher it in a one paragraph summary of genetic biology.

Genes come in packages called chromosomes. (But not all DNA is in the chromosomes - I'll get to the mitochondrial exception later). Diploid cells involve a set of pairs of chromosomes, one of each pair originating from each parent. Thus, for over 99% of we humans, our cells consist of 23 chromosome pairs, 46 chromosomes in all. Meiosis is the process in which such a diploid cell splits in two (in effect, though it's not so simple) forming cells which each have just one chromosome of each pair. These are the gametes, which are examples of haploid cells (containing single rather than paired chromosomes). The gametes of a female are called eggs, whilst the gametes of a male are called sperm. In humans, 22 of the 23 chromosome pairs are homologous, i.e., each chromosome within a pair, one originating from the mother and one from the father, contain the same genes at the same positions. However, the chromosomes which originate from, say, the father, are not the same as the father's chromosomes (ditto, the mother). This is because during meiosis genetic material from one of the pair of homologous chromosomes 'crosses-over' to the other of the pair, thus creating an entirely new combination of alleles in the gametes' chromosomes. An allele is a particular variant of a given gene, so that allele is to gene as isotope is to element. The 23rd pair are the sex chromosomes which are not homologous, being denoted XX and XY for female and male humans respectively, with Y being physically a relatively small chromosome. Note that this is not universally the case, for example in birds the male is the homomorphic sex (ZZ) and the female heteromorphic (ZW), and Z is the larger chromosome. Experts will know that there are a myriad of exceptions to this brief outline, but further details are not appropriate here. Lecture ends.

So that is what is meant by sexual reproduction. And sexual reproduction necessarily involves two types of individual in a given species: male and female – right?

Wrong.

So far I have not defined what 'male' and 'female' mean – and sexual reproduction does not necessarily require sexual dimorphism. If the two gametes which fuse to form the zygote are of comparable size and shape, they are said to be isogamous – in which case the terms 'male' and 'female' are either undefined or arbitrary or simply do not apply.

Overwhelmingly, plant and animal species are anisogamous: the two gametes are very different in size. The female is defined as the phenotype (individual) which produces the large gamete – the egg. The male is defined as the phenotype which produces the small gamete – the sperm. The sperm is little more than a package of genetic material with a distribution mechanism. The egg, on the other hand, comes complete with the infrastructure and nutrients required ultimately to form a complete diploid cell, the zygote. Eggs tend to be immobile, but sperm mobile. The sperm goes to the egg. This is as true in plants as in animals, wind-blown pollen being the male haploid gametes, the sperm.

The big question is "why"? Why did sex, and in particular anisogamous sex leading to sexually dimorphic individuals, evolve at all? You might think that such a basic question would have been answered long ago. But it has not been. To quote Paul Cox, Ref.[3],

"The evolution of anisogamy, one of the major evolutionary riddles to remain unsolved in the nineteenth and twentieth centuries, emerges into the twenty-first century as potent a mystery as ever. The prevalence of anisogamy in the animal and plant kingdoms – with isogamy characterizing only a few algal species – is an astonishing testament of the evolutionary ascendency of anisogamy as a robust evolutionary solution."

Indeed – but how come?

In truth this modest admission of ignorance belies the great deal that is known about the evolution of sex. Indeed, there are a number of hypotheses which, perhaps between them, probably provide the answer. Before reviewing the possible answers, though, let's make sure the problem is understood.

Some organisms can reproduce by parthenogenesis, i.e., asexually so that an individual creates offspring without the involvement of any other individual. It is fairly common in lower creatures. The phenomenon will be familiar to anyone who has kept stick insects – their numbers grow alarmingly quickly, despite all being female. Often the offspring are clones of the single parent, but, surprisingly, not always. In automictic parthenogenesis a haploid ovum is first made by meiosis, thus permitting genetic crossover to occur.

Why would evolution favour sexual reproduction over parthenogenesis? Sexual reproduction produces one offspring for every pair of individuals, whereas parthenogenesis would allow both individuals to reproduce, creating two offspring. This is the two-fold cost of sexual reproduction. Would it not be more efficient, and hence be preferentially selected by evolution, to deploy parthenogenesis in all species?

Actually, there is an easy way for sexual reproduction to avoid this two-fold evolutionary cost and that is by adopting reproductive hermaphrodites. Each individual could be fertilised by the other, and both would bear children (or lay fertilised eggs, as appropriate). So the advantages of genetic mixing between two individuals could be retained but two individuals would produce two offspring, just as for parthenogenesis.

This observation makes the original question even harder. It is now necessary to explain specifically why sexual dimorphism (hence anisogamy) is such a successful evolutionary strategy when the male cannot produce a child. In addition to this arithmetical two-fold cost, there is also the disadvantage that dimorphic sexual reproduction requires the male and female to physically find each other (or, at least, their gametes need to do so – think pollen) apparently introducing further inefficiency.

We can phrase this as a radical feminist might: "what use are males?"

Let's look at some older hypotheses before getting to the main event.

The Tangled Bank

The "tangled bank" is a convenient label for a class of theories stretching back to Darwin (the name originating from a throwaway paragraph of his). Essentially these theories claim that the benefit of sexual reproduction lies in its enhancement of genetic variation, because sex involves the mixing of genes from two parents (in additional to the mixing of genes of each parent via cross-over). I dare say this is what the lay person most commonly still believes. The problem with this idea is that it's wrong. To quote the review, unambiguously and helpfully titled "Sex reduces genetic variation", Gorelick & Heng write, Ref.[4],

"For over a century, the paradigm has been that sex invariably increases genetic variation, despite many renowned biologists asserting that sex decreases most genetic variation. Sex is usually perceived as the source of additive genetic variance that drives eukaryotic evolution vis-à-vis adaptation and Fisher's fundamental theorem. However, evidence for sex decreasing genetic variation appears in ecology, palaeontology, population genetics, and cancer biology."

Moreover, the theory has some obvious flaws in terms of what it predicts. In Ref.[5] John Cartwright writes, referring to the tangled bank hypothesis,

"The theory would predict a greater interest in sex among animals that produce lots of small offspring that compete with each other. In fact, sex is invariably associated with organisms that produce a few large offspring, whereas organisms producing small offspring frequently engage in parthenogenesis."

More directly Gorelick & Heng, Ref.[4], have this to say,

"...sex acts like a coarse filter, weeding out major changes, such as chromosomal rearrangements (that are almost always deleterious), but letting minor variation, such as changes at the nucleotide or gene level (that are often neutral), flow through the sexual sieve. Sex acts as a constraint on genomic and epigenetic variation, thereby limiting adaptive evolution. The diverse reasons for sex reducing genetic variation (especially at the genome level) and slowing down evolution may provide a sufficient benefit to offset the famed costs of sex."

Rather than sex increasing genetic variation, it decreases it – but this can be a good thing in terms of getting rid of harmful mutations. However, Gorelick & Heng's optimism that this might provide "a sufficient benefit to offset the famed costs of sex" has not withstood scrutiny. The tangled bank does not, on its own, provide a complete explanation of how sexually dimorphic species either evolved or are evolutionarily stable.

The Red Queen Hypothesis

The Red Queen hypothesis recognises that organisms are not in an environment which is static. In particular they are being attacked by parasites which themselves evolve rapidly. There is an arms race between the species and its parasites, both reacting to counter the latest move of the other. So, it takes all the running an organism can do to keep in the same place. More accurately, what is hypothesised is a sort of dynamic equilibrium in which both the species and its parasites evolve at equal rates. In 1993 Matt Ridley published a book on the evolution of sex which was titled, "The Red Queen", so he must have been sold on the idea.

However, it now looks unlikely that The Red Queen hypothesis can be the whole explanation of how anisogamous sex can overcome its two-fold cost. Some studies do indeed produce results consistent with the hypothesis, such as Ref.[6]. But such results would appear to be specific to particular circumstances, not a general phenomenon. Thus Otto and Nuismer, Ref.[7], conclude,

"The Red Queen hypothesis posits that sex has evolved in response to the shifting adaptive landscape generated by the evolution of interacting species. Previous studies supporting the Red Queen hypothesis have considered a narrow region of parameter space and only a subset of ecological and genetic interactions. Here, we develop a population genetics model that circumscribes a broad array of ecological and genetic interactions among species and derive the first general analytical conditions for the impact of species interactions on the evolution of sex. Our results show that species interactions typically select against sex. We conclude that, although the Red Queen favours sex under certain circumstances, it alone does not account for the ubiquity of sex."

Recombination as Gene Error / Mutation Purging

We have seen, from Gorelick & Heng, Ref.[4], quoted above, that sex can act as a coarse filter, removing the more serious genetic defects. For example, Paland and Lynch, Ref.[8], concluded that their results *"support the hypothesis that sexual reproduction plays a prominent role in reducing the mutational burden in populations"*. However, the same conclusion does not hold for the gradual accumulation of more minor genetic defects. The hypothesis that sexual reproduction might also purge such accumulations of minor defects is usually associated with the name Alexey Kondrashov, Ref.[9]. He concluded,

"If the deleterious mutation rate per genome per generation is greater than 1, then the greater efficiency of selection against these mutations in sexual populations may be responsible for the evolution of sex and related phenomena."

The trouble is that mutation rates are actually almost certainly smaller than 1 per genome per generation, see for example Refs.[10,11]. So once again it seems that sex, through recombination and sharing of genes, is not enough to overcome its apparent two-fold cost.

It's Not Just Recombination

So where does this leave us? It leaves us, as Mary Jane West-Eberhard, Ref.[12], put it succinctly, with *"the paradox of sex, whose maintenance by recombination alone has not been convincingly demonstrated in theory or in fact."*

It would appear that sex itself – which is gene recombination and sharing – does not provide a mechanism sufficient to offset the two-fold cost of sexual dimorphism. So, if it isn't the sex part, is it the dimorphism part? Does the existence of two distinct phenotypes, the two sexes, provide the mechanism driving sufficient evolutionary benefit?

The answer would appear to be "yes".

West-Eberhard, Ref.[12], expresses it thus, *"if you concentrate on the social aspects of sex, you can see males and females as two divergent, complementary morphs, mutually dependent alternative phenotypes that are similar to the queens and workers of social insects in their mutual dependence; neither can reproduce without the other."*

So now I turn to explanations based on social behaviour rather than gene recombination and sharing. Whilst these social explanations emerge as being the more significant, it should be borne in mind that recombination does confer benefit – just not enough to offset the two-fold cost of sex, and hence not sufficient to explain the evolution of sex on its own. However, the complete explanation of the origin and evolutionary stability of sexual reproduction probably involves both aspects in combination.

Maintenance of Sex Versus Evolution of Sex

Before proceeding, and in the interests of completeness, it is useful to distinguish between two problems: how sexual reproduction evolved, and why it remains stable against further evolutionary changes ("maintenance"). Mary Jane West-Eberhard, Ref.[12], graphically illustrates the difference thus,

"The factors responsible for the functional design of a trait are not necessarily those responsible for its maintenance at high frequency: sports utility vehicles were originally designed for rugged off-road use, but they are maintained at high frequency in many parts of the world for quite different reasons, such as to display signs of wealth and to serve as armoured shields against injury in traffic accidents."

Her view is that sex is maintained as a developmental trap, a mere legacy of selection past, hence a phenomenon quite independent of its evolution. She summarises her thesis thus,

"Sexual reproduction is maintained as an adaptive legacy of sexually selected and other male manipulations that have produced a reproductive dependence of females on males."

From this perspective, sexual reproduction is merely a bad habit, long past its ancient evolutionary usefulness. It echoes the earlier quote from Lukas

Schärer, Ref.[2], that "*the male sex can be seen as a parasite of the investment by the female sex*".

An analogue of this hypothesis is non-linear optimisation. It is infamously the case that an automated search for the minimum of a function can get stuck in a local minimum which is very different from the global minimum that is wanted. The local minimum is stabilised (maintained) even though it is the wrong solution. Indeed, purely mathematical, game-theoretical, models can 'explain' the stability of dimorphic sexual reproduction, see for example Alexander Feigel's bullishly titled "Sex Is Always Well Worth Its Two-Fold Cost". However, it would be an act of faith to assume the assumptions of such models represent reality.

Social Sexual Selection and Mutation Load

And so to the main event. Social sexual selection is beginning to emerge as the mechanism of greatest significance in realising the advantage of sexual reproduction. West-Eberhard, Ref.[12], expresses it thus,

"(Sexual reproduction has) a 'eugenic' function – that is, sexual behaviour, such as female assessment of males, is testing for good survival genes. You see female choice and male-male competition as ways of screening for the genetic quality of potential mates in the struggle for survival and ecological success. Agrawal and Siller assigned sexual selection another kind of eugenic function that depicted it as a way of placing the burden of mutation disadvantage on males. By this idea, which we can call "mutational cleansing", the cost of selection against deleterious mutations falls mainly on the more strongly sexually selected sex, usually the males, and this may help to compensate the cost of sex to females."

It should be noted that this is not West-Eberhard's preferred hypothesis; her views have already been discussed, above. But the quote is useful for its inclusion of the term "mutational cleansing". It is also useful because it seems to be the emerging favourite perspective.

As if in answer to the feminists' question "what use are men?", Steve Moxon in Ref.[14] expresses it thus,

"In contrast to females, the job of the males is for their genes to be radically exposed to natural selection, so that those males displaying, relatively, some form of deficiency or less than prowess, through possession of a sub-optimal, below average, or a simply not pre-eminent genome, are identified for weeding out, to take with them their deleterious genetic material, which thereby is eliminated from the local gene pool."

This overall process, continues Moxon, has been dubbed the male genetic filter by the pioneering biologist and computer engineer Wirt Atmar in his key 1991 paper "On the Role of Males", Ref.[15]. Atmar's conclusion is,

"A primary reason for the existence of males in a bisexual species may be to act as a pre-zygotic filter of genetic defects. Males appear to be an auxiliary sexual caste that may be culled at less cost to the reproductive success of a species than by allowing both maternal and paternal lines of inheritance to be culled uniformly. A variety of genetic and behavioural mechanisms promote and exaggerate a general physiological fragility in male animals not apparent in females."

Atmar goes on to cite intrasexual male violence as the mechanism by which this culling is achieved. However Moxon, Ref.[14], has a more nuanced, and more convincing, take on how the culling is achieved, namely through the agency of male hierarchies (addressed briefly below). Quoting Moxon again,

"The extra purging of deleterious genetic material from the gene pool through the male half of the lineage is sufficient to more than compensate for sexual reproduction requiring two parents to make each offspring rather than just the one needed in sexual reproduction (the famous two-fold cost of sex)."

To put it simply and brutally, the biological purpose of males is to be disposable. It always was, across all species it seems. One might say that the social disposability of men in our society is an echo of its evolutionary, genetic origins. This is the bottom of the rabbit hole.

So much for the statement of the hypothesis that males act as a genetic filter of mutations, but what about the evidence? In addition to Moxon's arguments, in a 2009 paper, Ref.[16], Whitlock and Agrawal observe that,

"Healthy males are likely to have higher mating success than unhealthy males because of differential expression of condition-dependent traits such as mate searching intensity, fighting ability, display vigour, and some types of exaggerated morphological characters. We therefore expect that most new mutations that are deleterious for overall fitness may also be deleterious for male mating success. From this perspective, sexual selection is not limited to influencing those genes directly involved in exaggerated morphological traits but rather affects most, if not all, genes in the genome. If true, sexual selection can be an important force acting to reduce the frequency of deleterious mutations and, as a result, mutation load. We review the literature and find various forms of indirect evidence that sexual selection helps to eliminate deleterious mutations. However, direct evidence is scant, and there are

almost no data available to address a key issue: is selection in males stronger than selection in females?"

This appears to leave the matter unresolved. However, since 2009 there have been a number of papers which do indeed supply evidence that sexual selection acts more strongly on males. I cannot do a thorough review of the literature in a short non-specialist review, even if I had the competence, but a sample of what was emerging when I wrote the original article in 2017 is as follows.

Lumley et al, (2015), Ref.[17], wrote,

"Reproduction through sex carries substantial costs, mainly because only half of sexual adults produce offspring. It has been theorized that these costs could be countered if sex allows sexual selection to clear the universal fitness constraint of mutation load. Under sexual selection, competition between (usually) males and mate choice by (usually) females create important intraspecific filters for reproductive success, so that only a subset of males gains paternity. If reproductive success under sexual selection is dependent on individual condition, which is contingent to mutation load, then sexually selected filtering through 'genic capture' could offset the costs of sex because it provides genetic benefits to populations. Here we test this theory experimentally by comparing whether populations with histories of strong versus weak sexual selection purge mutation load and resist extinction differently. After evolving replicate populations of the flour beetle Tribolium castaneum for 6 to 7 years under conditions that differed solely in the strengths of sexual selection, we revealed mutation load using inbreeding. Lineages from populations that had previously experienced strong sexual selection were resilient to extinction and maintained fitness under inbreeding, with some families continuing to survive after 20 generations of sib × sib mating. By contrast, lineages derived from populations that experienced weak or non-existent sexual selection showed rapid fitness declines under inbreeding, and all were extinct after generation 10. Multiple mutations across the genome with individually small effects can be difficult to clear, yet sum to a significant fitness load; our findings reveal that sexual selection reduces this load, improving population viability in the face of genetic stress."

So Lumley *et al* essentially support the male genetic filter hypothesis. Mallet et al. (2011), Ref.[18], wrote,

"Sex differences in the magnitude or direction of mutational effect may be important to a variety of population processes, shaping the mutation load and affecting the cost of sex itself......Mutation-accumulation (MA) experiments provide the most direct way to

examine the consequences of new mutations......We therefore investigated the effects of 50 generations of X-chromosome mutation accumulation on the fitness of males and females derived from an outbred population of Drosophila melanogaster. Results: Fitness declined rapidly in both sexes as a result of MA, but adult males showed markedly greater fitness loss relative to their controls compared to females expressing identical genotypes......Conclusions: Our data helps fill a gap in our understanding of the consequences of sexual selection for genetic load, and suggests that stronger selection on males may indeed purge deleterious mutations affecting female fitness."

Again this is supportive of the male genetic filter hypothesis, as is the 2012 paper by Roze and Otto, (2012), Ref.[19], extracts from whose Abstract are,

"Anisogamy is known to generate an important cost for sexual reproduction (the famous "twofold cost of sex"). However, male-female differences may have other consequences on the evolution of sex, due to the fact that selective pressures may differ among the sexes....it has been suggested repeatedly that sexual selection among males may help to purge the mutation load, providing an advantage to sexual females. However, no analytical model has computed the strength of selection acting on a modifier gene affecting the frequency of sexual reproduction when selection differs between the sexes. In this article, we analyse a two-locus model using two approaches......We find that costly sex can be maintained when selection is stronger in males than in females, but acts in the same direction in both. Complete asexuality, however, evolves under any other form of selection."

Further support for the male genetic filter hypothesis is provided by McGuigan et al, (2011), Ref.[20], and by Maclellan et al, (2009), Ref.[21]. However, it would be wrong to give the impression that this view is unanimous – or even that there is, as yet, a consensus. For example, in July 2012, Arbuthnott and Rundle Ref.[22], came to the opposite conclusion in a paper whose title is indicative: *Sexual selection is ineffectual or inhibits the purging of deleterious mutations in Drosophila melanogaster.*

My amateur impression is that the male genetic filter idea is certainly respectable, and probably currently the lead contender as an explanation of the net benefit of anisogamous sexual reproduction despite the latter's famous two-fold cost. However, there does not have to be a single mechanism which provides the entire benefit. It is clear that recombination effects alone do provide some of the benefit, though not enough. There are, however, two further strands to the argument in favour of the male genetic filter hypothesis: preferred male gene expression and the ancient breeding ratio, which we look at next.

Preferred Male Gene Expression

The purging of gene errors through the preferred culling (or childlessness) of males is of benefit to the species as a whole, both males and females. This would be the case even if genes originating from both parents were expressed equally. But another emerging fact appears to be that more of an offspring's genes originating from the male are expressed than those of female origin. ("Expression" in this context refers to the allele of the homologous gene pair which is actually "used", i.e., has an effect on the phenotype, the individual). This will make the male genetic filter mechanism even more effective.

One feels for the radical feminist. The thought that half their genetic material, the very stuff of their bodies, derives from a man must be disgusting to them. Well, in terms of expression, it's actually rather more than half.

The key paper is Crowley, et al, (2015), Ref.[23]. Their work was on mice, but they have reason to expect it to be applicable to humans. Their main finding was, "a new genome-wide parent-of-origin allelic imbalance favouring the paternal allele". Despite some technical language, the reader will grasp the import of the following extracts from the paper,

"Imprinted genes were 1.5 times more likely to be expressed from the paternal than the maternal allele. This observation is consistent with the observation that paternal expression predominates in brain, while maternal expression predominates in placenta. To test whether this asymmetry in parent-of-origin effects extends beyond imprinted genes, we estimated the parent-of-origin effect in each cross and each sex separately. We found that 54–60% of genes show higher expression from the paternal allele, significantly different from the expectation of 50%.....Among the 19 autosomes, 15 have a higher proportion of genes whose neighbour has the same parental skew than expected by chance.

We can calculate a rough estimate of the number of genes with paternal over-expression, simply by taking the difference between the number of genes with higher paternal minus higher maternal expression. For example, for female CAST/EiJ × PWK/PhJ reciprocal hybrids, there are 1,652 more genes with allelic imbalance in favour of the paternal allele (6,790 paternal minus 5,138 maternal over-expressed genes).....the excess of genes with paternal over-expression ranges between 938 and 2,500.....However, this likely represents an underestimate because, while we have high power to identify classical imprinting, we lack sufficient power to identify all genes with modest parental overexpression, while correcting for multiple testing."

To emphasise the import of this, Moxon, Ref.[14], wrote,

"We now know that mammals express more genetic variance from the father. So imagine that a certain kind of mutation is bad. If inherited from the mother, the gene wouldn't be expressed as much as it would be if it were inherited from the father."

In other words, it's more important to get good genes from the male, so evolutionary pressure acts more severely on the male. The excess of male genes which are expressed amplifies the male genetic filter mechanism of gene mutation purging.

In another 2015 paper, *Sexual selection drives evolution and rapid turnover of male gene expression*, Harrison et al, Ref.[24], note that *"the profound and pervasive differences in gene expression observed between males and females, and the unique evolutionary properties of these genes in many species, have led to the widespread assumption that they are the product of sexual selection and sexual conflict.... our results highlight the power of sexual selection to act on gene expression differences and shape genome evolution"*.

Ancient Breeding Ratio

Finally, a piece of evidence which might be the smoking gun. There is reason to believe that, if you could compile a list of all your ancestors going back 50,000 or 100,000 years, twice as many of them would be women as men. This remarkable conclusion is often expressed in this form: on average since ancient times, about 80% of women bore children, but only about 40% of men had progeny. Clearly, if true, this supports the hypothesis of a male genetic filter in which only the fitter portion (~40%) of every male cohort gets to breed. Sexual selection, by female choice and male hierarchies (or premature death) prevents lesser men reproducing at all.

This remarkable conclusion originates from genetic studies reported first in 2004 by Wilder, Mobasher and Hammer, Ref.[25]. It is, obviously, indirect. The paper analyses gene sequence variances in local populations. By concentrating on the non-recombining part of the Y-chromosome DNA, genetic variance generated by the male line only is determined. Similarly, by concentrating on mitochondrial DNA, genetic variance generated by the female line only is determined. (Mitochondrial DNA does not reside in the chromosomes and is inherited from the mother alone). If genetic changes occur at some fixed rate per generation, then genetic variance provides a means of gauging the time to the most recent common ancestor (TMRCA).

But it turns out that the mitochondrial DNA variance is double that for non-recombining Y-chromosome DNA. This seems to suggest that the TMRCA for males is only half that for females – which makes no sense. But actually it is not calendar years which matters, it is the number of individuals contributing to the breeding process. Wilder *et al* conclude that the effective male breeding population, averaged over ancient times, was only half that for females.

A potential alternative explanation for the differing male-female genetic variances was suggested, namely the far higher rate of female migration due to the cultural practice of patrilocality (or exogamy) in which the woman moves to live with her husband's family upon marriage. However, this was addressed by another paper from Wilder et al, Ref.[26], whose title is all you need to know: *Global patterns of human mitochondrial DNA and Y-chromosome structure are not influenced by higher migration rates of females versus males.*

Similar studies have been carried out since 2004 but without essential contradiction, as far as I am aware. It would be interesting to examine the historical evidence for (or against) the idea that 80% of women but only 40% of men had progeny (noting that the DNA evidence relates mostly to prehistory). Matt Ridley, Ref.[27], attributes the following view to Laura Betzig, Ref.[28],

(In medieval Christendom) *"the phenomenon of monogamous marriage and polygamous mating was so entrenched that it required some disinterring. Polygamy became more secret, but it did not expire. In medieval times, the census shows a sex ratio in the countryside that was heavily male-biased because so many women were 'employed' in the castles and monasteries. Their jobs were those of serving maids of various kinds but they formed a loose sort of 'harem', whose size depended clearly on the wealth and power of the castle's owner. In some cases, historians and authors were more or less explicit in admitting that castles contained 'gynoeciums', where lived the owner's harem in secluded luxury."*

Ridley adds, *"meanwhile, many medieval peasant men were lucky to marry before middle age and had few opportunities for fornication".* And further, *"a feudal vassal's son had a good chance of remaining childless, while his sister was carried off to the local castle to be the fecund concubine of the resident lord".*

I cannot vouch for the historical accuracy of this view, though it does conveniently align with the (ancient) DNA evidence. It would be interesting to make a more detailed historical study.

In passing I cannot resist addressing a spurious claim that has been touted around the popular press, namely that the Y-chromosome is shrinking and destined to disappear. It is remarkable the variety of forms which misandry can take – or perhaps it is just wishful thinking by the radical feminists. Anyway, it is not so. The claims were about as scientific as the utterances of Valerie Solanas. The findings of Rozen *et al*, Ref.[29], were *"at odds with prominent accounts of the human Y chromosome's imminent demise"*. In any case the geneticists who were the source of this misinformation were predicting the Y-chromosome's demise only in 10 million years, not a timeframe which causes me much unease. But even that is incorrect, being based on Y-chromosome gene loss which occurred tens of millions of years ago. In contrast, I quote,

"During the 6,000,000 years since divergence of the chimpanzee and human lineages, the chimpanzee Y chromosome has lost the function of four X-degenerate genes, possibly as a result of increased specialization for spermatogenesis. By contrast, the human Y chromosome has not lost any X-degenerate genes during the same 6,000,000 years. Our present findings show that, in addition, X-degenerate gene content in the overwhelming majority of human Y lineages has changed little since the last common ancestor of modern human Y chromosomes, ~100,000 years ago. Indeed, the results reported here imply that purifying selection has been effective in stabilizing and maintaining the amino acid sequences of the human MSY's X-degenerate proteins during this period. In combination with previous studies, our findings conclusively refute models of precipitous genetic decay in human Y-chromosome lineages."

The Male Hierarchy

The male genetic filter mechanism can only work if males with 'good genes' mate preferentially. But how is sexual selection to accomplish this preference for males with "good genes"? Females choose, and so females' choice must reflect the genetic quality of the males in question. But how can females tell which men have "good genes" as opposed to "poor genes"? In birds this is often achieved through the bright plumage of male birds, the peacock being the ultimate example. And in some cases pure physicality makes the matter unambiguous: the male who successfully mates is the one left standing after they battle it out.

But in humans the matter is more complex. There are many male hierarchies. Being physically imposing is just one, and one of the least significant: these days powerful men rarely have bulging muscles. Wealth and social status are the chief determinants of the male hierarchy in human societies, and these are virtually independent of physique – for men, that is.

Female hypergamy – mate choice on the basis of male wealth or status - is an important part of the male genetic filter in action. This illustrates how these biological matters manifest as social behaviours. This is why this lengthy chapter is so relevant to the rest of this book and its predecessor, *The Empathy Gap*.

It is worth noting that there was a long-standing dispute about whether female choice need be correlated with the quality of the male's genes, in any objective sense. A point of view normally associated with Ronald Fisher is that any "fashion" amongst females for a particular male characteristic can become self-sustaining. If a female bucks the fashion trend she is likely to have male offspring who are unfashionable, and hence who are less likely to mate, thus compromising her gene line. However, the male genetic filter hypothesis requires that female choice really is correlated with the genetic quality in the male – or, rather, that the deselected males are those in whom the genetic defects are concentrated and ripe for purging.

The purpose of the male hierarchy (or hierarchies) is to provide the female with a ready-made ranking which, the hypothesis claims, is correlated with genuine genetic quality. Such a linear hierarchy is achieved through transitive pair-wise ordering, as explained by Moxon, Ref.[14], who wrote,

"Dominance is adaptive stressing and ranking of males in the service of allocating reproduction by differential self-suppressed fertility."

The male dominance hierarchy is therefore the perfect tool for implementing the male genetic filter.

In pair-wise conflicts or assessments, only males behave in a manner which takes account of previous outcomes so as to form a linear dominance hierarchy. Moxon opines that such dominance hierarchies are unique to males because the neural functionality which supports the formation of such a hierarchy is specific to the SRY gene on the Y-chromosome (see van den Berg et al, Ref.[30]).

I will not attempt to address female hierarchies except to note that they will inevitably be of a different kind from male hierarchies if the male genetic filter hypothesis is correct (see Ref.[14]). In the language of the men's movement, men seek power to gain access to sex, whereas women seek sex to gain access to power.

For men, ranking exacerbates conflict, writes Moxon, because it's worth fighting for. In contrast, ranking based on violence is unnecessary, and actually undesirable, in females because injury is best avoided and there is little to gain by taking the risk. This explains why most violence is male-on-male, since its purpose is to establish the male hierarchy. Male-on-female violence is an aberration because it risks injury to the limiting factor in reproduction (the female) and hence is counter-evolutionary. This is why it is socially prohibited. Female-on-male violence is neutral in evolutionary terms and is probably an epiphenomenon of female control of the male via the pair-bond. However, both directions of inter-sex violence are atypical.

If the male genetic filter hypothesis is correct, male violence, and in fact all forms of male competitiveness, are ultimately for the benefit of the whole species, and for the benefit of females in particular as it provides them with a mechanism for ensuring the genetic strength of their own offspring. This is why it is misleading to regard the male sex as parasitic upon the reproductive investment by the female sex. The broader truth is that the male's investment comes in a different form and at a different time.

Male Culling

Failing to be sufficiently high in the male hierarchy can lead to a man failing to reproduce. However, there is another way in which the male genetic filter can operate: by premature death. Seager, Farrell and Barry, Ref.[31], remind us of the greater health risk to males, including as a foetus or young child before lifestyle issues become relevant,

"In a British Medical Journal article called 'The fragile male', Ref.[32], the many ways in which men are biologically more vulnerable than women are highlighted. The male foetus is at greater risk than the female of virtually all medical complications (e.g., cerebral palsy) and developmental disorders (e.g., autism). Perhaps it is the height of irony then for males

unthinkingly to be expected to be the more resilient sex, showing that sex and gender differences operate from the moment of conception and in some unexpected ways the differences favour the female."

Perhaps not irony. Perhaps an evolved strategy to place extra survival pressures on males as part of the male genetic filter? The conclusions of the BMJ article, Ref.[32], are clear,

"The disadvantages of the male are usually seen as socially mediated. Even from conception, before social effects come into play, males are more vulnerable than females. Social attitudes about the resilience of boys compound the biological deficit. Male mortality is greater than female mortality throughout life. The causes are a mixture of biological and social pressures: we need to be aware of both in order to promote better development and health for boys and men."

A couple of extracts from Matt Ridley's The Red Queen, Ref.[27], indicate the hormonal component of greater male vulnerability to disease,

"There seems to be something about steroid hormones that unavoidably depresses the immune defence. This immune effect of testosterone is the reason that men are more susceptible to infectious diseases than women, a trend that occurs throughout the animal kingdom. Eunuchs live longer than other men, and male creatures generally suffer from higher mortality."

And Ridley quotes Marlene Zuk, *"males are thus necessarily more vulnerable to disease as they acquire the accoutrements of maleness".*

At birth, in the UK, male babies outnumber female babies, the sex ratio at birth being 1.054, so that 51.3% of newborn babies are male and 48.7% are female. And yet, in the population as a whole, only ~49% of people are male and ~51% are female – as our former Chief Medical Officer, Dame Sally Davies, seemed to take delight in reminding us, Ref.[33]. This turnaround occurs because, before the age of 84, there are ~37,000 more deaths of males than females per year. Moreover, the excess of the male death rate over the female death rate occurs in every age range, from tiny babies to age 84. And the percentage excess of male over female deaths is not just one or two percent, but several tens of percent in every age range. Men are 44% more likely to die before age 75 than women.

And yet for many years the UK Government has had a Women's Health Strategy but refused to countenance a Men's Health Strategy, ministers producing all sorts of spurious rationalisations for why not. But now we know the real reason why not: it is because the acceptance of male disposability is an evolved trait. Thankfully, as I write, there has been some movement on this issue, thanks to tireless efforts by a range of groups and individuals. In November 2023 the UK government announced that "a Men's Health Ambassador would be appointed", Ref.[34]. It remains to be seen whether this successfully delivers benefit for men.

Conclusion

At the very least I hope I have given the lie to the sentiment that "the male sex is parasitic on the investment in reproduction by the female sex". This may be refuted even without invoking the not-insignificant issue of resource provisioning and protection. The male genetic filter is a high price paid by men as a class to maintain the genetic integrity of the species. It appears that more than half of men in antiquity did not have the opportunity to be parasitic upon women's reproductive investment. And yet the sacrifice of these men is the key aspect of the male genetic filter hypothesis. To reiterate my initial claim...

The evolutionary purpose of males is to be disposable.

In genetic terms, the male contribution to reproduction, which balances the female's greater obvious investment, is the high risk of being surplus to requirements.

Patriarchy, you will note, can have no relevance to a man not within a family.

But are present day social disadvantages of men and boys truly to be seen as a consequence of this ancient biological *weregild*? Or is it mere analogy or poetic echo? The answer, I think, is that female choice and male hierarchies are still very much in place. Female hypergamy shows no signs of ameliorating.

Indeed, we might ask whether the entire male gender script, Ref.[31] (be a fighter and a winner, be a provider and a protector, retain mastery and control over your feelings) is actually an enactment in the social sphere of the male genetic filter – with the added bonus that these behaviours are also beneficial to the rest of society?

It is reasonable to suppose that the male hierarchy / female choice mechanism would be implemented, in a species with high cognitive function, via evolved sex-dependent psychologies. Since males are, in effect, seeking female approval, this naturally leads to male deference towards females but a critical attitude of females towards males. It also naturally gives rise to intra-male competition (as opposed to co-operation). In fact, Moxon argues, the critical view of men will extend to men themselves, as a means of policing any tendency an individual may have to cheat and "dishonestly signal" his status on the hierarchy. Indeed, policing the honest operation of the male hierarchy is stressed as central by Moxon.

Inevitably, then, men are judged by harsher standards than women, because the judging of men is a key evolutionary requirement, whereas judging women is not – beyond, of course, indicators of youth and health, the correlates of fertility. Moxon wrote,

"That, in root biology, males are obliged to mutually contest in order to earn sexual access, is bound to have major ramifications in psychological and social terms: males are seen as having to earn regard, otherwise they are presumed to be worthless….. Women would have to behave conspicuously badly to earn disapproval from males; otherwise, invariably they are well regarded…..All kinds of normal behaviour by males may be tendentiously interpreted as actually or potentially 'anti-social' in some way, and males come to be held responsible – blamed – for their own policing."

John Gray, Ref.[35], reminds us that we are animals and any inclination to regard ourselves as having risen above our animal natures is conceit and self-delusion. If the male hierarchy / female choice mechanism is an inherited psychological trait, it will not be easily ignored. And in as far as traditional pair-bonding habits have been socially undermined by feminism, so the male hierarchy / female choice tendency must manifest in other forms. Women are now discouraged from reliance upon males and their 'privilege' hierarchy. So how is women's innate tendency to judge males based on their hierarchical rank to find expression? Is this the psychological origin of much of the endemic misandry? Is the anti-male culture on campuses, the rise of "misogyny" hate crimes, and the myriad of man-shaming tactics actually subconscious attempts by women to exercise their evolved right to criticise men – but now stripped of any positive connotations, divorced from its original purpose of examining male rank for the purposes of reproduction?

References

[1] Barry, J. (2022). *Beyond 'male privilege'. An interview with Rick Bradford (aka Will Collins), author of The Empathy Gap*. 30 June 2022.

[2] Schärer L. (2023). *Origins of Sexual Reproduction (lecture slides)*. Zoological Institute, University of Basel, 18 October 2023. (See slide 29).

[3] Togashi, T., and Cox, P.A. (eds) (2011). *The Evolution of Anisogamy: A Fundamental Phenomenon Underlying Sexual Selection*. Cambridge University Press, 14 April 2011. (For an extract see *here*).

[4] Gorelick, R., and Heng, H.H.Q. (2010). *Sex Reduces Genetic Variation: A Multidisciplinary Review*. Evolution International Journal of Organic Evolution, 20 November 2010.

[5] Cartwright, J. (2008). *Evolution and Human Behavior: Darwinian Perspectives on Human Nature*. Bradford Books. 31 July 2008.

[6] Morran, L.T. et al (2011). *Running with the Red Queen: Host-Parasite Coevolution Selects for Biparental Sex*. Science 333(6039), 216-218, 8 July 2011.

[7] Otto, S.P., and Nuismer, S.L. (2004). *Species Interactions and the Evolution of Sex*. Science 304(5673), 1018-1020, 14 May 2004.

[8] Paland, S., and Lynch, M. (2006). *Transitions to asexuality result in excess amino acid substitutions*. Science 311(5763), 990-992, 17 February 2006.

[9] Kondrashov, A.S. (1988). *Deleterious mutations and the evolution of sexual reproduction.* Nature 336(6198), 435-440, 1 December 1988.

[10] Denver, D.R., et al (2005). *Mutation Rates, Spectra and Hotspots in Mismatch Repair-Deficient Caenorhabditis elegans*. Genetics 170(1) 107-113, 1 May 2005.

[11] Keightley, P.D., and Eyre-Walker, A. (2000). *Deleterious Mutations and the Evolution of Sex*. Science 290, 331-333, 13 October 2000.

[12] West-Eberhard, M.J. (2005). *The maintenance of sex as a developmental trap due to sexual selection*. The Quarterly Review of Biology, 80(1) 47-53, March 2005.

[13] Feigel, A. (2009). *Sex Is Always Well Worth Its Two-Fold Cost*. PLOS ONE 7 July 2009.

[14] Moxon, S. *Sex Differences Explained. From DNA to Society: Purging Gene Copy Errors*. New Male Studies Publishing – Monograph, November 2016.

[15] Atmar, W. (1991). *On the Role of Males*. Animal Behaviour, 41(2) 195-205, February 1991

[16] Whitlock, M.C., and Agrawal, A.F. (2009). *Purging the Genome with Sexual Selection: Reducing Mutational Load through Selection of Males*. Evolution: International Journal of Organic Evolution 63(3) 569-582 March 2009.

[17] Lumley, A.J., et al (2015). *Sexual selection protects against extinction*. Letter to Nature 522, 470–473, 18 May 2015.

[18] Mallet, M.A., et al (2011). *Experimental mutation-accumulation on the X chromosome of Drosophila melanogaster reveals stronger selection on males than females*. BMC Ecology and Evolutionary 11, 156, 6 June 2011.

[19] Roze, D., and Otto, S.P. (2012). *Differential selection between the sexes and selection for sex.* Evolution: International Journal of Organic Evolution, 66(2) 558-574, February 2012.

[20] McGuigan, K., et al (2011). *Reducing mutation load through sexual selection on males*. Evolution: International Journal of Organic Evolution, 65(10) 2816-2829, 28 June 2011.

[21] Maclellan, K., et al (2009). *Sexual selection against deleterious mutations via variable male search success*. Evolutionary Biology, 5(6) 795-797, 23 December 2009.

[22] Arbuthnott, D., and Rundle, H.D. (2012). *Sexual selection is ineffectual or inhibits the purging of deleterious mutations in Drosophila melanogaster*. Evolution: International Journal of Organic Evolution, 66(7) 2127-2137, 1 July 2012.

[23] Crowley, J.J., et al (2015). *Analyses of Allele-Specific Gene Expression in Highly Divergent Mouse Crosses Identifies Pervasive Allelic Imbalance*. Nature Genetics, 47(4) 353-360, 2 March 2015.

[24] Harrison, P.W., et al (2015). *Sexual selection drives evolution and rapid turnover of male gene expression*. Proc Natl Acad Sci USA, 112(14) 4393-8, 23 March 2015.

[25] Wilder, J.A., Mobasher, Z., and Hammer, M.F. (2004a). *Genetic Evidence for Unequal Effective Population Sizes of Human Females and Males*. Molecular Biology and Evolution, 21(11) 2047–2057, November 2004.

[26] Wilder, J.A., et al (2004b). *Global patterns of human mitochondrial DNA and Y-chromosome structure are not influenced by higher migration rates of females versus males*. Letter to Nature Genetics 36, 1122–1125, 19 September 2004.

[27] Ridley, M. (1994). *The Red Queen: Sex and the Evolution of Human Nature*. Penguin, 6 October 1994.

[28] Betzig, L.L. (2008). *Despotism and Differential Reproduction: A Darwinian View of History*. Aldine Transaction, 30 April 2008.

[29] Rozen S., et al (2009). *Remarkably little variation in proteins encoded by the Y chromosome's single-copy genes, implying effective purifying selection*. Am J Hum Genet 85(6) 923-928, December 2009.

[30] van den Berg, W.E., et al (2014). *Sex-specific mechanism of social hierarchy in mice*. Neuropsychopharmacology 40(6) 1364-72, 3 December 2014.

[31] Seager, M., Barry, J., and Farrell, W. (2016). *The Male Gender Empathy Gap: Time for Psychology to Take Action*. New Male Studies, 5(2) 6-16, 2016.

[32] Kraemer, S. (2000). *The fragile male*. The British Medical Journal, 321:1609, 23 December 2000.

[33] Collins, W. (2016). *The Health of the 51%: Women*. The Illustrated Empathy Gap, 3 April 2016.

[34] Bunn, S., and Ramsay, D.A. (2023). *Men's Health*. UK Parliament POST Research Briefing, 12 December 2023.

[35] Gray, J. (2003). *Straw Dogs: Thoughts on Humans and Other Animals*. Granta Books, 1 Sept. 2003.

48. Emotion and the Pair-Bond

The human pair-bond is one of a handful of key evolutionary adaptations which allowed an otherwise rather pathetic animal to dominate the planet. Here I argue that emotion – and specifically the emotionality of men – was crucial to the evolution of the pair-bond. However, before this can be argued it is necessary to understand what we mean by "emotion" and how emotions themselves evolved. The chapter ends with a deconstruction of the oft-repeated, feminist inspired, falsity that men are emotionally inadequate.

Original posted on: <u>*11 December 2016*</u>.

48.1. Introduction and Motivation

It is a familiar claim that only a small percentage of people in the UK identify as feminists. And a far smaller percentage still would declare their opposition to feminism. This gives some people a falsely optimistic perspective that a strong majority of the public are "neutral". But that is a very misleading picture if one is concerned about issues facing men and boys. Unfortunately, the vast bulk of people, more than 90% I would guess, are gynocentric. It is adequate for our present purposes to define "gynocentric" as meaning "exhibiting the gender empathy gap". If it were not for this overwhelming gynocentric majority, which comprises both sexes equally, the feminist lobby would not have gained such influence.

Effectively addressing the systemic disadvantage of men and boys is synonymous with eradicating the empathy gap. So – and this must be faced – there is a problem with 90% of the population. That's why it *is* a problem.

The role of political ideologies in feminism is well-known. However, gynocentrism is not politically based but is a phenomenon of social psychology. We have already seen its evolutionary origins via male disposability and the male genetic filter mechanism in chapter 47. The reader may already be sceptical about how significant such a purely biological process can be in a species with an advanced level of rational cognition and sophisticated social structures. The implicit question is how the underlying genetic predisposition becomes instantiated in social psychology. An obvious place to start the investigation is with the human pair-bond in its natural state. Emotion plays the starring role.

Indeed, it is actually the nature of emotion which initially concerned me most. Much criticism is levelled (generally rightly) at those who are inclined to think too much with their feelings. Yet human social psychology is guided far more by emotion than reason, whether one approves of the fact or not. I confess I was partly motivated to think about these matters by irritation. A woman of my acquaintance looked me in the eye and smiled sweetly as she told me how emotionally stunted men are. Annoyance is an emotion, isn't it? This chapter is my reply. A corollary of my argument is that the human race would not exist without male emotionality.

Throughout this chapter I have in mind the natural, or evolved, pair-bond. This has been traduced in the feminist world, but that is not my concern here. The status of the pair-bond now, in the modern world, is not addressed. Throughout I use 'pair-bonding' to mean a long-lasting monogamous heterosexual partnership for the primary purpose of mating and successful raising of children to adulthood.

48.2. Emotion and Rationality

What are emotions? What are emotions for? Why did emotions evolve?

I am not so arrogant as to imagine I can do justice to these enormous questions. Here I merely make some elementary observations about emotions, the purpose of which is ultimately to clarify some aspects of contemporary gender issues.

One view is that emotions evolved to be cognitive shortcuts. To quote David Matsumoto, Ref.[1],

"The emotions humans experience today emerged (or were naturally selected) in our evolutionary history as rapid information processing systems that helped us deal with the environment and events that occurred. That is, emotions evolved to help us cope with events and situations that had consequences for our immediate welfare. If humans didn't have emotions, we wouldn't know when to attack, defend, flee, care for others, reject food, or approach something useful, all of which were helpful in our evolutionary histories."

"In fact emotions-as-information-processing-systems are extremely adaptive because they allow us to take immediate action without thinking. There simply is not enough time to think through the consequences of every single event that elicits an emotion. Emotions evolved to allow us to rapidly, efficiently, automatically, and unconsciously react to the world without thinking, and prepare us to act (or react) appropriately."

To paraphrase: emotions are like programming a hot-key on your keyboard with a macro.

From this perspective, emotions could be consistent, in principle, with logical reasoning. But emotions have two crucial advantages: they are far quicker to process than conscious analysis and they avoid going through the same laborious rational analysis time after time. No doubt this perspective is correct for some emotions.

On the other hand, emotion is often presented as being in opposition to rationality. In popular culture it is common to align extremely high levels of rationality with emotional coldness – think Mr Spock. Similarly, emotional floridity is often aligned with irrationality: an overly emotional person may present as unreasoning. These extreme caricatures encourage us to regard rationality and emotiveness as antithetical. I shall claim that in some important instances, this is precisely the truth – and actually essential.

But there is a paradox here. *Homo sapiens* are simultaneously uniquely developed in terms of both rational cognition and also in terms of emotional range, depth and expressiveness. If rationality and emotiveness are antithetical, why are both uniquely well developed in the same species?

I will argue that this is no coincidence. On the contrary, whilst rationality and emotiveness are indeed often in counterpoint, they necessarily coevolved. I shall argue that our emotional capacity evolved in proportion to our capacity for reasoning because of the very fact that they are (sometimes) required to be oppositional. It is suggested that the evolution of key emotional attributes is intimately related to the evolution of altruistic behaviours. Since altruistic behaviours are to the detriment of the individual, such behaviours are – from a purely selfish perspective – irrational.

When discussing altruistic behaviours, the benefits to the individual's gene line are proffered as the underlying causality. Indeed, this is correct, as long as one is focussed on the distal cause (i.e., the ultimate, or root, cause). But what about the proximate cause – the motivation for the individual to behave in a manner conducive to genetic advantage even when it is disadvantageous to the individual? In such discussions, proximate causes are often either ignored or conflated with distal causes.

Consider the man who saved his son from the river but at the cost of drowning himself. What was the reason for his action? Was it because he was optimising the propagation of his gene line? Or was it because he loved his son? The answer is: both. But was his behaviour learnt behaviour? No, his behaviour, and the emotion which promoted it, must be innate because the first answer ties it to evolution.

The argument to be amplified in this chapter can be summarised thus…

Emotions provide a trick by which the genotype cons the phenotype into behaviours which benefit the genotype despite being detrimental to the narrow self-interests of the individual. Emotions provide a proximate cause of phenotypical behaviour whose distal cause is genotypical success. In other words, emotions provide a mechanism for altruistic behaviours which promote gene line propagation. The emotions involved in such cases, and their induced behaviours, must be innate because they are evolved. Emotions also provide a rationalisation of instinctive behaviours.

48.3. What are Emotions?

Humans experience a wide range of feelings. Examples are being happy, sad, fearful, angry, surprised, disgusted, contemptuous, tired, bored, sleepy, excited, hungry, ashamed, enthused, proud, embarrassed, jealous, despairing, etc. etc. I will not attempt a complete list. These phenomena tend to be referred to as "emotions". More strictly, though, these feelings are just one part of the associated emotional complexes, namely the affective part. (Nor, in psychological parlance, are emotions the only affective phenomena).

Quoting David Matsumoto, Ref.[1],

"Feelings are an important part of everyone's psychology because they are our private readouts of internal processes, informing us without words how we evaluate the world around us and events that happen to us, and what may be going on in our bodies. They are windows to our souls. And, feelings and emotion are aspects of mental life that all humans have a lifetime of access to, and a lifetime of contemplating the proper words to describe nuances of an inner physiological state or sensation. Thus it is not surprising that people lump 'emotions' and 'feelings' all together in one messy category."

But emotions are not just feelings. Here is a possible definition of what is meant by "emotion", again quoting Matsumoto, Ref.[1],

"Emotions are transient, bio-psycho-social reactions designed to aid individuals in adapting to and coping with events that have implications for survival and wellbeing. They are biological because they involve physiological responses from the nervous system, and prime skeletal muscle activities. They are psychological because they involve specific mental processes required for elicitation and regulation of response. And they are social because they are often elicited by social interactions, and have meaning to those interactions."

So, emotions are social, psychological, physiological and motivate action.

Having made these clarifications, it will not be necessary for our present purposes to be so exacting. The key facet of emotions which I wish to emphasise here is their role in motivating behaviours. Indeed, the very etymology of "emotion" suggests this connection. Nico Frijda in *The Laws of Emotion*, Ref.[2], writes,

"If an event has no repercussion on an individual's inclination to act, one will hesitate to call it an emotion…"

It is this connection between emotion and behaviour which is central to my thesis in this chapter. If emotions did not influence the physical world via behaviour then they could not influence evolution. And if they did not influence evolution, emotions could not have evolved. However, concentrating upon the role of emotions in motivating behaviours does not imply that all emotions have such an impact on all occasions. Frijda completes the above sentence as follows,

"….except perhaps in the case of emotions evoked by art."

Aesthetically induced emotions we may safely dismiss as secondary or artificial – the designation as 'art' rather gives the game away. An analogy is with the role of hunger, and the pleasure of eating, in causing an organism to seek and devour food. The pleasure of eating having been established to promote this survival-related function does not prevent the subsequent pursuance of the pleasure of eating for its own sake – and the promotion of culinary skills as an art.

Matt Ridley in *The Origins of Virtue*, Ref.[3], reinforces the more typical point that,

"Emotion rather than reason (is) the wellspring of human motivation."

48.4. Emotions as Rationalisations of Instinctive Behaviour

Instincts are behaviours which are automatic and almost irresistible. Instinctive behaviours arise without the need for conscious deliberation. Indeed, an individual may find it extremely difficult, or impossible, to modify instinctive behaviours. How, then, is an organism with a highly developed rational cognitive capacity, replete with cultural and moral pretensions, to react to apparently being controlled by crass instincts?

Our consciousness deludes us into believing that our conscious "I" is in charge. It is certainly not in charge of everything. Our conscious selves would be overwhelmed if faced with the need to maintain all our autonomic bodily functions. The nightmare of having to concentrate in order to keep one's heart beating whilst also keeping breathing would be short lived because the neglect of the myriad biochemical processes in one's lungs, liver, kidneys, stomach, pancreas, thyroid, pituitary, etc., would quickly be terminal. But we can (and do) remain ignorant of all this autonomic control in favour of concentrating only upon 'external' issues. It would be harder for our conscious selves to ignore our overt behaviours as an organism. It would be disconcerting (to the conscious mind) if one found oneself constantly doing things without any apparent reason.

Take, for example, eating. In terms of the functional requirement to ingest nutrients, and hence to survive long enough to raise offspring, evolution might just as well have made seeking and devouring of food purely instinctive, devoid of any motivation which could be apprehended by the conscious mind. This is indeed the course taken in the case of lower organisms without sufficient cognitive capacity to be distressed by such a situation. But if that were the route taken by evolution in the case of *Homo sapiens*, my conscious mind would be bemused by my own actions. Why, I would wonder, am I spending all my time hunting down these roots and berries and then sticking them in my mouth and swallowing them? The emotion of hunger and the pleasure of eating provide the consciousness with a comprehensible impetus towards, and reward for, action in finding and devouring food. I know why I hunt those roots: it's because I'm hungry and I like eating. But actually, it isn't. That's a con.

To be more precise: hunger is the proximate cause of the impulse to eat, but its distal cause is genetic. Your genes have created hunger as their means of coercing the phenotype to adopt behaviours which optimise their propagation.

For a conscious mind with highly developed rationality, a causal narrative must be provided to 'explain' instinctive behaviours, to avoid massive cognitive dissonance. Strictly, the explanation is bogus. The affective part of emotion is a stick or carrot which provides a cogent reason for the action taken. I eat to avoid the stick which is the unpleasantness of hunger and to achieve the carrot which is the pleasantness of eating. Without these emotions I would have no obvious (rational) reason to eat.

The distal reason for your endeavour to keep yourself fed is, of course, to achieve successful reproduction via the expedient of remaining alive. But one does not think to oneself, "I must obtain nutrients so that my biological processes remain in good condition until I fulfil my prime directive of reproduction" despite this being the underlying causality. You just feel hungry and want to eat.

The impulse to eat, which evolves as an instinct, cannot be permitted to act entirely subconsciously in creatures which entertain the conceit of self-control. In these circumstances, affective emotion is a sop to the consciousness to maintain the illusion that it is in charge.

48.5. The Evolution of the Cooperation of Enlightened Self-Interest

There is no mystery as to how cooperative behaviour arises in those cases where there is an eventual benefit to both involved individuals, albeit possibly delayed. It is merely a case of enlightened self-interest. However, even in this case the propensity to delay gratification may require a high degree of cognition, though not always (e.g., successful vampire bats being magnanimous with their stock of blood).

The evolution of cooperation is sometimes presented as paradoxical, but really it is not. The prisoners' dilemma is the archetype of cooperative behaviour presented as a game-theoretical paradox. Details are unimportant but the essence of game-theoretical situations like the prisoners' dilemma is as follows. Suppose two individuals, A and B, each have a choice of two behaviours which we will label as "cooperating" and "declining". They are obliged to make their choice in ignorance of the other party's choice. If both individuals choose to "cooperate" they will both benefit more than if they both "decline". However – and this is the rub – if A "cooperates" but B "declines" then B benefits even more than if both cooperated, whilst A gets totally trashed, gaining even less benefit than if both declined. Thus, the combination in which A "cooperates" but B "declines" is the most beneficial for B but the least beneficial for A.

Cold rationality and the assumption of selfish action leads to A deciding to decline – because whatever B decides, A does better by declining. But B deploys the same reasoning. The result is that both decline. This is the so-called Nash equilibrium. But by both declining, both do less well than they would have done had both cooperated. This is the paradox of the purely game-theoretical situation, the defining essence of which is that the two individuals have no prior knowledge of how the other party is likely to behave. Herein lies the shortcoming of this overly simplistic situation as a model of human behaviour.

The crazy logic of the Nash equilibrium can be broken if both individuals are willing to trust each other. The art of cooperative behaviour is to tap into the potential for both individuals to benefit by cooperating. But this requires A to trust that B will indeed cooperate, and vice versa. If A trusts B but the dastardly swine reneges on the agreement ("declines"), A gets trashed and B laughs all the way to the bank. But if trust is mutual, both benefit compared to if mistrust is mutual.

The situation changes in the cases of iterated games, that is, if pairs of individuals 'play' each other repeatedly. The good news is that conditional cooperation is then what emerges, and not just when games of this type are played by humans. Simulations on computers also tend to evolve similar strategies to humans. The key to breaking the Nash equilibrium is that individuals must be recognisable and that individuals retain a memory of other individuals' past behaviour. In the myriad of 'deals' of which social interactions consist, your reputation goes before you.

Thus, a strategy which does well is to cooperate until the other person declines, and thereafter decline with that person. Many refinements are possible which may do slightly better, but the essence of a good strategy aligns well with the human tendency to trust those who have proved trustworthy before but to mistrust those who have betrayed your trust previously ("tit for tat").

Note that the evolution of cooperation depends crucially on the ability to recognise individuals, as well as to retain a memory of their behaviour. Hence the highly pronounced human ability to recognise individual people by their faces. Trust requires recognition. [This, incidentally, is why it is natural – and rational – to mistrust someone who wears a mask which conceals their identity].

Note that the evolution of cooperative behaviour is naturally tied to the evolution of general cognitive capacity – 'big brains' – because of the necessity to recognise individuals and to retain knowledge of their past behaviour.

However, where cooperative behaviour benefits the parties involved, albeit perhaps after some delay, only rational cognitive function is strictly necessary, not emotional capacity. This is illustrated starkly by observing that the same strategies evolve in computer simulations (devoid of any emotion) as in experiments on human participants (e.g., see Ref.[4]).

This does not mean that emotions play no role in cooperative behaviour in humans. It may very well be that your decision to trust, or not to trust, someone is based upon a 'feeling' you have about them. This is an example of emotion acting as a cognitive shortcut. Such considerations become dominant if you have had no previous dealings with the individual in question. You may not have come across the individual before, but you may be able to recognise that he is "of your tribe" – or not, as the case may be. At this point the issue of cooperation intersects with the issue of in-group preference, or its lack, issues of great importance in the sociology of gender but beyond the scope of this chapter.

However, the lesson here is that, whilst cooperative behaviour may be emotionally enhanced in practice, in principle cooperative behaviour does not require emotional involvement when cooperation leads to mutual benefit. I make this point to emphasise the difference between cooperation of the enlightened self-interested type and genuine altruism, to be discussed next.

48.6. The Evolution of Altruism

Altruism differs from cooperation of the enlightened self-interest type because, in true altruism, the individual accrues no benefit at all, even long term. In general the true altruist will actually suffer as a result of his actions. How, then, can altruism arise?

The answer is simple: behaviours evolve to benefit the continuance of the gene line, not the individual organism. By virtue of inherited behavioural characteristics, the individual organism favours actions which promote the chances of his, or her, gene line prospering. This is the tautology of evolution, by which reproductive success breeds more reproductive success. Altruism at the level of the individual is selfishness at the level of genes.

Some might react to this with dismay. Does this not undermine the virtue of self-sacrifice? As Matt Ridley, Ref.[3], paraphrasing Hamilton and Trivers, puts it,

"The relationships between parents and offspring, or between mates, or between social partners, (is) not one of mutual satisfaction, but one of mutual struggle to exploit the relationship."

This apparently cynical pronouncement makes Malthus seem positively cheery. But, in truth, it applies to the genes in question, not the people. And if genuine altruism arises spontaneously from selfish genes, is it not rather miraculous? From dross comes forth gold.

But there is, as yet, something missing from this description of how altruism arises in the case of species with advanced cognitive function. Merely instinctive impulses to self-sacrifice will be resisted by organisms with sufficient understanding to do so. As we have seen already, instincts are best rendered palatable to thinking creatures via a proximate causal narrative provided by emotions.

In the case of altruistic, self-sacrificial, behaviour, there is a further necessary function of emotion: it provides the motivation. Recall that cooperative behaviour is explicable provided that there is mutual benefit. But in the case of altruistic, self-sacrificial, behaviour there is no benefit to the individual, only disbenefit. Yes, there is benefit to the gene line. But that does not directly, of itself, provide a motivation for the individual to self-sacrifice. A mother does not sacrifice herself for her child because she rationalises to herself that this is the optimal strategy for ensuring genetic propagation. She does it out of love. It is emotion which provides the motivation for altruistic behaviour in organisms with highly developed cognition. In lower animals altruism may be implemented 'directly' via instincts, so the individual is unaware of any motivation. But human self-awareness and cognitive capacity would lead to the vetoing of self-destructive impulses if no compelling emotional narrative were provided to motivate it. Without emotions, altruism would not have evolved in humans.

In anthropomorphic language, emotions are a trick used by selfish genes to coerce the individual organism into behaviours beneficial to gene line propagation even though possibly harmful to the individual.

Emotions provide the proximate cause of altruistic behaviours whose distal cause is evolutionary.

I cannot emphasise this too strongly. Without emotions there would be no altruistic behaviour in humans. Rationality alone cannot give rise to altruism because the perfectly rational organism has no allegiance to the gene line *per se*. This is why (some types of) emotions evolved: because they are a mechanism for selfish gene propagation. It is also why emotional capacity evolved in proportion to rational cognitive function, because the former stands (in such cases) essentially in opposition to the latter.

The Calvinist might opine that a virtuous act is not truly virtuous if done for the selfish gain of emotional satisfaction. As Ridley puts it, Ref.[3],

"the more you truly feel for people in distress, the more selfish you are being in alleviating that distress. Only those who do good out of cold, unmoved conviction are 'true' altruists."

But evolution doesn't care for these Protestant scruples. If the act in question promotes the gene line, then the associated emotional satisfaction is the reward offered in the game-theoretical deal that is evolution. Ridley's reinforces the point,

"Emotion rather than reason (is) the wellspring of human motivation. The desire to escape or avoid guilt…is a human universal, common to all people in all cultures."

Ah, yes – guilt. There's much more needs saying about the destructive force of misapplied guilt, but that's a subject for another day. Quoting Kagan, Ridley writes.

"Construction of a persuasive basis for behaving morally has been the problem on which most moral philosophers have stubbed their toes. I believe they will continue to do so until

they recognise what Chinese philosophers have known for a long time: namely, that feeling, not logic, sustains the superego."

Driving home the message, a quote from Nico Frijda, Ref.[2],

"Voluntary control of cognitive capacities allows letting reality – full reality, including long term consequences – to be what determines emotion. They allow emotions to be elicited not merely by the proximal, or the perceptual, or that which directly interferes with one's actions, but by all that which in fact touches on one's concerns, whether proximal or distal, whether occurring now or in the future, whether interfering with one's own life or with that of others."

Finally, recall how the pleasure of eating, originally evolved to motivate the physical sustenance of the organism, has become sought after in its own right, divorced from its initial purpose (to the detriment of our waistlines). So it can be with the emotional states promoting altruistic behaviour. While the essential role of (some types of) emotion is to provide the individual with the motivation required to be self-sacrificial under conditions which benefit the gene line, such morally laudable behaviour might become an established pattern, independent of genetic value. Thus, Ridley paraphrasing Frank, writes, *"genuine goodness is the price we pay for having moral sentiments – those sentiments being valuable because of the opportunities they open in other circumstances."* So, forget the prognostications of moral philosophers, our ethical conceits are by-products of devious arrangements put in hand by the blind operation of evolution in order to maximise the selfishness of genes.

And yet virtue is still virtue.

And that the virtue of virtue is found not to reside in its atoms, the genes, is of no greater significance than the fact that the merits of Michelangelo's David cannot be discovered in calcium carbonate molecules.

Nor does an evolutionary origin of moral behaviours preclude there also being a transcendent origin. The transcendent may work through the mundane. Indeed, this is a commonplace.

48.7. Evolution of the Pair-Bond

So we come to the main event: the role of emotion in human pair-bonding. Before we get to the emotional (proximate) bit, what about the genetic (distal) pressure towards human pair-bonding?

Homo sapiens have a very strong tendency to pair-bond, in which the male remains in a close relationship with the mother well beyond birth, providing resources whilst the child is developing, and generally extending to several births. In its post-civilisation incarnation this is the nuclear family, but more generally would have been as part of an extended family or kin group. The reason why evolution produced pair-bonding in humans is not hard to rationalise, though there are a number of theories which may be either in competition or complementary. I have summarised these in extremely brief note form in the Appendix to the original post based on a short review of the literature carried out in 2016, Ref.[6]. This Appendix is concerned with the distal causes, for which it is necessary that there be a benefit of pair-bonding to both the male and the female gene lines. That there must be such a genetic benefit is certain, else humans would not pair-bond.

A key issue is the extended period over which human children remain physically dependent on adults. This in turn is related to our No.1 attribute, our big brains. As a result, human children need 14 years or more of being looked after. How could a primitive woman find enough food, etc., for a string of children for so many years on her own?

The matter is not trivial because primates' offspring also have a protracted maturation but primate species rarely pair-bond. Nor are fathers the only available allomothers (alternative carers). They may not be the most significant allomothers in some cases. And even if paternal provisioning were the correct hypothesis, the degree of evolutionary benefit conveyed by the male being a stable resource provider depends upon the rate of childhood mortality should he not do so, and this will be particular to the ecological niche within which the species in question operates.

For our present purposes the genetic drivers for pair-bonding are actually irrelevant. They must exist. And whatever these drivers are, they must be proximately motivated by emotion since the process of reproduction is altruistic: reproduction is of no selfish value to the parents if emotion be ignored. Nevertheless, I make some observations regarding mating strategies for completeness.

As discussed in some detail in chapter 47, Moxon, Ref.[5], and others stress the importance of male hierarchies in providing the female with a guide to the genetic quality of male suitors. They emphasise the importance of the "male genetic filter" whereby the failure of low ranked males to mate is the means by which weak genes are purged.

Potential benefits of pair-bonding to the female gene line, amplified further in the Appendix to the original post, include,

- Provisioning;
- The opportunity to form a lasting mating partnership with a reasonably ranked male (in particular, a higher ranked male than she might command later as her fertility falls);
- Protection from insemination by a lesser ranked male;
- By exploiting sexual crypsis, the opportunity to mate with a higher ranked male than would be willing to form a permanent partnership, whilst remaining in a provider-protector relationship with the lesser ranked male (cuckolding).

Benefits to the male gene line include the following,

- Immediate access to a female of high fertility in return for a commitment to be faithful when her fertility falls;
- Access for mating many times during the menstrual month, thus defeating sexual crypsis;
- Securing access to a female long term would be beneficial for a mid or low ranked male compared to 'proceeding in hope', especially if females were scarce;
- Greater certainty of paternity (mate guarding).

Whilst the details of the evolution of human pair-bonding raises many questions not yet subject to consensus (see for example Allison Guy, Ref.[7] and the range of views summarised in the Appendix to the original post and in my literature review, Ref.[6]), nevertheless human pair-bonding is certainly an ancient innovation, and the case for paternal investment improving offspring survival is reasonably strong (see Ref.[6]) despite the contrary indication from the likes of Ref.[8] (see the original post's Appendix for a discussion).

So much for the distal, genetic, cause of pair-bonding. But what about its motivation to the individual, the proximate cause?

The desire to have sex is an instinct. The desire to have children is also an instinct (at least in women) and the distinction between these two things has become evident now that contraception is widely used. As with other instincts in humans, sex and reproduction come complete with an emotional narrative which provides a proximate motivation and 'explanation' of these behaviours. Let's call it love. For references see the whole oeuvre of romantic literature and music.

The two sexes are not the same: there is a crucially important asymmetry – namely that only females have a uterus and mammary glands. There is therefore a huge difference between the sexes as regards their investment in reproduction. The mother is committed to nine months of energy-sapping gestation followed by the hazardous experience of childbirth. The father has zero investment in these processes. The game-theoretical deal is therefore the provision of child gestation and nurturing services in exchange for male resource provision during and after the birth – or in the provision of quality 'purged' male genes, due to preferential selection of a reasonably highly ranked male.

Moxon, Ref.[5], argues that the male's investment occurs *before* sex, in striving to become high ranking enough to be the chosen mate. Women are sex objects; men are success objects. Men choose women for their appearance of fertility (through the proxy of visual attractiveness) whereas women choose men for their genetic quality (through the proxy of status on a male hierarchy).

That there must have been evolutionary pressure in favour of this is clear. But we are concerned now with the proximate causes: what prompts men and women to pair-bond and reproduce? As always the answer is the associated complex of emotions.

But reproduction and pair-bonding are not merely cooperative behaviours: they are altruistic behaviours. Emotions aside, there is no benefit to the individual mother in producing children, nor is there benefit to the individual father in provisioning or being glued to a female. So the emotions which prompt these behaviours could not, even in principle, be replaced by rational cognition – as they could with cooperative behaviours of the enlightened self-interested kind. Emotions are the *sine qua non* of the human pair-bond. Who would have thought it?

In short, mothers nurture their children because they love them, and fathers provide resources for their wives and children because they love them.

Clearly, I deserve an award for this momentous discovery.

Sarcasm aside, you may replace the word "love" by whatever emotional complexes you might wish. But however you dress it up, these inherited psychological tendencies – these innate emotional configurations – are the proximate causes of behaviours which implement *Homo sapiens'* evolutionary mating strategy. And these emotional states must be innate, because, by definition, they are driven by evolution.

To quote Finkel and Eastwick, Ref.[9]

"Scholars are converging on the view that the primary mechanism through which evolution increased paternal investment was a deep emotional bond between the mother and the father of young children [see paper for references]. This bond motivates mothers and (of particular relevance to the present discussion) fathers to develop a long-term relationship predicated on mutual love and affection, and it would have had the additional benefit of helping mothers of young children acquire high-quality food and protect their food stores against theft."

But note that the essential role of emotion as the proximate cause of pair-bonding applies regardless of whether provisioning plays any part in the process – in fact, regardless of what mating strategies apply.

I would add a further driver of men's involvement in pair-bonding: the role that stable families play in promoting stable large scale social structures. See, for example, chapter 62 for the significance of men's patriarchal role in families for the stability of human society itself. This aspect seems to have escaped the notice of evolutionists. But is it not reasonable to suggest that pro-social behaviours would benefit gene propagation?

The innate nature of these emotional predispositions sounds a warning. If social pressures were to result in a decline in pair-bonding – and they have – nevertheless the evolved, innate, emotional drivers will still operate. The result is a social structure which is in conflict with individuals' psychology. Quoting Lynn Miller and Stephanie Fishkin, Ref.[10],

"We would argue that humans, over vast stretches of human history, were adapted to experience responsive caregivers, both fathers and mothers. When humans do not encounter this social environment as offspring, this lack of fit between what humans were adapted for and what they encounter is likely to have a number of emergent outcomes. Chief amongst these may be the impaired ability to trust and feel that one can get close to and dependent

on others. Control for such insecure individuals may instead be achieved through emotional withdrawal or attempts to dominate others."

This is not good.

48.8. The asymmetric pair-bond

The pair-bond is bidirectional, but its two directions are different: it is asymmetric. The fundamental reason for the asymmetry is that, in the mating deal in question, the man and the woman are putting up different wares for sale. This is true whichever of the factors outlined in section 7 you may choose to believe is most significant. In the exposition below I shall concentrate, for clarity, on the assumption that male provisioning is the main function of the pair-bond. However, essentially the same points apply whatever the most significant drivers may be.

The pair-bond asymmetry results from the unequal investments the two partners make in the gestation, birth and nurturing of their children. Women's investment is huge; men's trivial (ignoring the male "success investment" prior to copulation). Women will therefore tend to be rather careful about their choice of mate. Their investment in reproduction is very burdensome, and it would be unfortunate to make such an investment for the sake of either poor paternal genetic material or for a father who is likely to renege on his obligations as resource provider.

The asymmetry of the male-female bond is manifest by the man being committed to provide resource, whilst the woman expects to receive resource. Thus, in respect of resource provision, the man is behaving altruistically whereas the woman is not. Alternatively, if it is the man's genetic quality which is key to the mating strategy, then it is a man's striving to prove his quality via the male hierarchy which is his burden. In either case, the male effort to secure mating opportunities is not to his benefit as an individual. It follows that the male bonding to the female **must** be emotionally based. The reverse is not the case. The mother's altruistic contribution, on the other hand, is the production of a child. So the mother-to-child bond is necessarily emotionally based. Both these bonds are directional; they are naturally asymmetric because the service provision which has given rise to them is one-way.

Evolution dictates that it is fecundity that a man will look for in a potential mate (whether he knows it or not). Thus a man will favour females showing clear secondary sexual characteristics, indicative of maturity, and youth, because fertility declines with age. That'll be young women with breasts – so not too young. Men tend to be criticised in our culture for preferring young women with breasts, and yet the opposite would be perverse.

Men are attracted by appearance. Female beauty is strongly related to indicators of general health, another (subliminal) sign to the male of likely fertility. And finally, female beauty is neotenous: an attractive woman's face retains characteristics of that of an infant. This may be because the adult-infant bond formed first in evolution, and the male-female bond was partly modelled to mimic it. As Finkel and Eastwick, Ref.[9], note *"it appears that, in the genus Homo, pair-bonds were scaffolded on top of infant-caregiver attachment bonds."*

But what of female-to-male bonding? The above argument implies that this will not necessarily be emotionally based – though that does not preclude emotional adjuncts arising. The main concern of the woman will be to ensure that she is investing wisely. Caution will be her watchword. She will wish to test her suitor as to his reliability. "Commitment" is the word which most neatly captures her concern – and it is no accident that women today will often criticise men for their lack of it. Yet men are far less likely to criticise a woman for lack of commitment. Is this because women are naturally so very committed? I suggest it is more likely to be because the word "commitment" does not capture very well the woman's obligation. The deal the man is signing up to is not the woman's commitment exactly, but the production of children. The one-sided concern over commitment simply reflects the directionality of the male-female bond. [I am oversimplifying all this for clarity. It is all more nuanced in truth. In particular, resource provision is not the only function served by the pair-bond. For example, pair-bonded individuals serve as robust safe havens and secure bases for each other, a benefit to both parties].

This quote from Finkel and Eastwick, Ref.[9], exemplifies in particular the female perspective,

"In Western cultures today, it takes about two years for a full-fledged pair-bond to form… However, the process of developing a potential pair-bond begins much sooner than that, sometimes in the first moments of interaction with a partner one finds romantically

intriguing. People experience this proto-pair-bonding as a form of attachment-related anxiety regarding the potential partner – as agreement with self-report items like 'I need a lot of reassurance that this person cares about me' and 'I feel uncertain about this person's true feelings for me.'"

Matt Ridley, Ref.[3], puts it bluntly,

"Emotions are mental devices for guaranteeing commitment."

Whilst Fletcher et al, Ref.[11], opine that,

"Romantic love is a 'commitment device' for motivating pair-bonding in humans"

The point I am labouring here is that the female-to-male bond consists primarily in encouraging and confirming the male-to-female bond. The female-to-male bond is a secondary phenomenon, whereas the male-to-female bond is the primary emotional requirement for the altruistic arrangement of resource provision (or any other mating strategy resulting in pair-bonding). The pay-off to the man comes with the production of children, in relation to which the female behaves altruistically and is emotionally bonded to the child.

The provision of resources to women will naturally be according to their requirements. And a woman's acquiescence will be conditional upon demonstrations of the man's commitment, such as present giving and a willingness to provide as directed. The outcome of pair-bonding is therefore that women feel entitled to control men and have men treat them with gentleness and consideration. Women expect men to sacrifice themselves for their benefit, and men do too. Such expectation and entitlement is evolved behaviour. It is the nature of pair-bonding. There is no equality in evolution. What we have here is the evolution of matricentrism, the empathy gap and male disposability. So, if this perspective is correct, it is inappropriate to cast over these behaviours a pejorative pall because our existence depends upon them.

Since the nature of the pair-bond causes women to exercise control over male effort, it follows that women will tend to become the arbiters of what is "good". In other words, because the needs of the woman attain primacy in the motivation of the man, this has led to a ceding of moral authority to the woman.

My contention is that a man's transference of moral authority to a woman transcends romantic love and becomes a permanent feature, not only of that relationship but of men's relationships with women in general. This places the man in a subservient position, maintained, not by any external agency, but purely by evolved psychological inclination. This is surely very familiar to most men. It underlies the instinct to protect women. It is the reason for men's great reluctance to upset women. It is the reason why the accusation of misogyny has such power. It is the reason why women advocating on behalf of men possess a moral legitimacy which no man is authorised to possess. And it is also the enabler of feminism which consists essentially of an exploitation of this innate bias. My position is that this female moral authority is deeply atavistic, a psychological deferral by men which has coevolved with pair-bonding.

The asymmetry of the pair-bond therefore has enormous ramifications. This asymmetry is a key aspect of the traditional gendered society, being the basis of the domestic authority of women (the truth of which has been obscured by the false idea of oppressive patriarchy). But these innate psychological dispositions – particularly women's moral authority – also give rise to the pathologies of feminism when deployed inappropriately outside the family context. And whether an individual person, man or woman, can resist the feminist narrative depends upon the extent to which their rationality can triumph over their emotional predispositions which have become inappropriate in the modern world.

48.9. Which emotions contribute to the pair-bond?

Workers in the area of emotion usually distinguish a certain class of emotions, called 'basic emotions'. Basic emotions are defined as those which we share with our primate ancestors. (Some people believe many animals, such as dogs, Ref.[12], also share a capacity for these basic emotions). The basic emotions include anger, contempt, disgust, fear, happiness, sadness, and surprise, and the emotional sub-categories which fall into these general descriptions. Note that these are not the sort of emotions that one would imagine contributing to pair-bond formation. Indeed it would be inconsistent with the argument of this article if they did, because primate species do not pair-bond, with only one or two rare exceptions The basic emotions probably evolved as cognitive shortcuts, as described previously.

What about the emotions involved in pair-bond formation, which I have argued evolved in a very different manner – specifically to facilitate altruism? The alert reader will note that all I have demonstrated is that the male-to-female bond is emotionally based – not necessarily that the emotions in question are benign. Given that their end-product is altruistic, it would be peculiar if the emotional drivers were exploitative, though not logically impossible. By labelling said emotions as "love", with all that word connotes, I have implied that the emotions which induce the bonding are not merely benign but laudable. Indeed, "love" – especially if extended to its Christian sense – is virtually synonymous with genuine altruism. In its more restricted, romantic, sense, the male-to-female bond consists of those feelings of tenderness towards females which overwhelm a male at puberty. Relevant emotional terms are "affection", "tenderness", "adoration", "devotion", "longing", "concern", "sympathy", "compassion", "desire", "passion", even "worship" – and, yes, "sexual lust". These things are what it feels like inside to be a male product of an evolutionary strategy based on pair-bonding.

To most people, even now, the claim that pair-bonding is driven by love would hardly need defending. But we live in benighted times. Feminists are not in the habit of using the word "love". And those for whom the very concept of love has become alien are surely in a state of spiritual destitution.

The feminist position is that the pair-bond – at least in the institutionalised form of marriage – was created by men entirely for their own benefit. It consists of men using their superior physical and financial power to control and oppress women. It is never explained why men should want to do this. The implication is that we men simply like doing so. In other words, feminist patriarchy theory is essentially the claim that all men are sociopaths.

Now one can refute this based (as a man) on one's own lived experience. Alternatively, one can refute it based (as a man or a woman) on one's knowledge of many men. Are they all such monsters? And one can refute it based on one's own observations of married couples. Wives are always downtrodden, are they? Some are, most aren't. Many are clearly the dominant partner. And as for long-term marriages – are they the ones where the husband is most controlling, or the ones where the husband is most compliant?

But even if we were to accept that all men are indeed sociopathic monsters whose main purpose in life is the oppression of the very people upon whom they depend for emotional succour, feminist patriarchy theory still makes no sense. It makes no sense because it fails to explain how such a view can be consistent with resource provision, which is the essence of the male-to-female bond whose nature is in question. Bullies are not noted for giving gifts to their victims – especially on an habitual, indeed, reliable, basis, sustained over decades. Of course, feminists would claim that resource provision is just financial control. Even if you are inclined to disbelieve in paternal provisioning as significant in the evolutionary origin of the pair-bond, there is no doubt that it became significant.

And whatever the truth of the ancient mating strategies behind pair-bonding, it remains the case that it is essentially altruistic behaviour by the man. The perfectly selfish male would have nothing to gain by pair-bonding if the emotional drivers are ignored – the gain is only genetic.

And if power and control were a man's only interest, how does this explain monogamy exactly? Surely it is the tournament model of mating strategy, adopted by other primates, which best exemplifies power and control. And in this model the most powerful alpha male does most of the mating and most males do none. This is what an oppressive patriarchal culture (in the feminist sense) looks like, I suggest – not monogamy. And if monogamy has weakened somewhat of late, under whose tutelage has that happened? The transition from the tournament model to the pair-bond is surely a move *away* from physical power and male control of female fertility.

48.10. Emotion and Gender

The role of emotion in the asymmetric pair-bond is the main burden of this post. But by way of a coda before closing I make one final remark about emotionality in males in contrast to that in females.

It is striking that the male-to-female bond depends specifically on a *male* emotional response. I say 'striking' because, in some quarters, male emotional capacity is regarded as considerably muted compared to that of females. The key socio-sexual attribute of *Homo sapiens* would appear to have been made reliant on the weaker of the two vessels. Men, we are constantly told by the popular media, have poorer emotional intelligence than women. Indeed, so atrophied is men's emotional functionality, we are told, that some have referred to it as *Normative Male Alexithymia*. Now alexithymia is actually a clinical condition in which the sufferer has a severe deficit in emotional processing such as is found in cases of traumatic brain injury, severe autism, or post-traumatic stress disorder. The *Normative Male Alexithymia* hypothesis is exemplified by Ronald Levant who wrote in Ref.[13],

"One of the most far-reaching consequences of male gender-role socialization is the high incidence among men of… the inability to identify and describe one's feelings….men are genuinely unaware of their emotions. Lacking this emotional awareness, when asked to identify their feelings, they tend to rely on their cognition to try to logically deduce how they should feel. They cannot do what is automatic for most women – simply sense inwardly, feel the feeling, and let the verbal description come to mind."

(See also Ref.[14]). I don't suppose Dr Levant regards himself as an emotional cripple. He has, after all, presented himself as an expert on the subject. It's those other men. (Men who take the feminist line on castigating men invariably are presenting themselves as the One Good Man who is the exception).

Ronald Levant is a former president of the American Psychological Association (APA), the august institution which produced the guidance for psychological practice with boys and men which, at least in its initial form, was little more than misandric feminist theory (see *The Empathy Gap* section 17.5 for a discussion).

The *Normative Male Alexithymia* hypothesis is essentially the claim that men are emotionally broken, an hypothesis which sits neatly alongside the concept of toxic masculinity, a belief in the sociopathic patriarchy monster, and the persistent trend to regard women as the ideal to which men should aspire. For the opposing viewpoint see, for example, Ref.[15].

I might be reticent about demurring from such expert opinion as Dr Levant's were it not for the fact that even an extremely cursory dip into the literature appears to suggest that the empirical evidence is not actually supportive of men's emotional stupidity. Astoundingly, it seems that some people are unable to distinguish between emotion and the display, or expression, of emotion. This is most odd. I was raised to believe that people who wear their heart on their shirt sleeve are probably shallow. I was raised to believe that still waters run deep. Could it be that our society has now become so reduced that it can no longer stretch even as far as such folk wisdom?

Looking back at the definition of emotion we note the following defining characteristics,

- emotions are related to feelings;
- emotions are related to physiological responses;
- emotions motivate behaviours which are often of social significance.

I draw your attention to the absence from this definition of any essential requirement for emotion to be displayed or expressed, whether verbally or in any other way made manifest to observers.

Take, for example, this Finnish study, Ref.[16], which found that men assessed against the Toronto Alexithymia Scale scored higher than women on "difficulty in describing feelings", but there was no gender difference in scores on "difficulty in identifying feelings".

Men's emotional stance may be described as stoical. In Ref.[17] Jason Thompson wrote,

"Stoic individuals are not impaired in their ability to interpret emotion, rather, they have chosen resistance to entertain, act out, and discuss emotional matters. In fact stoic resisting of emotional impulses **requires** *an ability to identify one's emotions in order to go about reducing their effects."*

Stoicism is not to be confused with repression of emotions (which consists of brushing unwanted emotions under the carpet of the subconscious, possibly with detrimental effects). The elision of stoicism with repression is probably the source of much of the criticism of men's emotional habits.

The original Stoic philosophy did indeed teach that self-control and fortitude were virtues, and specifically because they are a means of overcoming destructive emotions. Stoicism also emphasised the importance of reason and clear judgment, but it did not seek otherwise to denigrate positive emotions. It has been said that the true religion of Victorian England was not Christianity but Stoicism. And it seems to be laudable rather than the opposite if this is indeed a fair description of men's nature.

Thompson goes on to critique Levant's thesis regarding *Normative Male Alexithymia*, concluding that,

"Whilst Levant may be right in his claim that men are generally less skilled than women in their ability to describe feelings, he is demonstrably incorrect in claiming that men are less able to identify specific feeling states in self or others in the true clinical sense of alexithymia. Here it would seem that Levant has failed to discriminate between the separate factors of (1) identifying and (2) describing feelings. The majority of alexithymia studies reveal that males are equally able to identify feelings in self and others, but occasional studies show that males are less able, or willing, to provide lengthy descriptions of the feelings they have successfully identified. What this means is that, like women, men can equally identify feelings such as jealousy, hatred, anxiety, fear, sadness, love, joy, envy and the like but they may not indulge a longer verbal description, preferring instead to thoughtfully act to modulate the intensity of emotions. This "action empathy" is in no way inferior to verbal empathy, and either of these responses typically employed by males or females can successfully modulate emotional arousal to desired levels."

There are many hypotheses which one can offer as to why men tend not to display or express emotions so readily as women. Poorer verbal dexterity might be one. Or the fact that the expression of strong emotions in men might carry the risk, in some situations, of promoting violence. But gender role is the most likely explanation, though this may be either innate or socially conditioned. In particular, displaying emotions relating to their own distress does not sit well with the social requirement that men should accept male disposability without demur. But the key, I suspect, is men's translation of emotion into action – as opposed from display – as alluded to by Thompson, above.

If what we are told is true, gender roles – be they evolved or socially constructed – promote male hyper-agency and female hypo-agency. But recall that the purpose of emotions is to motivate action. In whom is the emotion which is felt by a hyper-agentic male intended to promote action? Why, in himself, for he is the hyper-agent. What need has he, then, to display or express an emotion of which he is well aware? He merely translates the motivation directly into action. But in whom is the emotion which is felt by a hypo-agentic female intended to promote action? Why, in someone else, of course, for she herself is not an agent. So, for the female hypo-agent, it is essential to display, express and communicate said emotion unto whatever agent might be in the vicinity. From this perspective, the purpose of female emotion is to promote action in another. Female emotion acts indirectly;

male emotion acts directly. And only the former is necessarily visible to an observer through display or expression.

The hyper-agent simply has no need to display emotion – only to act upon it. So it is inappropriate to criticise the hyper-agent (men) for their lack of emotional display. And, in any case, a man displaying emotions of distress is far less likely to be rewarded with assistance than a woman in the same circumstances. What encouragement is there then, either evolutionary or socially constructed, for a man to be emotionally open? To paraphrase Warren Farrell, by displaying his need for help, a man forfeits his right to it.

The evolution of the human pair-bond, so crucial to human social structures, is wholly dependent upon specifically men's emotionality.

References

[1] Matsumoto, D. (2009). *The Origin of Universal Human Emotions*. San Francisco State University, 2009.

[2] Frijda, N.H. (2009). *The Laws of Emotion*. Routledge, 25 September 2006.

[3] Ridley. M. (1996). *The Origins of Virtue*. Penguin edition, 30 April 1998. (First edition 31 October 1996).

[4] Poundstone, W. (1993). *Prisoner's Dilemma: John Von Neumann, Game Theory, and the Puzzle of the Bomb*. Anchor Books, 1 Jan. 1993.

[5] Moxon, S. *Sex Differences Explained. From DNA to Society: Purging Gene Copy Errors*. New Male Studies Publishing – Monograph, November 2016.

[6] Collins, W. (2016). *Extracts from the literature on the origin of human pair-bonding and the significance of paternal provisioning*. December 2016.

[7] Guy, A. (2013). *Did Monogamy Make Us Human?* Next Nature, 13 August 2013.

[8] Sear, R., and Mace, R. (2008). *Who keeps children alive? A review of the effects of kin on child survival*. Evolution and Human Behavior 29(1) 1-18, January 2008.

[9] Finkel, E.J., and Eastwick, P.W. (2015). *Attachment and pairbonding*. Current Opinion in Behavioral Sciences 3, 7–11 June 2015

[10] Miller, L., and Fishkin, S. (1997). *On the Dynamics of Human Bonding and Reproductive Success: Seeking Windows on the Adapted-for Human-Environmental*

Interface. In Evolutionary Social Psychology by J.A.Simpson & D.T.Kenrick (Eds.), pp.197–235 (1997), Mahwah, NJ: Erlbaum. (See item 9 of Ref.[6]).

[11] Fletcher, G.J.O., et al (2015). *Pair-Bonding, Romantic Love, and Evolution: The Curious Case of Homo sapiens*. Perspectives on Psychological Science 10(1):20-36 January 2015.

[12] Anonymous (2011). *Dogology: Pet Problems, Jealousy Between Dogs and Pets Health Care*. 22 February 2011.

[13] Levant, R.F., and Pollack, W.S., editors (1995). *New Psychology of Men*. Basic Books, 1 June 1995. (See pages 238-9).

[14] Levant, R.F. (1996). *The new psychology of men*. Professional Psychology: Research and Practice 27(3) 259-265, June 1996.

[15] Wright, P., and Elam, P. (2017). *Red Pill Psychology: Psychology for Men in a Gynocentric World*. Academic Century Press, 26 September 2017.

[16] Salminen, J.K., et al (1999). *Prevalence of alexithymia and its association with sociodemographic variables in the general population of Finland*. Journal of Psychosomatic Research, 46(1) 75-82, January 1999.

[17] Thompson, J. (2009). *Emotionally Dumb: An Overview of Alexithymia*. Soul Books, 16 July 2009.

49. Male and Female Brains

Feminists are determined to spread the view that there are no innate differences of significance between the sexes. Consequently, the feminist axis constantly asserts that there are no structural differences between male and female brains. Actually there are, in the sense of statistically significant differences in the distributions of characteristics. But it is often the case that research which reveals such differences is nevertheless presented by those with feminist sympathies as if the opposite were the case. One such instance is examined here. I have not attempted to update the article from its January 2016 original, so there will be many more recent studies now.

Original posted on: 4 January 2016.

On 5th December 2015 the New Scientist ran an article titled *Brains are not male or female*, and subtitled *First analysis of the whole brain suggests gender distinctions are often meaningless*. I thought this rather curious because it seemed to conflict with what I had read previously about sex differences in brain structure.

The study which was being reported by New Scientist was Ref.[1]. The lead author was Daphna Joel, professor of psychology at Tel Aviv University. Here I make a few observations regarding the gender political leaning of Ref.[1] and the New Scientist article. I then examine the findings of Ref.[1] as well as the findings of an earlier study of sex differences in brain structure. My contention will be that the findings support substantial sex differences in brain structure, and this applies as much to Ref.[1] itself as to the earlier study, notwithstanding the spin put on the matter by New Scientist and Ref.[1].

The Gender-Political Spin

New Scientist told us that the findings of Ref.[1] suggest that *"we all lie on a continuum of what are traditionally viewed as male and female characteristics"* and that *"the study is very helpful in providing biological support for something we've known for a long time – that gender isn't binary"* (quoting psychologist Meg Barker of the Open University).

But the mindset behind the article is betrayed by this quote from Gina Rippon, professor of cognitive neuroscience at Aston University,

"This blow to the myth of distinct male and female brains is welcome. A key barrier to equality is crumbling, thanks to a new imaging study which blows away the idea that male and female brains are distinct."

Oh dear. It is so wrongheaded to suggest that equality of opportunity or equality of respect require indistinguishability. Difference is no barrier to equality if equality is understood in these terms. To quote Steven Pinker, from *The Blank Slate*, Ref.[2],

"There is, in fact, no incompatibility between the principles of feminism* and the possibility that men and women are not psychologically identical. To repeat: equality is not the empirical claim that all groups of humans are inter-changeable; it is the moral principle that individuals should not be judged or constrained by the average properties of their group. In the case of gender, the barely defeated Equal Rights Amendment put it succinctly: "Equality of Rights under the law shall not be denied or abridged by the United States or any state on account of sex". If we recognise this principle, no one has to spin myths about the indistinguishability of the sexes to justify equality. Nor should anyone invoke sex differences to justify discriminatory policies or to hector women into doing what they don't want to do."

*By "feminism" Pinker means "equality feminism", not the dogmatic assertion of gender feminists that gender is socially constructed – which is what he is arguing against.

But the above quote from Gina Rippon reflects the feminist doctrine that gender is a social construct. From this perspective, any disparity in outcome can only be due to societal disadvantage – because men and women are actually the same and any differences in aptitude or preference are culturally imposed. The purpose of the feminist dogma of socially constructed gender is to permit all disparities of outcome to be interpreted as due to societal disadvantage – thus legitimising affirmative or corrective action. As well as being incorrect, the fundamental dishonesty of this position is betrayed by such corrective actions only ever applying to situations where the underrepresentation is of a favoured in-group – not heterosexual white males.

Studies showing sex differences in brain structure do not create a "barrier to equality", understood as Pinker sensibly describes it, but they do create a problem for the credibility of feminist dogma. The lead author of Ref.[1], Daphna Joel, did not require the analysis of Ref.[1] to decide that brains are not male or female. She had already decided this and gone into print some four years earlier, Ref.[3]. (See also Ref.[4] and her 2012 TEDx talk, Ref.[5]).

The New Scientist article quotes Joel thus,

"We separate boys and girls, men and women, all the time."

No, we don't – but they often separate themselves. Modern life tends to mix the sexes together. Most people attend mixed-sex schools, mixed-sex colleges or universities, and work in a mixed-sex work environment (albeit not necessarily 50/50). But when this mixing of sexes is not enforced, the sexes often spontaneously segregate themselves. Here's an example. My study window overlooks the walkway back to town from the local secondary school. What I see at school closing time are groups of boys and, separately, groups of girls, walking back home. These sex-segregated groups occur naturally despite the boys and girls having spent all day in mixed-sex classes, and having done so from the age of 5. Very occasionally there will be a mixed-sex group – usually just a pair – but on the whole the sexes spontaneously segregate despite their co-ed upbringing.

Ref.[1] is tainted with the same gender political spin evident in the New Scientist article. It reports the significance of the study being as follows,

"Sex/gender differences in the brain are of high social interest because their presence is typically assumed to prove that humans belong to two distinct categories not only in terms of their genitalia, and thus justify differential treatment of males and females."

Really? Who is using sex as a justification for differential treatment of males and females? Not those of us who believe the sexes are indeed different. The 2010 Equality Act notwithstanding, or perhaps because of it, the DIE programme is precisely a spurious justification for treating people differently according to sex or race – and DIE is the creation of intersectional feminism. Hypocrisy, anyone?

The truth is exactly the opposite of the assertion in the above quote. The brain structure study of Ref.[1] is being spun to imply no sex differences, because – if there are indeed no sex differences – then inequalities of outcome, e.g., in employment sectors, can be interpreted as discriminatory and hence justify 'affirmative', or corrective, action. In truth it is the claim of sex indistinguishability which facilitates differential treatment of males and females – such as all-women shortlists, targets for women on corporate boards, and huge public expenditure on encouraging women into STEM...and now the DIE policies. Logically, such concerns should be reciprocated where men are in the minority, but they are not. Because the purpose of this whole narrative is to lend spurious justification to prejudice.

A 2014 Meta-Analysis (Ref.[6])

Before we look at what Ref.[1] actually reports, let's take a look at a study from the previous year, Ref.[6]. This work, by authors from Cambridge, Oxford and elsewhere, was the first meta-analysis of sex differences in human brain structure. A total of 126 articles were included in the meta-analysis, using established methodologies to find all relevant studies published between 1990 and 2013 in an unbiased way. The data covered brains from individuals as young as birth to 80 years old. A quantitative review of these brain imaging studies which addressed sex differences was carried out using sophisticated statistical techniques to establish significance. The study was restricted to grey matter and the parameters employed were local grey matter volume and local grey matter density. The objective was to identify any significant sex differences in the maps of grey matter volume or density across brain regions. The results are shown in Figures 49.1 and 49.2.

Extensive sex differences are readily apparent. The report concludes,

On average males have larger total brain volumes and specifically larger ICV (12%), TBV (11%), Cb (10%), GM (9%), WM (13%), CSF (11.5%) and Cbl (9%) absolute volumes than females. (See Ref.[6] for these acronyms)

As regards these differences being congenital, rather than a product of upbringing, the report notes that data were skewed to older ages but nevertheless concludes,

We found that across a wide age range, from new-borns to individuals over 80 years old, differences in overall brain volumes are sustained between males and females.

The report stops short of making claims regarding the behavioural or clinical implications of the observed sex differences in brain structure, but notes that,

Regional sex differences in volume and tissue density include the amygdala, hippocampus and insula, areas known to be implicated in sex-biased neuropsychiatric conditions. Together, these results suggest candidate regions for investigating the asymmetric effect that sex has on the developing brain, and for understanding sex-biased neurological and psychiatric conditions.

With this background established, let's turn to Ref.[1].

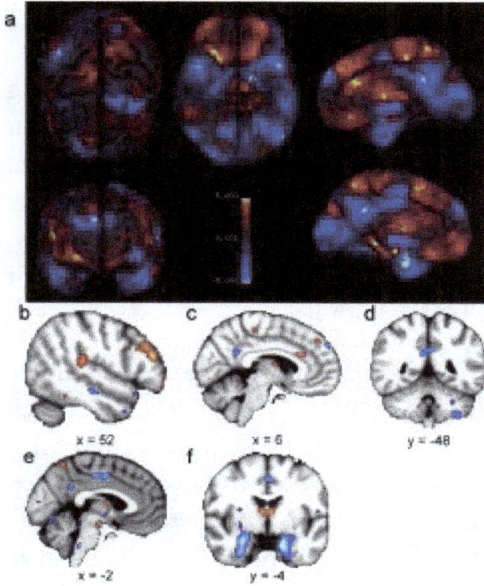

Figure 49.1: Sex differences in grey matter volume. Female > Male in red, and Male > Female is in blue (from Ref.[6])

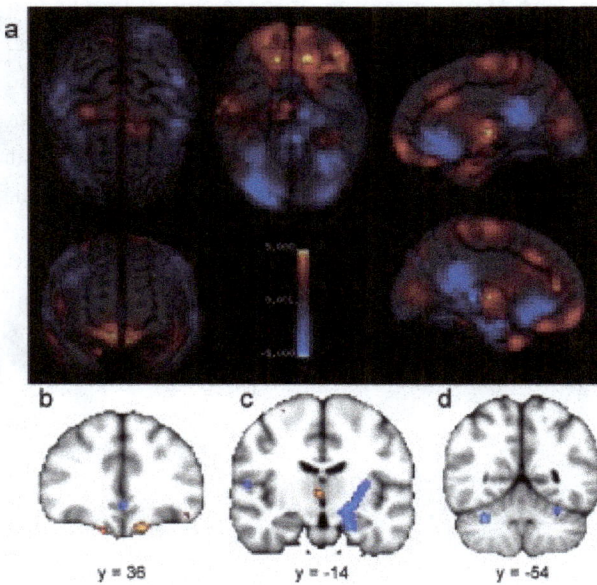

Figure 49.2: Sex differences in grey matter density. Female > Male in red, and Male > Female is in blue (from Ref.[6])

The Findings of Ref.[1]

Like Ref.[6], the work of Joel et al, Ref.[1], draws on a number of existing reports of MRI scans. Ref.[1] uses a far smaller number of independent studies, only 6 compared with 126 in Ref.[6]. However, Ref.[1] includes data on white matter as well as grey matter, and also includes brain connectivity ('connectome') data as well as volume and density data. Most importantly, Ref.[1] concentrates on the male/female characteristics over a number of features *for single individuals*, which Ref.[6] did not do.

Having identified a number of features which showed clear male-female differences, Ref.[6] then defines a 'degree of maleness or femaleness' for each of these features. The core of the study is to present a 'signature' (my word) for each individual, defined as the set of maleness/femaleness scores for each of these features. These 'signatures' are then compiled together for the whole dataset of individuals. Note that this exercise is possible only because features were found which show clear correlations with sex. The results are shown in Figures 49.3 and 49.4. (Apologies to readers who are colour-blind, but these Figures are copied from the original publication).

Consider firstly Figure 49.3. Each horizontal line of these colour blocks is a single individual. The more pink a pixel is, the more female that brain feature; the more blue it is, the more male. So a single multi-coloured horizontal line is the 'signature' for that individual. The two blocks represent all the results for females (left) and males (right) stacked together. So, you can see that many females have some blue (male) bits, and many males have some pink (female) bits. But the overall picture is that – wait for it – females are predominantly female and males are predominantly male: the left block comes across as fairly pink and the right block as fairly blue. Who would have thought it?

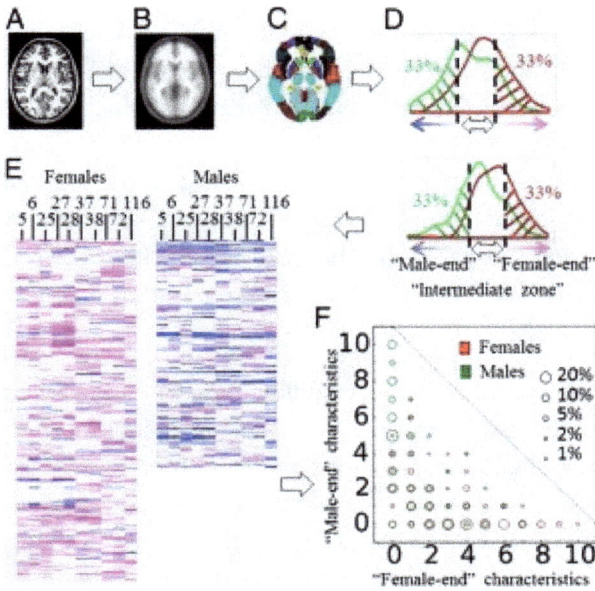

Figure 49.3: From Joel et al, Ref.[1], Fig.1.

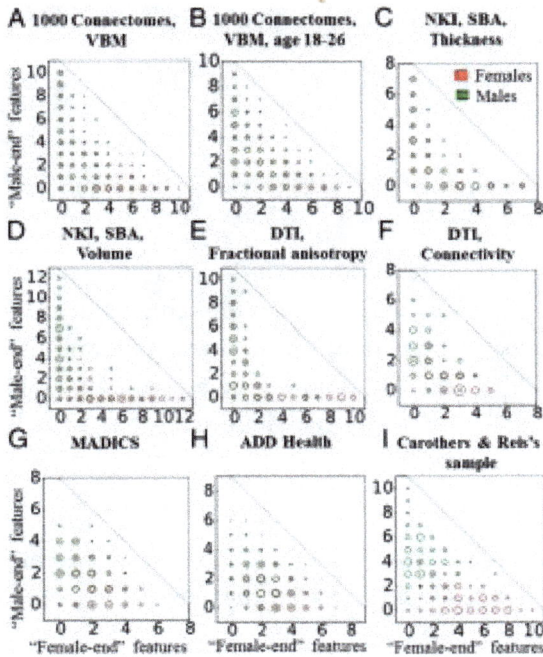

Figure 49.4: From Joel et al, Ref.[1], Fig.2

The same result is illustrated in a different manner by Figure 49.4. These plot "femaleness" on the x-axis, and "maleness" on the y-axis, the overall outcome being the sum of the number of individual features which show femaleness or maleness. The pink dots or circles denote female subjects, and the green denote male subjects. The size of the circle indicates the number of individuals at that x,y position. All these plots indicate the same broad result: very few, if any, females are at the extreme male end of the spectrum (top left corner), and very few, if any, males are at the extreme female end of the spectrum (bottom right corner).

Most males have middling maleness but below-middling femaleness, and vice versa. Most people have a mixture of characteristics. Being male is associated with a predominance of male characteristics, not with the complete absence of female characteristics – and vice-versa. The plots show this at a glance, with the bottom-right looking predominantly pink and the top left looking predominantly green.

This is completely unsurprising. The results of Ref.[1] indicate clear sex differences in brain structure, consistent with the results of Ref.[6], albeit a statistical rather than deterministic relationship in both cases.

What *is* surprising is the spin put on these results in Ref.[1]. One conclusion drawn in Ref.[1] is,

"Although there are sex/gender differences in the brain, human brains do not belong to one of two distinct categories: male brain/female brain."

This conclusion is valid only in the sense that some males' brains have equally many male and female features, and some females share the same number of male and female features as males. But this does not necessarily permit the conclusion that the brains are "the same", a point to be amplified below. Moreover this conclusion elides the obvious, that there is a clear overall difference in the distributions of brain features by sex.

Given a brain, a neuroscientist might not be able to tell if it were male or female. But if you gave the neuroscientist a large number of randomly sampled brains, he would get the sex right most of the time. Even New Scientist admits as much.

But the spin adopted in Ref.[1] is that, in order for brain structure to conform to the dimorphic view of gender, the result would have to be that all males were extreme males, and all females extreme females. In other words, the fact that individuals have a spectrum of characteristics is claimed to undermine the fundamental binary. The implicit claim is that the conventional (i.e., non-feminist) perspective would require all males to have a high maleness score in every feature, and all females to have a high femaleness score in every feature. On the plots of Figure 49.4, males would need to occur only at a maleness score of 10 and a femaleness of zero, and vice-versa.

But this is preposterous. It is surely a straw man argument. I doubt that anyone of scientific credibility, even those embracing the idea of binary gender, would have expected such a thing. In terms of *function*, that is in terms of skills and behaviours, the sexes do not differ so greatly that there is no overlap in their distribution of attributes. Males may be somewhat better at maths on average, and females somewhat better at verbal skills on average, but a female mathematician vastly exceeds in mathematical ability that of the average man, and an accomplished male author far exceeds the articulacy of the average woman. This is obvious. If it is obvious in terms of function, why should one not expect the same in brain structure?

To quote Steven Pinker again,

"Many psychological traits relevant to the public sphere, such as general intelligence, are the same on average for men and women, and virtually all psychological traits may be found in varying degrees among the members of each sex. No sex difference yet discovered applies to every last man compared with every last woman, so generalisations about a sex will always be untrue of many individuals. And notions like 'proper role' and 'natural place' are scientifically meaningless and give no grounds for restricting freedom."

So even those who espouse the importance of statistical, though not deterministic, distinctions between the sexes do not use it to "justify differential treatment of males and females".

In contrast to the above, sensible, perspective, the extreme male versus extreme female idea, a view which no one holds, might lead to all males being completely illiterate and all females completely innumerate, or some such silliness. Yet Joel et al manage to smuggle in this implication, concluding,

"The lack of internal consistency in human brain and gender characteristics undermines the dimorphic view of human brain and behaviour and calls for a shift in our conceptualization of the relations between sex and the brain."

Here "lack of internal consistency" simply means people with a mix of male and female brain features. The straw man is the pretence that there is any credible alternative view to knock down. And the fact that all people have a mix of characteristics, a fact understood well before neuroscience by the likes of Jung and Freud, does not require any "shift in our conceptualizations" whatsoever. Joel et al continue,

"Specifically, we should shift from thinking of brains as falling into two classes, one typical of males and the other typical of females, to appreciating the variability of the human brain mosaic."

which, on the face of it, is fair enough. But there is a logical fallacy here which needs to be exposed.

We have no idea how brain structure translates into function (skills, attributes, personality, psychology, etc.). Joel et al have fallen into the trap of assuming that if a set of features (label them $x, y, z, \ldots$) are all correlated with maleness, then the more of these features are 'male' the more male the overall result will be. In maths speak, they have unwittingly snuck in an assumption of linearity. But different parts of the brain interact, do they not? And in a crucial manner, essential to their basic function. If we can speak of an overall maleness at all, it is virtually inevitable that it will be a highly non-linear function of the individual features, x, y, z.

Suppose we normalise these parameters so that 0 represents 'male' and 1 represents 'female'. Let's start by looking at just two parameters, x and y. It is a simple matter to dream up a non-linear function, f, of x and y, which we interpret as the overall 'maleness' which results from the two features in combination and which is such that f has the following properties,

Holding y fixed results in f being positively correlated with x, as required

Holding x fixed results in f being positively correlated with y, as required

Setting $x = y = 0$ results in $f = 0$ ('full maleness')

Setting $x = y = 1$ results in $f = 1$ ('full femaleness')

And yet, setting $x = y = 0.5$ does not result in $f = 0.5$, nor anything close to a person equally balanced between male and female as you might expect, but $f = 0$ and so a fully male person!

Such a function is simply $xy|1 - x - y|^{\frac{1}{2}}$.

No, I don't pretend that's a credible value for f. It merely illustrates the danger of assuming that the outcome of two features being present together must be a linear combination of the outcomes for the features separately. Computers are built of non-linear gates, and the firing of a single neuron is essentially non-linear. The triviality of the above function compared with the massive complexity of brain interactions only serves to emphasise the naivety of the implicit linearity assumed in the reasoning of Ref.[1].

But it gets worse. Consider now four features, x, y, p and q normalised as before, and consider the outcome function,

$$f = 0.1xy|1 - x - y|^{\frac{1}{2}} + 0.9pq|1 - p - q|^{\frac{1}{2}}$$

This function illustrates another flaw in the logic of Ref.[1]. It is a sensible function in that it fulfils the above requirements of positive correlation, and $f = 0$ when $x = y = p = q = 0$, and $f = 1$ when $x = y = p = q = 1$. In Ref.[1], to assess overall maleness, the number of features exhibiting maleness is counted. Thus, the outcome for $x = y = 0, p = q = 1$ is tacitly assumed to be the same as that for $x = y = 1, p = q = 0$ since both have the same total score. But the above function is different for these two inputs. In the former case we get $f = 0.9$ (strongly female) and in the latter case we get $f = 0.1$ (strongly male).

In short, the assumption that the outcome for a particular combination of features which individually correlate with maleness/femaleness can be judged by simple linear summation of the individual feature scores is, at best, unproved and, in all probability, wrong. Consequently, the conclusion of Ref.[1] that,

"Our results demonstrate that....human brains cannot be categorized into two distinct classes: male brain/female brain"

is challengeable even assuming all the reported results are correct (which I don't doubt). But things get worse still when Ref.[1] strays into the overtly gender political, as in the conclusion,

"At the social level, adopting a view that acknowledges human variability and diversity has important implications for social debates on longstanding issues such as the desirability of single-sex education and the meaning of sex/gender as a social category."

I have no problem at all with acknowledging – in fact, I'd say, valuing – human variability and diversity. But, whatever your opinion on single-sex education might be, you would have to be incredibly foolhardy to argue the point based on our current knowledge of brain structure. And I am far from convinced that Ref.[1] has any impact on our perception of "sex/gender as a social category". It's a pity because Ref.[1] is an interesting piece of science blighted by a presentation which gives it a gender political spin which is unnecessary.

And as for New Scientist hinting that this is the basis of a "genderless future" – no, it isn't – though it would be a jolly good thing if New Scientist adopted a politically genderless editorial policy, an ideal from which it now deviates regularly. (This article predates my final break with New Scientist reported in chapter 45).

References

[1] Joel, D., et al (2015). *Sex beyond the genitalia: The human brain mosaic,* PNAS 112(50) 15468-73, 15 December 2015.

[2] Pinker, S. (2003). *The Blank Slate: The Modern Denial of Human Nature.* Penguin, 5 June 2003.

[3] Joel D. (2011). *Male or female? Brains are intersex.* Frontiers in Integrative Neuroscience, 5, 57, 1-5, September 2011.

[4] Joel, D. (2014). *Sex, Gender, and Brain, A Problem of Conceptualization.* In Gendered Neurocultures: Feminist and Queer Perspectives on Current Brain Discourses, S. Schmitz and G. Höppner (eds), Zaglossus, Verlag 1 April 2014.

[5] TEDxJaffa (2012). *Daphna Joel - Are brains male or female?* 8 October 2012.

[6] Ruigrok, A.N.V., et al. (2014). *A meta-analysis of sex differences in human brain structure.* Neuroscience & Biobehavioral Reviews 39, 34-50, February 2014.

50. Unconscious Bias and the IAT

The Implicit Association Test (IAT) has been telling virtually everyone that they are unconsciously racist and sexist – however much they may protest otherwise. Is it science, or is it just another stick to beat us with?

Original posted on: 17 June 2017.

50.1. The Implicit Association Test (IAT)

Back in the days when I still listened occasionally to mainstream radio, specifically on 17 May 2017, BBC Radio 4's *All In The Mind* programme was on the subject of Unconscious Bias, Ref.[1]. So was the same station's *Analysis* programme on 11 June 2017, Ref.[2]. The latter focussed on the Implicit Association Test (IAT), which is the subject of this chapter. If Ref.[2] does not remain available online, a transcript of the major points can be found in Ref.[3].

If you want to 'prove' that all men are misogynists and all white people are racists, then the Implicit Association Test (IAC) is a gift from the Gods. Or perhaps I should say it's more like the Delphic oracle – damnably treacherous and never what it seems.

Ostensibly, the IAC can be used to test "implicit" or "unconscious" bias against any chosen out-group. It works like this, using the race IAT as an example. You are shown words and faces. The words may be positive ones ("wonderful", "friendship", "joyous", "celebrate") or negative ("pain", "despise", "dirty", "disaster"). In one part of the process you have to press a key whenever you see either a black face or a bad word, and press another key when you see either a white face or a good word. Then it switches round: one key for a black face and good words, another for white faces and bad words. Sounds easy? The snag is you've got to hit the appropriate key as fast as possible. The computer measures your speed.

Your implicit bias against (say) blacks is revealed by taking longer on average when positive words are accompanied by a black person's face, as compared with when positive words are associated with a white person's face (and being quicker to associate negative words with a black face).

What sort of time difference are we talking about? Typically about 0.2 of a second.

Note that whilst I shall refer to the use of the IAT as a measure of racial bias, this is not because I wish to address the race issue. It is merely because the IAT has been used so extensively in this context, especially in the USA. My interest is in the reliability of the test to measure what it purports to measure – bias against the out-group, whatever the out-group.

The furore surrounding the IAT is that it claims to show that racism, or sexism, or whatever, is far more widespread than people think. Take someone who insists he is entirely unbiased, as egalitarian or as "progressive" as you might wish, but such people are, nevertheless, exposed as closet racists, or misogynists, by the test. Matin Durrani, then editor of Physics World, had this disconcerting experience. The March 2016 edition of Physics World, the monthly journal of the UK Institute of Physics, was given over entirely to diversity in physics. (Initiatives by the Institute of Physics and the Institution of Mechanical Engineers to enhance the profile of women in physics and engineering are common, as I reviewed in Ref.[4]). The IAT confidently informed Matin that he had a "strong automatic preference for white people compared with black people". He was mortified, of course. (Matin's father is Pakistani, his mother is German, he was raised in Birmingham and he presided over the wokefication of Physics World).

Poor Matin fared no better on the gender test. This time the IAT asked him to link male and female words with arts and science related words. Shock horror! He was informed that he had a "a strong association of male with science and female with liberal arts compared with vice-versa". The misogynist swine! (I'm tempted to add that if he had been driven strictly by data on student numbers he should, of course, have preferentially associated women with both arts and sciences, Ref.[5]).

There are other psychology tests which purport to measure implicit bias, but the IAT has become by far the dominant tool used by psychologists. It was developed by Anthony Greenwald and Mahzari Banaji of Harvard. You can take the test yourself on the Project Implicit website, Ref.[6]. Apparently, by June 2017, some 18 million people had taken the test on-line. By now it will be far more.

The IAT has become difficult to avoid. Unconscious bias posters were appearing in universities in early 2016 and over the next five years or so became ubiquitous in all Anglophone universities and large corporations.

You may recall Hilary Clinton claiming implicit anti-Black bias by the police in her election campaigning in 2016. She claimed there was a need to retrain the police because of this, Ref.[7]. By 2017 the IAT was "having an enormous impact on public discourse", to quote Radio 4's *Analysis* programme.

Any tool which claims to weed out the racists and misogynists amongst us, and can also be deployed as part of a diversity training programme and sold to companies for solid cash, is going to catch on fast. It did. By 2017, diversity training was claimed to be an $8 billion per year industry in the USA, and by then the UK was following suit.

A spokesman for KPMG at Canary Wharf told the *Analysis* programme that all staff had taken implicit bias training. He said, "implicit bias can get in the way of us being a truly inclusive and diverse company. Encouraging diversity makes good business sense – it improves the company's bottom line". (You'll have seen the data. No? Me neither).

It was inevitable that I would take a close look at the IAT. After reiterating the claims being made for the IAT, I indulge in a little neuroscience to explain what's actually going on in the test. Then I focus my artillery on the veracity of the test and its purported interpretation.

50.2. Claims for the IAT

The key feature of the IAT is that it measures reactions under severe time pressure. This is why it is referred to as a test of "implicit", or automatic, bias. The subject does not have time for any measured thought. For this reason it is also referred to as a test of unconscious bias; the subject does not have time for consciousness to operate. The interpretational leap is then made that this automatic, or implicit, or unconscious bias – obtained essentially as a reflex action without time for thought – reveals your true nature. As one of the contributors to the *Analysis* programme put it, "what we see coming through is your genuine implicit attitudes", i.e., you don't have time to "cover it up".

To quote from the introduction to the 2013 book *Blindspot: Hidden Biases of Good People*, Ref.[8], by the originators of the IAT, Banaji and Greenwald,

"The automatic White preference expressed on the Race IAT is now established as signalling discriminatory behaviour. It predicts discriminatory behaviour even among

research participants who earnestly (and, we believe, honestly) espouse egalitarian beliefs. That last statement may sound like a self-contradiction, but it's an empirical truth. Among research participants who describe themselves as racially egalitarian, the Race IAT has been shown, reliably and repeatedly, to predict discriminatory behaviour that was observed in the research."

We will see below that both those claims – that the IAT is "reliable and repeatable" and that it "predicts discriminatory behaviour" – are unsubstantiated, contentious and probably false. In an Appendix to the book, Banaji and Greenwald, wrote,

"...given the relatively small proportion of people who are overtly prejudiced and how clearly it is established that automatic race preference [as measured by the IAT] predicts discrimination, it is reasonable to conclude not only that implicit bias is a cause of Black disadvantage but also that it plausibly plays a greater role than does explicit bias in explaining the discrimination that contributes to Black disadvantage."

Pause to consider how bold is this claim: that a reflex reaction occurring unconsciously in a small fraction of a second is responsible for the *majority* of actual racial disadvantage. That such reflex reaction is generally overruled by subsequent measured thought (as evidenced by the admitted fact that a *"relatively small proportion of people are overtly prejudiced"*) seems not to count. It's almost as if they were looking for a stick to beat us with.

In short, the IAT provides a massive boost for Critical Race Theory.

In 2017 Banaji and Greenwald had been lobbying for implicit bias to be taken into account in the criminal courts (see Ref.[9]). I can readily believe that Blacks are treated more harshly in the criminal courts, just as men are, but I'm not convinced that the IAT is the right vehicle to use to address it.

Are these claims for the IAT valid, or is science being co-opted to provide a veneer of respectability for the approved sociopolitical narrative?

50.3. Morality: Fast and Slow – A Little Neuroscience

We are in the realms of morality. Were it not for racism and sexism being regarded as morally reprehensible we would have far less interest in whether a given individual displayed these characteristics. Whilst people may appeal to the pragmatic benefits of avoiding racism and sexism, it would be untrue, I believe, to assert that practical disbenefits are the reason for one's pejorative opinion of racism and sexism. The claims that increasing diversity automatically leads to improved company performance, for example, would probably not arise if it were not for the received moral narrative. Indeed, in truth, the claim is an inducement to enact diversity which is actually motivated socio-politically.

Traditionally, discussions of morality have been taken to be philosophical, addressing questions such as whether there are moral absolutes, for example. But there is another approach to morality which is more tractable, and addresses different questions. In this approach one accepts that morality is an aspect of human behaviour, and hence that the relevant disciplines are psychology and neuroscience. There have been several excellent books published in the last few years which provide the lay person with a good grounding in how productive the psychological approach to studying morality can be, see for example Refs.[10-12].

Studying the phenomenology of moral decision-making leads rather quickly to the conclusion that moral opinions are not entirely rational. Greene, Ref.[12], makes extensive use of variants of a "trolley scenario" to dissect the structure of moral decisions. No doubt you are familiar with the initial version of the vignette, as follows.

You are on a footbridge over a railway line. Ahead you see five workmen on the line. Behind you, and bearing down upon the men, you see a runaway trolley. The workmen's vision of the trolley is obscured and it is clear to you that they are going to be killed. Beside you on the bridge is a man wearing a large backpack. If you push him off the bridge and into the path of the runaway trolley you will save the lives of five men at the cost of one. Do you push him off? You may assume that it is clear that you yourself would not be sufficient to stop the trolley, so a noble self-sacrifice would not work. You can also assume that pushing the man off the bridge would save the other five lives with virtual certainty.

Most people would not push the man off the bridge.

However, change the scenario to this: there is no other man on the bridge. Instead, there is a side-track off the main line, the points for which are operated by a lever next to you on the bridge. But there is one workman on the branch line (whose vision of the trolley is also obscured). If you throw the switch you can save five lives at the cost of killing the single man on the branch line.

Most people would indeed throw that switch.

And yet, rationally, those two situations are functionally identical. Both involve you taking action which you know will cause the death of one man, deliberately to save five. So why the difference in moral judgment? It is not as if the death of the unfortunate sacrifice is any different, e.g., a fast painless death versus a slow agonising death. The mechanism of the death is the same in both cases: being run over by the trolley.

A computer could surely not distinguish between the cases, and yet people do – very clearly.

This illustrates the motivation behind the "dual process" hypothesis of moral cognition.

What follows is woefully over-simplified, but inevitably so if I am to avoid straying too far from my subject matter. The phenomenology of scenarios like the trolley problem suggests that there are two processes at work in moral decision making: a rapid process which is emotionally based and a slower process which is more rational. Indeed, one of the key functions of emotions is to act as cognitive shortcuts (see chapter 48). It's no good working out slowly what that lion might be about to do by debating rationally on the use to which those teeth might be put. Instead, the reaction by any species which has succeeded in evolving is "fear-so-run", cutting out the fatally slow rational middleman.

In order to be fast, the emotional moral process has to be of particularly simple cognitive form. To explain certain variants of the trolley scenario, Greene hypothesises that the fast emotional process can address only a single linear causal sequence. Any event which happens on a logical branch in the causal sequence is ignored by the fast moral process (so Greene hypothesises). The necessary cognitive simplicity of the rapid emotional moral response is something I'll come back to in the context of the IAT.

I close this section by noting that the dual process hypothesis gains credibility when neurological correlates are also considered. Again this is really woefully over-simplified, but here goes...

The brain is not so modular in its operation that one can identify a single region which carries out rational deduction and another which causes emotional responses. However, there are indeed areas of the brain which respond more over emotional issues, and others which respond more to rational calculation. This can be established by testing subjects using fMRI (functional magnetic resonance imaging). The correspondence between brain region and cognitive process can be established by getting the subject to perform a calculation or view pictures which induce an emotional response whilst in a scanner. Emotional response is correlated with increased activity in the ventromedial prefrontal cortex (VMPFC), as well as the amygdala. In contrast, rational cognition is correlated with increased activity in the dorsolateral prefrontal cortex (DLPFC).

Subjects can then be scanned whilst being asked to make moral judgments of the 'trolley problem' type. So, does increased activity in these areas correspond as the dual process hypothesis would suggest, with emotionally driven decisions exciting the VMPFC and amygdala more, but cold rational decisions being related to DLPFC excitation? Yes, they do.

50.4. The Evolution and Interaction of the Two Morality Modes

Some elementary considerations of the evolution of human social dynamics helps rationalise the emergence of a dual process morality. The social structure of humans is unique. No other species forms such huge societies of cooperative, but unrelated, individuals. (Termites, and Hymenoptera such as bees, wasps and ants, are not an exception as all the individuals in their hives or colonies are siblings). A key ingredient in facilitating cooperative behaviour in human societies is morality, i.e., a shared view of what behaviour is correct or incorrect.

Humans cannot survive alone, so cooperation within your own tribe is essential. On the other hand, cooperation between different tribes may either be desirable or not. Depending upon game theoretic considerations, it might be beneficial to exploit or aggress against another tribe. Alternatively, cooperation with the other tribe may be mutually beneficial, just as cooperation between individuals within your own tribe is generally beneficial.

Within-tribe recognition, and the associated positive moral bias, can therefore be implemented in the fast, emotionally based neural process. Cooperation within the "in group" is the default setting. But cooperation with a member of an out-group is more problematic. This requires rational cognition because contingent factors must be taken into account to decide how to treat a "foreigner". There's not much benefit in being nice to some bloke who's about to stick his spear in you. On the other hand, there may well be mutual benefit in trading with said "foreigner" if, after due reflection, he appears friendly.

The fast, emotional moral process (VMPFC-amygdala) therefore flags a negative response as the default setting for a "foreigner", this being a means of referring the decision "up the management" to the slower rational moral process (DLPFC). If the emotional response is sufficiently strong, the more measured process may never activate ("spear raised – fear/attack/run"). But if the VMPFC-amygdala response is mild, being triggered solely by the recognition of an out-group member rather than by an overt threat, the higher management (consciousness) is engaged to make a rational decision.

In short, the emotionally based fast morality is for the purpose of ensuring automatic cooperation between "me" and "us", whereas the slow, rationally based morality implements an option to cooperate (or not) between "us" and "them".

All this is again ridiculously over-simplified, but I think it's a first order approximation to what happens. And it does rationalise the existence of a dual process moral mechanism. Is it valid, then, to castigate ourselves for negative fast-process VMPFC-amygdala responses to an out-group member occurring in ~0.2 seconds if they are subsequently over-ruled by rational-cognitive responses? No, it is not.

Greene in Ref.[12] gives an example of the interplay of the two processes observed experimentally,

"Kevin Ochsner and colleagues showed people pictures that elicit strong negative emotions (e.g., women crying outside a church) and asked them to reinterpret the pictures in a more positive way, for example, by imagining that the crying women are overjoyed wedding guests rather than despondent mourners. Simply observing these negative pictures produced increased activity in our old emotional friends, the amygdala and the VMPFC. By contrast, the act of reappraising the pictures was associated with increased activity in the DLPFC. What's more, the DLPFC's reinterpretation efforts reduced the level of activity in both the amygdala and the VMPFC.

It appears that many of us engage in this kind of reappraisal spontaneously when we encounter racial out-groups. Wil Cunningham and colleagues presented white people with pictures of black people's and white people's faces. Sometimes the pictures were presented subliminally – that is, for only 30 milliseconds, too quickly to be consciously perceived. Other times the faces were presented for about half a second, allowing participants to consciously perceive the faces. When the faces were presented subliminally, the black faces, as compared with the white faces, produced more activity in the amygdala of the white viewers. What's more, the effect was stronger in people who had more negative associations with black people as measured by an IAT.

All of the participants in this study reported being motivated to respond to these faces without prejudice, and their efforts are reflected in their brain scans. When the faces were on the screen long enough to be consciously perceived, activity in the DLPFC went up, and amygdala activity went down, just as in Ochsner's emotional regulation experiment. Consistent with these results, a subsequent study showed that, for white people who don't want to be racist, interacting with a black person imposes a kind of cognitive load.

Thus, we see dual-process brain design not just in moral judgment but in the choices we make about food, money, and the attitudes we'd like to change. For most of the things that we do, our brains have automatic settings that tell us how to proceed. But we can also use our manual mode to over-ride these automatic settings, provided that we are aware of the opportunity to do so and motivated to take it."

50.5. Criticisms of the IAT

In January 2017, Jesse Singal published two excellent reviews of the IAT. The first addresses the race issue, Ref.[13], but is also an accessible introduction to the literature for the lay person: *Psychology's Favorite Tool for Measuring Racism Isn't Up to the Job*. The second addresses gender bias, Ref.[14]. Both are recommended reading. The criticisms of the IAT from within the psychology community were extensive, and this had been the case for many years before 2017, Refs.[15-17] being further examples.

In Ref.[15], after outlining the raging academic dispute between the pro-IAT and anti-IAT camps, John Tierney pointedly concludes, *"If they can't figure out how to get along with their own colleagues, how seriously should we take their advice for everyone else?"*

50.5.1 What does the IAT Measure?

One can reasonably question what the association between words and pictures in the IAT means. An association between black faces and negative words is universally interpreted as meaning the person in question thinks badly of black people. Well, for a start, the word "thinks" here is inapplicable. The IAT detects reflex reactions over timescales too short for "thought", understood as a rational-cognitive process.

All we can say is that people associating black faces with negative words have a fast VMPFC-amygdala response which refers the issue upwards for further rational consideration. The IAT itself tells us nothing about the subsequent rational process. Is this enough to imply racism? I think not. Consider a society in which people are schooled assiduously to avoid anti-black racism. This is likely to lead to a learnt VMPFC-amygdala response in which the association of black faces and negative words would indeed flag the need for careful further consideration – exactly as is commonly observed. In other words, the apparently racist IAT response may sometimes be exactly the opposite.

This point can be explained in a different way. Recall that the essence of the VMPFC-amygdala response is its speed. Its speed is accomplished by being computationally (cognitively) very simple – perhaps so simple that its response is virtually a binary switch. If so, it is reasonable to suppose that all 'negative' associations would produce the same response. So, what if a group – say Blacks – were associated socially with disadvantage, oppression, victimization, and discrimination. The VMPFC-amygdala response might well conflate these negatives with the negative words deployed in the IAT ("lazy", "dirty", "disaster", etc). So, an IAT result which is being interpreted as indicating racial bias could equally be indicating a recognition of racial disadvantage, a diametrically opposite interpretation. Ref.[18] reports an experiment demonstrating this very effect.

50.5.2 Hating Yourself

As early as 2010, in an article titled, *I Don't Actually Hate Myself: Why Harvard Is Wrong About Bias*, Ref.[19], the openly gay journalist, John Cloud, was surprised to be told that, following his IAT, "Your data suggest a slight automatic preference for Straight People compared to Gay People". He observed, "My results might mean I'm self-hating, although I'm not exactly sure what I could do to be gayer. Wear a tiara to work?".

Cloud also quotes Maia Szalavitz as having noted that, "48% of African Americans who take the test also show a bias against themselves". Are we to conclude that self-ism is as prevalent as other-ism? But the paradox of "hating yourself" disappears if you accept, as argued in Section 50.5.1, that the IAT can be a measure of perceived disadvantage rather than perceived inferiority. Or, alternatively, if the IAT results are rather random. If so, there would be a reproducibility problem.

50.5.3 Reproducibility

One of the major criticisms of the IAT is its very poor reproducibility. A proposed measure of anything is obviously suspect if a second, third and fourth test produce substantially different results. With the IAT, they do tend to.

A measure of test reproducibility (or reliability) is the coefficient of multiple correlation, r. (For a single repeat test this is just the usual Pearson correlation coefficient). If $r = 1$ then the test result is precisely and consistently reproducible. If $r = 0$ then testing is merely producing random numbers. Ref.[20] gives the following guidance on the degree of confidence one can have in a test against r value,

- 0.9 and greater: excellent reliability
- Between 0.9 and 0.8: good reliability
- Between 0.8 and 0.7: acceptable reliability
- Between 0.7 and 0.6: questionable reliability
- Between 0.6 and 0.5: poor reliability
- Less than 0.5: unacceptable reliability

Jesse Singal, Ref.[13], tells us,

"The IAT's architects have reported that overall, when you lump together the IAT's many different varieties, from race to disability to gender, it has a test-retest reliability of about r = 0.55. *By the normal standards of psychology, this puts these IATs well below the threshold of being useful in most practical, real-world settings."*

But it gets worse. The value $r = 0.55$ derives from the IAT's proponents. Singal reviews estimates of r from other sources. Generally they are not better than $r = 0.4$ or thereabouts. So, even setting aside what an IAT result might mean (if anything), the IAT does not meet the criterion to be a sound measurement of anything. Quoting Singal again,

"What all these (r) numbers mean is that there doesn't appear to be any published evidence that the race IAT has test-retest reliability that is close to acceptable for real-world evaluation. If you take the test today, and then take it again tomorrow — or even in just a few hours — there's a solid chance you'll get a very different result. That's extremely problematic given that in the wild, whether on Project Implicit or in diversity-training sessions, test-takers are administered the test once, given their results, and then told what those results say about them and their propensity to commit biased acts."

50.6. Does the IAT Predict Behaviour?

So, finally to the main event: does an IAT tell us anything about a person's behaviour? If not, then who cares about the IAT? If the IAT tells you that you have a bias against blacks or against women, but these claims are not born out in actual behaviour, then the claims of Greenwald and Banaji for their test are invalid. Behaviour is, in truth, all that matters.

In psychology, a single piece of research, published as a single journal paper, tends to be unreliable. At least the 100 studies considered in the review of Ref.[21] proved to be so – with only between one third to one half of reported significant effects being reproducible. It is important, therefore, to amalgamate many individual studies in meta-analyses in order to extract any reliable features. After years of tussle between pro-IAT and anti-IAT academics, the outcome seems to have been decided: the original architects of the IAT, Greenwald and Banaji, effectively conceded in 2015. Jesse Singal, Ref.[13], wrote,

"The psychometric issues with race and ethnicity IATs, Greenwald, Banaji, and Nosek wrote, 'render them problematic to use to classify persons as likely to engage in discrimination.' In that same paper, they noted that 'attempts to diagnostically use such measures for individuals risk undesirably high rates of erroneous classifications.' In other words: you can't use the IAT to tell individuals how likely they are to commit acts of implicit bias. To Blanton, this is something of a smoking gun: 'This concession undermines the entire premise of their webpage,' he said. 'Their webpage delivers psychological diagnoses that even they now admit are too filled with error to be meaningful.'"

Yet this zombie test was still being touted around to corporations in 2017, with ever increasing zeal, and this continued for years thereafter (and perhaps still does, in 2024?). Certainly there remains no shortage of websites where the test is promoted and where the test can be taken online. This is easy to understand: it produces results in conformity with the approved narrative and helps consolidate the employment security of all those people employed in the DEI industry. That it is scientifically unsound is merely business as usual for this axis.

50.7. Sexism and the IAT

There are even more question marks over the IAT when applied to gender than when applied to race. There is also a difference in the nature of such tests. In the race IAT, the associations in question relate to words which are indisputably negative or indisputably positive. In the gender IAT – at least as usually applied – the associations are with 'career related' words versus 'family related' words. There is nothing intrinsically positive or negative about either in this case (unless, of course, you are ideologically inclined to regard domestic roles as inferior – bit of a giveaway, that).

But even leaving that aside, there are puzzling aspects of the IAT as applied to gender. As Greg Mitchell and Phil Tetlock put it in Ref.[9],

"One particularly puzzling aspect of academic and public dialogue about implicit prejudice research has been the dearth of attention paid to the finding that men usually do not exhibit implicit sexism while women do show pro-female implicit attitudes."

Mitchell and Tetlock opine that *"these findings are contrary to the common finding on IATs of the historically advantaged group being favoured by members of both the advantaged and the disadvantaged groups"*. But these authors' puzzlement is simply due to their assumption as to which gender is advantaged. Had they permitted themselves to entertain the notion that women are the more advantaged sex, their difficultly would vanish. That this thought did not occur to them we may attribute to cultural bias – ironically.

Referring to Mitchell and Tetlock's observation, Singal, Ref.[13], wrote,

"This appears to be a pretty robust finding, and if you translate it into the same language IAT proponents speak elsewhere, it means men don't have implicit sexism and are therefore unlikely to make decisions in an implicitly sexist manner (women, meanwhile, will likely favour women over men in implicitly-driven decision-making). Even weirder, when you

switch to IATs geared at evaluating not whether the test-taker implicitly favours men over women (or vice versa), but whether they are quicker to associate men versus women more with career, family, and similarly gendered concepts, the IAT somewhat reliably evaluates women as having higher rates of implicit bias against women than men do."

This quote refers to the IAT results shown in Figure 50.1. In view of the preceding criticisms of the IAT, one cannot be confident that Figure 50.1 is a reliable indication of implicit gender bias. Nevertheless, it is comical that the psychology professionals appear utterly baffled by a result that any member of the men's movement would have anticipated: the bias is against men, whereas women are preferred.

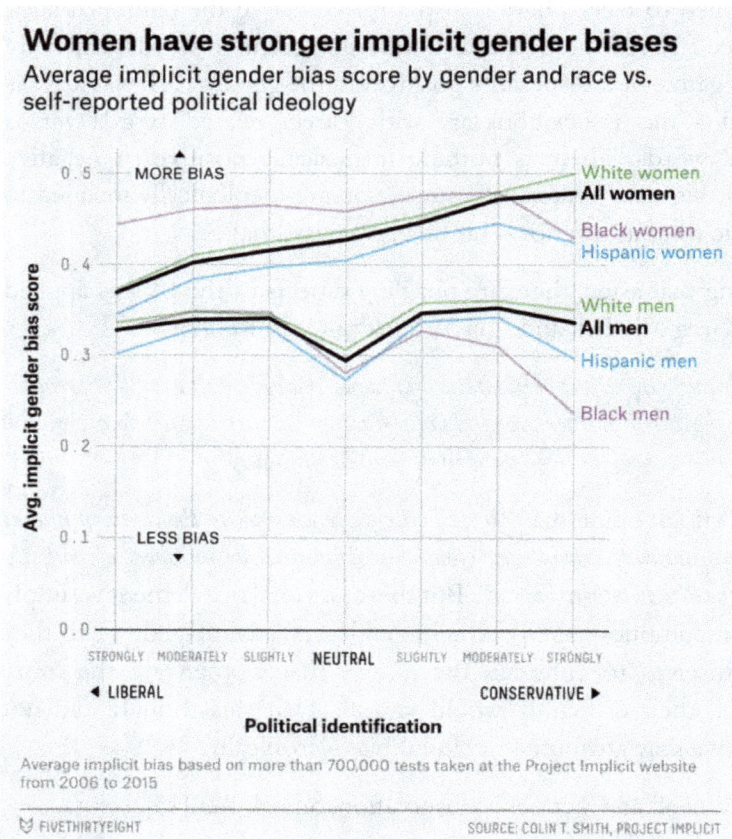

Women have stronger implicit gender biases
Average implicit gender bias score by gender and race vs. self-reported political ideology

Average implicit bias based on more than 700,000 tests taken at the Project Implicit website from 2006 to 2015

FIVETHIRTYEIGHT   SOURCE: COLIN T. SMITH, PROJECT IMPLICIT

Figure 50.1: Data from Colin T Smith, Implicit Project. It shows the IAT results for average implicit gender bias based on over 700,000 tests taken at the Project Implicit website, Ref.[6].

458

Figure 50.1 apparently shows that women are more gender biased than men. A further result is that women's implicit gender bias varies with political opinion, whereas men's does not. But I give a health warning: having discredited the IAT in the context of race, it risks inconsistency to believe its results are reliable in the context of gender. However, the two cases are treated differently, as explained in the text, so this may not be as inconsistent as it appears.

In June 2017 Ref.[22] reported the results of experiments which have a bearing on the interpretation of the IAT. This work does not study bias, but simply factual error. Subjects were required to press one button or another according to whether a briefly illuminated X appeared on the left or the right of the screen. Their speed and accuracy were the outcome measures. They were asked to focus on a + sign in the centre of the screen, but this + sign was replaced for a fraction of a second by an arrow pointing either to the left or the right. This arrow might correctly point towards the X, or incorrectly point the opposite direction. The arrow acts as a misdirection, potentially causing the subject to waste time checking for the X in the wrong place. The clever aspect of the experiment was that two different timings for the duration of the arrow were used: 33 milliseconds and 400 milliseconds. The former is subliminal – too short for the subject to be consciously aware there had been an arrow at all. The 400 millisecond arrow would, however, be consciously perceived. When the arrow was shown subliminally, subjects took longer to respond because they were unable to prevent themselves looking in the direction of the (not consciously perceived) arrow. Even when the arrow pointed incorrectly 88% of the time, subjects were still unable to ignore it when it was presented subliminally. In contrast, subjects responded faster when the arrow was consciously perceivable because they were able to learn to disregard it. Are we to interpret this as meaning that humans are "unconsciously stupid"? This would be the analogue of the widespread misinterpretation of the IAT in the race or gender cases. Clearly what it actually means is that the aspect of human cognition which leads to the ability to learn from experience requires conscious perception (a significant finding, and the purpose of the paper). This therefore requires stimuli to persist long enough for conscious perception to be triggered.

References

[1] BBC Radio 4 (2017a). *The Everyday Effect of Unconscious Bias*. All in the Mind, 17 May 2017, 15:30.

[2] BBC Radio 4 (2017b). *Implicit Bias*. Analysis, 11 June 2017, 21:30.

[3] BBC News (2017). *Implicit bias.: Is everyone racist?* 5 June 2017.

[4] Collins, W. (2015). *STEM v Teaching*. The Illustrated Empathy Gap, 5 January 2015.

[5] Collins, W. (2017). *Higher Education Entrance by Sex 2016*. The Illustrated Empathy Gap, 5 June 2017.

[6] Project Implicit (2011). *Online Implicit Association Test*.

[7] Clinton, H. (2016). *Clinton on implicit bias in policing*. The Washington Post, 27 September 2016.

[8] Banaji, M.R. and Greenwald, A.G. (2013). *Blindspot: Hidden Biases of Good People*. Delacorte Press, 12 February 2013.

[9] Lilienfeld, S.O., and Waldman, I.D., editors (2017). *Psychological Science Under Scrutiny: Recent Challenges and Proposed Solutions*. Wiley-Blackwell, 3 January 2017. A relevant extract can be read here.

[10] Haidt, J. (2013). *The Righteous Mind: Why Good People are Divided by Politics and Religion*. Penguin, 2 May 2013.

[11] Bloom, P. (2018). *Against Empathy: The Case for Rational Compassion*. Vintage, 1 February 2018.

[12] Greene, J. (2015). *Moral Tribes: Emotion, Reason and the Gap Between Us and Them*. Atlantic Books, 5 March 2015.

[13] Singal, J. (2017a). *Psychology's Favourite Tool for Measuring Racism Isn't Up to the Job*. New York Magazine, The Cut, 11 January 2017.

[14] Singal. J. (2017b). *Maybe Clinton Lost Because of Implicit Sexism, but the Implicit Association Test Can't Prove It*. New York Magazine, 24 January 2017.

[15] Tierney, J. (2008). *In Bias Test, Shades of Gray*. The New York Times, Science, 18 November 2008.

[16] Singal, J. (2018). *Psychology's favourite tool for measuring implicit bias is still mired in controversy*. The British Psychological Society, 5 December 2018.

[17] Nagai, A. (2017). *The Implicit Association Test: Flawed Science Tricks Americans into Believing They Are Unconscious Racists*. The Heritage Foundation, 12 December 2017.

[18] Uhlmann, E.L., et al. (2006). *Are members of low status groups perceived as bad, or badly off? Egalitarian negative associations and automatic prejudice*. Journal of Experimental Social Psychology 42(4) 491-499, July 2006.

[19] Cloud, J. (2010). *I Don't Actually Hate Myself: Why Harvard Is Wrong About Bias*. Time Magazine, Psychology, 12 October 2010.

[20] Study.com (undated). *Test-Retest Reliability | Definition, Importance & Examples*.

[21] Open Science Collaboration (2015). *Estimating the reproducibility of psychological science*. Science 349 (6251) 28 August 2015.

[22] Travers, E., et al (2017). *Learning Rapidly about the Relevance of Visual Cues Requires Conscious Awareness.* Quarterly Journal of Experimental Psychology, June 2017.

Section 10

Relationships

51. Marriage is Dead

Should a young man today get married? In being asked that question one is in a cleft stick as explained in chapter 37 of Ref.[1].

Original posted on: 4 July 2020.

While everyone was focussed on covid and the Domestic Abuse Bill, the Divorce, Dissolution and Separation Act 2020, Ref.[2], was slipped quietly through Royal Assent on 25th June 2020.

This is the Act that has been dubbed the No-Fault Divorce Act. Well, *de facto* we have had no-fault divorce for a long time, though this Act does indeed consolidate it. However, the even more substantive purpose of the Act is to make divorce unilateral. These are the key parts of the Act which make both no-fault and unilateral action clear…

"(1) Subject to section 3, either or both parties to a marriage may apply to the court for an order (a "divorce order") which dissolves the marriage on the ground that the marriage has broken down irretrievably."

"(3) The court dealing with an application under subsection (1) must – (a) take the statement to be conclusive evidence that the marriage has broken down irretrievably, and (b) make a divorce order."

Admirably clear. The word "either" in (1) means that just one of the couple can apply for the divorce, simply making a statement of irretrievable breakdown. Neither reasons nor evidence of anything are required. A unilateral statement of irretrievable breakdown really means nothing more than "I want to leave the marriage". Clause (3) states that the court MUST take that statement as conclusive evidence (i.e., no-fault, no reason, no evidence) and then MUST make a divorce order.

There is a cooling-off period within the Act which, in most circumstances, will mean that a divorce is final after 26 weeks from initial application. A confirmation that the applicant wishes to proceed is required 20 weeks after initial application. The unilateral nature of the new divorce provision is reiterated at this point: *"in the case of an application that is to proceed as an application by one party to the marriage only, that party has confirmed to the court that they wish the application to continue"*.

If that confirmation is forthcoming, a provisional divorce order is made and this will become final in a further 6 weeks. It cannot be contested.

The best spin one can put on this is that marriage is now pointless. What was once a solemn covenant which could not be "put asunder" is now as easy to cancel as a magazine subscription. It is the final triumph of the feminist policy on marriage.

The point of a contract is to tie the two parties into an agreement which neither party can withdraw from unilaterally. This is the case whether one considers legal contracts or contracts which are "policed" by social disapprobation. Marriage, as it is now legally instantiated, is no longer a contract.

The purpose of marriage was to tie fathers into an obligation to provide for their children. The "deal" of the traditional marriage arrangement was that, in return, men acquired social status and respect and achieved security in their position as fathers with a close involvement in the lives of the children they were supporting.

This is what has been destroyed.

In its place we have a temporary arrangement into which children may be born. Following its dissolution, other legal arrangements typically continue to oblige the father to provide financially for the children, and perhaps the mother, whilst often being denied meaningful involvement in the lives of those children. (It can happen with the sexes reversed, but that is overwhelmingly less frequent). This common occurrence is extremely distressing to all involved (markedly increasing suicide rates) and diminishes the likely outcomes for the children.

Motherhood is a secure status; it is unambiguously defined by biology. Fatherhood is a social status that requires social reinforcement and defence if it is not to cease to exist. Traditionally, fatherhood received the triple protections of, (i) strong social disapprobation of sex, and hence children, outside marriage, (ii) legal protection of marriage in its original form, with divorce being difficult and rare, (iii) unambiguous moral backing by religious authorities. These have all been smashed.

Beyond the sentiment of passing attraction to the opposite sex, what more substantive reason does a young man now have to get married?

There is none. For men, marriage is now the acceptance of duty and obligation in return for nothing.

This is unfortunate as it is bad for everyone: men, women and children. For men, under traditional conditions, the acceptance of the responsibilities of being a family man were a valid path to a more meaningful life.

One must also acknowledge the rise of women in educational attainment and hence in employment, which, combined with natural hypergamy, has severely reduced the pool of men they would consider suitable marriage partners. Whilst at the other end of the socioeconomic spectrum, where parents are reliant upon benefits, the system can make it financially advantageous for the mother to not take a partner, married or otherwise (see Ref.[3]).

The architects of these changes lack the wisdom to perceive that, in destroying traditional, inviolate marriage, they have also dissolved the glue that holds society itself together. Increasingly young people live alone, with every prospect of this being permanent.

The truly nasty part of this contrivance is that the reality of it is kept from young men and young women until they find out the hard way.

It is a moral obligation to continue the attempt to correct this broken system, to restore balance and fairness, through argument and reason. But those who place all their faith in such docile responses have failed to learn the lessons – not just of the last 50 years – but the ongoing lessons of legislation that has been passed over the last few years.

Should there be a mass outbreak of understanding among young women, they have the moral and social power to make change happen. Unfortunately, this seems a forlorn hope at present.

As for young men, the lack of in-group preference in men means there will never be coordinated "political" counteraction. The only card that men have to play is to withdraw on an individual basis, deciding for their own reasons that there will be no marriage, no cohabitation, no babies and perhaps not even any intimate relations at all. If coordinated, this would be a "marriage strike". That would be fully justified. People who go on strike want to work, but striking is the workers' only weapon against unacceptable conditions. However, it will not be coordinated and so would be essentially MGTOW, but by young men who may never have even heard the term.

In case there is any misunderstanding, let me clarify. I am in favour of (real) marriage. It is the cornerstone of a thriving society and is the path to a responsible life, for both sexes. I am married myself. My relationship with my wife started nearly half a century ago when the world was a different place, and mores were correspondingly different. You could not assume that your potential spouse would have a comparable outlook today, and the odds are highly adverse. What is on the table now is not marriage but a trap in the name of marriage. Real marriage is dead and the disintegration of our society is the result.

References

[1]   Collins, W. (2022). *The Destructivists*. Principia Publishing Unlimited, 20 February 2022.

[2]   UK government (2020). *Divorce, Dissolution and Separation Act 2020*.

[3]   Collins, W. (2020). *The Utter Ignorance of White Knight Politicians*. The Illustrated Empathy Gap, 21 June 2020.

52. Feminism Against Progress

This long chapter is a review of the 2023 book Feminism Against Progress by Mary Harrington, Ref.[1]. The review originally appeared as two blog posts. Harrington's book followed 2022's The Case Against The Sexual Revolution by Louise Perry, Ref.[2]. Both books make the "discovery" that feminism has been bad for women – specifically that a life of libertine sexual freedom is not a route to happiness for women. Instead, they advocate for sexual restraint via more-or-less-traditional marriage. Both authors have, in effect, demonstrated the likely truth of Geoff Dench's suggestion that the ancient matriarchs were probably the original architects of so-called patriarchy. They have done so by rediscovering the rewards of "patriarchy" for women themselves. Not willing to let go of the feminist label entirely, Harrington now refers to herself as a Reactionary Feminist. This is after having lived a life in which she "liberalled as hard as it is possible to liberal".

There is a vogue for books on the theme of "feminism is bad for women" at present. The End of Woman by Carrie Gress (2023, Ref.[3]) is another. That one majors on the disturbing history of feminism and its early leading lights (already familiar to people from the men's movement and well covered by Janice Fiamengo). Gress's "reactionary" take on "liberal" feminism is that it has abolished real women entirely by making the male life the norm for everyone. None of these books reference Gabrielle Kuby's 2012 German book The Global Sexual Revolution (English translation 2015, Ref.[4]) which addresses precisely these destructive effects of sexual licence and does so with far greater political depth, emphasising the roots of the phenomenon in the globalist powers.

What all of Refs.[1,2,3] have in common with each other, and with feminism, is that scant concern is evident for males or for the depth of the damage wrought on men and boys by feminism over the last 60 years. As a result, they all fail to realise that even women may no longer have the power to reverse what they have wrought. Many men may now be too wary of women to have any interest in cooperating with them in any form. In short, whilst these authors may have appreciated, finally, that feminism is bad for women, their gynocentrism remains undisturbed. They have yet to understand that the patriarchy has indeed been smashed, but what smashing the patriarchy actually means is awakening men from the enchantment of gynocentrism. Once that spell is lifted, women today lack the magic to replenish it.

Originals posted on: 25 March 2023 and 28 March 2023.

Contents

Because this chapter is so lengthy, I offer a contents list to its sections below,

- Power and the Critical Poison
- Serving the Interests of the Elites
- The Unacceptably Ignored
- The Law in History
- Work & Pay in History
- Patriarchy is Theatre
- Male Dissident Opinion
- Are Men Human?
- The Destruction of Marriage
- The TERF Tendency
- Trans and Feminism
- Conclusion

Introduction

This is a review of *Feminism Against Progress* by Mary Harrington, Ref.[1].

Read all about it! Feminist discovers the sexes are not the same!

Are we supposed to be grateful for this revelation?

But wait – there's more…

Feminist discovers that the patriarchy was not all bad for women!

WHAT??

And…and…

Progress (as in "Progressive") is not actually a good thing for women!

Crucify her! Off with the heretic's head!

OK, I apologise. I should not descend to such sarcasm. But really, it's hard to take.

It's as if a lunatic who has insisted for decades that he's Napoleon suddenly writes a book chastising us all for believing it.

Err…we didn't, Mary.

The thrust of *Feminism Against Progress* is that feminism took a wrong turn in promoting "progress". However, Harrington interprets "progress" as having an extremely restricted scope. Her "progress" is identified with "women's liberation" and that is equated with a particular type of "freedom". That "freedom" became defined as following men into the path of wage-slavery. I cannot fault the exposure of that semantic trick…except that it's hardly news to some of us, Mary. You just wouldn't listen.

Don't blame us, if, having stolen men's clothes, you discover they are just labourers' donkey jackets. And, no, Mary, this is not mere *schadenfreude*. My reaction has deeper foundations. Nor is it based merely on conservative dogma.

Shockingly, Harrington has discovered by personal experience that she has a deep emotional connection with her child, that caring for said child is a rewarding experience, and that being a stay-at-home mother is (wait for it) actually quite pleasant.

How many more of these bombshells can there be?

Sorry.

I'll be serious now. The book is important enough to have provoked my undivided attention.

The Overview

There is much to commend this book, but equally as much to condemn it. Harrington's analysis of how feminism has harmed women is correct, as are her ideas for reversing these harms. This is no small thing; let us recognise that.

My condemnation of the book is that the harms to men and boys go unrecognised. I must immediately expand upon that because people will point out that the book contains a whole chapter on the desirability of allowing men their own single-sex spaces. They will also draw attention to passages here and there exposing how boys and young men are falling behind in education, how childless women working full-time are now out-earning men, and even the relationship between divorce and the high rate of male suicide. But do not be fooled. Harrington's concern over issues impacting men arises solely from the position that it affects men's subsequent ability to function efficiently for the benefit of women. It is not based on a perspective that men might, simply by virtue of their humanity, be deserving of some concern (let alone equal concern). The humanity of men has no presence in this book.

Gynocentrism is the loam out of which all feminisms grow.

Mary Harrington's gynocentrism remains firmly in place.

The red flag is, of course, that Harrington still considers herself a feminist. She has had to invent yet another variant of feminism, Reactionary Feminism, to do so. In truth, Harrington is simply a gynocentrist, as are all feminists, of every stripe.

Anyone who remains happy to call themselves a feminist, irrespective of any adjectival rider, has failed to accept responsibility for the destruction they have wrought upon our world. It is not possible to internalise that responsibility and still to find the title "feminist" tolerable.

In the first instance it was the destruction of men, but you cannot poison half a well. The destruction of men has now matured into the inevitable destruction of our society as a whole, other than a few elites. Harrington rightly emphasises this, though from a relentlessly female perspective. Nevertheless, this is a crucially important theme as it correctly identifies feminism as a central driver of the authoritarianism which is now emerging globally. Harrington deserves credit for this also.

She acknowledges that there is a great deal of explicit reference in feminist literature to the obliteration of the heterosexual two-parent family as a specific policy objective. That there was an historical counterpoint between that "liberation" wing of feminism and a "caring" feminism is something I will have to take on trust, though I was not aware of any "caring" feminism. What Harrington identifies, rightly, is that the "freedom" feminism which triumphed has led, inexorably, to the elite feminism which she dubs the Meat Lego Gnostic tendency. The mechanism by which this has happened is social atomisation.

Harrington admits that "we'll need to reckon with some of feminism's unpaid debts, and to take more of a realistic stance on where the limits to individual freedom really are". Agreed, but, as yet, she has fallen woefully short of acknowledging all those debts, or the grave extent of their destructiveness.

The ejection of men from the family severs the main bond that holds men into society more widely. But what we, along with Harrington, have discovered is that the hyper-liberal "freedom" tendency leads ultimately also to the dissolving of the mother-child bond: the apogee of social atomisation. Feminists complacently imagined they could weaponise the establishment to make fathers optional and remain safe themselves. They supped with the Devil using a short spoon. *Schadenfreude* would indeed be tempting, but inappropriate given that we are all in the same boat.

The resulting social atomisation inevitably leads to authoritarianism. In short, feminism has functioned as the gateway to globalist technocratic totalism, exactly as I argue in *The Destructivists*, Ref.[5]. We are all alone, now – and at exactly the time we need to be united against the common technocratic-globalist threat. In this I concur with Harrington. And this is extremely important.

The Proposed Policy Objectives

Perhaps the most intellectually impressive aspect of the book is Harrington's identification that the toxic effects of "freedom" (or liberalism) result from the lack of constraints upon it. I must point out that the much-vilified Melanie Phillips explained this very cogently in the 1990s with *All Must Have Prizes* and *The Sex-Change Society*, Refs.[6,7]. Liberalism is a powerful drug which, whilst desirable in moderation, becomes worse than the disease if taken without restraint. The conservative moral dimensions of loyalty, authority and sanctity are central to the constraints upon individual freedom which are essential to ensure that liberalism remains within its beneficial boundaries. Otherwise moral usurpation will morph liberalism into libertinism and licentiousness. (See *The Destructivists*, Ref.[5], for amplification of these matters).

In this context, Harrington suggests three constraints to which we should freely subject ourselves…

Firstly, the reinstatement of single-sex spaces.

Secondly, that sex (in the sense of sexual activity) should be made "properly consequential again". This means refusing to accept the current jaded perspective of sex "as a low consequence activity". In my words: acknowledging that there is no such thing as casual sex.

Thirdly, the "post-romantic case for marriage" should be made, thus opposing the vision of that institution merely as "a vector for self-fulfilment".

She adds to these that women should challenge "the centrality of abortion and birth control to our sexual culture".

I agree with all that. Passionately so. Again Harrington deserves considerable credit for emphasising that these factors are central and essential.

She is careful to throw some criticisms at conservatives, lest she become identified with them. In view of the above, clearly enunciated, programme, that precaution will be entirely inadequate. As she well knows, the treatment meted out to apostates is inescapable. Being willing to brave it is something for which Harrington, once again, deserves to be applauded.

Power and the Critical Poison

Referring to feminism under the term "obsolete mindset", Harrington writes,

"Our biggest obstacle is an obsolete mindset that deprecates all duties beyond personal fulfilment, and views intimate relationships in instrumental terms, as means for self-development or ego gratification, rather than enabling conditions for solidarity. This radical reordering of women's politics, women's priorities and even our bodies to the interests of the market, in the name of 'freedom', has racked up a growing mountain of uncounted costs and unpaid debts. As the mother of a young daughter, I look at that growing mountain of deferred repayment, and the growing chorus of resentment from groups that gather outside feminist filter bubbles, and I worry about her future should we face the ideological equivalent of a subprime crisis."

This is right but horribly inadequate. She has identified, correctly, that feminism (albeit codified as "freedom") has harmed women and stands to harm her daughter. The problem, and it is no small problem, is that she is relentlessly gynocentric. She would have profited much from having a son. She would, I think, be even more concerned for him. What feminism has done to boys requires explicit recognition and clear contrition. There can be no Truth and Reconciliation without the truth, the full truth. But she writes,

"The postmodern worldview I'd learnt at university encodes a deep pessimism about how inescapable power is from human relations at both small and large scale. My experiences seemed to underline this hypothesis. I found myself wondering: if this really is inescapable,

whether as our cultural legacy or a fact of the human condition, does it really make sense to treat power relations as bad? Why not just accept that they're a fact of life?"

It's not a matter of accepting that human relations are inescapably about power, Mary – it's a matter of appreciating that it is not so. Cynicism is not obligatory. She writes,

"I am still a feminist, in the sense that I care about women's interests and think these are often sidelined."

I am not a feminist because I care about the interests of men, women and children and because I think that the interests of men and of children have been sidelined a great deal more than those of women, and that this has been done knowingly for the ostensible, but misguided, benefit of women. I am not a feminist because it is intrinsically sexist and destructive. Harrington continues,

"...crucially, though I have some questions about the direction critical theory has taken since my university days, I'm deeply shaped by some of its insights. It's clear enough to me that language does shape meaning, and more broadly, that memes really do help to structure reality."

Hmm. Paddling in the epistemological shallows will not do. A little knowledge is a dangerous thing.

I suggest that "having some questions" is not an adequate response to an ideology which is now poised to drive Western civilisation into extinction (and Critical Theory *is* an ideology). That topic is too huge to be addressed here. For now, please note that the postmodern / Critical Theory position on language and power is epistemological dilettantism. It is superficial to the point of naivety, not a great insight. It is cynicism and resentment repackaged as something of intellectual depth. It is a fraud.

I doubt that I was much older than eight or so when I first spotted that a dictionary was the embodiment of circular logic. But even then I was not so foolish as think that that invalidated the meaning of words. On the contrary it implies that meaning ultimately lies beyond words, the opposite of the postmodernist position. A true study of epistemology takes one into deep waters where we shall not venture. However, I could reasonably observe that postmodernism is the rubbishing of the greatest minds of Western philosophy by very much smaller minds.

But there is a simpler, more pragmatic, reason to reject the cynical postmodernist position that all is power. Observe that postmodernism requires one to embrace an inescapable nihilism, and to throw away everything of true value in the process. But one simply does not need to adopt such a position. Instead, observe that there **are** things of true value – accessible through everyday experience (the apogee of which is immanence). It is easy to discern what these things of true value are: they are all those things which Critical Theory is destroying (truth, beauty, love, religion, an ethical orientation based upon pursuit of the genuine virtues, and an education which promotes all these things via enculturation and humility in the face of past achievements – see *The Destructivists*, Ref.[5]).

In the context of the power of the sexes, and on a more observational and less theoretical level, Harrington writes of a medieval wife "more than holding her own" in a dialogue with her husband and notes that women have always had their own resources of social power, e.g.,

"The ethnologist Susan Carol Rogers supports this view in her study of power dynamics between men and women in agrarian communities…Rogers shows that in practice women in such communities wield considerable informal power, via channels such as control of information or the ability to inflict public loss of face." (Harrington is here referring to Ref.[8])

Quite. The reality of gender relations is that women often possess decisive social and moral power. Yet feminism has denied this as a cool strategy to have yet more power devolve to them – as recompense for their claimed powerlessness. The reality of the last 60 years is that a balance of power has been replaced by a crushing of men, and boys, wrought deliberately by feminism. I say again: this has to be acknowledged before reconciliation is possible. Again I acknowledge that Harrington has admitted that which must be admitted, namely that women always had considerable moral power. It remains only to acknowledge also that feminism has abused that power.

Serving the Interests of the Elites

Harrington is right to see the cyborg, transhumanist, technocratic movement as deeply inimical to human wellbeing. She rightly identifies the "technologically enabled liberation" as a threat that has "formed the centrepiece of a war on relationships of all kinds that has accelerated radically since the digital revolution". She is also right to align this with the "advancing process of social atomisation under liberalism" and to identify its "far-reaching consequences" and its likely "howlingly dystopian" vista (though I baulk at the inevitable "particularly for women").

We did warn you. Feminism has encouraged women to abandon the individual "patriarch", which, in the great majority of cases is a loving relationship, for the state super-patriarch. The latter is notably parsimonious, not at all loving, and totally crap at fatherhood. But worse: when women align with the state super-patriarch it hands female social and moral power over to the elites.

Harrington is also right to note that the progressives' progress "though conceived of as an idealistic project, in practice this largely serves the corporate interests". But again I baulk at the "three centuries of struggle". This is gynocentric focus. In truth, it took the whole of human history until about one hundred years ago to achieve democracy, and this was achieved for men and women at almost the same time on an historical timeframe. The main difference is that men had been engaged in that struggle for many centuries before Harrington's three. Those were the true Centuries of Oppression, Ref.[9], which involved massive loss of male lives.

Social atomisation is the necessary, and probably sufficient, precursor to authoritarianism (see Ref.[10]). Harrington aligns feminism with the emergence of atomisation thus. "In both China and the West, then, feminist viewpoints emerge in tandem with technological advancement and social atomisation...But if the causal relationship between feminism and atomisation is complex, what's indisputable is its deep implication in what it seeks to remedy". Again Harrington deserves credit for getting that right.

She observes that the effects of pursuing individualist "freedom" has not been beneficial. Instead "it dissolves social codes developed over millennia to manage such patterns, and reorders the still-existing patterns to the logic of the market. And while the result may sometimes benefit a subset of wealthy, high-status women in the West, the class interests of this group are increasingly at odds with those of, not just many men, but also the young, women with fewer resources, and women who are mothers". Harrington may seek to distance herself from conservatives but this is as clear a statement of the conservative position as one could wish for.

The Unacceptably Ignored

Harrington is right that the destruction of the family was the gateway for the rest of the faux-progressive breakdown of our society.

But it will not do.

It will not do, Mary Harrington, to ignore the devastation that feminism has wrought upon men, boys and children generally – and thence to everyone.

Admittedly she does not ignore it entirely; she is explicit about several issues for which feminism is culpable – but nevertheless relentlessly motivated only by the consequent harms to women. I would not expect a complete exposition of all the male disadvantages, which, after all, took me 676 pages to address in *The Empathy Gap*, Ref.[11]. However, there are two topics which I would consider the minimum necessary acknowledgement of what feminism has done. These are the cruel, wholesale and deliberate severing of fathers from their children, and the weaponising of "violence against women and girls" by denial of comparable female culpability. Those two things are inextricably linked.

Ignoring these issues would be unacceptable if they were historical. But they are not historical. They are not only still prevalent, but increasingly so. They are not only increasingly prevalent, but the feminist establishment is pushing ever more to undermine any residual elements of justice, with no end in sight. But it is not only justice but any semblance of humanity at all that has been lost.

Every year in England and Wales some 60,000 fathers are obliged to go to court to attempt to obtain "contact" with their own children (and the usage "contact" is an obscenity in itself). In most cases these fathers' only crime is to no longer be their female ex-partner's favourite person. Half of them will be subject to allegations of domestic abuse, often rape or child sexual abuse. Most of these allegations are false, and everyone involved in the process knows it. Yet these fathers are obliged to submit to the distinctly untender mercies of a system which is institutionally sexist. The level of trauma these men undergo is extreme (I have data), this occurs in bulk, and our culture cares only about Violence Against Women and Girls. The humanity of men, because they are men, counts for nothing. This is why I am so sensitive to the absence of any recognition of men's humanity in your book, Mary.

Yes, there are some men who really are villains. But I can assure you that there are as many mothers who are just as dangerous to their children, but far less likely to have their "contact" challenged by the courts. About one-quarter of fathers involved in contested child contact cases will, at some time during the process, experience suicidal ideation. Five percent will attempt suicide. We know that the death rate of payees into the Child Maintenance System is abnormally high compared to people of the same age and sex in the general population – and these are overwhelmingly men.

I acknowledge that Harrington does note the correlation of men's suicide with divorce, and the lack of such association for women. But the process by which this happens is still in place, and getting worse. It will not do.

The outcome for the men who survive the family court gauntlet and obtain "contact" is, if they are amongst the lucky ones, every other weekend and maybe one day in between – perhaps including one or two overnight stays. This is what fathering is often reduced to now, for the lucky ones. And having survived several years of trauma – and perhaps been denied any contact – our media and our politicians delight in referring to such men as "deadbeat dads". Generally they are not deadbeat, but often they are either dead or beat.

So, why would young men wish to continue with the enterprise of fathering children? Recognition of this little problem is a massive hole in Harrington's policy plan which I'll address further below. The genie may not easily be persuaded back into the bottle.

And I have not even mentioned the worst of it: the destructive effects of fatherlessness on children which is well-known and supported by a vast academic literature.

While the catastrophic effects of the destruction of the two-parent family is a central theme in the book, Harrington fails to be fully forthcoming about the extent of feminism's responsibility for it. After admitting there is no shortage of quotes from second wave feminism's writings relating to the objective to destroy the nuclear family, Harrington asks "do the conservatives who blame feminism for a thinning social fabric, hollowed-out families and collapsing birth rate have a point?" She answers "yes and no". She flatly claims, "there's nothing monolithic about the association between the women's movement and a rejection of familial ties or social norms".

This is evasion and a re-writing of history. It will not do. The sins squarely attributable to feminism must be recognised and acknowledged before Harrington's own project can come about. There are many examples of feminist lobby groups being the dominant force behind primary legislation which undermined, and has now completely annihilated, meaningful marriage. Feminist lobbying – and the embedding of ardent feminist ideologues in positions of power – are the mechanisms directly responsible for giving women the ability to wipe fathers out of their children's lives. This is not even history. The feminist slaughter of fathers actively continues – and not just against fathers. The feminist animus is aimed at all males. A couple of examples from the UK will suffice.

In 2014, feminist-controlled charities together with well-placed feminists in parliament successfully neutralised the threat (as it was to them) of a rebuttable presumption of equal shared parenting after parental separation appearing in primary legislation. This was accomplished by ensuring that the "experts" who were consulted were of suitable ideological persuasion. They proceeded to grossly misrepresent the research literature to the Ministry of Justice, and all thereafter. The associated weaponising of Violence Against Women and Girls (VAWG) has turned the family courts in England and Wales into an arena in which a perfectly decent father, who has done nothing wrong, has to prove he is not a danger to his own children. True, this asymmetry in the treatment of men and women in the family courts is partly an innate bias. But feminism has traded upon this bias mercilessly. See *The Woozling of Shared Parenting* for the full story, Ref.[12].

Nor will it do, Mary Harrington and Louise Perry, to continue to blame men alone for child abuse, even when that focuses on the danger of a stepfather, or casual boyfriend who is not the biological father (what Harrington terms the "Cinderella effect"). You are perfectly correct to identify the families of unmarried mothers as being at particular risk, but it is not only from men. It is the mothers themselves who are the greater risk to their children (see Ref.[11] sections 9.2.7 and 9.2.8). It is about time this was acknowledged by feminists. The lack of that acknowledgement is yet further evidence of gynocentric focus, to the detriment of children. It will not do.

The bigger picture in regard to the weaponising of VAWG is the serious undermining of several fundamental principles of justice, Ref.[13]. Moreover, the feminist drive in this direction is far from over. They will not rest until juries are removed from rape trials – the last defence of an innocent man – and there are feminist MPs in parliament who support just that. That there are, at least, hundreds, and perhaps thousands, of innocent men in prison convicted on sexual offence charges is beyond doubt. But feminism recognises no such thing as an "innocent man". There is no shortage of documentary evidence to that effect too. And please do not plead you are not "that kind of feminist", Mary. The only kind of feminist that counts are those who have been successful in bringing these things about.

A more recent example is the final step in the destruction of marriage. This *coup de grâce* was enacted by the *Divorce, Dissolution and Separation Act 2020* (see chapter 51) which came into force in April 2022. It was billed as a no-fault divorce Act, but, in truth, we have had that in all but name for decades. The new Act establishes divorce as a unilateral action which cannot be contested and which is automatic upon application – one only has to wait for 26 weeks to pass. So, when Harrington refers to our current marriage arrangements as a "contract" this is incorrect. It is not even a contract. The essence of a contract is that it ties two parties into a binding agreement which neither party can legally withdraw from unilaterally. Marriage can now be annulled as easily as cancelling a magazine subscription, and it can be done by one of the spouses without the agreement of the other. Be in no doubt that the easy passage of this Bill through both houses of parliament was because very few MPs or Peers will say boo to the feminist hegemony. Are we to believe that the powerful lobby which has made this their declared objective for half a century was not the main driver behind its accomplishment?

Real marriage, which Harrington appears to support as the way forward (as do I), is a solemn covenant which is mutually binding and lifelong. What is now called "marriage" is merely a mockery of real marriage. There is no real marriage now; it does not exist. Nor is it within the gift of individuals to create real marriage in isolation, because it is the key feature of the institution that the solemn vow is made publicly and regarded as permanent by society, and that both the legislature, and preferably also a religious authority, recognise and endorse it as a joining together "until death us do part".

The Law in History

Harrington notes, correctly, that the law of coverture and its precursors in medieval law were not all to women's disadvantage, as ill-informed feminists might believe. She illustrates this via coverture's shielding of women from "legal and economic exigencies". It worked both ways. Property ownership under coverture was not quite the patriarchal monopoly that is sometimes claimed, and legal non-existence could prove very useful to women who decided to exploit it (not least the avoidance of imprisonment). One could make the case that the advantages of coverture to women outweighed the disadvantages, see chapter 1.

In the context of not wanting to reverse feminism, Harrington declares she has "no wish to be banned from voting". I cannot but be irritated. It is frankly ignorant. Feminism had scant involvement in winning the vote for women, and the suffragettes none whatsoever. See Ref.[9] for the true story of The Vote. This is one of the many feminist myths that must be corrected before there can be a healing of what feminism has wrought over the last 60 years.

Work and Pay in History

Harrington's vision for a desirable future is essentially a return to the era of domestic trade. In as far as it would be possible, I concur. There is, however, a massive problem. Harrington's ignoring of it would seem to emanate from the feminists' marked tendency, not only to ignore the male perspective, but also to be completely blind to what men **do**.

You cannot do work at home when it is fundamentally work that takes place elsewhere!

It is still the case, and always will be the case, that men do almost all the work that involves interaction with inanimate matter. Being a tradesman means working in other people's houses, or other sites away from their own homes. And I refuse to be browbeaten into writing a sex-neutral version of "tradesman". I often hear women farmers referenced in books or in interviews. Indeed, women outnumber men massively in agricultural sciences at college. However, living in the country, I also see farmers working in the fields, on a daily basis. They are always men. Always.

Harrington is right to point to the industrial revolution as a process which alienated both men and women from their domestic environment – simply by removing them from it for most of their waking hours. For men, this would not be easy to reverse because it is not only factories which remove men from their homes but almost all work done by working-class men. Harrington writes,

"When conservatives call for a return to 'traditional' family life, but mean by this a return to some variant of 'separate spheres'. . . this misses the fact that such forms of family life are not 'traditional' at all, but distinctively modern."

I suppose Harrington would class me as conservative, though I regard myself as a radical. However, this is not news to me. It is feminists who, condescendingly, refer to men as unable to adjust to the loss of their "traditional jobs in factories and heavy industry". Excuse me, Mary, why do you burden me with this silliness? I refer you to my 26 part series *Centuries of Oppression*, Ref.[9], which depicts both the medieval agrarian and domestic trade eras. I know very well that the era of working in factories has been but an historical blip.

In critiquing Friedan and Greer, Harrington notes that they both envisage *"a world where some unspecified other does all the dull, sticky drudgery that keeps the world of freedom and selfhood turning"*. Unfortunately, under "dull, sticky drudgery" Harrington refers only to the mothering of children. It is staggering the extent to which work which is not merely dull and sticky, but laborious, dirty and dangerous, is invisible to her because it is done almost exclusively by men. Moreover, such work is crucial to sustaining both the world of "freedom and selfhood" *and* the world of caring mothers. No one gives men any choice, nor, it seems, any recognition. Worse, our contribution is rebranded as economic oppression.

Quoting an historian, she writes that some jobs *"became 'women's work' precisely because they were compatible with keeping an eye on small children. Textile production, for example, was a largely female occupation for some 20,000 years, until the Industrial revolution"*. Well, that may be true for most of those 20,000 years (do we know?), but it was certainly untrue in the era of the handloom to which Harrington goes on to allude. It is worth making a lengthy digression here because it illustrates the broader issues about the historical sex-segregation of paid work.

Handloom weavers were of both sexes, but men predominated – not women, as Harrington implies. From the medieval period to the first decades of the nineteenth century, skilled handloom weaving was the province of men due to the Craft and Trade Guilds creating a *de facto* closed shop requiring would-be handloom weavers to serve an apprenticeship. These proto-unions helped secure a living wage from the trade, sufficient for a man to keep a family – which was the functional definition of "men's work". The "putting-out" system, to which Harrington refers, predominantly involved male handloom weavers.

Once the steam-driven mills opened, with their power looms, the business of weaving ceased to be so skilled, and fewer weavers were required due to the vastly greater productivity of the power looms. Hence – responding to the iron law of labour supply and demand – wages in the mills fell. Men follow the money. They have to if they have a family to support. The mills became full of women on low wages. Do note: the wages were not low because the workers were women; the workers were women because the wages were low. (Either way, it was, of course, exploitation by the new mill owners and the resulting relationship with the Chartist movement and with Marx and Engels I will pass over).

The prices available to the remaining handloom weavers therefore fell also, and handloom weaving became a byword for poverty – whereas previously it had been a profitable trade. (Silas Marner, in George Elliott's eponymous novel, was a handloom weaver – deliberately to be redolent of poverty to a Victorian readership. Ditto Stephen Blackpool in Dickens' *Hard Times*). Consequently, the proportion of women in the (now dying) handloom trade increased. Yet even by 1838 the majority were still men, just. Actual numbers of hand loom weavers, disaggregated by sex, in 1838 Norwich can be found in Ref.[14] Contrary to Harrington's implication, women did not cease to be the majority of weavers when the industrial revolution introduced the mills. Quite the reverse: it was men who ceased to be the majority of weavers at that time, whilst women ***became*** the majority then, but in the mills.

As a Lancastrian, this has resonance with my own family history. My wife's grandmother – the last of 12 children (all with rickets) – was born in the Victorian era. She started in the mill in Atherton, Lancashire, at age 12, receiving no pay for the first year. These matters are not ancient history but were the actual lives of people I knew as a young man. There ***is*** such a thing as progress, Mary. Having children free of rickets (vitamin D deficiency) is one. Denying this is both cynical and demonstrably false. It's just that your perspective on "progress" is hopelessly restricted.

The displaced men, the former handloom weavers, followed the money and moved into mining and digging tens of thousands of miles of canal and railroad by hand; tougher work but better pay. And not work that women would ever do.

One of the many jibes directed at men in the feminist era has been the claim that men find it hard to adjust to new employment environments – generally justifying the claim by reference to the loss of their "traditional" jobs in factories. Utter nonsense, of course. Because men have always been obliged to follow the money, due to family commitments, it follows that men must always be ready to move into new work areas as old ones become less economically attractive.

To call factory work "traditional" is staggeringly myopic. The era of domestic trades (of which weaving was just one of many trades, all dominated by men) was longer than the factory era by far, growing rapidly as serfdom died out around the time of the Black Death. And the periods of industry and domestic trades together constitute a mere blip in history compared with the 10,000 years in which economic activity was massively dominated by agriculture and its ancillary functions of food production. And that, I suppose I must add, was but a recent innovation compared to the evolutionary period of hundreds of thousands of years of *Homo sapiens'* hunter-gatherer lifestyle.

However…Harrington is perfectly correct to point the finger at the industrial revolution as a catastrophe for family life. It was every bit as catastrophic for men as for women – and ultimately more so. The advantage of the era of domestic trades was that there was no distinction between home and workplace. And this was just as true for the men involved as the women. The Master Craftsman was the head of a small business, which not only brought the wife and children into active participation, but would also include apprentices, journeymen and female domestic help. The Master's wife was, typically, the undisputed Second-in-Command. In fact, so fearsome were many such Masters' wives that, in practice, they ruled entirely. Running the household budget, and hence rations, was a powerful position. Many apprentices' Articles explicitly required obedience to the Master's wife, by name, not just the Master himself. Consequently, in this period, there was a mingling of the economic and domestic activities. Much the same goes for agriculture, at least for those married, where the place of work was usually on their doorstep. The exceptions were the itinerant, seasonal, male labourers, usually unmarried.

Are Men Human?

In discussing Dorothy Sayer's essay *Are Women Human?*, Harrington writes that women sought to "become human on the same terms as men". This was being asserted, I believe, in the very limited context of employment – as if one's job defines one's humanity. More broadly, women would not be pleased if their humanity was as circumscribed as men's. I have already noted above that, in Harringtons's book, men's humanity is notable by its absence. I recall, many years ago, a poster campaign in Canada in which the posters asserted "men's rights are human rights". All the posters were defaced and the word "wrong" scrawled across them. To complete the syllogism, then, we conclude that men are not human.

Harrington identifies the feminist rejection of the caring role as being their attempt to assert their "humanity", or personhood. Predictably, criticism is then levelled at men for being unwilling to pick up their share of the caring. My own experience of attempting to do so was not a happy one. My wife made it very clear that, whilst I was indeed expected to contribute to nappy changing, baby minding and getting up in the middle of the night, on no account should I entertain any independent notions of what needed doing or when. I was to be only the under-nursery-maid…with an unacknowledged side-line in providing all the family's income.

This fierce policing of the childcare role by mothers, to ensure it remains their monopolistic domain, is noted by Harrington in another context: "*In one 1985 essay, Ruth Wallsgrove describes her experience as a childless feminist woman doing her best to support mothers with childcare, but frustrated that such women 'want support, on their terms' but at no cost to the bond they have with their children: 'they don't want to share'*". I suspect it is common for fathers to meet with this resistance – though that will not stop the mothers later turning around to complain that their men do not do enough to help them. Fathers have to work out for themselves how to fit their fathering into the interstices left by the mother.

This may, I suspect, be ultimately for the good as it forces upon fathers a truly complementary role which is actually crucial. But if that perspective is correct, it follows that the mothering role really is best done by the mother.

Patriarchy as Theatre

The term "patriarchy" is used by feminists in two distinct ways: to indicate a man being the head of the household, and also to indicate that men are dominant in the world of business, politics and other external affairs. Here I am concerned with the first usage: the individual patriarch in the family setting.

The feminist conception of marriage as being an arrangement to facilitate a man's desire to dominate (oppress) his female partner arises, I think, from a profound failure to understand male psychology – coupled with a remarkable blindness to the real nature of family dynamics. Men have an innate drive to protect and provide resources for women. Hence, marriage is an altruistic action for men. But respect is also very important for men, and being in a position of servitude does not fit well with that requirement. This conflict is resolved by patriarchy – when properly understood. For patriarchy is essentially a piece of theatre. It is a means of providing status to the role of protector and resource provider. By assigning status to the role, men are encouraged to fulfil it. But that formal status does not negate the underlying reality that, in truth, the woman is the power in her own home. The human pair-bond crucially involves the man ceding moral authority to his female partner. By this means her requirements become his duty to fulfil; this is part of the mechanism of resource provision. Some quotes from the late sociologist Geoff Dench are worth repeating on this issue,

"The frog (Dench's metaphor for the unattached man), *knowing no dependents, is largely self-sufficient in his pool, and can find little reason to abandon freedom and precious playing time just to become a domestic help. To be tempted from the pleasures of the forest, men need to be flattered by an important sounding title, and by the hint – which becomes absurd as soon as it is examined closely – that all of this business of child rearing and reproducing society is in some way being done for them and takes place under their indispensable management. Want to be my helper? Well, maybe; I'll let you know. How about head of household, domestic monarch? Now that's more like it!"*

"Patriarchal exaggeration of men's importance obscures the deeper power of women, and behind the theatre of male dominion the palace holds many secrets."

487

The patriarchy that feminism has been so busy smashing was created as a device to encourage men into commitment to a role which is essentially altruistic. In other words, the purpose of patriarchy is to benefit women. Here's Dench again,

"Patriarchy is a system that may well have been largely devised and promoted by primordial matriarchs in order to even out the burden on their children."

In that context we can interpret Harrington's suggestion that we should return to a traditional type of marriage arrangement as a rediscovery of what feminist women had forgotten, but what their ancient forebears had previously brought about – for their benefit.

Harrington writes, *"It's some time now in the West since we abandoned actual 'patriarchy'…efforts to 'smash' this nebulous thing appear only to have moved the goalposts in terms of where and how it manifests. And this is because most of what flies under the 'patriarchy' banner in the 21ª century is simply those ineradicable sex differences that return, like zombie caricatures of themselves, in a hyper-liquid market society"*. She hits the target, but nowhere near the bullseye. She has not yet grasped, or will not concede, that the theatre of patriarchy was always for women's benefit, and also of women's construction. Moreover, the "patriarchy banner" was only ever a label applied by feminists, not the rest of us.

Male Dissident Opinion

Feminists seeking to critique the "manosphere" (whatever that is) are generally keen to hang around on forums for Incels or PUAs or MGTOW. They seem less keen to engage with the serious – and often highly academic – milieu of the main men's movement itself. The latter includes people who are content to be regarded as men's rights activists, or advocates, plus many people who are less happy with that label but broadly sympathetic to the calls for the male disadvantages to receive greater acknowledgement. Harrington's book joins the list of feminist writings which implicitly dismiss the morally and intellectually valid men's movement by critiquing only Incels, PUAs and MGTOW – the latter being peripheral to the larger movement and the former two being no part of it at all. The only mention of "men's rights activism" in the book is this,

"The siren call of atomisation comes from everywhere, and legitimises itself in many ways: girl-power self-actualisation and embittered men's rights activism, for example, are

mirroring ideologies driving the same decline into loneliness and mutual hostility. For both these perspectives, marriage is tantamount to prostitution: a fake contract that enables exploitation of one sex by the other."

I am an MRA. Who are you, Mary Harrington, to harangue me in this way, with your new-found evangelism? I am an MRA who is in the same – and only – relationship which has now lasted nearly half a century, married for over 40 of them. I am the living embodiment of the lifestyle your recent conversion now lauds as society's salvation (rightly). You, on the other hand, Mary, with your self-confessed degenerate history and neophyte "reaction" should be a little more humble. You also need to be more cautious about your tendency to project, another perennial failing of the feminist.

The best interpretation I can put on this is ignorance: you failed to do your homework, Mary. You either know nothing of the men's movement – in which case you should not speak of it – or you have deliberately misrepresented it.

But as for the attitude towards marriage of many who call themselves MRAs, that requires a separate discussion which exposes exactly what that institution is, was and needs to be.

The Destruction of Marriage

The great weakness in Harrington's proposed resurgence of "real marriage" (my term) is how it can be brought into existence. Harrington has nothing to say about the systematic dismantling of real marriage by feminist activism over many decades, and its embedding in primary and secondary legislation by an overwhelmingly feminist establishment.

It is easy to smash – be it the patriarchy or anything else. It is not so easy to rebuild. Harrington needs to understand that the disempowering of men through their being rendered unnecessary to the family was very easily accomplished precisely because such changes worked with the grain of the establishment's natural tendency to aggregate power to itself. We will not find it so easy to work against the authoritarian establishment's resistance to reinstate meaningful marriage.

There is an unacknowledged assumption in Harringtons' strategy which originates in her failure to appreciate the male perspective. She assumes that men will continue to want to marry. Frankly, under existing conditions, they would need to be very badly informed, or unusually risk tolerant, to want to do so. Harrington should note that this opinion comes from a man who has been in the same relationship for half a century and married for over 40 of them. But my relationship started in different times, among people with a different perspective on life, and when marriage was a different institution. If I were a young man in our society as it now is, with our legislation as it now is, and knowing what I do, I would not marry or cohabit or father children. What you are up against, Mary, is not mere emotionally based reluctance. You are espousing the benefits of an arrangement which has been systematically legislated out of existence.

No one has a map of the road back. But it will clearly be long.

Men's increasing reluctance in respect of family life is because it is now far too precarious to be a sensible choice. That is simply a correct evaluation as things stand.

Add to this the great difficulty that men (or boys) now have in achieving any relationship with a female – who seem to have become akin to unexploded bombs - and the disastrous scenario is complete. When a man (or a boy) can be vilified even for the most polite attempt to introduce himself to a female, and when a man (or a boy) can be placed on the sex offenders register for touching a female on the shoulder, any chance of relationship is dead in the water for most men. Why should one even take the risk? What's in it for us?

And then there's the economic ascendancy of women and their natural hypergamy and choosiness which ensures that 20% of men on dating apps get all the attention – to the point of creating a sexual glut for that minority of men. Women thereby create commitment-phobic men whilst simultaneously creating the lack of "good men" by the simple expediency of ignoring them – and then pouring opprobrium upon their heads if they have the temerity to speak up in the "manosphere" (a term which is itself derogatory).

The TERF Tendency

One concern I have with Harrington's "conversion" is that too large a part of it is motivated by the second-wave, so-called trans-exclusionary radical feminist (TERF), reaction to trans. The TERFs (or "gender critical feminists" as Harrington prefers) have found themselves suddenly with out-group status, not something to which they are accustomed. (I will admit to a spot of *schadenfreude* here). Harrington does, at least, acknowledge that the trans monster is a creation of feminism (about which TERFs are in denial), although even Harrington attempts to quarantine the blame by confining it to the "freedom feminism" from which she now finds it convenient to distance herself. Her lingering allegiance with this axis may be evident in, for example, this advice in respect of activism,

"The approach taken by gender-critical feminists should serve as a template for reactionary feminist politics across the board."

I doubt that she means being beaten up like Posie Parker – or perhaps she does?

A puissant mechanism for bringing about a change in the nature of marriage along the lines we both desire might be a resurgence in men's power in the matter. One means by which this might come about is via a cheap, readily available, reliable, convenient and easily reversible male contraceptive – and one whose side effects were sufficiently minor not to detract from its widespread use. Such a power of men over women's fertility could be a game-changer. Under these conditions, men could make viable sperm available only upon their terms – and those terms should include security of involvement in a child's life.

Trans and Feminism

Harrington is rather good at describing the likely origins of the sudden, and huge, increase in the incidence of young people identifying as trans. Her anecdotes, whilst not constituting a scientific study, confirm what I suspected but had never researched. Male-to-female trans, Steven, "found puberty distressing". He testified that, "As a white man, I was directly responsible for all of the oppression experienced by women and people of colour. I was fourteen years old and had never been in a fight in my life or said a racist or misogynistic word to anyone, but I believed that the circumstances of my birth made me a monster". Are the TERF-types listening? You created the trans debacle, not MRAs as you preposterously claim. That's as clear a statement of "third wave intersectional feminism drove me trans" as you could wish for.

The same conclusion applies to female-to-male trans, Helena. Being raised in the "hyper-sexualised and pornified" world of sex-positive "freedom feminism" terrified her. She concluded "I must not have really been meant to be a girl, because if I was, this wouldn't all be so scary and confusing". Tragic, isn't it?

Both Steven and Helena were made unable to handle what was happening to them in puberty, as a direct result of the appalling postmodern-Critical narrative in which they had been marinated by school and media and politics. Both ended up hating their bodies as the apparent source of their monstrousness. Steven was terrified of what testosterone was doing to him, and also terrified that he was turning into an example of the toxic masculinity he had always been taught to despise.

The trans monster was created by feminism. Feminism created the theoretical possibility of trans by severing sex from gender – and, in fact, creating the word "gender" in its modern usage. But worse, feminism also provided the impetus behind individual boys and girls wanting to transition.

Girls, under feminism, have been raised to believe they live in a rape culture in which every male is a predator, just waiting to pounce on them given the ghost of a chance. On the other hand, girls have also been raised to believe boys have it easy, drifting through life without a care in the world. No wonder so many girls want to ditch a life of constant danger for one it which (as they believe) they will be powerful and privileged and without fear. Helena thought that "transition would transform her into 'this outgoing male jock archetype' who would be 'handsome, have lots of friends, and love life'". Such a misconstruing of life as a male under feminism would be funny if it weren't so sad.

Boys, in contrast to what girls imagine, have actually been raised to believe that, when puberty strikes, they will turn into the monsters that they have persistently been told all men truly are. Not surprisingly, then, given the cataclysmic power of pubescent hormones, some boys think that is exactly what is happening to them. Male puberty, Harrington tells us, is now viewed as hostile and poisonous to enough boys that there is a tee-shirt slogan "I survived testosterone poisoning".

And yet, despite the extent of the devastation that feminism has wrought across the whole of society, still it is held to be reprehensible to declare oneself against feminism – and virtually obligatory for politicians to declare their allegiance to an ideology long since proved to be terminally corrosive. Humans, eh?

Harrington wrote,

"The principal advocates for this movement, wittingly or not, are those progressive knowledge-class women who are still net beneficiaries of the war on embodiment. But while feminism has provided much of the moral cover for this dystopian possible future, I am not saying this is all women's fault. The technological and cultural shifts that got us here happened slowly, and every step made sense on its own terms."

Hmm. I'm not impressed by that evasion. The moral smokescreen provided by feminism was (in true moral usurpation style) the key driver which gave advances in technology the direction of travel as regards its social implications. Technology itself is neutral, Mary.

Conclusion

Reaction to the book provokes one to clarify what the men's movement is trying to achieve. My position is, and always has been, that we do not want to return to a traditionalist world. The men's movement is not merely conservative (though many of its adherents happen to be). The men's movement is actually radical. This is not appreciated by any feminists, nor by the public at large. The radical element lies in the movement's opposition to gynocentrism. This immediately rules out the traditional world, which was as gynocentric as our present world.

However, there is much common ground with Harrington: sufficient common ground upon which to build an alliance. But a deal breaker must be the priority given to re-establishing fathers' security of meaningful paternity. Without that it all collapses into hot air.

The second, and closely related, condition must be the acknowledgement of the reality of gynocentric bias (by whatever name) which skews concern to women and girls and responsibility to men and boys. Unless this is replaced by empirically sound balance, men will – and should – continue to walk away.

The third condition must be the recognition that women, even women in traditional domestic caring roles, are not, and never have been, powerless. The influence of female moral, and hence social, power must be explicitly recognised. The importance of this lies in this moral power, allied to gynocentrism, being the true foundation of feminism. If it continues unrecognised, the excesses of feminism and all that it brings with it will re-emerge.

A fourth condition must be the acknowledgement of the gynocentric bias of the Violence Against Women and Girls narrative, followed by putting that weapon beyond use.

To say that success in implementing these changes will not be easy is a massive understatement. Harrington notes that it will not be straightforward politically for it's likely to come at some cost to those women who benefit from the "progressive" agenda, that is the elite women: quote *"This class may need to lose some measure of the benefits that such 'equality' and 'progress' has afforded them. Suggesting they do so is likely to provoke, to put it mildly, a defensive reaction. And this class of women currently has the mic."*

Harrington's fighting talk about wresting the (feminist) movement from the "sterilised steel claws of the Fourth Industrial Revolution" is a joy to read, but we have yet to forge a force capable of defeating the transnational Woke Industrial Complex (for more of which see The *Destructivists*, Ref.[5]).

References

[1]   Harrington, M. (2023). *Feminism Against Progress*. Forum, 2 March 2023.

[2]   Perry, Louise. (2022). *The Case Against the Sexual Revolution*. Polity, 16 May 2022.

[3]   Gress, C. (2023). *The End of Woman: How Smashing the Patriarchy Has Destroyed Us*. 15 August 2023.

[4]   Kuby, G. (2105). *The Global Sexual Revolution: Destruction of Freedom in the Name of Freedom*. English translation, LifeSite (Angelico Press) 2015.

[5]   Collins, W. (2022). *The Destructivists*. Principia Publications Unlimited, 20 February 2022.

[6]   Phillips. M. (1997). *All Must Have Prizes*. Little, Brown, 3 April 1997.

[7]   Phillips, M. (1999). *The Sex Change Society: Feminised Britain and the Neutered Male*. The Social Market Foundation (28 Oct. 1999).

[8] Rogers, S.C. (1975). *Female forms of power and the myth of male dominance: A model of female/male interaction in peasant society*. American Ethnologist 2(4) 727-756, November 1975.

[9] Collins, W. (2017). *Centuries of Oppression: The Road to 1918*. YouTube 8 October 2017.

[10] Desmet, M. (2022). *The Psychology of Totalitarianism*. Chelsea Green Publishing, 23 June 2022.

[11] Collins, W. (2019). *The Empathy Gap*. LPS Publishing, June 2019.

[12] Collins, W. (2018). *The Woozling of Shared Parenting*. The Illustrated Empathy Gap, 12 November 2018. (Alternatively see *The Empathy Gap*, Ref.[11], section 12.3).

[13] Collins, W. (2019). *Gender Bias and Erosion of UK Criminal Justice*. YouTube 25 April 2020.

[14] History Pieces (undated). *Handloom Weavers in Mid-Nineteenth Century Norwich*.

53. Prejudice: Boys in School

The prejudice starts in school, and not just by the teachers.

Original posted on: 12 February 2023.

In September 2014 I wrote an article, Ref.[1], about the organised intention to promote the image of schoolboys as sexual predators (on that occasion in the context of compulsory Sex and Relationship Education). It ended thus,

"Only boys are acknowledged as potential abusers. One shudders at the totalitarian mentality behind the phrase "adequate interventions" – not for boys who have done anything, but for those who are deemed "at risk" of doing something – as judged, one presumes, by people with suitably approved ideological purity. It is presented to us as a fact that more abuse will be reported. It will. The very process will ensure it and is intended to do so. God help our boys. They will be forced to play the role of the bourgeoisie in our very own Cultural Revolution."

It is now in full swing.

Hard data is not available and never will be as long as the prejudice prevails to prevent its collection. But news reports are beginning to appear which are exposing what is happening in schools. The dominant narrative will, of course, continue to be that girls are at constant, severe and ever-escalating risk from sexually rapacious boys. That the boys may be aged 13 (or even younger) makes no difference. They have the indelible mark of Cain, a penis, and their original sin cannot ever be expunged.

In July 2022 an anonymous mother wrote an article for a newspaper titled *My son's innocent teenage fumblings saw him branded a rapist*, Ref.[2]. I urge you to read it in full. The key points are as follows.

The story is recounted by a mother who withheld her name out of fear for her son. She had other sons too, and observed that, *"throughout their young lives they have routinely been told by their young female friends that they 'hate men' and that 'all men are rapists'. So fevered has the atmosphere among young women become that today something as innocent as a male tapping you on the shoulder can be construed as assault."* Do not doubt it. A teacher recently committed suicide over something that trivial because it led to a court case, Ref.[3].

One of this mother's sons was 13 when he was sent a topless photo by a schoolgirl. With another girl he had been involved in "*saucy texting and some mutual touching*". There was zero question of full-blown sex taking place and all the behaviour was mutual and consensual, as far as the boy was aware. But one of the girls' mothers found the material on her daughter's phone and complained to the school. The boy's mother then discovered the truth about our society. She wrote,

"*...the stark difference between the treatment of girls and boys became evident, to my son's lifelong cost. The girls, who were equally culpable, as sending nude photographs is both an offence and against the school rules, were dealt with discreetly. A quiet word was had with them and their parents and that was an end to it. Conversely, my son, who'd never been in trouble before, was suspended for two days, the final step before expulsion. The school's rationale was that the other pupils would see this as 'justice'.*"

Moral authority, do note, was delegated to children.

A merciless campaign of intimidation and bullying by other school pupils followed. The boy was called a 'rapist', a 'nonce' and told he should be castrated. He was urged to kill himself on a daily basis. He was attacked by a mob in the playground and was threatened with stabbing. Lurid rumours started that he had locked multiple girls in cupboards and raped them. Later, one of the girls decided to call the police and accuse the boy of sexual assault. The boy was told by an acquaintance that it was because she was 'feeling bored'. A month later, a girl who had been friends with the boy for years accused him of sexual assault after he touched her on the back to get her attention. Once again, writes his mother, "*his teachers reacted aggressively by hauling him out of his lesson, thereby cementing his reputation as a predator and destroying any scant chance he had to resume a normal life at school*". The boy's emotional well-being inevitably crumbled under this assault. His friends deserted him; nothing he said or did made any difference, he was a 'rapist' in the eyes of his entire school.

During the investigation that followed, the police told the boy's parents that they were being inundated with similar calls from teenage girls "whipped into a frenzy by the MeToo movement". Lawyers the parents consulted confirmed an exponential rise in allegations against young schoolboys in the past few years.

The anonymous mother subsequently discovered that two of her girlfriends' sons had had similar experiences: *"One had been ostracised by all his friends and had to move away from the area after an ex accused him of rape after he started a new relationship. Another had his picture plastered on a website with the smear of "rapist" next to it, for much the same reason."*

Data to quantify the prevalence of such cases are not available, as far as I am aware. But it is becoming clear, just from newspaper reports, that this appalling targeting of boys is not rare. In March 2021, Sarah Rodrigues had a piece in the Telegraph titled, *As a mother of sons, this is scaring me*, Ref.[4]. She wrote that, as lockdowns ended, many of the country's adolescent boys were not so much excited about returning to school as frightened. The reason was the thousands of allegations being made on Everyone's Invited. The prevailing atmosphere was of fear.

Rodrigues recounts several examples. One was of a teenage boy arriving at his sixth form college to a chorus of screams from girls, others hissing or spitting. This was due to some story about him circulating on social media platforms. He never went back. His friends immediately deserted him, having been threatened with 'cancellation' otherwise. Teenage boys are now concluding that it's safer to stay at home. Rodrigues rightly raises the issue of allegations which only follow the end of a relationship – which seems common. Last week's fully engaged bit of fun is today's retrospective sexual assault.

The Rodrigues article was followed in the newspaper by a piece by Pravina Rudra reminding us (I paraphrase) not to forget that it is the boys who are the little shits, and the girls who are the real victims. Just in case you were in danger of confusion. Articles like Rodrigues' are always immediately neutralised.

In February 2023, The Sunday Times had an article by Sian Griffiths, *Why MeToo fallout is wrecking the lives of schoolboys*, Ref.[5], which begins to shed some light on the issue of prevalence. It reports the testimony of highly experienced psychotherapist, Julie Lynn-Evans. Her clients used to be teenage girls with eating disorders or self-harming issues. But for the last six months they have been exclusively boys – boys who have been ostracised, punished or even expelled for behaviour that she describes as little more than clumsy teenage fumbling. Many have done nothing wrong. Her testimony involves words like "serious", "dangerous" and "not justice". Some of the boys are suicidal. Clearly all of them are extremely severely impacted or they would not be seeing a psychotherapist.

The article quotes a criminal defence lawyer who has worked with dozens of boys subject to these allegations, which generally first appear on Everyone's Invited or the *Whisper* app. None have resulted in convictions. Some involve such things as "brushing up against someone in the lunch queue". Give me strength. On that basis I was sexually assaulted multiple times daily for six years...and that's not counting primary school.

The process is the punishment, and that punishment follows automatically upon allegation. The facts are irrelevant. It is not even very relevant if a prosecution finds "not guilty" in court. By that time the boy's education has been seriously disrupted for a protracted period, usually over a year, he has been ostracised and vilified, he is seriously depressed, even suicidal, and the family generally has to move away because the boy's life will go on being intolerable despite any "not guilty" verdict. The trauma these boys undergo is underestimated by society. They are often left fearing to restart education or to go to university, and may become too fearful ever to go within ten yards of a girl ever again – and possibly boys too.

Who is the one hurt here? Was it the girl who was merely touched (or voluntarily provided a topless photo of herself) and was subsequently the recipient of everybody's concern and protection, perhaps enjoying the attention and envy of her school friends? Or was it the boy who was universally vilified, urged to kill himself, lost all his friends, was subject to mob aggression and further groundless accusations, ultimately obliging his family to move away?

In future life, will it be the girl or the boy who will be frightened of risking intimacy with the opposite sex? Who has truly been damaged, by intense harm in the short term, and perhaps chronic harm throughout life?

Who are the villains here?

What are the causes of this behaviour by young teenage girls?

Girls of that age are testing their newly acquired power over boys. It was ever thus. Girls used to be content to break hearts; now, it seems, they want to destroy a boy's entire existence. There appears to be no remorse when the consequences of their accusations become clear. Quite the opposite.

Girls of that age are also keen for attention, especially if the attention involves sympathy or admiration. Both of those objectives can be fulfilled by making fashionable allegations against a boy. And this perennial inclination is now exacerbated by our victimhood culture, which provides a bonus in terms of status to the alleged victim. Girls presenting as sexual assault victims will be met only with sympathy, concern, and positive encouragement by all authority figures.

Then there's the mobbing. Another girl, envious of the attention a "victim" is getting (or perhaps just bored) decides to join in. What better than to accuse the same boy? Everyone will believe it immediately, he's a known rapist after all.

Then there are the mobs of boys. Schoolboys were always ready, *Lord Of The Flies* fashion, to be merciless towards the excluded. They too are fearful; fearful of being the next for the treatment. And so they learn the quisling response of allyship, the cowards. I hope there are exceptions.

But we must also acknowledge that some girls (not all) are genuinely fearful of boys – which is not to say that such fear is well founded. How could they not be fearful when they have been raised to believe they live in a rape culture? That preposterous narrative continues to go from strength to strength. It is incredibly damaging to both sexes, driving a wedge between them. Every boy, they have been taught to believe, is just waiting for an opportunity to pounce on them. That boys might be motivated by feelings of tenderness towards girls is not something they have ever heard. Females have always been rather ignorant of the inner life of males, and ignorance has now given way to wild falsity.

The role of our therapeutic educational system contributes strongly to girls' fear. They have been taught to prioritise their feelings over factual evidence, and this plays to a natural tendency. Regrettably, there is truth in the oft-made claim that we have raised a generation of snowflakes. And let us not overlook that girls are also now raised to be prejudiced.

There is, perhaps, a deeper psychological reason too. Girls and young women have a need to feel protected. Yet their distancing from males of their own age, encouraged by the mantras of the "strong independent woman" – and perhaps fatherlessness too – have removed the source of protection. But the innate feeling of need of protection remains. To rationalise this feeling, a cause must be attributed to it. The dangerous predatory male fits the bill. In short, boys become the victims of irrational, innate female psychology.

But let us not forget the simpler and more direct explanation: that some girls are just wicked. The "mean girl" phenomenon is real, and boys have zero chance against mean girls. As Erin Pizzey has said in the context of mixed-sex DV refuges, "no way, the women would eat the men alive". Quite.

Everyone's Invited facilitates these behaviours – and is intended to do so. It not only provides an easy vehicle for allegations, analogous to #MeToo, but also is a further conduit for the narrative on rape culture. The strapline of the organisation is *"Everyone's Invited is the leading activist and educational organisation tackling rape culture in the UK"*. They particularly target schools and universities.

One can see a pattern of future behaviour emerging from this. Unjust treatment of young men accused of sexual assault has been increasingly a feature of university life for many years. Men are not even safe at the gym now, Ref.[6]. The false allegations of sexual assault that are made in adult life are the natural extension and outcome of behaviours reinforced by society via the schools at an earlier age. Five years ago I did a brief review of such false allegations in the UK and identified the reasons (see chapter 8).

And, no, I don't believe the above remarks will apply to all girls. I fully expect there are many who understand very well what is really going on. But like the neutral boys, sticking one's neck out in a school environment would be courting the mob to turn on you. And so both sexes learn to bite their tongues about disgraceful behaviour out of fear and self-interest. It will serve them well in later life in our culture now.

But I have addressed only the causes of the girls' keenness to make allegations. There is another dimension to this phenomenon, namely the active encouragement of these behaviours from every direction in society. The #MeToo phenomenon has been highlighted as one cause. One of the things that drives me to distraction is that, even in the articles quoted above, it remains obligatory to display concern for the girls. For example, the psychotherapist Lynn-Evans stated, *"I like #MeToo and would like to give the woman who started it an award'*. Incredibly, someone working with the fallout from this monstrous movement has failed completely to recognise whence it has come. Similarly, the anonymous mother in the first piece included the following in her account,

"Of course, any girl should feel able to complain about physical contact that makes her feel uncomfortable."

"Let me be clear: I abhor the fact that violence against women is still such a problem in our society. It breaks my heart every time I read about the latest young woman who has been attacked, raped and even murdered on our streets. I've always taught my sons to respect women and make sure their female friends get home safe. I fervently believe girls have the right to call out bad behaviour and be listened to."

"I had never brooked sexism in my house, yet found myself questioning my own mothering skills. Had I not hammered home the importance of treating girls respectfully?"

This is how hard it is to escape gynocentrism even for a mother defending her – let's be frank about this – her **abused** son. She should have been demanding that mothers raise their daughters to understand the importance of treating boys with respect. What chance is there of anyone ever imposing such an obligation on girls? None.

Instead we have the empathy gap on steroids, with callous behaviour by girls being rewarded instead of punished. This is the nub of the problem: total failure of moral authority. There are no adults in the room anymore.

The #MeToo phenomenon has been highlighted as a driver of this accusatory culture, but this has merely given further impetus to the feminist mantras which go back at least 50 years (and actually far longer). If ordinary schoolgirls are now saying they hate all men and all men are rapists, then it is hardly irrelevant to note that feminists have been writing exactly that in their tracts for over half a century. It is hardly irrelevant that the feminist perspective is obligatory in the whole education system.

This is not to say that all teachers are feminist zealots (though some are). Many teachers are the victims of this ideologically based intolerance. Teachers too have allegations made against them – sometimes women teachers too. But that is to be expected in an ideologically driven process, essentially totalist in nature. No one is safe. The ideology holds everyone in its sway, even those who seem to be its chief progenitors.

For example, teachers may have limited freedom of action following allegations from pupils, such as those recounted above. Government statutory advice on required action following allegations was updated in September 2022, Ref.[7]. This stemmed from the earlier *"rapid review of sexual abuse in schools and colleges"*, Ref.[8], carried out by Ofsted in 2021, and this in turn was a response to the launch of Everyone's Invited, Ref.[9]. The advice describes anyone accused of any sexual misdemeanour as a 'perpetrator' and recommends that schools remove them from any classes or spaces they share with the 'victim'. The advice also states, "staff should be aware it is more likely that girls will be the victims of sexual violence and sexual harassment and more likely it will be perpetrated by boys".

The government guidance is all about safeguarding, yet it is clear that the actions of schools failed catastrophically to safeguard the accused boys in the above cases. The reason is the endemic prejudice that is blind to girls' situational aggression and equally blind to harms against boys. We are culturally unable to recognise who is the victim and who is the villain.

What this example of government guidance demonstrates is that, (i) these draconian, and prejudiced, policies are promulgated top-down by government, but also that, (ii) their origin can lie in a private initiative by a single individual or small group of individuals. This can only occur if the spark created by a small group falls into the dry tinder of a pre-existing prejudicial environment which extends through official bodies and into government.

But the killer observation is this: if there is such widespread concern that girls are subject to rampant sexual abuse at school, where are the calls for girls to be educated separately? I hear none.

If the authorities – and parents and girls themselves – really believed the narrative which they all so gleefully promulgate, why are they not calling for girls to be educated separately from boys?

This suggests that, at some level, they know the truth – which makes them complicit in this monstrous injustice.

This mirrors what has been happening in universities for many years. On the one hand the narrative claims that universities are the epicentre of a rape culture. On the other hand, neither young women themselves, nor their parents, show any reluctance regarding young women's continuing attendance at universities in ever increasing numbers.

In contrast, I hear plenty of calls for boys to be educated separately, including from myself. Which sex, then, is truly at risk?

There will never be calls for single sex education from the feminists because that would defeat their purpose because their purpose is not the protection of females. Their purpose is the control of males, which is why feminism has focussed relentlessly on the eradication of all-male spaces. The feminists want males to be firmly under their thumb at all times so they can vent their lust for endlessly vilifying all things male. If women and girls are collateral damage in that campaign of prejudice, well that's too bad. And so schoolgirls are now collaborating with a process which will lead to their own undoing in later life: a culture in which young men increasingly have no interest in intimate relations with them.

References

[1] Collins, W. (2014). *Dear Nicky*. The Illustrated Empathy Gap, 30 September 2014.

[2] Anonymous (2022). *My son's innocent teenage fumblings saw him branded a rapist, hounded out of school and left sobbing in emotional agony, his anonymous mother reveals*. Mail Online, 28 July 2022.

[3] McAnally, A. (2023). *Respected teacher, 53, who was accused of assault while confiscating a mobile phone from a pupil 'takes her own life' days before her trial*. Mail Online, 11 February 2023.

[4] Rodrigues, S. (2021). *As a mother of sons, this is scaring me*. The Telegraph, 30 March 2021.

[5] Griffiths, S. (2023). *Why MeToo fallout is wrecking the lives of schoolboys*. The Sunday Times, 5 February 2023.

[6] Kennedy, K. (2023). *The toxic women of gym TikTok: Who's the real victim in their viral videos?* The Spectator, 7 February 2023.

[7] Department for Education (2022). *Keeping children safe in education 2022 Statutory guidance for schools and colleges*. 1 September 2022.

[8] Ofsted (2021a). *Review of sexual abuse in schools and colleges*. 10 June 2021.

[9] Ofsted Press Release (2021b). *Ofsted's review of sexual abuse in schools and colleges*. 7 April 2021.

54. The Decline of Intimate Relationships

Here I look at the data for England and Wales on marriage and cohabitation, and also a recent Pew Research survey of dating and relationship status in the USA. Add to this evidence the comments left by readers of the latter research and we see a picture of a broken society, a society broken by the wedge driven between the sexes. What might have caused that?

Original posted on: 10 March 2023.

For those who would lament the decline of intimate relationships, there are disconcerting signs of this in the younger age range (under 30). My review of marriage and cohabitation data is effectively an introduction to the Pew survey which seems to provide the clearest picture of the declining interest in intimate relationships amongst the under-30s. But most revealing are the comments left by viewers of a CNN programme which presented the findings of that Pew survey. I include a sample of those comments at the end of this article. They suggest a picture of a broken society.

Readers will be aware of the declining popularity of marriage. The extent of this decline may be gauged from the number of marriages annually or from the marriage rate, defined as the number of marriages per year per 1,000 in the unmarried population. The upper graph in Figure 54.1 shows the decline in the number of marriages annually, whilst the lower graph shows the even steeper decline in marriage rate terms. For men, the peak marriage rate, in 1972, was 84 per year per thousand unmarried men. By 2019 this had dropped to 18.6 per thousand, barely more than one-fifth of its peak rate.

However, I caution you against falling into the same trap of misinterpretation that I fell into myself initially. The steep decline in marriage rate is partly a result of people getting married later. Because of that, the percentage of people who are unmarried has increased. Since the number of unmarried people serves as the denominator in the definition of marriage rate, this drives down the marriage rate – and this would be the case even if the percentage of people who marry eventually remained the same. Statistics, eh? One needs to be careful.

On the other hand, the absolute number of marriages provides an under-estimate of the extent of the decline in the popularity of marriage when the overall population has been increasing. A better measure of the current popularity of marriage is simply the percentage of people who are married (in which I include civil partnerships). This is given by Figure 54.2.

Number of opposite-sex marriages and rates, England and Wales, 1929 to 2019

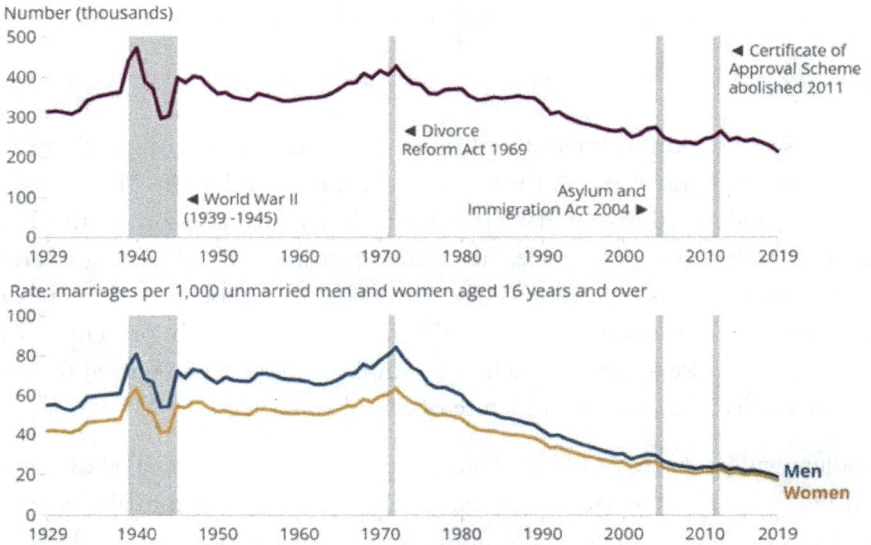

Source: Office for National Statistics – Marriages in England and Wales

Figure 54.1: Taken from Ref.[1]

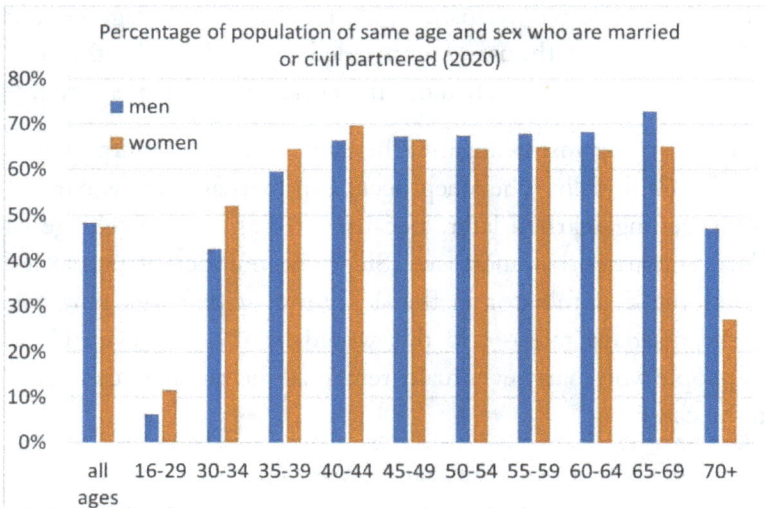

Figure 54.2: Taken from Ref.[1] (data for England and Wales)

This provides a rather different picture for those in midlife to just over retirement age (40 to 69), for which about 65% to 70% are currently married.

However, far fewer people in their early 30s are married, and an extremely small percentage of the under 30s. Is this merely because people are getting married later, or will this cohort persist in remaining unmarried as they age? In other words, does it indicate a new disinclination to marry at all, ever? Later marriage will certainly account for some of it, but there are signs that a genuine turning away from marriage is also occurring among the young.

One needs to be slightly careful of the data in the 16 – 29 age range. One would hardly expect many 16- or 17-year olds to be married (and this has just been made illegal in the UK, Ref.[2]). This will bias down the percentage married in the 16 – 29 age range. On the other hand, it is worth recalling that, 50 years ago, most women were married with children in their 20s. (My cousin was married as soon as she turned 16 and was pregnant soon after. 55 years later she remains happily married, to the same man, and has a close family).

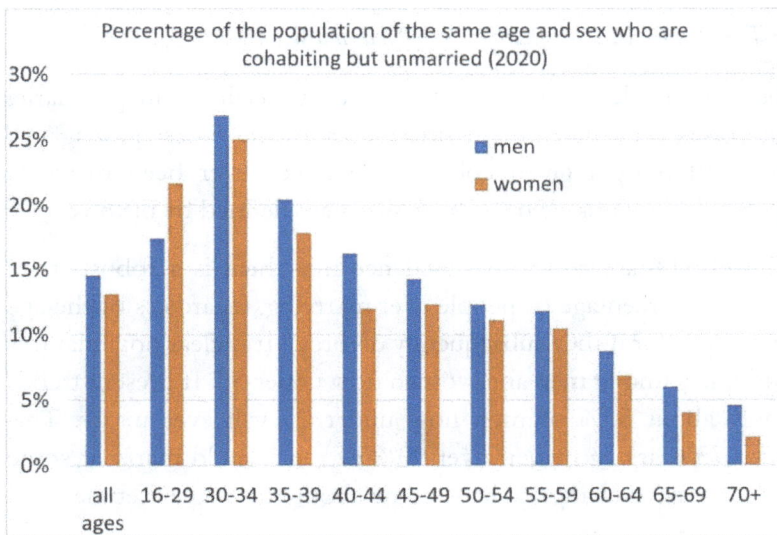

Figure 54.3: Taken from Ref.[1] (data for England and Wales)

Figure 54.3 shows the number of people cohabiting, but unmarried, as a percentage of the population of the same age and sex. Figure 54.4 shows the number of people cohabiting or married, as a percentage of the population of the same age and sex. Between the ages of 30 to 69 roughly 70% to 80%

of the population have a live-in intimate relationship. This raises a question as to whether the decline of intimate relationships is indeed real, or just an aspect of such relationships being delayed to later life.

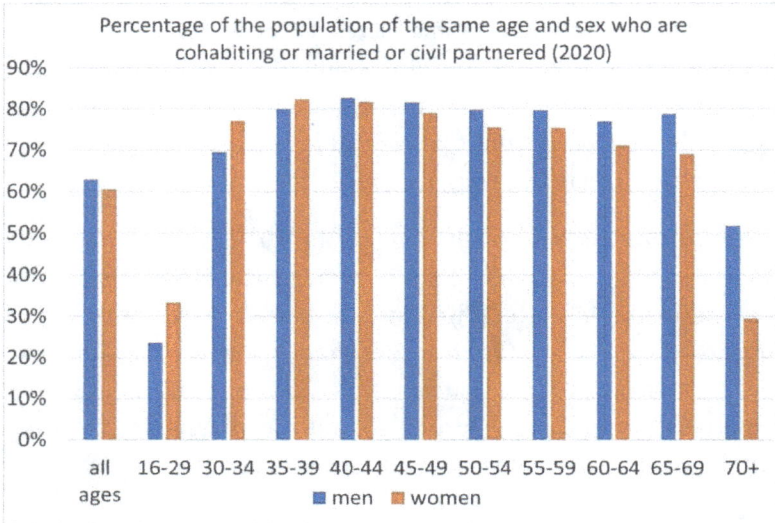

Figure 54.4: Taken from Ref.[1] (data for England and Wales)

One key piece of evidence that marriage is truly declining in popularity amongst the young is provided by Figures 54.5 and 54.6. These plot against year the proportion of a given cohort who have "ever been married" (regardless of current status), where the cohorts are defined by birth year.

Figure 54.5 and 54.6 are conclusive evidence that there is a robust trend towards a smaller percentage of people ever marrying, regardless of the age at which they do so (or if they subsequently divorce). It is clear now that this trend is continuing among men and women now under-30. If present trends continue, only about 50% of men now under 25 will ever marry. This contrasts with 75 years ago when over 90% of men would marry at some time. This is a dramatic change to have come about in a single lifetime.

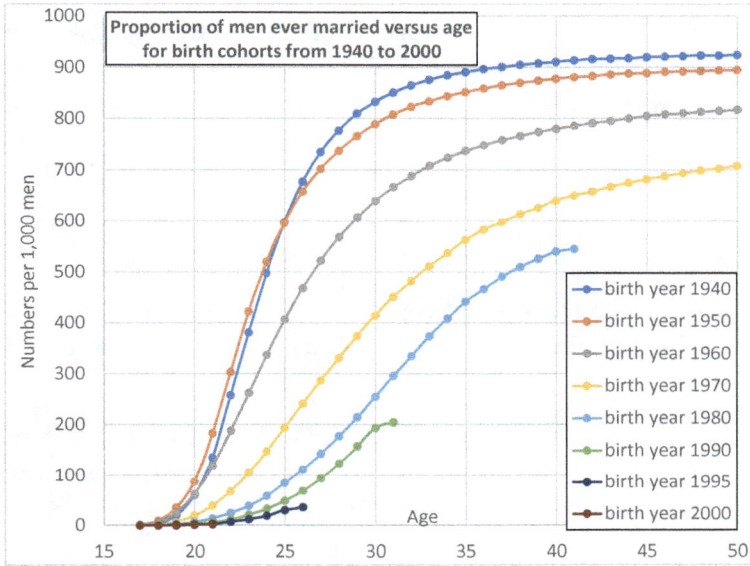

Figure 54.5: Proportion of Men Ever Married Versus Age: Different Birth Cohorts Compared (data from Ref.[3])

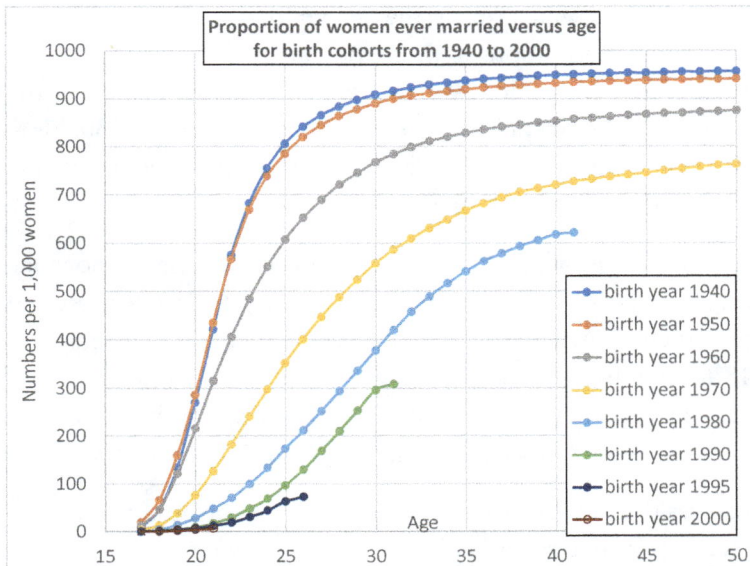

Figure 54.6: Proportion of Women Ever Married Versus Age: Different Birth Cohorts Compared (data from Ref.[3])

And that brings us to the Pew Research survey in the USA, Ref.[4]. The term "single" is used here to mean "not married, not living with a partner and/or not in a committed romantic relationship". The key results were,

- 63% of men in the age range 18 to 29 in the USA are single, compared with 34% of women.

- Across all ages, 32% of men in the USA are single.

- Across all ages and both sexes, of people who are single, most (57%) are not currently looking for a relationship of any kind – not even casual dating.

- The proportion of single men in the USA who are not looking for an intimate relationship of any kind, not even dating opportunities, has increased substantially from 39% in 2019 to 50% in 2022.

- The proportion of single women in the USA who are not looking for an intimate relationship of any kind, not even dating opportunities, has increased slightly from 62% in 2019 to 65% in 2022.

This paints a picture in which even the active desire for an intimate relationship is disappearing amongst those not already "sorted". This is especially the case for the under-30s, though not exclusively. And the phenomenon appears to be of epidemic proportions for men under 30. Note that the Pew data relates to being inactive even in seeking dating opportunities, even for casual hook-ups.

To this one can add the growing evidence of the decline in the proportions of people having sex (penile-vaginal intercourse) in, say, the last year. Ref.[5] reports a large survey of Americans which revealed that the percentage of people aged 18 to 49 who have not had sex at all in the last year increased from 23% in 2009 to 28% in 2018. Of those having sex, the frequency has declined. Trends amongst adolescents also indicate reduced frequency of sex.

There was a discussion of these Pew survey results on the American news outlet CNN, Ref.[6] (rather remarkably). Many issues were raised, mostly quite sensible, though, inevitably, porn got blamed. I don't think so. I doubt that porn drives less interest in relationships. The causality is, I suspect, the reverse: failing access to relationships drives interest in porn. "Online misogyny" also got blamed (I suspect this is a contractual obligation at CNN) especially from "people masquerading as men's advocates". (To paraphrase:

the decline in intimate relations is my fault, apparently). However, the fact that the issue was aired on CNN, and in a largely sympathetic manner, is novel and welcome.

The phenomenon of young men in particular checking out of relationships may not come as a surprise to parents of sons or daughters in their 20s or 30s. My own sons, aged 36 and 38, are not married nor in relationships. Of my 12 nephews and nieces, all in their 30s or 40s, just three are married, four are cohabiting, and five are unpartnered, and this has been a long-standing condition. There are just three grandchildren. Together with my wife, my siblings and my wife's siblings and their partners, if any, this amounts to 13 in the "grandparent" generation who have had between them 14 children, now all over 30. And these 14 adult 'children' have, so far, resulted in just three grandchildren. Whilst there is likely to be some more to come (maybe), my own extended family's fertility is currently running at a rate woefully below replacement.

The reasons for this declining interest in seeking a relationship, even a casual one, will be many and varied. But the reactions to the CNN programme, as judged by the comments left, are salutary. The overwhelming bulk of the comments were left by men. They paint such a picture that I have listed a large proportion of the comments below. There were a few along the lines "I have found a great girlfriend/wife, etc", but only a very few in proportion. There were also a few comments from women, some of which described their own despair at finding a suitable partner. But the selection below is a fair representation of the overwhelming bulk of the comments – and include all those with the largest numbers of "likes". You will see that there are certain comment themes which occur over and over again...

- The adverse impact of social media in replacing real-life social interactions;
- The skewed effects of online dating apps from which only the top 20% of men get any interest;
- The poisonous, stressful up-hill struggle that is the dating scene, especially modern women's unrealistic demands;
- That dating is too expensive for many men to afford now, since the man is still expected to pay for everything;
- Men's fear of losing everything in divorce;
- Men's fear of false allegations;

- That the whole business of relationships is a huge amount of effort, expense and risk for little reward.

Of course, I know that viewers' comments do not constitute science. But has "science" as it is currently practiced in the academy elicited men's reasons for checking out of relationships? Pouring opprobrium on incels doesn't count. The self-pitying few who take to the internet to whine are merely symptomatic of the vastly greater number of the genuinely disenfranchised whose voice is revealed here.

Do bear in mind that the comments were taken from a CNN programme – which one might not expect to draw an audience especially sympathetic to men. This makes the resulting comment stream even more revealing. The comments paint a picture of a society which is broken. The usual culprits will, of course, interpret all this as misogyny. No, this is the world that feminism has created, a world of atomised, lonely young people with soaring rates of mental ill-health. A world in which a large and growing proportion of young men have given up on women. It was predictable. It was predicted.

The Comments taken from Ref.[6] on 8 March 2023

- I gave up on dating because I was tired of being made to feel both like an ATM and a therapist. (3,500 upvotes)
- I'm 43 and I've noticed this shift gradually over the last 20 years. Social media has filled the gap of social needs of many rather than actually going out and having meaningful relationships, either romantically or platonically. There is a reason we have an anxiety and depression problem in this country. A lot of people have become shut-ins and some (not all of them) haven't developed the social skills to function in a public setting and that brings a lot of anxiety to some. (1,600 upvotes)
- I can't imagine dating in the digital age. It must be a nightmare. (833 upvotes)
- Having been brought up in Mexico of an American mother and Mexican father and exposed equally to both cultures, I have always noticed that emotional bonds between people in the US are much, much weaker. People don't have wide social circles. Their nonchalant attitude toward people they should feel close to, and just how they greet them, the lack of interest in their lives, is astounding. (747 upvotes)

- I'm a 39 year old single man with no kids. I have no interest in dating anymore because I don't see the benefit in doing so. I've worked so hard to get where I'm at financially. I can't imagine getting married, then a divorce and seeing half of everything that I worked so hard for go out the window because she's not happy. I no longer want kids either. I'm just tired of dealing with the lies and games, bad attitude, the manipulation, being a stepdad to her kids, being looked at as a wallet and not a person. I'm done! I finally have peace, I'm stress free, no drama, I can save more, invest more, do anything I want to now. I'm much happier single compared to being in a relationship. I'm not sure if this will change for me 3-5 years from now but as of right now, I don't want to be bothered. (674 upvotes)
- The recent rent exploits are putting the final nail in this coffin – how can a young man afford to pay rent, college loans, and everything else, and still have money to go out and socialize. A single short evening at a bar can cost $50 – these days that is basically all the money many people have left in their budget after paying the bills. Even if you meet a girl, that night – you can't even afford to take her out again…(631 upvotes)
- Yep I'm a trucker and I'm 24 and feel so alone sometimes. I cry and I feel better but it never goes away. No one cares. (581 upvotes)
- This problem – how social media has affected socializing – will seemingly only continue to get worse and worse. You can't put social media back in the bottle. As a 27 year old guy, I already noticed this trend when I was a senior in high school, back in 2014. Everyone was on their smartphones and not talking in "social gatherings". 9 years later, things have only gotten worse regarding this. You don't see neighbours, people in coffee shops, or those at events socialize. Nobody talks anymore. (572 upvotes)
- I'm 49, and I feel very sorry for the younger generations. I think mine was the last that had genuine fun and community. (536 upvotes).
- This is not limited to young people, and it's time to recognize the fact that there is a very large portion of people in this world that fight every day to find reasons to go on living. (515 upvotes)
- Spent my entire 20s being depressed and thinking I needed a girl in my life. But once I realized happiness comes from within, I stopped looking for someone else to make me happy. You also become stronger and more attractive and feel a sense of self-worth. Don't worry about what

women want, care about what you want! and let women do what they do. You just might discover how great life can be and people will flock towards that energy, men, women and everything in between alike. (503 upvotes)

- The last time I had a girlfriend was when I was 18, for about 3 months (I don't know if you count that as a relationship). I'm 30 now and I haven't been in a relationship since then. I've gone on some dates and let me tell you, it's exhausting. I'm not upset at my situation. I'm just tired. I eventually realized I don't need someone else to be happy. I also kind of developed a fear of approaching women because I'm afraid I might be labelled a creep or be falsely accused of sexual harassment/assault. I don't think this is a big deal because there are worse problems I could be dealing with. I still have a roof over my head and food in my belly. I accept my situation and count my blessings every day. I understand deep down most people want love (including myself) but I also understand that life doesn't always make sense or goes the way you want it to. (491 upvotes).
- As a single early 30s guy, I've lost almost all hope of having a family. Can't seem to afford anything more than a room in a house. I can't find an actual home, and I can see 10 years from now having serious issues mentally, assuming this keeps up. (458 upvotes)
- So glad I saw this report. I am sixty and physically disabled with cerebral palsy. I worked my way though college, learned to drive, and held different jobs. All of that was a cakewalk compared to dating. I have found my social outlet via volunteering. It is truly amazing the type of people you meet. I used to read for the visually impaired on the radio and had an absolute blast doing it. I now volunteer at a local hospital three days a week and totally enjoy it. (438 upvotes)
- I'm in my mid 30s and have been single for a couple of years now. I've had 2 serious long-term relationships and had had my heart broken twice. There was also a lot of baggage and drama brought into my life with those relationships. I'm terrified to date. I don't want any drama or someone else pointing out how I'm ineffectively meeting their needs (even though I gave everything I had in the last relationship). Every now and then I think that I should put myself back into the dating pool due to societal pressures, but my life is peaceful alone. My peace is everything. (421 upvotes)

- Dating apps have pretty much ruined real-life dating. The algorithms they use are broken. Before these apps it was easier to just meet people in a bar or club and strike up a conversation. Now you notice that not many people really talk outside of their social circles when in the real world. Improving income or level of education doesn't solve the root cause. (397 upvotes)

- I'm single, I'm older and I just cannot handle dating anymore. It's way too stressful. (393 upvotes)

- Mid 30s here. Childless, debt free, stress free and living alone. Dateless and really don't care. I have lived frugally for so long that I have more money in the bank than I know what to do with. I moved to one of the lowest cost-of-living areas in 2016 so I could save even more money. My hobbies and smoking weed is what keeps me going. Disregard what society tells you, live however you see fit. You'll be dead one day and none of this will even matter. (380 upvotes)

- As a guy married for twenty one years, I never cheated, never hung out in the bars with the guys, never once hit her, made good money and provided a beautiful home, and helped produced two beautiful and successful children. But it was never good enough. She chose to cheat on me, divorce me, and to finally marry a city sewer worker, who was an alcoholic and beat her up. She is now divorced from him too. After having another girlfriend for 13 years who could never commit to anything, I give up. I'd rather put my efforts into something that provides benefits. (351 upvotes)

- Stay single. That's my advice. Almost all my friends that married are now divorced, having to start all over again financially. The ones that never seem to manage life on their own chase another partner, calling it "love" every time – but are just whitewashing sleeping around. They are afraid of being alone, and it must be terrible. Even worse is to stay in a bad marriage for economic reasons. That's a prison sentence. Be free, I say, value your single status and stay true to yourself. (350 upvotes)

- Dating is really expensive. Women don't often appreciate how tough it can be to pay for it all. And I'm saying this as a woman. A cheap date is still around $50 per person. Times two, for just one date a week, and that's $400 a month. That's your groceries or your car maintenance. Cost of living is crazy now, so dating can have you living paycheck to paycheck, eat up your savings, or put you in debt for someone who may or may not be all that into you. Women look to men to have their back and secure their future, and that puts so much pressure on men. When they have a hard time with it, women lose interest and act like the dude is a loser. Men don't want to keep feeling like failures in the eyes of attractive women and all of their judgmental girlfriends. It *is* depressing to feel like love and starting a family is out of your reach. So, it's no wonder men would rather work, stay home, save their money and their self-esteem as single men. (311 upvotes)

- I gave up on dating in my late 20s because it felt like being like a dog chasing mating opportunities. Ton of work with too little reward. Primitive, stupid, and making you feel stupid for doing it. 10 years later, I still see that as a very wise decision (even though I doubted myself a couple of times, during a few years, and re-tried dating). (303 upvotes)
- Today's American women have a really skewed set of requirements for men. I went on a date with a girl who said she only eats out at fancy restaurants. She makes $42k a year. She then hinted at a $1,500 Gucci purse for her birthday too. Too many looking for sugar daddies, not partners. (234 upvotes)
- I'm 27 and haven't dated or been in a relationship my whole life so far. I have been trying dating apps this past year but they are absolutely useless, I can hardly ever get any likes or matches. As far as trying to meet women in real life, it seems useless too because people are not friendly to strangers. (222 upvotes)
- The underlying implication is that you have to be in a relationship to be happy. Many of us have found that we're perfectly happy being single, and we're under less social pressure to be in relationships than we were in past generations. (219 upvotes)
- The older I've gotten (now 45), the happier I've become doing my own thing. I got burned out on the dating apps (online dating was a bit easier before it went mobile). I recently bought a small place in a downtown neighbourhood so that has taken up most of my time along with my hobbies. There's tons of good looking eligible people out there I think but when I go to my favourite spots for a drink or a burger, I see that single people aren't going to these places. Then there's the whole notion that if you ask a woman out and she deems you below her standards, you're a creep and will end up in a TikTok video. (210 upvotes)

- I stopped dating at 19, currently 30 and haven't been in a relationship since. I made a conscious choice back then to stop dating because I wanted to find myself and what I wanted. I realized I was happier alone. Women being hypergamous makes dating a constant game of trying to prove oneself with very little actual payoff. I came to the conclusion that there are four main reasons to be in a relationship: 1. pleasure (can be achieved without a partner); 2. companionship (can be achieved through a pet); 3. help around the house (can be achieved with a roommate, family, or hired help); 4. reproduction (I honestly couldn't care less). (202 upvotes)
- The important thing to note here is that young men aren't just failing to find romantic relationships, they're failing at finding any sort of relationship. 1 in 7 young men don't have any close friends. It was 1 in 33 for the previous generation. Human beings have lost their sense of community, and it's affecting young men the most because women do have some built-in solidarity through political and social movements. Young men don't. (201 upvotes)
- I'm 26, never been in what I'd call a relationship, and never had sex. It's definitely not easy, most of the time I feel like I don't even belong on this planet. People certainly don't go out of their way to make you feel valued. Being black on top of being a man, it can seem like the whole world hates you. But, I'm too stubborn to just give up at this point, for better or for worse. That feeling of being picked last — or not at all — doesn't feel good, so I've simply decided to 'improve my draft stock' so to speak. I've decided to just focus on myself, learn as many skills as possible, invest in my body and mind, and draw nearer to God. Essentially I'll make myself such a valuable human being, that it'll be hard for anyone to pass on me — be it a woman, job, business opportunities etc. At some point, the right ones will notice. I'm bound to find success at some point, right? (187 upvotes)
- I'm 40 and I gave up on dating and relationships because I spent the past 20 years of my life trying to find love and realized that none of those women truly loved me. I kept at it for 20 years because women would say "pick better" or "you haven't found the right one". The hard truth is there are no unicorns. The only woman that truly loved me for me was my mother, may her soul rest in peace. Now I'm in a loving

517

relationship with myself. All the love and energy I used to give to women now I give it to myself. (167 upvotes)

- I'm 50, single and never been married. Yes, women are picky but I'm imperfect and I do have my many flaws so it's totally understandable. My focus now is being a more loving and kind person, being of assistance to the young and elderly and being more useful to my congregation. We live in imperfect conditions but we can still experience inner peace. (161 upvotes)

- As a 19 year old guy about to be 20 living in the centre of this I guarantee the number of suicides and overdoses are going to increase. I see how bad it is. I live every day in isolation, my only social life is my therapist, and talking to my friends on the phone. I have tried to make friends, and I have tried in the dating world. I am not sure why but this world just loves to kick you when you are already down. (156 upvotes)

- I lived in San Francisco 1992-95 when I was in my late 20s and met women through newspaper, magazine and alternative weekly personals. Online personals didn't exist yet. It was an unpleasant experience. All of my dates were snotty, shallow, materialistic, flaky, deceitful and neurotic. For those reasons, I didn't even score once. The fact that I am a college graduate and was gainfully employed and financially secure with a personal net worth in seven figures didn't help me. All my dates had unrealistic expectations. I think San Francisco is a dating cesspool. I later decided that I don't need a woman to be happy, they actually caused me more problems and heartache. (156 upvotes)

- I spent my 20's trying not to starve to death. I was 30 when I met my daughter's mom. She divorced me immediately after getting pregnant, fed my kid a narrative resulting in her not talking to me to this day, and has continued to milk me financially for 18+ years (293 days left). I'm nearly 50 now and I think lots of younger men saw guys like me and their own dads live miserable lives and have decided it's not for them. It's less painful, and cheaper, to be miserable alone. You've been telling us we are useless and not needed for anything other than the check we are forced to send every month for so long, we totally believe it at this point. Put that in your National Birth-rate and smoke it. (135 upvotes)

- It's got nothing to do with age. The point is that the whole dating game has totally changed in about 2019-20 when it started to become nearly impossible for a normal man not being in the top 20% to get into a relationship. Whether you are 20, 30, 40 or 50 – if you are single today, you have a high chance of remaining single. (115 upvotes)

- What I find funny is how none of these conversations – in the mainstream press – are focused on why it is important to encourage these young men to become better people to help ***them***. It is always focused on how the growing number of lonely and discarded young men will hurt the society around them. Nobody cares about those young men until it is a problem for everyone else. Hell, they still sneak the talking point that "Men have had a head start for 300,000 years" in there, signalling the idea that patriarchy was a consistent evil until they "corrected" it. Until we change that attitude and start focusing on helping young men because these young men f****** ***deserve*** to be helped and encouraged we're not going to go anywhere. (100 upvotes)

- Dating as a man nowadays is pretty tough, unfortunately. Women are so incredibly picky these days due to online dating because it makes women always think that they can find someone better. I have most things that women tend to look for in a man yet I'm still single and okay with that. It isn't worth trying because dating tends to not go anywhere these days. I only date women that ask me out or make very very clear hints that they want to date because those women are showing that they might not be a waste of time, money, and emotions. It isn't worth it for men to chase these days. (100 upvotes)

- I think most young men have just given up. My single son wants to meet a good woman, settle down and have kids, but cannot see himself taking on the responsibilities of being a husband and father with the current society and financial troubles.

- I'm 37, I live alone and haven't been in a meaningful relationship in 7 years. On a scale of mediocre to very attractive I probably fit between mediocre and slightly handsome. But what I lack in looks I make up for in conversation. I haven't had sex in two years, and to be honest it was probably pity sex from her, because we were both lonely on New Years. Majority of the women I've conversed with aren't interested in a traditional relationship anymore. They want men who will be fine with their overwhelming social media presence and fluid sexual ambiguity. Finding a woman that isn't obsessed with Tik Tok, Instagram and snap stories well into her mid 30's is rare. That is absolutely scary!

- I'm 31 and have been single since my ex and I broke up in 2016. I was interested in dating for a few years afterward but it was too much of a hassle and I grew to like being single. The cons of a relationship far outweigh the pros.

- I am 33 years old female from Brazil, South America. I participated in an exchange program in the US when I was 18 years old. Already at that time, as a foreigner, I found American women very critical and acidic towards men. I'm not saying that Latin American culture is ideal, our culture is more sexist, but I also don't think the way most American women treat men is healthy.

- I'm 37 and have been married for 12 years, but I would say the thing that helped me as a young man was going to a social gathering every week (church). As a shy and introverted person normally I think it's important to put yourself out there whether you feel like it or not. Join a social group if you can. I worry about the young ones out there.

- As a female who's never really dated or been in a relationship (i.e., asexual)....I feel for men today, and women as well. It seems relationships are rarely genuine and most of them are transactional. Even myself, who doesn't want to date or have sex with anyone, still engages in romance/smex through fiction, fan shipping and imaginative pursuits. If I were to put myself out there then I'd want something meaningful, magnetic and passionate: people who'd really give a damn. Most people unfortunately don't. We live in a selfish era of history. Everything is superficial.

- I'm not 6 feet tall, I don't have 6 pack abs, and I don't have a 6 figure income. The vast swaths of women in America don't want me, so I gave up trying when I was 20 years old. That was 16 years ago and I've long accepted that things are only going to get worse. Women seem to have no problem all sharing the tall, rich, and attractive dude and complaining about him cheating with 10 other women. This is the world women wanted.

- I'm 30 and single and stopped dating. Unlike everyone else though, I did have a girlfriend previously pre-pandemic, and I was seeing someone last year. Nothing worked out because I either fell out of love, or I made mistakes and felt I couldn't recover from them. I genuinely think it's better for me to stay single, I'm neither boyfriend nor husband material. I wish society would leave us alone in this choice.

- The thing that struck me was the friendlessness. I think we need to promote men making friends with each other in a wider variety of settings (outside of sports and drinking). Maybe what we need are more public spaces and organized social activities? (*WC comment: Feminism has systematically, and with deliberate intent, eliminated all male-only spaces. Consequently, men's lack of same-sex socialising is, in part (not entirely) a result of feminism*).

- Thank you all for actually taking the time to report on this issue. It's real and no one thinks it's "cool" to care about men's issues. Or even believe that men have any issues. Men are just looked at as the toxic incel patriarchy that are holding women back from being more man-like. It would be kind of funny if it weren't so real and rampant.

- Women are too much hassle. You have to make the first move and get rejected hundreds of times, plan the dates, navigate her emotional labyrinth while meeting her stringent modern female standards. You have to do all the work. Once you get to your 30's you are stuck with obese single mothers.

- Nowadays if you happen to like your coworker, your friend, or even just a random person you met at a social function, and you "make a move" to see if they would be interested in you, it's now this awkward social environment where the other person doesn't know how to respond to your advances or automatically thinks you're a creep or something. People can't just vibe with each other and test the waters, take a little risk. I say this as a 20 year old man. It sucks, really. It can be so lonely when the expectation of society is that you simply do not interact with anyone. Heaven forbid actually complimenting someone or trying to be interesting and see if they like you too.

- (*WC comment: There is a large public poster in the main shopping centre in Bristol, UK, which lists the prohibitions which men are expected to respect in regard to their interactions with women, in order not to be guilty of misogyny or "violence against women". One of these is complimenting a woman. It is indubitably true that feminism has driven a wedge between the sexes very effectively. Young women seem to be unaware of how men have been confined – essentially by women themselves – in a situation where initiating any relationship with the opposite sex is so fraught with risk that it is no longer worth the effort or potential downside. The reason why so many young women are unaware of this is the empathy gap: a radical inability to place themselves in the position of men*).

- There's two major reasons (for the decline in interest in relationships). First, a lot of men have determined that it's not in their interest to be in a relationship considering the way society is. It's just one giant double standard. You can't expect your girlfriend to do any housework whether she works or not, you're expected to pay for everything whether she works or not, but she gets to keep all her money for herself. When she's done using you, she gets all the advantages in court to your children or your finances. She can also make a false accusation against you whenever she feels like it which will automatically be believed, etc. It's a mixture of 1950s patriarchy and modern feminism, taking all the features of each one that disadvantages men and leaving behind all the ones that disadvantage women or make them equal. The second reason is that men are not doing well in modern capitalism. Our wages are much lower and society doesn't care, so we're just going straight downhill. At the same time, women are completely unwilling to adjust to that new reality. They're still expecting a guy with a huge income along with all kinds of other prince charming fantasy traits, and they refuse to except anything less, and are encouraged to do so. It's pretty basic stuff.

- I'm 41 and have no kids, no girl, no one. I'm so used to being alone and ignored by women, I'm used to it and now I've got that I don't care when it comes to women because I've been single for so long. I'm happy and contented being single and I see no point in getting a woman. Besides they have that cold hearted attitude.

- The things that women find attractive in men are also things they can accomplish for themselves without a man. For example: a house, car, career, financial stability, status, etc. All of these can be accomplished by a woman without a man. Men, and the things that make them attractive, are separable from each other in the eyes of women, and many of these women are questioning why they should bother with a man at all when they can essentially fulfil these roles for themselves. I believe that's the reason we see so much open hatred and misandry towards men these days. Women don't need men, and female nature has a way of dehumanizing the men they don't need.

- I am 36. I find contentment in living a solitary life as a man. My past experiences have revealed that the presence of women in my life often invites needless drama and complexities. Moreover, the family court system's shortcomings have left me with a sense of disenfranchisement as a father. In light of these circumstances, I see little incentive to pursue romantic relationships. Instead, I prefer to find solace in my own company, engage in personal hobbies, and avoid the emotional strains and grievances that often accompany relationships.

- How many men, beginning in elementary school, have been falsely accused of something by a female? And then faced consequences for something they didn't do? That is a big reason young and older men will avoid women. It's a huge gamble to be sociable with women in the office. So many men don't. Human Resources (HR) will protect women at all costs even if the allegation is "sketchy" at best. Once a man leaves the office, why would he think he was safer or his chances of being treated well and respected were better? In American society they're not. Ignoring and avoiding women is a self defence mechanism for men who value their reputation and hard-earned assets.

- We've eliminated men-only spaces, incentivized women to leave relationships, and have told men for years that if you don't meet a laundry list of requirements/expectations you aren't worth investing time in a relationship with….and we wonder why men are saying no to relationships all together?

- Women view 80% of men 'unattractive'. Not by character, personality, ethics, morals, demeanor, style… it's by physical appearance. So right off the bat, without any consideration to a man's character he is deemed unworthy of attention. That is one of the major causes of this situation. And it will get worse. If society does not address this, there is going to be a horrible impact to all of us as a whole. Everyone will feel the effects and it won't be pretty.

- At 25 I'm starting to accept I just might be single forever and I'm ok with that. My life is peaceful and I focus on my purpose. I will not entertain or give a woman my resources. Every man I know who is married tells me not to get married or all they do is complain about how their wives are causing stress. All in all, I cannot take the risk of welcoming a woman into my life especially in America.

- I'm a 56 year old male and never been on a date. There are some people who are always left without a chair when the music stops. God, life, fate, the universe… whatever you call it plays favourites and there is nothing those of us who are cursed can do about it.

- I'm a manager in the I.T. world and never in my life seen so many young men single. When I talk to these young men they just don't want the hassle of dealing with modern women, so they gave up on women. A lot of these young men are six figure earners and hang out with other men that feel the same way they do; going out driving their fast cars, golfing, riding motorcycles, and things like that.
- (*From a woman*): I have heard many men in their thirties and forties say they don't want to get married because if it does not work out they do not want to have to pay alimony, or lose their house or half of their pensions or 401k. Men will not lose what they work for their entire life if they do not get married.
- Since a look, a touch, a word, a thought, is now a prosecutable sexual assault, men are saying to themselves "why bother?" I'd like to have someone at my side, but the financial, legal and emotional costs are far too high. Not only do women earn a lot more money than they used to, they want to get your money, too. Being alone has simply become the way to go.

A couple from mothers…

- Any parent of teen or young adult males has seen this coming for years. It's incredibly sad.
- I feel so bad for my son. He's a toddler now but my worry is that relationships will become more of a thing of the past by the time he's an adult. Almost like he will be looking for the love of his life and his crush will just be looking to destroy his self-esteem.

References

[1] Office for National Statistics (2022). *Marriages in England and Wales: 2019*. Dataset published 19 May 2022.

[2] Daily Mail (2023). *Marriage age rises from 16 to 18 today under new law which aims to protect children from forced weddings including non-legally binding 'traditional' ceremonies*. Mail Online, 27 February 2023.

[3] Office for National Statistics (2023). *Marriages in England and Wales*. 2022 Dataset published 11 May 2023 (Tables 14a,b).

[4] Gelles-Watnick, R. (2023). *For Valentine's Day, 5 facts about single Americans*. Pew Research Centre, 8 February 2023.

[5] Herbenick, D., et al. (2022). *Changes in Penile-Vaginal Intercourse Frequency and Sexual Repertoire from 2009 to 2018: Findings from the National Survey of Sexual Health and Behaviour*. Archives of Sexual Behaviour 51, 1419–1433, (2022), 19 November 2022.

[6] CNN (2023). *Why the rate of single men in the US looking for dates has declined*. YouTube, 25 February 2023.

Section 11

Books: Reviews, Extracts, Authors

55. A Gentleman's Guide

This is a review of the 2021 book "A Gentleman's Guide to Manners, Sex and Ruling the World" by Stephen Baskerville.

Original posted on: *24 August 2021*

This book is rather wonderful. It is a book whose time has come. It will be hard for the gender-fluid denizens of Wokeville to believe that a work so fearlessly Incorrect can still be written. Its true nature will be entirely beyond their grasp. Oh dear, what a pity, never mind.

The delight of the book for me is its sly humour. A gentleman, I dare say, should be willing – on occasion, but judiciously – to deploy such humour in the service of matters of deadly seriousness. So it is here. Anyone wishing to cock their own particular snook at the relentlessly Correct could learn from this masterly example…such as,

"While a gentleman might not be greatly aroused by the spectre of global warming, it has been observed that he will not neglect to take any measures necessary to ensure the comfort of his hunting hounds."

The apoplexy induced in many by this insouciant disregard for all that is currently regarded as holy is cathartic to contemplate.

Dr Baskerville explains the difference between his work and the deluge of instructions to men, invariably stemming from women's complaints against us. This book, he tells us, is about the logic behind the rules, though he does not disregard the importance of Good Form. You may usefully take advice from many sources, he advises, on *"how to fit a suit, pass the dishes at a dinner party, or do battle with a crocodile"* and, he adds, *"while you are at it, it may be time to consider dispensing with the tattoos and body piercings and backward baseball caps."* (Ugh! The thought!).

Grammarians will be delighted to find an ally in Dr Baskerville: *"Your appearance will be a challenge you must live up to (or, because a gentleman always uses correct grammar, up to which you must live)".*

There is much sound advice, such as *"never argue with a fool because a third party does not know which one is the fool".*

There are examples aplenty of the art of the elegant put-down, such as when quoting Jean-Jacques Rousseau, "*I can only meditate when I am walking. When I stop, I cease to think*", to which Baskerville adds, "*Given that his pensées were the main inspiration behind the French Revolution, it might have been better for everyone if somebody had offered him a lift*". I think the author lets Rousseau off lightly – arguably he is also culpable for Wokeness and many points in between, too,.

As an atheist I am not sure I am entitled to express vigorous agreement with the following, though I do so anyway: "*Any church where the presiding clergyperson is a woman is almost certainly more of a political outfit than a real church and is best avoided, unless you wish to be harangued about your proclivity for domestic violence and rape.*"

And speaking of religion, here's a passage which illustrates the inseparability of the gentlemanly from the numinous, but in the same beguiling humorous tone deployed throughout: "*It has been said that 'a gentleman believes in God because by and large he is confident that God believes in him'. This irony is not so flippant as it might sound. Religious beliefs – at least the best ones – impel us to obey the rules not simply because otherwise bad consequences will ensue, including serious punishments to ourselves. At some point, we at least try to obey because gradually we come to feel that to do so is to act in ways that are consistent with the logic of the universe. There is no better preparation for being a gentleman.*"

However, it is not all fun and games, poking at the conceits of our critics. There is a hard core to this book. It concerns how we men – we aspiring gentlemen – should be responding in this age of misandry. It is, I fear, a message whose importance will vie with its likelihood to be misunderstood. This message becomes most emphatic in the last chapter, wherein the author instructs that we should "stop rebelling", but the message is presaged here and there throughout. I indulge in a long quote by way of illustration,

"*Nowadays, when men as a group have fallen to about the lowest status in their history, it might be worth considering the value of taking the moral high ground and rising above the sordid pursuit of individual 'empowerment', the finger-pointing, and victim-mongering, and seek a code of conduct that is more elevated than that of others...*

...a gentleman must not be afraid of being hated, and one of the gentlemanly qualities that is most difficult to put into practice is how to respond to reproaches, insults, criticism, and hatred. You might recall that the seminal figure of the religion that shaped the ideal of a

modern gentleman – Jesus – provided precisely such a model of how to respond, not with vitriol, bitterness, and reciprocal anger…but with humility and sacrifice."

Continuing the serious tone, Dr Baskerville reminds us of a generic characteristic of failing empires: *"When the ruling ethic deteriorates, and before the empire collapses altogether, the administration degenerates into an oppressive bureaucratic tyranny, with the functionaries expanding their turf and making business for themselves by creating the problems they are supposed to be solving."* The reader will think of his or her own examples. The author is clear in this book and in his other works that the deterioration of the ethic in the West is due, in the main, to feminism and the sexualisation of politics. The claims of feminists that they are oppressed, *"rationalises ever-increasing power for politicians, judges, lawyers, and functionaries"*.

As an atheist it is discomforting to acknowledge that Baskerville is right when he opines: *"It is no accident that the status of men has deteriorated directly alongside the status of religion. In societies where religion is still respected, men are still respected."* This is a sentiment which will attract severe criticism in the context of the Taliban's recent ascendancy in Afghanistan – but there are religions and then there are religions.

Dr Baskerville's view on sex, marriage and family is deeply and unapologetically traditional. But he recognises that our culture is now replete with feminist women. His advice is simple: avoid them. The following advice will rankle with both sides in the (so-called) sex war: *"You must accept the responsibility to protect and provide for any woman. It is therefore critical to choose a woman who acknowledges this and accepts the traditional rules and division of labour, rather than one who asserts her 'equality' (another meaningless word in the relations between the sexes). The bottom line: avoid such women."* When it becomes a war between men and women, he reminds us, men lose. This is why it is a cardinal principle for a gentleman never to compete against a woman. (And, I would add, an innate instinct in men to avoid such unfair competition – unfair because men will always lose, society will see to that).

"By all means", writes Baskerville, *"join the MGTOW men and abstain from sex with my blessing, but while you are at it, at least direct your boycott at a constructive purpose: to marginalise bad women, encourage good women, and possibly even – despite your professed intentions – find one of the latter to marry"*. He rightly warns MGTOW against throwing the gentlemanly baby out with the feminist bathwater:

"While you may have other, valid, reasons for a life of celibacy, if you resort to it from fear, you will have largely disqualified yourself from being a gentleman." One cannot accuse Baskerville of being fearful. One wonders whether it will be the feminists or the extreme-MGTOW who will scrag Baskerville first.

The tough message, gentlemen, is that, despite rampant injustice, the particular *noblesse oblige* applicable to the *gentilhomme* is just this: *"You are the end of the road, the buck stops with you. It is you who must build our institutions again from scratch"*. I did say the book had a hard core. *"The moment you put away your rebellion is the moment you will assume your rightful place and begin to rule. Like it or not, the ball is now in your court. Actually, the ball is always in your court….No one ever said that ruling the world would be easy"*.

References

[1] Baskerville, S. (2021). *A Gentleman's Guide to Manners, Sex and Ruling the World*. Sophia Institute Press, 30 July 2021.

56. Captain Cuttle and Jack Bunsby

In 2021 I started pursuing a project to reread the whole of Dickens (in 2024 the project continues with undiminished enjoyment). I thought this extract from my review of Dombey and Son was interesting as an illustration of behaviours which we might have thought modern.

Original posted on: 4 May 2021.

This extract from my review of Charles Dickens' *Dombey and Son* is not at all off-topic, quite the contrary as you will see. One of the foundations of the feminist mindset is a distorted view of history as unrelenting oppression of women. Academic history is poor at exposing the nature of intimate relations in the past. Even so-called social histories tend to be written on a large scale, not the personal scale. As a consequence, perhaps the best guide to relations between the sexes in the past can be found in novels, which have the advantage of focusing on the personal and the intimate.

That novels are, obviously, works of fiction, is not as significant an objection as it might first appear. Authors would deploy character types which their audience would readily recognise. That Lady Catherine de Bourgh did not exist outside the pages of *Pride and Prejudice* is irrelevant to the accuracy of her depiction as representative of a type of powerful dowager. Readers of the time would be familiar with real-life examples. Dickens' *Dombey and Son* is particularly illustrative as its main theme is Mr Dombey's appalling disdain for his daughter in favour of his son, so it is ostensibly a novel which might appeal to feminists – except that the reader is clearly expected to find Mr Dombey monstrously unnatural. However, be that as it may... here is an extract involving two minor characters which gives us an insight into the historical realities of what we would now call domestic abuse.

Captain Cuttle and Jack Bunsby

Captain Cuttle, retired old sea captain, is one of those irresistibly endearing Dickens characters, as simple as he is staunch, the salt of the earth – or, rather, a salt of the sea in this case. Here is Dickens' description, *"No child could have surpassed Captain Cuttle in inexperience of everything but wind and weather, in simplicity, credulity, and generous trustfulness. Faith, hope and charity shared his whole nature among them."*

The captain's difficulties with his landlady, the termagant widow Mrs MacStinger, is an object lesson in domestic abuse, illustrating that there is no need for any intimate relationship for this term to apply. Captain Cuttle was, simply put, terrified of Mrs MacStinger who had a hold over him that we can understand as coercive control. The Victorians clearly had no trouble recognising the phenomenon, though perhaps no specific term for it. At one point we read the captain explaining his recent absence, saying: *"We had some words about the swabbing of these here planks, an she — in short', said the Captain, eyeing the door and relieving himself with a long breath, 'she stopped my liberty.'"*

The captain's flight from the abusive Mrs MacStinger did not relieve him of this fear. Rather, now lodging in old Sol Gay's shop, he remained fearful whenever he ventured out, in case he should run into her. *"The Captain never dreamed that in the event of his being pounced upon by Mrs MacStinger in his walks it would be possible to offer resistance. He felt it could not be done. He saw himself, in his mind's eye, put meekly in a hackney-coach, and carried off to his old lodgings. He foresaw that, once immured there, he was a lost man: his hat gone; Mrs MacStinger watchful of him day and night."* How much clearer could a case of coercive control possibly be?

Captain Cuttle's greatly respected friend Bunsby also suffered under the hand of a controlling landlady, and we intuit that Dickens must have had some first-hand experience of the breed. Relating to Bunsby's removal of the gangway which led to his dwelling on a boat, we read: *"That the great Bunsby, like himself (Cuttle), was cruelly treated by his landlady, and that when her usage of him for the time being was so hard that he could bear it no longer, he set this gulf between them as a last resource."*

Alas, poor Bunsby. Having had the goodness to retrieve the captain's trunk from his previous dwelling with Mrs MacStinger, Bunsby becomes ensnared as her next victim. This, too, is typical of a modern-day serial abuser.

The main theme of *Dombey and Son* may be the sexist treatment by Dombey of his daughter, but Dickens repeatedly reminds us throughout the book that, not only is this an aberrant behaviour specific to Mr Dombey but, if any more widely characteristic of popular sentiment, is confined to the bourgeoisie. The lower orders, we are reminded at many points, experienced very different conditions as regards relations between the sexes. So, the feminists do not get this story all their own way. And certainly not in this particular extract.

In a scene towards the end, Captain Cuttle runs across his old friend Jack Bunsby now securely captured by Mrs MacStinger. They are on their way to church to be wed. Captain Cuttle is justifiably alarmed, not least because Bunsby's demeanour does not speak of voluntary action. Here they are nearing the altar,

"'Jack Bunsby,' whispered the Captain, 'do you do this here of you own free will?'

Mr Bunsby answered, 'No'.

'Why do you do it, then, my lad?' inquired the Captain, not unnaturally.

Bunsby, still looking, and always looking with an immovable countenance, at the opposite side of the world, made no reply.

'Why not sheer off?' said the Captain.

'Eh?' whispered Bunsby, with a momentary gleam of hope.

'Sheer off', said the Captain.

'Where's the good?', retorted the forlorn sage. 'She'd capter me agen'.

'Try!' replied the Captain. 'Cheer up! Come! Now's your time. Sheer off, Jack Bunsby.'

Mr Bunsby merely uttered a suppressed groan.

'Come!' said the Captain, nudging him with his elbow, 'now's your time! Sheer off! I'll cover your retreat. The time's a flying. Bunsby! It's for liberty. Will you once?'

Bunsby was immovable.

'Bunsby!' whispered the Captain, 'will you twice?'

Bunsby wouldn't twice.

'Bunsby!' urged the Captain, 'it's for liberty; will you three times? Now or never!'

Bunsby didn't then, and didn't ever; for Mrs MacStinger immediately afterwards married him.

One of the most frightful circumstances of the ceremony to the Captain, was the deadly interest exhibited therein by Juliana MacStinger; and the fatal concentration of her faculties, with which that promising child, already the image of her parent, observed the whole proceedings. The Captain saw in this a succession of man-traps stretching out infinitely; a series of ages of oppression and coercion, through which the seafaring line was doomed."

57. In Praise of Richmal Crompton

Few authors managed to prick English middle-class conceits quite so effectively as Richmal Crompton in her series of Just William books. Such conceits being archetypal, the stories are still relevant despite dating from the year after World War One.

Original posted on: <u>14 August 2016</u>.

This is another review that you might have thought wildly off-topic. It isn't. And savour this moment. I am unlikely to sing the praises of a suffragette again very soon.

I was not a great reader as a child – I was a boy, after all. I did read several of the *Just William* books, though. I loved them. My experience was the common one. I went right off them when I discovered that Richmal Crompton was a woman. Clearly, my misogyny set in early. But it wasn't misogyny, of course. (I doubt that a 10-year-old boy is capable of such a thing). No, it was shock. Shock at the realisation that an adult woman understood me so well. Because I **was** William Brown, you see – or I would have been had I been possessed of his chutzpah.

William Brown, like Richmal Crompton, was raised in a middle-class English home when the English middle classes were properly bourgeois. The constant references to the Brown household's domestic staff may grate upon the modern reader. But the *William* stories are all about exploding social pretentions. It is remarkable how well they stand up despite the huge changes in our society since the first story appeared in 1919. The same types of characters are to be found infesting today's world as they did a century ago. And they are still eminently in need of having their conceits pricked. The fact that the *William* stories remained unchanged in nature during the 50 years they were being written is testament to the timelessness of the psychologies involved. Throughout, William remained stubbornly 11 years old.

William himself is the star, and he is a conceit-free zone. He stands in glorious contrast to the cast of pompous adults against whom he is in permanent opposition. Admittedly, his ethics are somewhat elastic, but in the important things he has admirable standards. The phrase 'loveable rogue' was surely invented especially for William Brown.

Which brings me to the burden of this chapter. The affection in which Richmal Crompton holds her little hero shines forth on every page. There is no trace of toxic masculinity here – though, heaven knows, William's exploits might provide adequate ammunition for such a thesis. Moreover, the contrast between the former suffragist and a modern feminist could hardly be more stark when Crompton exposes some specifically female character flaws.

We need to pinch ourselves on occasion as a reminder that what we are reading was penned by the adult female Richmal Crompton, and must therefore reflect her own understanding – and, we suspect, her own opinion too. Crompton's understanding of small boys is all the more remarkable in view of her having had no children of her own, remaining unmarried all her life. There's no trace here of any desire to redefine masculinity: only to record its juvenile foibles.

The contrast between the warmth which Richmal Crompton displays towards William, an attitude towards boys which was once normal, and the vilification poured upon boys today makes my heart bleed. But, to the books…

William's *bête noire*, Violet Elizabeth, is not introduced until the fifth book in 1925, some six years after the first story was published. In the story *The Sweet Little Girl in White*, William has been obliged by his mother to meet Violet Elizabeth. This is their opening skirmish…and it contains more truth about the male-female power dynamic than all the feminist texts ever written…

"Whath your name?' said Violet Elizabeth.

She lisped? She would, thought William bitterly, with those curls and those skirts. She would. He felt at any rate relieved that none of his friends could see him in the unmanly situation – talking to a kid like that – all eyes and curls and skirts.

'William Brown' he said, distantly, looking over her head as if he did not see her.

'How old are you?'

'Eleven'

'My nameth Violet Elizabeth'

He received the information in silence.

'I'm thix.'

He made no comment. He examined the distant view with an abstracted frown.

'Now you muth play with me.'

William allowed his cold glance to rest upon her.

'I don't play little girls' games', he said scathingly. But Violet Elizabeth did not appear to be scathed.

'Don' you know any little girlth?' she said pityingly. 'I'll teach you little girth gameth', she added pleasantly.

'I don't want to', said William. 'I don't like them. I don't like little girls games. I don't want to know 'em.'

Violet Elizabeth gazed at him open mouthed.

'Don't you like little girlth?' she said.

'Me?' said William with superior dignity. 'Me? I don't know anything about 'em. Don't want to.'

'D-don't you like me?' quavered Violet Elizabeth in incredulous amazement. William looked at her. Her blue eyes filled slowly with tears, her lips quivered.

'I like you', she said. 'Don't you like me?'

William stared at her in horror.

*'You – you **do** like me, don't you?'*

William was silent.

A large shining tear welled over and trickled down the small pink cheek.

'You're making me cry', sobbed Violet Elizabeth. 'You are. You're making me cry, 'cause you won't say you like me.'

'I – I do like you', said William desperately. 'Honest – I do. Don't cry. I do like you. Honest.'

A smile broke through the tear-stained face.

'I'm tho glad', she said simply. 'You like all little girth, don't you?' She smiled at him hopefully. 'You do don't you?'

William, pirate and Red Indian and desperado, William woman-hater and girl-despiser, looked round wildly for escape and found none.

Violet Elizabeth's eyes filled with tears again.

'You do like all little girth, don't you?', she persisted with quavering lip, 'You do, don't you?'

It was a nightmare to William. They were standing in full view of the drawing-room window. At any moment a grown-up might appear. He would be accused of brutality, of making little Violet Elizabeth cry. And, strangely enough, the sight of Violet Elizabeth with tear filled eyes and trembling lips made him feel that he must have been brutal indeed. Beneath his horror he felt bewildered.

'Yes, I do', he said hastily, 'I do. Honest I do.'

She smiled radiantly through her tears. 'You with you wath a little girl, don't you?'

'Er — yes. Honest I do', said the unhappy William.

'Kith me', she said raising her glowing face.

William was broken. He brushed her cheek with his."

Brilliant. Coercive control, anyone?

I trust I have no need to labour the significance of this extract nor to defend further the claim that this chapter is not off-topic. The mass psychological delusion which feminism has exercised upon the world rests upon a narrative of female powerlessness and their oppression by powerful men. You need to be very naive to think so. Or very Machiavellian to pretend to do so. In truth, feminism's tyranny of feigned powerlessness plays to exactly the same power dynamic as illustrated above by the six-year-old Violet Elizabeth. The finer feelings of the male target — call it chivalry or just common decency — are used against him. He is left "*feeling he must have been brutal indeed, and beneath his horror he feels bewildered*". In other words, moral blackmail based on gaslighting.

Underwriting this psychological coercion lies an Ultimate Authority. In the case of Violet Elizabeth this is the adult world. In the case of feminism, it is the state. While female power was confined to the domestic and social worlds, men were free to control their own lives in the 'external' world of work. There was thus a balance of power between the two worlds and the two sexes. But when women entered the 'external' world in comparable numbers, they brought their domestic power with them and deployed it there too – propelled by feminist theory but really powered by innate psychosexual proclivities.

The reason why feminism has been able to sweep across the globe within my lifetime is because the body politic is no more able to counter female social power than was William in the above extract. The body politic can raise no effective immune response to feminism, because feminism presents itself as women's wishes and the arrangements of the 'external' world were designed to deliver those wishes, not to frustrate them. Feminism is therefore not self-limiting. The analogy with cancer is very apposite.

The story ends with Ginger lamenting that Violet Elizabeth's involvement has spoiled their day…

"'Girls always do', said William. 'I'm not going to have anything to do with any ole girl ever again.'

' 'S all very well sayin' that', said Douglas who had been deeply impressed that morning by the inevitableness and deadly persistence of the sex. 'S all very well sayin' that. It's them what has to do with you.'"

Violet Elizabeth's dearest wish is to be included in The Outlaw's games – and, of course, to control them completely. Here's the beginning of 1964's *Violet Elizabeth's Party*…

"'She's still coming', said Ginger, throwing a hasty glance behind him.

'Let's dodge into the wood an' throw her off the scent', suggested Henry.

'We've tried that', said Douglas with a hollow laugh. 'It's never been any good yet.'

'Let's hide somewhere', said Ginger.

'That's never been any good either', said Douglas with another hollow laugh.

'No, she's as many eyes as an octopus', said William morosely.

'Let's try it anyway', said Henry. 'Come on.'

They dodged into the wood and hastened down the narrow path.

Ginger glanced back. The small resolute figure of Violet Elizabeth could be seen winding its way behind them through the trees.

'She's still coming', he said.

'Let's run', said Douglas.

*'Gosh, I'm not goin' to run away from her', said William with spirit. 'I'm not goin' to run away from a kid like that. She'd start thinkin' no end of herself if we ran away from her. She'd think we were **scared** of her.'*

'Well, we are', said Henry simply."

Yep, that's about the size of it.

And why would they be scared of her? Because she's powerless?

Violet Elizabeth is in particularly fine form in *Mrs Bott and the Portrait* (1964). Perhaps we should not be too hard on her. She was, after all, the product of her mother, the ogress Mrs Bott. The self-proclaimed *true* gentry despised none more than the *nouveau riche*, and the more the latter aspired to ape their "betters" the more they were despised…

"Mr Bott sighed. He had suspected for some time that his wife was due for another outbreak of social ambition."

On this occasion Mrs Bott has a yen for portraiture. They need to persuade Violet Elizabeth to sit. There's no doubting in this story what Richmal Crompton thinks of Violet Elizabeth's character.

"Would you like to have your portrait done, love?' said Mrs Bott.

Violet Elizabeth's small red tongue performed an adroit circular lick that encompassed the entire surface of her ice lolly.

'Will you give me a nithe prethent if I do?' she said.

For all her air of angelic sweetness Violet Elizabeth was a calculating child.

'We'll see', said Mrs Bott. 'We'll see if you're a good little girl and sit still'.

'I don't want to thit thtill', said Violet Elizabeth.

She gave another circular lick to the lolly and the remaining fragment detached itself from the stick and fell onto the parquet floor.

'Pick that up', said Mr Bott.

'I don't want to pick it up', said Violet Elizabeth. 'I'll thquath it'.

She ground the piece of ice into the parquet with a miniature sandal.

'Now don't give her exhibitions*, Botty', said Mrs Bott, seeing an expostulation quivering on her husband's tongue. *she means inhibitions.

'She's givin' 'em to me', said Mr Bott.

Violet Elizabeth licked the wooden stick clean then put it among her curls behind her ear and turned her attention to the subject under discussion.

'Who'th going to paint it?' she said.

'Well, that's the question, love', said Mrs Bott. 'There's Archie Mannister and there's this nephew of Mrs Lane's that's coming to stay with her. Seems he's an artist, too. So we've got to make up our minds between them.'

Violet Elizabeth fixed limpid blue eyes on her parent. They held their usual expression of wondering innocence, but her mind was working quickly. She was not an unintelligent child and she saw the possibilities of the situation.

Those youthful desperadoes, known as The Outlaws – William, Ginger, Henry and Douglas – used Archie's cottage and garden as their playground. Archie was so vague and absent-minded that they could turn his garden into a Red Indian camp, raid his larder, and use his studio as the cockpit of an aeroplane, without his even realising that they were present. There were occasions when he suddenly noticed them and drove them in exasperation from the scene, but the occasions were few. The result was that William and his friends cherished for Archie a deep and ardent loyalty. They would, Violet Elizabeth knew, go to any lengths to secure the portrait commission for Archie. And it was the greatest desire of her heart to be accepted by the Outlaws as their playmate, to join in their games and accompany them on their lawless expeditions over the countryside.

So far all her efforts had been in vain. They continued to treat her with contempt and derision, to eject her when she tried to join them, to ignore her threats, her tears, her blandishments. And suddenly she saw a way of gaining her ends. The fact that Archie's rival was a member of the Lane family added piquancy to the situation. For Hubert Lane was William's inveterate foe. She would be able to play one off against the other to her heart's content.

*'Now will you promise to be a good little girl and have your portrait done?' coaxed Mrs Bott. 'Then I'll give you a **lovely** present.'*

But Violet Elizabeth had lost interest in the present. She was after bigger game. She maintained her air of wondering innocence.

*'I will if it'th a **nithe** painter', she stipulated. 'I couldn't thit thtill if it wathn't a nithe one.'"*

Upon gaining her parent's agreement that she, Violet Elizabeth, should choose the artist...

"Drunk with the sense of power, Violet Elizabeth gambolled gleefully through the French window."

The situation developed exactly along the lines that Violet Elizabeth had hoped. News soon leaked out in the neighbourhood that Violet Elizabeth had been given the choice of artist. William immediately accosted her in order to sing the praises of Archie in emphatic tones.

"Violet Elizabeth gave him a smile of radiant sweetness.

'I'd like to come and play Red Indianth in the woodth with you, William', she said.

'All right', he said ungraciously. 'You can come tomorrow.'"

The next time Violet Elizabeth emerged from the Hall gates Hubert Lane was waiting for her. Hubert was fat and smug with a large oily smile. He carried a box of chocolates.

"'I thought you'd like these, Violet Elizabeth ' he said, baring his teeth in the oily smile. 'They're the most expensive in the shop.'

Violet Elizabeth fluttered her eyelashes at him."

"'Thank you for the chocolatth, Hubert. I like chocolate, Hubert. An' I like lollypopth and caramelth and pear dropth and thugar mithe and jelly babieth and candy floth', said Violet Elizabeth."

"There followed for Violet Elizabeth a period of bliss that surpassed her wildest dreams. The lust for power that lives in every six-year-old breast found ample and almost incredible outlet. As William's squaw she bossed and bullied and nagged and tormented."

"Hubert rang the changes on chocolates, lollypops, sugar mice, jelly babies, caramels and pear drops – and Violet Elizabeth found fault with everything he brought. Still intoxicated by the sense of power, she flung her weight about, tossing her curls, elevating her small nose, keeping him running backwards and forwards to the sweet shop, draining every last penny of his pocket money, lavish though it was. Hubert's smug face began to wear an anxious, driven look.

And the Outlaws fared even worse. Ruthlessly, Violet Elizabeth organised their games. Where before she had been rigorously excluded, she now lorded it as squaw, exploress, and highwaywoman. She insisted on having the chief part in every game they played. She even forced them to play an outrageous game of her own invention featuring the Outlaws as courtiers and herself as Queen."

Invasion of male space, anyone? And, of course, abuse of power. Crompton herself uses the word 'power' three times in this short extract. I cannot recall her ever describing William as possessed of power. On the contrary, the stories are generally about William battling against the unwelcome powers of others, sometimes adult power, sometimes not. I'll not regale you with the further twists and turns of the plot, though you may rest assured that Archie gets the commission in the end.

Young men are invariably portrayed by Crompton as love struck, pathetic fools – and none so pathetic than those who are in love with William's sister, Ethel. We read in *William and the Hoop-la Stall* (1964),

"William shook his head compassionately. He couldn't understand what Ethel's many admirers saw in her but, though willing to exploit them in every possible way, he pitied as well as despised them."

Middle-aged women, on the other hand, feature as unassailable powers whose wills cannot be challenged head-on but can only be successfully countered by craft and subterfuge – the arts to which William is wholeheartedly dedicated. For example, again in *William and the Hoop-la Stall,*

"Everyone knew what Mrs Monks was. Beneath her bland exterior lay a will power and tenacity of purpose that brooked no opposition. Her tactics were simple. She selected her victim, issued her orders and thereafter ignored protests, resistance and even open rebellion.

'Why didn't you jus' say no?', queried William.

'I did', said Archie."

In *William and the Psychiatrist* (1964) we find William having a mid-life crisis. It's not surprising; by this time he has been 11 for some 45 years. He clearly understands his allotted role as a doer of deeds...

"'Here I am', he muttered, 'gettin' older an' older every year an' done nothin' yet to make the world ring with my name. Gosh! I haven't even started. I bet Christopher Columbus was thinkin' out how to discover America when he was my age. I bet that Watt man that invented steam had started boilin' kettles. There's not much time left. I've got to start soon.'"

So William sets up as a psychiatrist, perhaps because he's tried everything else by this time: "Mental Trubbles Kured. Threppence Eech". He soon gets his first patient who explains his problem...

*"'Amanda. My fiancée', said Mr Peaslake, fixing his eyes gloomily in front of him. 'At least, she **was** my fiancée, but in this letter I've just received she breaks off the engagement. She's coming this evening to return my presents. She has to come in person with her car because one of them's a spin dryer and she can't very well post it. I thought she'd be pleased with the spin dryer, but she said it showed a lack of imagination. She said that all my presents showed a lack of imagination. I knew, of course, that she found me – disappointing in many ways. She says I lack the vital spark. But this letter – well, it's shattered my world to its foundations. I realise that I'm not worthy of her – she's so vibrant and alive – but I simply can't face life without her.'*

'Well, I think you're jolly lucky gettin' rid of her', said William. 'They're all bossy. Gosh! Even when they seem all right at first, they always turn out bossy before they've finished an' they get bossier an' bossier an' bossier.'"

Tut, tut, William – or, rather, Richmal – that's a banned word, don't you know. But let me not give you the impression that William was immune to feminine charms. Here he is in *The Fall of the Idol* (1922) having a crush on his teacher, Miss Drew,

"There was a faint perfume about her, and William, the devil-may-care pirate and robber-chief, the stern despiser of all things effeminate, felt the first dart of the malicious blind God. He blushed and simpered."

"Malicious", eh, Miss Crompton? An interesting choice of word. So smitten is William that he actually starts doing his homework. Alas, William goes on in the story to lose faith in his beloved due to her fickleness in floral preferences.

Joan, the dark-haired girl next door, figures frequently – sometimes in the guise of William's admirer ("*To Joan, William was a godlike hero. His very wickedness partook of the divine*", in *William's Christmas Eve*, 1922) – sometimes as the target of William's desire to impress (as in *The Rivals*, 1922). And girls often feature as William's partners in crime (e.g., the delightfully laddish Dorita in *William and White Satin*, 1922) or as the beneficiaries of his schemes, as the following two examples illustrate.

These final examples serve to emphasise Crompton's positive portrayal of William, and by implication a positive portrayal of masculinity (albeit here in its juvenile form).

We are never in any doubt that William's heart is in the right place, regardless of sex. In *William's Christmas Eve* we find our hero being importuned by a little guttersnipe named Sheila. Stung though William is to be verbally attacked in such a manner, and by such a one, he cannot help but be impressed by little Sheila's command of street language and her positive pride in her father's imprisonment. "*Softie! Swank!*" she calls after him, but not before she has revealed her dream that Father Christmas will deliver a sumptuous Christmas dinner this year. "*I tol' you it was rot', says William. 'There isn't any Father Christmas*". But the episode prays on William's mind…

"William had a strong imagination. When an idea took hold upon his mind, it was almost impossible for him to let it go. He was quite accustomed to Joan's adoring homage. The scornful mockery of his auburn-haired friend (i.e., Sheila) was something quite new, and in some strange fashion it intrigued and fascinated him. Mentally he recalled her excited little face, flushed with eagerness as she described the expected spread. Mentally also he conceived a vivid picture of the long waiting on Christmas Eve, the slowly fading hope, the final bitter disappointment. While engaging in furious snowball fights with Ginger, Douglas and Henry, while annoying peaceful passers-by with well-aimed snow missiles, while bruising himself and most of his family black and blue on long and glassy slides along the garden path, while purloining his family's clothes to adorn various unshapely snowmen, while walking across all the ice (preferably cracked) in the neighbourhood and being several

times narrowly rescued from a watery grave – while following all these light holiday pursuits – the picture of the little auburn-haired girl's disappointment was ever vividly present in his mind."

So William, with the help of the ever-adoring Joan, sets out to provide the desired Christmas feast – succeeding admirably and earning punishment from his family as a result (well, he did steal their food). Overly saccharine, blatant pathos? Yes, of course. But that is not the point. The point is the portrayal of a positive masculinity: William's compassion and conscience, and the determination to translate these into action.

The May King (1922) provides another example of William championing the cause of a deserving girl, in this case in preference to one less deserving. The class is to have a May Queen. The less deserving candidate...

"...Evangeline Fish began to canvass for votes methodically. Evangeline Fish was very fair, and was dressed always in that shade of blue that shrieks aloud to the heavens and puts the skies to shame. She was considered the beauty of the form...

Evangeline Fish was elected May Queen by an overwhelming majority. She was, after all, the beauty of the form and she always wore blue. And now she was to be May Queen. Her prestige was established forever. 'Little angel', murmured the elder girls. The small boys fought for her favours. William began to dislike her intensely. Her voice, and her smile, and her ringlets, and her blue dress began to jar upon his nerves."

"It was not until a week later that William noticed Bettine Franklin. Bettine was small and dark. There was nothing 'angelic' about her. William had noticed her vaguely in school before and had hardly looked upon her as a distinct personality. But one recreation in the playground he stood leaning against the wall by himself, scowling at Evangeline Fish. She was surrounded by a crowd of admirers, and was prattling to them artlessly in her angelic voice.

'I'm going to be dressed in white muslin with a blue sash. Blue suits me, you know. I'm so fair.' She tossed back a ringlet. 'One of you will have to hold my train and the rest must dance round me. I'm going to have a crown and...'. She turned round in order to avoid the scowling gaze of William in the distance.

William had discovered that his scowl annoyed her, and since then he had given it little rest. But there was no satisfaction in scowling at the back of her well-curled head, so he relaxed his scowl and let his gaze wander around the playground. And it fell upon Bettine. Bettine was also standing by herself and gazing at Evangeline Fish. But she was not scowling. She was looking at Evangeline Fish with wistful envy. For Evangeline Fish was 'angelic' and a May Queen and she was neither of these things. William strolled over and lolled against the wall next to her......"

Bonding is instantly established through the exchange of gifts. ("*William plunged his hands into his pockets and brought out two marbles, a piece of clay and a broken toy gun. 'You can have 'em all', he said in reckless generosity*").

"'*She'll look ever so beautiful when she's a May Queen', opined Bettine.*

'*You'd look nicer', said William.*

Bettine's small pale face flamed.

'*Oh, no!', she said.*

'*Would you like to be May Queen?*'

'*Oh, yes!', she said.*

'*Umm', said William.*

'*I'd hold your train if you was goin' to be queen', he volunteered.*

'*I wouldn't want you to hold my train', she said earnestly. 'I'd — I'd — I'd want you to be May King with me'.*

'*Yes. Why don't they have May Kings?', said William, stung by this insult to his sex.*

'*Why shouldn't there be a May King?*'"

No prizes for guessing how the story subsequently unfolds. William discovers Evangeline's weak spot — her greed for cakes — and uses it against her. Inveigling her to a massive feast of cakes and pastries, Evangeline is fatally delayed whilst William and Bettine steal the show as King and Queen of the May. It ends, "*Bettine, standing on the platform with William's hand holding hers and the maypole dancers dancing around her, was radiant with pride and happiness. Evangeline Fish in the woodshed was just beginning the last currant cake.*"

For those readers who are bewildered as to why I included this homage to Richmal Crompton in a book on gender politics, let me reprise the reasons — there are two. The modern world has little love for laddishness. Yet only a very short time ago even a never-married, childless, ex-suffragette was able to appreciate its positive aspects and regard even juvenile masculinity with genuine affection and appreciation. This is how far we have sunk. But secondly, I wished to provide elementary examples of the nature of gender-related social power as so aptly performed by Violet Elizabeth. Would anyone dare present a six-year-old girl in such a manner now?

References

[1] Crompton, R. (mostly 1922 to 1928) *Just William Collection, Richmal Crompton, 10 Books*. Macmillan Children's Books, 13 August 1999. This is a collection of 10 books with the earliest stories. There were 38 William books in all, the last being posthumously published in 1970.

[2] McVeigh, J. (2022). *Richmal Crompton, Author of Just William: A Literary Life*. Palgrave Macmillan, 31 Mar. 2022.

58. Orwell's Preface Revisited

George Orwell wrote a Preface to Animal Farm which was not published until after his death. Here I reproduce extracts from it in an updated form that, today, might duplicate publishers' reluctance to publish.

Original posted on: <u>16 November 2014</u>.

Orwell wrote a Preface to "Animal Farm" which did not appear in early editions. It was discovered only in 1972, some 27 years after the book's original publication in 1945, and many years after the author's death. It explains the contemporary context. At the end of the second world war, when "Animal Farm" was first published, criticism of the Soviet Union was politically and culturally unacceptable. Many people at the time thought the book should not have been published at all. Indeed, it was rejected by four publishers. The Preface explains the informal, but nevertheless pervasive, censorship which prevailed at the time. It is easy to see why the publisher declined to include it in the early editions. This chapter consists of extracts from Orwell's Preface. You will see that I have crossed out some words and replaced them with others. Consequently, you can read it as an historical account or one of current relevance: you will be struck immediately by just how relevant. The full Preface can be found in Ref.[1]. Below I break with the convention of the rest of the book and leave off the italics in this long extract (any italics are my own commentary).

Extracts from Orwell's Preface

The chief danger to freedom of thought and speech at this moment is not the direct interference of the Ministry of Information or any official body. If publishers and editors exert themselves to keep certain topics out of print, it is not because they are frightened of prosecution but because they are frightened of public opinion. In this country intellectual cowardice is the worst enemy a writer or journalist has to face, and that fact does not seem to me to have had the discussion it deserves.

The sinister fact about literary censorship in England is that it is largely voluntary. Unpopular ideas can be silenced, and inconvenient facts kept dark, without the need for any official ban.

So far as the daily newspapers go, this is easy to understand. But the same kind of veiled censorship also operates in books and periodicals, as well as in plays, films and radio. At any given moment there is an orthodoxy, a body of ideas which it is assumed that all right-thinking people will accept without question. It is not exactly forbidden to say this, that or the other, but it is 'not done' to say it, just as in mid-Victorian times it was 'not done' to mention trousers in the presence of a lady. Anyone who challenges the prevailing orthodoxy finds himself silenced with surprising effectiveness. A genuinely unfashionable opinion is almost never given a fair hearing, either in the popular press or in the highbrow periodicals.

At this moment what is demanded by the prevailing orthodoxy is an uncritical admiration of ~~Soviet Russia~~ feminism. Every-one knows this, nearly everyone acts on it. Any serious criticism of ~~the Soviet régime~~ feminist orthodoxy, any disclosure of facts which the ~~Soviet government~~ feminista would prefer to keep hidden, is next door to unprintable. And this nation-wide conspiracy to flatter ~~our ally~~ one sex takes place, curiously enough, against a background of ~~genuine~~ presumed intellectual tolerance.

For though you are not allowed to criticize ~~the Soviet government~~ feminism, at least you are reasonably free to criticize ~~our own~~ everything else. Hardly anyone will print an attack on ~~Stalin~~ a feminist, but it is quite safe to attack ~~Churchill~~ anyone who opposes it.

The servility with which the greater part of the English intelligentsia have swallowed and repeated ~~Russian~~ feminist propaganda from ~~1941~~ the 1960s onwards would be quite astounding if it were not that they have behaved similarly on several earlier occasions (!). On one controversial issue after another the ~~Russian~~ feminist viewpoint has been accepted without examination and then publicized with complete disregard to historical truth or intellectual decency. (*At this point Orwell cited a specific instance – by the BBC, surprise! Insert your own contemporary example, there is no shortage*).

Factions which the ~~Russians~~ feminists were determined to crush were recklessly libelled in the English leftwing press, and any statement in their defence even in letter form, was refused publication. At present, not only is serious criticism of ~~the USSR~~ feminist dogma considered reprehensible, but even the fact of the existence of such criticism is kept secret in some cases.

Any large organization will look after its own interests as best it can, and overt propaganda is not a thing to object to. One would no more expect ~~the *Daily Worker*~~ *Herizons* to publicize unfavourable facts about ~~the USSR~~ feminism than one would expect the *Catholic Herald* to denounce the Pope. But then every thinking person knows ~~the *Daily Worker*~~ *Herizons* and the *Catholic Herald* for what they are. What is disquieting is that where ~~the USSR~~ feminism and its policies are concerned one cannot expect intelligent criticism or even, in many cases, plain honesty from Liberal writers and journalists who are under no direct pressure to falsify their opinions. ~~Stalin~~ Feminism is sacrosanct and certain aspects of ~~his policy~~ its dogma must not be seriously discussed.

There was a huge and almost equally dishonest stream of ~~pro-Russian~~ pro-feminist propaganda, and what amounted to a boycott on anyone who tried to discuss all-important questions in a grown-up manner. You could, indeed, publish ~~anti-Russian~~ anti-feminist books, but to do so was to make sure of being ignored or misrepresented by nearly the whole of the highbrow press. Both publicly and privately you were warned that it was 'not done'. What you said might possibly be true, but it was 'inopportune' and 'played into the hands of' this or that reactionary interest.

The English intelligentsia, or a great part of it, had developed a ~~nationalistic~~ sexist loyalty towards ~~the USSR~~ feminism, and in their hearts they felt that to cast any doubt on ~~the~~ its wisdom ~~of Stalin~~ was a kind of blasphemy. ~~Events in Russia and events elsewhere~~ The doings of feminists and the doings of others were to be judged by different standards.

But now to come back to this book of mine. The reaction towards it of most English intellectuals will be quite simple: 'It oughtn't to have been published'. The English intelligentsia, or most of them, will object to this book because it traduces ~~their Leader~~ feminism and (as they see it) does harm to the cause of progress. If it did the opposite they would have nothing to say against it, even if its literary faults were ten times as glaring as they are. The success of, for instance, the Left Book Club over a period of four or five years shows how willing they are to tolerate both scurrility and slipshod writing, provided that it tells them what they want to hear.

The issue involved here is quite a simple one: Is every opinion, however unpopular – however foolish, even – entitled to a hearing? Put it in that form and nearly any English intellectual will feel that he ought to say 'Yes'. But give it a concrete shape, and ask, 'How about an attack on ~~Stalin~~ feminism? Is *that* entitled to a hearing?', and the answer more often than not will be 'No'. In that case the current orthodoxy happens to be challenged, and so the principle of free speech lapses.

One of the peculiar phenomena of our time is the renegade Liberal. Over and above the familiar Marxist claim that 'bourgeois liberty' is an illusion, there is now a widespread tendency to argue that one can only defend ~~democracy~~ equality by totalitarian methods. If one loves ~~democracy~~ equality, the argument runs, one must crush its enemies by no matter what means. And who are its enemies? It always appears that they are not only those who attack it openly and consciously, but those who 'objectively' endanger it by spreading mistaken doctrines. In other words, defending ~~democracy~~ equality involves destroying all independence of thought.

This argument was used, for instance, to justify ~~the Russian purges~~ banning men's groups in universities. The most ardent ~~Russophile~~ feminists hardly believed that all ~~of the victims~~ men were guilty of all the things they were accused of, but by holding heretical opinions they 'objectively' harmed the (feminist) régime, and therefore it was quite right not only to ~~massacre~~ silence them but to discredit them by false accusations.

These people don't see that if you encourage totalitarian methods, the time may come when they will be used against you instead of for you.

But where had these people learned this essentially totalitarian outlook? Pretty certainly they had learned it from the Communists themselves! (*I deliberately changed no words there*). Tolerance and decency are deeply rooted in England, but they are not indestructible, and they have to be kept alive partly by conscious effort. The result of preaching totalitarian doctrines is to weaken the instinct by means of which free peoples know what is or is not dangerous.

It is important to realize that the current ~~Russomania~~ uncritical acceptance of feminism is only a symptom of the general weakening of the western liberal tradition. Had the Ministry of Information chipped in and definitely vetoed the publication of this book, the bulk of the English intelligentsia would have seen nothing disquieting in this. Uncritical loyalty to ~~the~~

~~USSR~~ feminism happens to be the current orthodoxy, and where the supposed interests of ~~the USSR~~ feminists are involved they are willing to tolerate not only censorship but the deliberate falsification of history. To name one instance (*here I might replace Orwell's example with "the myth that votes for women were won by the suffragettes" or with the "myth of centuries of oppression of women"*).

And this tolerance of plain dishonesty means much more than that admiration for Russia happens to be fashionable at this moment. Quite possibly that particular fashion will not last. For all I know, by the time this book is published my view of the Soviet régime may be the generally-accepted one. But what use would that be in itself? To exchange one orthodoxy for another is not necessarily an advance. The enemy is the gramophone mind, whether or not one agrees with the record that is being played at the moment. (*I left that paragraph unchanged because its very meaning is that a society which was willing to be slavishly devoted to the totalitarian Soviet regime has proved equally willing to be slavishly devoted to the totalitarian feminist regime.*)

Intellectual freedom is a deep-rooted tradition without which our characteristic western culture could only doubtfully exist. From that tradition many of our intellectuals are visibly turning away. They have accepted the principle that a book should be published or suppressed, praised or damned, not on its merits but according to political expediency. And others who do not actually hold this view assent to it from sheer cowardice.

I know that the English intelligentsia have plenty of reasons for their timidity and dishonesty, indeed I know by heart the arguments by which they justify themselves. But at least let us have no more nonsense about defending liberty against ~~Fascism~~ the patriarchy. If liberty means anything at all it means the right to tell people what they do not want to hear. It is the liberals who fear liberty and the intellectuals who want to do dirt on the intellect: it is to draw attention to that fact that I have written this Preface.

Plus ça change, plus c'est la même chose, n'est-ce pas?

References

[1] Orwell, G. (1945). *Animal Farm: A Fairy Story*. Edition including, in two Appendices, Orwell's proposed Preface and the Preface to the Ukrainian Edition. Penguin Classics, new edition, 7 September 1989.

59. Revisiting the Road to Wigan Pier

This chapter is a review of Orwell's 1937 book The Road to Wigan Pier, which was a depiction of working-class life in northern England at the height of the Great Depression. Here I draw out from that book Orwell's views on socialism and how they were to change.

Original posted on: 29 March 2017.

You can read *The Road to Wigan Pier* free online at Gutenberg-Australia, Ref.[1].

Wigan Pier was a coal landing jetty on the Leeds-Liverpool canal where it passed through Wigan. It is an ironic appellation, Wigan's pier bearing no more relation to a seaside pier than a lump of coal to a diamond. The pier does not actually feature in the book at all, for the simple reason that it had been demolished some years before Orwell visited Wigan. You, dear reader, would be luckier if you visited Wigan today for the pier has been rebuilt – perhaps because the locals got fed up with tourist types asking the way to something which did not exist. I wouldn't bother making a special trip if I were you.

Whatever Wigan might be like today, it was not beautiful in 1936. But, as a Mancunian, and hence on the Lancastrian side of the Pennines and thus in opposition to Yorkshire by long tradition, I note Orwell's remark,

"Even Wigan is beautiful compared with Sheffield. Sheffield, I suppose, could justly claim to be called the ugliest town in the Old World."

But enough frivolity. Writing in 2017, I had just re-read *The Road to Wigan Pier* for the first time since I was a teenager. Orwell's book is a valuable historical record of working-class lives in the north of England at the height of the Great Depression of the 1930s, particularly those of miners and their families. Though published in 1937, the book describes Orwell's visits to northern working towns in the spring of 1936 (by the end of 1936 Orwell was in Spain). This is the pre-World War Two Orwell, and hence the Orwell before Animal Farm (1945) and Nineteen Eighty-Four (1949). You need to be aware of the date because when Orwell uses the phrase 'pre-war' he is referring to World War One.

If you have never read an account of the working conditions of coal miners at that period, you should – and Orwell is as good a source as any. Simply put, the sheer physical arduousness of the work would be unsustainable by men today, even men used to labouring. British coal mines were generally very deep. Once underground a miner would need to 'travel' to the coal face – a distance of up to 3 miles along an excavated tunnel mostly little more than around four feet high. This 'travel' had to be undertaken doubled-up, with the back almost horizontal. You will appreciate why miners were generally small men. But the time taken for this 'travelling', typically between one and three hours daily, was unpaid. The miners' working day began only upon reaching the coal face where he would hack away for some seven and a half hours on top of his 'travel' time. Orwell himself 'travelled' only one mile, a comparatively short 'travel', but was barely able to manage it and was certainly not capable of then putting in a full day's labour – even had he otherwise been capable of doing a miner's job, which he was not. And all this is done in the heat and blackness of a deep mine with the ever-present threat of roof falls and death.

Orwell emphasises the extent to which all aspects of life in Britain were dependent upon coal, and hence upon the miners.

*"You and I and the editor of the Times Literary Supplement, and the nancy poets and the Archbishop of Canterbury and Comrade X, author of "Marxism for Infants" – all of us **really** owe the comparative decency of our lives to poor drudges underground, blackened to the eyes, with their throats full of coal dust, driving their shovels forward with arms and belly muscles of steel."*

But *The Road to Wigan Pier* is also a rare account of working people's daily lives; their homes, their eating habits, their poverty, their standards. It is an account of the class divide which, at that time, was still absolute. It is the book in which Orwell describes himself, with admirable precision, as lower-upper-middle class. Whilst he was invariably taken as a toff by those he was anthropologising, Orwell barely earned as much as they did. On this 'genteel poverty' Orwell is particularly good. He describes a sinking mass of the middle class, left stranded by the decline in the British national fortune after World War One, whose class status depended entirely on education, pretension and 'appearances', the latter accomplished in the teeth of secret poverty.

On the one hand, 1936 cannot be regarded as ancient history: it is within the lifetime of people still living. On the other hand, 1936 is as distant from the present as it is from Wordsworth. Well it might be, for the conditions of life in the UK now bear little relation to those times, whatever people may insist. And yet, despite being a mere single lifetime distant, already the truth of those times – as described by Orwell – is submerged beneath the propaganda of 'the historical oppression of women'. No. If you must have history in a sound bite it was this: the oppression of the many by the few. And both the many and the few consisted of both sexes.

Women and children used to work down the mines too, but the Victorians put a stop to that in 1842 – the nasty old patriarchs!

There were to be some changes in Orwell's politics between the 1930s and the 1940s, and not only because of the cataclysm of World War Two. *The Road to Wigan Pier* sees Orwell as a socialist apologist. It is not hard to understand why given the conditions of the working class he describes in the book. Moreover, Orwell was already aware in early 1936 of the growing menace of fascism in Europe. He literally fought against fascism in Spain from late 1936 to June 1937 (*Homage to Catalonia*, Ref.[2], refers). Orwell's view in early 1936 is summed up thus,

"At this moment we are in a very serious mess, so serious that even the dullest-witted people find it difficult to remain unaware of it. We are living in a world in which nobody is free, in which hardly anybody is secure, in which it is almost impossible to be honest and to remain alive."

"There is no chance of righting the conditions I described in the earlier chapters of this book, or of saving England from Fascism, unless we can bring an effective Socialist party into existence. It will have to be a party with genuinely revolutionary intentions, and it will have to be numerically strong enough to act..... In the next few years we shall either get that effective Socialist party that we need, or we shall not get it. If we do not get it, then Fascism is coming."

He was wrong on that point, of course. Fascism was defeated without the need of a socialist polity.

If I recall *Homage to Catalonia* correctly, his experience in the Spanish civil war caused Orwell to believe that socialism really could work – thus revealing his earlier doubts about the matter – though it was also Orwell's experiences in

Spain that made him an ardent anti-Stalinist. For Orwell was a realist and was never a great fan of Marxist theory, and still less of those who espoused it. In addition to the urgency of thwarting the fascist threat, Orwell clung to socialism only because he could see no other way of affecting a change in the appallingly degraded conditions in which the bulk of humanity lived – and he was convinced that there was no economic necessity for it. He placed the blame squarely on the class system, as a good socialist would. But for Orwell it was all about mass poverty.

"Socialism means the overthrow of tyranny, at home as well as abroad…the profoundest philosophical difference is unimportant compared with saving the twenty million Englishmen whose bones are rotting from malnutrition."

In regard to philosophical differences (for which read "Marxist doctrines"), Orwell opined *"the time to argue about them is afterwards"* – after the elimination of endemic poverty and the defeat of fascism, that is. With the benefit of hindsight, Orwell's socialism seems remarkably naive – the perennial failing of the good man – and all the more so given his crushingly incisive insights into the nature of collectivist totalitarianism just a few years later. In 1936 he thought that,

"All that is needed is to hammer two facts home into the public consciousness. One, that the interests of all exploited people are the same; the other, that Socialism is compatible with common decency."

Orwell was never one to bang on about dialectical materialism or other Marxist doctrines. He knew too much about working men to confuse Marxist theory with reality.

*As for the philosophic side of Marxism, the pea-and-thimble trick with those three mysterious entities, thesis, antithesis, and synthesis, I have never met a working man who had the faintest interest in it. It is of course true that plenty of people of working-class **origin** are Socialists of the theoretical bookish type. But they are never people who have **remained** working men; they don't work with their hands, that is. They belong either to the type I mentioned in the last chapter, the type who squirms into the middle class via the literary intelligentsia, or the type who becomes a Labour MP or a high-up trade union official. This last type is one of the most desolating spectacles the world contains. He has been picked out to fight for his mates, and all it means to him is a soft job and the chance of 'bettering' himself. Not merely while but **by** fighting the bourgeoisie he becomes a bourgeois himself. And meanwhile it is quite possible that he has remained an orthodox*

Marxist. But I have yet to meet a **working** *miner, steel-worker, cotton-weaver, docker, navvy, or whatnot who was 'ideologically' sound.*

It was not just as regards Marxism that the working man was politically uninvolved. Orwell notes,

"I happened to be in Yorkshire when Hitler re-occupied the Rhineland. Hitler, Locarno, Fascism, and the threat of war aroused hardly a flicker of interest locally, but the decision of the Football Association to stop publishing their fixtures in advance (this was an attempt to quell the Football Pools) flung all Yorkshire into a storm of fury."

Indeed, the working class seemed to be just as in need of consciousness raising as they had been when they frustrated Robert Tressell so, Ref.[3]. People will accept almost anything if it's all they have ever known – at least they did when TV was not around to make them envious of others.

"Talking once with a miner I asked him when the housing shortage first became acute in his district; he answered, 'When we were told about it', meaning that till recently people's standards were so low that they took almost any degree of overcrowding for granted. He added that when he was a child his family had slept eleven in a room and thought nothing of it, and that later, when he was grown-up, he and his wife had lived in one of the old-style back to back houses in which you not only had to walk a couple of hundred yards to the lavatory but often had to wait in a queue when you got there, the lavatory being shared by thirty-six people. And when his wife was sick with the illness that killed her, she still had to make that two hundred yards' journey to the lavatory. This, he said, was the kind of thing people would put up with 'until they were told about it'."

Orwell regarded the middle-class leftist zealots as an embarrassment. He is amusingly politically incorrect (not that there was any inhibition at the time), referring derisively to vegetarians, the temperance movement ("fruit-juice drinkers"), pacifism and a host of other holy cows, including feminism. Here's some lovely rants,

"It would help enormously, for instance, if the smell of crankishness which still clings to the Socialist movement could be dispelled. If only the sandals and the pistachio-coloured shirts could be put in a pile and burnt, and every vegetarian, teetotaller, and creeping Jesus sent home to Welwyn Garden City to do his yoga exercises quietly!"

"The first thing that must strike any outside observer is that Socialism, in its developed form is a theory confined entirely to the middle classes. The typical Socialist is not, as

tremulous old ladies imagine, a ferocious-looking working man with greasy overalls and a raucous voice. He is either a youthful snob-Bolshevik who in five years' time will quite probably have made a wealthy marriage and been converted to Roman Catholicism; or, still more typically, a prim little man with a white-collar job, usually a secret teetotaller and often with vegetarian leanings, with a history of Nonconformity behind him, and, above all, with a social position which he has no intention of forfeiting. This last type is surprisingly common in Socialist parties of every shade; it has perhaps been taken over en bloc from the old Liberal Party. In addition to this there is the horrible – the really disquieting – prevalence of cranks wherever Socialists are gathered together."

"One sometimes gets the impression that the mere words 'Socialism' and 'Communism' draw towards them with magnetic force every fruit-juice drinker, nudist, sandal-wearer, sex-maniac, quaker, 'nature cure' quack, pacifist, and feminist in England."

I love that "secret teetotaller with vegetarian leanings" (speaking as an unreconstructed beer drinking carnivore myself). And as for the so-called left being dominated by the middle class, what resonance that has today. Orwell is scathing about what we would later call "champagne socialists". He sees through their pretensions to the unchanged class disdain beneath.

"Look at Comrade X, member of the CPGB* and author of "Marxism for Infants". Comrade X, it so happens, is an old Etonian. He would be ready to die on the barricades, in theory anyway, but you notice that he still leaves his bottom waistcoat button undone. He idealizes the proletariat, but it is remarkable how little his habits resemble theirs. Perhaps once, out of sheer bravado, he has smoked a cigar with the band on, but it would be almost physically impossible for him to put pieces of cheese into his mouth on the point of his knife, or to sit indoors with his cap on, or even to drink his tea out of the saucer. I have known numbers of bourgeois Socialists, I have listened by the hour to their tirades against their own class, and yet never, not even once, have I met one who had picked up proletarian table-manners. Yet, after all, why not? Why should a man who thinks all virtue resides in the proletariat still take such pains to drink his soup silently? It can only be because in his heart he feels that proletarian manners are disgusting. So you see he is still responding to the training of his childhood, when he was taught to hate, fear, and despise the working class." (*CPGB = Communist Party of Great Britain).

Orwell was equally scathing about Socialist literature. Here is a passage in which he reveals that, in early 1936, he was still ignorant about the situation in Russia.

"If one faces facts one must admit that nearly everything describable as Socialist literature is dull, tasteless, and bad.....Every writer of consequence and every book worth reading is on the other side. I am willing to believe that it is otherwise in Russia – about which I know nothing, however – for presumably in post-revolutionary Russia the mere violence of events would tend to throw up a vigorous literature of sorts. But it is certain that in Western Europe Socialism has produced no literature worth having ....The real Socialist writers, the propagandist writers, have always been dull, empty windbags – Shaw, Barbusse, Upton Sinclair, William Morris, Waldo Frank, etc., etc....I do think it a bad sign that it has produced no songs worth singing."

Orwell is frequently critical of Soviet-worship in *The Road to Wigan Pier*. However, it appears that his education about the true nature of Stalin's Russia only really started in 1937 in Spain. Naively he imagined that the leftist forces in Spain would be united against the fascists. Essentially by chance he happened to join a militia (the POUM) which, though Marxist and hence fighting the fascists, was also an anti-Stalinist communist party. He would, initially, have been equally content to join the Soviet-supported, communist-run International Brigades. But Stalin had his own agenda in Spain, and he did not take kindly to interference. That the POUM was also Marxist was of little significance to Stalin. He decided to eliminate them. In May 1937, Orwell in his POUM militia was attacked, not by the fascist forces he had gone to Spain to fight, but by the Soviet controlled forces which he had thought were allies. Thus were Orwell's eyes opened and the author of the post-World War Two books was born.

But the reader should not imagine that the Orwell of *Animal Farm* and *Nineteen Eighty-Four* had relinquished his socialism. He is reputed to have written, after Spain, *"At last I really believe in Socialism which I never did before"*. And many years later, *"Every line of serious work that I have written since 1936 has been written, directly or indirectly, against totalitarianism and for democratic Socialism, as I understand it"*.

In respect of socialist literature, though we must largely agree with Orwell, he is perhaps being a little harsh. What about *The Ragged Trousered Philanthropists*, Ref.[3], for heaven's sake? And what about Greenwood's *Love On The Dole*, Ref.[4], published four years earlier and also a response to the mass unemployment of the 1930s? *Love On The Dole* addresses the same issues as *The Road to Wigan Pier*, but does so through emotionally engaging fiction. Like the theme of *Love On The Dole*, Orwell also recognised the significance of the working class being willing to marry whilst unemployed, a habit which struck the middle classes as evidence of irresponsibility. Moreover, in contrast to today in which the benefit system actively encourages such "irresponsibility", Orwell noted in 1936,

"There is just this to be said for the unemployment regulations, that they do not discourage people from marrying. A man and wife on twenty-three shillings a week are not far from the starvation line, but they can make a home of sorts; they are vastly better off than a single man on fifteen shillings.

A working man does not disintegrate under the strain of poverty as a middle-class person does. Take, for instance, the fact that the working class think nothing of getting married on the dole. It annoys the old ladies in Brighton, but it is a proof of their essential good sense; they realize that losing your job does not mean that you cease to be a human being. So that in one way things in the distressed areas are not as bad as they might be. Life is still fairly normal, more normal than one really has the right to expect. Families are impoverished, but the family-system has not broken up."

This is one very significant way in which the present is worse than the 1930s: the family system **has** broken up, especially in the lower socioeconomic classes. This is particularly worth noting because, whilst the beneficial changes since the 1930s can be attributed to science and technology, this disbeneficial change must be laid squarely at the door of politics. Orwell was wrong about socialism being the answer to mass poverty. He had the Romantics' negative view of the 'machine age', and so he failed to predict that science and technology (and trade) would provide the route out of poverty for the masses, not socialism.

To consolidate this picture of the benefits of marrying in 1936, regardless of unemployment, Orwell notes,

"The life of a single unemployed man is dreadful. He lives sometimes in a common lodging-house, more often in a 'furnished' room for which he usually pays six shillings a week, finding himself as best he can on the other nine (say six shillings a week for food and three for clothes, tobacco, and amusements). Of course he cannot feed or look after himself properly, and a man who pays six shillings a week for his room is not encouraged to be indoors more than is necessary. So he spends his days loafing in the public library or any other place where he can keep warm. That keeping warm is almost the sole preoccupation

of a single unemployed man in winter. In Wigan a favourite refuge was the pictures, which are fantastically cheap there. You can always get a seat for fourpence, and at the matinee at some houses you can even get a seat for twopence. Even people on the verge of starvation will readily pay twopence to get out of the ghastly cold of a winter afternoon. In Sheffield I was taken to a public hall to listen to a lecture by a clergyman, and it was by a long way the silliest and worst-delivered lecture I have ever heard or ever expect to hear. I found it physically impossible to sit it out, indeed my feet carried me out, seemingly of their own accord, before it was half-way through. Yet the hall was thronged with unemployed men; they would have sat through far worse drivel for the sake of a warm place to shelter in."

And here are a couple of interesting insights into class distinctions, one into gender roles and one regarding the pressure of aspiration,

"A working-class bachelor is a rarity, and so long as a man is married unemployment makes comparatively little alteration in his way of life. His home is impoverished but it is still a home, and it is noticeable everywhere that the anomalous position created by unemployment — the man being out of work while the woman's work continues as before — has not altered the relative status of the sexes. In a working-class home it is the man who is the master and not, as in a middle-class home, the woman or the baby."

and,

"I have seen just enough of the working class to avoid idealizing them, but I do know that you can learn a great deal in a working-class home, if only you can get there. The essential point is that your middle-class ideals and prejudices are tested by contact with others which are not necessarily better but are certainly different. Take for instance the different attitude towards the family. A working-class family hangs together as a middle-class one does, but the relationship is far less tyrannical. A working man has not that deadly weight of family prestige hanging round his neck like a millstone. I have pointed out earlier that a middle-class person goes utterly to pieces under the influence of poverty; and this is generally due to the behaviour of his family — to the fact that he has scores of relations nagging and badgering him night and day for failing to 'get on'."

Despite some incongruous disparaging remarks about birth control, Orwell makes the following observation which is surely bang on the money.

"Even if you live in a back-to-back house and have four children and a total income of thirty two shillings and sixpence a week from the PAC*, there is no need to have unemptied

chamber-pots standing about in your living-room. But it is equally certain that their circumstances do not encourage self-respect. The determining factor is probably the number of children. The best-kept interiors I saw were always childless houses or houses where there were only one or two children; with, say, six children in a three-roomed house it is quite impossible to keep anything decent."

*PAC stands for "Public Assistance Committees". These were introduced in 1934. This was the first time that unemployment benefit had been paid nationally via taxation. Prior to that the "poor relief" funded by local rate payers was still in operation as it had been for centuries. The huge demand for unemployment assistance due to the 1930s depression was responsible for the switch to national funding for the first time. With the benefit of hindsight this was a significant shift to more centralised state power, though at the time it was simply essential. The PAC-controlled dole was strictly means tested. If people on benefits today are aggrieved at having to "sign on" every month (or provide evidence of job-seeking), take a look at the practice in 1936...

"The Means Test is very strictly enforced, and you are liable to be refused relief at the slightest hint that you are getting money from another source. Dock-labourers, for instance, who are generally hired by the half-day, have to sign on at a Labour Exchange twice daily; if they fail to do so it is assumed that they have been working and their dole is reduced correspondingly."

In 2017, when this review was written, the so-called 'bedroom tax' had been causing discontent. This was, and still is, a reduction in Housing Benefit payable to people who live in a housing association or council property that is deemed to have one or more spare bedrooms. This often hits non-resident fathers hard, as family court orders often require a non-resident parent to have a spare bedroom if they wish their child(ren) to stay with them overnight. Housing Benefits may also be reduced, or stopped completely, if partners decide to live together. This feature of the current system leads to much cohabitation being kept quiet or being effectively discouraged. Here is the 1936 equivalent,

"The most cruel and evil effect of the Means Test is the way in which it breaks up families. Old people, sometimes bedridden, are driven out of their homes by it. An old age pensioner, for instance, if a widower, would normally live with one or other of his children; his weekly

ten shillings goes towards the household expenses, and probably he is not badly cared for. Under the Means Test, however, he counts as a 'lodger' and if he stays at home his children's dole will be docked. So, perhaps at seventy or seventy-five years of age, he has to turn out into lodgings, handing his pension over to the lodging-house keeper and existing on the verge of starvation. I have seen several cases of this myself. It is happening all over England at this moment, thanks to the Means Test."

What is forgotten today is the revolutionary ambiance which was all-pervasive after World War One. Not only were the workers and the intelligentsia 'Bolshie', but the feeling was common amongst the 'posh' classes too, especially the young. Of the workers, Orwell writes,

"Immediately after the war, the English working class were in a fighting mood. That was the period of the great coal strikes, when a miner was thought of as a fiend incarnate and old ladies looked under their beds every night lest Robert Smillie* should be concealed there....The men who had fought had been lured into the army by gaudy promises, and now they were coming home to a world where there were no jobs and not even any houses. Moreover, they had been at war and were coming home with the soldier's attitude to life, which is fundamentally, in spite of discipline, a lawless attitude. There was a turbulent feeling in the air. To that time belongs the song with the memorable refrain: There's nothing sure but the rich get richer and the poor get children." *Robert Smillie was the Arthur Scargill of his day, a miner's trade union leader.

Of the upper-middle classes Orwell writes,

"But those years, during and just after the war, were a queer time to be at school, for England was nearer revolution than she has been since or had been for a century earlier. Throughout almost the whole nation there was running a wave of revolutionary feeling which has since been reversed and forgotten, but which has left various deposits of sediment behind. Essentially, though of course one could not then see it in perspective, it was a revolt of youth against age, resulting directly from the war. In the war the young had been sacrificed and the old had behaved in a way which, even at this distance of time, is horrible to contemplate; they had been sternly patriotic in safe places while their sons went down like swathes of hay before the German machine guns. Moreover, the war had been conducted mainly by old men and had been conducted with supreme incompetence.

By 1918 everyone under forty was in a bad temper with his elders, and the mood of anti-militarism which followed naturally upon the fighting was extended into a general revolt against orthodoxy and authority. At that time there was, among the young, a curious cult of hatred of 'old men'. The dominance of 'old men' was held to be responsible for every evil known to humanity, and every accepted institution from Scott's novels to the House of Lords was derided merely because 'old men' were in favour of it. For several years it was all the fashion to be a 'Bolshie', as people then called it. England was full of half-baked antinomian opinions. Pacifism, internationalism, humanitarianism of all kinds, feminism, free love, divorce-reform, atheism, birth-control – things like these were getting a better hearing than they would get in normal times."

Sounds familiar, especially if one reads "male, stale and pale" for "old men". And this passage also has resonance with today's ignorant espousal of Marxism by our youth,

"One day the master who taught us English set us a kind of general knowledge paper of which one of the questions was, 'Whom do you consider the ten greatest men now living?' Of sixteen boys in the class (our average age was about seventeen) fifteen included Lenin in their list. This was at a snobbish expensive public school, and the date was 1920, when the horrors of the Russian Revolution was still fresh in everyone's mind."

I have speculated previously, Ref.[5], that the British Establishment's fear of revolution at the end of World War One might have been part of the motivation behind the 1918 Representation of the People Act. This was the Act which gave the vote to all men (aged 21 and over) and all women (aged 30 and over) for the first time. This Bill was debated in parliament in 1917, the year of the Russian revolution, which started in the ranks of the Russian army. It is not unreasonable to suppose that parliament's previous reluctance to extend the franchise might have been overcome, in part, by fear of the contagion of revolution spreading to Britain, especially after the horrors of the World War One trenches. Orwell's words lend some support to the thesis. However, whatever fears inhabited the minds of the ruling classes, it is unlikely that the workers were for violent revolution. At least, any revolutionary fervour was easily quelled...

"It is quite likely that fish-and-chips, art-silk stockings, tinned salmon, cut-price chocolate (five two-ounce bars for sixpence), the movies, the radio, strong tea, and the football pools have between them averted revolution."

Bread and circuses, I guess.

The physical, as well as emotional, effects of the war were still in evidence. On witnessing a parade of Guards, Orwell laments dolefully,

"Where are the monstrous men with chests like barrels and moustaches like the wings of eagles who strode across my childhood's gaze twenty or thirty years ago? Buried, I suppose, in the Flanders mud. In their place there are these pale-faced boys who have been picked for their height and consequently look like hop-poles in overcoats – the truth being that in modern England a man over six feet high is usually skin and bone and not much else. If the English physique has declined, this is no doubt partly due to the fact that the Great War carefully selected the million best men in England and slaughtered them, largely before they had had time to breed."

Ah, male privilege.

And those who are into gender-scripts may wish to contemplate whether they should be focussing on class-scripts instead, at least in 1936, as Orwell remarks,

"Having to do everything at other people's convenience is inherent in working-class life. A thousand influences constantly press a working man down into a passive role. He does not act, he is acted upon."

And finally, you may find current resonance in Orwell's summing up,

"If you present Socialism in a bad and misleading light – if you let people imagine that it does not mean much more than pouring European civilization down the sink at the command of Marxist prigs – you risk driving the intellectual into Fascism."

"We have got to admit that if Fascism is everywhere advancing, this is largely the fault of Socialists themselves. Partly it is due to the mistaken Communist tactic of sabotaging democracy, i.e., sawing off the branch you are sitting on; but still more to the fact that Socialists have, so to speak, presented their case wrong side foremost. They have never made it sufficiently clear that the essential aims of Socialism are justice and liberty."

No, George, and they still haven't – and, even if they did, one doubts that the reality would ever be more than a mockery of those aims.

And finally – do you recall Orwell mockingly referring to "Comrade X, author of 'Marxism for Infants'"? Well, a book published in 2017 by MIT Press is *Communism for Kids*, Ref.[6].

References

[1] Orwell, G. (1937). *The Road to Wigan Pier*. Linked is the Penguin Classics edition, 26 April 2001, or read it free online at Gutenberg Australia.

[2] Orwell, G. (1938). *Homage to Catalonia*. Linked is the Penguin Classics edition, 3 January 2013.

[3] Tressell, R. (1914). *The Ragged Trousered Philanthropists*. Linked is the Wordsworth Classics edition, 9 April 2012.

[4] Greenwood, W. (1933). *Love on the Dole*. Linked is the Vintage Digital edition, 4 September 2008.

[5] Collins, W. (2014). *Universal Suffrage in the UK*. The Illustrated Empathy Gap, 10 December 2014. (For the videos of this history see *Centuries of Oppression: The Road to 1918*).

[6] Adamczak, B. (2017). *Communism for Kids*. Translated by Jacob Blumenfeld and Sophie Lewis, The MIT Press, 24 March 2017.

60. The Bostonians

Here I present some extracts from the Henry James novel The Bostonians. It is remarkable how the nature of feminism today was already established in the 1870s, evidence perhaps that we are looking at innate proclivities of evolutionary heritage.

Original posted on: <u>*31 May 2022*</u>.

In The Fiamengo Files 2.0 (TFF2.0), Ref.[1], Janice Fiamengo focussed on early feminism, from the late eighteenth century, through the nineteenth century and up to the second wave. In one TFF2.0 video, Ref.[2], she acquaints us with the relevance of *The Bostonians* in this respect. This is the Henry James novel that depicts the views of feminists in 1870s America. You may wish to watch Janice's video first.

Published in 1886, *The Bostonians* was set around 1874 and hence rather nearer to the end of the American Civil War (1865). I find the denouement of the novel rather unconvincing, despite James being classed as a "realist". I suspect that designation relates to his representations of the details of social mores and the everyday minutiae of life, rather than plot credibility. Plots were to James merely the coat hangers on which the interesting clothing was hung, and coat hangers are not there to be noticed.

This book, then, is about feminism in (to use the UK designation) the mid-Victorian era. It is set in the fashionable circles of Boston and New York. Several ardent feminists appear in the book, but the main protagonists are Olive Chancellor and her protégée Verena Tarrant. We have become accustomed to the most active feminists being of the bourgeoisie, and Olive is a fine example. She is moneyed to the degree that she lives in considerable elegance without the inconvenience of having to think about money at all, something which dominates the lives of most of us, less privileged folk. Olive's antagonist is Basil Ransom. To consolidate his oppositional status he is from the South, a former Confederate soldier. But his chief sin (next, of course, to being male) is to be conservative – by modern standards disconcertingly so.

There is a lesson there immediately. As we shall see, the feminist views expressed by Olive and Verena and others in the novel are perfectly in accord with modern feminism. But few modern conservatives would be as hardline as Basil Ransom. Over time the entire political spectrum has moved to the left.

Novels can be a rich source of knowledge about social attitudes in the past. That the plots are fictional does not detract from the author's need to present characters who would be recognisable to readers of the time, and that necessarily imbues factuality. In that spirit I do not intend to attempt any further review of the book, but wish merely to present quotes which illustrate the nature of feminism as it was in fashionable circles in the USA around the 1870s/80s. Quotes can be assumed to be Olive Chancellor speaking (or thinking), unless otherwise stated or clear from the context. In parentheses are my observations. Perhaps the most remarkable is the one featured last in this list, where Basil Ransom speaks for Henry James, one suspects.

****

"She thought him very handsome as he said this, but reflected that unfortunately men didn't care for the truth, especially the new kinds, in proportion as they were good-looking. She had, however, a moral resource that she could always fall back upon; it had already been a comfort to her, on occasions of acute feeling, that she hated men, as a class, anyway."

(Do note the "new kinds of truth", we're accustomed to that now).

"Olive Chancellor regulated her conduct on lofty principles, and this is why, having tonight the advantage of a gentleman's protection, she sent for a carriage to obliterate that patronage....he belonged to a sex to which she wished to be under no obligations."

(Yet when I tell people that feminism isn't about equality, it's about making women independent of men, even after two centuries of being told this clearly by feminists themselves, they still don't believe it).

"'Are you against emancipation?' she asked, turning a white face on him...their vehicle stopped with a lurch. Basil Ransom got out; he stood at the door with an extended hand, to assist the young lady... 'You hate it!' she exclaimed...She alighted without his help."

"'Don't you believe, then, in the coming of a better day – in its being possible to do something for the human race?'... 'Well, Miss Olive,' he answered... 'what strikes me most is that the human race has got to bear its troubles.' 'That's what men say to women, to make them patient in the position they have made for them.' 'Oh, the position of women!'

Basil Ransom exclaimed. 'The position of women is to make fools of men. I would change my position for yours any day,' he went on. 'That's what I said to myself as I sat there in your elegant home.'" (Ransom was hard pressed financially).

(As if to illustrate what true emancipation and equality looks like, James includes the character Doctor Mary Prance – throughout referred to as Dr Prance. She is a no-nonsense medical scientist and practical doctor, with no time for feminism – or fashionable froth of any kind. Elsewhere in the novel James refers to "lady" journalists as irritating a particular male journalist by their tendency to get their "copy" into print in preference to his. Later, Olive muses to herself about Verena, noting that "the fact that the girl had grown up among lady-doctors, lady-mediums, lady-editors, lady-preachers, lady-healers, women who, having rescued themselves from a passive existence, could illustrate only partially the misery of the sex at large." James is clearly signalling here that female professionals were already a commonplace, even if less so than today. Recall this was 150 years ago.)

(Of Mrs Farrinder, one of the leading feminists of the day): "*She lectured on temperance and the rights of women; the ends she laboured for were to give the ballot to every woman in the country and to take the flowing bowl from every man.*"

(In the UK at this date, and hence before the Third Reform Act of 1884, 67% of men over 21 did not have the parliamentary vote. Over 90% of men earned their living through manual labour of a severity that few men today could tolerate. They had no choice, there was no welfare state. Just saying).

(Of the type of people attending a society gathering at which there was to be a feminist speech): "*Basil Ransom wondered who they all were; he had a general idea they were mediums, communists, vegetarians.*"

(I love that lumping together of "mediums, communists and vegetarians". It reminds me of Orwell in *The Road to Wigan Pier*, referring with coruscating derision to "fruit juice drinkers" and "prim little (socialist) men" who are "secret teetotallers with vegetarian leanings" creeping home to Welwyn Garden City to do their yoga exercises. Ha! *Plus ça change!*).

"*...she (Olive) would do something to brighten the darkness of that dreadful image that was always before her, and against which it seemed to her at times that she had been born* *to lead a crusade – the image of the unhappiness of women. The unhappiness of women! The voice of their silent suffering was always in her ears, the ocean of tears that they had shed from the beginning of time seemed to pour through her own eyes. Ages of oppression had rolled over them; uncounted millions had lived only to be tortured, to be crucified. They were her sisters, they were her own, and the day of their delivery had dawned. This was the only sacred cause, this was the great, the just revolution. It must triumph, it must sweep everything before it; it must exact from the other, the brutal, the blood-stained, ravening race, the last particle of expiation!"*

(This hyperbole, one has to assume, is not James' own opinion. Rather he was recording here the sort of rhetoric that was current, or else how could he have come up with it? It is precisely the voice of modern feminism – and indicates, I believe, that this extremity of perspective, including the demand for 'expiation', springs from a common psychological source).

(Olive): *"'It would be the greatest change the world had seen; it would be a new era for the human family, and the names of those who had helped to show the way and lead the squadrons would be the brightest in the tables of fame. They would be names of women weak, insulted, persecuted, but devoted in every pulse of their being to the cause, and asking no better fate than to die for it.' It was not clear to this interesting girl in what manner such a sacrifice (as this last) would be required of her, but she saw the matter through a kind of sunrise-mist of emotion…"*

(Note the psychological pull being described here is the same in feminism today – victim mentality disorder and the euphoric 'fix' which victimhood confers upon the addict via its "authenticity, innocence and an aura of admirable courage", to quote Janice Fiamengo again.)

(Ransom musing on Verena Tarrant's speech): *"…it was all about the gentleness and goodness of women, and how, during the long ages of history, they had been trampled under the iron heel of man. It was about their equality – perhaps even (he was not definitely conscious) about their superiority. It was about their day having come at last, about the universal sisterhood, about their duty to themselves and to each other."*

(Verena Tarrant): *"'When I look around me at the world, and the state that men have brought it to, I confess I say to myself, well, if women had fixed it this way I should like to know what they would think of it. When I see the dreadful misery of mankind and think of the suffering of which at any hour, at any moment, the world is full, I say that if this is the best they can do by themselves, they had better let us come in a little and see what we can do. We couldn't possibly make it worse, could we?'"*

(Yes – much, much worse. These are the sentiments of the pampered, lacking all appreciation for those by whom their world is maintained.)

"Olive asked her (Verena) where she had got her 'intense realisation' of the suffering of women; for her address…showed that she, too (like Olive herself), had had that vision in the watches of the night. Verena thought a moment….then she inquired, always smiling, where Joan of Arc had got her idea of the suffering of France….She said to her visitor that whether or no the angels came down to her in glittering armour, she struck her as the only person she had yet encountered who had exactly the same tenderness, the same pity, for women that she herself had…it was the only thing in all the world she cared for, the redemption of women."

(Ransom speaking, with tongue in cheek, of Verena's speech, attempting to ingratiate himself): *"I know what your ideas are – you expressed them last night in such beautiful language; of course you convinced me. I am ashamed of being a man; but I am, and I can't help it, I'll do penance any way you may prescribe."*

(Ransom speaking again of Verena's speech, now more seriously): *"Do you really believe all that pretty moonshine you talked last night? I could have listened to you for another hour, but I never heard such monstrous sentiments, I must protest – I must, as a calumniated, misrepresented man. Confess you meant it as a kind of reductio ad absurdum – a satire on Mrs Farrinder?"*

(Ransom again): *"Do you really take the ground that your sex has been without influence? Influence? Why, you have led us all by the nose to where we are now! Wherever we are, it's all you. You are the bottom of everything.' 'Oh, yes, and we want to be at the top,' said Verena".*

(Olive musing on two young gentlemen visitors): *"It was amazing how many ways men had of being antipathetic; these two were very different from Basil Ransom, and different from each other, and yet the manner of each conveyed an insult to one's womanhood. The worst of the case was that Verena would be sure not to perceive this outrage – not to dislike them in consequence. There were so many things she hadn't yet learned to dislike, in spite of her friend's earnest efforts to teach her. She had the idea vividly (that was the marvel) of the cruelty of man, of his immemorial injustice; but it remained abstract, platonic; she didn't detest him in consequence."*

(This is feminism, not just as man-hating, but as taught man-hating).

(Olive): *"Yes, I am hard; perhaps I am cruel; but we must be hard if we wish to triumph. Don't listen to young men when they try to mock and muddle you. They don't care for you;*

they don't care for us. They care only for their pleasure, for what they believe to be the right of the stronger."

(Olive to Verena): *"Promise me not to marry!"*

(Olive): *"No man that I have ever seen cares a straw in his heart for what we are trying to accomplish. They hate it; they scorn it; they will try to stamp it out whenever they can. Oh yes, I know there are men who pretend to care for it; but they are not really men, and I wouldn't be sure even of them!"*

(Poor male feminists – not really men, ha!)

(Olive): *"Any man that one would look at – with him, as a matter of course, it is war upon us to the knife."*

(Why does Olive find attractive men to be the particular enemy? Because the psychological origin of feminism is based essentially in female sexuality).

(Olive): *"She considered men in general as so much in the debt of the opposite sex that any individual woman had an unlimited credit with them; she could not possibly overdraw the general feminine account."*

(Now that is feminist patriarchy theory to a tee – any amount of female preferencing is just the striving for an equality that will never be reached, and all disadvantages imposed on men, however extreme, are always fully justified and always leave men still privileged).

(Olive): *"She had never pretended to deny that the hope of fame, of the very highest distinction, was one of her strongest incitements...A person who might have overheard some of the talk of this possibly infatuated pair would have been touched by their extreme familiarity with the idea of earthly glory."*

"Mrs Luna (Olive's sister) declared that if she must be trampled upon – and very likely it was her fate – she would rather be trampled upon by men than by women, and that if Olive and her friends should get possession of the government they would be worse despots than those who were celebrated in history."

(Indeed – there have always been women who knew well how dangerous is feminism.)

"Miss Chancellor had no difficulty in persuading herself that persons doing the high intellectual and moral work to which the two young ladies in Charles Street were now

committed owed it to themselves, owed it to the groaning sisterhood, to cultivate the best material conditions."

(Of Verena's suitor, Mr Burrage): *" 'Well, he is greatly interested in our movement': so much Verena once managed to announce; but the words rather irritated Miss Chancellor, who, as we know, did not care to allow for accidental exceptions in the great masculine conspiracy."*

(Of Olive and Verena): *"They read a great deal of history together, and read it ever with the same thought – that of finding confirmation in it for this idea that their sex had suffered inexpressibly, and that at any moment in the course of human affairs the state of the world would have been so much less horrible...if women had been able to press down the scale. Verena was full of suggestions which stimulated discussions; it was she, oftenest, who kept in view the fact that a good many women in the past had been entrusted with power and had not always used it amiably, who brought up the wicked queens, the profligate mistresses of kings. These ladies were easily disposed of between the two, and the public crimes of Bloody Mary, the private misdemeanours of Faustina, wife of the pure Marcus Aurelius, were very satisfactorily classified. If the influence of women in the past accounted for every act of virtue that men had happened to achieve, it only made the matter balance properly that the influence of men should explain the casual irregularities of the other sex."*

(So familiar! There really is nothing new in modern feminism, is there? Except that it is now the establishment.)

"...our young friends had a source of fortifying emotion...This consisted in the wonderful insight they had obtained into the history of feminine anguish. They perused that chapter perpetually and zealously, and they derived from it the purest part of their mission. Olive had poured over it so long, so earnestly, that she was now in complete possession of the subject...she reminded Verena how the exquisite weakness of women had never been their defence, but had only exposed them to sufferings more acute than masculine grossness can conceive. Their odious partner had trampled upon them from the beginning of time, and their tenderness, their abnegation, had been his opportunity."

"...it was women, in the end, who had paid for everything. In the last resort the whole burden of the human lot came upon them; it pressed upon them far more than on others, the intolerable load of fate. It was they who sat cramped and chained to receive it; it was they who had done all the waiting and taken all the wounds. The sacrifices, the blood, the tears, the terrors were theirs. Their organism was in itself a challenge to suffering, and men had practiced upon it with an impudence that knew no bounds. As they were the weakest

most had been wrung from them, and as they were the most generous they had been most deceived."

"...she (Verena) was not so hungry for revenge as Olive, but at the last...she quite agreed with her companion that after so many ages of wrong...men must take their turn, men must pay!"

"'I advocate equal rights, equal opportunities, equal privileges. So does Miss Chancellor,' Verena added, with just a perceptible air of feeling that her declaration needed support.' 'Oh, I thought what she wanted was simply a different inequality – simply to turn out the men altogether,' Ransom said. 'Well, she thinks we have great arrears to make up. I do tell her, sometimes, that what she desires is not only justice but vengeance, I think she admits that', Verena continued."

"As he went on with Verena he asked her about the Women's Convention, the year before; whether it had accomplished much work and she had enjoyed it. 'What do you care about the work it accomplished?' said the girl. 'You don't take any interest in that.' 'You mistake my attitude. I don't like it, but I greatly fear it.' In answer to this Verena gave a free laugh. 'I don't believe you fear much!' 'The bravest men have been afraid of women' (said Ransom)."

"'I suppose it was very exciting – your convention,' Ransom went on, in a moment, 'the sort of thing you would miss very much if you were to return to the ancient fold.' 'The ancient fold, you say very well, where women were slaughtered like sheep! Oh, last June, for a week, we just quivered! There were delegates from every State and every city...'"

(Note that such mass feminist rallies were taking place in the 1870s – and, of course, Seneca Falls was 1848. We can assume these would have been attended only by bourgeois women; working class women could not afford such frivolities. Recall again what the plight of the majority of British men was at this time: disenfranchised beasts of burden).

"The Memorial Hall of Harvard consists of three main divisions....the third, the most interesting, a chamber high, dim, and severe, consecrated to the sons of the university who fell in the long Civil War....they lingered longest in the presence of the white, ranged tablets, each of which, in its proud, sad clearness, is inscribed with the name of a student-soldier. The effect of the place is singularly noble and solemn, and it is impossible to feel it without a lifting of the heart. It stands there for duty and honour, it speaks of sacrifice and example, seems a kind of temple to youth, manhood, generosity. Most of them were young, all were in their prime, and all of them had fallen... 'It is very beautiful – but I think it is very

dreadful!' This remark, from Verena, called him (Ransom) back to the present. 'It's a real sin to put up such a building to glorify a lot of bloodshed. If it wasn't so majestic, I would have it pulled down.'"

(Recall that Ransom had fought on the other side, and yet he regarded this monument with the utmost respect, not as a challenge or a rebuke. Verena, in contrast, goes on to claim that when women had the conduct of affairs they would "reason so well they would have no need to fight – they would usher in the reign of peace". You've heard that one before, haven't you?)

"...she (Olive) asked him about his mother and sisters, what news he had from the South. 'Have they any happiness?' she inquired, rather as if she warned him to care not to pretend they had."

"'Ah, don't be rough with me,' he said, in his soft Southern voice; 'don't you remember how you knocked me about when I called on you in Boston?' (Olive replies) 'You hold us in chains, and then, when we writhe in our agony, you say we don't behave prettily.'"

(Ransom, thinking of Verena's speech): *"'Certain phrases took on a meaning for him – an appeal she was making to those who still resisted the beneficent influence of the truth....there were those whose prejudice was stronger and more cultivated, pretended to rest upon study and argument. To those she wished particularly to address herself; she wanted to waylay them, to say, 'look here, you're all wrong; you'll be so much happier when I have convinced you.'... 'Do you think any state of society can come to good that is based upon an organised wrong?'"*

(No)

(From Verena's speech): *"...the precious sovereign remedy, of which society insanely deprives itself – the genius, the intelligence, the inspiration of women...The heart, the heart is cold, and nothing but the touch of woman can warm it, make it act. We are the Heart of humanity...Try us and you'll see – you will wonder how, without us, society has ever dragged itself even this distance – so wretchedly small compared to what might have been...I shall not touch upon the subject of men's being most easily influenced by considerations of what is most agreeable and profitable to them; I shall simply assume that they are so influenced, and I shall say to them that our cause would long ago have been gained if their vision were not so dim...It they had the same quick sight as women, if they had the intelligence of the heart, the world would be very different now...you would find grass and trees and flowers that would make you think you were in Eden...There would be generosity, tenderness, sympathy, where there is now only brute force and sordid rivalry. But you really do strike me as stupid even about your own welfare!"*

(You'll be getting the point by now – the entire psychological orientation of feminism as we know it today was in place 150 years ago – and presumably long before that. Basil Ransom's view of Verena's speech was that "from any serious point of view it was neither worth answering nor worth considering". He then reflects on "the crazy character of the age in which such a performance as that was treated as an intellectual effort". Quite.)

(Ransom, after a bad-tempered exchange with Olive): *"He turned away, with the sense that it was really insufferable, her attempt always to give him the air of being in the wrong. If that was the kind of spirit in which women were going to act when they had more power!"*

(Unfortunately, yes, it was to be.)

(Olive to Verena): *"I'll tell you what is the matter with you – you don't dislike men as a class!"*

"It was nothing new to Verena that if the great striving of Olive's life was for justice she yet sometimes failed to arrive at it in particular cases."

(Exactly)

(Olive to Verena in reply to her wish to talk to Ransom to convince him of their case, arguing that she had right on her side): *"What is that – for a man? For what was their brutality given them, but to make that up?'"*

(Ransom speaking to Verena in perhaps the most remarkable passage in the book): *"There has been far too much talk about you, and I want to leave you alone altogether. My interest is in my own sex; yours evidently can look after itself. That's what I want to save.' 'To save from what?' she asked. 'From the most damnable feminisation! I am so far from thinking, as you set forth the other night, that there is not enough women in our general life, that it has long been pressed home to me that there is a great deal too much. The whole generation is womanised; the masculine tone is passing out of the world; it's a feminine, a nervous, hysterical, chattering, canting age, an age of hollow phrases and false delicacy and exaggerated solicitudes and coddled sensibilities, which, if we don't soon look out, will usher in the reign of mediocrity, of the feeblest and flattest and the most pretentious kind that has ever been. The masculine character, the ability to dare and endure, to know and yet not to fear reality, to look the world in the face and take it for what it is…that is what I want to preserve, or rather, as I may say, to recover; and I must tell you that I don't in the least care what becomes of you ladies while I make the attempt!'"*

(Well said, Mr James. The author has Ransom note that the rejection of the ideas expressed in that last quote by leading periodicals "was certainly not a matter for surprise". It seems one could not talk openly about countering male feminisation even 150 years ago! Perhaps anticipating some trouble publishing, despite this being his eighth novel, James has Ransom say "editors are a mean timorous lot, always saying they want something original, but deadly afraid of it when it comes". It seems that goad did the trick, though James' reputation by that time would have helped.)

References

[1] Fiamengo, J. (2021). *Why I Am Still An Anti-Feminist: TFF 2.0*. The Fiamengo Files 2.0, 27 December 2021.

[2] Fiamengo, J. (2022). *Nineteenth-Century Novelist Henry James Predicted Twentieth-Century Feminism*. The Fiamengo Files 2.0, 5 May 2022.

61. The Power: A Review

This is a review of The Power, a novel by Naomi Alderman. To this day I cannot see what the author was trying to achieve, other than the most brutal confession of a lust for torturing men.

Original posted on: <u>16 January 2018</u>.

The book in question is Ref.[1], winner of the 2017 Bailey's Women's Prize for fiction. It asks the question "what if the power to hurt were in women's hands?" and answers it very clearly indeed.

Now I'm frightened. But it's not only the book that I find frightening. It is more the reaction of many women to it in the real world which terrifies. The author's own position, too, seems paradoxical.

It's not what you'd call fine writing, but if you are happy to judge a book by its page turning qualities, then this is a good book. My own personal criterion of quality is whether you find yourself thinking about a book for some days after reading it. *The Power* by Naomi Alderman passes that test also.

But I didn't say it was *nice*. It's not *nice*. It's really very nasty. It's odd, isn't it, that the safe space and trigger warning generation seems simultaneously to have sensibilities so jaded, so inured to depictions of violence, that the datum of normality is on an ever-escalating upward ratchet. The resolution of this paradox is that novels of this type have one foot in the world of computer games. No great insight is required to make this observation given that Naomi Alderman also writes game scripts. This hybrid of novel-cum-game potentially allows the gamer's cartoonish levels of violence to be imported into the novel format, to the detriment of the novelistic element, in my opinion. To an antediluvian brought up on the gentility of Austen, Dickens, George Elliot and E.M.Forster, it is all horribly brutish.

Is it a feminist novel? I was almost poised to declare it an anti-feminist novel. How can the violent excesses of the second half of the book be regarded as presenting female power in a favourable light? Unfortunately, those in thrall to the feminist lens can do so, it seems. *The Power* was reviewed on a Radio 4 book programme a month or two back. Owen Jones opined that it was "*a fascinating dissection of the Patriarchy – it's a satire on Patriarchy*". Err, no. It isn't. Mr Jones proceeded to treat us to the familiar feminist line on VAWG. But the book is about female violence upon men – and this is not allegorical, it is *essentially* about female violence upon men. Was it my imagination, or was the female presenter a little embarrassed by Jones's take on the book? She expressed her view as being *"whoever has the power is going to abuse it"*. That is certainly very much closer to the mark. But I get ahead of myself. Let's get to the plot…

Adolescent girls suddenly acquire The Power – the ability to send high voltage shocks from their fingers and electrocute others. Quickly it spreads to all women. Alderman's book examines the consequences of this change for society.

Spoiler alert! Synopsis follows. If you are thinking of reading the book you might wish to do so now, before proceeding.

The book opens with thugs breaking into Roxy's house and killing her mother and sticking Roxy in a cupboard. Turns out it was Roxy's Dad that sent the thugs to bump off her Mum, but we don't know that yet. Also, it turns out later that Roxy was sexually abused (surprise!) by her piano teacher, so her Dad cut his balls off, as one does. Roxy discovers her ability to electrocute, and soon all adolescent girls do too. From them it spreads to all women. A man in a supermarket oppresses a girl by asking her to smile, so he gets zapped. Had it coming, the bastard. That's the start of The Day of the Girls. Domestic violence figures soar, boys get segregated for their own safety, girls start to fight each other. Girls with feeble power are mocked and shamed.

By chapter two we have The Power also being used by girls to sexually stimulate boys. Yes, there's going to be lots and lots of The Power being used to execute sexual violence, as well as plain vanilla frying of brains and such.

Mixed race Allie was orphaned and passed around many foster homes. Her foster 'Dad', Mr Montgomery-Taylor, sexually abuses her (surprise!), so, obviously, the menz darn well deserve what they've got coming. But that biblical voice in Allie's head is a little worrying.

We have some delightful vignettes such as seven policemen beating a woman to within an inch of her life (one sees it all the time), thus further legitimising what the menz have got coming. By chapter seven the Saudi women are on the rampage. They want sex, and they're going to get it by raping men. But we all know what vile misogynistic scum the Saudis are, so that's OK too, you must agree. (No, you MUST agree). In the blink of an eye, masses of cities all over the world are being run by gangs of women "mostly freed from sexual slavery" (which legitimises anything, including near obliteration of the human race, as we'll see).

Ricky, one of Roxy's Dad's mobsters, gets raped by three women. *"Down there it was just burned flesh, fern pattern on the thighs, pink and brown and raw red and black. Like a Sunday roast"*. Roxy and the girls take revenge (role reversal). Tunde nearly gets raped too, but is saved by other women (more role reversal).

Jocelyn is a nice girl, really – but a little uncontrolled. *"His scalp crisps under her hand. He screams. Inside his skull liquid is cooking. Delicate parts are fusing and congealing. The lines of power are scarring him, faster than thought. She can't hold it back. It's not a good way to go. She didn't mean to do it"*.

Roxy takes over the Mob and also becomes an international big wheel via the leadership of Allie who is now Mother Eve. Mother Eve can now use The Power to heal and to control people's thoughts and actions. Pretty darn cool superpower. She's still being guided by her biblical voices. She declares God to be a woman, that *"woman rules over man"*, and that lesbianism is preferable. This all seems vaguely familiar.

We are constantly reminded that men are vile and deserve all the worldwide extreme violence they get, such as,

"This is a place men come when they want a woman they can use without law or licence, discard without censure."

"There are eight of them, four women, four men, all mid-twenties....Bankers. One of the men already has his hand up one of the women's skirt."

"We don't have to ask ourselves who is on the side of justice when we meet the brave fighters of Bessapara – many of whom were trafficked women, shackled women, women who would have died alone in the dark."

"There was a time that a woman could not walk alone here....now they (i.e., men) will know that they are the ones who should not walk out of their houses alone at night. They are the ones who should be afraid."

A quote with a large number of highlights showing on my Kindle is "*The only wave that changes anything is a tsunami. You have to tear down the houses and destroy the land if you want to be sure no one will forget you.*" Bear that in mind when it comes to debating whether feminists might truly think it worthwhile destroying the planet and sending humans back to the Neolithic period in order to achieve their feminist Utopia. And be worried.

There are no straight white males in the book who are not vile. Tunde is about the only non-vile male in the book, but he's a black Nigerian, so that's OK. Oh, and Jocelyn's friend Ryan, but he's indeterminate on the gender spectrum, so that's OK too. Daniel, the archetypal straight white 'powerful' male politician is an egomaniac. Margot hates him and covets his job. More of them shortly.

Once the pogrom of men has started (but the media are covering it up) Tom makes a plea on-air about the need to protect men. Gets sacked.

At the simplest level, *The Power* is a tale of feminist wish-fulfilment. One can imagine the author finding writing it a visceral pleasure. I'm sure that the appeal of the book to many feminist readers will be simply this revenge-porn aspect. ("*As I began to read this futuristic tale I was nodding and going YESS, when the young girls first discover their power, like when Wonder Woman kicks ass....... the book certainly packs a punch, makes you think, makes you dream, makes you tingle and makes you wonder: what if?*" reviewed by The Feminist Library, Ref.[2]). I spent the first half of the book hoping there would be more to it than that. There wasn't. But it got worse.

It seems women are not entirely lovely. Increasingly through the second half of the book, the women's invariably gratuitous violence becomes impossible to defend, surely even to someone of feminist sympathies. At least, you would think so. Disconcertingly, though, it would appear that women in the real world react differently – of which more shortly.

After her power kicks in, Margot's political career really takes off. It seems the public didn't mind her zapping her opponent on live TV. She becomes a sexual predator and starts to lie blatantly to further her career, selling out for power and money. (For all of which read "just like a man" – more role reversal). "*Later, in the hotel, she buys a couple of drinks for one of the junior guys from the American embassy in the Ukraine. He's attentive – well, why wouldn't he be? She's going places. She rests her hand on his firm young ass as they ride the elevator together up to her suite.....she could lick the flesh straight off his bones, there's always more blokes where he came from; they're ten a penny. Especially if she were President".*

Tatiana becomes leader of Bessapara by the simple expedient of killing her husband, then goes full-on Stalin-Mao-Pol-Pot but worse. Men must be under the guardianship of a woman and have papers to prove it. Men may not gather. *"They are rounding up the men without papers. They go away for 'work detail' but they do not return".*

"The young man swallows. 'I'm sorry', he says. 'Did I tell you to speak?' she (Tatiana) says..... 'Needs to be taught some manners', says one of the women.....Tatiana plucks the bottle of brandy from the young man's hands....A glass of this is worth more than you....She drops it to the floor. The glass smashes.... 'Lick it up', she says.....There are glass fragments among the brandy......He kneels down and begins to tongue the floor."

"The police here no longer investigate the murder of men...if a man is found dead it is presumed that a vengeance gang had given him his proper reward for his deeds in the time before. Even a young boy....a boy who is only fifteen now — what could he have done in the time before?"

"There are accounts on Tom Hobson's website of things happening in Bessapara that Jos can't really believe. Torture and experiments, gangs of women on the loose in the north near the border, murdering and raping men at will."

Roxy saves Tunde and Tunde saves the now-Powerless Roxy. They both witness the utter horror of mass rapes, torture and murder of men by gangs of militarised feral women who attack refugee camps for the purpose, high on drugs which enhance their power further. There are graphic depictions of this sadistic sexual violence perpetrated by women.

"You are weak and we are strong. You are the gift and we are the owners. You are the victim and we are the victors. You are the slave and we are the masters. You are the sacrifice and we are the recipients......And when she killed him it was ecstasy."

"He will not stop screaming. Two of the women take him by the throat and send a paralysis into his spine. One squats on top of him. She pulls off his trousers. He is not unconscious.....The woman cups his balls and dick in her palm.....She puts her head to one side, makes a sad face at him. She might as well have said in any language in the world 'What's the matter? Can't get it up?'....The woman sitting on the man's chest applies her palm to his genitals.....He's still doing muffled screaming.....His cock comes up like a salute, like they always do......She holds his balls, tugs on them once, twice,

just as if she were giving him a treat, and then jolts him fiercely, right through the scrotum. It'd feel like a glass spike, driven straight through.....He screams, arches his back. And she unbuttons the crotch of her combat trousers and sits on his cock. Her mates are laughing now and she's laughing herself as she pumps herself up and down on him. She's got her hand firmly planted in the centre of his stomach, giving him a dose every time she thrusts up with bunched thighs."

"There is no sense in what is done here this day. There is no territory to be gained, or a particular wrong to be avenged, or even soldiers to be taken. They kill the older men in front of the younger with palms to the faces and the throat, and one shows off her special skill of drawing crude effects upon the flesh with the tips of her fingers. Many of them take some of the men, and use them, or simply play with them.....They do it because they can."

"...they have the arm off. The others are at his legs, and his neck, and the other arm....Like the wind stripping leaves from a tree, so inexorable, so violent.......they get his head off, and at last he is quiet, their fingers dark with his blood......."

So what happened to "if women had the power the world would be a place of peace and perfection"? It's clear that Alderman is not portraying women as demonstrating a responsible and constructive use of power, is she?

Well, it's clear to me. Staggeringly, it is not to others. I watched several YouTube videos of women reviewing the book. You might have expected these reviewers to have found the women's violence against men as salutary. You might have expected some conclusion to be drawn, such as 'power corrupts' or something along those lines. You might have expected the extremity of the violence to at least be recognised as reprehensible. But no. Staggeringly, more monstrous by far than the book itself, these women reviewers saw nothing untoward. The words these women used to describe the book were "fun", "exciting", "fulfilling", "satisfying". One said, *"I did feel like I wanted to get back at men for the pain inflicted on women"*. The nearest another managed to come to condemnation of brutal mass murder of men by women was that it was *"disconcerting the decisions people make"*. Do note the use of the gender-neutral word "people" there.

Another woman reviewer said, *"For me it showed the depth of pain that these women felt about what men had done to them and that was the important point"*. Most of the men in question were attempting to flee, in refugee camps. Deconstruct the sentiment behind that remark. Do you recall those social experiment videos on YouTube in which a woman is violent to a man in public – and the public reaction is to assume that the woman is the real victim because the bloke must have done something to deserve it? Well, that woman's comment is exactly in that tradition. Some women – is it the majority? – simply cannot interpret a woman as being responsible for her own violence against a man. It would seem their psychology compels them always to hold a man, or men in general, as culpable for their own victimisation – even when the level of women's gratuitous violence is as extreme as imaginable and comes within an ace of obliterating the entire human race. Still the prejudice holds. Still the slaughtered men in this nasty tale are the villains in the eyes of ordinary female reviewers.

One woman reviewer declared the MRA bloggers represented in the book made her really angry and actually complained that there were no male allies in the book. That's right, whilst women were busy around the globe electrocuting men to death in the most extreme sadistic manner, this woman seems still to think that men should be supporting their noble cause. And *that* is what is truly terrifying; not so much this nasty book itself, but what it has helpfully revealed about female psychology. The phrase "empathy gap" is too mild to encompass this horror. What hope can there be?

There is a toxicity abroad in our society, but it isn't masculinity.

The best advert for MGTOW I have yet come across is the reaction of "ordinary" women reviewers to this book.

Immediately before the denouement, the global conflict which results in Cataclysm, Allie perceives the fraudulence of the militant women's supposed moral legitimacy.

Mrs Montgomery-Taylor, it turns out, was the prime mover behind her husband's sexual abuse of Allie. And not only Allie but a succession of children. When Allie finally learns of this, she realises the skew in her own perception, that the simplistic 'men bad, women good' won't cut it. *"to denounce her would be to denounce everything. If she roots this out, she roots out herself. Her own roots are rotten already. And with this she is undone"*. At last, Allie questions her inner voice. Is it not, after all, the unimpeachable voice of rectitude and justice? *"I keep meaning to ask. Who are you? I've wondered for a while. Are you the serpent?"*

Tellingly the voice attempts to exonerate itself thus: "*The whole point of me was to keep things simple for you, you see? That's what you wanted. Simple feels safe. Certainty feels safe.*"

This is the most important passage in the book. It exposes as clearly as Alderman dares the appeal of an ideology based on cognitive minimalism. Eliminating moral dilemmas at a stroke, women are always blameless whatever they do. But Allie has finally realised that this is not reality.

"*Who's bad and who's good? Who persuaded the other to eat the apple? Who has the power and who's powerless?*" asks the voice. "*It's more complicated than that.....You people like to pretend things are simple, even at your own cost.*"

Allie silences the voice for ever – but goes right on with her jihad in any case. This is the nature of tragedy. She tells her followers, "*the apocalypse is near at hand and only the righteous will be saved, she can call the world to a new order. The end of all flesh is near, because the Earth is filled with violence. Therefore, build an ark. It will be simple. That is all they want.*" It is hard to read this as anything other than an admonishment.

Roxy is not keen on apocalypse. She says to Mother Eve, "*But you know what's going to happen. We'll bomb them and they'll bomb us and it'll spread out wider and wider....the women will suffer as well as the men, Evie. The women will die just as much as the men will if we bomb ourselves back to the stone age. And then we'll be in the stone age....And then there will be five thousand years of rebuilding, five thousand years where the only thing that matters is: can you hurt more, can you do more damage, can you instill fear?*"

"*And then the women will win*", replies Allie.

But what sort of a "win" is it, Alderman implicitly asks? Near obliteration of the human race, with the mass suffering which is implied, followed by a return to the Neolithic. After 5,000 years re-running human history what we end up with (according to Alderman) is just like now – except with the sex roles reversed. So in what way is anything improved?

Monstrously, those whose worldview is that men are currently powerful and privileged may actually regard this as a win for women. I'm not even sure of Alderman herself. It seems that the loopier feminist could read the whole book without thinking the planet-wide violence against men had gone too far. Anything – anything – is justified, even putting the human race back 5,000 years, in order to achieve feminist Utopia.

Based on its contents alone I would have been inclined to praise the book (though not its reviewers) for illustrating how destructive female violence would be if they were gifted such a Power. Given the premise, I think Alderman has the subsequent course of events bang on – at least as far as the Cataclysm. Exactly what would happen during history#2, and what sort of society would emerge in 5,000 years, is another matter. That, I suspect, she has wrong.

However, I am very conflicted regarding what Ms Alderman herself intended. Could it be that she thought near-global death and trashing humans back to the Neolithic was a price worth paying to achieve a society just like our present society, but with women "on top"? If she were reincarnated at that time, she would be *so* disappointed at how not-on-top that turns out to be! (In 2018 I added to that sentence "ask Norah Vincent", Ref.[3] – alas, no longer possible as she has subsequently died). There are reasons to be concerned that Ms Alderman inclines rather more to the revenge-porn position than the salutary-tale-of-corrupting-power perspective. For example, she has explained her motive for writing the book in interviews thus,

"I got onto the Tube and saw a poster for some movie, a thriller, where the main image was a beautiful woman crying. It was also what I was doing: waking up crying, feeling that I might break into pieces. It felt like the culture we live in was saying: 'Good. That's what you should be doing. We like it. We find it sexy'." (Ref.[4])

"Hey, that crying that you're doing right now, carry on with that, that's sexy, that's great. We love it when women cry. We love it when women suffer. Do more of that. Hey, it's really attractive." I just started thinking furiously on this Tube train about what I would have to do, or what would have to change in the world for me to be sitting opposite a poster of a really beautiful, attractive man crying." (Ref.[5])

I simply do not recognise what she is claiming here. We (i.e., men) love it when women suffer? We find it sexy? No, this is simply false as well as a horrible calumny. I believe that men and women generally react the same way to seeing a woman cry – namely with sympathy and concern. Why does Ms Alderman think differently? Her view of men is wildly at odds with empirical reality; it seems to be a product of her own mind.

In the book, Margot, daydreaming in a political meeting with the hated Daniel and others, thinks, *"She could kill them. That is the profound truth of it......Nothing that either of these men says is really of any great significance, because she could kill them in three moves before they stirred in their comfortably padded chairs....The power to hurt is a kind of wealth"*. What does this tell us about Naomi Alderman? Does she think that men sit around musing on how easily they could kill women? Disturbingly this is indeed the basis of feminist patriarchy theory: that men dominate in society by physical violence upon women – real or threatened. But I know, via my lived experience as well as empirical evidence, that it is untrue – wildly, monstrously untrue.

It is difficult to decide whether Alderman is deliberately exposing the unacceptable extremes of feminism, or glorying in contemplating their fruition. I am prevented from working it out by Poe's Law. Take, for example, this extract, supposedly characterising the emerging consensus amongst the increasingly murderous women,

"How many men do we really need?...Men are dangerous. Men commit the great majority of crimes. Men are less intelligent, less diligent, less hard-working, their brains are in their muscles and their pricks. Men are more likely to suffer from diseases and they are a drain on the resources of the country. Of course we need them to have babies, but how many do we need for that? Not as many as women....Maybe one in ten."

A TV presenter reacts to this with the words, *"I blame those men's rights people; they're so extreme, they've provoked this kind of response."*

What am I to make of this given that, here in the real world, the suggestion that males would be best reduced to around one-in-ten has been a staple of radical feminism for decades Ref.[6]? And, in truth, it took decades for even a small number of men to have the temerity to object to views suggesting they should be culled. Is Alderman just winding us up in suggesting that radical feminism was a reaction to the men's movement, rather than the reverse? I cannot tell, but, lamentably, I think not – I think she means it.

In the book Alderman has Jocelyn describe UrbanDox's web site as "horrible" for observing that what is happening is a *"holy war between men and women"* – and yet this war has been declared *de facto* by women the world over "because they could" – and is explicitly holy to Mother Eve and her followers. Yet she refers in the book to *"the men's movement, and...their particular conspiracy theories"*. But how can Alderman refer to men's concerns –

in the book – as being a conspiracy, given that shortly most people in the world are to die in the Cataclysm?

And what can we infer about the consistency of Alderman's position in real life? In an interview, Ref.[7], she used almost the same words of the real world: *"Men's rights activists spread conspiracy theories in online forums whose rhetoric is sickeningly familiar"*. If I am sickening, Ms Alderman, what words are left to describe your book and, even more so, women's reaction to it?

References

[1] Alderman, N. (2016). *The Power*. Viking, 27 October 2016.

[2] O'Mahoney, S. (2017). *Review of 'The Power' by Naomi Alderman*. The Feminist Library, 27 July 2017.

[3] Vincent, N. (2006). *Self-Made Man: My Year Disguised as a Man*. Atlantic Books, 14 Sept. 2006.

[4] Jilani, S. (2016). *Naomi Alderman interview: 'The book's not mine anymore, the rights are sold'*. Independent, 28 October 2016.

[5] Krishna, S. (2017). *Q&A: Naomi Alderman on her electrifying work of feminist sc-fi, 'The Power'*. Los Angeles Times, 27 October 2017.

[6] Roberts, C. (2003). *Male-Bashing and a Foreboding of the Future*. ifeminists, 12 August 2003.

[7] Rutherford, A. (2016). *Role Reversal: Naomi Alderman on The Power*. The Skinny, 24 October 2016.

62. Of Frogs And Men

This is an obituary, of sorts, of the late Professor Geoff Dench who died on 24 June 2018. Specifically, I recall the significance of his 1996 book "Transforming Men". Dench was amongst the first to identify social decline with the decline of men and to denounce feminism as the cause.

"Most commentators still seem hugely reluctant to link this collapse of men openly to the rise of feminism" – In memoriam, Geoff Dench (1940 – 2018)

Original posted on: 9 July 2018.

In 1996, Professor Geoff Dench, who died on 24 June 2018, published the book *Transforming Men*, Ref.[1]. He did not choose the title himself. Dench used the fairy story *The Frog Prince* as an allegory for gender relations in the West. There is a curious consilience with what was contemporary in 2018, and Jordan Peterson comes into it. But first, Dench's argument – starting with the fairy story itself…

A young princess, still very much a child, who spends all her time playing, ventures outside the palace grounds and enters the wild forest beyond. Her golden ball, which she values above all else, falls into a pool (or well) and sinks from view, leaving her heartbroken.

To her surprise a frog appears and speaks to her, offering to retrieve her ball for her if she promises to be his friend. In her childish grief for the lost ball, and carelessly disregarding the future, she agrees. So the frog restores her ball to her.

The princess returns to the palace, where she is later embarrassed by the frog who has followed her, and who now insists on her keeping the promise of friendship. She is reluctant, but her father, the King, insists that she honour her commitment.

So, the frog is allowed to participate in the civilised activities of the palace, such as eating at the table and sharing the princess's food. After contact has become more intimate, variously expressed as the princess kissing the frog, or allowing him to sleep on her pillow (with the result, in some versions, that she begins to feel more friendly towards him), the frog turns into a prince.

He declares that this is in fact his original and true form, and that by befriending him the princess has removed from him the spell of an evil witch. They marry – for the princess has now matured – and go off in a gold coach to live at the prince's own castle.

In what way did Dench interpret this fairy story as an allegory for gender relations? Dench was a social anthropologist and naturally comes at the matter from that perspective. For Dench the key anthropological problem for a society to solve is how to make constructive use of men. Think primates: the males are a law unto themselves. Or, rather, a lawlessness. They make less contribution to the troop than males in human societies. There is, of course, no pair bonding amongst most primates; no paternal resourcing. Arguably, the anthropological inventions of family and society are key to the evolutionary success of *Homo sapiens*. Not that Dench would express it in that way.

But he certainly argued strongly for the crucial importance of family. And families include fathers, and fathers mean patriarchy. Aargh! But Dench did not understand patriarchy in the feminist sense – namely a conspiracy by men to oppress and exploit women. For Dench, patriarchy was a piece of theatre, a subterfuge expressly designed to tie men into familial relationships whose purpose was twofold: to extract benefit from men whilst minimising the threat of men reverting to a feral state. From this perspective, patriarchy is closer to an exploitation of men by women rather than the reverse. This aligns with my own view as expressed in *The Empathy Gap*, Ref.[2], though Dench would not have taken my evolutionary approach to it.

So, to the interpretation of the story. A frog is a feral male – or a free male, if you will: a male who is not a patriarch, a family man. A prince is a male bound into society via family – and society (or the 'moral economy') is predominantly female. As a boy, and a member of a family, a male starts as a prince. As he becomes mature, however, he becomes independent and loses his initial status as a prince. He is no longer accepted by female society and has become a frog. Most adolescent males know what it is to be a frog. It is specifically female society which rejects the young man, so, in the myth, it is a witch – the analogue of female society – which casts the spell which turns him into a frog.

To re-enter society – to become once again a prince – the frog must avail himself of female magic for a second time. To this end he must perform some service of great value to a princess. That done, the princess becomes locked into an obligation which – it is notable – the King, the existing patriarch, enforces. The externally enforced obligation is essential, because the princess is initially repulsed by the frog.

The allegory makes explicit female power over men: to turn them into frogs, or frogs into princes. The presumption of the story is that any frog must prefer to become a prince. But the twist for our times is that a frog may prefer to remain a frog, despite the dangers of the forest. Being a prince sounds grand, but actually means duty and obligation, in contrast to the freedom of the forest. And as for the modern princess, she is no longer so keen on transforming frogs, and her patriarch, the King, has been usurped by his wife, the Queen, who does not enforce the old rules. As Dench writes,

"Girls no longer want to be dependent, even nominally; and boys are losing hope of being turned into princes. It is time to re-write the story as a fin-de-millennium lament, or even a horror story. In it the princess refuses to accept the loathsome frog as a partner after all. Her power to perform good magic is thereby wasted; and the original spell of the witch, far from being broken, remains unchecked and grows in strength. Soon the princess's father, the King, abdicates and turns back into a monstrous and malevolent frog himself, and starts abusing the inhabitants of the palace. Bereft of leadership, the kingdom slips into feuding and chaos, its citizens selfish and unruly; and the forest of individual desire starts to encroach upon the formerly meticulous and orderly palace gardens."

Patriarchy was only ever a piece of theatre, a con, and the status of prince in part illusion and in part reward. Surely the witch and the princess were playing for the same team, working the prince-frog-prince scam. In which case, was the "prince", who was never truly a prince, never truly a frog either?

In a curious resonance of frogs, current in 2018, enter Pepe (remember him?). And enter Kek, who, in ancient Egyptian mythology, was the deification of the concept of primordial darkness. Enter Jordan Peterson and Jonathan Pageau, on whom the relevance of *The Frog Prince* is not lost, as made explicit in their discussion of the metaphysics of Pepe, Ref.[3]. In *The Frog Prince* the choice of frog as the creature into which the prince is turned is appropriate because, herpetophiles aside, frogs are generally perceived as physically repulsive, especially to beautiful, self-regarding princesses. But there is something deeper here. The frog is a mythological archetype. Being amphibian, the frog mediates between two states of being. Water represents chaos, and frogs being at home in water, are the emissaries of chaos. The explosion of popularity of the Pepe meme saw the ubiquitous frog deployed to represent absolutely anything. Being the emissary of the primordial, Pepe naturally inclines to the glorification of misrule. As Jonathan Pageau has explained, Ref.[4], the universal applicability of the Pepe meme is because, as a manifestation of chaos, it can instantiate anything. Chaos is at the same time nothing and everything. A frog is empowered to pull a specific instantiation out of the infinite potential of chaos, such as a golden ball from a pond.

So much for metaphysics and mythology. What follows are extracts from Dench's *Transforming Men* (in italics), interspersed with my commentary.

Patriarchy

Feminists will say that patriarchy hurts men too. But I would say that patriarchy was designed primarily to "hurt" men, or, to be more precise, to control men. That is essentially Dench's position,

"Patriarchy is a system that may well have been largely devised and promoted by primordial matriarchs in order to even out the burden on their children."

"Patriarchal exaggeration of men's importance obscures the deeper power of women, and behind the theatre of male dominion the palace holds many secrets."

"The whole plot existed first in the mind of the witch. It was, I suspect, the mothers who conjured up the prince in their efforts to turn men into more reliable helpers; and it is the arrangements they invented which feminism now seeks to blame on men."

"It seems very likely that feminist promulgation of ideas that family life mainly serves men, and that women are "doing it all for men", is in part, at least, a reworking of traditional devices for exerting more leverage over men. The appearance of male control and benefit is a cover which permits women considerable moral power in practice. Hera, goddess of marriage and a jealous wife, is also the power behind the throne."

One sees here the origins of the instinct of women towards victimhood. The creation of the patriarchal illusion provided the basis for feminist women to claim victimhood. It has long been the case that such victimhood, or seeming subservience, worked as the source of women's moral leverage.

"What 'The Frog Prince' and its ilk have done in the past is to sell the path of matrimony and responsible fatherhood. Patriarchal cultures teach boys that their nature is evil and they must rebuild themselves around a sense of duty."

"By rejecting men and allowing them back on terms acceptable to themselves as major guardians of the general interest, women in concert act as filters for a natural resource which would otherwise at best be lost to society, and at worst pose dangers."

These extracts express Dench's view of patriarchy: that it provides a semblance of authority to men in return for the reality of men's service to benefit women and society generally. But feminists are dismantling patriarchy without knowing what it is they're dismantling…

"The frog, or knight, is free to wander following his fancy, and needs to recognise no frontiers. But a prince belongs to the land and his subjects."

"The frog, knowing no dependents, is largely self-sufficient in his pool, and can find little reason to abandon freedom and precious playing time just to become a domestic help. To be tempted from the pleasures of the forest, men need to be flattered by an important sounding title, and by the hint – which becomes absurd as soon as it is examined closely – that all of this business of child rearing and reproducing society is in some way being done for them and takes place under their indispensable management. Want to be my helper? Well, maybe; I'll let you know. How about head of household, domestic monarch? Now that's more like it."

"Western society is sliding away from patriarchy and from the control over men which it gave."

People will observe that feminism has freed men more than it has freed women. Yes, but it is a freedom men did not ask for.

Feminism and The Left

"The merger of public and private, which perhaps is reaching its fullest expression to date in the phenomenon of political correctness, is I believe rooted in sixties popular Marxism, which created perfect conditions for the germination of statist feminism."

"In a few years time, when it has all come down to earth with a bump, statist feminism may be remembered chiefly as an ideology which simply failed to understand how to manage men. The real fairy story will turn out to be its idea that women's lot can be improved through movement towards explicit gender equality."

Unfortunately, in respect of "in a few years time", this optimistic prediction has not come to pass. Nearly 30 years since Dench wrote those words the pigeons have yet to come home to roost and "explicit" equality (equality of outcome, equity) is a stronger political drive than ever.

"Women have succeeded in mobilising state institutions to carry out or even take over some of the management of men which was previously pursued, discreetly, within the home; and

the feminised state, as it blossoms, is revealing itself as a continuation of the moral economy by other means."

I think this is spot on. Feminism insists that women should exercise the same control over public spaces as they have always traditionally done in the domestic arena.

"A crucial analytic mistake on the Left, which has misled feminist thought for the last generation, is to overlook that collectivism cannot just operate in a soup of romanticised consensuality but does actually need to be grounded in a firm recognition and acceptance of individual obligations."

"State providing as a matter of routine soon creates a victim culture in which all but the richest people feel that, far from owing the community anything, they deserve more from it. This deprives the mass of citizens of the elementary self-respect which they need to have in order for a moral economy to operate."

"Immersion in a group helps to avoid existential angst and brings men within the magic circle of creation and communal renewal. But it is essential to remember that entry to this promised land requires highly personalised, long-term obligations. This is something which the libertarian Left, still getting it wrong after all these years, signally fails to take on board. The idea that the state can "help" families by relieving people of their personal responsibilities is just incredibly inept."

"The feminisation of the state launches a new offensive in the gender war. It is now an orthodoxy that one of the primary duties of the state is to protect women's interests against men. Anna Coote and her colleagues (1990) write that fathers are no longer essential to the economic survival of family units. And Polly Toynbee (1989) can calmly incite women to forget about fatherhood and just look to the state for all the provisions needed to enable them to have careers and operate effectively without men. Quoting Toynbee: 'What it (the state) can do is shape a society that makes a place for women and children as family units, self-sufficient and independent'."

"It would not be overstating the case too much to suggest that it is the need of feminists for socialism which has kept the Left going for the last decade or longer. For as a theory of how society works it is surely discredited now. Economic systems which give so little prominence to individual incentives and responsibilities are not competitive. They are now surviving in the world......by dint of political correctness, which treats attempts to unravel the social accounting of welfare as tantamount to the rape of defenceless women. But looking

the other way will not prevent the current welfare state system from collapsing as a result of its own contradictions. Feminists have built their new palace on sand."

The welfare state hasn't collapsed yet, but it still seems likely as Western nations are increasingly looking bankrupt.

"What the expanding concept of state provision effectively does is to end up serving and sanctifying a lower interest, that of the individual, who is now the unit of entitlement and consumption, unhampered by any tedious obligations or sense of mutuality which could set a boundary for both aspiration and disappointment. Feminism is thus heavily implicated in the creation of....'egotistical socialism', the practice whereby citizens grab benefits for themselves with no regard for the common good...... This betrays survival on the Left of an astonishing naiveté concerning what the outcomes and implications of welfarism are generally likely to be......The lower we go economically, welfarism sooner or later bids to become regarded as the call of first resort, and proves destructive of interpersonal relations and commitments which seem less worth maintaining, and is liable to lead claimants into traps of dependency where the state is the only possible source of support. Family networks of reciprocity, the base of the moral economy, have atrophied as the welfare state has bloomed."

Responsibility / Irresponsibility, 'The Forest' / Failure-to-Launch

"As feminist discourse erodes the family man role model, there is not much else for a lad to aspire to."

"What men need is demands upon them to make them grow up."

This is Jordan Peterson's message. The radical element in the MHRM will choke on the idea that men need to be encouraged to "grow up", but perhaps we should be considering whether there is an alternative to the traditional interpretation of "demand" which is equally beneficial in terms of providing meaning in life.

"A man who does not become a provider in one way or another fails to become a proper adult, and faces reduced life chances in almost every dimension. The community cares little about such men, because they make little input to it; and in turn this renders them prone to self-neglect."

This is an expression of "men are human doings, not human beings". Some may baulk at being told that a failure to perform the provider role will prevent them being "a proper adult". Better to say, as I think was intended, that a life of irresponsibility will prevent you being a proper adult. The question then is whether a meaningful, responsible life is possible for men independent of the traditional provider model. I say it is. And it is in this possibility becoming manifest in the bulk of men that the demise of feminism lies.

"The fundamental public duty of any able-bodied citizen is to minimise calls on community resources both by being self-reliant where he or she can, and through helping out family members too, in order to limit the use made of state help. Communities would soon get overdrawn without families."

How shockingly conservative!

"A man's pride and independence may be greater than his need for domestication. This underlines men's original power, very different from and far older than patriarchy, of being freer than women to walk away from relationships and situations that don't suit them….it is this raw power of men to care less than women which brings about patriarchy, rather than vice-versa. While one aspect of this cultural response to male offhandedness is to denigrate irresponsibility as childish, or a place of banishment and eventual failure – the forest – this probably will not be enough to convince all men. Some carrot is needed as well, some pull factors as well as push."

This is the MGTOW tendency, which, in Dench's view, patriarchy was invented by women to discourage by offering a carrot: the formal appearance of greater power and authority than was, in fact, the case.

"The language of belonging is responsibility; the sign of grace is responsiveness to the needs of others; and the first commandment is not to be independent or allow it in others."

This is Dench's take on the female perspective. "*The first commandment is not to be independent*" may be seen as the origin of women's in-group preference.

"It is children who ultimately are the main ingredient in the transformation of men."

"Looked at this way, dependants are a lifeline, the ultimate antidote to anomie."

"Surely dependants, for men and women equally, represent the primary means of attaching to society, and of realising a sense of fulfilment and moral worth. We are always being told by feminists that this is why many single mothers decide to have children. Why should this

apply only to women? Accepting responsibility for others gives one a right to be there oneself. Women qualify very easily for this and they should not dismiss too haughtily as a drive for power the efforts of men to abandon excessive individualism and to experience, hopefully, some release from the endlessness of desire."

The feminist interpretation of the role of the father in the family is a caricature of power and control. Their consequent determination to oust men from the family is synonymous with disenfranchising men from society generally and so is particularly cruel. A reconnection of men with society independent of women is essentially the MGTOW project, though whether it is possible on a large scale remains to be seen.

The Plight of Men

"The simple fact that women have children while men don't has more than enough immediate social consequences to render sexual equality a chimera and a delusion."

"Princes are passé and the frog is now inheriting the world. Male adolescents are as heavily burdened with feelings of guilt and isolation as ever; but they are no longer being shown a way out."

"It is significant that men's competitiveness is highly generalised, even pervasive. This is perhaps partly an adaptation for survival in chaos...To be certain of winning approval, and thereby getting out of the forest, it is important to be the best at whatever it is which is being valued and judged....The boys or men in the forest are not the ones who set the rules, or who decide what society will reward....the prizes are partly sexual and the operative community values which govern approval and define what life is for are widely felt by men to be female."

Note Dench's description of the forest as "chaos". This paragraph expresses a key concept: that the much-derided male competitiveness and hierarchies arise, not from toxic masculinity, but as the only means males have of acceptance into society. This is why the following is so accurate...

"When I see Susie Orbach arguing that men should take emotional responsibility for themselves and find a masculinity that is more fulfilling and less precarious it looks like Royalty telling the masses to eat cake. It's just not relevant to men's objective situation, which is more insecure than women's."

Added to men's difficult social position is their weakness over sex...

"The more powerful men's sexual impulses are, the stronger the bargaining position of women, and the smaller men's chances of coming together in a mutually regulatory system at the expense of women."

This is an oblique acknowledgement that men have little or no in-group preference. (Of course not, they have competition instead).

In a nod to fathers' rights, and the efforts of groups like FNF and F4J, Dench writes,

"These fathers know that they need their families. But they are not making much impact, and at the level of general principles, in the public arena, the overwhelming mood, blending feminism and traditional sentiments, is that if women want to exclude men they should be allowed to."

"If you want to wind up a feminist, talk about children's rights."

Christianity

It's not necessarily about God, silly...

"A male priesthood is no less important...The most important areas of church regulation are precisely those dealing with the place of men in the moral community...The theatrical officiation of a male priest in policing rules of the family is symbolically very significant....This is what makes the tomfoolery of Bishops in western churches who have been supporting the full ordination of women so extraordinary and hard to understand. Do they really not see or care that a church without a male senior priesthood loses its social relevance and is doomed to a speedy decline?.....What these debates have ignored above all is that male priesthood is a crucial symbolic prop to fatherhood in society generally; and the most obvious effect of more and more senior female officiants will be to give colossal endorsement to the idea that men are not really needed anymore."

Another bullseye. The anthropological origins of religious rites, or magical rites, was to give men their own source of significance to offset women's biologically gifted magic in respect of reproduction. Undermining key all-male spaces such as these is vandalism of a magnitude that will be civilisation destroying.

Men's Emotions

In one of my favourite passages, Dench tells of a young man, probably with Asperger Syndrome, who had been prosecuted for hacking into dozens of computer systems. The press had a field day mocking the lad for his alleged inability to express his emotions. Dench writes,

"But why should he have to talk about his emotions? They're his after all; if he did come out with them other people might well find them unacceptable, or use them against him in some way. Men's silence may well have something to do with the fact that male feelings are much more likely to prove unacceptable than those of women, which is why men say 'ask me no questions and I'll tell you no lies'. So let him button up. Emotional espionage has to be resisted. He knows what he feels and he can talk about it if and when he wants to. Keep right on, son. Don't let them grind you down."

Elsewhere Dench observes,

"That is perhaps why so many otherwise resolute men seem so weak-kneed and tongue-tied in female company. They are suppressing their emotions in the hope of staying in charge of themselves."

Female Moral Force

"Men are primed in all cultures to be responsive to women's needs and wishes, and to the values espoused by women. Feminism has confused this impulse considerably by introducing the notion that women would prefer to do for themselves many of the things which men were traditionally expected to do for them; and a half hearted New Chivalry has consequently tried to articulate around the paradoxical project of helping women to be more independent of men."

This is another key observation. When men ceded moral authority to women, back in the mists of evolutionary time, no limits were placed on what direction women's demands might take. This evolved proclivity – call it chivalry or gynocentrism or the empathy gap or simply female moral force, as you prefer – was initially related to optimising reproductive success, as all evolved adaptations are. But it can be deployed for whatever purposes women desire; men are programmed to assist. It is a psychosocial pathology which has always been inherent in *Homo sapiens*, but lay dormant while social, economic and technological conditions kept women predominantly within the domestic sphere.

"Female power seems magical to men because it is not vested in individuals but arises out of collective support and moral cohesion."

This is another nod to the power of female in-group preference which men underestimate. Conversely, feminism over-estimates male power due to failing to appreciate that men lack in-group preference. Patriarchy, in the feminist sense, is not only false but impossible.

"Women's voices, organised through a multitude of voluntary associations and committees, living fragments of the female church, have tremendous moral force to endorse or condemn public policies…political correctness in the public arena (is) currently exerting even greater secular influence. It is wielding the traditional moral power of the female church but in a new and particularly overt manner. I would expect this to be self-defeating quite quickly as it tries to monopolise influence by combining both formal and informal power, which men will not see as equitable and be happy to play along with for long."

Absolutely bang-on. This again alludes to the attempt by feminism to extend the informal female power of the domestic realm into the formal world of affairs and work, thus leaving men subservient in both. Unfortunately, most men still fail to perceive what is happening, being perpetually bamboozled by the narrative of female disadvantage. It remains to be seen whether the majority of men will "play along with it" indefinitely.

Doubling-down on Feminist Failure

In respect of equal division of domestic labour, especially in the context of childcare, Dench noted,

"I have heard or know of extremely few (cases) where the mother did not, sometimes in spite of conscious efforts to restrain herself, continue to see herself as the better judge of her children's needs, so that the father sooner or later realises that he could not be an equal parent, merely a helper, who had to follow instructions carefully."

"All except the most devoted and idealistic of New Men must be aware by now that the deal is spurious and that their actual position in any non-patriarchal household will be as mother's little helper. The idea of equal parenting is a dodo. It is no use women saying that men have to show that they can be trusted. That is all humbug."

Spot on, once again.

"Merging the private and public realms is arguably leading towards the collapse of much more than the boundary between them, and perhaps is about to show us just how reliant the whole social fabric still may be on gendered social divisions. Feminist canards may soon be coming home to roost."

Unfortunately, that "soon" continues to prove optimistic.

"If feminists do face up to this situation at all it is usually in the scornful language of emasculation. Men deprived of breadwinner status, they will say with mock sympathy, feel emasculated. (Poor things; but really that is not our problem, their smiles will add). This is not however a situation which deserves such easy displays of hauteur. It is something which arises out of the relative positions of men and women in dependency chains, and is a matter of dehumanisation rather than emasculation."

Correct. And that's how the H got into MHRM.

"Many middle-class workaholics fending off female competition are too busy to be actively caring fathers, while working-class benefit-drones on the other hand are too demoralised and dehumanised to be much use even though they have time on their hands. Equal opportunities have helped to let both categories off the hook and both are learning to survive outside patriarchy. Radical feminists then come along and use them as manifest justifications for writing men even further out of their script for the future. A self-perpetuating vilification of men is in progress."

"From this perspective, the new art of publicly bad-mouthing men seems in very dubious taste. Many men are now caught in a classic vicious circle of degradation and exclusion. They neither receive any respect from anyone but their closest buddies, nor do they have any real chance to win it."

Quite.

"Most men still do not feel under too much attack. But at the bottom of society there is a growing lump.....who are unemployed and probably unemployable, unfulfilled, have no self-respect because they know they are despised, and who have little incentive to be nice to anyone, even or especially women."

Yes, it is the lower socioeconomic groups which are being trashed most. That's why the association of feminism with "the left" is such an egregious fraud.

"A fast growing library of studies....have all identified a core of irresponsible and purposeless men at the centre of our current social malaise......a rising tide of male early mortality and suicide, high long term unemployment, the deterioration in academic performance of boys even in science subjects...and arguably the formation of right-wing nationalist movements across Europe giving a sense of belonging to otherwise unattached and unlovable young men, have all been linked in some way to the erosion of the male breadwinner role."

"Predictably, most commentators still seem hugely reluctant to link this collapse of men openly to the rise of feminism."

"The more men crumble and fade into the scenery, the easier it is for women to succeed. They are the ones piling up a monopoly of virtue."

In the context of the British Afro-Caribbean community, Dench wrote,

"There is a history waiting to be written here of the disservice done by white middle-class women, in helping to promote absent fatherhood, to an economically hard-pressed group which collectively desired and certainly needed stronger families if it was going to establish itself properly in this country. Instead it is now the scene of massive demoralisation. The fate of the black prince is a serious warning to the rest of us."

Finally, another key passage which presages, perhaps, sex and relationship education, hate crimes, false allegations, #MeToo, etc., and laments their destructive effect,

"The sixties alliance of feminism with the state is finally beginning to bear unholy fruit in a big way. For what seems to be happening now that women are moving strongly into the public realm is that traditional interpersonal networks for organising the moral economy, like the family, are being supplanted by depersonalised, abstract processes in the public domain. The phenomenon of political correctness is an aspect of this, as it involves traditional female evaluation of men, but channels its judgments through public institutions, especially the media, backed up by the police, rather than using them to inform and control particular personal ties."

In short, in exchange for formal power, feminism has gifted the state with women's moral power and has thus contributed in large measure, and arguably initiated, the rising authoritarianism we now see across the whole Western and Anglophone world.

References

[1] Dench, G. (1996). *Transforming Men: Changing Patterns of Dependency and Dominance in Gender Relations*. Link is to the Routledge edition of 27 April 2018.

[2] Collins, W. (2019). *The Empathy Gap*. LPS Publishing, June 2019.

[3] Peterson, J.B. (2017). *The Metaphysics of Pepe with Jonathan Pageau*. Jordan B Peterson YouTube channel, 4 January 2017.

[4] Pageau, J. (2017). *Supplement to the Metaphysics of Pepe Interview with Jordan Peterson*. Jonathan Pageau YouTube channel, 4 January 2017.

Section 12

Culture

63. Hylas and the Nymphs

There are far too many examples of feminist idiocy to spend one's time commenting on many of them. But I couldn't resist in this case because it exposes their ignorance so beautifully.

"Those who see ugly meanings in beautiful things are corrupt without being charming" (Oscar Wilde).

Original posted on: 3 February 2018.

Hylas and the Nymphs, J.W.Waterhouse, 1896. Image from Wikimedia Commons, Ref.(1)

Until a few days before my original blog article, the above painting by J.W.Waterhouse hung in the Manchester Art Gallery. But then it vanished, to be replaced by a disorderly collection of post-it notes. This is more like valid art, the gallery appears to think. But not their visitors. Not judging by the contents of said post-it notes.

The 1896 painting depicts an episode from Greek myth, *Hylas and the Nymphs*. The pre-Raphaelite painting usually hangs in a room of 19th century art called 'In Pursuit of Beauty'. But Clare Gannaway, the museum's curator of contemporary art, has called the 'In Pursuit of Beauty' collection a cause for "embarrassment", Refs.[2,3]. Gannaway said that recent anti-sexual harassment campaigns such as Time's Up, Ref.[4], and #MeToo, Ref.[5], had an influence on the decision to remove the painting. She said, *"For me personally, there is a sense of embarrassment that we haven't dealt with it sooner. Our attention has been elsewhere."*

She added *"it wasn't about denying the existence of particular artworks."* Hmm. The truth is they thought the painting sexist, demeaning and objectifying of women and were disturbed by its (apparent) depiction of female pubescent nakedness.

The gallery insisted it was not banning the picture but simply wanted to provoke debate – to "prompt conversations about how we display and interpret artworks" and how to make them "relevant" in the twenty-first century.

Why should a painting be relevant to the benighted twenty-first century? Anyway, as it happens, this one is – and I'm happy to oblige you with the tale. You will soon see why I am taking up your time with this matter, which appears to be merely the latest bit of feminist nonsense. There is a delightful twist in this tale, though the imbeciles who do this sort of thing know nought of it.

Hylas was one of the Argonauts. As merely the son of a King, Hylas must have felt rather socially inferior as so many of the crew of the Argo were sons of Gods. Not having the status of a celebrated Hero, poor Hylas, a mere mortal boy, was destined to be one of those who did not survive the adventures of the Argonauts. At least – he didn't return.

It is said by some sources that Hera, the Queen of Heaven, was behind it. That it was she who put the nymph, Dryope, to the task of kidnapping Hylas. What the poor boy had done to anger the Goddess is not recorded. But one does not need to be a genius to work it out. Hera was renowned for her jealousy and resentment of other lovers of her husband and brother, Zeus - and, of course, their bastard offspring – of whom Heracles was one.

Hera was to dedicate herself to the torment of Heracles for the duration of his mortal life (and who knows what thereafter). His every adventure was plagued by the revengeful Goddess.

Heracles's favourite was none other than Hylas, the golden boy. The great demi-God and Hero raised Hylas as a warrior and as his personal assistant. Oh dear, poor Hylas. What tragedy to be both mortal and the favourite of one permanently the target of Hera. And how like the spiteful Goddess

Queen to strike at his favourite, the Hero himself being harder to damage directly.

So it was that when Hylas went to fetch water from the river he was ensnared. The chief culprit was the nymph Dryope, operating in accord with Hera's will. Hylas knew nothing of nymphs. As he bent down to fill his pitcher he heard silvery voices, calling, calling. He bent lower and two slender white hands suddenly rose from the black water and pulled him in. He was in the power now of Dryope and her sisters. His fate was sealed and Hylas was never seen again by mortal man.

So distraught was Heracles that he spent days on end searching for his companion. So long, in fact, that the Argo sailed without him.

And what of the art gallery's request: to make this myth relevant to the twenty-first century? You see, it already is. Any follower of Jordan Peterson knows that myths appeal to Archetypes, and hence are timeless.

Hera is the great Matriarch, the Goddess of women and marriage; the Great Sacred Cow. She is the seat of female power, the Earth Mother. The nymphs are a mechanism of her power, namely sexual power expressed as the visible female form and hence wielding power over men in the form of their desire. Thus, Hera and the nymphs together represent gynocentric power over men.

Hera was not only a sworn enemy of Heracles, she was also jealous of the purely male bond between Heracles and his Hylas. Such a thing is a challenge to gynocentric power and must be broken. The nymphs, the manifestation of desire, are the means by which Hera breaks the male bond, depriving Heracles of his golden boy, and depriving Hylas of his father-mentor.

The story is allegorical and of particularly apposite contemporary relevance. It tells of the breaking of male companionship by jealous gynocentric power. Think destruction of male spaces.

Look closer and you will see that this myth, this picture which these fools have chosen to challenge, is a warning to men of the very thing being played out by #MeToo and the Presidents Club, Ref.[6]. It warns that alluring female pulchritude may be a trap set to divide and conquer men.

I am confident that this was not the conscious intention of those responsible for the painting's removal. Is this, then, just a stupendous irony? Or is it a case of the wicked being betrayed by their own subconscious?

Oh, and incidentally, Hylas and the Nymphs is a theme that has been put in paint by other artists too – including female artists. Check out Henrietta Rae's version. Clearly a case of internalised misogyny.

References

[1] Wikipedia Commons. *https://upload.wikimedia.org/wikipedia/commons/b/bd/Waterhouse_Hylas_and_the_Nymphs_Manchester_Art_Gallery_1896.15.jpg*

[2] BBC News (2018). *Gallery denies censorship after removing Victorian nymphs painting*, and also *Curator defends removal of 'uncomfortable' nymph painting*. 1 February 2018.

[3] Hooton, C. (2018). *Painting of naked nymphs removed from Manchester Art Gallery to provoke debate about women in art*. Independent, 2 February 2018.

[4] The Telegraph (2018). *Stars to wear black to the Baftas in Time's Up anti-harassment protest*. 1 February 2018.

[5] The Telegraph (2017). *#Metoo: Thousands of women identify themselves as victims of sexual harassment or assault with 'me too' hashtag*. 16 October 2017.

[6] The Presidents Club Charitable Trust had been raising money for charities for 33 years when men attending their annual dinner in London were accused of sexual harassment. The resulting controversy led to the charity being shut down. See for example *this Wiki account*.

64. The Anatomy of Our Decline

There is no limit to the social destruction that we will permit in the name of protecting women, no sacrifice too great for the altar of gynocentrism.

Original posted on: 2 November 2017.

Ah, gender! It's a hall of mirrors, full of misdirection.

You must forgive me if I have not followed the details of all this #MeToo business and the 'revelations' of mass sexual victimisation of women in parliament. I don't do social media, I am not a regular reader of newspapers, and, even in 2017, I could write "I haven't watched TV for years". The only exception was BBC's Newsnight on 1 November 2017, Ref.[1]; a distressing experience which reconfirmed the wisdom of my normal practice. But one would have to be living on the moon not to have heard the gist of it. I understand one woman is still recovering from the trauma of a man putting his hand on her knee 15 years ago. I believe another woman is alleging rape "at a social event". Hmm, one might have hoped that, by 2017 even without #MeToo, men would have got the message that having sex with a woman who has been drinking is not legally advisable, Ref.[2].

Despite my best attempts to isolate myself from the horror, I keep hearing feminist types telling us that "it's not about sex, it's about power". Yes, indeed – but I disagree as to who has the power. I'm a simple-minded chap. I suggest that he who is forced to resign over a matter of supreme triviality is not the one with power. I suggest that the group of people whose behaviour is to be modified, constrained, dictated and controlled is not the group with power. *"Men's greatest weakness is their facade of strength, and women's greatest strength is their facade of weakness"* (Ref.[3]). What we are looking at here is an exercise in bullying, made possible by gynocentrism. But it is bullying with a purpose, and that purpose is the furtherance of female power. It is the most disgusting spectacle to witness.

I do wonder, if sexual abuse is defined as "unwanted touching of a sexual or suggestive nature", what proportion of men have been sexually abused? I have a suspicion it might be most men, though probably few men will ever have registered it as abusive, and perhaps not even sexual. I can offer some personal experiences which are clear cut. Be warned, this is not going where you think.

I was strikingly pretty as a young man, though seeing me now you would be forgiven for being incredulous. On two occasions in my early twenties I had my bottom very firmly tweaked by a 'gang' of Amazonian women who appeared to be prowling the street for that express purpose. I assumed at the time it was a gender-political statement. But possibly it was simply sexual. This was outside UCL (University College London), so I presume they were students of some sort.

Most people would regard my other experience as more significant. This happened at primary school when I was about eight. A number of boys from my class, perhaps about eight or ten of us, were paraded in the headmistress's office. She was there with a woman 'friend'. We were told to strip to our underpants. One at a time we had to approach the headmistress' desk, where she put her hand down our underpants and fondled our testicles. We had then to walk to the other side of her desk where her female 'friend' also fondled our testicles. That was it. We got dressed and returned to class.

Of course, this may have been a medical examination to check that our testicles had descended, and the 'friend' might have been a nurse. I cannot recall anything of the sort being said. At that age, we would not necessarily be told anything – one just needed to obey. However, that explanation does not legitimise the headmistress getting in on the act, does it?

Aren't I brave in speaking out about this abuse?

No, is the answer, in case you were in any doubt.

Some people opine that men's rights advocates are simply indulging in victimhood Olympics. Some people say that men's rights advocates are just another type of snowflake. No doubt you, dear reader, have much the same impression of my foregoing tale. Ah, the misdirection!

Let me make this absolutely clear. My purpose is exactly the opposite.

You see, my "dreadful experience" completely failed to ruin my life. It didn't even ruin my day. In fact, not the slightest frisson of trauma was inflicted upon me, either then or later. It was just a bit weird. Clearly it must have registered as a bit weird or I would not even remember it.

But get real. The average eight-year-old boy is poked about at will by any adult woman who wishes to do so. Perhaps things are different now, but that's certainly how it was in that era (I'm talking circa 1962). As a wee boy I sported a mass of tight ginger curls. I hated my hair. Not so the local matrons. It was a common experience for me to have women I didn't know come up to me on the street and run their hands through my ringlets, going goo goo about my lovely hair (yuck!). As far as I was concerned the ball-feeling incident was much the same thing – the only difference being that that happened only the once.

So my message to the poor traumatised female researchers and Members of Parliament is, frankly, to man up. I don't expect a terribly high standard of manliness, mind you. Just as manly as I was at eight, that'll do.

But this is more misdirection. You see, these female MPs and researchers were not really traumatised any more than I was. It is widely appreciated – not least by many women – that these complainants are playing the victim. It is acknowledged that victimhood confers advantage.

Sensible women commentators deplore this victimology, observing that it presents women as feeble and needy rather than as strong and independent. Seeking victimhood status is seen by these sane women as disempowering rather than empowering. Well, yes indeed – as long as one confines attention to the impact on an individual woman. But, for women as a class, it is a power strategy, as I shall argue below. Unfortunately, it doesn't matter how many Sarah Vines, Ref.[4], Julia Hartley-Brewers, Ref.[5], Kathy Gyngells, Ref.[6], or Joanna Williams, Ref.[7], speak out about this parliamentary madness. I'm afraid the monster is out of control.

Andrea Leadsom, then Leader of the House of Commons, told MPs she would be "*setting the bar significantly below criminal activity*". She went on to say, Ref.[4], that all people are deserving of our respect and "*your age, gender or job title should have no bearing on the way you are treated in a modern workplace, and nobody is an exception to that*". But, Andrea, I think you meant to say that childcare work is an exception, didn't you? After all, you are the woman who said (in parliament) we should not hire men in childcare work because they may be paedophiles, Ref.[8]. That sounds rather like gender "having a bearing on the way men are treated in the workplace", doesn't it? Or perhaps you just meant that all women, not all people, are deserving of our respect?

But, readers, this is yet more misdirection. There is a broader dynamic at work here than merely victimology, one that makes sense in terms of power-seeking behaviour. Let me approach this obliquely with a short digression.

It has long been the case that male teachers avoid being alone with a female pupil. They will keep the classroom door wide open if such a condition becomes unavoidable. Kato Harris advised men not to go into teaching, Ref.[9], the risk of false accusation being so great. It is standard advice to university lecturers to keep their office door open when meeting female colleagues (let alone female students), Ref.[10]. In the workplace more generally, since 2017 especially, men have become increasingly reticent about their interactions with female staff, for fear of accidentally provoking an accusation of some sort. Invariably when journalists or professional sources report on this phenomenon, the blame is heaped on men for being misogynists, Refs.[11,12,13]. That Guardian journalists can only conceptualise men's reaction to the hostile environment imposed on them by interpreting it as "women being punished for #MeToo" is a measure of their catastrophic lack of empathy for men's predicament – which feminists themselves have created. That men are in genuine and understandable fear only emerges in comments left by men themselves, Ref.[14].

In particular, it is not so much a brave man as a foolish man who attempts to date a female colleague. The days of the office romance are over. You may, like Mike Spence, Ref.[15], be accused of misogyny if you openly admit to any reluctance to meet a female colleague socially. But the irreversible fact is that few men are now willing to take the risk of asking a female colleague out. Inevitably, instead of this being seen as the result of long-standing policing of male behaviour, the complaint is now that women's career prospects are being harmed by men becoming more distant.

Calls are beginning to be made for men to be 'trained' in how to interact with women in the workplace. So, having absorbed the lesson of what they must *not* do, men are now to be instructed in what they *must* do. What is not forbidden will be compulsory. The end result will be that those men with any remaining self-respect will increasingly withdraw from such environments. The space becomes female in nature by a process of making men uncomfortable to be there.

Do you see the social dynamic at work here? What we are seeing in parliament is the same. For sensible women to decry the disempowering nature of victimhood is to fail to appreciate the implicit strategy. This is a power play. All feminism is a power play, it always was. The objective is to convert male spaces into female spaces, and hence to control everything. Let me spell it out.

The social dynamic of a male space is different from that of a female space. The former is based on hierarchy and competition. Generally, it is inaccurate to refer to this as a 'dominance hierarchy', this being more relevant to other primates than to *Homo sapiens*. In man, it is generally some form of competence hierarchy which is significant, and this may give rise to a hierarchy of authority. In contrast, female spaces tend to be organised around consensus and mutual caring and support with less overt competition (though there may well be concealed competition). Roy Baumeister, Ref.[16], has argued that the female group dynamic can only function within small to medium sized groups. He argues that the male group dynamic is essential to form the very large social structures essential for the creation of culture and societies larger than hunter-gatherer societies. Whether that is correct or not, it seems clear that male and female group dynamics are different.

What happens, then, when a few women enter a male space? They are obliged to function within the male dynamic, which (for some women) will feel unnatural to them and may be perceived as discriminatory. But when the proportion of women in a formerly male space becomes sufficiently large, a female sub-dynamic will naturally form. In parliament, the broad, cross-party coalition of feminists is part of this female sub-dynamic. Inevitably there will be conflict between the two coexisting dynamics, simply because they are incompatible.

We have seen repeatedly over the last few decades that the female dynamic expands and tends to drive out the male dynamic (e.g., the decline of male teachers). Male spaces are transformed into female spaces. Why? The answer is simply gynocentrism. Men are intrinsically inclined to oblige women, whereas women have no intrinsic inclination to oblige men. On the contrary, women are inclined to simply insist that men should assist women. In this context that means, paraphrasing Geoff Dench, that men should undertake "the paradoxical project of helping women to not need men". Women have strong in-group preference which powerfully assists their group interests, whilst men have no in-group preference. This asymmetry has its origin in the evolution of the human pair-bond. This behavioural asymmetry coevolved with the species and is made possible by the male disposability inherent in anisogamous sexual reproduction (see chapter 47).

The term "gynocentrism" sounds very pejorative. But it should be understood simply as the constellation of emotionally based behavioural characteristics which underpin the human pair-bond and, by extension, relations between the sexes generally. If you thought that sex was all there was to it, think again. Gynocentrism underpins inter-sex interactions even when there is no sexual attraction on either side at all.

So now we have put the "abuse" of women in parliament in perspective. You should not be misled by the details of the current debacle. You should view it as part of a process. This process exerts pressure on men to change to accommodate women's social dynamic, pressure which is not resisted because men's gynocentric nature impels them to acquiesce. This episode will be one of many in which parliament is gradually converted to a female space. At no point will there be any question as to whether this is a good thing. Gynocentrism provides the direction of change, not functionality.

So you now see why those sensible women who have spoken out have not grasped the whole picture when they focus only on the disempowering effect of victimhood. Victimhood may seem to disempower an individual woman, but it is part of the gynocentric mechanism which leads to increasing female power *en masse*. This is accomplished by the drive for an increasingly dominant female social dynamic via the destruction of the male dynamic through a process of shaming.

Whence cometh the social power which drives the ascendency of the female over the male dynamic? It is important to appreciate that this power does not originate in victimhood. The victimhood acts merely as a trigger or switch. The power is already in place, implicit in ancient gynocentrism. As an analogy consider turning on a light. It is naïve to think that the switch causes the illumination. No, the real cause is the national network of turbogenerators which, via a sequence of transformers, causes a permanent 240 volt potential difference over the terminals of the light switch. Gynocentrism is the national grid; victimhood is just the switch.

Consequently, victimhood stimulates a beneficial societal response only when triggered by a member of an identity group with pre-existing moral cachet. Thus, victimhood works for women, and ethnic minorities, and the LGBT minorities, because their moral entitlement has been constructed in advance. But claims of victimhood would bring no rewards of societal support for men, or conservatives, or white people as a whole, because these identity groups have been morally disenfranchised by decades of conditioning.

I labour this point as a rebuttal of the claim that is levelled at men's rights advocates that they are indulging in victimhood Olympics. On the contrary, MRAs discover very early that the reaction to the male disadvantages is that no one cares – there is no reservoir of moral cachet to be tapped for men. So victimhood is not an applicable strategy for men (thankfully).

So why do MRAs bang on about male disadvantages, then? What is the point? Well, I guess reasons vary. Some men come to the view that there is indeed no point and become MGTOW. This is a perfectly rational response. Unfortunately, it leaves other men – and boys – to their fate. Others make strenuous attempts to address a specific issue on behalf of male victims, be it domestic abuse or child contact or sexual offences against males, etc. What these groups have in common is lack of funding.

For my part the motivation is, firstly, that I believe there is intrinsic merit in truth – though truth can be a slippery fish to catch. My second motivation is to shine a light on gynocentrism itself. In other words, to illustrate the empathy gap – which is just the other side of the same coin as gynocentrism. It is the empathy gap which precludes any advantage in victimhood for men.

The current pogrom is not just in Hollywood and in the UK parliament. This mass exercise in denouncing and shaming is spreading everywhere, driven by social media. There had already, in 2017, been male suicides in the Vancouver club scene as a result, Ref.[17]. There will be more*. It may be your club, your workplace, your town next. It may be you next.

*Four days after posting the original blog article, the former Welsh government minister and Labour MP, Carl Sargeant, who had been suspended following allegations of misconduct, was found dead at his home,

Ref.[18]. 611 days later Sargeant's death was formally confirmed as suicide, Ref.[19].

Carl Sargeant died without ever knowing who had made allegations against him. We still don't know officially, and if I did I could not publicise the name. This is how easy it is to kill a man with complete impunity. The allegations were of "unwelcome attention, inappropriate touching or groping of women". Is there anyone on the planet who has not experienced "unwelcome attention"? Sargeant was summarily dismissed as a government minister. One cannot avoid the suspicion that the allegations were politically motivated. His family's response to the inquest was extremely critical of the then-First Minister (of Wales), and sources have referred to the "murkiest side of Welsh politics", Ref.[20]. Sargeant wasn't told anything about the accusations against him. No one knows their veracity. No investigation was ever carried out to test them.

Where will all this end? I don't know. Moreover, fascinating though it is to attempt to understand what is happening, no amount of understanding will divert this historic process from its course – whatever that is.

So here I am on the deck of the Titanic, intent on studying closely the hydrodynamics of shifting buoyancy. Well, what else is there to do? We are all in the same boat, but unfortunately one side seems to think that smashing the other end of the boat will be beneficial. Human life rarely rises much above the level of farce, so at least our decline has the merit of genuine tragedy.

References

[1] Justice for Men and Boys (2017). *BBC Newsnight: The Problem with Men*. 2 November 2017.

[2] Platell, A. (2017). *Platell's People: From Little Big Lies to Broadchurch and Doctor Foster to Fearless, why do the makers of TV dramas hate men?* The Daily Mail, 7 October 2017.

[3] Farrell, W. (1993). *The Myth of Male Power*. Linked is the 21st anniversary edition, on Kindle. *See also the original here, from Simon & Schuster*, 1 August 1993.

[4] Vine, S. (2017). *If this hysterical Westminster witch hunt is what a world run by women looks like, count me out*. The Daily Mail, 1 November 2017.

[5] Hartley-Brewer, J. (2017). *Julia Speaks Out Over Michael Fallon Reports*. TalkTV, 31 October 2017.

[6] Gyngell, K. (2017). *Of course, sex assaults are deplorable. But this hysteria is out of proportion, says Conservative Woman co-editor Kathy Gyngell*. The Daily Mail, 30 October 2017.

[7] The Liberty Belles (2017). *The Liberty Belles in Conversation with Joanna Williams*. The Liberty Belles YouTube channel, 31 October 2017.

[8] Stone, J. (2016). *Andrea Leadsom says men should not be hired to do childcare as they may be paedophiles*. Independent, 15July 2016.

[9] Harris, K. (2017). *Abuse Lottery: Deputy head Kato Harris falsely accused of raping pupil claims men working at school are 'playing the lottery' in trying to avoid sex claims*. The Sun, 11 May 2017.

[10] Academia (2015). *When is it appropriate to close your office door when meeting with a student?*. 8 April 2015.

[11] Philipps, C., and Tsatsas, N. (2017). *Male Bosses Avoid Being Alone with Women at Work*. HRDirector, 17 November 2017.

[12] Mahdawi, A. (2019). *Men now avoid women at work – another sign we're being punished for #MeToo*. The Guardian, 29 August 2019.

[13] Marks, G. (2019). *When men are afraid to interact with women at work, it harms the whole company*. The Guardian, 5 September 2019.

[14] Quora (undated). *I have heard many men say that they are now afraid to talk to women. Has #metoo had any negative effects on women in the workplace?* Answers from individual readers, various dates.

[15] Herman, L. (2017). *If Mike Pence Won't Even Have Dinner With Women, He Probably Shouldn't Tell Us What to Do With Our Bodies*. Glamour, 31 March 2017.

[16] Baumeister, R.T. (2010). *Is There Anything Good about Men?: How Cultures Flourish by Exploiting Men*. Oxford University Press, 12 August 2010.

[17] Davison, D. (2017). *The Death of Vancouver Nightlife*. Diana Davison YouTube channel, 30 October 2017.

[18] Hawkes, S. (2017). *'Sex Pest' Death Riddle: Axed Labour minister Carl Sargeant 'begged party chiefs to tell him sex pest allegations' before 'he took his own life'*. The Sun, 9 November 2017.

[19] Gittins, J. (Senior Coroner for North Wales). *Inquest on death of Carl Sargeant*. 11 July 2019.

[20] Hemming, J. (2019). *How the inquest into Carl Sargeant's death cast light on the 'murkiest' side of Welsh politics*. NorthWalesLive, 11 July 2019.

65. The Silence of the Dogs

This is by way of a coda for the last chapter, specifically about why male MPs were so quiet about the pogrom being conducted on them at the time by women members.

Original posted on: <u>6 January 2018</u>.

In November 2017, Kathy Gyngell published an article in TCW (then known as The Conservative Women) titled *The Silence of the Males*, Ref.[1]. I wrote a response which I did not initially publish. But when TCW re-published Mrs Gyngell's original piece in January 2018, I took the opportunity to finally publish my response. I suggest you read Ref.[1] first; it is excellent.

In the context of the ongoing parliamentary pogrom of male MPs by female MPs claiming misdemeanours of one form or another, Kathy Gyngell asked *"Where's their protest? Will they not speak out even in self-defence?"*

Only Mrs Gyngell's surprise surprised me.

"Is it their innate chivalry? Do they not like contradicting women? Or are they genuinely scared?", she further asked.

Yes, yes and yes.

As regards fear, there are many examples of men being sacked for voicing even the mildest of heretical opinions. There is a reason why men's rights advocates "live on the internet", often using pseudonyms, or are older men and safely retired. (*C'est moi, cet homme*).

Male privilege is indeed a myth. So is male power. It always was. Except for a very few.

What is power?

Is the muscle-bound oaf powerful because he can, briefly, intimidate you? Do the truly powerful typically sport the finest physique? Yet feminists, obsessed with domestic and sexual violence, conflate muscles with power. Or they pretend to do so. Misdirection?

Is the family man working a 55-hour week to support a family actually just a bully – a wielder of patriarchal control through "financial coercion" as feminists insist? Or is this more misdirection? Are bullies noted for giving gifts to their victims – persistently for years?

Then what is power?

Power is the ability to impose your will on others.

The war lord, or criminal gang, may impose their will on others by violence. But this power strategy is used infrequently and has largely been neutralised by the rise of state power. The law modifies people's actions, to a degree, and the state can impel compliance since it wields the credible threat of overwhelming force.

But people's behaviour, and indeed the very stability of society, is mostly controlled by a common perception of what is right and what is unacceptable. This is the social morality. It is not the absolute morality of the religious or certain moral philosophers. Social morality differs between cultures. Most importantly, social morality is mutable.

The ability to mould the precepts of accepted social morality is by far the most puissant strategy for those seeking power.

And feminism is all about power. It always was.

Feminism is a psychosocial pathology. Specifically, it is a corruption of social morality for its own ends, as a power strategy.

If you want an image of feminism it is this: a dog owner viciously beating her dog – to a chorus of applause.

Imagine a large powerful dog – a beast who could make mincemeat out of his mistress. But he does not. He cowers under the onslaught of blows and does not attack back. Why? Because countless generations of selective breeding have moulded his behaviour. The dog is psychologically incapable of attacking his human abuser.

Men are also the product of selective breeding. The selection is done by women because women are the gatekeepers of sex. The right of a woman to choose with whom she mates is sacrosanct. This is proved by the perceived heinousness of rape – which is precisely the violation of that right. As a result, over deep genetic time, only 40% of men left progeny, compared with 80% of women, see chapter 47.

One of the key evolutionary adaptations of *Homo sapiens* is the formation of long-term pair-bonds. This phenomenon, shared by extremely few other primates, is key to the species' evolutionary success, and hence coming to dominate the planet. The glue which binds this pair-bond is a complex of emotions (see chapter 48). Contrary to the now-popular belief that males are emotionally stunted, the emotional complex underpinning the crucial pair-bond is primarily within the male – since it is the male whose behaviour is altruistically modified. An emotional basis is essential to drive altruistic behaviour: the phenotype is conned by the genotype via the intermediary of emotional triggers. This is the foundation for what is perceived as morally "good" becoming defined by what is good for the family. And, as far as the male is concerned, a convenient cognitive shortcut for "what is good for the family" becomes "what is good for the woman". This remains the societal presumption to this day, as embodied by the family courts, even when the individual man has reason to perceive the fallacy of it, when the mother stands between him and his children.

So it came to be that, millennia ago, men ceded moral authority to women – because men were selected on that basis.

When gynocentric power was deployed to preference the family, it acted as a highly successful evolutionary adaptation. But feminism is gynocentric power misapplied to preference women in the external, formerly male, world of affairs. It is power being deployed without responsibility. Worse, neither the body politic nor the body social have any means to counter it.

Just pause for a moment to consider how absolute is the power to define what is regarded as morally correct, and what is not. This control over the moral narrative is hegemonic power indeed. It blows my mind that it goes unnoticed. But covert action is part of its power structure because it acts directly within the evolved psychology of both sexes.

In short, men are bred to be gynocentric and women expect it.

I suspect that almost no women have the faintest clue just how men's gynocentric mindset controls their actions. Men are generally not aware of it themselves. Take my own case. Modesty aside, I dare say I am quite well informed about the wealth of factual evidence which confirms the litany of male disadvantages. Despite that, my logic module exists in a perpetual state of war with my gynocentric emotion module. The latter screams 'nasty misogynist' at me constantly. The former responds with more facts, but to no avail. I have my own, inescapable, internal feminist.

There are just two things you need to know about sexual dynamics. First, the key attribute of inter-sex dynamics is that men are terrified of female disapproval (because women define the moral right). Second, the key feature of intra-sex dynamics is that women have strong in-group preference whereas men have no in-group preference. As a result, men have no choice but to be self-reliant. Men's strength is their self-reliance. Men's weakness is their self-reliance.

So, Kathy Gyngell should not be surprised that the dogs will not fight back. They just can't. Oh, the odd one may do so. But such a dog proves thereby that he is a vicious beast who must be put down, and quickly. The dogs cannot unite and mount a coordinated counterattack on humans. It is unthinkable.

In January 2018 I wrote, "The female onslaught upon men will not slacken, it will intensify. There will be no coherent counter to it. A few suicides will make no difference. Our society can tolerate mass male death with equanimity. Because of men's lack of gender-based joint action, they can respond only as individuals. An individual can respond to an attack by an army only by withdrawing, not by counterattack. Men will increasingly withdraw. The economy will weaken as young males fail to see any point in continued striving in a society which provides only sticks and no carrots. Their increasing withdrawal will be mocked, Ref.[2], and their lack of motivation chided, Ref.[3], but to no avail in a society which can only demand their performance but give nothing back in return, not even the minimum of respect. Women will reap the usual rewards of getting what you wished for." This is now underway, as outlined in chapters 53 and 54.

References

[1] Gyngell, K. (2018). *2017 Revisited – November: The silence of the males*. The Conservative Woman, 5 January 2018.

[2] Anonymous reporter (2016). *Meet the men who hate women so much that they have vowed never to sleep with them again*. The Daily Mail, 27 September 2016.

[3] Walker, P. (2018). *White working-class boys should be more aspirational, says Labour minister*. The Guardian, 3 January 2018.

66. After the Culture War

The culture war was lost; long live the rebellion.

Original posted on: 10 July 2020.

Even four years after I originally wrote this, I continue to observe that some people believe we are still fighting the culture war. It is debatable whether we ever fought the culture war. We certainly are not now. The culture war was lost years ago. Yet some good people are inclined to think we are still fighting that war – rather like those (seemingly not apocryphal) Japanese soldiers who were still emerging from the jungle 20 years after World War Two.

I do not mean to be unkind, especially to those few who put in the effort to pushback against the narrative, however forlornly. These endeavours remain essential. But it is important to appreciate the reality of our position.

Let me convince you by extending the war analogy. Suppose the enemy has invaded your country and is now occupying every city, every town, every village. Suppose national government and local government are in their hands, as are the news media, the police forces, the judiciary, the armed forces and even the schools and universities. Would you be prepared to concede that the war was lost?

Ah, you say – but *I* am still fighting!

Of course, even when a war is lost there may be a resistance movement. But it is important to understand that we are a few scattered dissidents. We are a resistance movement operating within an occupied country.

You may think this is mere semantics; that I am splitting hairs. I think not. I think it is important regarding what activism is worth pursuing, and what can realistically be expected to be achieved.

What exactly do we mean by "culture war"? The culture war is (was) a replacement of one moral system by another. It is (was) a war over what is regarded as right or wrong. The enemy "occupation" is an occupation of our minds by an alternative moral system. It is an occupation of the (ostensible) moral high ground.

The mechanism underlying this moral usurpation is addressed in chapters 68 and 69 (and in greater detail in Ref.[1]). The minds of the public – or, at least, large swathes of the public – have been occupied. We dissidents are the ones who have resisted the brave new morality (or have discovered its corruption by hard experience).

The terrible power of moral takeover is that it subverts the democratic process. The democratic process fails if a large proportion of the public is seriously misled. Moral usurpation facilitates misleading the public. This can be done with great conviction by leaders because many of them have been misled themselves (though some are more knowing and cynically exploit the opportunities presented).

The other feature of the falsity now passing as ethical is that it involves a moral hierarchy. This is betrayed by the creeping tendency for true democracy to be replaced by rule by "the people who know best". We saw this in parliament in 2019 with the declared intention of a huge proportion of MPs to act contrary to a clear plebiscite (on Brexit) – because they knew better than us "deplorables". Melanie Phillips pointed to the same phenomenon years ago when, being disturbed by The Guardian's tendency to be – let us say, misleading – she was given to understand that such an attitude was unsophisticated, Ref.[2]. The *cognoscenti* knew that they were operating in the interests of "the Greater Good" or "the Broader Truth" – broader, that is, than anything so plebeian as actual truth.

Let me give you a couple of examples of the elite usurpers overruling us plebs. In the debates on the Divorce, Dissolution and Separation Act, 2020 (addressed in more detail in chapter 51) it transpired that a public consultation on the matter had been totally ignored because it gave the wrong result. It is worth repeating what Baroness Eaton said during the second reading of the Bill in the Lords, Ref.[3],

"I am also concerned by the way in which the Government appear to have dealt with the consultation process that preceded the Bill. Consultations are intended to ensure that the Government have listened to the public and adjusted their proposals in the light of the concerns expressed. In the consultation on divorce reform, 80% of those who responded did not agree with the proposal to replace the five facts demonstrating that a marriage had irretrievably broken down with a notification process. A mere 17% were in favour of the proposed change.

Furthermore, 83% of those who responded disagreed with the Government's proposal to remove the ability of a spouse who does not want divorce to contest the assertion that their marriage has irretrievably broken down, while only 15% supported the plans. Can the Minister please explain how much of the consultation was taken into consideration, because this appears to conflict with the process that the Government are taking forward? I have serious concerns that the Bill will have negative consequences for families."

Lord Farmer made the same observation, noting that the Ministry of Justice had simply dismissed the strength of feeling in response to its own consultation.

Here's another example. In an interview on The Glass Blind Spot, Richard Lucas, leader of the Scottish Family Party, told of public meetings where civil servants were promoting the case for hate crimes and hate speech but receiving an overwhelmingly negative response from the public, Ref.[4]. When asked what message the civil servants would take away from the meeting they replied "we need to communicate better with people what this is about". Here again we see the unshakeable mindset that "those who know best" are right, and if the public do not agree then the public simply need to be better instructed – or ignored.

This is the same mindset that has a Women and Equalities Committee and cannot be brought to understand that the title is a contradiction. It is the same mindset that appoints an all-feminist Family Justice Review Panel and excludes all representatives of fathers, and then reacts to complaints by adding further feminist members – as if to teach us a lesson. It is the same mindset that leads to a Public Bill Committee which invites witnesses only from feminist organisations. It is crucial to appreciate that those in charge do not perceive these things as bias or prejudice; they are just and laudable within the purview of the new culture – the culture that has come about because we lost the culture war.

Any dissent on these matters can now only be interpreted as *your* moral error, which is why we meet with such angry responses.

The acquisition of power by capturing the (ostensible) moral high ground in this way is not new. Religions have been doing it for millennia. And it tends to be forgotten that the power of kings used to be morally based. Kings used to claim that they ruled by divine assent. It is hard for us to get our heads around the fact that this was accepted by most of the populace. Even in revolutionary times, the revolting peasants tended to believe that the king was being misled by wicked advisers, rather than culpable himself. One is naturally inclined to try to salvage one's moral perspective.

The Cromwellian civil war can also be interpreted as a culture war, as it was essentially a war between opposing religious views. I am hardly the first to note the psychic similarity between woke intolerance and Puritanism.

No one will have difficulty regarding a religious establishment or a power hierarchy centred on an absolute monarch as being cultural structures. Our brave new moral order is also a culture, defined by its own scriptures: social justice mantras, DEI, ESG, obligatory "pride" in LGBTQ and everything associated with the equalities industries, political correctness and identity politics. And like the earlier culturally appropriated moralities, its true purpose is to support the elites in their privileged position.

This is why it is pointless to approach the centres of power as a supplicant. You are asking them to dismantle the structures upon which they have built, not only their sense of self and self-worth, but also their material benefits. You will always be regarded as scum so that they can continue to be regarded as virtuous and deserving.

The practical significance of these observations relates to what activism is worth pursuing, and why. Direct campaigning and lobbying against unfair legislation or policies is valuable, in fact essential. But its purpose is not to effect change. Its purpose is to act as a rallying cry to the uncorrupted. Its purpose is to continually reconfirm the validity of our own moral position. To effect change is another matter. For that, greater subtlety, even subversion, is required – and far greater ambition – and a far, far longer timescale.

References

[1] Collins, W. (2022). *The Destructivists*. Principia Publications Unlimited, 20 February 2022.

[2] Phillips, M. (2018). *Melanie Phillips on why she left the Left*. Speakers Action Group YouTube channel, 15 March 2018.

[3] Eaton, Baroness (2020). *Divorce, Dissolution and Separation Bill [HL], Volume 801*. Hansard record of the House of Lords, 5 February 2020.

[4] Lucas, R. (2020). *Richard Lucas on Hate Speech*. The Glass Blind Spot YouTube channel, 6 July 2020.

67. Alessandro Strumia's CERN Talk

This incident now reads like just another instance of the cancellation of someone brave enough to tell the truth. It's now merely the same-old-same-old, which, of course, makes it far worse.

Original posted on: 3 October 2018.

Oh dear, in September 2018 Professor Strumia, Professor of Physics at Pisa University, got himself into a spot of bother. No doubt you heard. The good professor (oops, sorry, bad professor – very, very bad physics professor) gave a talk at CERN's first workshop on High Energy Theory and Gender, 28 September 2018. He claimed that men were being disadvantaged in physics, not women. Shocking stuff, you must agree. No – you **must** agree. He was immediately dismissed from CERN and the University of Pisa issued him with a public sanction, Ref.[1]. The slides of his talk were immediately deleted from the CERN servers. You'd think the chaps (and chapesses, of course) at CERN would know the internet is forever, what with their having invented it an' all. I've saved his slides for posterity (Ref.[2]).

The slides were written in a type of physics-joke terminology, making references to fashionable physics theories. I'm not about to try to explain what spontaneously broken symmetries are, or the significance of terms like M-theory. Suffice it to say that he establishes himself as a nerd of the physics variety. He seems to have declared himself a conservative, too. Clearly, he was intent on self-destruction.

The talk was delivered during a conference specifically about gender in high energy physics. So, Strumia's talk was directly relevant. However, it would appear that this was the sort of conference at which only one opinion was ever going to be acceptable. To be fair (someone has to be) it might have been possible to broach the main subject matter of Strumia's talk without actually being kicked off the site – perhaps escaping with merely being ostracised and spat at a little. But, whilst I didn't hear him speak, I can imagine his first few slides would have been delivered in full-on physicist-Aspie bluntness.

A pity, really. Perhaps an opportunity lost – though maybe it's just what he wanted, and must have expected. And I could guess that the motivation might have been frustration – the frustration born of decades of male physicists being chastised for their sexism and being accused of disadvantaging female physicists at every turn. If so, it is surely a frustration – even a concealed anger – which many male physicists (indeed, men generally) must share by now. There are just so many decades of unjustified blame one can absorb.

"Physics was invented and built by men" is the quote which the press are mostly using. You'd have to be very Asperger indeed not to anticipate flak from that one. *"Highly offensive"* came the chorus. Well, highly predictable response, anyway. Is it true, though? Well, decreasingly so since the mid-twentieth century. But as an extremely good approximation before that you can't argue with it, albeit with very notable exceptions.

The obvious exception is Madame Curie, whom Strumia notes in his talk – she of the two Nobel prizes. But the No.1 female physicist for me, by a country mile, is Emmy Noether (even though she was strictly a mathematician, and equally notable in that capacity). Noether's Theorem is the most stunning theorem in the whole of mathematical physics. For God's sake don't tell the feminists. We'll never hear the end of it. Especially the bit about having to lecture at Erlangen without pay and at Gottingen under the name David Hilbert. Shh! Quiet!

Mary Somerville is worth a mention, though I struggle to think of a discovery to attach to her name (no doubt someone will remind me). She was one of those to speculate about the existence of Neptune before it had been observed, but she is not the one usually credited with Neptune's theoretical prediction (several men competing for that honour).

There were a number of female astronomers, of which Caroline Herschel (sister and assistant of William) is noteworthy, though only as an observer not a theoretician. She was an accomplished observer though, having been brought up in the art by her brother. She bagged eight comets, using a telescope specially built for her by her brother, plus several nebulae which were not in the existing catalogues. There seems to be a mini tradition of sister-astronomers, another one being Sophia Brahe, though she may have been only Tycho's assistant rather than an observer in her own right – history does not record.

Of all the stories of female scientists being diddled out of their just recognition by the patriarchy, such as Jocelyn Bell Burnell, that of Lise

Meitner is the most valid. Co-discoverer with Otto Hahn of nuclear fission, only Hahn was awarded the Nobel Prize. Meitner has a far greater claim to unjustified neglect than the much-vaunted Rosalind Franklin (see chapter 40) though one must be cautious about assuming that sex was the reason. A great many contributors to discoveries fail to win Nobels which are awarded instead to others – and most of those also-rans are men. And as for Mileva Einstein-Marić, the stories about her contributions to relativity are preposterous nonsense (see chapter 42). Like Emmy Noether, Meitner's principal misfortune was not so much being female as being Jewish in Nazi Germany, from which they both had to flee in the 1930s. Both women received plentiful accolades in their later careers, however, as did Bell Burnell.

Jocelyn Bell Burnell, FRS, was later to be made a Dame and to become both president of the Royal Astronomical Society and president of the Institute of Physics, not to mention, in 2018, winning the $3M Special Breakthrough Prize in Fundamental Physics. The prize money for that award is more than twice that of a Nobel Prize. The main reason was her discovery of pulsars way back in the 1960s, for which she missed out on a Nobel, so the later award must be regarded as deliberate compensation.

After the middle of the twentieth century, female physicists become more plentiful – and I'm not going to attempt any summary of that. But back at CERN…

What hasn't surfaced in the press is that one of the things Strumia had been doing at CERN is developing a novel algorithm for assessing scientific achievement based on citation analysis. The substantive part of his talk was based on this work, which (I guess) deserved serious consideration. It's worth updating my original post at this point to inform you that Strumia's analysis was eventually published in a peer-reviewed journal, Ref.[3]. In the following pages of the same issue, the journal also published a string of critical commentaries on the article, followed by Strumia's responses to those commentaries, Ref.[4]. That the commentaries were published on the same day as the original article implies that the journal editors must have sent the draft article to selected persons, inviting them to contribute a commentary. One suspects the editors lacked the courage to publish Strumia's analysis, even two and a half years after the initial controversy, without accompanying negative commentaries to neutralise it.

But one of the published commentaries was authored by popular physics vlogger Sabine Hossenfelder, Ref.[5]. Her short piece was not as negative as perhaps the journal expected from a female physicist. Here are extracts,

"Strumia's major finding is that, on average, women write fewer papers than men, their papers are less cited than those written by men, and they are hired with lower bibliometric indicators based on these measures. His findings are significant and robust. My collaborators Tobias Mistele, Tom Price, and I have been able to reproduce the bibliometric results with the same database and with a different database of the same disciplines."

"Studies such as Strumia's, of course, cannot reveal the origin of the existing gender differences, and the question of what measures of scientific impact are useful is a loaded one, even leaving aside gender. Still, works such as his allow us to understand better what the current situation is and what impact our policies have had, if any... Maybe the most surprising thing about Strumia's analysis is that it wasn't done sooner."

Hossenfelder's last point is revealing. The answer to it, as perhaps she realised, is that such analyses are extremely unwelcome. It's the sort of truth that gets you chucked out of CERN and sanctioned by your employer.

Strumia observed that Hossenfelder was the only one of the commenters who works in fundamental physics, Ref.[4].

In his talk, Strumia also quoted some familiar results from Swedish studies on gender and career choice, which undoubtedly are relevant to the subject matter of the conference. What he was referring to was the so-called gender paradox in careers: the more gender equal a society, the greater the degree of gender segregation in employment. Of course, you have to believe in social constructivism to regard this as a paradox. For the rest of us (i.e., most of us) it is entirely unsurprising that men and women, given sufficient freedom, will gravitate to different occupations by choice, simply due to innate differences in preference. In contrast, where there is less freedom and greater economic pressure, you will tend to get (say) a greater proportion of women engineers – simply because financial considerations oblige women to enter professions which pay, rather than occupations motivated more by personal preference. I dare say that Chinese women are not intrinsically more interested in engineering than western women: they just need the cash and it isn't so readily available in Chinese social science research. The reality of the so-called gender employment paradox was being advertised in the mainstream press even before Strumia's talk, e.g., Ref.[6], and you can read more about it in *The Empathy Gap*, Ref.[7].

In 2018 we had the usual predictable commentary on the Strumia affair. In the Telegraph, Lindsay Nicholson had a piece titled *Physics does have a women problem – and it's not rocket science to work out why*, Ref.[8]. There is nothing in the article to justify the claim that physics does have a woman problem, and so "working out why" does not even arise. This is a cheap journalistic trick. Unless you have your wits about you, the message conveyed by the title sticks, despite it being given no substance by the article itself.

The most amusing thing about the article is that the author appears unaware that she herself provides an illustration of preference being the origin of unequal numbers of the sexes in many occupations. Lindsay Nicholson took astrophysics at university (apparently mainly to annoy the nuns at her convent school). She declares herself to have been of middling ability – until she discovered "the joys of the student newspaper – and the union bar". Fair enough, but she also says she was offered several jobs, at least one in a technical field (as a rocket scientist, no less). But she preferred to become a journalist. Surprise, surprise. Then she goes on to lament the continuing low percentage of women in science. Who is the more responsible for that: she or I – or Alesandro Strumia? (Women are the majority of pure science undergraduates in the UK, by the way, and have been for over 17 years, Ref.[9]).

Nicholson writes,

"Although I wasn't the best in my class at University College London – that honour went to an absurdly tall skinny boy who couldn't make eye contact. I wasn't the worst either – that was a rugby player who later switched to engineering."

I am offended! Offended, I say! Who would not be offended by her outrageous appeal to the stereotype of the Asperger-nerd gawky male physicist? Too easy a target from the Olympian heights of her female glamour and fine social adjustment. And was she sneering, or jealous? And why "boy" not "man"? And why is it acceptable to reference his physical appearance? We men have been forbidden from referring to adult females as "girls", or making derogatory comments about their physical appearance, for 50 years. And is it just me – or is she assuming that we will make the appalling *faux pas* of assuming the rugby player in question to have been male?

Shocking stereotyping! That's a remarkable number of double standards to cram into one sentence.

Nicholson ends with these two remarkable claims,

"The definition of physics is that it is the science of measurement."

Err, no it isn't. The science of measurement is called metrology. Ye Gods, what dork could possibly think that that was an adequate definition of physics?

"Professor Strumia – as a physicist – should remember that the scientific aptitude of the male versus the female brain is not something that can be objectively measured."

That's a big claim, and contrary to the findings of neuroscience (see chapter 49). Moreover, it is almost a denial that psychology is objective and hence scientific. Psychologists – over to you to defend your discipline.

But all this is beside the point. Nicholson's title stated that physics does have a woman problem – but then failed to address the matter at all. So, let's take a quick look at just that. By coincidence, the same day the Alessandro Strumia affair broke, the latest Physics World flopped through my letterbox. It was the thirtieth anniversary edition of the Institute of Physics' house journal, though that's of no great relevance. Here to hand, then, is a ready exemplar of the woman problem in physics. Let's just take a look at how the male hegemony of Physics World manifests the patriarchy at its most blatantly misogynistic. Let's see how women are ignored.

In the original blog article I included all the pictures of people which occur in the magazine, both in ads and articles. I make the final score 14 photos of men and 17 of women. Not a bad effort for a subject which is about 85% male – if your objective is to redress the imbalance, that is. Most of the men were non-white, by the way. The photos in the article about graduate careers in physics were: three women and two non-white men. I've left out those little inset pictures of authors that you sometimes get. In that context note that 12 authors were men and just five were women. Shocking! Something must be done! (Though why momentarily escapes me). The editorial staff is a different matter: two men and four women.

One of the women pictured was the President of the Institute of Physics at the time, by the way (Dame Julia Higgins). The current president (as of

February 2024 and since 2021) is also a woman, Sheila Rowan. Dame Jocelyn Bell Burnell was the president in two periods from 2008 to 2011.

Other things of note in this issue of Physics World included two articles on diversity in physics, particularly as regards women in physics, occupying a whole page. Most of another page was devoted to Jocelyn Bell-Burnett's donation of her $3M prize money to create new graduate studentships for under-represented groups in physics, including women.

The president of the Institute of Physics (Julia Higgins) had a three-page article reviewing how physics had changed over the preceding 30 years. Higgins was one of those responsible for setting up the Athena project in the 1990s (see Ref.[10]). Most of the article does not concern gender, but a great deal did, including positive action. She's in favour. Examples: if a shortlist does not contain women – go back and put some in. And this admission: "If you look at nominations for fellowship of the Royal Society, we do work proactively to make sure women get nominated". The sexism from which she reports having suffered were two instances of being mistaken for a secretary (probably decades ago). The sexism to which she confesses, from her position of authority, was a persistent and deliberate preferencing in hiring/advancement based on sex. Moreover, this was contemporary behaviour, not ancient history. Was she more sinned against or more the sinner?

The letters page is of interest also. It was not a normal letters page, though. It was a hand-picked selection of the most witty or pithy letters over the last 30 years. The correspondents' names indicate 33 men, 3 women and one indeterminate. One of the women co-authored a letter with a man concerning a (whimsical) suggestion for particle nomenclature. Their affiliations were schools of psychology and English. One of the other women correspondents wrote to make reference to an article on Women In Physics and to complain about an invitation to a college reunion which was extended also to her wife. The last woman correspondent wrote to inform us that Brian Cox was not on TV because he knows physics but because he's pretty (which she found distracting, poor thing). Change that to any female TV presenter and see if such a letter would get published – let alone chosen as one of the best letters in 30 years. Double standards? I think so. But my point is that none of the women's letters were about physics. I suspect the editors tried very hard to find letters from women, but these were all they could come up with. I have noticed a familiar dominance of letters to Professional Engineering by men, far more emphatic than the 85% one might expect from the gender proportions of engineering students.

One issue of Physics World hardly constitutes a scientific study, though I can confirm there is nothing unusual about the issue in question (apart from being the thirtieth anniversary issue). So, you can ask yourself which of the following two propositions seems best to fit the evidence from Physics World,

- That physics is a misogynistic institution which neglects to portray women in physics and does little to encourage women in physics, or,
- That physics as an institution bends over backwards to include women in physics and does an enormous amount to neutralise any adverse stereotyping.

The latter is the case, of course, and has been for decades. I have already noted in chapter 45 that the editor-in-chief of New Scientist has been Emily Wilson since April 2018 (and still is as of February 2024), with unfortunate effects. The president of CERN between 2013 and 2015 was a woman, Professor Agnieszka Zalewska, and shortly after Strumia's talk was again a woman, Ursula Bassler, 2019 – 2021. And in the year of Strumia's presentation, 2018, a woman, Donna Strickland, was one of the winners of the Nobel Prize, Ref.[11]. In 2020 there was another female winner of the physics Nobel, Andrea Ghez, and in 2023 another, Anne l'Huillier.

It has been decades since any physicist or engineer could use the male pronoun in print. For some of us it has been a lifetime of this accommodation, but without the accusations of discrimination ever letting up – in fact they have only become worse. And, of course, without any reciprocation. The invention of "unconscious bias" is a clever ruse to ensure you can have no escape from the endless blame, whatever you think, whatever you say, and however you behave.

After decades of ceaseless unjustified blaming of men who could do no more than they were doing, frustration and resentment becomes inevitable. Alessandro Strumia's approach may have been cack-handed. And the price paid for this is that he has gifted the prevailing gender narrative with more fuel for its protestations of offence and endemic misogyny. Unfortunately, there is scant evidence that a more diplomatic approach would be more effective. So those of us who dissent from the approved perspective of perpetual male privilege are forbidden from speaking at all. The frustration, resentment and anger can only fester in increasingly disgusted silence. This is unhealthy.

But there is worse. In all those decades there has been absolutely no reciprocation. I covered this as regards education in *STEM v Teaching* nearly ten years ago, Ref.[12]. Men are increasingly aware of the disadvantage to their own sex, including in matters of employment (though this is by no means the worst area). Women dominate in many areas of employment, including many professions. Women dominate in virtually all areas which deal with people rather than things, including education, healthcare and social work. And males are disadvantaged in education, healthcare and issues addressed by social workers. It's about time the juxtaposition of those two observations was promoted to a position of political prominence.

The endless castigation of the institutions of physics and engineering needs to stop. There is nothing further that men can do to "assist" women in these areas. Further protestations will only feed increasing resentment and generate more Alessandro Strumias. In contrast, there is a great deal that women can, and must, do to assist men in other areas – because, so far, they have done nothing. There has been no recognition that reciprocation is required. The spotlight of criticism needs to be turned upon the gendered aspects of people-oriented sectors. The partisan double standards which prevail at present are now being perceived – and resented – by an increasing number of people, of both sexes. But a situation has been cultivated in which it is forbidden, on pain of ostracism or sacking, from expressing the resulting anger and disgust at the approved hypocrisy. And this unfortunate social situation is amplified by the opportunistic purveyors of a poisonously divisive politics.

References

[1] University of Pisa (2019). *Ethical sanction against Prof. Alessandro Strumia*. Issued by the Academic Senate of the University of Pisa on 18 January 2019 (original in Italian).

[2] Strumia, A. (2018). *Slides of Alessandro Strumia's presentation*. First CERN Workshop on High Energy Theory and Gender, 28 September 2018.

[3] Strumia, A. (2021). *Gender issues in fundamental physics: A bibliometric analysis*. Quantitative Science Studies. 2(1), 225–253. 8 April 2021.

[4] Strumia, A. (2021). *Reply to commentaries about 'Gender issues in fundamental physics: A bibliometric analysis'*. Quantitative Science Studies 2(1): 277–287, 8 April 2021.

[5] Hossenfelder, S. (2021). *Analyzing data is one thing, interpreting it another*. Quantitative Science Studies 2(1): 273–274, 8 April 2021.

[6] Tom Whipple, T. (2018). *Patriarchy paradox: how equality reinforces stereotypes*. The Times, 15 September 2018.

[7] Collins, W. (2019). *The Empathy Gap*. LPS Publishing, June 2019 (section 7.3.4).

[8] Nicholson, L. (2018). *Physics does have a women problem – and it's not rocket science to work out why*. The Telegraph, 1 October 2018.

[9] Bradford, R. (2021). *Women's Dominance in Higher Education in the UK*. File Note based on UCAS data, 6 July 2021.

[10] Collins, W. (2019). *The Empathy Gap*. LPS Publishing, June 2019 (section 2.8).

[11] The Nobel Prize Committee (2018). *Nobel prize for physics 2018*. The Royal Swedish Academy of Sciences, 2 October 2018.

[12] Collins, W. (2015). *STEM v Teaching*. The Illustrated Empathy Gap, 5 January 2015. (See also *this article on Academia*).

Section 13

Moral Usurpation

68. Behold, The Neo-Bourgeois Morality Vampires

This blog article was my first foray into a theory of moral usurpation. It is interesting that this appeared just days before The Empathy Gap was published as it indicates that I was, by then, already becoming more concerned with general politics, rather than only gender politics. It was to be another 32 months before the complete theory appeared in book form, The Destructivists, Ref.[8]. Readers with a specific interest in these ideas will find this article both a suitable introduction to that book and also complementary to it as there are some themes here which were not addressed in the book.

However, it was not until I wrote The Destructivists that I appreciated the full structure of what I there call the Woke Industrial Complex. Nor did I, until then, appreciate the algorithmic similarities with Gramscianism, though the theory of moral usurpation adds the key moral ingredient which is essential in understanding the appeal and rapid contagion of "Woke". After five years' mature reflection I remain of the view that the ideas propounded in The Destructivists are the correct sociopsychological basis of the "progressive" perspective which now afflicts us.

"A system of morality which is based on relative emotional values is a mere illusion, a thoroughly vulgar conception which has nothing sound in it and nothing true". (Socrates).

Original posted on: 3 June 2019.

In this piece I abandon my usual obsession with data and indulge in a little theorising. There comes a point when one must do so. Empiricism alone does not enlighten. The scientific method is conjecture and refutation (or, to those who are happy to disrespect Popper on the grounds of pragmatism, conjecture and validation). The empirical evidence is the judge, but there must be some putative theory which is in the dock. This set of brief notes presents a theory of how our present polarised politics has arisen, its psychological basis and how this supports a power structure.

I acknowledge Ben Cobley's *The Tribe*, Ref.[1], as the source of the terms "System of Diversity" and "The Administration", and the associated ideas (the book is strongly recommended). However, that the mechanism by which the System derives its power is the annexation of the perceived moral high ground is my spin, as is the idea that The Administration is the neo-Bourgeoisie in an emerging new class structure.

The Generic Process of Removing Your Freedom

There is a temptation to blame the occurrence of tyrannous regimes on unusual evil, the unusual evil being embodied in an individual, or small group of individuals. But an unusually evil individual is not necessary, and is certainly not sufficient, for tyrannies to arise. In a democracy, it is also required that the regime is empowered by a substantial level of popular support, at least in the early days before fear takes over as the controlling mechanism. This popular support is not the result of great evil of heart becoming widespread, but results from mundane and universal character flaws. The tragedy is that these humdrum psychological predispositions can be inveigled to bolster wickedness. This may proceed from ignorance, but such ignorance may be more wilful than blameless.

The process seems always to be the same. An out-group is distinguished from the in-group. The out-group is blamed for all the ills of society. The appeal to the in-group is based on two factors: flattery and resentment. These are the mundane character flaws in question. The in-group is flattered by being told they are superior to the out-group. Their resentment is generated by being told that they are being, and have always been, badly used by the out-group. The out-group is said to enjoy greater wealth and power at the in-group's expense, and perhaps also to abuse them in other ways. For the process to work it is not necessary that the flattery and resentment are factually well founded: it is only necessary that the in-group believe it. What the out-group believes is of no consequence.

It never seems as clear as that when the process is in play. The superficial details differ enough to disguise each new instance of the phenomenon. The driving resentment is presented as a moral crusade, and hence laudable, not a character flaw. And the associated flattery is hard to resist. What's not to like when you are encouraged to bask in the warm glow of superiority whilst being told that you are owed benefits due to other people's past misdemeanours? It's so much more attractive than being told you are a sinner, and that you are owed no more than you owe others. The snag is that the former leads to division, injustice, tyranny and social collapse.

The observations which follow lay out how "progressive", feminist, faux-leftist politics manifest this process. Though I acknowledge that I lean heavily on Ref.[1], the emphasis on moral aspects is my own. I start with the four keys to understanding, followed by a set of brief notes expanding on how it all works.

The "Progressive" Class System

The first key to understanding what's going on is to realise that the "progressive", feminist, faux-leftist system is actually a class system (which is why I write "faux-leftist"). Hence it is correctly called a regressive system, and bears little relation to the true left as it might have been understood by trade unionists a century ago. This essay explains the structure of this brave new class system and its psychological basis. For reasons that will become apparent, I follow Cobley in referring to this as the "System of Diversity". The adherents of this System of Diversity I will refer to as "progressives", the inverted commas being essential in view of their commonly regressive true nature.

It is worth adding that, like all class systems, those who consider themselves the superior caste are the new snobs who despise the rest of us, Ref.[2]. We are the hoi polloi, the rabble, the uneducated possessors of "low information". We are the basket of deplorables. In contrast, the snobs are the "anointed", to use Thomas Sowell's excellent term, Ref.[3]. They are the neo-Bourgeoisie.

Power

The second key to understanding our present predicament is to realise that the "progressives" have genuinely embraced postmodernism and relegated truth to a subsidiary position, if not abandoned it entirely. Instead, they are obsessed with power. So obsessed are they that in the British Psychological Society's appalling document *Power Threat Meaning Framework*, Ref.[4], power is the key factor in their proposed diagnostic system for mental disorders. But what is power? (No marks for "the rate of doing work", sorry physicists). Power, in the sociological sense, is the ability to impose your will on others. The System of Diversity is also a System of Power. This is inevitably discriminatory as those with power are distinct from those over whom power is exercised. However, all social structures involve power hierarchies. The issue is their legitimacy (representativeness) and the degree to which the nominally less powerful have the sanction of removing power from the powerful (called "democracy").

Social Morality

The keystone in the arch of power that is the System of Diversity is *Homo sapiens'* innate inclination to adhere to a social moral code. It is remarkable that humans form extremely large societies of unrelated individuals who get along in reasonable harmony and cooperation. One of the ingredients which make this possible is a set of conventions regarding what is acceptable and what unacceptable, a social morality, which the bulk of people abide by voluntarily and without policing. Defaulters are discouraged largely by social censure. Whilst severe cases may need to be dealt with by criminal proceedings, a decent society needs recourse to such measures only relatively rarely. A congenial society runs on the near-universal adoption of social moral conventions. But this social morality need not be the absolute morality of which philosophers and theologians speak. Clearly not, for social moralities are mutable: different cultures have differing moral codes (ignorance of which can get a stranger into trouble).

Moral Legitimising

The final key to understanding the System of Diversity is to appreciate how our social moral code has been subverted to imbue the "progressive" elite, the neo-Bourgeoisie, with power. As outlined above, the generic process rests always on clearly defined in-groups and out-groups. A route to ensuring that the in-group is flattered and the out-group denigrated is to align in/out group status with moral deserts. The mutability of social morality then provides a mechanism to align your preferred groups as "in-groups". In the same way, groups from whom you wish to withhold power may be aligned as "out-groups" by negative moral representation. The former is facilitated by moral vampirism (below), whilst the latter is facilitated by denigratory propaganda.

The basis of the "progressive" system therefore depends crucially on moral relativism.

The out-groups are first defined as those from whom you wish to take power. The in-groups are any readily identifiable groups which are distinct from, and may be presentable as opposed to, the out-groups. Only after the group status is defined is the process of imbuing them with positive or negative moral characteristics embarked upon.

Capture of the educational and media institutions is key to carrying out the programme of moral manipulation. Once captured, success is assured. To illustrate just how effective it can be, suppose an in-group were to carry out an extreme atrocity on a mass scale. Perhaps (as a purely hypothetical example) murdering and raping many hundreds of an out-group, filming the event and making the video available for all to see. You might imagine that the status of this in-group as occupying the moral high ground could not survive the universal knowledge of this atrocity. You would be wrong. They can continue to be presented as victims, not villains, without missing a beat. This is the power of moral usurpation.

Entering the Institutions and Obtaining Political Support

Those who would acquire power in a democratic State have a problem. By visibly holding power they are clearly privileged. But the privileged are not those who naturally command popular sympathy and hence electoral support. There are two solutions to this conundrum: the aspiring politician can be a spokesperson for a class which does inspire sympathy, or he/she can contrive to acquire power without being elected. Even democratic states have means by which power can be acquired without a popular mandate. This can be via the permanent executive, the civil service or similar function, or via the judiciary, or other roles of significant influence. Achieving power in this manner offers the advantage of remaining invisible. The phenomenon of the *éminence grise*, the power behind the throne, has many historical instantiations. (The example I gave in June 2019 was Martin Selmayr, you can probably think of many current examples). Less dramatically, society consists of many professional positions ("the institutions") which carry substantial levels of influence obtained without election but through promotion or appointment. The System of Diversity operates here to preference "progressive" in-groups.

However, the route of invisibility is inapplicable to elected politicians. They must cultivate a constituency who will support them in elections. They are, after all, supposed to be merely representatives. How are politicians seeking election to acquire popular support? The traditional way was for politicians to present their case, stating their proposed policies and arguing for their benefits. No doubt their claims would have lots of spin, exaggeration, unjustified assumptions and ignored disbenefits. But at least such an approach provided the basis for debate, focussed around policies. The "progressives" have adopted a different strategy to obtain political support. They have commandeered the social morality and corrupted it to their purpose. This is the process that I called moral vampirism in 2019, but which I now refer to as moral usurpation. I now explain what it is.

Moral Usurpation

Recall that social morality is a natural proclivity which strongly encourages alignment of opinion, a basic attribute of humans and a central aspect of evolved social cooperation. The existence of such a proclivity provides a great opportunity if you are in the business of acquiring popular support. If your political pitch happens to align with an existing moral position then you're on a winner. But, more cunningly, what if you exploit the mutability of social morality to realign popular morality in a manner which suits your political purpose? If this can be done you will have achieved a short cut to extremely strong political support.

Moral usurpation first requires the in-groups and out-groups to have been defined. As explained above, this dichotomising into identity group status precedes the moral preferencing of the in-group and the moral denigration of the out-group. The ostensible justification for such alignment is therefore fraudulent, but that does not diminish its power to garner popular support.

Moral vampirism, as one aspect of the whole moral usurpation strategy, consists of identifying and aligning all such sources of moral succour with the in-groups, whilst, if possible, preventing the out-groups from being positively morally associated. The simplest and most pervasive example is victimhood. Moral succour is naturally associated with victims, whilst perpetrators are undeserving. For example, we have the ceaseless narrative about "violence against women and girls". In the context of the in-group "women" and the out-group "men", this supports the moral stance "women good, men bad". It is the simplicity of the message which is part of its popular appeal.

I first became aware of the use of moral vampirism in the context of the women's peace camp at Greenham Common in the 1980s. The camp was promoted as a protest against nuclear missiles stored at the Greenham Common base. Men who turned up early in the peace camp's history were asked to leave. The reason for this rejection of men, as stated at the time, was that the presence of men might provoke violence. It was a rather obvious rationalisation. It was clear to me that the camp presented the women with a perfect PR opportunity to align the moral right with women. Inside the base, on the other side of a high wire fence, were men – virtually exclusively men – with weapons of mass destruction. Outside, in their primitive benders, were women, mothers who stood for peace not killing. The "women good, men bad" narrative could hardly be clearer, and there were great optics to go with it.

Here we also see the attraction of infantilising moral issues. An effective public relations image requires simplicity of message. Good PR is not served by close examination of the issues, either moral or military. The desirability, or otherwise, of national defence, and how it might best be accomplished, was not recognised as a discussion which needed to be had. Killing was bad, and the peace camp mothers presented it specifically as the killing of children. Any possibility of moral dilemma was obliterated, implicitly declared nugatory and never explicitly discussed.

It is telling that the camp was not presented as a feminist enterprise at the time. But since then, many feminists have acknowledged that the camp marked a key event in their feminist awakening. The "awakening", I suggest, actually consisted largely of the discovery of how delightful it was to be able to bask in the warm glow of moral purity and export all badness to the "others". This was one of the many steps in consolidating the in-group status of women and the out-group status of men.

Another example of moral vampirism is the Green Party. The Green Party is floridly feminist and hard left. Yet the Greens are (at least in theory) a conservationist movement. Given the etymological equivalence of "conservation" and "conservative", one might have thought that the Green movement should be part of the Conservative political axis. And as for being aligned with sex, why should the Greens be so aligned at all? Logically, the feminist-leftist nature of the Green Party makes no sense. The explanation is that, some decades ago, environmental issues acquired a patina of moral correctness. The reason is clear enough: trashing the planet is bad, saving the planet is good. (Recall that this is the level of simplicity at which moral cachet works best). As soon as Green issues became established as a source of moral probity, it was naturally targeted by the morality vampires, ever hungry for another source of moral succour. The morality vampires are the "progressives", and especially the feminists.

Both men and Conservatives are out-groups, so both had to be excluded from partaking in the moral succour of the Green movement. The annexation of the Green Party by the feminist faux-left serves the purposes of aligning the moral credentials of "Greenness" with the approved "progressive" in-groups whilst encouraging the eviction of the out-groups from the movement and hence from the associated moral benefit. One feels for men with Green sympathies: many have been obliged to leave their natural political home because the Greens have become so appallingly anti-male. You think I exaggerate?

Take a look at the image linked in Ref.[5]. It is a picture of then-Green Party leader, Natalie Bennett, holding a sign declaring her patch on a camp site at Glastonbury to be a "mansplaining free zone". Mansplaining is an overtly sexist appellation. The phenomenon to which it refers is not specific to men. Feminist women have been femsplaining what it's like to be a man for decades, e.g., Ref.[6] to give one example out of hundreds. Any male MP declaring a space a "femsplaining free zone" would have committed career suicide, would immediate lose the whip and be deselected. Bennett was given a peerage in Theresa May's 2019 resignation honours.

The functional purpose of the Greens within the System of Diversity is to harvest the moral cachet associated with greenness and allocate it to approved in-groups. So, out-groups had to be ejected or disenfranchised from recognition as Greens (unless adopting the correct Administrative opinions, see below). This is why the Greens went uber-feminist. It is part of the system of moral fraudulence.

The System of Diversity and the Neo-Bourgeoisie

The System of Diversity is the power structure which results from advertising and promoting the claims of the chosen in-groups for preferencing on the basis of their moral deserts. The elite class which performs the function of enacting this preferencing is what Cobley calls the Administration, Ref.[1]. The Administrators are well educated, high achievers in positions (or heading towards positions) in which they are able to exert influence to deliver on this preferencing of the in-groups (whilst neglecting the out-groups). But the Administrators also achieve their elite positions by espousing the cause of the in-groups, thus benefiting both from vicarious moral positioning and from enjoyment of the in-groups' support, e.g., in elections. This could be a description of any process of political representation. But it is pernicious compared with "honest" politics in several ways,

- It is deliberately divisive, being based on denigration and disadvantaging of the out-groups;

- The out-groups are chosen as those whom the System Administrators wish to disempower, not on the basis of their disempowerment being justified or even beneficial to society;

- The moral claims of the in-groups are exaggerated by the Administration, and sometimes dishonest, especially in comparison with the out-groups whose parallel claims are ignored or denied;

- The Administrators promote and maintain the above system of prejudice because it is the source of their own power and elite status, whilst the members of the in-groups acquiesce to being Administered because they benefit from the system, both materially and in terms of implied moral purity, at no cost to themselves;

- The Administration's total control of the (perceived) moral high ground leads to control of the institutions, including the legislature, academia, the media and the judiciary, thus robbing the out-groups of any voice to protest and also undermining justice.

The parallels with Marcuse's Repressive Tolerance are clear, Ref.[7]. But Repressive Tolerance is based on an explicit division of policies into those of left or right political leaning. To be enacted requires widespread active popular support, which weakens its likelihood of occurrence without some additional ingredient to make it popular. But the System of Diversity is instantiated at the popular level by control of the moral sense, and morality is an innate human proclivity. The manipulation of the moral sense is the true basis of this brave new System of Diversity. And because it appeals to an innate proclivity, it has been possible to infect large swathes of the public, perhaps even the majority.

Basing a political system on morality may seem desirable. But it is not at all desirable when the moral sense has been corrupted by appeal to people's baser instincts, levering only their desire for preference and ready acceptance of the wickedness of others. The System of Diversity is based on division. It is the latest form of the oldest and most effective strategy in the book: divide and conquer.

The Administrators are the "progressive", feminist, faux-leftist elite: they are the neo-Bourgeoisie. Their power structure is founded on manipulation of popular perceived morality via moral vampirism and moral infantilism.

There is nothing dramatically new about an Administrative intelligentsia attaining bourgeois status by representing a Labour-preferred group. In the 1930s Orwell wrote of,

"…the type who squirms into the middle class via the literary intelligentsia, or the type who becomes a Labour MP or a high-up trade union official. This last type is one of the most desolating spectacles the world contains. He has been picked out to fight for his mates, and all it means to him is a soft job and the chance of 'bettering' himself. Not merely while but by fighting the bourgeoisie he becomes a bourgeois himself."

Moral Infantilism and Intolerance

In the System of Diversity all moral issues are decided and clear. Preferencing of the in-groups is morally right, QED. Disadvantaging the out-groups is morally justified. Insert here your favourite radical feminist anti-male quote by way of illustration. It is legitimate to hate all men, or kill all men, and men may benefit from being falsely accused, etc, etc. Women, on the other hand, cannot be sexist and never lie. One need never struggle over any of these things. "Man bad, woman good" decides everything immediately.

One of the attractions of this moral infantilism is that it minimises cognitive load. A great boon for the adherent of moral infantilism is that one need never agonise over a moral dilemma ever again. Everything is now black and white, absolutely clear and unambiguous. Every issue – and ultimately every person – will wear a black hat or a white hat. Every issue is decided in advance. This is analogous to religious obedience where a priestly class tells the masses what is right and wrong in every case: no need for them to think at all. In fact, independent thinking is very much to be discouraged.

The method for establishing your over-simplified position as the unchallengeable moral right is strident intolerance of alternative opinion. All attempts at opposition are met with explicit outrage, a signal to all that moral certainty is being asserted. Even factual evidence, unopposed by any contrary information, can be defeated by the simple expedient of lashings of outrage.

All that is necessary is to refuse to be deflected by anything, and simply to repeat endlessly the same claim of moral certainty. The strategy of presenting your position as one of moral certainty is that any opponent is immediately branded despicable, thus reinforcing your case. Some examples,

- Immigration: No reasoned debate addressing pros and cons is possible. To even tolerate a discussion about immigration is to be a racist, Islamophobic, alt-right bigot. Arguments that immigration is financially beneficial to the country are given prominent circulation; contrary financial arguments are not.

- Gay marriage: No public debate was had over what marriage means, or what the adoption of same-sex marriage would mean in terms of changing the meaning of marriage for everyone. Instead, opposing same-sex marriage is merely labelled as unacceptable bigotry. Accept it or shut up and hopefully die soon.

- The EU: After four years or so of non-stop media coverage around Brexit, almost nothing was said about the central issue of democratic self-determination or justified concerns about being ruled from abroad by unelected bureaucrats over whom we have little or no influence and cannot remove from office. Instead, raise these issues and one is immediately branded a "little Englander", a xenophobe or a Fascist. Where was the discussion about the Lisbon Treaty? Where was the discussion about how Ursula von der Leyen got her job as President of the European Commission?

- Disadvantages to men & boys: Listen they will not. The placement of moral rectitude with females has already been decided and male disadvantages can only be things that men and boys bring upon themselves. QED.

The In-Groups and Out-Groups

Without being exhaustive, the in-groups include women and girls, blacks and ethnic minorities, Muslims, non-heterosexuals and trans.

The out-groups include men and boys, whites, conservatives, Christians and heterosexuals.

As regards how the System operates, the division into in- and out-groups has an element of arbitrariness: the key thing is division itself. However, the out-groups tend to be those who are perceived as privileged and powerful, whilst the highest-ranking in-groups arise due to the relative ease with which a moral case can be created for them. The case need not be valid, only easy to sell.

In case of doubt, my own position is opposition to the System itself. I am opposed to any form of identity politics, not merely an advocate of an alternative preferred identity group. (See chapter 14 of *The Destructivists*, Ref.[8], for a game theory demonstration of how identity politics is inevitably catastrophic, or Ref.[9] for the published academic paper).

The division into deserving and undeserving groups is the Original Sin from which all the injustices of the System of Diversity flow. Judging people as privileged, or else deserving of preference, based on identity group membership is a profound moral corruption. The only basis for justice is to judge people on their individual merits. What is now called "social justice" is injustice. In the System of Diversity, this "social justice" is the driving force of a power structure whose basic methodology is divide and conquer.

At the heart of it all is moral infantilism.

System Management, Group Representatives and Immigration

A complex web of identity group Representatives acts as the interface between the in-groups and the Administrators. For example, Imams or Muslim councillors may act as Representatives for their local Muslim community. Muslims and immigrant communities have a very strong bias towards voting Labour. Representatives may boast that they can "deliver" block votes, thus giving such Representatives considerable power with the Administrative class. In return, the Administrators will protect their interests as a preferred group. This is the trading of power for power.

The claims that the Blair government encouraged immigration to boost the Labour vote would appear to be true. The Administration and Representation of these communities is one of the processes of the System of Diversity.

The Purpose of the Administration

The purpose of the Administration is to maintain the System of Diversity, and thereby to maintain their elite position. The System is maintained by protecting the perceived deserving status of the in-groups. One task of the Administration is to remind us constantly that all spaces, everywhere and at all times, are racist, sexist, misogynistic, homophobic, Islamophobic and transphobic. The actual benefits, or disbenefits, to individual in-group members is of less importance than maintaining the System itself, based mainly on perception, because it is the System which is the power structure.

Indeed, it is preferable never to make any real progress with genuine issues which affect the in-groups because such real progress would diminish their worth as a source of moral probity. Women must be perceived as remaining oppressed. That women in the West are actually the most privileged creatures ever to walk the planet is a truth that must be rigorously suppressed from being perceived because it would undermine the use of feminism as a moral smokescreen.

As for the in-group members, groupthink and a sense of belonging and social approval encourage conformance. The System offers members protection of their identity status, but not authority. Authority is vested in Representatives and Administrators. For fixed identity groups, membership is the default position. Apathy is on the side of the System. To opt out requires proactive dissent. A key function of the Administration is to ensure that dissenters are discomforted, by denigration and perhaps punitive action, such as sacking or false accusation. In contrast, there is great comfort in conforming to in-group identity expectations, including holding the approved political opinions. It becomes part of one's social persona. The discomfort of the dissenter is therefore also enacted socially.

Male feminists

Male feminists take great delight in trashing masculinity. They write whole books on the subject. This is puzzling when you first come across it. Some people explain the phenomenon by claiming that these men are using their feminist credentials to get into women's knickers ("sneaky fucker" syndrome). But a parallel phenomenon occurs when white professors, of either sex, express a desire to see white people fall and fade ("all I want for Christmas is white genocide"). Another example is a white female feminist who goes on a demo bearing banners which read "fuck white feminism". These examples are not so easily explained in the same way. However, all cases are simply explained once the central importance of the Administration in the System of Diversity is appreciated.

The generic means by which a member of an out-group can attain a positive persona, and indeed, status, within the System is to become an Administrator. In all the above examples, the people in question, who appear to be denigrating themselves, are actually bidding for Administrator status. By their striking adoption of right-think they atone for their immutable identity sin, becoming the One Good Man (or the One Good White). Hence they distance themselves from the common run of reprehensible men (or whites). Their born-again moral posturing gains its strength by contrast with the rest of their tribe. The lesson which these phenomena should teach us is how shallow is the progressives' self-knowledge.

White Ribbon is another example of men bidding for Administrator status. It is essentially self-aggrandisement.

Parallels with the British Colonial System

The operation of the System of Diversity in respect of its trading power to community Representatives for assistance with managing their identity group is uncannily similar to how the British Empire managed the colonies. The Raj was run by the British with a preposterously small number of men given the size of India. This was accomplished by devolving authority to Maharajas, Nabobs and other local officials, leaving the British only with the task of overseeing the system as a whole, ensuring that its component parts kept within their allotted roles. The similarity is also noted by Cobley. The System of Diversity is a colonial system within our own shores. The irony is amusing given the progressives' ostensible adoption of militant anti-colonialism.

Abandoning the Working Class

In the UK the beginnings of the System of Diversity can be traced to the early 1980s. I have mentioned Greenham Common which started in 1981 and became most active in 1983. But this was specific to feminism. The origins of the more general political process which became the System of Diversity probably stems from the 1984/5 miners' strike. Mrs Thatcher so decisively defeated the miners that the power of the working-class man, via the trades unions, was broken. The chemotherapy killed not just the tumour, but also the patient. The power infrastructure of the trades unions and the Labour party remained, but now shorn of their previous source of moral legitimacy. The trades unions spent the rest of the 1980s regrouping. Whether deliberately or by happenstance they arrived at an alternative source of moral legitimacy: that of women, of racial minorities, and later of LGBT. The existing infrastructure of the trades unions and the Labour party, now a political system looking for a cause, alighted on these alternatives as their new *raison d'être*. This was the rise of the equalities industry. This, I suspect, was also the origin of the System of Diversity in the UK. It was always, at least in part, for the purpose of continuing the employment of trade unionists and Labour party MPs who morphed into the Administrators of Diversity.

This is the point at which the left became the faux-left as the new "progressives" abandoned the working-class male because he no longer served as a source of power. Cobley reminds us that feminists such as Harriet Harman do not merely see the Labour party as a suitable home for feminists. Harman regards the Labour party as simply the political wing of feminism, and subsidiary to it. How much further could the working man have fallen? Feminists have completely co-opted his main vehicle for political representation. For this reason, the working class is not a chosen in-group, instead enjoying, at best, no particular Identity status. But the innate snobbery of the neo-Bourgeoisie renders the working classes as low information deplorables and hence an effective out-group. Ownership of a white van is tantamount to a confession of fascism.

To any person keen to forge a new political movement, the working class is the constituency which is up for grabs. In fact, the term "working class" (which I don't like anyway) is too narrow. Many of the less well-paid middle class fall into the same neglected category with no effective representation at present. Brexit has made this obvious. A powerful movement could be forged from the combination of the working class (or the less wealthy) with the men's movement and the remaining true social conservatives. These are all out-groups so they might align naturally under opposition to the System of Diversity which disadvantages them all.

Abandoning Conservatism?

I have hinted above that the Conservative party has ceased to represent real conservatism. The reason is that the System of Diversity and its moral vampire apparatchiks have been so successful in annexing all perceived sources of moral legitimacy that the Conservatives were left looking like the nasty party. Unfortunately, the Conservative Party made the fatal error of thinking that this could be rectified by aping the faux-left. This led to the disheartening spectacle of Theresa May's Labour-lite election manifesto (and things have only got worse since). It points to a total failure to understand how the System of Diversity works. The Conservatives, as a leading out-group, cannot benefit from copying policies or opinions from the system designed to delegitimise them. By doing so, they have delegitimised themselves.

The way forward is, as declared above, an alliance between those with true conservative principles and the broad working class, or less well off, plus the men's movement. The System of Diversity itself must be challenged, not appeased. This essay serves to motivate targeting that challenge at the false, infantile morality upon which the whole edifice of deceit is based.

The New Class System

In the System comprising the Administrative elite, the web of Representatives, and the identity group members, we have an echo of older class systems: the ruling elite, the middle class and the working class. In the feudal system, the elite was maintained by birth, by property ownership and by force. In the industrial system, the new elite arose by control of capital and by ownership of the means of production. In the System of Diversity, the new elite attains power by control, and subversion, of perceived moral deserts, embedded via selective preferencing. In the feudal system the force was military. In the industrial system the force was financial. In the System of Diversity the force is moral. Those who exercise control over this System are the neo-Bourgeoisie, the new owners of the factories of false morality.

The System of Diversity and Globalism: Natural Allies

The feminist position on the gender pay gap is propaganda whose aim is to get women working more paid hours. Whether this is what women themselves want is not their concern. The Administrative level feminists want to increase their power by increasing the power of their administered group, in this case by increasing women's financial significance. In this they align with government objectives, for whom more paid working hours means more tax revenue and increased GDP. Business interests are similarly aligned with this: more workers, more profit. And this all works at the international level also. Hence, the World Economic Forum, the EU, the UN, the IMF, are all aligned with this feminist objective of increased working hours.

A similar logic applies for immigrants. Putting more workers where the Western economy can put them to work is beneficial to the business and political classes for the above reasons. More parochially, immigrants provide a ready supply of cheap labour. But we have already seen how the System of Diversity and the Labour Party benefit from immigration. Hence, once again the interests of the System of Diversity and of international business and international politics coincide.

The Media and Misleading the Public

The mainstream media are almost entirely of the "progressive" class. Their ability to decide what constitutes news, and how it is expressed, gives them *carte blanche* to impose one-way propaganda upon the public. The result is that the public have a very distorted view about many issues. Favoured identity groups are reported only in terms which present them in a positive light, with only rare exceptions when this might be detected and rebound upon them. Similarly, issues relating to the out-groups are preferentially reported when issues provide an opportunity to portray them in a poor light, and disadvantages to the out-groups are rarely reported at all. Where the media are obliged to report something which goes against their narrative, control over programme content is invariably used to neutralise its impact by immediately following up with material which resets the imbalance in the "correct" direction.

The good propagandist never lies. But as the System has matured and become arrogant in its power, outright untruths are to be heard frequently. It is not always clear if the reporters believe what they report but have been misled by unreliable sources. The "progressive" bubble generates its own falsities spontaneously, and these are accepted uncritically as long as they conform to the narrative.

More egregious still are the so-called academics who are dedicated to advocacy research. Advocacy research starts from the desired conclusions and ensures that those conclusions are duly reached. It can look just like genuine research, with lots of data and valid analysis methodologies. It may require a great deal of effort to expose it as biased and worthless. Bioethicist Brian Earp has a great phrase "the unbearable asymmetry of bullshit". By this he refers to the fact that it can take far more effort to expose advocacy research than it took to produce it in the first place. This gives the producers of this biased material a massive advantage. This unfortunate situation is promoted by funding agencies which are "progressive" and hence only fund people or institutions whose work can be relied upon to produce the "correct" outcome. As a result there is now so much advocacy research that there is a danger the social sciences are being destroyed completely. Certainly, the lay person has no ready way of knowing what is valid from what is bullshit. They look the same to the non-expert. Science has always been dependent upon the honesty of scientists. The physical sciences have held out longer, but are expected to fall too.

Recalling the importance of moral claims for the operation of the System of Diversity, the key element in capturing the (apparent) moral high ground is to mislead the public as to where the moral high ground actually lies.

The Willingly Misled

The propagandists of the System of Diversity find that their seed falls on fertile ground. It is unsurprising when the gospel being preached is one of villainous others robbing ***us*** of our rightful bounty. It is not hard to convince people that they have been diddled and that they deserve better. Divisiveness is an easy sell. In the case of feminism it is particularly easy due to innate gynocentrism and a host of other psychological inclinations which it would be too long a digression to expound (but see Ref.[8], chapters 20 and 21).

It is less obvious why the out-groups are happy with a message which paints them as the villains. But here again both innate psychology and existing moral principles assist the process. The lack of male preferencing by other men (what I would call a lack of in-group preference were it not for the terminological confusion) is a major enabler. Since women have natural in-group preference but men do not, a policy of female preferencing (and male neglect) is easy to sell to both. The reverse would be extremely difficult in the modern world. Similarly, whatever one's view of history, the present reality is that Christians and heterosexuals are highly tolerant and accepting of non-Christians and non-heterosexuals. Policies which favour non-Christians or gays are readily accepted. There is no pushback along the lines of "what about us?", because that would be regarded as bad form. The out-groups have adopted a view that fairness will prevail. They are only now beginning to realise that the discriminations against them are belligerent and deliberate, not accidental.

For the recalcitrant, a battery of words like sexist, racist, misogynist, Islamophobe, homophobe, Nazi and "white supremacist" are available. These terms are deployed as weapons against the enemies of the System. Few members of the public are acquainted with the word "misandrist", and we are told that women cannot be sexist and blacks cannot be racist. This is an indirect way of telling us that the weapons "sexist" and "racist" are not permitted to be deployed against the in-groups.

Hence the division into in-groups and out-groups aligns with the grain of popular acceptance. Consequently, when the propagandists inundate us with stories of the wickedness of the out-groups and the victimisation of the in-groups, we are primed to accept them uncritically. We are the willingly misled because the truth goes against the grain of our preconceptions.

The System of Diversity Drives Inequality

This is a big topic to which I cannot do justice here. However, the key issue is that merely because the Administrative class purports to speak for the in-groups does not mean they have the interests of these groups at heart. The System is a power structure, driving power to the Representative and Administrative classes. It is parasitic upon genuine disadvantage, rather than dedicated to relieving it. Consequently, even the in-groups cannot be assured of benefit, for all they are explicitly preferenced in policy. In fact, it is worse than that because the Administrative class are invested in maintaining any genuine disadvantages to the in-groups because this provides the source of their apparent legitimacy.

The position of the working class is worse still. The System's policies drive increasing inequality to the detriment of the working class. The collapse of marriage is far more prevalent in the working class, and this drives poverty amongst single mothers as well as social isolation for men. The downward pressure on male earnings through leveraging the pay gap narrative and due to declining male education also drives increasing inequality. Feminists may be pleased about this male decline, but that is surely ignorance regarding its consequent effect on women. The reason is the money syphon. Men have always earned more than women, but women have always been primarily responsible for spending. Partly this occurs due to marriage or cohabitation. But it also occurs via the redistribution of tax revenue by the benefit system. In short, when men earn less, women end up with less to spend. The System is driving this by disadvantaging men. The System fails to recognise that men and women are in the same boat because feminist philosophy is to force the sexes into different boats which do not exist.

Why don't Feminists Attack Muslim Attitudes to Women?

Many people express puzzlement that feminists do not criticise traditional Muslim attitudes to women, ostensibly an obvious patriarchal target. But such people make the mistake of thinking that feminism is about the protection of women. No, feminism is a political strategy. At the Administrative level, feminism is primarily concerned with maintaining the flow of power to themselves which results from the moral force associated with both administered identity groups, i.e., both "women" and "ethnic or religious minorities". To have in-fighting between administered groups would challenge the System. Hence such internecine strife is suppressed at the Administrative level. In short, the purpose of feminism at the Administrative level is to protect the System of Diversity and its associated power structure, not primarily to uphold the true interests of women. The identity group "women" serves their purpose; the Administration is not the servant of this identity group, rather it is its overseer.

Why are MPs Almost All Feminists?

Every generation of elites must solve the problem of justifying themselves anew. Time was that the justification was that rulers ruled and others did not because it was "the natural order ordained by God". This specious justification gradually, over many centuries, morphed into a representative legislature and a democratic process. Unfortunately, you can fool most of the people most of the time, so the democratic system is not foolproof. The manipulation of the moral sense has proved highly effective in steering the voting public.

The System of Diversity is now in place. To deny being a feminist is to speak against the System. This will not be tolerated and is discouraged by immediate condemnation using the harshest of terms. You will be declared a danger to women. This is not good PR, especially for an MP whose job depends upon a popular vote. Moreover, the System reigns supreme in parliament – and indeed in virtually all the institutions – and so failing to conform is career terminal. Or it was. Some small cracks may be starting to appear. For a time Dominic Rabb appeared to be an exception, but the System ultimately removed him from office.

Why has the Judiciary become Feminist/Progressive?

For the same reason. The instantiation of the System as the (apparent) moral high ground makes resistance problematic. Judges, being human, like to bestow mercy, but only upon those for whom the prevailing popular prejudice, i.e., the social morality, has deemed worthy. Conversely, in line with the same prejudice, judges will consider it their duty to enact retribution where the prevailing social mores so directs. All this is not only their natural inclination but is also laid down in formal guidance published by the Judicial College, Ref.[10].

Why have Private Companies also become Feminist/Progressive?

For the same reason again. Senior managers, and indeed most staff, have absorbed the promulgated messages regarding whose causes are valid and whose not. And just as the judiciary also has a formal document to instruct them on precisely who is deserving, so do corporations have a formal process of enforcement. This is ESG, the Environment, Social and Governance corporate credit score (taken up in more detail in the next chapter).

What's All This Trans Business About?

Moral vampirism requires a constant supply of moral succour. The trans issue provides another source of moral succour. It could be anything. Any group which can be presented as disadvantaged and deserving assistance is grist to the System's mill. Remember that the System Administrators garner power from their role as overseers of morally deserving groups. They don't have to truly care about the people in question. Trans, gays, women, Muslims

– they are fodder for the operation of the System whose true purpose is the power hierarchy which advantages the Administrators.

Is the System of Diversity stable?

In a reasonably free society, no. The System of Diversity can be stable long-term only in a tyranny. Barring tyranny, systems based on making individuals subsidiary to identity group membership are intrinsically unstable, being subject to endless schism (see Ref.[9]). The good news is that such systems will eventually blow themselves out. The bad news is that, by then, the social and economic damage is likely to be very grievous, and perhaps fatal to the culture.

Should we be Reassured that only a Small Minority Identify as Feminists?

No.

It should be clear from the preceding schema that activists identifying as feminists are broadly those bidding for Administration or Representative status. But the identity group which is being administered includes the mass of women, by default. Feminist Administrators therefore speak in women's name because too few women actively and vociferously speak out against them doing so. But it's worse than that. A large proportion of people have adopted the brave new morality which teaches that preferencing the identity-based in-groups is the definition of social justice.

Church and State

The Administrator class can use its status as the controller of Identity, and hence as the guardian of social justice, to mould new moral stances in respect of language and behaviour. Thus, the politically dominant class can impose its ethics upon us all. This used to be accomplished through the Church. But the established Church has now been captured by the System of Diversity and hence acts as yet another arm of the System's moral hegemony. Thus the new "church" is the System itself, and church and State are closer than ever.

Where do Censorious Students Fit into this System?

People try to reassure me that the antics of the NUS and other censorious students are not representative of the overwhelming majority of students. Should I be reassured? Why do the majority of students not kick out these bigots who refuse permission for men's groups and who shut down speaking events that the university has already approved? Why should I be comforted that the activist zealots are only a small minority when the majority can be relied upon to be apathetic and do nothing to stop them? Why should I not expect national politics to be another example of the same phenomenon, with the small but highly vocal minority calling all the shots? And why should I not expect that national politics, and all that flows from it, to become ever more extreme as today's activist students become tomorrow's MPs? What sort of society can we expect when these closed-minded, semi-thugs acquire power?

Quite what is in the minds of these activist students defeats me. But two factors can be identified. The first is that they will be sensitive to their relative privilege and anxious to atone for it. Evidence in favour of this perspective is that such activism tends to be more common at the most elite universities and colleges. The escape route offered to the nascent elites is to join the Administration. By espousing the cause of the deserving in-groups, one's sins as an otherwise privileged person may be expiated. Hence, the second factor is that these censorious students are in training as new Administrators, the neo-Bourgeoisie in waiting.

The Punishment for Dissent

Dissenting from the approved views of The System does not result in debate over who is right. This must be avoided because the shallowness of the System's position will not bear much scrutiny. For people who are full-on dissidents (MRAs, real conservatives) the approach is *ad hominem*. No need to say that Nigel Farage is wrong, and still less to analyse why he's wrong; he is a repugnant racist, and that's all that's needed. People who hold views contrary to the correct victimhood perspective of the in-groups are personally vile, by definition.

I was taken to task for voting for Ann Widdecombe in the EU elections, the knee-jerk response being "you can't have voted for her, she's a fascist!". She's an elderly woman and a Christian conservative who does not say the right things about LGBT. It's no good observing that fascists are people who rove the streets in gangs beating people up and asking whether that's really a good description of Ann Widdecombe. The mind invaded by this contagious moral infantilism is closed. Lamentably, the moral infantilism and associated intolerance has been adopted by the masses – at least the bulk of the middle class, anyway.

Intolerance plays an important role in the virulence of the contagion. To avoid being berated yourself you'd better adopt the views that the lovely people hold. If you know what's good for you. But it's not done so crudely that the moral blackmail is apparent. Instead, the invariable hostility which greets dissenting voices discourages you from doing the same. This is the self-censorship of political correctness. But worse, the relentless personal attacks on dissenters leads you to interpret dissident views in terms of personal failings of those holding them. Most people simply have no strong reason to resist the easiest response: to adopt the approved perspective. It's easy, it minimises cognitive load, it makes everyone think you're a good person, it avoids trouble, and there's no downside…other than the eventual destruction of the whole culture that sustains you. This compliance with a moral narrative, contravening which meets with powerful social disapprobation, is precisely what the human moral disposition was evolved to do.

The System of Diversity as Situational Aggression against Out-Groups

Roy Baumeister's 1997 book *Evil: Inside Human Violence and Cruelty*, Ref.[11], is focussed on the mind and motivation of perpetrators of physical violence, but it is remarkable how apposite are many of Baumeister's findings when considered in the context of the progressives' attitude towards the out-groups. One only needs to reinterpret Baumeister's observations in terms of out-group denigration, or situational aggression. It seems that the "progressive" attitude towards the out-groups is very similar to the attitude of the physically cruel and violent towards their victims. For example,

"A common solution to the problem of justifying one's aggression is to depict the enemy as evil."

"A very powerful benefit of demonising the enemy is that all misfortunes and suffering on both sides can be blamed on the enemy.…What the good side suffers is the fault of the evil

side. By the same token, whatever the evil side suffers is also its own fault, because it brought it on itself by means of its evil activities."

Compare those points with the feminist view that the "patriarchy" is responsible for women's disadvantages, and also that "patriarchy hurts men too".

Feminists tend to interpret relatively benign words or actions by men as sexist and stemming from male sexual entitlement. By comparison, Baumeister observed that the most aggressive people tended to see hostility when it wasn't really there: *"they interpreted relatively innocuous and agreeable interactions as attempts to dominate others aggressively"*. Are we to conclude that this feminist tendency is related to their own aggression?

Baumeister even makes some observations which are explicitly critical of the identity political mindset, on which remarks I close this chapter,

"The history of hate crimes does not offer either whites or blacks much basis for claiming moral superiority......Both have proved the fallacy of thinking that you are entitled to special respect on the basis of your race; society may work better if people try to earn respect as individuals, by their virtuous acts and achievements."

"The incorporation of racial conflict into the myth of pure evil suggests one risk in the current American rush to categorise everyone by race and gender. The more people become sensitive to these differences, the more easily they will fall into the us-against-them mentality, and the more readily the myth of pure evil will be passed onto the other side. The more people are pushed to be constantly aware of differences, the harder it may be for them to get along. In the history of the world, increased recognition of differences between groups has led more often to conflict and violence than to peaceful cooperation and sharing. America is now making a dangerous gamble on the opposite result."

References

[1] Cobley, B. (2018). *The Liberal left and the System of Diversity*. Imprint Academic, 1st July 2018.

[2] Embery, P. (2020). *Despised: Why the Modern Left Loathes the Working Class*. Polity, 27 November 2020.

[3] Sowell, T. (1996). *The Vision Of The Anointed: Self-Congratulation As A Basis For Social Policy*. Basic Books, 28 June 1996.

[4]   British Psychological Society (2018). *Power Threat Meaning Framework (PTMF)*. 17 January 2018.

[5]   Datoo, S. (2015). *Mansplainers Are Offended By Natalie Bennett's Opposition To Mansplaining*. BuzzFeed News, 6 July 2015.

[6]   Asher, R. (2016). *Man Up: Boys, Men and Breaking the Male Rules*. Harvill Secker, 2016. (Linked is the Vintage edition, 4 May 2017).

[7]   Marcuse, H. (1969). *Repressive Tolerance*. In A Critique of Pure Tolerance by R.P.Wolff, B.Moore and H.Marcuse, Boston: Beacon Press, 1969, pp. 95-137.

[8]   Collins, W. (2022). *The Destructivists: How moral usurpation is being used to control us and change every aspect of our lives without our consent*. Principia Publications Unlimited, February 2022.

[9]   Bradford, R.A.W. (2018). *Group Extinction in Iterated Two Person Games with Evolved Group-Level Mixed Strategies*. The Journal of Mathematical Sociology, 43(4), 195-212, 2019.

[10] Judicial College. *The Equal Treatment Bench Book*. Latest edition February 2021 with April 2023 revisions.

[11] Baumeister, R.F. (1996). *Evil: Inside Human Violence and Cruelty*. W.H.Freeman & Co Ltd, 15 October 1996 (linked is the Kindle edition, Holt Paperbacks, 14 April 2015).

69. The Currencies of Moral Usurpation: Athena Swan, DIE and ESG

In chapter 68 I introduced the idea of moral usurpation. For a more systematic account of moral usurpation read The Destructivists, Ref.[1], or watch the videos linked as Refs.[2,3,4]. The original blog article on which this closing chapter is based followed the publication of The Destructivists and adds some relevant commentary to it, in particular in relation to how Athena Swan, DIE and ESG are specific manifestations of the moral usurpation process. I would emphasise particularly that ESG is moral usurpation applied at the highest levels of corporate finance and is a key factor in the globalist push towards "stakeholder capitalism" after the Chinese model.

Original posted on: 18 May 2022.

"Currencies"?

A "currency" is a means of exchange or the quality of being generally accepted. An elision of these interpretations is my meaning here.

In *The Destructivists*, Ref.[1], I explain how a manipulated moral standing can be used as a power trading currency within a triumvirate of elite power centres, the Woke Industrial Complex. Although I borrowed that term from Vivek Ramaswamy, Ref.[5], I use it with an enhanced meaning. The enhancement is the addition of moral standing as a form of power. This is the cornerstone of the idea of moral usurpation. Without the addition of moral power into the mix, the full triumvirate structure of the Woke Industrial Complex cannot be fully understood. In particular, the contagiousness and popularity of Wokeness would remain mysterious. The focus on moral usurpation elucidates these key features of our current predicament.

Whilst other forms of power are indisputable – such as the control of police forces, the ability to create laws, the access to large amounts of cash, or the control of the media – you might feel in contrast that "moral standing" is a rather nebulous commodity. Can moral standing really be traded effectively as a "currency" like those other forms of power?

In this post I expand upon how moral currencies are, in practice, manifest in very concrete terms. These examples serve to illustrate how hyper-elite players – those who stand to gain power as a result – coercively manage the adoption of these "moral currencies".

Currencies Manifest as Processes

One needs to distinguish between the knowing actors (the generally invisible hyper-elites) and the masses of willing employees, and other involved individuals, who probably believe they are doing good in the world. We shall look at Athena Swan, DIE (Diversity, Inclusion and Equity), and ESG (Environmental, Social and Corporate Governance). These examples of moral currencies deploy highly systematised processes to impose coercively their desired instruments of control (viz power) via the faux morality of moral usurpation.

Athena Swan

In the UK, Athena Swan was originally dedicated to advancing women's careers in Higher Education and research, initially in STEMM subjects but then also more broadly, see Ref.[6]. However, Athena Swan now embraces the broader DIE agenda.

Athena Swan is part of the Equality Challenge Unit (ECU), formally a private charity. It is funded by educational granting bodies, universities, professional scientific institutions and government departments. A large proportion of these funds originate from central government with the result that a nominally independent charity actually promotes the policies of a political agenda. This promotion is coercive.

Athena Swan operates a system of awards, the achievement of which depends on demonstrating compliance, in practice not just in theory, with the objectives of the DIE agenda. These awards relate to specific departments in specific universities. Failure to achieve a suitable award will result in your department failing to get research funding. In short, hire women, blacks and LGBTQ or get no money.

Athena Swan, like DIE generally, discriminates openly against white males – promoting the interests of everyone but. This betrays the political, rather than empirical, motivations which lie behind it, because white males (together with black Caribbean males) are the bottom of the heap as regards access to university (see chapter 28).

DIE (Diversity, Inclusion and Equity)

My change to the usual order of the three initials from DEI to DIE is deliberate, Ref.[7].

In the wider world, especially that of employment, the DIE agenda has been well embedded in practice for many years. Rather than a formal body promoting the agenda, it was promoted initially through the action of moral usurpation and the resulting moral coercion. Most large corporations voluntarily adopted quotas for the employment of women, BAME (Black, Asian and Minority Ethnic) and LGBTQ – the latter two invariably in excess of their prevalence in the general population. In respect of sex, the legally obligatory gender pay gap reporting is one particular coercive mechanism deployed in this area.

As we will see, the true purpose of DIE is not to be nice to women or blacks or gays, but to disempower those holding power (white males) and to undermine meritocracy (which is a barrier to imposing other employment criteria, such as obedience to the System).

DIE within the corporate world is now subsumed into the broader ESG programme.

ESG

ESG stands for Environmental, Social and Corporate Governance.

The Corporate Finance Institute, Ref.[8], defines ESG as "the framework for assessing the impact of the sustainability and ethical practices of a company".

ESG is to corporations what a social credit score is to individuals, Ref.[28]. It serves the same purpose: control by an authoritarian elite in the guise of social responsibility and moral loveliness.

The "social" part of ESG consists mostly of DIE subsumed within this larger programme. The "Governance" part is largely "corporate Wokeness". The "Environmental" part is dominated by the climate change agenda. All these things are classified under "sustainability", though without any coherent reason why. However, that buzz word serves to clearly link ESG to the UN's Agenda 2030, Ref.[9]. ESG is the mechanism for coercively imposing Agenda 2030 in the corporate world.

The impact of ESG or DIE on a corporation's bottom line can be argued either way. Sometimes it is claimed that ESG is financially beneficial. But if reality breaks through, that's OK because it only enhances the corporation's moral standing if they take a financial hit for the sake of social benefit. Those who are behind the ESG initiative do not care if individual corporations find the process financially beneficial or damaging. Their purpose is neither the financial health of individual businesses nor even the progress of the agendas ostensibly promoted by ESG. Their purpose is to harness corporate financial power and to place the reins in their own hands.

I amplify below how ESG is being enacted and what lies behind it.

The Appeal of these "Moral Currencies" to the Elites and the Public

It is worth itemising in brief the great appeal of these initiatives...

- Always be aware that the true purpose of these initiatives is not to support that which is overtly promoted, but to undermine or destroy that which they are designed to eclipse (men, whites, meritocracy, Christianity, corporate independence). And the true purpose of that is to obtain control by wresting it from the hands of those very people they denigrate. This key issue is amplified below.

- The hyper-elites do not principally want money. They already have that. They want power – which means control. This requires removing the disobedient from positions of influence where they might be disruptive. This is what cancel culture is.

- By loudly supporting causes which have been successfully, but often fraudulently, positioned on the moral high ground, the elites expiate their privilege-guilt and replace it with a glow of apparent loveliness.

- DIE and ESG are presented as socially and morally desirable. Why would you oppose "sustainable development"? Consequently, the unknowing majority of those involved in the business are keen to support such initiatives, and so the elites gain full employee engagement.

- The same applies to the public at large. The top-down approach of DIE and ESG is joined in a pincer movement by the bottom-up approach which creates zealots via the education systems. There is a ready supply of the morally infantilised whose mission, in their minds, is social justice.

But these people, who are most vociferous in seeing fascism everywhere, are actively engaged in its promotion.

The Purpose of DIE/ESG is Authoritarian Control

DIE

The objective of the DIE agenda is not primarily to be nice to women or ethnic minorities but to undermine meritocracy. Why? Because once hiring and promotion based on meritocracy is abandoned the way is clear to favour people based on something else. And whilst this "something else" is ostensibly related solely to identity groups (which is bad enough) in practice the way is clear to smuggle into the process other considerations – such as preferencing those who are likely to be compliant or helpful to other agendas.

If the society in question has an active social credit score system, then that social credit score can be used to decide upon hiring and promotion whilst appearing to be above board. After all, a valid "social credit" would be expected to reflect such desirable factors as Diversity, Inclusion and Equity. In practice, certain identity groups will indeed be favoured as well as the system serving the purposes of covert control.

In the case of universities or corporations, the creation of Diversity Officers provides the ideal opportunity for the ideologically aligned to be hired into positions of considerable influence. This is essentially entryism, but now boosted from within.

ESG

As DIE is to individuals, so ESG is to corporations.

The purpose of ESG is not solely (or even primarily) to promote "sustainability", or any of the environmental, social or governance issues advertised, but to undermine the conventional "corporate meritocracy" based on commercial success.

Some commentators will focus only on how ESG has replaced purely commercial motivations by Wokeness. But this misses the point. Whilst the Wokeness is an end in itself for the infantilised zealots who play a key role in driving the ESG process, it is merely a by-product as far as the controlling hyper-elites are concerned. The true purpose of ESG is to bring the corporate financial engine under the control of the authoritarian and unaccountable elite "stakeholders" (in the Klaus Schwab sense, see Appendix C of Ref.[1]).

Just as DIE smashes individual meritocracy, so ESG smashes corporate meritocracy. By this I mean that ESG undermines independent companies operating in a free market and subject only to a commercial standard of success. ESG replaces corporate meritocracy with a very unfree system in which the standard of success, upon which access to investment funds are based, is subject to control by unaccountable bodies who are then able to impose their own agenda. By this means the economic engine becomes yoked to an authoritarian government-stakeholder axis.

As Vivek Ramaswamy has noted, Ref.[5], once corporations cease to have profit and shareholder value as their motivation, how can one know *what* is controlling them? (The Appendix to this chapter expands upon the dangers of corporate power in political hands, based on Ramaswamy). The "merit" of corporations used to be measured by their bottom line; but ESG is changing that. Now corporations are being judged on their ESG scores – the corporate equivalent of a social credit score.

"Who cares?", you might think. Well, you should care because the corporations themselves do. Why? Because the ESG system is being imposed upon them by those on whom they are reliant for investment cash and operating capital – the banks, hedge funds, investment and asset management institutions, especially the latter.

"Go Woke, go broke" is misleading. The asset management companies ensure that the reality of the funding environment in which corporations now operate is that *failure* to go Woke will ensure they go broke. If an individual business ends up going broke, perhaps as a consequence of going Woke, that is just collateral damage as far as the hyper-elite authoritarian players are concerned.

The major asset management companies and investment funds are likely to expect companies seeking capital to have an ESG Policy in place, as they will also have themselves. The situation is similar to that for charities (in the UK) seeking grants. Virtually all the trusts and foundations which provide charitable grants will expect a charity to have a suite of policies in place before any application for a grant will be considered (such as safeguarding policies, health & safety policies, environmental policies, equal opportunities policy, complaints and grievance policies, etc.).

Here are some examples of the ESG policies and ESG funds, etc., of asset management companies: Goldman Sachs, Ref.[13], Morgan Stanley, Ref.[14], Blackrock, Ref.[15], Renaissance Technologies, Ref.[16], Man Institute, Ref.[17], AQR Capital Management, Ref.[18], Sigma Capital Group, Ref.[19], Nuveen Investment Management, Ref.[20].

How ESG is Imposed on Companies

It comes from the top down. At the international level it is the United Nations and its satellites like the World Economic Forum (WEF) and the World Bank which drive the policy at the highest level. The loan strategy of the World Bank reflects the UN's Sustainable Development Goals, i.e., Agenda 30. Recall that ESG is a key component of the UN's overarching Agenda 30, Ref.[9]. Each nation state will then have its own national-level implementation of ESG as an obligation.

In the UK, the Financial Conduct Authority (FCA) has laid down its expectations in respect of ESG in considerable detail, Ref.[10]. Given that the FCA is the business regulator in the UK, their expectations have the power of "compelling advice". To quote the FCA's ESG policy: *"As a regulator, we can set requirements and supervise proactively to promote firm behaviour in line with our expectations".*

In November 2002 the FCA's ESG strapline was, *"Our environmental, social and governance (ESG) strategy sets out our target outcomes and the actions we expect to take to deliver these. Our aim is to support the financial sector in driving positive change, including the transition to net zero".*

It is clear that this is a government requirement on the FCA, which stated in 2022, *"the Government has raised the level of its ambition, confirming a carbon emissions reduction target of 78% of 1990 levels by 2035. The Government's policy direction has triggered policy and regulatory measures to green the financial system"* and *"...the Government has also raised its expectations of regulators. In our latest remit letter, received in March 2021, the Chancellor set a clear expectation that we should 'have regard' to the Government's net zero commitments in all our regulatory activities".*

In December 2021, the FCA published two policy statements finalising its climate-related financial disclosure rules for asset managers and other financial companies. Under FCA regulation such companies will have to disclose how they take climate-related risks and opportunities into account in managing investments, Ref.[11].

Another channel through which government "sustainability" directives are to be imposed on companies are the Sustainability Disclosure Requirements. The Department of Business and Trade have already published the UK government's framework to create Sustainability Disclosure Standards, Ref.[12]. The Sustainability Disclosure Requirements (SDR) are rules that require companies to report on their impact on the climate and environment. The SDR will require firms to substantiate their sustainability claims and may involve independent verification.

Ref.[12] makes clear that the UK's Sustainability Disclosure Standards will be modelled on those of the International Sustainability Standards Board (ISSB), with an intention for the Secretary of State for Business and Trade to endorse these standards by July 2024. The creation of the ISSB was announced at COP26, the 2021 UN Climate Change Conference in Glasgow. This is an example of one of many routes by which UN policies become adopted as national policies and hence imposed upon businesses. In short, it is an example of one of many routes by which UN Agenda 30, Ref.[9], will ultimately impact you, via the constraints imposed on companies.

The Financial Muscle of the Asset Management Companies

The financial power of the asset management companies can be gauged by the total value of the assets they manage. The league table varies annually (and also depending on what source one uses), though Blackrock has been top of every list for some time. In 2023 according to one source the top 20 asset management companies were (together with the total value of their managed assets),

1. Blackrock ($9.09 trillion)
2. Vanguard ($7.60 trillion)
3. Fidelity Investments ($4.24 trillion)
4. State Street ($3.60 trillion)
5. Morgan Stanley ($3.13 trillion)
6. JP Morgan Chase ($3.01 trillion)
7. Goldman Sachs ($2.67 trillion)
8. Crédit Agricole ($2.66 trillion)

9. Allianz ($2.36 trillion)
10. Capital Group ($2.30 trillion)
11. Amundi ($2.10 trillion)
12. BNY Mellon ($1.91 trillion)
13. UBS ($1.83)
14. PIMCO ($1.80 trillion)
15. Edward Jones Investments ($1.70 trillion)
16. Deutsche Bank ($1.49 trillion)
17. Invesco ($1.48 trillion)
18. Legal & General ($1.48 trillion)
19. Bank of America ($1.47 trillion)
20. Franklin Templeton ($1.42 trillion)

To put these huge sums of money in context, the GDP of the USA in 2023 was $27.4 trillion, while that of the UK was £2.27 trillion ($2.86 trillion). Hence, Blackrock alone is managing assets worth over three times the UK GDP and one-third of the USA's GDP. The total assets being managed by the top five asset management companies exceeds the GDP of the USA. Each of the top 12 asset management companies is managing assets worth more than the GDP of Russia.

If the asset management companies were countries with a GDP equal to the above figures, Blackrock and Vanguard would be ranked third and fourth in terms of all countries' GDP, after the USA and China only.

Of those top 20 asset management companies, 14 are registered in the USA, two in France, two in Germany, one in Switzerland and one in the UK. Legal & General, registered in the UK, is managing assets worth half the entire UK GDP.

The political process, both international and national, in enacting the ESG elements of the UN's Agenda 30 via the asset management companies, has acquired control over the whole corporate world.

What the Asset Managers Reveal

If you browse the material provided online by the asset managers you will see evidence of the coercive aspects of the ESG agenda. For example, the Man Group, Ref.[17], tell us that *"exclusions lists are a basic method to incorporate ESG"*. In other words, "comply or you go on the funding blacklist". As for "impact on returns" we read, "*there is evidence that some G metrics have a real impact on returns. The picture is more mixed for the E and S*". You can see that same observation in several of Refs.[13-20]. The oft-repeated claim that ESG is financially beneficial is simply false. But the ESG lobby is unconcerned as that is no part of their true agenda.

Similarly, in the videoed panel discussion linked at Ref.[21] you will hear references to "*if companies are not willing to engage in these issues we may choose not to invest*". They unashamedly prefer "*women led businesses*" and groom aligned persons for seniority, referring to "*bring up the next generation of leaders*". This is how corporations go Woke: the senior management are selected into a cadre at an early stage of their career (grooming).

The impetus for corporations to adopt ESG is clear, due to the coercive influence of the funders. But what exactly is in it for the asset managers themselves? The answer is several things,

- First and foremost, recall that the asset management companies are subject to political and legislative obligations, via regulators and enforceable standards, as discussed above, i.e., this is a top-down phenomenon.

- The hyper-elites within the asset management institutions achieve their desired control over the corporations. One suspects that, ultimately, this control over the corporations is intended to be shared with their political masters (think CCP).

- This control is further enhanced because ESG scores themselves can very easily be manipulated – and, like social credit scores, actually measure obedience to the System, rather than being a genuine metric of social benefit.

- The funding institutions do very well financially out of it too.

In contrast to the corporations themselves, who are obliged to take this medicine, ESG-constrained funds have been tremendously lucrative to the financial institutions and their stakeholders (i.e., the hyper-elites) at the heart of this radical shift in corporate governance. According to the Heartland Institute, Ref.[22], in 2022,

"*...it is BlackRock, the world's largest private asset manager, that has stood to gain the most. BlackRock holds a stake in almost every public company with its $7.4 trillion in* *assets under management, and it has leveraged its size and diversification to fully reap the benefits of ESG investment. BlackRock's iShares Global Clean Energy ETF is one of the largest ESG funds in the world....Is it a coincidence that BlackRock is run by Larry Fink, who has largely spearheaded the stakeholder takeover and is a board member of the World Economic Forum, one of the leading advocates of ESG?"*

As for an individual company's ESG score, it is fairly meaningless. Ref.[22] reports that, as of 2022,

"A recent paper aggregating evidence from more than 1,000 studies on ESG performance found "studies use different scores for different companies by different data providers. One study analyzing six prominent ESG ratings agencies noted that each of the six companies employs different category scopes, different measurement of those categories, and different assigned weights to those categories. Additionally, a rater's overall subjective view of a firm was found to influence the rater's assessment."

"There truly is no objective, uniform ESG model. ESG scores are often subjectively determined and typically depend on potentially biased self-reporting from large corporations."

This is the ambiguity that the International Sustainability Disclosure Standards are intended to remove. Whether such Standards will have the beneficial effect of preventing the reduction of a company's ESG score due to "incorrect politics" remains to be seen. One example of that is Tesla. As one of the world's most significant manufacturers of electric vehicles, Tesla should have a high ESG score. It does not, quite the opposite. You would have to be very naïve not to associate this with Elon Musk's outspoken anti-Wokeness and his purchase of Twitter followed by the revelations about Twitter which Musk then released, Ref.[23].

However, as of now, ESG ratings are rather a random mess. According to Ref.[24] from Two Sigma, one of the main ESG funders,

"ESG ratings are all over the place. In the investment industry, it's well-known and researched that ESG ratings differ substantially by provider. Dimson, Marsh, and Staunton found that 'companies with a high [ESG] score from one rater often receive a middling or low score from another rater' and that correlations between ESG ratings from various providers were minimal."

The video linked at Ref.[25] tells of a history in which ethical investing was initially promoted by left-leaning individuals with a personal experience of the 1930s depression, the McCarthy era and the Vietnam war. Whatever view one might have regarding the desirability of ethical investing, these originators were at least honest in what they were doing and trying to achieve. But the video ends by observing that there are now only a few niche investment funds which promote this honest form of ethical investing. It refers to "dubious practices" by the current ESG-driven funders (cue Al Gore). The video ends on the note that ESG funding, rather than being socially beneficial, can "make things even worse". One of the originators of ethical investing referred to the transition to ESG as "making success the mother of defeat", noting that the "little people" had disappeared from the picture under ESG.

In short, ESG is actually the moral usurpation of the original purpose of ethical investing.

It's worth noting that the video referred to above (Ref.[25]) was made by Bloomberg which is itself an ESG funder. Another Bloomberg video, *ESG Ratings Are Not What They Seem*, Ref.[26], promotes the same message – stating that ESG ratings can be the exact opposite of what people think they are. It focusses on trashing the market leader in ESG scoring, MSCI. If you are a true believer in the climate change narrative then you'll be disappointed by what this video reveals. Whilst the talk around ESG is replete with references to climate change and carbon emissions, it seems that they don't figure much in actual ESG scores. Instead, this video argues that the ESG score is more a reflection of the impact of the world on the corporation rather than the reverse. Quote, *"the idea that investing in these funds is doing anything to make the world better – it's really, really hard to see how that's the case"*.

Allow me to repeat one of the key features of the generic moral usurpation strategy: it does not truly assist those whom it ostensibly supports, because it is invested in using victims as a source of moral smokescreen to conceal unrelated purposes. It would be contrary to these true interests to alleviate victims of their problems as this would diminish their usefulness as a moral smokescreen.

The video ends with a statement that Bloomberg LP (the parent company of Bloomberg News) does itself *"compete to sell sustainability ratings and data to money managers"*. Even more remarkably they note that Bloomberg LP has a partnership with MSCI, whose operation they just trashed. Moreover, it is clear from the video that all they see wrong with the current system is that the ESG ratings should truly promote the climate change agenda, rather than merely pretending to do so. I guess this is why these videos are still available (as of March 2024).

Ref.[27] is another video, this time of a former Blackrock Chief Investment Officer, who testifies that ESG investing is neither useful simply as an investment tool nor is there any evidence that it is beneficial to the causes it appears to support. Again he comes at it from a mindset that we really should be reducing carbon emissions and that ESG just doesn't do it. The important point, though, is that ESG is basically fraudulent, irrespective of the separate issue of the need, or otherwise, for carbon reductions.

Conclusion

There is a certain amount of scepticism within the financial system in regard to ESG, but this generally focusses on the inadequacy of the ESG ratings or the cash value that ESG investment products have for the funders.

The greater threat in respect of ESG and DIE, and indeed feminism, is recognised by relatively few commentators. This threat is that these movements or initiatives implement the moral usurpation mechanism in order to transfer power into the hands of political actors.

And yet a political system in which authoritarian social policies are allied to the economic power of the corporations is the stuff of which CCP-style fascism is composed. This is the threat which lies behind ESG, revealed most clearly when ESG is interpreted as the corporate analogue of social credit systems.

Appendix: The Danger of Corporate Power in Political Hands

This Appendix summarises some pertinent observations from Vivek Ramaswamy, Ref.[5]. For example,

"Our contemporary understanding of capitalism is influenced by a little-appreciated intellectual feud between Milton Friedman and Klaus Schwab. In September 1970, Friedman famously wrote in The New York Times Magazine that the purpose of the corporation was to pursue profit. He argued that 'the doctrine of 'social responsibility' in business, if 'taken seriously' would extend the scope of the political mechanism to every

human activity'. He warned that its proponents were 'preaching pure and unadulterated socialism' and 'undermining the basis of a free society'.

Yet as Friedman argued for shareholder primacy, other prominent economists organised against him. In 1973, Schwab, the World Economic Forum executive chairman, wrote the 'Davos Manifesto' calling for a new 'Code of Ethics for Business Leaders'. Executives were no longer simply to seek a return on investment for their shareholders, Schwab declared, but to 'serve' their workers and employees, as well as societies, and to harmonize the different interests of the stakeholders.....''

"It was to be left to a class of capitalist leaders to decide just what that meant. So every January they met at a ski resort in Davos, Switzerland, to pontificate about 'ethical capitalism'''.

Elsewhere Ramaswamy notes that,

"Society gave corporations superpowers. Foremost among them was the gift of limited liability. In return, society demanded that companies use that power for only a narrow set of activities – namely to make products and services – to prevent them from wielding too much power in our politics and other non-commercial spheres of our lives."

He goes on to note,

"Advocates of classical capitalism like Milton Friedman...ignored the way in which limited shareholder liability would create titanic corporate monsters with power heretofore unimagined, offering no coherent theory for how society should constrain the power of these monsters outside the marketplace.

By contrast, advocates of stakeholder capitalism were correct to acknowledge a social contract between shareholders and society in which shareholders owe something back to society in return for the great gift of limited liability. They were also correct to recognize that the social contract was one which demanded restraint from corporations. They erred only in surmising that this social contract was 'implicit' and that corporate restraint was about tamping down the pure pursuit of profit. To the contrary: if limited liability was the quid from society, the mandate to maximise shareholder value was the quo from corporations."

I commend the following further observation by Ramaswamy to your closest attention in the context of what ESG is doing to release corporate power into the hands of political and self-serving unaccountable actors,

"The requirement to maximise profits wasn't just about protecting shareholders, as Milton Friedman types had assumed. **It was about protecting the rest of society from a Frankensteinian corporate monster.** *That's why we keep the monster trapped in the cage of capitalism: to protect democracy and other civic institutions from a monster that, once unleashed, would exercise more power than any business or person ever should."* (His emphasis).

Ramaswamy goes on to opine that the great gift of limited liability should be confined to companies pursuing purely commercial objectives, i.e., maximising profit. Where corporations, including funders, choose to pursue other objectives – even if dressed up as "social responsibility" – they should lose the protection of limited liability. Their directors and shareholders will then be personally exposed to the resulting financial liability. This would kill ESG dead at a stroke.

References

[1] Collins, W. (2022). *The Destructivists: How moral usurpation is being used to control us and change every aspect of life without our consent*. Principia Publications Unlimited, 20 February 2022.

[2] Collins, W. (2021). *My presentation at ICMI21: Moral Usurpation*. William Collins YouTube video, 20 December 2021.

[3] Men Are Good (2022a). *What Connects Feminism to the Global Elite & How Can We Fight It?* A chat with Tom Golden and Janice Fiamengo, Men Are Good YouTube channel, 19 January 2022.

[4] Men Are Good (2022b). *The Destructivists*. A chat with Tom Golden and Janice Fiamengo, Men Are Good YouTube channel, 11 May 2022.

[5] Ramaswamy, V. (2021). *Woke Inc*. Swift Press, 23 August 2021.

[6] Collins, W. (2015). *Athena Swan*. The Illustrated Empathy Gap, 1 March 2015.

[7] Peterson, J. (2022). *D-I-E Must Die*. Jordan Peterson YouTube channel, 19 January 2022.

[8] Corporate Finance Institute (undated). *ESG (Environmental, Social, & Governance)*. Accessed 3/3/24.

[9] United Nations Department of Economic and Social Affairs (2015). *Transforming our world: the 2030 Agenda for Sustainable Development*. The United Nations policy adopted at the Sustainable Development Summit on 25 September 2015.

[10] Financial Conduct Authority (2022). *A strategy for positive change: our ESG priorities*. 21 November 2022.

[11] Linklaters (2021). *FCA finalises TCFD disclosure rules for FCA regulated asset managers and standard listed companies*. 21 December 2021.

[12] Department for Business and Trade (2023). *UK Sustainability Disclosure Standards*. 2 August 2023.

[13] Goldman Sachs (2021). *The Evolution of ESG Financing*. 13 April 2021.

[14] Morgan Stanley (2023). *Environmental and Social Policy Statement*. August 2023.

[15] Blackrock (2024). *ESG Funds*. Accessed 3 March 2024.

[16] Renaissance Technologies (2023). *Sustainability Report*. July 2023.

[17] Man Institute (2021). *ESG Investing*. March 2021.

[18] AQR Capital Management (2022). *Environmental, Social, Governance*. 2022.

[19] Sigma Capital Group (2022). *ESG Upholding Values*. 2022.

[20] Nuveen Investment Management (2023). *ESG Growth Models*. 9 December 2023.

[21] NYU Stern Center for Sustainable Business (2019). *ESG and Impact Investing Across Asset Classes with Goldman Sachs*. 23 April 2019.

[22] Justin Haskins, J., and McPherrin, J. (2022). *Understanding Environmental, Social, and Governance (ESG) Metrics: A Basic Primer*. The Heartland Institute, 1 February 2022.

[23] Neuburger, T. (2023). *All Twitter File Links, Aggregated*. 7 February 2023. An alternative source is *here*. You can read an account of the Twitter File issue in Wikipedia but beware of bias.

[24] Botte, A., Nigro, M., and Cohen, D. (2021). *Street View. What is ESG? Depends on Whom You Ask*. 21 May 2021.

[25] Bloomberg Originals (2021). *Where ESG's $35 Trillion Explosion Really Came From*. Bloomberg Originals YouTube channel, 13 December 2021.

[26] Bloomberg Originals (2021). *ESG Ratings Are Not What They Seem*. Bloomberg Originals YouTube channel, 20 December 2021.

[27] CNBC Television (2021). *ESG investing doesn't work: Former BlackRock CIO*. CNBC Television YouTube channel, 17 November 2021.

[28] Wikipedia (2024). *Social Credit System*. Accessed 3 April 2024.

Acronyms Used in the Text

APPG – All-Party Parliamentary Group

BAME – Black, Asian and Minority Ethnic

BIGI – Basic Index of Gender Inequality

CAFCASS - Children and Family Court Advisory and Support Service

CCP – Chinese Communist Party

CPGB – Communist Party of Great Britain

CPS – Crown Prosecution Service

CSEW – Crime Survey for England & Wales

DA – Domestic Abuse

DAPN – Domestic Abuse Protection Notice

DAPO – Domestic Abuse Protection Order

DBS – Disclosure and Barring Service

DfE – Department for Education

DIE – Diversity, Inclusion, Equity (normally rendered DEI)

DLPFC - Dorsolateral Prefrontal Cortex

DPP – Director of Public Prosecutions

DV – Domestic Violence

DWP – Department of Work and Pensions

ECHR - European Court of Human Rights

EHRC - Equality and Human Rights Commission

ESG – Environmental, Social, and (corporate) Governance

EVAWGC - End Violence Against Women and Girls Coalition

EU – European Union

F4J – Fathers 4 Justice

FCA – Financial Conduct Authority

FGM – Female Genital Mutilation

fMRI – functional Magnetic Resonance Imaging

FNF – Families Need Fathers

FNF-BPM Cymru – Families Need Fathers - Both Parents Matter Cymru

FoI – Freedom of Information

FTE – Full Time Equivalent

GBH – Grievous Bodily Harm

GDP – Gross Domestic Product

GGGI – Global Gender Gap Index

GMS – General Medical Service

HMCTS (HM Courts & Tribunals Service)

IAT – Implicit Association Test

IC – Istanbul Convention

IMF – International Monetary Fund

Incel – Involuntary Celibate

IPA – Intimate Partner Abuse

IPV – Intimate Partner Violence

ISSB – International Sustainability Standards Board

J4MB – Justice for Men & Boys

JCQ - Joint Council for Qualifications

KC – King's Counsel

KPMG – An English company, the initials derived from Klynveld Peat Marwick Goerdeler

KS2 – Key Stage 2

LGBTQ – Lesbian, Gay, Bisexual, Transgender, Queer

MGM – Male Genital Mutilation

MGTOW – Men Going Their Own Way

MHRM – Men's Human Rights Movement

MOJ – Ministry of Justice

MRA – Men's Rights Activist / Advocate

MRI – Magnetic Resonance Imaging

NAPAC - National Association of People Abused in Childhood

NHS – National Health Service

NRM - National Referral Mechanism

OCD – Obsessive Compulsive Disorder

OML – Other Modern Languages

ONS – Office for National Statistics

PA – Parental Alienation or Partner Abuse

PAC – Public Assistance Committees (the forerunner of unemployment benefit)

PCC – Police & Crime Commissioner

PHSO - Parliamentary and Health Service Ombudsman

PTSD – Post-Traumatic Stress Disorder

PUA – Pick-Up Artist

QC – Queen's Counsel

RSE – Relationship and Sex Education

SAT – Standard Attainment Test

SCR – Serious Case Review

SDR - Sustainability Disclosure Requirements

SNP – Scottish National Party

SPA – State Pension Age

SRE – Sex and Relationship Education (now RSE)

SSRN - Social Science Research Network

TERF – Trans-Exclusionary Radical Feminist

TFF – The Fiamengo Files (videos by Janice Fiamengo)

UCL – University College London

UN – United Nations

UNCRC – United Nations' Convention on the Rights of the Child

USAPP – United States of America Politics and Policy

VAWG – Violence Against Women and Girls

VMPFC - Ventromedial Prefrontal Cortex

WEC – Women and Equalities Committee

WEF – World Economic Forum

WASPI - Women Against State Pension Inequality